Lecture Notes in Computer Science 14258

Founding Editors

Gerhard Goos
Juris Hartmanis

Editorial Board Members

The series Lecture Notes in Computer Science (LNCS), including its subseries Lecture Notes in Artificial Intelligence (LNAI) and Lecture Notes in Bioinformatics (LNBI), has established itself as a medium for the publication of new developments in computer science and information technology research, teaching, and education.

LNCS enjoys close cooperation with the computer science R & D community, the series counts many renowned academics among its volume editors and paper authors, and collaborates with prestigious societies. Its mission is to serve this international community by providing an invaluable service, mainly focused on the publication of conference and workshop proceedings and postproceedings. LNCS commenced publication in 1973.

Lazaros Iliadis · Antonios Papaleonidas ·
Plamen Angelov · Chrisina Jayne
Editors

Artificial Neural Networks and Machine Learning – ICANN 2023

32nd International Conference on Artificial Neural Networks
Heraklion, Crete, Greece, September 26–29, 2023
Proceedings, Part V

Springer

Editors
Lazaros Iliadis ⓘ
Democritus University of Thrace
Xanthi, Greece

Antonios Papaleonidas ⓘ
Democritus University of Thrace
Xanthi, Greece

Plamen Angelov ⓘ
Lancaster University
Lancaster, UK

Chrisina Jayne ⓘ
Teesside University
Middlesbrough, UK

ISSN 0302-9743 ISSN 1611-3349 (electronic)
Lecture Notes in Computer Science
ISBN 978-3-031-44191-2 ISBN 978-3-031-44192-9 (eBook)
https://doi.org/10.1007/978-3-031-44192-9

This Springer imprint is published by the registered company Springer Nature Switzerland AG
The registered company address is: Gewerbestrasse 11, 6330 Cham, Switzerland

Paper in this product is recyclable.

Preface

The European Neural Network Society (ENNS) is an association of scientists, engineers and students, conducting research on the modelling of behavioral and brain processes, and on the development of neural algorithms. The core of these efforts is the application of neural modelling to several diverse domains. According to its mission statement ENNS is the European non-profit federation of professionals that aims at achieving a worldwide professional and socially responsible development and application of artificial neural technologies.

The flagship event of ENNS is ICANN (the International Conference on Artificial Neural Networks) at which contributed research papers are presented after passing through a rigorous review process. ICANN is a dual-track conference, featuring tracks in brain-inspired computing on the one hand, and machine learning on the other, with strong crossdisciplinary interactions and applications.

The response of the international scientific community to the ICANN 2023 call for papers was more than satisfactory. In total, 947 research papers on the aforementioned research areas were submitted and 426 (45%) of them were finally accepted as full papers after a peer review process. Additionally, 19 extended abstracts were submitted and 9 of them were selected to be included in the front matter of ICANN 2023 proceedings. Due to their high academic and scientific importance, 22 short papers were also accepted.

All papers were peer reviewed by at least two independent academic referees. Where needed, a third or a fourth referee was consulted to resolve any potential conflicts. Three workshops focusing on specific research areas, namely Advances in Spiking Neural Networks (ASNN), Neurorobotics (NRR), and the challenge of Errors, Stability, Robustness, and Accuracy in Deep Neural Networks (ESRA in DNN), were organized.

The 10-volume set of LNCS 14254, 14255, 14256, 14257, 14258, 14259, 14260, 14261, 14262 and 14263 constitutes the proceedings of the 32nd International Conference on Artificial Neural Networks, ICANN 2023, held in Heraklion city, Crete, Greece, on September 26–29, 2023.

The accepted papers are related to the following topics:

Machine Learning: Deep Learning; Neural Network Theory; Neural Network Models; Graphical Models; Bayesian Networks; Kernel Methods; Generative Models; Information Theoretic Learning; Reinforcement Learning; Relational Learning; Dynamical Models; Recurrent Networks; and Ethics of AI.

Brain-Inspired Computing: Cognitive Models; Computational Neuroscience; Self-Organization; Neural Control and Planning; Hybrid Neural-Symbolic Architectures; Neural Dynamics; Cognitive Neuroscience; Brain Informatics; Perception and Action; and Spiking Neural Networks.

Neural applications in Bioinformatics; Biomedicine; Intelligent Robotics; Neuro-robotics; Language Processing; Speech Processing; Image Processing; Sensor Fusion; Pattern Recognition; Data Mining; Neural Agents; Brain-Computer Interaction; Neuro-morphic Computing and Edge AI; and Evolutionary Neural Networks.

September 2023

Lazaros Iliadis
Antonios Papaleonidas
Plamen Angelov
Chrisina Jayne

Organization

General Chairs

Iliadis Lazaros   Democritus University of Thrace, Greece
Plamen Angelov   Lancaster University, UK

Program Chairs

Antonios Papaleonidas   Democritus University of Thrace, Greece
Elias Pimenidis   UWE Bristol, UK
Chrisina Jayne   Teesside University, UK

Honorary Chairs

Stefan Wermter   University of Hamburg, Germany
Vera Kurkova   Czech Academy of Sciences, Czech Republic
Nikola Kasabov   Auckland University of Technology, New Zealand

Organizing Chairs

Antonios Papaleonidas   Democritus University of Thrace, Greece
Anastasios Panagiotis Psathas   Democritus University of Thrace, Greece
George Magoulas   University of London, Birkbeck College, UK
Haralambos Mouratidis   University of Essex, UK

Award Chairs

Stefan Wermter   University of Hamburg, Germany
Chukiong Loo   University of Malaysia, Malaysia

Communication Chairs

Sebastian Otte   University of Tübingen, Germany
Anastasios Panagiotis Psathas   Democritus University of Thrace, Greece

Steering Committee

Stefan Wermter   University of Hamburg, Germany
Angelo Cangelosi   University of Manchester, UK
Igor Farkaš   Comenius University in Bratislava, Slovakia
Chrisina Jayne   Teesside University, UK
Matthias Kerzel   University of Hamburg, Germany
Alessandra Lintas   University of Lausanne, Switzerland
Kristína Malinovská (Rebrová)   Comenius University in Bratislava, Slovakia
Alessio Micheli   University of Pisa, Italy
Jaakko Peltonen   Tampere University, Finland
Brigitte Quenet   ESPCI Paris, France
Ausra Saudargiene   Lithuanian University of Health Sciences,
                                           Lithuania
Roseli Wedemann   Rio de Janeiro State University, Brazil

Local Organizing/Hybrid Facilitation Committee

Aggeliki Tsouka   Democritus University of Thrace, Greece
Anastasios Panagiotis Psathas   Democritus University of Thrace, Greece
Anna Karagianni   Democritus University of Thrace, Greece
Christina Gkizioti   Democritus University of Thrace, Greece
Ioanna-Maria Erentzi   Democritus University of Thrace, Greece
Ioannis Skopelitis   Democritus University of Thrace, Greece
Lambros Kazelis   Democritus University of Thrace, Greece
Leandros Tsatsaronis   Democritus University of Thrace, Greece
Nikiforos Mpotzoris   Democritus University of Thrace, Greece
Nikos Zervis   Democritus University of Thrace, Greece
Panagiotis Restos   Democritus University of Thrace, Greece
Tassos Giannakopoulos   Democritus University of Thrace, Greece

Program Committee

Abraham Yosipof	CLB, Israel
Adane Tarekegn	NTNU, Norway
Aditya Gilra	Centrum Wiskunde & Informatica, Netherlands
Adrien Durand-Petiteville	Federal University of Pernambuco, Brazil
Adrien Fois	LORIA, France
Alaa Marouf	Hosei University, Japan
Alessandra Sciutti	Istituto Italiano di Tecnologia, Italy
Alessandro Sperduti	University of Padua, Italy
Alessio Micheli	University of Pisa, Italy
Alex Shenfield	Sheffield Hallam University, UK
Alexander Kovalenko	Czech Technical University in Prague, Czech Republic
Alexander Krawczyk	Fulda University of Applied Sciences, Germany
Ali Minai	University of Cincinnati, USA
Aluizio Araujo	Universidade Federal de Pernambuco, Brazil
Amarda Shehu	George Mason University, USA
Amit Kumar Kundu	University of Maryland, USA
Anand Rangarajan	University of Florida, USA
Anastasios Panagiotis Psathas	Democritus University of Thrace, Greece
Andre de Carvalho	Universidade de São Paulo, Brazil
Andrej Lucny	Comenius University, Slovakia
Angel Villar-Corrales	University of Bonn, Germany
Angelo Cangelosi	University of Manchester, UK
Anna Jenul	Norwegian University of Life Sciences, Norway
Antonios Papaleonidas	Democritus University of Thrace, Greece
Arnaud Lewandowski	LISIC, ULCO, France
Arul Selvam Periyasamy	Universität Bonn, Germany
Asma Mekki	University of Sfax, Tunisia
Banafsheh Rekabdar	Portland State University, USA
Barbara Hammer	Universität Bielefeld, Germany
Baris Serhan	University of Manchester, UK
Benedikt Bagus	University of Applied Sciences Fulda, Germany
Benjamin Paaßen	Bielefeld University, Germany
Bernhard Pfahringer	University of Waikato, New Zealand
Bharath Sudharsan	NUI Galway, Ireland
Binyi Wu	Dresden University of Technology, Germany
Binyu Zhao	Harbin Institute of Technology, China
Björn Plüster	University of Hamburg, Germany
Bo Mei	Texas Christian University, USA

Brian Moser	Deutsches Forschungszentrum für künstliche Intelligenz, Germany
Carlo Mazzola	Istituto Italiano di Tecnologia, Italy
Carlos Moreno-Garcia	Robert Gordon University, UK
Chandresh Pravin	Reading University, UK
Chao Ma	Wuhan University, China
Chathura Wanigasekara	German Aerospace Centre, Germany
Cheng Shang	Shanghai Jiaotong University, China
Chengqiang Huang	Huawei Technologies, China
Chenhan Zhang	University of Technology, Sydney, Australia
Chenyang Lyu	Dublin City University, Ireland
Chihuang Liu	Meta, USA
Chrisina Jayne	Teesside University, UK
Christian Balkenius	Lund University, Sweden
Chrysoula Kosma	Ecole Polytechnique, Greece
Claudio Bellei	Elliptic, UK
Claudio Gallicchio	University of Pisa, Italy
Claudio Giorgio Giancaterino	Intesa SanPaolo Vita, Italy
Constantine Dovrolis	Cyprus Institute, USA
Coşku Horuz	University of Tübingen, Germany
Cunjian Chen	Monash, Australia
Cunyi Yin	Fuzhou University, Singapore
Damien Lolive	Université Rennes, CNRS, IRISA, France
Daniel Stamate	Goldsmiths, University of London, UK
Daniel Vašata	Czech Technical University in Prague, Czech Republic
Dario Pasquali	Istituto Italiano di Tecnologia, Italy
David Dembinsky	German Research Center for Artificial Intelligence, Germany
David Rotermund	University of Bremen, Germany
Davide Liberato Manna	University of Strathclyde, UK
Dehao Yuan	University of Maryland, USA
Denise Gorse	University College London, UK
Dennis Wong	Macao Polytechnic University, China
Des Higham	University of Edinburgh, UK
Devesh Jawla	TU Dublin, Ireland
Dimitrios Michail	Harokopio University of Athens, Greece
Dino Ienco	INRAE, France
Diptangshu Pandit	Teesside University, UK
Diyuan Lu	Helmholtz Center Munich, Germany
Domenico Tortorella	University of Pisa, Italy
Dominik Geissler	American Family Insurance, USA

DongNyeong Heo	Handong Global University, South Korea
Dongyang Zhang	University of Electronic Science and Technology of China, China
Doreen Jirak	Istituto Italiano di Tecnologia, Italy
Douglas McLelland	BrainChip, France
Douglas Nyabuga	Mount Kenya University, Rwanda
Dulani Meedeniya	University of Moratuwa, Sri Lanka
Dumitru-Clementin Cercel	University Politehnica of Bucharest, Romania
Dylan Muir	SynSense, Switzerland
Efe Bozkir	Uni Tübingen, Germany
Eleftherios Kouloumpris	Aristotle University of Thessaloniki, Greece
Elias Pimenidis	University of the West of England, UK
Eliska Kloberdanz	Iowa State University, USA
Emre Neftci	Foschungszentrum Juelich, Germany
Enzo Tartaglione	Telecom Paris, France
Erwin Lopez	University of Manchester, UK
Evgeny Mirkes	University of Leicester, UK
F. Boray Tek	Istanbul Technical University, Turkey
Federico Corradi	Eindhoven University of Technology, Netherlands
Federico Errica	NEC Labs Europe, Germany
Federico Manzi	Università Cattolica del Sacro Cuore, Italy
Federico Vozzi	CNR, Italy
Fedor Scholz	University of Tuebingen, Germany
Feifei Dai	Chinese Academy of Sciences, China
Feifei Xu	Shanghai University of Electric Power, China
Feixiang Zhou	University of Leicester, UK
Felipe Moreno	FGV, Peru
Feng Wei	York University, Canada
Fengying Li	Guilin University of Electronic Technology, China
Flora Ferreira	University of Minho, Portugal
Florian Mirus	Intel Labs, Germany
Francesco Semeraro	University of Manchester, UK
Franco Scarselli	University of Siena, Italy
François Blayo	IPSEITE, Switzerland
Frank Röder	Hamburg University of Technology, Germany
Frederic Alexandre	Inria, France
Fuchang Han	Central South University, China
Fuli Wang	University of Essex, UK
Gabriela Sejnova	Czech Technical University in Prague, Czech Republic
Gaetano Di Caterina	University of Strathclyde, UK
George Bebis	University of Nevada, USA

Gerrit Ecke	Mercedes-Benz, Germany
Giannis Nikolentzos	Ecole Polytechnique, France
Gilles Marcou	University of Strasbourg, France
Giorgio Gnecco	IMT School for Advanced Studies, Italy
Glauco Amigo	Baylor University, USA
Greg Lee	Acadia University, Canada
Grégory Bourguin	LISIC/ULCO, France
Guillermo Martín-Sánchez	Champalimaud Foundation, Portugal
Gulustan Dogan	UNCW, USA
Habib Khan	Islamia College University Peshawar, Pakistan
Haizhou Du	Shanghai University of Electric Power, China
Hanli Wang	Tongji University, China
Hanno Gottschalk	TU Berlin, Germany
Hao Tong	University of Birmingham, UK
Haobo Jiang	NJUST, China
Haopeng Chen	Shanghai Jiao Tong University, China
Hazrat Ali	Hamad Bin Khalifa University, Qatar
Hina Afridi	NTNU, Gjøvik, Norway
Hiroaki Aizawa	Hiroshima University, Japan
Hiromichi Suetani	Oita University, Japan
Hiroshi Kawaguchi	Kobe University, Japan
Hiroyasu Ando	Tohoku University, Japan
Hiroyoshi Ito	University of Tsukuba, Japan
Honggang Zhang	University of Massachusetts, Boston, USA
Hongqing Yu	Open University, UK
Hongye Cao	Northwestern Polytechnical University, China
Hugo Carneiro	University of Hamburg, Germany
Hugo Eduardo Camacho Cruz	Universidad Autónoma de Tamaulipas, Mexico
Huifang Ma	Northwest Normal University, China
Hyeyoung Park	Kyungpook National University, South Korea
Ian Nabney	University of Bristol, UK
Igor Farkas	Comenius University Bratislava, Slovakia
Ikuko Nishikawa	Ritsumeikan University, Japan
Ioannis Pierros	Aristotle University of Thessaloniki, Greece
Iraklis Varlamis	Harokopio University of Athens, Greece
Ivan Tyukin	King's College London, UK
Iveta Bečková	Comenius University in Bratislava, Slovakia
Jae Hee Lee	University of Hamburg, Germany
James Yu	Southern University of Science and Technology, China
Jan Faigl	Czech Technical University in Prague, Czech Republic

Jan Feber	Czech Technical University in Prague, Czech Republic
Jan-Gerrit Habekost	University of Hamburg, Germany
Jannik Thuemmel	University of Tübingen, Germany
Jeremie Cabessa	University Paris 2, France
Jérémie Sublime	ISEP, France
Jia Cai	Guangdong University of Finance & Economics, China
Jiaan Wang	Soochow University, China
Jialiang Tang	Nanjing University of Science and Technology, China
Jian Hu	YiduCloud, Cyprus
Jianhua Xu	Nanjing Normal University, China
Jianyong Chen	Shenzhen University, China
Jichao Bi	Zhejiang Institute of Industry and Information Technology, China
Jie Shao	University of Electronic Science and Technology of China, China
Jim Smith	University of the West of England, UK
Jing Yang	Hefei University of Technology, China
Jingyi Yuan	Arizona State University, USA
Jingyun Jia	Baidu, USA
Jinling Wang	Ulster University, UK
Jiri Sima	Czech Academy of Sciences, Czech Republic
Jitesh Dundas	Independent Researcher, USA
Joost Vennekens	KU Leuven, Belgium
Jordi Cosp	Universitat Politècnica de Catalunya, Spain
Josua Spisak	University of Hamburg, Germany
Jozef Kubík	Comenius University, Slovakia
Junpei Zhong	Hong Kong Polytechnic University, China
Jurgita Kapočiūtė-Dzikienė	Vytautas Magnus University, Lithuania
K. L. Eddie Law	Macao Polytechnic University, China
Kai Tang	Independent Researcher, China
Kamil Dedecius	Czech Academy of Sciences, Czech Republic
Kang Zhang	Kyushu University, Japan
Kantaro Fujiwara	University of Tokyo, Japan
Karlis Freivalds	Institute of Electronics and Computer Science, Latvia
Khoa Phung	University of the West of England, UK
Kiran Lekkala	University of Southern California, USA
Kleanthis Malialis	University of Cyprus, Cyprus
Kohulan Rajan	Friedrich Schiller University, Germany

Koichiro Yamauchi	Chubu University, Japan
Koloud Alkhamaiseh	Western Michigan University, USA
Konstantinos Demertzis	Democritus University of Thrace, Greece
Kostadin Cvejoski	Fraunhofer IAIS, Germany
Kristína Malinovská	Comenius University in Bratislava, Slovakia
Kun Zhang	Inria and École Polytechnique, France
Laurent Mertens	KU Leuven, Belgium
Laurent Perrinet	AMU CNRS, France
Lazaros Iliadis	Democritus University of Thrace, Greece
Leandro dos Santos Coelho	Pontifical Catholic University of Parana, Brazil
Leiping Jie	Hong Kong Baptist University, China
Lenka Tětková	Technical University of Denmark, Denmark
Lia Morra	Politecnico di Torino, Italy
Liang Ge	Chongqing University, China
Liang Zhao	Dalian University of Technology, China
Limengzi Yuan	Shihezi University, China
Ling Guo	Northwest University, China
Linlin Shen	Shenzhen University, China
Lixin Zou	Wuhan University, China
Lorenzo Vorabbi	University of Bologna, Italy
Lu Wang	Macao Polytechnic University, China
Luca Pasa	University of Padova, Italy
Ľudovít Malinovský	Independent Researcher, Slovakia
Luis Alexandre	Universidade da Beira Interior, Portugal
Luis Lago	Universidad Autonoma de Madrid, Spain
Lukáš Gajdošech Gajdošech	Comenius University Bratislava, Slovakia
Lyra Puspa	Vanaya NeuroLab, Indonesia
Madalina Erascu	West University of Timisoara, Romania
Magda Friedjungová	Czech Technical University in Prague, Czech Republic
Manuel Traub	University of Tübingen, Germany
Marcello Trovati	Edge Hill University, UK
Marcin Pietron	AGH-UST, Poland
Marco Bertolini	Pfizer, Germany
Marco Podda	University of Pisa, Italy
Markus Bayer	Technical University of Darmstadt, Germany
Markus Eisenbach	Ilmenau University of Technology, Germany
Martin Ferianc	University College London, Slovakia
Martin Holena	Czech Technical University, Czech Republic
Masanari Kimura	ZOZO Research, Japan
Masato Uchida	Waseda University, Japan
Masoud Daneshtalab	Mälardalen University, Sweden

Oleg Bakhteev	EPFL, Switzerland
Olga Grebenkova	Moscow Institute of Physics and Technology, Russia
Oliver Sutton	King's College London, UK
Olivier Teste	Université de Toulouse, France
Or Elroy	CLB, Israel
Oscar Fontenla-Romero	University of A Coruña, Spain
Ozan Özdenizci	Graz University of Technology, Austria
Pablo Lanillos	Spanish National Research Council, Spain
Pascal Rost	Universität Hamburg, Germany
Paul Kainen	Georgetown, USA
Paulo Cortez	University of Minho, Portugal
Pavel Petrovic	Comenius University, Slovakia
Peipei Liu	School of Cyber Security, University of Chinese Academy of Sciences, China
Peng Qiao	NUDT, China
Peter Andras	Edinburgh Napier University, UK
Peter Steiner	Technische Universität Dresden, Germany
Peter Sutor	University of Maryland, USA
Petia Georgieva	University of Aveiro/IEETA, Portugal
Petia Koprinkova-Hristova	Bulgarian Academy of Sciences, Bulgaria
Petra Vidnerová	Czech Academy of Sciences, Czech Republic
Philipp Allgeuer	University of Hamburg, Germany
Pragathi Priyadharsini Balasubramani	Indian Institute of Technology Kanpur, India
Qian Wang	Durham University, UK
Qinghua Zhou	King's College London, UK
Qingquan Zhang	Southern University of Science and Technology, China
Quentin Jodelet	Tokyo Institute of Technology, Japan
Radoslav Škoviera	Czech Technical University in Prague, Czech Republic
Raoul Heese	Fraunhofer ITWM, Germany
Ricardo Marcacini	University of São Paulo, Brazil
Riccardo Renzulli	University of Turin, Italy
Richard Duro	Universidade da Coruña, Spain
Robert Legenstein	Graz University of Technology, Austria
Rodrigo Clemente Thom de Souza	Federal University of Parana, Brazil
Rohit Dwivedula	Independent Researcher, India
Romain Ferrand	IGI TU Graz, Austria
Roman Mouček	University of West Bohemia, Czech Republic
Roseli Wedemann	Universidade do Estado do Rio de Janeiro, Brazil

Rufin VanRullen	CNRS, France
Ruijun Feng	China Telecom Beijing Research Institute, China
Ruxandra Stoean	University of Craiova, Romania
Sanchit Hira	JHU, USA
Sander Bohte	CWI, Netherlands
Sandrine Mouysset	University of Toulouse/IRIT, France
Sanka Rasnayaka	National University of Singapore, Singapore
Sašo Karakatič	University of Maribor, Slovenia
Sebastian Nowak	University Bonn, Germany
Seiya Satoh	Tokyo Denki University, Japan
Senwei Liang	LBNL, USA
Shaolin Zhu	Tianjin University, China
Shayan Gharib	University of Helsinki, Finland
Sherif Eissa	Eindhoven University of Technology, Afghanistan
Shiyong Lan	Independent Researcher, China
Shoumeng Qiu	Fudan, China
Shu Eguchi	Aomori University, Japan
Shubai Chen	Southwest University, China
Shweta Singh	International Institute of Information Technology, Hyderabad, India
Simon Hakenes	Ruhr University Bochum, Germany
Simona Doboli	Hofstra University, USA
Song Guo	Xi'an University of Architecture and Technology, China
Stanislav Frolov	Deutsches Forschungszentrum für künstliche Intelligenz (DFKI), Germany
Štefan Pócoš	Comenius University in Bratislava, Slovakia
Steven (Zvi) Lapp	Bar Ilan University, Israel
Sujala Shetty	BITS Pilani Dubai Campus, United Arab Emirates
Sumio Watanabe	Tokyo Institute of Technology, Japan
Surabhi Sinha	Adobe, USA
Takafumi Amaba	Fukuoka University, Japan
Takaharu Yaguchi	Kobe University, Japan
Takeshi Abe	Yamaguchi University, Japan
Takuya Kitamura	National Institute of Technology, Toyama College, Japan
Tatiana Tyukina	University of Leicester, UK
Teng-Sheng Moh	San Jose State University, USA
Tetsuya Hoya	Independent Researcher, Japan
Thierry Viéville	Domicile, France
Thomas Nowotny	University of Sussex, UK
Tianlin Zhang	University of Manchester, UK

Tianyi Wang	University of Hong Kong, China
Tieke He	Nanjing University, China
Tiyu Fang	Shandong University, China
Tobias Uelwer	Technical University Dortmund, Germany
Tomasz Kapuscinski	Rzeszow University of Technology, Poland
Tomasz Szandala	Wroclaw University of Technology, Poland
Toshiharu Sugawara	Waseda University, Japan
Trond Arild Tjostheim	Lund University, Sweden
Umer Mushtaq	Université Paris-Panthéon-Assas, France
Uwe Handmann	Ruhr West University, Germany
V. Ramasubramanian	International Institute of Information Technology, Bangalore, India
Valeri Mladenov	Technical University of Sofia, Bulgaria
Valerie Vaquet	Bielefeld University, Germany
Vandana Ladwani	International Institute of Information Technology, Bangalore, India
Vangelis Metsis	Texas State University, USA
Vera Kurkova	Czech Academy of Sciences, Czech Republic
Verner Ferreira	Universidade do Estado da Bahia, Brazil
Viktor Kocur	Comenius University, Slovakia
Ville Tanskanen	University of Helsinki, Finland
Viviana Cocco Mariani	PUCPR, Brazil
Vladimír Boža	Comenius University, Slovakia
Vojtech Mrazek	Brno University of Technology, Czech Republic
Weifeng Liu	China University of Petroleum (East China), China
Wenxin Yu	Southwest University of Science and Technology, China
Wenxuan Liu	Wuhan University of Technology, China
Wu Ancheng	Pingan, China
Wuliang Huang	ICT, China
Xi Cheng	NUPT, Hong Kong, China
Xia Feng	Civil Aviation University of China, China
Xian Zhong	Wuhan University of Technology, China
Xiang Zhang	National University of Defense Technology, China
Xiaochen Yuan	Macao Polytechnic University, China
Xiaodong Gu	Fudan University, China
Xiaoqing Liu	Kyushu University, Japan
Xiaowei Zhou	Macquarie University, Australia
Xiaozhuang Song	Chinese University of Hong Kong, Shenzhen, China

Invited Talks

Developmental Robotics for Language Learning, Trust and Theory of Mind

Angelo Cangelosi

University of Manchester and Alan Turing Institute, UK

Growing theoretical and experimental research on action and language processing and on number learning and gestures clearly demonstrates the role of embodiment in cognition and language processing. In psychology and neuroscience, this evidence constitutes the basis of embodied cognition, also known as grounded cognition (Pezzulo et al. 2012). In robotics and AI, these studies have important implications for the design of linguistic capabilities in cognitive agents and robots for human-robot collaboration, and have led to the new interdisciplinary approach of Developmental Robotics, as part of the wider Cognitive Robotics field (Cangelosi and Schlesinger 2015; Cangelosi and Asada 2022). During the talk we presented examples of developmental robotics models and experimental results from iCub experiments on the embodiment biases in early word acquisition and grammar learning (Morse et al. 2015; Morse and Cangelosi 2017) and experiments on pointing gestures and finger counting for number learning (De La Cruz et al. 2014). We then presented a novel developmental robotics model, and experiments, on Theory of Mind and its use for autonomous trust behavior in robots (Vinanzi et al. 2019, 2021). The implications for the use of such embodied approaches for embodied cognition in AI and cognitive sciences, and for robot companion applications, was also discussed.

Challenges of Incremental Learning

Barbara Hammer

CITEC Centre of Excellence, Bielefeld University, Germany

Smart products and AI components are increasingly available in industrial applications and everyday life. This offers great opportunities for cognitive automation and intelligent human-machine cooperation; yet it also poses significant challenges since a fundamental assumption of classical machine learning, an underlying stationary data distribution, might be easily violated. Unexpected events or outliers, sensor drift, or individual user behavior might cause changes of an underlying data distribution, typically referred to as concept drift or covariate shift. Concept drift requires a continuous adaptation of the underlying model and efficient incremental learning strategies. Within the presentation, I looked at recent developments in the context of incremental learning schemes for streaming data, putting a particular focus on the challenge of learning with drift and detecting and disentangling drift in possibly unsupervised setups and for unknown type and strength of drift. More precisely, I dealt with the following aspects: learning schemes for incremental model adaptation from streaming data in the presence of concept drift; various mathematical formalizations of concept drift and detection/quantification of drift based thereon; and decomposition and explanation of drift. I presented a couple of experimental results using benchmarks from the literature, and I offered a glimpse into mathematical guarantees which can be provided for some of the algorithms.

Reliable AI: From Mathematical Foundations to Quantum Computing

Gitta Kutyniok[1,2]

[1]Bavarian AI Chair for Mathematical Foundations of Artificial Intelligence, LMU Munich, Germany
[2]Adjunct Professor for Machine Learning, University of Tromsø, Norway

Artificial intelligence is currently leading to one breakthrough after the other, both in public life with, for instance, autonomous driving and speech recognition, and in the sciences in areas such as medical diagnostics or molecular dynamics. However, one current major drawback is the lack of reliability of such methodologies.

In this lecture we took a mathematical viewpoint towards this problem, showing the power of such approaches to reliability. We first provided an introduction into this vibrant research area, focussing specifically on deep neural networks. We then surveyed recent advances, in particular concerning generalization guarantees and explainability methods. Finally, we discussed fundamental limitations of deep neural networks and related approaches in terms of computability, which seriously affects their reliability, and we revealed a connection with quantum computing.

Intelligent Pervasive Applications for Holistic Health Management

Ilias Maglogiannis

University of Piraeus, Greece

The advancements in telemonitoring platforms, biosensors, and medical devices have paved the way for pervasive health management, allowing patients to be monitored remotely in real-time. The visual domain has become increasingly important for patient monitoring, with activity recognition and fall detection being key components. Computer vision techniques, such as deep learning, have been used to develop robust activity recognition and fall detection algorithms. These algorithms can analyze video streams from cameras, detecting and classifying various activities, and detecting falls in real time. Furthermore, wearable devices, such as smartwatches and fitness trackers, can also monitor a patient's daily activities, providing insights into their overall health and wellness, allowing for a comprehensive analysis of a patient's health. In this talk we discussed the state of the art in pervasive health management and biomedical data analytics and we presented the work done in the Computational Biomedicine Laboratory of the University of Piraeus in this domain. The talk also included Future Trends and Challenges.

Contents – Part V

A Multi-Task Instruction with Chain of Thought Prompting Generative Framework for Few-Shot Named Entity Recognition

WenJie Xu and JianQuan OuYang[✉]

Xiangtan University, Xiangtan, China
oyjq@xtu.edu.cn

Abstract. Few-shot Named Entity Recognition (NER) is the task of identifying new named entities using only a small number of labeled examples. Prompt-based learning has been successful in few-shot NER by using prompts to guide the labeling process and increase efficiency. However, previous prompt-based methods for few-shot NER have limitations such as high computational complexity and insufficient few-shot capability. To address these concerns, we propose a multi-task instruction framework called CotNER for Few-shot NER, which utilizes a chain-of-thought prompting generative approach. We introduce two auxiliary tasks, entity extraction and entity recognition, and integrate reasoning processes through chain-of-thought prompting. Our approach outperforms previous methods on various benchmarks, as demonstrated by extensive experiments.

Keywords: Chain of Thought · Multi-Task Instruction

1 Introduction

Named Entity Recognition (NER) is a fundamental task in natural language processing (NLP) that aims to identify significant information from raw text, such as people, locations, organizations, and so on. NER is often seen as a specific sequence labeling problem, where models built upon pre-trained language models (PLMs) have recently achieved significant improvements. A large number of neural network approaches based on PLMs have shown promising ability on the NER task. The current well-established approach to dealing with NER is to use PLMs combined with several NER paradigms trained on large corpora, such as the label classifier paradigm [3], machine reading comprehension paradigm [15], and unified generative paradigm [32]. However, the annotation resources for token labeling are often rare and expensive in the real world. Few-shot NER aims to recognize novel-class named entities based on only a few labeled examples. Thus, few-shot NER has garnered great attention in recent years [1,21].

L. Iliadis et al. (Eds.): ICANN 2023, LNCS 14258, pp. 1–15, 2023.
https://doi.org/10.1007/978-3-031-44192-9_1

A recent line of work investigates the setting of few-shot Named Entity Recognition by using Prompt Learning (PL) methods [1, 2, 11] and metric learning-based approaches [9, 29, 33, 34]. Prompt-based methods are proposed to exploit the knowledge of PLMs more effectively [1, 17]. PL is typically used to comprehend sentence-level problems by decoding a specific identifier of an input. However, adapting PL to token-level tasks where the class of each token must be recognized is difficult. **TemplateNER** [2], inspired by PL, applies manual templates to few-shot NER, which must enumerate all probable spans and propagate several times for each input. This method is inelegant and time-consuming. **BARTNER** [32] proposes a pointer-based seq2seq architecture that transforms NER subtasks into a unified sequence generation task and predicts entities from the input sentences and corresponding type indexes. **LightNER** [1] adds prompt-tuning to BARTNER's attention mechanism, providing new parameters to the attention layer as soft prompts and achieving promising improvements in low-resource scenarios.

Metric learning-based techniques have been observed to efficiently address few-shot NER challenges relative to the traditional TemplateNER. The core principle of this paradigm focused on acquiring a similarity metric that gauges semantic relations between samples for both query example and support example. However, significant domain gaps limit the effectiveness of these techniques due to their lack of adaptability to new domains. In other words, these techniques may fail to effectively incorporate information from the provided support samples.

Chain-of-Thought Prompting [30] introduces the concept of giving language models the ability to construct a coherent chain of thought-a set of intermediate reasoning processes that leads to the final solution to a problem. This paper proposes a multi-task instruction with a chain-of-thought prompting generative framework for few-shot NER, named CotNER, inspired by Chain of Thought. We reformulate the NER task as a natural language generation problem and design descriptive instructions for the source sentence. These instructions enable the model to understand different tasks, employ an option mechanism that includes all candidate entity categories as output space constraints, and build a chain of thought that leads to the final solution of a problem. Additionally, we introduce two auxiliary tasks, entity extraction (EE) and entity typing (ET). EE requires the model to decode only the entity names and learn to collect boundary information more accurately. ET's goal is to forecast only entity types and improve the PLM's knowledge of type semantics.

In summary, this paper makes three main contributions:

- We propose a multi-task instruction with chain of thought prompting generative framework for few-shot NER called CotNER, which solves the problem of few-shot NER with multi-task instruction and chain of thought prompting.
- Proposing two auxiliary tasks that improve the ability to capture entity boundaries and enhance understanding of type semantics.
- Conducting experiments on five different few-shot NER benchmarks across various domains, demonstrating that CotNER achieves highly competitive performance.

Table 1. An example of the simplest 2-way 1-shot setting, which contains two entity classes and each class has one example (shot) in the support set $\mathcal{S}$. Different colors indicate different entity classes.

Target Types $\mathcal{Y}$	[person-actor], [art-film]
Support set $\mathcal{S}$	(1) *Leonardo DiCaprio*[person-actor] has starred in many acclaimed films over his illustrious career
	(2) The science fiction thriller *Inception*[art-film] earned widespread critical acclaim for its original screenplay
Query Set $\mathcal{Q}$	In the biographical drama The Wolf of Wall Street, Leonardo DiCaprio delivered an Oscar-worthy performance
Expected output	In the biographical drama *The Wolf of Wall Street*[art-film], *Leonardo DiCaprio*[person-actor] delivered an Oscar-worthy performance

2 Task Definition

Given an input sequence $\boldsymbol{x} = \{x_i\}_{i=1}^{L}$ consisting of L tokens, an NER system is tasked with producing a label sequence $\boldsymbol{y} = \{y_i\}_{i=1}^{L}$, where each x_i denotes the i-th token, and $y_i \in \mathcal{Y} \cup \{0\}$ represents the label for x_i. Here, $\mathcal{Y}$ refers to the set of predefined entity classes, while 0 signifies non-entities.

The present study focuses on the standard N-way K-shot setting, as introduced in [6]. An instance of this scenario, involving a 2-way 1-shot episode, is depicted in Table 1. During the training phase, we examine training episodes $\mathcal{E}_{train} = \{(\mathcal{S}_{train}, \mathcal{Q}_{train}, \mathcal{Y}_{train})\}$ that are derived from labeled data within a source domain context. The support set, $\mathcal{S}_{train} = \{(\boldsymbol{x}^{(i)}, \boldsymbol{y}^{(i)})\}_{i=1}^{N \times K}$, comprises support samples, while $\mathcal{Q}_{train} = \{\boldsymbol{x}^{(j)}, \boldsymbol{y}^{(j)}\}_{j=1}^{N \times K'}$ represents the query set. Furthermore, $\mathcal{Y}_{train}$ specifies the entity class set, with $|\mathcal{Y}_{train}| = N$.

During the testing phase, we consider novel episodes $\mathcal{S}_{new} = \{(\boldsymbol{x}^{(i)}, \boldsymbol{y}^{(i)})\}_{i=1}^{N \times K}$ which are constructed analogously to those of the training set, but with target domain data. In the few-shot NER task, a model trained based on $\mathcal{S}_{train}$ must utilize the support set $\mathcal{S}_{new} = \{(\boldsymbol{x}^{(i)}, \boldsymbol{y}^{(i)})\}_{i=1}^{N \times K}$, which belongs to a novel episode $(\mathcal{S}_{new}, \mathcal{Q}_{new}, \mathcal{Y}_{new}) \in \mathcal{E}_{new}$, in order to make predictions regarding the query set $\mathcal{Q}_{new} = \{\boldsymbol{x}^{(j)}\}_{j=1}^{N \times K'}$. Notably, $\mathcal{Y}_{new}$ represents the entity class set associated $\mathcal{S}_{new}$ and $\mathcal{Q}_{new}$, and is of cardinality N. It should be emphasized that for any $\mathcal{Y}_{train}$ and $\mathcal{Y}_{new}$, their intersection is an empty set, indicated by the symbol $\mathcal{Y}_{train} \cap \mathcal{Y}_{new} = \emptyset$.

3 Methodology

In this section, we introduce the overall framework of our proposed CotNER. Figure 1 show the overall framework. We convert NER tasks to sequence-to-sequence (seq2seq) tasks and integrate chain of thought prompting methods. We propose two auxiliary tasks, named entity extraction and entity typing, which

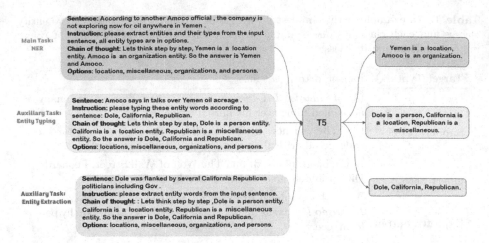

Fig. 1. Overview of our CotNER framework.

help the model to better identify the entities for both the boundary and the type.

We reformulate the NER challenge in the seq2seq form and solve it by fine-tuning T5 [24] to better transfer and leverage the knowledge obtained in pre-trained language models.

Specifically, each input consists of the four fields shown below:

- Sentence: the raw input sentence
- Instruction: Instructions are available in three forms, corresponding to each task. For the entity extraction task, the instruction is *please extract entity words from the input sentence*. For the entity typing task, the instruction is *please typing these entity words according to sentence:* . After the colon, add the entities collected from the entity extraction task. For the main task, the instruction is *please extract entities and their types from the input sentence, all entity types are in options*.
- Chain of Thought: Lets think step by step, x_i is a/an y_i entity, so the answer is x_i.
- Options: all entity types C.

The framework have three tasks, one primary and two auxiliary tasks. Each task has 4 components. Specifically, for the entity occurrence $\langle S, I, C, O \rangle$, we convert it to the natural language form using the template: x_i is a/an y_i and join all the transformed entity occurrences to form an output sentence (Separated by a comma and terminated by a dot).

Uniquely, we have devised two methods for populating the category 't' in the template. One method uses tokens or phrases that represent 't', such as using dual tokens like 'book title' to represent the entity category 'book_title'. The alternative approach is to use synthetic tokens that represent 't', such as using a single token <book_title> to represent the entity category "book_title". These novel tokens are added to the token vocabulary of pre-trained language models, while their embeddings are randomly initialised during the fine-tuning phase. In the course of our analytical experiments, we have compared the two methods and discovered interesting results.

Auxiliary Tasks: In order to enhance the performance of the model, we propose two auxiliary tasks, namely entity extraction and entity typing, which enable the model to capture more boundary information of entities and deepen the understanding of entity type semantics.

For the entity extraction task, we train the model to extract entities from the input sentences. The instruction is *"Please extract entity words from the input sentence"*. Inspired by Chain of Thought Prompting [12,30], and combined with the specificity of the NER task, we provide chain-of-thought prompting to the model along with the instruction. The entity extraction task only needs to extract entities and does not focus on the type of entities. Experiments show that this can significantly improve performance.

For the entity typing task, the model is trained to type the given entity occurrences in the sentence. Specifically, the instruction is *"Please type these entity words according to the sentence:"*. The colon is followed by the result of the entity extraction task. This promotes the model to create more correct category labels while preserving entity occurrence generation accuracy in the primary NER job, hence enhancing NER performance.

Chain-of-Thought Prompting: In principle, chain-of-thought prompting allows models to decompose multi-step problems into intermediate steps, which means that additional computation can be allocated to problems that require more reasoning steps. Chain-of-thought reasoning can be readily elicited in sufficiently large off-the-shelf language models simply by including examples of chain-of-thought sequences into the exemplars of few-shot prompting.

4   Experiments

4.1   Datasets

We conducted experiments to evaluate our proposed approach on two datasets.

Few-NERD [6]. Few-NERD contains 8 coarse-grained types, 66 fine-grained types, 188,200 sentences, 491,711 entities and 4,601,223 tokens. FewNERD consists of two tasks: Few-NERD-INTRA and Few-NERD-INTER. In **Few-NERD-INTRA**, the entities in the training set (source domain), validation set, and test set (target domain) all belong to different coarse-grained types. In **Few-NERD-INTER**, only the fine-grained entity types are mutually exclusive across different sets.

Cross-Dataset. We use CoNLL-2003 [25] as the rich-resource domain. Following the settings in [35] and [10], we utilize the Massachusetts Institute of Technology (MIT) Restaurant Review [19], MIT Movie Review [16], and Airline Travel Information Systems (ATIS) [8] datasets as cross-domain low-resource datasets.

4.2   Baselines

Regarding Few-NERD, our novel approach is pitted against an array of cutting-edge models, including ProtoBERT [26], ESD [29], CONTAINER [4], NNShot [31], StructShot [33], and methods from [6], BARTNER [32], and LightNER [1].
   In the realm of Cross Dataset, our groundbreaking technique is subjected to a rigorous evaluation process that encompasses Template [2], BARTNER [32], LightNER [1], InstructionNER [28], as well as two other noteworthy methodologies: LC-BERT and LC-BART, which employ traditional sequence labeling methods for named entity recognition implemented with BERT and BART technology, respectively.
   1) NNShot [31] is a simple method based on token-level nearest neighbor classification. **2) StructShot** [33] adopts an additional Viterbi decoder based on NNShot. **3)TemplateNER** is a method proposed by [2], which uses a BART-based seq2seq structure model to type all the enumerated spans by completing the human-designed template in line with the cloze task. **4) ESD** [29] is a span-level metric learning approach that enhances prototypical networks by employing inter-span and cross-span attention for improved span representation and designing multiple prototypes for the O label. **5) LightNER** [1] has a similar architecture with BART, but they introduce a prompt-guided attention mechanism, which is the only tuned module in the training process. **6) InstructionNER** is a multi-task instruction-based generative framework for few-shot NER. **7) Cot-NER** is trained without auxiliary task and $CotNER_{EE/ET/EE,ET}$ is trained with the ET/EE/both auxiliary tasks and $CotNER_{EE,ET,cot}$ is trained with both auxiliary tasks with Chain-of-Thought Prompting.

4.3   Implementation Details

We implement our approach with PyTorch 1.12.0[1]. We use the T5v1.1-large[2] model. The released version 1.1 of T5-large, which is pretrained on C4 only without mixing in the downstream tasks.We train all models for 1,000 steps and choose the best model with the validation set. We use a batch size of 8, maximum sequence length of 512, and a dropout probability of 0.2. The learning rate of the Adam optimizer is set to $2e-5/5e-5$, and the decoding beam search size is set to 2 to ensure more stable results and faster decoding speeds.

---

[1] https://pytorch.org/.
[2] https://huggingface.co/google/t5-v1_1-large.

4.4   Evaluation

For evaluation on Few-NERD, we use episode evaluation as in [6] and calculate precision (P), recall (R), and micro F1-score (F1) across all test episodes. For evaluation on Cross-Dataset, we calculate P, R, and F1 within each episode, then average the results over all episodes, as in [9]. For all results, we report the mean and standard deviation based on five runs with different seeds.

Table 2. F1 scores with standard deviations on Few-NERD for both inter and intra settings. [†] denotes the results reported in [6]. The best results are in **bold**.

Models	Intra				Inter			
	1–2-shot		5–10-shot		1–2-shot		5–10-shot	
	5 way	10 way	5 way	10 way	5 way	10 way	5 way	10 way
ProtoBERT[†]	23.45±0.92	19.76±0.59	41.93±0.55	34.61±0.59	44.44±0.11	39.09±0.87	58.80±1.42	53.97±0.38
NNShot[†]	31.01±1.21	21.88±0.23	35.74±2.36	27.67±1.06	54.29±0.40	46.98±1.96	50.56±3.33	50.00±0.36
StructShot[†]	35.92±0.69	25.38±0.84	38.83±1.72	26.39±2.59	57.33±0.53	49.46±0.53	57.16±2.09	49.39±1.77
CONTAINER	40.43	33.84	53.70	47.49	55.95	48.35	61.83	57.12
ESD	36.08±1.6	30.00±0.70	52.14±1.5	42.15±2.6	59.29±=1.25	52.16±0.79	**69.06±0.80**	64.00±0.43
Ours	**43.66±0.50**	**36.75±0.75**	**55.36±0.60**	**49.56±0.45**	**61.10±0.55**	**54.20±0.49**	62.01±0.50	**66.50±0.42**

Table 3. F1 score on three datasets under different shot settings. The value in brackets represents the standard deviation. The best results are in **bold**, "*" indicates our reproduction results.

Methods	MIT Movie			MIT Restaurant			ATIS		
	10	20	50	10	20	50	10	20	50
Baselines									
LC-BERT	25.2	42.2	49.6	21.8	39.4	52.7	44.1	76.7	90.7
LC-BART	10.2	27.5	44.2	6.3	8.5	51.3	42.0	72.7	87.5
Template	37.3	48.5	52.2	46.0	57.1	58.7	71.7	79.4	92.6
BARTNER*	41.1	54.0	67.7	44.0	56.0	64.0	77.7	86.1	93.4
LightNER	41.7	57.8	73.1	48.5	58.0	62.0	76.3	85.3	92.8
InstructionNER	65.7	70.1	74.7	58.9	66.1	71.1	90.6	93.0	95.3
Our implementations									
CotNER	65.1 (1.2)	72.2 (0.4)	74.1 (0.7)	60.7 (0.6)	67.2 (0.4)	72.4 (0.4)	91.9 (0.4)	92.2 (0.4)	94.1 (0.5)
CotNER+ET	65.9 (1.1)	73.3 (0.6)	75.6 (0.2)	61.1 (0.4)	69.2 (0.7)	72.8 (0.9)	91.5 (0.2)	94.1 (0.3)	**95.3** (0.6)
CotNER+EE	68.3 (1.4)	71.8 (0.4)	77.1 (0.6)	61.4 (0.8)	68.5 (0.7)	73.2 (0.9)	91.5 (0.4)	93.3 (0.2)	93.4 (0.4)
CotNER+ET,EE	67.3 (2.1)	74.1 (1.6)	76.7 (0.6)	62.9 (0.6)	70.1 (0.8)	74.1 (0.7)	92.1 (0.4)	93.0 (0.1)	94.6 (0.3)
CotNER+ET,EE,Cot	**69.1 (1.5)**	**75.3 (1.2)**	**78.7 (0.7)**	**63.5 (0.8)**	**71.3 (0.7)**	**75.6 (0.9)**	**92.4 (0.4)**	**94.6 (0.1)**	93.1 (0.5)

4.5   Results

Table 2 and Table 3 show the comparison results between our method and previous state-of-the-art methods for Few-NERD and Cross-Dataset, respectively. We can draw the following conclusions: 1) Our novel approach surpasses its predecessors by a significant margin, with performance improvements that reach up to 7.08 F1 scores on Few-NERD (intra, 5 way 1–2shot), and 3.4 F1 scores on MIT Movie. These results are a testament to the efficacy of our approach. 2) In Few-NERD, the overall performance of the Intra scenario is inferior to that of the Inter scenario. This is attributable to the inherent challenge posed by Intra, wherein coarse-grained types differ between train/dev/test sets. Nevertheless, despite these challenges, our approach consistently achieves satisfactory effectiveness. These results suggest that our method is capable of adapting to novel domains in which both coarse-grained and fine-grained entity types are unseen. 3) CotNER+ET,EE,Cot achieves a 3.4, 5.2, and 4 improvement on F1 score and an average improvement of 4.6, 5.2, and 4.5 on F1 score in MIT Movie and MIT Restaurant datasets. The results show that by converting the task into natural language instructions with options and Chain of Thought Prompting, our approach demonstrates strong generalization capabilities, effectively minimizing the impact of insufficient data.

4.6   Ablation Analysis

To evaluate the contributions of various components in the proposed approach, we present the following variants and baseline models for ablation study: 1) CotNER+ET, which adds the entity typing task. 2) CotNER+EE, which adds the entity extraction task. 3) CotNER+ET, EE, which adds both the entity extraction task and the entity typing task. 4) CotNER+ET, EE, Cot, which adds entity extraction task, entity typing task, and Chain of Thought Prompting.

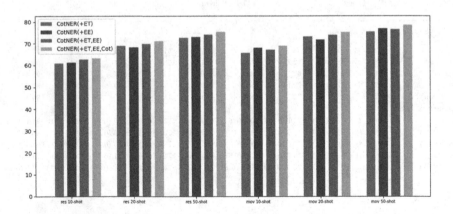

Fig. 2. Performance comparison between T5-natural and InstructionNER on.

Table 3 illustrates the contributions of each component in our proposed approach. Generally, eliminating any of them will result in a decrease in performance. We can also draw some in-depth observations as follows: 1) CotNER+ET, EE, Cot outperforms ours CotNER+ET, EE indicate that exploring the information contained in support examples with the proposed Chain of Thought Prompting brings performance gains for few-shot transfer. 2) CotNER+ET, EE outperforms CotNER indicate that two auxiliary tasks bring performance gains for few-shot transfers.

Auxiliary Tasks. Table 3 and Fig. 2 shows that using ET, EE auxiliary tasks, and Chain of Thought Prompting can further enhance the performance of InstructionNER in low-resource NER settings. Specifically, in typical low-resource settings of 10/20/50 shot, our models achieved an average improvement of 4.6/5.2/4.5% points in F1 score on the MIT Restaurant dataset. Entity extraction and typing enable the model to capture more details about entities and provide a deeper understanding of entity type semantics. Auxiliary tasks can deliver huge performance gains. We noticed a decrease in performance when we combined the ET and EE tasks. We believe the cause of this is the reduced data size ratio between the main task and the auxiliary tasks, which is now 1:2 with the introduction of ET and EE. This may introduce some noise to the main task.

Chain of Thought Prompting. Table 3 and Fig. 2 shows that adding Chain of Thought Prompting performs better than not adding them. This shows that the addition of auxiliary tasks to the Chain of Thought Prompting is effective and can bring performance gains to the T5 model. Chain-of-thought reasoning can be identified in large language models by including examples of chain-of-thought sequences in the few-shot prompting exemplars. This method of prompting can help the model generate a more comprehensive understanding of the natural language task at hand. By providing the model with a deeper understanding of the language, it can be better equipped to recognize the tendencies and patterns of chain-of-thought reasoning. This, in turn, allows the model to draw on its understanding of language to accurately predict the results of a chain-of-thought sequence. In addition, providing examples of chain-of-thought sequences in the few-shot prompting exemplars provides a clear, transparent understanding of the model's behavior and explains how it arrived at a particular result. This is an invaluable tool for improving the accuracy and robustness of language models, as it enables researchers to better understand the nuances of chain-of-thought reasoning and apply them to the development of more effective models.

Table 4. An analysis of errors in 5-way 1–2 shot on FewNERD-INTER indicates that "FP-Span" represents extracted entities with incorrect span boundaries, and "FP-Type" denotes entities that have correct span boundaries but are assigned incorrect entity types. The total number of erroneous predictions across both types is denoted by "Total."

Models	F1	Total	FP-Span	FP-Type
CotNER	**61.10**	**8.6k**	79.4%	20.6%
ProtoBERT	38.83	30.4k	86.7%	13.3%
NNShot	47.24	21.7k	84.7%	15.3%
StructShot	51.88	14.5k	80.0%	20.0%
ESD	59.29	9.4k	72.8%	27.2%

4.7   Error Analysis

To gain a detailed understanding of the types of errors made by the model, we divided the model prediction errors into two categories: FP-Span and FP-Type. As shown in Table 4, CotNER outperformed baselines and produced significantly fewer false positive prediction errors. Although FP-Span is the most common prediction error across all models, indicating the difficulty in locating the correct span boundary in few-shot NER, CotNER has a lower ratio of FP-Span errors compared to previous methods. We attribute this improvement to the auxiliary tasks of entity extraction and entity typing in CotNER, which played a crucial role in the model training process. Additionally, encouraging a logical sequence of thought during inference aided in improving the model's performance.

4.8   Label Semantic Analysis

As expounded in Sect. 3, there are two techniques employed for populating entity types in templates. The first involves utilizing natural language forms, whilst the second entails treating type words as synthesized tokens and subsequently integrating them into the vocabulary. CotNER can, quite intuitively, leverage the semantic information present in synthesized tokens to enhance the model's performance in low-resource scenarios. To thoroughly explore the impact of these strategies on CotNER's efficacy, we have crafted multiple experimental scenarios, spanning from 10-shot to fully supervised, on both the MIT Movie dataset and MIT Restaurant dataset. As illustrated in Fig. 3, our observations reveal that: 1) when synthesized tokens serve as entity types, the model's performance is worse in low-shot scenarios. 2) Curiously, however, when evaluating resource-rich settings, the strategy of using synthesized tokens outperforms all other strategies. We speculate that this outcome may be attributed to the following conjectures: 1) In low-resource scenarios, the semantic information inherent in the natural language form of synthesized tokens could aid in simulating latent knowledge obscured within the PLM and generating entity words with greater precision - a feat that synthesized tokens alone cannot accomplish. 2) Conversely, when adequate supervision signals exist, synthesized tokens gradually assimilate specific semantic relationships pertaining to the task at hand, whereas the original meanings of label words in natural language forms may impede the specialization process of these words.

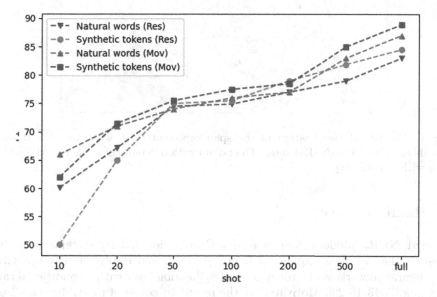

Fig. 3. F1 score on the MIT Restaurant (res) and the MIT Movie (mov) datasets using two different word type strategies under different shot settings.

4.9 Visualizations

This section culminates in an exploration of how CotNER acquires the semantic space's representations. We selected a 5-way 5–10 shot episode data from FewN-ERD Inter at random and generated a visualization using the t-SNE toolkit. Figure 4 evidences that CotNER adeptly clusters representations of corresponding entity classes while diffusing those of divergent ones. We further observed, owing to the proposed multi-task learning, that most erroneous results can be effectively distinguished from accurate ones.

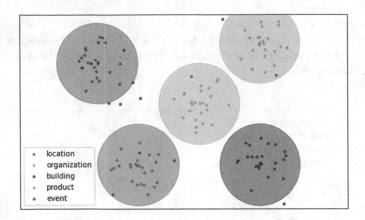

Fig. 4. The t-SNE visualization of the span representations with 5-way 5–10-shot episode data from Few-NERD Inter. The points with different colors denote the entity span with different types.

5   Related Work

Neural NER. Modern Named Entity Recognition (NER) systems typically consider the task as a sequence labeling problem and resolve it by employing deep neural networks and a token-level classification layer with a conditional random field [5,13,18,22]. Motivated by the recent successes of pre-trained seq2seq models, we have reformulated all three types of NER subtasks as a generation problem and proposed a pointer-based framework to inference entities as well as their type index using BART [15]. In this new formulation, we treat NER as a natural language generation task, requiring the model to generate entity names and corresponding types in the form of natural language. Furthermore, we have employed T5 as our base model instead of BART, as the pre-training task of T5 is to predict the sequence of corrupted tokens, which is more suitable for our purpose.

Meta-learning. Meta-learning also known as "learning to learn", aims to quickly train models to adapt to new tasks with minimal training samples. Prototype-based methods, which involve meta-learning, have recently become popular approaches in the field of low-resource NER. These methods are particularly useful for few-shot learning. There are typically three categories of meta-learning approaches: black-box adaptation-based methods [14], optimization-based methods [27], and metric learning-based methods [7]. Some approaches, such as MAML [7] and Reptile [23], are optimization-based. Their goal is to train a meta learner to optimize or adjust the optimization process.

Prompt-Based Few-Shot NER. Recently, more researchers have focused on a new fine-tuning paradigm called prompt-based learning. This new paradigm can utilize the knowledge learned in the pretraining stage to achieve better performance in few-shot scenarios. TemplateNER [2] proposed a time-consuming template-based BART for few-shot NER. Template-freeNER [20] proposed an entity-oriented method that fine-tunes the language model to predict class-related label words instead of the original words. This method was inspired by prompt tuning. LightNER [1] has incorporated continuous prompts into the self-attention matrix, resulting in a semantic-aware answer space that supersedes label-specific layers. However, the effectiveness of these methods heavily depends on the chosen prompt. The author notes that the performance difference can be significant based on the prompt used. Consequently, without a substantial validation set, their usefulness is limited for true few-shot learning. Unlike their approach, we inject task instructions, answer options, and Chain of thought prompting into the source sentences. This allows us to elicit more natural language knowledge from the pre-trained model in a few-shot setting.

6   Conclusion

In this paper, we redefine the task of sequence labeling as a problem of generation, and introduce an innovative multi-task instruction with Chain of Thought Prompting generative framework for few-shot NER. By constructing sentences rooted in descriptive task instructions, limited answer options, and chain of thought prompting, CotNER maximizes the utilization of semantic knowledge acquired by Pre-trained language models. Additionally, we integrate two supplementary tasks to empower the model with the capacity to capture more boundary information of entities and the semantics of types. Our experiments on several NER datasets consistently demonstrate the superiority of our method over other baselines, evidencing its efficacy in few-shot contexts.

Acknowledgments. This research has been supported by Key Projects of the Ministry of Science and Technology of the People Republic of China (2020YFC0832401).

References

1. Chen, X., et al.: LightNER: a lightweight tuning paradigm for low-resource NER via pluggable prompting. In: Proceedings of the 29th International Conference on Computational Linguistics, pp. 2374–2387 (2022)
2. Cui, L., Wu, Y., Liu, J., Yang, S., Zhang, Y.: Template-based named entity recognition using BART. In: Findings of the Association for Computational Linguistics: ACL-IJCNLP 2021, pp. 1835–1845. Association for Computational Linguistics, Online, August 2021. https://doi.org/10.18653/v1/2021.findings-acl.161, https://aclanthology.org/2021.findings-acl.161
3. Cui, L., Zhang, Y.: Hierarchically-refined label attention network for sequence labeling. arXiv preprint arXiv:1908.08676 (2019)
4. Das, S.S.S., Katiyar, A., Passonneau, R.J., Zhang, R.: CONTaiNER: few-shot named entity recognition via contrastive learning. In: ACL (2022)

5. Devlin, J., Chang, M.W., Lee, K., Toutanova, K.: BERT: pre-training of deep bidirectional transformers for language understanding. arXiv preprint arXiv:1810.04805 (2018)
6. Ding, N., et al.: Few-NERD: a few-shot named entity recognition dataset. In: Proceedings of the 59th Annual Meeting of the Association for Computational Linguistics and the 11th International Joint Conference on Natural Language Processing (vol. 1: Long Papers), pp. 3198–3213. Association for Computational Linguistics, Online (2021). https://doi.org/10.18653/v1/2021.acl-long.248, https://aclanthology.org/2021.acl-long.248
7. Finn, C., Abbeel, P., Levine, S.: Model-agnostic meta-learning for fast adaptation of deep networks. In: International Conference on Machine Learning, pp. 1126–1135. PMLR (2017)
8. Hakkani-Tür, D., et al.: Multi-domain joint semantic frame parsing using bidirectional RNN-LSTM. In: Interspeech, pp. 715–719 (2016)
9. Hou, Y., et al.: Few-shot slot tagging with collapsed dependency transfer and label-enhanced task-adaptive projection network. arXiv preprint arXiv:2006.05702 (2020)
10. Huang, J., et al.: Few-shot named entity recognition: a comprehensive study. arXiv preprint arXiv:2012.14978 (2020)
11. Huang, Y., et al.: COPNER: contrastive learning with prompt guiding for few-shot named entity recognition. In: Proceedings of the 29th International Conference on Computational Linguistics, pp. 2515–2527 (2022)
12. Kojima, T., Gu, S.S., Reid, M., Matsuo, Y., Iwasawa, Y.: Large language models are zero-shot reasoners. arXiv preprint arXiv:2205.11916 (2022)
13. Lafferty, J.D., McCallum, A., Pereira, F.C.N.: Conditional random fields: probabilistic models for segmenting and labeling sequence data. In: Brodley, C.E., Danyluk, A.P. (eds.) Proceedings of the Eighteenth International Conference on Machine Learning (ICML 2001), Williams College, Williamstown, MA, USA, 28 June–1 July 2001, pp. 282–289. Morgan Kaufmann (2001)
14. Lample, G., Ballesteros, M., Subramanian, S., Kawakami, K., Dyer, C.: Neural architectures for named entity recognition. arXiv preprint arXiv:1603.01360 (2016)
15. Li, X., Feng, J., Meng, Y., Han, Q., Wu, F., Li, J.: A unified MRC framework for named entity recognition. In: Proceedings of the 58th Annual Meeting of the Association for Computational Linguistics, pp. 5849–5859. Association for Computational Linguistics, Online, July 2020. https://doi.org/10.18653/v1/2020.acl-main.519, https://aclanthology.org/2020.acl-main.519
16. Liu, J., Pasupat, P., Cyphers, S., Glass, J.: Asgard: a portable architecture for multilingual dialogue systems. In: 2013 IEEE International Conference on Acoustics, Speech and Signal Processing, pp. 8386–8390. IEEE (2013)
17. Liu, Q., Lin, H., Xiao, X., Han, X., Sun, L., Wu, H.: Fine-grained entity typing via label reasoning. arXiv preprint arXiv:2109.05744 (2021)
18. Liu, T., Yao, J.G., Lin, C.Y.: Towards improving neural named entity recognition with gazetteers. In: Proceedings of the 57th Annual Meeting of the Association for Computational Linguistics, pp. 5301–5307 (2019)
19. Liu, Y., Meng, F., Zhang, J., Xu, J., Chen, Y., Zhou, J.: GCDT: a global context enhanced deep transition architecture for sequence labeling. arXiv preprint arXiv:1906.02437 (2019)
20. Ma, R., et al.: Template-free prompt tuning for few-shot NER. In: Proceedings of the 2022 Conference of the North American Chapter of the Association for Computational Linguistics: Human Language Technologies, pp. 5721–5732. Association

for Computational Linguistics, Seattle, United States, July 2022. https://doi.org/10.18653/v1/2022.naacl-main.420, https://aclanthology.org/2022.naacl-main.420

21. Ma, T., Jiang, H., Wu, Q., Zhao, T., Lin, C.Y.: Decomposed meta-learning for few-shot named entity recognition. arXiv preprint arXiv:2204.05751 (2022)

22. Ma, X., Hovy, E.: End-to-end sequence labeling via bi-directional LSTM-CNNs-CRF. arXiv preprint arXiv:1603.01354 (2016)

23. Nichol, A., Achiam, J., Schulman, J.: On first-order meta-learning algorithms. arXiv preprint arXiv:1803.02999 (2018)

24. Raffel, C., et al.: Exploring the limits of transfer learning with a unified text-to-text transformer. J. Mach. Learn. Res. 21(140), 1–67 (2020)

25. Sang, E.F., De Meulder, F.: Introduction to the CoNLL-2003 shared task: language-independent named entity recognition. arXiv preprint cs/0306050 (2003)

26. Snell, J., Swersky, K., Zemel, R.S.: Prototypical networks for few-shot learning. In: Guyon, I., et al. (eds.) Advances in Neural Information Processing Systems: Annual Conference on Neural Information Processing Systems, 4–9 December 2017, Long Beach, CA, USA, vol. 30, pp. 4077–4087 (2017). https://proceedings.neurips.cc/paper/2017/hash/cb8da6767461f2812ae4290eac7cbc42-Abstract.html

27. Vinyals, O., Blundell, C., Lillicrap, T., Wierstra, D., et al.: Matching networks for one shot learning. In: Advances in Neural Information Processing Systems, vol. 29 (2016)

28. Wang, L., et al.: InstructionNER: a multi-task instruction-based generative framework for few-shot NER. arXiv preprint arXiv:2203.03903 (2022)

29. Wang, P., et al.: An enhanced span-based decomposition method for few-shot sequence labeling. arXiv preprint arXiv:2109.13023 (2021)

30. Wei, J., et al.: Chain of thought prompting elicits reasoning in large language models. arXiv preprint arXiv:2201.11903 (2022)

31. Wiseman, S., Stratos, K.: Label-agnostic sequence labeling by copying nearest neighbors. arXiv preprint arXiv:1906.04225 (2019)

32. Yan, H., Gui, T., Dai, J., Guo, Q., Zhang, Z., Qiu, X.: A unified generative framework for various NER subtasks. arXiv preprint arXiv:2106.01223 (2021)

33. Yang, Y., Katiyar, A.: Simple and effective few-shot named entity recognition with structured nearest neighbor learning. arXiv preprint arXiv:2010.02405 (2020)

34. Yu, D., He, L., Zhang, Y., Du, X., Pasupat, P., Li, Q.: Few-shot intent classification and slot filling with retrieved examples. arXiv preprint arXiv:2104.05763 (2021)

35. Ziyadi, M., Sun, Y., Goswami, A., Huang, J., Chen, W.: Example-based named entity recognition. arXiv preprint arXiv:2008.10570 (2020)

ANODE-GAN: Incomplete Time Series Imputation by Augmented Neural ODE-Based Generative Adversarial Networks

Zhuoqing Chang[1] , Shubo Liu[1(✉)] , Zhaohui Cai[1], and Guoqing Tu[2]

[1] School of Computer Science, Wuhan University, Wuhan 430072, China
{changzhuoqing,liu.shubo,zhcai}@whu.edu.com
[2] School of Cyber Science and Engineering, Wuhan University, Wuhan 430072, China

Abstract. Missing data is a commonly encountered problems in time series analysis, impeding accurate data analysis. Various methods have been proposed to impute missing values, including statistical, machine learning, and deep learning approaches. However, these methods either involve multi-steps, neglect temporal information, or are incapable of imputing missing data at desired time points. To overcome these limitations, this paper proposes a novel generative framework for imputing missing data, named the Augmented Neural Ordinary Differential Equation-assisted Generative Adversarial Network (ANODE-GAN). ANODE-GAN utilizes a Variational AutoEncoder (VAE) module to maps an incomplete time series instance to fixed-dimension initial latent vectors, generates continuous-time latent dynamics, and finally decodes them into complete data. With the aid of an additional discriminative network, ANODE-GAN can produce complete data that is closest to the original time series according to the squared error loss. By combining the generator and discriminator, ANODE-GAN is capable of imputing missing data at any desired time point while preserving the original feature distributions and temporal dynamics. Moreover, ANODE-GAN is evaluated on real-world datasets with varying missing rates by conducting the imputation task. A set of rigorous experiments show ANODE-GAN outperforms baseline methods in terms of Mean Square Error (MSE).

Keywords: Incomplete Time Series · Generative Adversarial Networks · Augment Neural ODEs

1 Introduction

The past few decades have witnessed a surge in time series data, which has become ubiquitous across a diverse range of applications including finance, healthcare, environmental science, and transportation. Consequently, the analysis of time series has gained immense popularity. However, practical time series

L. Iliadis et al. (Eds.): ICANN 2023, LNCS 14258, pp. 16–27, 2023.
https://doi.org/10.1007/978-3-031-44192-9_2

data are easily trapped into the missing values problem due to sensor malfunctions, interruptions in data transmission, and human errors. Furthermore, some data are sampled at irregular frequencies for cost-saving purposes, such as blood pressure, heart rate measurements in the medical field. These incomplete time series data hinder the application of existing data analysis methods.

Generally, there are two approaches to processing incomplete time series data. The first and simplest approach involves omitting missing data that accounts for less than 15% of the total and making inferences using only the remaining data [2]. However, this method has significant limitations as it discards historical data and ignores potentially valuable hidden information [3]. The second two-stage methodology is a natural solution for this issue. The irregular timespan is divided into uniform intervals, and missing values are imputed or filled by statistical learning [4] or machine learning-based methods [5]. An adverse effect of this discretization is inevitably destroying the measurement timing information that might be informative about latent variables [6,7]. The additional data imputation method operates independently from subsequent data analysis, often leading to suboptimal results.

These issues can be tackled by incorporating time information directly into deep learning models to model the raw data more effectively. A small trick is to concatenate time information to the input of Recurrent Neural Networks (RNNs) [6,8]. Time interval information is further incorporated into the models, allowing them to learn changes in different sampling intervals, such as Gated Recurrent Unit with Decay (GRU-D) [7] and Bidirectional recurrent imputation for time series (BRITS) [9]. Generative Adversarial Networks (GANs) have gained a lot of notoriety. Strenuous efforts have been made to employ a bidirectional RNN in the generator network to learn the distribution of the incomplete data [10,11]. Another line of work attempts to optimize the noise input vector to make the generated sample obey the original distribution, which spends much time finding the best matched input vector [12]. An end-to-end GAN-based imputation model (E2GAN) is proposed to learn high-dimensional data distributions of incomplete time series by the auto-encoder strategy, which is effective to avoid the process of noise optimization [13]. Unfortunately, these methods are unable to impute missing data at desired time points.

This paper proposes a novel generative framework, called Augmented Neural Ordinary Differential Equation-assisted Generative Adversarial Network (ANODE-GAN), to overcome the aforementioned challenges. ANODE-GAN is designed based on a GAN network, consisting of a VAE-based generator and a discriminator. In the generator, a time-aware LSTM (TA-LSTM) learns to encode incomplete time series instance into fixed-dimension initial latent vectors by perceiving the impact of the previous observation. An Augmented Neural Ordinary Differential Equation (ANODE) infers continuous-time latent dynamics by utilizing the posterior distribution of the initial latent state. A fully connected network decodes the latent dynamics into a complete time series. Additionally, a fully connected layer serves as the discriminator to distinguish true from false elements. The generator not only spares no effort to learn continuous latent dynamics of time series and construct the complete time series data, but also deceives the discriminator. By using the generator and the discriminator, ANODE-GAN can automatically learn the original feature distributions and temporal dynamics from incomplete time series, generate latent states at any desired time points and reconstruct these temporal data. This model improves imputation accuracy by more effectively modeling latent dynamics, primarily due to the suitable encoder, stable flow learned from time series to continuous hidden dynamic in an augmented space, and the efficacy of additional discriminator network. The proposed method is evaluated on real-world datasets with varying missing rates. Extensive experiments indicate ANODE-GAN achieves superior imputation accuracy compared to existing methods.

To conclude, the contributions of this paper can be summarized as follows:

- This paper proposes a novel generative framework, ANODE-GAN, to address the issue of missing data in real-world time series data. The proposed framework is capable of imputing data at any desired time and simplifying the data imputation process.
- This is the first work that imputes missing data of incomplete time series by applying ANODEs to the GAN framework, the generator of which employs a TA-LSTM network to compute approximate posterior from partial observations and an ANODE to model more complex functions using simpler flows with improved stability and generalization.
- The ANODE-GAN model is applied to three real-world time series datasets with varying degrees of missing data for the purpose of imputation. Results demonstrate that this method outperforms existing methods in terms of imputation accuracy.

2   Proposed Method

This section presents the proposed ANODE-GAN algorithm to address the issue of incomplete time series analysis. As the framework is shown in Fig. 1, the algorithm is designed under the GAN network, which consists of a generator and a discriminator playing a min-max game [18].

2.1   Generator Network Architecture

A d-dimensional time series $X = \{x_1, x_2, \ldots, x_n\} \in R^{d \times n}$ is observed at $T = \{t_1, t_2, \ldots, t_n\}$, where t is the sampling timestep and x_t is the tth observation. Missing data happens sometimes. Missing values can be indicated by a mask matrix $M = \{m_1, m_2, \ldots, m_n\} \in \{1, 0\} \in R^{d \times n}$ with the same dimension, where m_t is 1 if x_t is revealed and 0 if x_t is missing.

The generator of proposed method is presented in Fig. 1, which is designed based on a VAE framework including a TA-LSTM encoder, an ANODE network and a fully connected decoder.

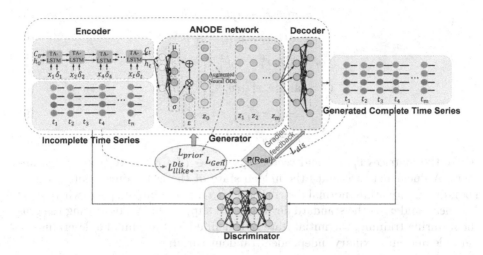

Fig. 1. The proposed ANODE-GAN framework. The generator generates complete data by learning the continuous-time latent dynamics of the incomplete time series. The discriminator employs a fully connected network to predict the truth probability.

Time information is especially important in incomplete time series. On one hand, the time points are closely related to missing rates, on the other, nonuniform time intervals clearly reflect the impact of the previous observation. The RNNs cannot handle nonuniform time interval between successive elements. Inspired by [14], TA-LSTM is employed as the encoder to learn the posterior distribution from partially-observed trajectories. It is of great significance to control the influential decay of the past observation on the current moment. It will introduce a time decay function $\beta(\delta_i^t)$ to modify memory cells, which is validated by previous works [14,19]. Compared with LSTM, the previous memory cell C_{t-1} is TA-LSTM is divided into a short-term memory C_{t-1}^S and a long-term memory C_{t-1}^L. $\beta(\delta_i^t)$ is used to decay the historical influence of the past data on C_{t-1}^S got through a linear network. C_{t-1}^L is obtained by interpolation of C_{t-1} and C_{t-1}^S. An adjusted previous memory $C_{t-1}^{'}$ is established by the sum of C_{t-1}^L and $\beta(\delta_i^t)C_{t-1}^S$. The rest of the calculation process is consistent with the traditional LSTM, only replacing C_{t-1} with $C_{t-1}^{'}$. The update function of TA-LSTM is summarized below:

$$\beta(\delta_i^t) = \frac{1}{\log(e + \delta_i^t)} \tag{1}$$

$$C_{t-1}^S = \tanh(\omega_s C_{t-1} + b_s) \tag{2}$$

$$C_{t-1}^L = C_{t-1} - C_{t-1}^S \tag{3}$$

$$C_{t-1}^{'} = C_{t-1}^L + \beta(\delta_i^t) \times C_{t-1}^S \tag{4}$$

$$f_t = \sigma(v_f x_i^t + u_f h_i^{t-1} + b_f) \tag{5}$$

$$i_t = \sigma(v_i x_i^t + u_i h_i^{t-1} + b_i) \tag{6}$$

$$o_t = \sigma(v_o x_i^t + u_o h_i^{t-1} + b_o) \tag{7}$$

$$\widetilde{C} = \tanh(v_c x_i^t + u_c h_i^{t-1} + b_c) \tag{8}$$

$$C_t = f_t * C_{t-1}^{'} + i_t * \widetilde{C} \tag{9}$$

$$h_t = o_t \circ \tanh(C_t) \tag{10}$$

where the matrices v_p, u_p, and vectors b_p for $p \in \{f, i, o, c\}$ are training parameters. A linear network maps the hidden state of the last moment into a corresponding multivariate normal distribution $\mathcal{N}(\mu_z, \sigma_z)$ in latent space, where μ_z is the mean and σ_z is the standard deviation. To support backpropagating the gradient during training, the initial state z_0 is defined by the sum of a deterministic variable and an auxiliary independent random variable ε.

$$z_0 = \mu_z + \sigma_z \circ \varepsilon \tag{11}$$

where $\circ$ defines the element-wise product and $\varepsilon \sim \mathcal{N}(0, I)$.

Recently, Neural ODEs have been flagged as a possible solution for the continuous-time dynamics modeling, describing the input to output variable transformation by a continuous representation of trajectory through a vector field defined by a neural network [15, 16]. Motivated by [17], ANODEs are used to generate latent states of any desired time $T^{'} = \{t_1, t_2, \ldots, t_n\}$, which use the additional dimensions in latent states to avoid trajectories intersecting each other. As presented in Fig. 1, the initial state learn from the last hidden state of TA-LSTM encoder is concatenated with a vector of zeros, which enables to learn more complex latent dynamics using simpler flows.

The continuous time latent states finally flow to another fully connected layer, which will decode the latent state to a generated data $X^{'}$.

The ANODE-GAN mainly performs the imputation task, which is designed based a VAE framework. The loss function of the generator includes two parts, one is Kullback-Leibler (KL) penalty $L_{prior} = D_{KL}[q_\phi(z \mid x) \parallel p_\theta(z)]$ and the other is the reconstruction error $E_{z \sim q_\phi(z|x)}[log p_\theta(x \mid z)]$. The following describes the total loss L_{Gen}.

$$L_{Gen} = -E_{z \sim q_\phi(z|x)}[log p_\theta(x \mid z)] + D_{KL}[q_\phi(z \mid x) \parallel p_\theta(z)] \tag{12}$$

2.2 Discriminator Network Architecture

The discriminator consists of three fully connected layers to learn a global contextual information. It aimed to identify whether each data in the completed time series is real or imputed rather than distinguish the whole completed vector is true of fake. To get an estimated probability that illustrates the degree of authenticity, *tanh* is used as the activation function in the first two layers and sigmoid activation function is adopted in the last layer. The discriminator updates a set of parameters that generates large probability when real data is encountered and low probability when false data is coming. Thus, the loss function of can be expressed as follows.

$$L_{Dis} = -(E[logD(X)] + E[log(1 - D(X^{'}))])$$ (13)

where D is the estimated mask probability of the discriminator. The discriminator attempts to make log output of prediction on real data close to 1 (the first term) and minizine the loss for imputed data (the second term).

The generator aims at the imputed data closer to the truth ones by fooling the discriminator D. The adversarial loss of generator can be calculated as follows:

$$L_{adv} = E[\log(1 - D(X^{'}))]$$ (14)

2.3 Training of ANODE-GAN

The total training loss of ANODE-GAN is expressed as the following shows.

$$L_{ANODE-GAN} = \lambda_G L_{Gen} + L_{adv}$$ (15)

where λ_G is hyper-parameter. The lose function can be trained by the BPTT algorithm. The ANODE-GAN provides an adversary strategy for incomplete time series imputation. The discriminator D is trained with the truth data and imputed completed data, and the mask matrix effectively provides supervision on the imputed data, making the generated data closer to the real data.

3 Experimental

In this section, the proposed ANODE-GAN method is evaluated on three real-world datasets with missing values. Results of this experiment are provided and further analyzed in details.

3.1 Datasets and Baseline Models

Three datasets including a Gas dataset, a GAMS dataset and an Electricity dataset are used to evaluate the proposed ANODE-GAN algorithm.

Gas Sensor Array Temperature Modulation Dataset[1]: The dataset contains 13 text files that corresponds to a different measurement day. Each file records a time-dependent multivariate response of 14 MOX gas sensors to the different gas stimuli every 0.3 s. The evaluation data selected in this paper is recorded on October 5, 2016, with more than 90,909 pieces of data.

---

[1] Gas sensor array temperature modulation Data Set. Available on: https://archive.ics.uci.edu/ml/datasets/Gas+sensor+array+temperature+modulation.

GAMS[2]: It is a public complete air quality dataset published by the gams Environmental Monitoring company (denoted as GAMS). The GAMS indoor data is selected in this paper, air quality of which is collected every minute between 2016/11/21 to 2017/3/28. CO_2, Humidity, PM10, PM2.5, Temperature, and Voc in GAMS are measured more than 130,000 times as independent variables.

Electricity[3]: It is a widely-used University of California Irvine (UCI) public dataset. The electricity consumption in kWh is recorded every 15 min between 2012/01/01 to 2014/12/31 for 321 clients, which has no missing data. The data in this paper is converted to express hourly consumption.

The proposed ANODE-GAN method is compared with the following baselines.

Gated Recurrent Unit (GRU) [1]: Gated Recurrent Unit. An improved version of RNN that is capable of capturing long-term temporal dependencies.

GRU-D [7]: A hidden state decay mechanism is introduced in the GRU model to deal with the missing data issue.

Time-Aware LSTM (T-LSTM) [14]: Another kind of LSTM that improves the internal structure to tackle the irregular time interval issue.

Latent ODE [15]: It is one of advanced imputation method based on VAE, where continues time latent states generated by neural ODEs according to the initial state learned from a RNN encoder will be decoded to impute the missing values.

ODERNN-VAE [16]: An additional ODE is used in the encoder to better learn the approximate posterior than RNN on sparse data.

ANODE [17]: An additional vector of zeros is concatenated with the initial state to avoid latent trajectories intersecting each other.

Adversarial Joint-Learning Recurrent Neural Network (AJ-RNN) [20]: It is GAN-based imputation method that trained in an adversarial and joint learning manner where a discriminator is introduced to minimize the negative impact of missing data in the generator.

3.2   Creating Missing Data

The missing data in this paper assumes the missing completely at random (MCAR) regime. For imputation task, this paper randomly drops out k percent of time series, where $p \in \{10, 20, \dots, 70\}$. The incomplete time series are imputed by the proposed ANODE-GAN method and comparison methods. MSE is used to calculated the imputation accuracy.

---

[2] GAMS Indoor Air Quality Dataset. Available on: https://github.com/twairball/gams-dataset.

[3] ElectricityLoadDiagrams20112014 Data Set. Available on: https://archive.ics.uci.edu/ml/datasets/ElectricityLoadDiagrams20112014.

3.3   Imputation Performance Comparison for Incomplete Time Series

In implementation, for all baseline models, batch size is 50, learning rate is 0.001, dropout rate is 0.5, and training epoch is 1500. The hyper-parameters λ_G of the generator is 1 for Gas and 0.5 for Gams and 0.3 for Electricity, which is determined based on the results of the ablation study below. The dimensionality of the latent states in Gas, Gams and Electricity is 30, 60, and 132. The ADAM algorithm is adopted to train all the networks. For all the experiments, input data are normalized with zero mean and unit variance, and 80% of dataset as selected as train set and the rest 20% as test set.

Table 1. The MSE results of ANODE-GAN and comparison methods on the Gas dataset.

Missing Rate (%)	GRU	GRU-D	T-LSTM	Latent ODE	ODERNN-VAE	ANODE	AJ-RNN	ANODE-GAN
0	.0565	.0482	.0144	.0321	.0224	.0195	.1004	.0166
10	.0703	.0624	.1076	.0166	.0170	.0199	.1171	.0169
20	.0962	.0737	.2031	.0162	.0164	.0177	.1162	.0153
30	.1250	.1153	.2961	.0246	.0226	.0345	.1403	.0161
40	.1614	.1518	.3892	.0223	.0211	.0281	.1442	.0159
50	.2017	.1907	.4818	.0285	.0194	.0206	.1468	.0165
60	.2572	.3056	.5799	.0259	.0275	.0251	.1675	.0160
70	.3245	.4011	.6742	.0290	.0287	.0286	.2377	.0165

Table 1 presents the imputation results on Gas dataset by using ANODE-GAN and baseline methods including GRU, GRUD, T-LSTM, Latent ODE, ODERNN-VAE, Augmented ODE, and AJ-RNN. The first column in Table 1 is missing rate that represents how many percent values are randomly dropped and other columns and other columns denote MSE results of corresponding imputation methods in terms of corresponding data missing rate. It can be observed that ANODE-GAN achieves the best imputation accuracy in high missing-rate cases. Additionally, imputation accuracy of most traditional methods worsens with increasing missing rate.

Conventional algorithms including GRU, GRU-D and T-LSTM gain relatively high imputation accuracy when missing rate is less than 10%. With higher missing rate, these methods cannot accurately infer the missing values, because they impute missing values by hidden state of previous moment. AJ-RNN does not generate imaginatively accurate imputation values, because it utilizes RNNs to model the captured data and cannot learn the distribution with missing values. Imputation results using ODE-based methods maintain good within varying missing rates. Such methods can model the original incomplete data distribution by a VAE structure and learn the continuous-time latent dynamics via an ODE model. The proposed method takes advantage of GANs to model the incomplete data distribution to generate more accurate imputed values.

Table 2 also presents the imputation performance on the Gams dataset using the proposed ANODE-GAN and various comparison methods. As expected, when the amount of missing data exceeds 10%, the proposed method wins others methods in most cases. This demonstrates that the augmented neural ODE coupled with an additional discriminative network has much higher utility for the missing data imputation.

Table 2. Performance (MSE) of imputation task using the Gams dataset.

Missing Rate (%)	GRU	GRU-D	T-LSTM	Latent ODE	ODERNN-VAE	ANODE	AJ-RNN	ANODE-GAN
0	.0058	.0060	.0050	.0484	.0478	.0531	.0933	.0481
10	.0473	.0448	.1059	.0457	.0461	.0532	.1002	.0477
20	.0908	.0886	.2110	.0497	.0506	.0538	.1138	.0483
30	.1367	.1275	.3105	.0528	.0577	.0717	.0957	.0514
40	.1804	.1752	.4182	.0557	.0546	.0580	.0982	.0535
50	.2329	.2216	.5195	.0526	.2322	.0575	.1073	.0513
60	.2831	.2639	.6280	.0598	.0669	.5689	.0971	.0577
70	.3306	.3081	.7198	.0623	.0596	.0657	.1227	.0543

Table 3. Performance comparison on different imputation models in the Electricity dataset with different missing rates.

Missing Rate (%)	GRU	GRU-D	T-LSTM	Latent ODE	ODERNN-VAE	ANODE	AJ-RNN	ANODE-GAN
0	.0917	.0922	.0835	.2176	.2363	.1896	.3417	.1836
10	.1281	.1598	.1936	.2134	.2681	.1643	.3230	.1667
20	.1635	.2169	.2955	.2548	.2741	.1806	.3071	.1669
30	.2031	.2349	.3946	.2401	.2826	.1905	.2887	.1858
40	.2539	.2770	.4886	.2160	.2408	.1713	.2846	.1691
50	.3164	.3329	.5729	.5937	.2456	.2187	.2884	.1811
60	.3935	.4142	.6571	.5448	.3467	.2405	.2757	.1780
70	.5048	.5274	.7431	.5929	.2540	.1803	.2889	.1773

In order to further verify the effectiveness of ANODE-GAN, the imputation task is also tested on a larger dataset with 321 dimensions. Table 3 shows MSE results tested on the Electricity dataset with different missing rates using ANODE-GAN and baseline algorithms. There is no doubt that the experimental results are consistent with the previous conclusion. The TA-LSTM is capable of learning the unequal time interval and effectively inferring the posterior distribution of irregularly-sampled time series data. The additional discriminative network makes the imputed complete time series closest to the original incomplete data. Furthermore, to present the efficiency of each module in the proposed method, ablation study will be presented in the latter part of this paper.

3.4   Model Analysis

Impact of Hyper-parameter

This paper explores the influence of hyper-parameter λ_G in the imputation task as presented in Fig. 2. The black line represents the MSE result of the imputation task of the hyper-parameter influence in the Gas dataset, and the red line and blue line are impact of the hyper-parameter on the Gams dataset and the Electricity dataset, respectively. The imputation performances vary with the change of hyper-parameter. Too large or too small hyper-parameter makes the MSE indicator rise. This indicates that the loss function of the discriminator makes great contribution to the imputation result. As can be seen, the blue curve reaches the bottom when λ_G is 0.1. The red and black curves get the lowest point when λ_G is 0.5 and 1. Specifically, the large dimension of the electricity dataset make loss of the generator L_{Gen} much larger than the loss of the discriminator L_{adv}, and the hyper-parameter need to reduce the L_{Gen} to make the adversarial network work when the imputation task is executed. On the contrary, the dimensions of Gams and Gas datasets are relatively small, and λ_G needs to be set a little larger. Conclusion can be drawn that it is necessary to adjust the loss proportion of generator and discriminator loss in order to maximize imputation accuracy of the ANODE-GAN method.

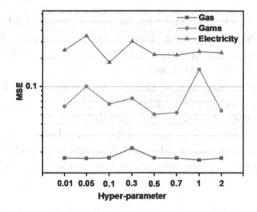

Fig. 2. The influence of hyper-parameter in the imputation task when missing rate is 50%. (Color figure online)

Ablation Study

An ablation study is provided to evaluate the insights and impact of the discriminator and the latent state augment of proposed models. Table 4 presents the imputation results on the Gas dataset, the Gams dataset and the Electricity dataset with a variety of missing rates (measured by MSE). The first ablated model is ANODE-GAN with no latent state augment (ANODE-GAN-no-augment) and the second is ANODE-GAN with no discriminator (ANODE-GAN-no-D). The last model is the proposed ANODE-GAN model. As expected, the discriminator and the latent state augment are of vital significance to missing data imputation. Evaluated on three datasets, the imputation accuracy decreases without the discriminator or latent augment.

Table 4. The ablation study of discriminator and latent state augment.

Model	Dataset	Missing Rate (%)							
		0	10	20	30	40	50	60	70
ANODE-GAN -no-augment	Gas	.0252	.0178	.0175	.0173	.0220	.0309	.0313	.0342
	Gams	.0458	.0572	.0522	.0684	.0623	.0513	.0630	.0612
	Electricity	.2891	.2895	.1677	.2525	.2768	.2505	.1949	.1803
ANODE-GAN -no-D	Gas	.0241	.0214	.0214	.0201	.0194	.0171	.0231	.0225
	Gams	.0484	.0464	.0542	.0570	.0598	.1526	.0685	.0710
	Electricity	.2745	.2321	.1679	.5990	.1839	.2365	.1894	.1778
ANODE-GAN	Gas	.0166	.0169	.0153	.0161	.0159	.0165	.0160	.0165
	Gams	.0481	.0477	.0483	.0514	.0535	.0505	.0577	.0543
	Electricity	.1836	.1667	.1669	.1858	.1691	.1811	.1780	.0543

4 Conclusion

This paper introduces a novel generative framework called ANODE-GAN, which is capable of imputing missing data at any desired time point. To the best of our knowledge, this paper is the first to use ANODEs in a GAN framework for data imputation. With an additional discriminative network, ANODE-GAN employs the KL penalty, the reconstruction error, and the adversarial loss to generate complete time series that are closest to the original incomplete data. Extensive empirical studies on real-world datasets show that the proposed method improves the accuracy of incomplete time series imputation. Investigating how to make combination of neural controlled differential equations and the GAN framework suitable for dealing with incomplete graph time series data remains to be done in the future work.

Acknowledgments. This work was supported by the Major Projects of Technical Innovation of Hubei Province under Grant 2018AAA046.

References

1. Qing, T., Fang, L., Yong, L., Denis, S.: Air pollution forecasting using a deep learning model based on 1D convnets and bidirectional GRU. IEEE Access **7**(5), 76690–76698 (2019)
2. Graham, J.W.: Missing data analysis: making it work in the real world. Annu. Rev. Psychol. **60**(1), 549–576 (2009)
3. Tian, W., Haoxiong, K., Alireza, J., Sheng, W., Mohammad, H.S., Shuqiang, H.: Missing value filling based on the collaboration of cloud and edge in artificial intelligence of things. IEEE Trans. Industr. Inf. **18**(8), 5394–5402 (2021)

4. Bengio, Y., Gingras, F.: Recurrent neural networks for missing or asynchronous data. In: 9th Conference on Neural Information Processing Systems (NeurIPS), vol. 8 (1995)
5. Hudak, A.T., Crookston, N.L., Evans, J.S., Hall, D.E., Falkowski, M.J.: Nearest neighbor imputation of species-level, plot-scale forest structure attributes from LiDAR data. Remote Sens. Environ. **112**(5), 2232–2245 (2008)
6. Lipton, Z.C., Kale, D., Wetzel, R.: Directly modeling missing data in sequences with RNNs: improved classification of clinical time series. In: Machine Learning for Healthcare Conference, pp. 253–270 (2016)
7. Che, Z., Purushotham, S., Cho, K., Sontag, D., Liu, Y.: Recurrent neural networks for multivariate time series with missing values. Sci. Rep. **8**(1), 1–12 (2018)
8. Choi, E., Bahadori, M.T., Schuetz, A., Stewart, W.F., Sun, J.: Doctor AI: predicting clinical events via recurrent neural networks. In: Machine Learning for Healthcare Conference, pp. 301–318 (2016)
9. Cao, W., Wang, D., Li, J., Zhou, H., Li, L., Li, Y.: BRITS: bidirectional recurrent imputation for time series. In: 32th Conference on Neural Information Processing Systems (NeurIPS), vol. 31 (2018)
10. Miao, X., Wu, Y., Wang, J., Gao, Y., Mao, X., Yin, J.: Generative semi-supervised learning for multivariate time series imputation. In: 35th Proceedings of the AAAI Conference on Artificial Intelligence (AAAI), vol. 35 (2021)
11. Gupta, M., Beheshti, R.: Time-series imputation and prediction with bi-directional generative adversarial networks. arXiv preprint arXiv:2009.08900 (2020)
12. Yoon, J., Jordon, J., Schaar, M.: Gain: missing data imputation using generative adversarial nets. In: 35th International Conference on Machine Learning (ICML), pp. 5689–5698 (2018)
13. Luo, Y., Zhang, Y., Cai, X., Yuan, X.: E^2GAN: end-to-end generative adversarial network for multivariate time series imputation. In: Proceedings of the 28th International Joint Conference on Artificial Intelligence (IJCAI), pp. 3094–3100 (2019)
14. Baytas, I.M., Xiao, C., Zhang, X., Wang, F., Jain, A.K., Zhou, J.: Patient subtyping via time-aware LSTM networks. In: Proceedings of the 23rd ACM SIGKDD International Conference on Knowledge Discovery and Data Mining, pp. 65–74 (2017)
15. Chen, R.T., Rubanova, Y., Bettencourt, J., Duvenaud, D.K.: Neural ordinary differential equations. In: 32th Conference on Neural Information Processing Systems (NeurIPS), vol. 31 (2018)
16. Rubanova, Y., Chen, R.T., Duvenaud, D.K.: Latent ordinary differential equations for irregularly-sampled time series. In: 33th Conference on Neural Information Processing Systems (NeurIPS), vol. 32 (2019)
17. Dupont, E., Doucet, A., Teh, Y.W.: Augmented neural ODEs. In: 33th Conference on Neural Information Processing Systems (NeurIPS), vol. 32 (2019)
18. Creswell, A., White, T., Dumoulin, V., Arulkumaran, K., Sengupta, B., Bharath, A.A.: Generative adversarial networks: an overview. IEEE Signal Process. Mag. **35**(1), 53–65 (2018)
19. Zhang, Y.: ATTAIN: attention-based time-aware LSTM networks for disease progression modeling. In: Proceedings of the 28th International Joint Conference on Artificial Intelligence (IJCAI), pp. 4369–4375 (2019)
20. Ma, Q., Li, S., Cottrell, G.W.: Adversarial joint-learning recurrent neural network for incomplete time series classification. IEEE Trans. Pattern Anal. Mach. Intell. **44**(4), 1765–1776 (2020)

Boosting Adversarial Transferability Through Intermediate Feature

Chenghai He[1,2,3], Xiaoqian Li[3], Xiaohang Zhang[3], Kai Zhang[3], Hailing Li[3], Gang Xiong[1,2(✉)], and Xuan Li[3(✉)]

[1] Institute of Information Engineering, Chinese Academy of Science, Beijing, China
{hechenghai,xionggang}@iie.ac.cn
[2] School of Cyber Security, University of Chinese Academy of Sciences, Beijing, China
[3] CNCERT/CC, Beijing, China
{hechenghai,lxq,zhangxiaohang,zhangkai,lihailing,lixuan}@cert.org.cn

Abstract. Deep neural networks are well known to be vulnerable to adversarial samples in the white-box setting. However, as research progressed, researchers discovered that adversarial samples can perform black-box attacks, that is, adversarial samples generated on the original model can cause models with different structures from the original model to misidentify. A large number of methods have recently been proposed to improve the transferability of adversarial samples, but the majority of them have low transferability. In this paper, we propose an intermediate feature-based attack algorithm to improve the transferability of adversarial samples even further. Rather than generating adversarial samples directly from the original samples, we continue to optimize existing adversarial samples to improve attack transferability. To begin, we calculate the feature importance of the original samples using existing adversarial samples. Then, we analyze which features are more likely to produce adversarial samples with high transferability. Finally, we optimize those features to improve the attack transferability of the adversarial samples. Furthermore, rather than using the model's logit output, we generate adversarial samples using the model's intermediate layer output. Extensive experiments on the standard ImageNet dataset show that our method improves transferability and outperforms state-of-the-art methods.

Keywords: Adversarial Attacks · Neural Network Models

1 Introduction

Many researchers have been drawn to neural network algorithms' sensitivity to adversarial samples as they have made breakthroughs in many computer vision fields, including image recognition [21], object detection [31], semantic classification [30], and face recognition [13]. Adversarial samples are generated by adding perturbations to the original samples, which has a devastating impact on the models [9,10,18]. The emergence of adversarial samples has triggered

L. Iliadis et al. (Eds.): ICANN 2023, LNCS 14258, pp. 28–39, 2023.
https://doi.org/10.1007/978-3-031-44192-9_3

two major research directions: the first is to improve the attack ability of the adversarial samples as much as possible [6, 8, 12, 17, 26], and the second is to strive to improve the model's defense capability against adversarial samples [1, 29, 32]. Similar to the relationship between the spear and the shield, the enhancement of one's ability will inevitably lead to the enhancement of the other's ability.

There are two types of adversarial attack algorithms: white-box attacks, in which the parameters and architecture of the model are accessible, and black-box attacks, in which the parameters and architecture of the model are unknown. Many algorithms for white-box adversarial attacks have been developed, including one-step gradient-based attacks [5, 25], iterative gradient-based attacks [14, 20], and optimization-based attacks [2], all of which have achieved excellent results in white-box attacks. Furthermore, adversarial samples generated using white-box attacks can sometimes successfully attack irrelevant models. This phenomenon is commonly referred to as "transferability".

In general, the black-box attack almost always has a lower success rate than the white-box attack, implying that the white-box attack overfits the source model [8]. Adversarial attack algorithms all strive to improve their attack capabilities, such as FGSM [5], which performs a one-step update along the gradient of the loss function, I-FGSM [14], which extends the FGSM attack algorithm, MI-FGSM [3], which incorporates the momentum method into I-FGSM, and DIM [27], TIM [4], SIM [16], which perform input transformation to improve the attack ability of the adversarial samples. However, the majority of them are not specifically designed for transferability.

Furthermore, most algorithms treat features of one sample equally without considering the difference in feature importance, which makes the adversarial samples generated based on those algorithms easier to overfit. In order to consider the importance of features in the process of generating adversarial samples, Wang et al. [26] propose the feature importance-aware transferable attack (FIA), which adapts random pixel dropping with a certain probability. If the model's logit output is more similar to the true label of the sample, the retained features are more important, and vice versa.

From another perspective, can we determine the importance of a feature by increasing or decreasing the value of the pixel, rather than dropping the pixel? And how can the pixel be altered to determine the importance of the feature?

This paper gets the feature importance by taking the derivative of the perturbation of the existing adversarial sample relative to the original sample on the output of the intermediate layer. Furthermore, the adversarial samples generated by the other adversarial attack algorithms cannot be expected to have optimal transferability, but the adversarial samples show the direction of optimization [8, 15].

Previous papers have proved that intermediate features of well-trained models are transferable [28], and perturbing the feature space of a deep model to generate more transferable adversarial samples [11, 12, 19].

Moreover, our experiments also show that one layer produces more transferable samples than another, and intermediate feature representations of deep learning models with fundamentally different architectures are highly similar.

The contributions of this paper are as follows:

- This paper proposes an innovative Intermediate Feature-based Attack (IFA) algorithm that improves the transferability of adversarial samples by adjusting the perturbation on pre-trained adversarial samples.
- This paper calculates the feature importance of the original samples to identify those features that are more likely to lead the model to misclassify, and then we use these features to improve the performance of the adversarial samples.
- This paper generates adversarial samples using the model output rather than the sample labels in order to achieve data-free. Even if we don't know the labels of the samples, we can also generate adversarial samples.
- Extensive experiments on various classification models show that the adversarial samples produced by the proposed IFA algorithm have better transferability than state-of-the-art transferable attack methods. The code is available at github.com.

2 Related Work

Let x be an original image, y be the true label of x, x' be an adversarial sample generated by another attack method for x and $f(x; \theta)$ be a classification model with parameters θ. Let $J(x, y; \theta)$ denote the loss function of a classification model f, $f_k(x)$ denote the k-th intermediate layer output, and $\mathcal{B}_\epsilon(x) = \left\{ x' : \|x - x'\|_p \leq \epsilon \right\}$ denotes the ℓ_p-norm ball centered at x with radius ϵ.

Fast Gradient Sign Method (FGSM) [5] is the first gradient-based attack algorithm, which performs the one-step update along the direction of the gradient of the loss function $J(x, y_{true})$.

$$x^{adv} = x + \epsilon \operatorname{sign}\left(\nabla_x J\left(x, y_{\text{true}}\right)\right) \tag{1}$$

Iterative Fast Gradient Sign Method (I-FGSM) [14] executes the FGSM attack algorithm T times with small step size and intercepts the adversarial samples to the valid range each time.

$$x_{t+1}^{adv} = \operatorname{Clip}\left\{ x_t^{adv} + \alpha \operatorname{sign}\left(\nabla_x J\left(\theta, x_t^{adv}, y\right)\right) \right\} \tag{2}$$

Momentum Iterative Fast Gradient Sign Method (MI-FGSM) [3] introduces the momentum method into the I-FGSM attack algorithm.

$$g_{t+1} = \mu \cdot g_t + \frac{\nabla_x J\left(\theta, x_t^{adv}, y\right)}{\left\|\nabla_x J\left(\theta, x_t^{adv}, y\right)\right\|_1}$$
$$x_{t+1}^{adv} = \operatorname{Clip}\left\{ x_t^{adv} + \alpha \operatorname{sign}\left(g_{t+1}\right) \right\} \tag{3}$$

Diverse Input Method (DIM) [27] applies random resizing and padding of the input samples with a certain probability and feeds the transformed samples into the classification model to improve the transferability of the adversarial samples.

Translation-Invariant Method (TIM) [4] adopts a set of images to calculate the gradient for the update. To further improve the efficiency of the calculation, TIM shifts the samples by small magnitudes and approximates the gradients.

Scale-Invariant Method (SIM) [16] discovers the scale-invariant property and computes the gradient of a set of samples, scaled by a factor of $1/2^i$ on the input image, to boost the transferability of the generated adversarial samples.

3   Methodology

3.1   Feature Importance

To get the feature importance, we use the k-th intermediate layer output $f_k(x)$, the logit output $f(x)$ and $f(x^{adv})$ to obtain the gradient w.r.t $f_k(x)$ as follows,

$$\Delta_k^{x,x^{adv}} = \frac{\partial l\left(f(x), f(x^{adv})\right)}{\partial f_k(x)} \tag{4}$$

where $l(\cdot, \cdot)$ denotes the similarity of the logit output of the model for x and x^{adv}. To improve the effectiveness of the algorithm, we also use aggregate gradient [12], which aggregates gradients from randomly transformed x, the formula is as follows,

$$\bar{\Delta}_k^x = \frac{1}{C} \sum_{n=1}^{N} \Delta_k^{x+(x'-x)\odot M_{p_d}^n}, M_{p_d} \sim \mathrm{B}\left(1 - p_d\right) \tag{5}$$

where M_{p_d} denotes a binary matrix with the same size as the input x, $\odot$ indicates the element-wise product, C denotes the size of ℓ_2-norm on the corresponding summation term, N indicates the number of random masks applied to x.

In our algorithm, $\bar{\Delta}_k^x$ denotes the feature importance, the larger the absolute value of $\bar{\Delta}_k^x$, the more likely the perturbation of this position pixel is to improve the adversarial transferability of the adversarial samples, and the sign of $\bar{\Delta}_k^x$ represent the direction of perturbation.

3.2   Adversarial Samples Generation

We regard the feature importance as a coefficient, and the output of the intermediate layer is used as an input, the loss of the adversarial samples can be obtained by the following function [26]:

$$\mathcal{L}\left(x^{adv}\right) = \sum\left(\Delta \odot f_k\left(x^{adv}\right)\right) \tag{6}$$

where Δ denotes $\bar{\Delta}_k^x$, and the same goes for the rest of this paper. And then, we aim to decrease the value of features with negative Δ and increase the value of features with positive Δ. Finally, we get the proposed objective function for the intermediate feature-based attack as follows.

$$\arg\max_{x^{adv}} \mathcal{L}\left(x^{adv}\right), \text{ s.t. } \left\|x - x^{adv}\right\|_{\infty} \leq \epsilon \tag{7}$$

To solve the above objective function, we slightly modified the existing gradient-based attack algorithm. Since there are already adversarial samples generated by other algorithms in our algorithm, the gradient of the existing adversarial samples can give us a rough direction to generate new adversarial samples, so we can use the gradient of the existing adversarial samples to calculate gradients. The formula is as follows.

$$\bar{g}_t = r\nabla_{\hat{x}_t^{adv}}\mathcal{L}\left(\hat{x}_t^{adv}\right) + (1-r)\nabla_{x'}\mathcal{L}\left(x'\right) \tag{8}$$

where r denotes the balance factor, $\nabla_{\hat{x}_t^{adv}}\mathcal{L}\left(\hat{x}_t^{adv}\right)$ denotes the gradient of the newly generated adversarial sample, and $\nabla_{x'}\mathcal{L}\left(x'\right)$ denotes the gradient of the existing adversarial sample.

3.3   Intermediate Feature-Based Attack

The Intermediate Feature-based Attack algorithm is summarized in Algorithm 1. The overview of the Intermediate Feature-based Attack algorithm is shown in Fig. 1.

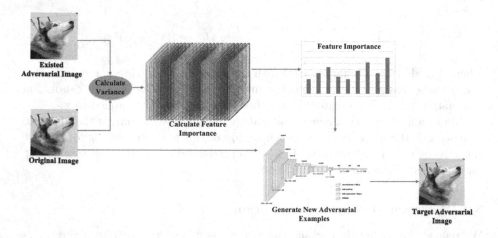

Fig. 1. Overview of Intermediate Feature-based Attack (IFA). Given an original image and existed adversarial image, calculate the variance between the original image and the existing adversarial image, and then calculate the gradients to serve as the feature importance. Finally, generating adversarial samples with higher transferability by optimizing important features.

Algorithm 1. Intermediate Feature-based Attack

Input: the original clean image x, the adversarial example x' generated for x by baseline attack, classification model f, intermediate layer k, perturbation probability p_d, ensemble number N in aggregate gradient, max perturbation ϵ, the number of iteration T, the decay factor μ, and the balance factor $r \in [0, 1]$.

Output: the adversarial samples x^{adv} with $\left\| x - x^{adv} \right\|_\infty < \epsilon$

1: $\Delta = 0, \alpha = \frac{\epsilon}{T}, g_0 = 0, x_0^{adv} = x$
2: **Obtain aggregate gradient:**
3: **for** $n = 0$ to $N - 1$ **do**
4:      $\Delta = \Delta + \Delta_k^{x + (x' - x) \odot M_{p_d}^n}$
5: **end for**
6: $\Delta = \frac{\Delta}{\|\Delta\|_2}$
7: **Construct optimization objective:**
8: $\mathcal{L}\left(x^{adv}\right) = \sum \left(\Delta \odot f_k\left(x^{adv}\right)\right)$
9: **Update x^{adv} by momentum iterative method:**
10: **for** $t = 0$ to $T - 1$ **do**
11:     $\hat{x}_t^{adv} = x_t^{adv} + \alpha g_t$
12:     $\bar{g}_t = r\nabla_{\hat{x}_t^{adv}} \mathcal{L}\left(\hat{x}_t^{adv}\right) + (1 - r)\nabla_{x'}\mathcal{L}\left(x'\right)$
13:     $g_{t+1} = \mu \cdot g_t + \frac{\bar{g}_t}{\|\bar{g}_t\|_1}$
14:     $x_{t+1}^{adv} = \text{Clip}\, p_{x,\epsilon} \left\{ x_t^{adv} + \alpha \cdot \text{sign}\left(g_{t+1}\right) \right\}$
15: **end for**
16: **return** x_T^{adv}

---

4 Experiments

To validate the effectiveness of our proposed algorithm, we will introduce the following aspects, *i.e.* experimental setup, comparison with gradient-based attacks, integrated with transformation-based attacks, and ablation studies.

4.1 Experimental Setup

Dataset. We evaluate our proposed algorithm on 1000 samples that were randomly chosen from the ILSVRC 2012 validation set [22]. All samples are resized to $299 \times 299 \times 3$.

Baselines. We compare our proposed algorithm with four attack methods, *i.e.* FGSM [5], I-FGSM [14], MI-FGSM [3], FIA [26]. To better evaluate our proposed algorithm, we also integrate our algorithm in an input transformation-based method, *i.e.* DIM [27], TIM [4], and SIM [16] and their combinations, SI-TIM, SI-DIM, and SITI-DIM, respectively.

Models. We generated adversarial samples based on four popular normally trained models, *i.e.* Inception-v3 (Inc-v3) [24], Inception-v4 (Inc-v4), Inception-Resnet-v2 (IncRes-v2) [23], Resnet-v2-101 (Res-101) [7], and corresponding ensemble adversarial trained models, *i.e.* ens3-adv-Inception-v3 (Inc-v3$_{ens3}$), ens4-Inception-v3 (Inc-v3$_{ens4}$), ens-adv-Inception-ResNet-v2 (IncRes-v2$_{ens}$) [25].

Attack Settings. We follow the model settings in [3] with the maximum perturbation $\epsilon = 16$, the number of iterations $T = 10$, the decay factor $\mu = 1.0$, the Gaussian kernel with size 7×7 for TIM, the transformation probability $p = 0.5$ for DIM, and the number of copies $m = 5$ for SIM. In the proposed IFA attack, the perturbation probability $p_d = 0.3$, the ensemble number $N = 30$, and the balance factor $r = 0.9$. The existing adversarial samples are generated by MI-FGSM [3]. The intermediate layer selected by each algorithm is consistent, *i.e.* Mixed_5b for Inc-v3 and Conv_4a for InRes-V2.

4.2   Comparison with Gradient-Based Attacks

To compare our proposed algorithm with the baseline methods more effectively, we use Inc-v3, Inc-v4, IncRes-v2, and Res-101 as the source model to attack the single models and the ensemble models respectively. The attack success rates, *i.e.* the misclassification rates of the input samples on the corresponding models, are shown in Table 1. Each row represents the results of adversarial samples generated by different attack algorithms on the same source model attacking normally trained models and adversarially trained models.

From Table 1, we can know that adversarial examples generated by our algorithm have better transferability, and our algorithm maintains high attack success rates under the white-box setting. For instance, using Inc-v3 to generate adversarial examples, most algorithms can achieve the attack success rates of approximately 100% under white-box attacks, but for black-box attacks, most algorithms achieve the attack success rates of less than 80% on Inc-v4, less than 70% on IncRes-v2 and less than 40% on Inc-v3$_{ens4}$ while our algorithm achieves the attack success rates of 84.6% on Inc-v4, 81.9% on Inc-Res-v2, and 49.2% on Inc-v3$_{ens4}$.

4.3   Integrated with Transformation-Based Attacks

Lin *et al.* [16] propose that combining SIM with TIM and DIM can greatly improve the transferability of adversarial samples. To further verify the effectiveness of our algorithm, we integrate our methods with various input transformation methods. We compare the attack success rates of TIM and DIM incorporating SIM, FIA, and our method denoted as SI-DIM, FIA-DIM, IFA-DIM (Ours), SI-TIM, FIA-TIM, IFA-TIM (Ours), SI-TI-DIM, FIA-TI-DIM, IFA-TI-DIM (Ours), respectively. All the results are shown in Tables 2, 3, and 4, respectively.

From the experimental results, we conclude that the adversarial samples generated by our algorithm achieve better transferability than other algorithms. For example, with Inception-v3 as the original model, the attack success rate of adversarial samples generated by IFA-DIM (Ours) is at least 1%–7% higher than other algorithms, the attack success rate of adversarial samples generated by IFA-TIM (Ours) is at least 2%–14% higher than other algorithms, the attack success rate of adversarial samples generated by IFA-TI-DIM (Ours) is at least

6%–9% higher than other algorithms. Such remarkable improvements show that our proposed method has higher effectiveness.

Table 1. Attack success rates (%) of adversarial attacks against the baseline models. The adversarial samples are crafted on Inc-v3, Inc-v4, IncRes-v2, and Res-101. * indicates the white-box model being attacked.

Model	Attack	Inc-v3	Inc-v4	IncRes-v2	Res-101	Inc-v3$_{ens3}$	Inc-v3$_{ens4}$
Inc-v3	FGSM	67.3*	25.7	26.0	24.5	10.2	10.4
	I-FGSM	100.0*	20.3	18.5	16.1	4.6	5.2
	MI-FGSM	100.0*	44.5	42.0	36.3	13.4	13.7
	FIA	98.3*	83.5	80.6	70.4	43.9	42.0
	IFA (Ours)	100.0*	84.6	81.9	75.2	45.0	49.2
Inc-v4	FGSM	26.5	52.2*	22.8	22.1	15.4	9.6
	I-FGSM	32.1	100.0*	18.4	19.4	5.1	6.1
	MI-FGSM	53.5	100.0*	43.1	39.4	14.5	15.4
	FIA	85.4	98.7*	81.1	72.3	49.7	43.1
	IFA (Ours)	87.8	99.4*	83.2	78.0	55.9	50.4
IncRes-v2	FGSM	27.2	20.2	41.9 *	23.6	9.5	9.1
	I-FGSM	33.4	25.2	98.2 *	20.2	6.8	6.4
	MI-FGSM	57.3	52.5	99.3 *	40.1	21.4	16.0
	FIA	81.1	77.5	89.2*	71.8	46.9	44.7
	IFA (Ours)	89.9	87.5	99.1*	81.9	64.2	56.7
Res-101	FGSM	36.4	31.2	30.0	78.1 *	14.9	13.3
	I-FGSM	31.4	25.3	23.1	99.3 *	8.7	8.5
	MI-FGSM	57.2	48.2	49.7	99.6 *	23.9	22.1
	FIA	85.3	81.1	77.8	96.8 *	61.4	60.3
	IFA (Ours)	85.4	82.8	79.6	99.7*	63.0	65.3

4.4 Ablation Study

In this section, we conduct ablation studies to explore the impact of the perturbation probability, ensemble number, and layer choice, respectively. To simplify the analysis process, we only consider the transferability of adversarial samples generated with Inc-v3 as the source model. The default parameters are the same as those in the experimental setup section.

On Perturbation Probability. The perturbation probability p_d affects the attack success rate of adversarial samples by affecting the computation of the feature importance. We set the perturbation probability to change from 0.1 to 0.5 with the step of 0.1 to generate adversarial samples and then attack the baseline models. All the results are shown in Fig. 2 (a), and when the perturbation probability value is set as 0.3, we can get the best result.

On Ensemble Number. The ensemble number N affects the attack success rate of adversarial samples by affecting the process of calculating gradient aggregation. We set the ensemble number to change from 5 to 40 with the step of 5 to generate adversarial samples and then attack the baseline models. All the results are shown in Fig. 2 (b). To balance performance with cost, we set the ensemble number $N = 30$.

Table 2. Attack success rates (%) on seven models by SIM, FIA, and our method integrated with DIM. * indicates white-box attacks.

Model	Attack	Inc-v3	Inc-v4	IncRes-v2	Res-101	Inc-v3$_{ens3}$	Inc-v3$_{ens4}$
Inc-v3	SI-DIM	98.9*	85.0	81.3	76.3	48.0	45.1
	FIA-DIM	99.7*	90.1	85.4	80.7	51.5	48.4
	IFA-DIM (Ours)	99.8*	91.6	87.9	83.2	52.8	51.3
Inc-v4	SI-DIM	89.3	98.8*	85.6	79.9	58.4	55.2
	FIA-DIM	91.4	99.3*	88.1	81.7	59.7	58.7
	IFA-DIM (Ours)	94.0	99.7*	90.7	86.4	61.6	60.3
IncRes-v2	SI-DIM	87.9	85.1	97.5*	82.9	66.0	59.3
	FIA-DIM	89.4	86.7	98.0*	87.1	70.5	62.5
	IFA-DIM (Ours)	90.2	88.4	97.0*	85.8	69.7	63.7
Res-101	SI-DIM	87.9	83.4	84.0	98.6*	63.5	57.5
	FIA-DIM	89.4	86.7	86.7	99.6*	67.7	59.4
	IFA-DIM (Ours)	91.9	89.0	89.6	99.8*	69.7	62.3

Table 3. Attack success rates (%) on seven models by SIM, FIA, and our method integrated with TIM. * indicates white-box attacks.

Model	Attack	Inc-v3	Inc-v4	IncRes-v2	Res-101	Inc-v3$_{ens3}$	Inc-v3$_{ens4}$
Inc-v3	SI-TIM	100.0*	71.8	68.6	62.2	48.2	47.4
	FIA-TIM	100.0*	76.4	69.4	68.7	54.7	54.1
	IFA-TIM(Ours)	100.0*	85.4	82.3	76.1	60.4	56.8
Inc-v4	SI-TIM	78.2	99.7*	71.9	66.1	58.6	55.4
	FIA-TIM	84.1	99.8*	74.1	69.7	61.4	60.1
	IFA-TIM(Ours)	88.7	99.7*	81.7	78.4	67.1	64.7
IncRes-v2	SI-TIM	84.5	82.2	97.8*	77.4	71.6	64.7
	FIA-TIM	88.1	85.7	98.8*	79.7	76.7	68.1
	IFA-TIM(Ours)	91.7	88.7	98.6*	84.8	79.6	75.4
Res-101	SI-TIM	74.2	69.9	70.2	98.7*	59.5	54.5
	FIA-TIM	77.4	71.4	77.5	99.8*	65.4	58.7
	IFA-TIM (Ours)	82.7	79.8	80.9	99.7*	66.9	64.3

Table 4. Attack success rates (%) on seven models by SIM, FIA, and our method integrated with TI-DIM. ∗ indicates white-box attacks.

Model	Attack	Inc-v3	Inc-v4	IncRes-v2	Res-101	Inc-v3$_{ens3}$	Inc-v3$_{ens4}$
Inc-v3	SI-TI-DIM	99.1*	83.6	80.8	76.7	65.2	63.3
	FIA-TI-DIM	99.7*	85.4	83.2	78.1	67.8	66.7
	IFA-TI-DIM (Ours)	99.9*	89.7	87.5	83.6	73.1	72.2
Inc-v4	SI-TI-DIM	87.9	98.7*	83.0	77.7	72.4	68.2
	FIA-TI-DIM	88.2	98.1*	84.2	78.9	74.1	69.7
	IFA-TI-DIM (Ours)	91.1	99.5*	88.4	83.5	75.7	72.1
IncRes-v2	SI-TI-DIM	88.8	86.8	97.8*	83.9	78.7	74.2
	FIA-TI-DIM	89.1	87.1	96.1*	85.4	80.5	77.8
	IFA-TI-DIM (Ours)	91.4	89.8	97.9*	86.9	83.1	79.2
Res-101	SI-TI-DIM	84.7	82.2	84.8	99.0*	75.8	73.5
	FIA-TI-DIM	87.6	85.8	87.4	98.7*	78.1	76.1
	IFA-TI-DIM (Ours)	90.7	86.8	88.9	99.9*	82.5	78.7

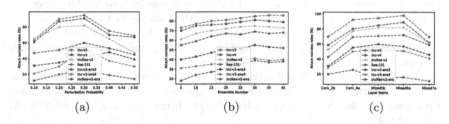

| (a) | (b) | (c) |

Fig. 2. (a)(b)(c) denote the attack success rates (%) on seven models with adversaries crafted by IFA on Inc-v3. (a) is for various perturbation probability, (b) is for various numbers of the ensembled samples, (c) is for different layers.

On the Layer Choice. Previous layers of the DNN may be building a base feature set that is often data-specific, and deep layers can get these extracted features to maximize the model's classification accuracy, but deep layers may make the features model-specific [11]. We generate adversarial samples with different layers, such as Conv_2b, Conv_4a, Mixed5b, Mixed6a, and Mixed7a, and then attack the baseline models. All the results are shown in Fig. 2 (c). When Mixed5b is selected, we can get the best result.

5 Conclusions

We proposed a novel method called the Intermediate Feature-based Attack algorithm (IFA) to improve the transferability of adversarial samples. The proposed IFA algorithm calculates the feature importance of the original sample based on the perturbation of the existing adversarial samples in comparison to the original samples and then optimizes the adversarial samples in the direction of the feature importance. Extensive evaluations show that the proposed IFA algorithm has much better adversarial transferability than the existing competitive algorithms. We hope that our IFA algorithm will shed light on potential adversarial attack directions.

Acknowledgements. This work is supported by the National Key R&D Program of China (No. 2021YFB3100600).

References

1. Bai, T., Luo, J., Zhao, J., Wen, B., Wang, Q.: Recent advances in adversarial training for adversarial robustness. In: Zhou, Z.H. (ed.) Proceedings of the Thirtieth International Joint Conference on Artificial Intelligence, IJCAI-2021, pp. 4312–4321. International Joint Conferences on Artificial Intelligence Organization, August 2021. https://doi.org/10.24963/ijcai.2021/591, Survey Track
2. Carlini, N., Wagner, D.: Towards evaluating the robustness of neural networks (2017)
3. Dong, Y., et al.: Boosting adversarial attacks with momentum (2018)
4. Dong, Y., Pang, T., Su, H., Zhu, J.: Evading defenses to transferable adversarial examples by translation-invariant attacks. In: Proceedings of the IEEE Computer Society Conference on Computer Vision and Pattern Recognition (2019)
5. Goodfellow, I.J., Shlens, J., Szegedy, C.: Explaining and harnessing adversarial examples (2015)
6. He, C., et al.: Boosting the robustness of neural networks with M-PGD. In: Tanveer, M., Agarwal, S., Ozawa, S., Ekbal, A., Jatowt, A. (eds.) Neural Information Processing, pp. 562–573. Springer, Cham (2023). https://doi.org/10.1007/978-981-99-1639-9_47
7. He, K., Zhang, X., Ren, S., Sun, J.: Deep residual learning for image recognition. In: 2016 IEEE Conference on Computer Vision and Pattern Recognition (CVPR), pp. 770–778 (2016). https://doi.org/10.1109/CVPR.2016.90
8. Huang, Q., Katsman, I., He, H., Gu, Z., Belongie, S.J., Lim, S.N.: Enhancing adversarial example transferability with an intermediate level attack. arXiv:abs/1907.10823 (2019)
9. Huang, Y., Kong, A.W.K.: Transferable adversarial attack based on integrated gradients. In: International Conference on Learning Representations (2022). https://openreview.net/forum?id=DesNW4-5ai9
10. Huang, Y., Chen, C.: Smart app attack: hacking deep learning models in android apps. IEEE Trans. Inf. Forensics Secur. **17**, 1827–1840 (2022). https://doi.org/10.1109/TIFS.2022.3172213
11. Inkawhich, N., Liang, K.J., Carin, L., Chen, Y.: Transferable perturbations of deep feature distributions (2020)
12. Inkawhich, N., Wen, W., Li, H.H., Chen, Y.: Feature space perturbations yield more transferable adversarial examples. In: 2019 IEEE/CVF Conference on Computer Vision and Pattern Recognition (CVPR), pp. 7059–7067 (2019). https://doi.org/10.1109/CVPR.2019.00723
13. Kim, M., Jain, A.K., Liu, X.: AdaFace: Quality adaptive margin for face recognition. In: Proceedings of the IEEE/CVF Conference on Computer Vision and Pattern Recognition (CVPR) (2022)
14. Kurakin, A., Goodfellow, I., Bengio, S.: Adversarial examples in the physical world (2017)

15. Li, Q., Guo, Y., Chen, H.: Yet another intermediate-level attack (2020). https://doi.org/10.48550/ARXIV.2008.08847, https://arxiv.org/abs/2008.08847
16. Lin, J., Song, C., He, K., Wang, L., Hopcroft, J.E.: Nesterov accelerated gradient and scale invariance for adversarial attacks (2020)
17. Lu, Y., et al.: Enhancing cross-task black-box transferability of adversarial examples with dispersion reduction (2019)
18. Luo, C., Lin, Q., Xie, W., Wu, B., Xie, J., Shen, L.: Frequency-driven imperceptible adversarial attack on semantic similarity. In: Proceedings of the IEEE/CVF Conference on Computer Vision and Pattern Recognition (CVPR) (2022)
19. Luo, X., Wu, Y., Xiao, X., Ooi, B.C.: Feature inference attack on model predictions in vertical federated learning. In: 2021 IEEE 37th International Conference on Data Engineering (ICDE), pp. 181–192 (2021). https://doi.org/10.1109/ICDE51399.2021.00023
20. Madry, A., Makelov, A., Schmidt, L., Tsipras, D., Vladu, A.: Towards deep learning models resistant to adversarial attacks. In: International Conference on Learning Representations (2018). https://openreview.net/forum?id=rJzIBfZAb
21. Muneeb, M., Feng, S., Henschel, A.: Deep learning pipeline for image classification on mobile phones. In: Proceedings of the IEEE/CVF Conference on Computer Vision and Pattern Recognition (CVPR), May 2022
22. Russakovsky, O., et al.: ImageNet large scale visual recognition challenge (2015)
23. Szegedy, C., Ioffe, S., Vanhoucke, V., Alemi, A.A.: Inception-v4, inception-ResNet and the impact of residual connections on learning. In: Proceedings of the Thirty-First AAAI Conference on Artificial Intelligence, AAAI 2017, pp. 4278–4284. AAAI Press (2017)
24. Szegedy, C., Vanhoucke, V., Ioffe, S., Shlens, J., Wojna, Z.: Rethinking the inception architecture for computer vision. In: 2016 IEEE Conference on Computer Vision and Pattern Recognition (CVPR), pp. 2818–2826 (2016). https://doi.org/10.1109/CVPR.2016.308
25. Tramèr, F., Kurakin, A., Papernot, N., Goodfellow, I., Boneh, D., McDaniel, P.: Ensemble adversarial training: attacks and defenses. In: International Conference on Learning Representations (2018). https://openreview.net/forum?id=rkZvSe-RZ
26. Wang, Z., Guo, H., Zhang, Z., Liu, W., Qin, Z., Ren, K.: Feature importance-aware transferable adversarial attacks (2022)
27. Xie, C., et al.: Improving transferability of adversarial examples with input diversity. In: Computer Vision and Pattern Recognition. IEEE (2019)
28. Yosinski, J., Clune, J., Bengio, Y., Lipson, H.: How transferable are features in deep neural networks? (2014)
29. Zhang, J., Zhu, J., Niu, G., Han, B., Sugiyama, M., Kankanhalli, M.: Geometry-aware instance-reweighted adversarial training. In: International Conference on Learning Representations (2021). https://openreview.net/forum?id=iAX0l6Cz8ub
30. Zhao, Y., Zhong, Z., Sebe, N., Lee, G.H.: Novel class discovery in semantic segmentation. In: Proceedings of the IEEE/CVF Conference on Computer Vision and Pattern Recognition (CVPR) (2022)
31. Zheng, Z., et al.: Localization distillation for dense object detection. In: Proceedings of the IEEE/CVF Conference on Computer Vision and Pattern Recognition (CVPR) (2022)
32. Zhou, D., et al.: Removing adversarial noise in class activation feature space (2021)

DaCon: Multi-Domain Text Classification Using Domain Adversarial Contrastive Learning

Yingjun Dai$^{(\boxtimes)}$ and Ahmed El-Roby

Carleton Univeristy, Ottawa, ON, Canada
yingjundai@cmail.carleton.ca

Abstract. Multi-Domain Text Classification (MDTC) aims to classify text from a specific domain based on knowledge learned from multiple other domains. Recent state-of-the-art approaches address the MDTC problem using a shared-private model design (i.e., a shared feature encoder and multiple domain-specific encoders) which requires massive amounts of labeled data. However, some domains in real-world scenarios lack sufficient labeled data, resulting in significant performance degradation when recent approaches are directly applied to these low-resource domains because all domain-specific features are set to zeros. In this paper, we propose DaCon, a novel MDTC approach that employs domain adversarial supervised contrastive learning to improve classification accuracy. In particular, DaCon uses supervised contrastive learning to align text classification features with respect to label information, pulling pairs of the same class together and pushing pairs of different classes apart in the embedding space and aligns features with respect to domain information through domain adversarial learning. We conduct experiments on the widely-used benchmarks FDU-MTL. Our results demonstrate that DaCon achieves state-of-the-art performance for MDTC with or without labeled data from the target domain.

Keywords: Multi-Domain Text Classification · Contrastive Learning · Domain Adversarial Training

1 Introduction

Text classification is of fundamental importance in natural language processing. It aims to classify new text into pre-defined classes and has been successfully applied in a range of applications, such as sentiment analysis [21] and spam detection [14]. Recently, with the rapid development of computational power, deep neural networks have shown their success in text classification and have gradually replaced traditional methods [1]. Compared with traditional methods, deep neural networks avoid human feature engineering. Therefore, those deep learning methods are data-driven and require a sufficient amount of annotated training data. However, in many real-life scenarios, some emerging domains may

L. Iliadis et al. (Eds.): ICANN 2023, LNCS 14258, pp. 40–52, 2023.
https://doi.org/10.1007/978-3-031-44192-9_4

have a limited amount of annotated data, and gathering a large number of reliable labels is expensive and time-consuming. Thus, the design of models that can effectively leverage all available resources and generalize well across multiple domains is crucial.

Multi-Domain Text Classification (MDTC) was proposed to address the problem of learning knowledge from multiple domains [11]. MDTC assumes labeled data exists for multiple domains but is insufficient for training an effective classifier for one or more emerging target domains. In the worst case, some emerging domains may not have any labeled data at all. MDTC aims to leverage all possible resources, including unlabeled data, to improve the classification accuracy across all domains. The shared-private paradigm, which extracts the features into two subspaces, is proposed by [2]. The shared feature extractor learns general features of all domains while the private feature extractors (one per domain) are trained for domain-specific features. Domain adversarial learning [8] is often used for extracting the domain-invariant features: the classifier maximizes the loss of domain classification on the shared features while minimizing the total loss for the label classification. However, extra mechanisms need to be implemented to ensure the domain classifier captures only domain-invariant features [5]. In scenarios where no labeled data for the emerging domain is available, the shared-private paradigm methods only feed the shared features to the classifier, and all domain-specific features are set to zeros [17,19], resulting in inferior accuracy compared to when labeled data for the target domain is available.

In this paper, we introduce DaCon, a domain adversarial supervised contrastive learning framework for multi-domain text classification. The key idea of DaCon is shown in Fig. 1. It aligns the text features from different domains in two aspects: 1) It adopts supervised contrastive learning to maximize the similarities between the positive pairs (instances with the same class label) and minimize the similarities between the negative ones. 2) A gradient reversal layer is placed before the domain classifier to regularize the learning of text representations which helps the learning of domain-invariant features. Supervised contrastive loss works by maximizing the similarity between samples from the same class and minimizing the similarity between samples from different classes in the shared representation space. This encourages the model to learn representations that are discriminative for the task at hand, while also being domain-invariant

Experimental results on the benchmark dataset show that our proposed method can outperform state-of-art MDTC approaches for domains with no labeled data and when labeled data is available.

The main contributions of this paper can be summarized as follows:

- We introduce DaCon, a contrastive learning based approach to solve the problem of Multi-Domain Text Classification. We implement a supervised contrastive layer on top of the feature extractor and use domain adversarial learning to obtain better domain-invariant features.
- We validate the effectiveness of our approach by running experiments on a benchmark dataset FDU-MTL under two settings (with and without labeled data in the target domain). Experimental results show that our approach outperforms the previous approaches.

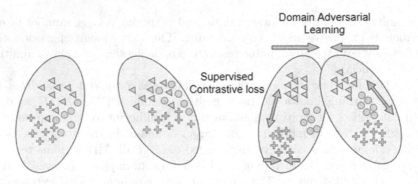

Fig. 1. The supervised contrastive layer pulls instances of the same class together and pushes instances of different classes apart in the embedding space. The domain adversarial module aligns the distribution of different domains.

2   The Overview of DACON

In this section, we first define the problem of Multi-Domain Text Classification. We then introduce the architecture of DACON in detail.

2.1   Problem Definition

In this paper, we investigate the Multi-Domain Text Classification problem, in which textual data originate from multiple domains. Assume that there are M source domains $\{D_i\}_{i=1}^m$. Let $\mathbb{L}_i = \{(x_j, y_j)\}_{j=1}^{l_i}$ denote the labeled data and $\mathbb{U}_i = \{x_j\}_{j=1}^{u_i}$ denote the unlabeled data in the i-th domain for the sample x_j. The MDTC problem seeks to allocate all possible resources to map the instance x in the target domain T to its corresponding classification label y.

2.2   The Architecture of DACON

In this section, we discuss the overview of DACON. In Sect. 3, we discuss our approach in more detail. Figure 2 shows the architecture of DACON. On the top channel, the input samples from the source domains are first sampled into batches before being passed to the data augmentation module (Sect. 3.1), which generates vectors, called views, for each original sample. The goal of data augmentation is to increase the number of training samples and generate pairs of positive and negative features for use in contrastive learning. The generated views are then fed into the encoder network (Sect. 3.2) for feature extraction. The encoder network maps the augmented views into representation vectors. The representation vectors represent the domain invariant features learned by the model, which are then fed into the label classifier and projection network simultaneously. The projection network (Sect. 3.2) further maps hidden representations to a lower-dimensional latent space. The supervised contrastive loss $\mathcal{L}_{SCL}$

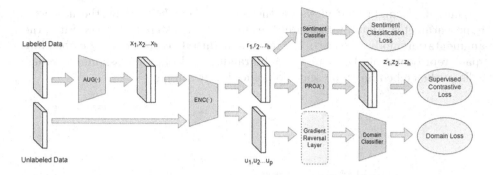

Fig. 2. The Architecture of DaCon. The augmentation network $Aug(\cdot)$ generates h views for the input sample which outputs $v_1, v_2...v_h$. The encoder network $Enc(\cdot)$ produces features, $r_1, r_2...r_h$, from the generated views. The h encoded representations are fed into a projection network $Proj(\cdot)$ and a label classifier simultaneously. The projection network outputs a k-dimension vector $z_1, z_2...z_h$ for each encoded feature. The supervised contrastive loss $\mathcal{L}_{SCL}$ is computed for the current batch. The sentiment classification loss $\mathcal{L}_{Sent}$ is computed for $r_1, r_2...r_h$. The unlabeled data are encoded and the resulted vector representations $u_1, u_2...u_h$ are passed into the domain classifier to compute the $\mathcal{L}_{Domain}$. The total loss $\mathcal{L}_{total} = \mathcal{L}_{Sent} + \alpha\mathcal{L}_{SCL} + \beta\mathcal{L}_{Domain}$ is used to back-propagate and update the model.

is computed based on the projected representations of the batch. A lower loss means samples with the same label lie closer together in the embedding space. In the other branch, the domain invariant features encoded by the encoder are fed into the classifier $\mathcal{C}_{tc}$ for sentiment classification. The sentiment classification loss $\mathcal{L}_{Sent}$ measures the difference between the predicted and actual labels of the samples. On the bottom channel, the unlabeled data samples are encoded using the shared encoder in the meantime. The encoded unlabeled data vectors are then passed into a domain classifier to compute the domain classification loss $\mathcal{L}_{Domain}$.

The objective of DaCon is to train a model that minimizes the weighted sum of the supervised contrastive loss, the sentiment classification loss, and the domain classification loss. This process aims to achieve high accuracy of classification for instances within the target domain.

3   The Details of DaCon

In this section, we present more details of each component in DaCon. Namely, the Augmentation Module, the Encoder Network, the Projection Network, the Domain Adversarial Learning Module, and the optimized loss function.

3.1   Data Augmentation Module

In DaCon, we apply dropout as our augmentation strategy. Each input sample $s = (x_{ij}, y_{ij})$ in the batch is passed to the dropout augmentation module h times to generate h augmented views for the input, where h is set by the user as a hyperparameter. Figure 3 illustrates the augmentation step in DACON. First, the augmentation module converts the text input into its corresponding embedding space representation. Dropout works by randomly dropping (assigning 0 value) cells in the embedding representation of an input sample.

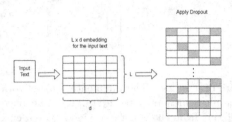

Fig. 3. The generation of views by applying Dropout to the text embedding

This augmentation step results in obtaining multiple different views (embeddings) for each input sample such that they all retain the same class of this input sample. The output views are then passed to the encoder network to extract the domain-invariant features of the augmented views.

3.2 Encoder and Projection Network

The purpose of the encoder is to extract domain-invariant features from the views. The views generated from the augmentation module are passed into the encoder $Enc(\cdot)$ to obtain the domain invariant representations r. The output of encoders can be denoted as:

$$r_1 = \text{Enc}(\hat{x}_1), r_2 = \text{Enc}(\hat{x}_2), \ldots, r_h = \text{Enc}(\hat{x}_h) \tag{1}$$

where $\hat{x}_1, \hat{x}_2, \ldots, \hat{x}_h$ are augmented views from the data augmentation module.

DACON is agnostic to the encoder being used, the encoding method can be a fully-connected convolutional neural network (CNN) or a transformer-based model. To demonstrate this, we run experiments with both approaches in Sect. 4.

Instead of computing the contrastive loss on the encoded vectors from the encoder directly, a projection network is further used to extract representations for contrastive learning to compare against each other. Using a projection network to reduce the dimensionality of the views has been shown to be effective [4] in semi-supervised contrastive learning for image classification.

The projection network $Proj(\cdot)$ is a multi-layer perceptron on top of the encoder network, which maps the domain invariant representations $r_1, \ldots, r_h$ into vectors that can be used for supervised contrastive learning to contrast against each other. The projection network outputs a k-dimensional vector for computing the supervised contrastive loss. The output of the projection network can be written as

$$z_1 = \text{Proj}(r_1), z_2 = \text{Proj}(r_2), \ldots, z_h = \text{Proj}(r_h) \tag{2}$$

3.3 Domain Adversarial Learning

The primary objective of adversarial adaptive methods is to regularize the learning process for source and target representations, reduce the distance between the source and target distributions, and thereby generate domain-invariant features.

The domain classification loss and sentiment classification loss can be written as:

$$u_j = \text{Enc}(x_j), \ where \ x_j \in \mathbb{U}_i \tag{3}$$

$$r_j = \text{Enc}(x_j), \ where \ x_j \in \mathbb{L}_k \tag{4}$$

where $\mathbb{U}_i$ and $\mathbb{L}_i$ are the set of all unlabeled samples of the i-th domain and all labeled samples of the k-th domain respectively.

$$p(y_d|u_j) = \text{MLP}(u_j) \tag{5}$$

$$p(y_j|r_j) = \text{MLP}(r_j) \tag{6}$$

where y_d is the domain label of the unlabeled sample u_j and y_j is the sentimental label of the sample y_j.

$$\mathcal{L}_{Domain}(\theta_f, \theta_d) = \sum_{j=1} -\log p(y_d|u_j; \theta_f, \theta_d) \tag{7}$$

$$\mathcal{L}_{Sent}(\theta_f, \theta_s) = \sum_{j=1} -\log p(y_j|r_j; \theta_f, \theta_s) \tag{8}$$

where θ_f, θ_s, and θ_d are the learnable parameters of the encoder, the sentiment classifier, and the domain classifier respectively.

At learning time, the model learns a set of parameters of θ_f that maximize the domain classification loss, while simultaneously learning the sets of parameters θ_s and θ_d that minimize their respective classification losses. We apply a Gradient Reversal Layer (multiply the gradients by a negative value during backpropagation) [8] before the domain classifier to achieve the min-max optimization.

3.4 Contrastive Loss Function

The supervised contrastive learning [9] extends self-supervised contrastive learning in a fully supervised setting. The use of supervised contrastive loss encourages the source and target domain representations to be closer together in the latent space, thereby necessitating the model to learn domain-invariant features for the user from the source and target domain.

In Multi-Domain Text Classification, labeled data for source domains are available. The supervised contrastive loss can be used to fully leverage the labeled data and produces better representations.

The supervised contrastive loss function takes the following form:

$$\mathcal{L}_{SCL} = \sum_{i \in I} \frac{-1}{|P(i)|} \sum_{p \in P(i)} log \frac{exp(z_i \cdot z_p/\tau)}{\sum_{a \in A(i)} exp(z_i \cdot z_a/\tau)} \tag{9}$$

where $z_i = \text{Proj}(\text{Enc}(\hat{x}_i))$, $P(i)$ is the set of indices of samples that form positive pairs with the sample i, $A(i) = I - \{\hat{x}_i\}$, the $\cdot$ symbol is the dot product, and the τ is a scalar hyperparameter called temperature.

3.5 Training Objective

The supervised contrastive loss $\mathcal{L}_{SCL}$ measures the current progress of the feature alignment. The loss is computed based on the projected representations of the batch using (9).

In DACON, the $\mathcal{C}_{tc}$ is a linear classification model which takes the text representation r as input and outputs the probability of the sample being a class y. The $\mathcal{C}_{domain}$ is another linear classification model that takes the input u and outputs the probability of an unlabeled sample belonging to a domain D. The cross-entropy loss is computed for the labeled samples using (8), and the unlabeled samples using (7).

The objective function of DACON is the weighted sum of the sentimental classification loss, supervised contrastive loss, and the domain loss. The model is optimized by minimizing the total loss $\mathcal{L}_{total}$.

$$\mathcal{L}_{total} = \mathcal{L}_{Sent} + \alpha \mathcal{L}_{SCL} + \beta \mathcal{L}_{Domain} \tag{10}$$

4 Experimental Evaluation

In this section, we first introduce the experimental setup. We then present our experimental results on the benchmark dataset. Last, we present the ablation study and the hyper-parameters analysis.

4.1 Experimental Setup

Datasets. We evaluate our methods on a widely-used dataset for MDTC: the FDU-MTL [13]. The experiments are done under two settings: with and without labeled training data for the target domain. The FDU-MTL dataset contains raw text product reviews from Amazon for 14 domains (books, electronics, dvds, kitchen, apparel, camera, health, music, toys, video, baby, magazine, software, and sport) and 2 movie reviews domains (IMDB and MR). The number of samples in training, testing, and unlabeled data varies across domains, but are roughly 1600, 400, and 2000, respectively. We follow the setting of [17] and we randomly pick 200 samples from the training set as the validation set.

Comparison Methods. For the FDU-MTL dataset, we compare our method with a number of state-of-art methods in two different settings:

- Co-regularized adversarial learning (CRAL) [19]. The approach constructs two diverse adversarial training branches and punishes the disagreements between the two alignments based on the predictions of the unlabeled data.
- Conditional adversarial network (CAN) [17]. The approach conducts alignment on the joint distributions of domain-invariant features and predictions.
- Multinomial adversarial network (MANs) [5] with two different forms of loss functions, the least square loss (MAN-L2) and the negative log-likelihood loss (MAN-NLL). The approach follows the shared-private paradigm and is able to minimize the difference between multiple distributions simultaneously.
- Dual adversarial co-learning method (DACL) [16]. The approach follows the shared-private paradigm and conducts dual adversarial regularizations to align features across different domains.
- Robust Contrastive Alignment (RCA) [12]. The approach proposes to align text features of various domains into one embedding space.
- ASP-SC and ASP-BC [13]. The two models are single-channel model and bichannel model of adversarial multi-task learning.
- Weighting Scheme based Unsupervised Domain Adaptation framework (WS-UDA) and Two-Stage Training based Unsupervised Domain Adaptation (2ST-UDA) [6], which combine the source classifier to generate pseudo labels for target instances and exploits the generated pseudo labels for the training of a private feature extractor.

Implementation Details. In the experiment on the FDU-MTL dataset, we adopt a CNN-based feature extractor. The size of the convolutional kernel is (3, 4, 5) and the number of kernels is 200. The input to the convolutional layer is the pre-trained 300d fastText word embedding. The output of the projection network used for contrastive learning is a 256-dimensional vector. We choose the CNN-based feature extractor for the sake of fair comparison to the approaches that we compare since they use the same approach. We also did experiments with BERT as our encoder in the ablation study.

ReLU is used as the activation function. The dropout rate is set to 0.4. The batch size used for training is 16. We use Adadelta as the optimizer with a learning rate of 0.05 and $\rho = 0.95$. The temperature of contrastive learning τ is 0.07.

4.2   Evaluation of MDTC for with Labeled Instances

Table 1 shows the sentiment classification accuracy on the FDU-MTL dataset. The best results for each domain are written in bold. From this table, we have the following observations:

First, DACON achieves state-of-the-art performance in terms of the average accuracy scores across all domains. DACON outperforms the compared methods on 9 out of 16 domains.

Second, Although DaCon focuses completely on obtaining domain-invariant features as opposed to the existing methods with a shared-private paradigm, which make use of both domain-invariant and domain-specific features, DaCon still achieves superior results. More specifically, DaCon outperforms MAN-L2 and MAN-NLL by significant margins (i.e., absolute improvements of 1.7% and 1.5%) in terms of the averaged accuracy scores. DaCon also outperforms the recent state-of-art methods RCA, DACL, and CAN with at least 0.5%, which is a considerable improvement.

Table 1. MDTC accuracy (%) with labeled instances on the FDU-MTL dataset.

Domains	books	elec.	dvd	kitchen	apparel	camera	health	music	toys	video	baby	magaz	sofw	sports	IMDB	MR	AVG
MAN-L2	87.6	87.4	88.1	89.8	87.6	91.4	89.8	85.9	90.0	89.5	90.0	92.5	90.4	89.0	86.6	76.1	88.2
MAN-NLL	86.8	88.8	88.6	89.9	87.6	90.7	89.4	85.5	90.4	89.6	90.2	92.9	90.9	89.0	87.0	76.7	88.4
RCA	86.8	88.3	**89.8**	90.0	87.5	91.8	90.8	87.0	90.3	**90.8**	91.0	92.8	88.5	90.3	90.5	**78.5**	89.0
DACL	87.5	90.3	**89.8**	**91.5**	89.5	91.5	90.5	86.3	**91.3**	88.5	92.0	93.8	90.5	89.3	87.3	76.0	89.1
CAN	87.8	**91.6**	89.5	90.8	87.0	**93.5**	90.4	86.9	90.0	88.8	92.0	**94.5**	90.9	91.2	88.5	77.1	89.4
DaCon-CNN	**91.0**	88.8	88.8	90.5	**90.3**	92.3	**92.3**	**88.8**	91.0	90.5	**92.5**	92.0	**91.3**	**91.3**	**91.8**	76.0	**89.9**

4.3 Evaluation of MDTC Without Labeled Instances

The experimental results on FDU-MTL dataset are shown in Table 2. From the table, we have the following observations:

DaCon outperforms the compared methods on 6 out of the 16 domains and DaCon achieves state-of-the-art performance in terms of the average accuracy scores across all domains. We attribute this to the fact that DaCon adopts supervised contrastive learning to pull pairs of the same class together and push pairs of different classes apart in the embedding space, and domain adversarial training, which result in better domain-invariant features.

Table 2. MDTC accuracy (%) without labeled instances on the FDU-MTL dataset.

Domains	books	elec.	dvd	kitchen	apparel	camera	health	music	toys	video	baby	magaz	sofw	sports	IMDB	MR	AVG
ASP-SC	83.2	82.2	85.5	83.7	87.5	88.2	87.7	82.5	87.0	85.2	86.5	**91.2**	85.5	86.7	87.5	75.2	85.3
ASP-BC	83.7	83.2	85.7	85.0	86.2	89.7	86.5	81.7	88.2	85.2	88.0	90.5	88.2	86.5	86.7	**76.5**	85.7
CRAL	**88.5**	87.0	87.8	89.0	87.0	86.5	87.0	**85.8**	88.3	87.3	88.0	83.0	85.8	87.5	87.0	75.0	86.3
WS-UDA	84.6	87.9	**88.9**	88.7	**90.1**	**90.2**	87.8	84.3	89.1	**88.7**	87.4	86.6	88.4	88.2	88.7	74.6	87.1
2ST-UDA	86.3	**89.5**	88.5	89.3	89.5	89.1	88.5	84.1	89.0	87.5	89.0	88.8	88.8	**88.3**	88.3	73.3	87.4
DaCon-CNN	88.0	88.8	87.5	**89.5**	89.0	88.3	**89.5**	84.8	**89.3**	88.3	**89.8**	90.0	**90.3**	86.8	**88.8**	74.5	**87.7**

4.4 Model Analysis

Ablation Study. In this section, we study the effect of each component of DaCon. We conduct four experiments on the FDU-MTL dataset (with labeled target samples): 1) DaCon without the contrastive layer; 2) DaCon without the domain adversarial module; 3) DaCon without both the contrastive layer and the domain adversarial module; 4) DaCon with BERT-base as the encoder;

The results are shown in Table 3. We can see that all three variants have inferior performance compared to the full model, validating that all of these components contribute to the performance improvement of our model. In particular, the removal of the supervised contrastive layer degrades by a large margin (1.3%). DACON is also shown to be agnostic to the encoder used. When BERT-base is used as our encoder, it achieves an accuracy of 91.6% on average.

Table 3. Abalation Study with labeled instances

Domains	books	elec.	dvd	kitchen	apparel	camera	health	music	toys	video	baby	magaz	sofw	sports	IMDB	MR	AVG
DACON	91.0	88.8	88.8	90.5	90.3	92.3	92.3	88.8	91.0	90.5	92.5	92.0	91.3	91.3	91.8	76.0	**89.9**
w/o C	89.8	88.8	86.8	89.5	89.25	90.5	91.0	86.5	90.8	90.8	89.0	92.0	90.5	90.3	87.5	74.5	88.6
w/o D	90.0	88.3	88.0	90.3	89.0	90.0	91.8	88.0	90.3	90.0	93.0	93.5	92.3	90.8	90.5	75.3	89.4
w/o CD	88.3	87.3	88.3	90.3	88.5	91.0	90.3	87.5	89.3	90.3	89.8	91.5	89.8	90.3	88.5	73.5	88.4
DACON-BERT	92.3	92.0	89.5	92.8	92.3	93.3	94.3	91.0	93.3	89.8	93.3	94.7	93.8	91.8	86.3	85.0	91.6

Impact of Important Hyperparameters. In this section, we explore the impact of the hyperparameters (α and β) on our approach. These two hyperparameters are used to trade off different loss functions. We conduct hyperparameters analysis on the FDU-MTL dataset with labeled samples for the target domain. When evaluating one hyperparameter, the other one is fixed as 1. The experiment results are presented in Fig. 4. We report the average classification accuracy. It can be noted that the different values of α do not significantly influence the classification accuracy and DACON has better classification accuracy with smaller values of β.

(a) Classification accuracy with differnet α (b) Classification accuracy with differnet β

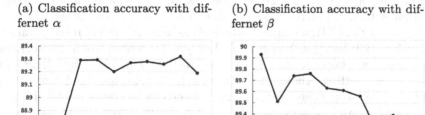

Fig. 4. Classification results of the hyperparameters study

5 Related Work

In this section, we review related work in two parts: multi-domain text classification, and contrastive learning.

5.1   Multi-Domain Text Classification

Text classification is a fundamental problem in natural language processing, which aims to assign documents with pre-defined labels. Multi-domain text classification is an extension to text classification, which leverages limited training data of different domains to improve the classification performance [11]. Currently, the mainstream methods of MDTC are based on neural networks. Bousmalis et al. [2] proposes a shared-private paradigm, where the model captures both domain-invariant features and domain-specific features to improve the discriminability. The shared-private paradigm methods are usually associated with adversarial learning. The Multinomial Adversarial Network (MAN) [5] minimizes the divergence between multiple probability distributions. Wu et al. [18] uses the shared-private paradigm and two mixup-based interpolation regularizations to improve the learned features. The conditional adversarial network(CAN) [17] aligns the joint distribution of the domain-invariant features and label predictions to improve the discriminability of the shared features. Li et al. [12] proposes a robust contrastive alignment and demonstrated that the accuracy of training one model for all domains can be competitive with methods that train a domain-specific model for each domain.

5.2   Contrastive Learning

Contrastive learning has achieved state-of-art performance in representation learning in recent years. It aims to learn an embedding space by pulling positive pairs together while pushing negative pairs apart. Positive pairs are drawn from applying data augmentation strategies to the input sample, whereas negative pairs are other different samples in the batch. Contrastive learning is a dominant component of self-supervised learning [3,7,10,20] and the learned representation is then transferred to downstream tasks with fine-tuning. Chen et al. [3] proposed SimCLR, a simple framework for learning visual representation using the InfoNCE loss [15]. Yan et al. [20] proposes a contrastive framework for sentence representation learning. It uses contrastive loss to fine-tune BERT in an unsupervised setting. Khosla et al. [9] extends the self-supervised contrastive learning to a fully-supervised setting, which effectively leverages the label information. Our approach utilizes the supervised contrastive loss and focuses more on learning better domain invariant features, thus it could generalize well on data from unseen domains.

6   Conclusion

In this paper, we proposed DaCon, a domain adversarial supervised contrastive learning framework for Multi-Domain Text Classification, which uses a supervised contrastive layer and a domain adversarial module on top of the encoded features. Our experimental results show that DaCon outperforms current state-of-art MDTC approaches using only domain-invariant features on the benchmark dataset.

References

1. Aly, R., Remus, S., Biemann, C.: Hierarchical multi-label classification of text with capsule networks. In: Proceedings of the 57th Annual Meeting of the Association for Computational Linguistics: Student Research Workshop, pp. 323–330 (2019)
2. Bousmalis, K., Trigeorgis, G., Silberman, N., Krishnan, D., Erhan, D.: Domain separation networks. In: Advances in Neural Information Processing Systems, vol. 29 (2016)
3. Chen, T., Kornblith, S., Norouzi, M., Hinton, G.: A simple framework for contrastive learning of visual representations. In: International Conference on Machine Learning, pp. 1597–1607. PMLR (2020)
4. Chen, T., Kornblith, S., Swersky, K., Norouzi, M., Hinton, G.E.: Big self-supervised models are strong semi-supervised learners. Adv. Neural. Inf. Process. Syst. **33**, 22243–22255 (2020)
5. Chen, X., Cardie, C.: Multinomial adversarial networks for multi-domain text classification. In: Proceedings of the 2018 Conference of the North American Chapter of the Association for Computational Linguistics: Human Language Technologies, Volume 1 (Long Papers), pp. 1226–1240 (2018)
6. Dai, Y., Liu, J., Ren, X., Xu, Z.: Adversarial training based multi-source unsupervised domain adaptation for sentiment analysis. In: Proceedings of the AAAI Conference on Artificial Intelligence, vol. 34, pp. 7618–7625 (2020)
7. Falcon, W., Cho, K.: A framework for contrastive self-supervised learning and designing a new approach. arXiv preprint arXiv:2009.00104 (2020)
8. Ganin, Y., et al.: Domain-adversarial training of neural networks. J. Mach. Learn. Res. **17**(1), 2030–2096 (2016)
9. Khosla, P., et al.: Supervised contrastive learning. Adv. Neural. Inf. Process. Syst. **33**, 18661–18673 (2020)
10. Kim, M., Tack, J., Hwang, S.J.: Adversarial self-supervised contrastive learning. Adv. Neural. Inf. Process. Syst. **33**, 2983–2994 (2020)
11. Li, S., Zong, C.: Multi-domain sentiment classification. In: Proceedings of ACL-08: HLT, short papers, pp. 257–260 (2008)
12. Li, X., et al.: A robust contrastive alignment method for multi-domain text classification. In: ICASSP 2022–2022 IEEE International Conference on Acoustics, Speech and Signal Processing (ICASSP), pp. 7827–7831. IEEE (2022)
13. Liu, P., Qiu, X., Huang, X.J.: Adversarial multi-task learning for text classification. In: Proceedings of the 55th Annual Meeting of the Association for Computational Linguistics (Volume 1: Long Papers), pp. 1–10 (2017)
14. Ngai, E.W., Hu, Y., Wong, Y.H., Chen, Y., Sun, X.: The application of data mining techniques in financial fraud detection: a classification framework and an academic review of literature. Decis. Support Syst. **50**(3), 559–569 (2011)
15. Oord, A.v.d., Li, Y., Vinyals, O.: Representation learning with contrastive predictive coding. arXiv preprint arXiv:1807.03748 (2018)
16. Wu, Y., Guo, Y.: Dual adversarial co-learning for multi-domain text classification. In: Proceedings of the AAAI Conference on Artificial Intelligence, vol. 34, pp. 6438–6445 (2020)
17. Wu, Y., Inkpen, D., El-Roby, A.: Conditional adversarial networks for multi-domain text classification. In: Proceedings of the Second Workshop on Domain Adaptation for NLP, pp. 16–27 (2021)
18. Wu, Y., Inkpen, D., El-Roby, A.: Mixup regularized adversarial networks for multi-domain text classification. In: ICASSP 2021–2021 IEEE International Conference on Acoustics, Speech and Signal Processing (ICASSP), pp. 7733–7737. IEEE (2021)

19. Wu, Y., Inkpen, D., El-Roby, A.: Co-regularized adversarial learning for multi-domain text classification. In: International Conference on Artificial Intelligence and Statistics, pp. 6690–6701. PMLR (2022)
20. Yan, Y., Li, R., Wang, S., Zhang, F., Wu, W., Xu, W.: ConSERT: a contrastive framework for self-supervised sentence representation transfer. arXiv preprint arXiv:2105.11741 (2021)
21. Yang, Q., Shang, L.: Multi-task learning with bidirectional language models for text classification. In: 2019 International Joint Conference on Neural Networks (IJCNN), pp. 1–8. IEEE (2019)

Exploring the Role of Recursive Convolutional Layer in Generative Adversarial Networks

Barbara Toniella Corradini[1,2(✉)], Paolo Andreini[1], Markus Hagenbuchner[3], Franco Scarselli[1], and Ah Chung Tsoi[3]

[1] Department of Information Engineering and Mathematics,
University of Siena, Siena, Italy
{paolo.andreini,franco.scarselli}@unisi.it
[2] Department of Information Engineering, University of Florence, Florence, Italy
barbaratoniella.corradini@unifi.it
[3] Faculty of Engineering and Information Sciences, School of Computing
and Information Technology, Wollongong, Australia
{markus_hagenbuchner,act}@uow.edu.au

Abstract. This paper aims to study the potentialities of incorporating recursive layers into Generative Adversarial Networks (GANs). Drawing inspiration from biological systems, in which feedback connections are prevalent, different studies investigated their impact on artificial neural networks. These studies have shown that feedback connections improve performance in tasks such as image classification and segmentation. Motivated by this insight, in this work we investigate whether also image generation can benefit from recursive architectures. To support our argument, we introduce a recursive layer into a standard generative architecture, specifically a Wasserstein GAN with gradient penalty (WGAN-GP), resulting in a novel model we refer to as the Looping Generative Adversarial Network (LoGAN). The performance of the LoGAN architecture is compared with the corresponding feedforward WGAN-GP both qualitatively and quantitatively. Preliminary experiments suggest that the use of recursive layers holds significant potential to generate higher-quality samples in GANs. The code is publicly available at https://github.com/bcorrad/LoGAN.

Keywords: Recursive neural networks · generative adversarial networks · Looping Generative Adversarial Network (LoGAN)

1 Introduction

Neural networks are traditionally based on feedforward architectures. This characteristic continues to dominate modern architectures such as Convolutional Neural Networks (CNNs) and Generative Adversarial Networks (GANs). Interestingly, those architectures are quite different from biological systems, where feedback and recursion are characteristic features [7]. Although the exact role played by those characteristics in the brain is still unclear, it is widely acknowledged that recursive dynamics are crucial for the learning process and the expressive capabilities of biological systems. Some conjectures have been made: recursion could fill parts of obstructed objects or implement a feedforward computation that repeats transformations several times [20].

Motivated by these insights, a new line of research aims at elucidating the relationship between the capability of artificial neural networks and the presence of feedback connections in their architectures. For example, the authors of [9] propose a simple recursive architecture called the Fully Recursive Perceptron Network (FRPN). It is shown that FRPNs can emulate multi-layer perceptrons (MLPs) with an arbitrary number of hidden layers and that they can perform better than traditional MLPs in tasks such as image classification. In [22], the authors reframe the concept of FRPN in CNNs, and introduce the Convolutional FRPN (C-FRPN). C-FRPNs utilise a CNN architecture with a novel internal layer called the Recursive Convolutional Layer (RCL). The authors of [19] explore a variety of architectures, termed ConvRNNs, to identify local recurrent cells and long-range feedback links that yield optimal performance in image classification tasks. These recent studies found that the introduction of recursive layers yields networks that perform better than their feedforward counterparts.

However, to the best of our knowledge, no research has been conducted on the integration of recursive layers into neural architectures for image generation. Generative neural networks are a class of machine learning models that aim to generate new data samples that resemble the distribution of a given training dataset. This paper focuses on GANs, generative architectures based on a competitive algorithm in which two agents are involved: a generator G and a discriminator D. G is trained to map a latent random variable $\mathbf{z} \in \mathbb{R}^Z$ to fake images $\tilde{\mathbf{x}} = G(\mathbf{z})$, while D aims to distinguish fake samples from real data. The GAN training is formulated as a min–max game between G and D.

This paper aims to investigate whether the integration of recursive units into a GAN can yield quantitative and qualitative benefits. Intuitively, the introduction of back connections may endow the generator with the capability of performing iterative tasks on static images, which is not feasible with traditional convolutions. To achieve such a goal, we have performed a preliminary study where an RCL is integrated into a popular generative neural network, namely a Wasserstein GAN with gradient penalty (WGAN-GP) [18]. We argue that the WGAN-GP represents a sensible middle ground between overly complex models that can be challenging to evaluate and may require significant computational resources, and overly simplistic models that lack significance. For example, state–of–the–art generative architectures such as diffusion models [12] are infeasible to train without overwhelmingly high computational resources. Our approach in using a WGAN-GP model facilitates the straightforward integration of new components, e.g., recursive layers, and their evaluations.

The proposed model, which is called Looping Generative Adversarial Network[1] (LoGAN), is compared with a feedforward generator on common benchmark datasets. The experiments reveal that LoGAN can generate images with more details and obtain a better Fréchet Inception Distance (FID). These results seem to validate the rationale behind incorporating back connections in generative architectures and suggest that back connections can play a significant role in generative models. While our results are still preliminary, the findings, nevertheless, provide a foundation that motivates future research on advancing generative methods via the introduction of recursive layers.

The rest of this paper is organized as follows: Sect. 2 gives an overview of relevant works that inspired our conjectures. Section 3 introduces the LoGAN architecture. The experimentation details are described in Sect. 4, and the results are presented and discussed in Sect. 5. Finally, Sect. 6 concludes the paper and provides an outlook for future research.

2   Related Works

The use of back connections in neural networks that process static data was first investigated in [9], where a novel architecture called Fully Recursive Perceptron Network (FRPN) is introduced. The FRPN comprises a fully connected layer with backlinks between all neurons. The state of each neuron is computed iteratively until stability or if a maximum number of iterations is reached. Experimental results demonstrate that FRPNs outperform traditional feed-forward networks in image classification.

Later, the Convolutional FRPN (C–FRPNs) has been proposed [22], which is a CNN with a novel internal layer called Recursive Convolutional Layer (RCL). The RCL is an extended version of the one-stage feedforward convolutional layer, incorporating feedback connections between the outputs and the inputs. In [24], authors have studied how the number of iterations affects the performance in image classification tasks. The ConvRNN is a generic model that allows the presence of both local recurrent cells and long–range feedback links [19]. The experimental analysis of a large number of ConvRNN architetcures have shown that, with appropriate choices of layer–local recurrent circuits and connectivity patterns with long–range feedback, ConvRNNs can achieve the same performance of much deeper feedforward CNNs but using many fewer units and parameters.

More generally, recurrent layers have broader applications in image analysis. For instance, in [1], a recurrent model called R2U–Net is proposed for image semantic segmentation, inspired by the popular U–Net architecture [21]. The R2U–Net replaces convolutional layers with recurrent convolutional units, resulting in improved performance compared to the standard feedforward U-Net.

GANs have gained increasing popularity from their introduction, achieving great success in image synthesis [2,6,14] and image-to-image translation [1,3,5].

---

[1] Some researchers in the literature use the term "recurrent" interchangeably with "recursive". In our work, we refer to our model as "looping" due to the incorporation of recursive units into a non–recurrent and non–recursive framework.

In this paper, the baseline is the WGAN–GP [18], which is a popular network that addresses common issues in generative networks, such as vanishing gradient and mode collapse. A vanishing gradient occurs when the discriminator learns faster than the generator, resulting in weak gradient feedback and lower–quality generated images. Instead, mode collapse affects the diversity of generated outputs, as the generator may get stuck in producing a limited set of outputs that easily fool the discriminator.

WGANs overcome these issues by approximating the Earth-Mover's distance instead of the Jensen-Shannon divergence used in the original GAN formulation [4]. Additionally, WGANs replace the discriminator with a critic that scores the plausibility of an image. WGAN-GP is an extension of WGAN that exploits a gradient penalty in order to enforce Lipschitz continuity [8].

Recently, much more complex generative models have been presented that have not been used in the experimentation of this paper in consideration of the expected huge computational burden and the expected difficulty of analysing the possible results in a preliminary study. For example, in [15], an architecture, called StyleGAN, has been proposed that allows to generate novel images combining characteristics of two or more input images. An improved version of StyleGAN is introduced in [16]. StyleGAN2 exploits progressive growing, where the generator starts with a low-resolution image and gradually increases the resolution during training, resulting in higher-quality images with more details. Additionally, StyleGAN2 incorporates an adaptive discriminator, which dynamically adjusts its architecture based on the generated images, leading to improved image synthesis quality and stability.

Finally, the introduction of diffusion models [23] provided a further important technique useful for the research field and, in particular, for conditional image generation. Diffusion models differ from GANs since they do not use a competitive algorithm for training, but they are based on probabilistic method that decomposes the image generation process in many small denoising steps. Interestigly, the success of those models seems to support the more general intuition, which also underlies our study, that the generation may be more efficient if the image is obatined by an iterative procedure instead directly by single step from the noise.

3 The LoGAN Model

This section presents the proposed LoGAN architecture, which embeds a Recursive Convolutional Layer (RCL) into a WGAN–GP architecture.

3.1 RCL: An Overview

An RCL [9] is a generalization of the classic one–stage feedforward convolutional layer with feedback connections between the outputs of the convolutional layer and its inputs. The basic structure of an RCL module is represented in Fig. 1a. The RCL is a recursive cell whose state is computed using a convolutional block, in which a convolution is followed by batch normalization and ReLU as a non-linear activation function. The state is back propagated to the input of the RCL with a back connection and concatenated (in the channel dimension) with the input of the RCL. Hence, at each iteration, the internal convolutional block of RCL processes a concatenation of the input and the internal state.

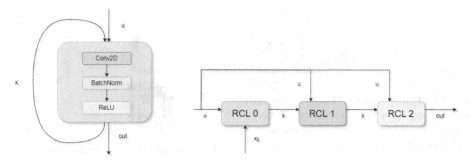

(a) RCL internal architecture   (b) Unrolled RCL architecture (3 iterations)

Fig. 1. RCL consists of a convolutional layer followed by batch normalization and a ReLU activation function (a). The feedback loop can be unfolded (b).

A more formal mathematical description of an RCL layer can be formulated as follows.

A convolution with weights $w_{i,j}, i = 1, 2, \ldots, N; j = 1, 2, \ldots, N$, operating on a $N \times N$ window on an input $u_{i,j}, i = 1, 2, \ldots, N; j = 1, 2, \ldots, N$ at position (s_1, s_2) is defined by

$$x_{s_1,s_2} = \sum_{i=-N/2}^{N/2} \sum_{j=-N/2}^{N/2} w_{i,j} u_{s_1+i,s_2+j} + b, \tag{1}$$

where x_{s_1,s_2} is the result of the convolution and the indexes s_1 and s_2 range over the entire input image.

In the case of the RCL, let u_{s_x,s_y} denote the vector of input feature maps at position s_x, s_y and $x_{s_x,s_y}(t)$ represent the vector of the state at time t at position s_x, s_y. Then, we have (Eq. 2)

$$x_{s_x,s_y}(t+1) = f\left(\sum_{i=-\frac{N}{2}}^{\frac{N}{2}} \sum_{j=-\frac{N}{2}}^{\frac{N}{2}} \alpha_{ij} u_{s_x+i,s_y+j} + \sum_{i=-\frac{N}{2}}^{\frac{N}{2}} \sum_{j=-\frac{N}{2}}^{\frac{N}{2}} \beta_{ij} x_{s_x+i,s_y+j}(t) + b \right), \tag{2}$$

where b is the neuron bias, and $\alpha_{i,j}, i = 1, 2, \ldots, n; j = 1, 2, \ldots, m, \beta_{i,k}, k = 1, 2, \ldots, n$ are the unknown weights of the kernel. The activation function $f(\cdot)$ can be one of the common function used in neural networks (e.g. sigmoids, ReLU).

An RCL with multiple iterations can be represented by an equivalent unrolled network, for example Fig. 1b shows the unrolled RCL for three iterations: At the first iteration, the convolutional layer takes the output provided by the previous layer (u) and feature maps having the same shape as u with all values set to zero (x_0). The peculiarity of RCL is that the dimension of the input does not change during the iterations, while the value of the state is updated. The input is fed to the RCL and the output is updated and referred to as x. At the next iteration, the input is formed by concatenating x and u.

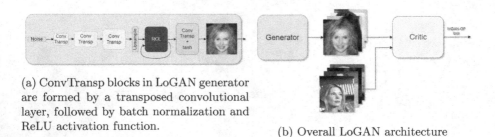

(a) ConvTransp blocks in LoGAN generator are formed by a transposed convolutional layer, followed by batch normalization and ReLU activation function.

(b) Overall LoGAN architecture

Fig. 2. LoGAN architecture

It is interesting to observe that the unfolded network is very similar to successful architectures for image classification, like resNet [10] and denseNet [13], where the input of the convolutional block is propagated with skip connections and combined with the output to subsequent processing stages. However, unlike resNet or denseNet, in an unfolded RCL the weights are shared by all layers.

3.2   Embedding RCL into WGAN–GP

The structure of LoGAN is based on a WGAN–GP (Fig. 2b): It consists of a generator and a critic that are trained in an adversarial manner. The main contribution of our work is that the WGAN–GP generator is modified by substituting one of the ConvTransp blocks with an RCL, which is composed of a transposed convolutional layer[2] followed by batch normalization and ReLU activation function.

The LoGAN is designed for an easy evaluation of the impact of the RCL compared to the WGAN–GP baseline. The generator architecture, shown in Fig. 2b, consists of a series of upsampling modules that increase spatial resolution while reducing the number of channels. More specifically, the RCL module is inserted after three ConvTransp blocks. RCL is preceded by a nearest neighbour interpolation up–sample layer that doubles the input resolution. The output of the RCL is then fed into a final transposed convolutional layer with hyperbolic tangent activation.

---

[2] Transposed convolutions [25] compute the matrix transpose of a regular convolutional layer, swapping the effect of the forward and the backwards pass as a result. They allow to use a smaller input and to learn its larger representation (as the weights are learnable).

4   Experimentation

This section compares the proposed approach with the baseline by introducing the datasets Sect. 4.1 and describing the experimental setup Sect. 4.2.

4.1   Datasets

The experiments are performed on two datasets for image generation.

CelebFaces Attributes (CelebA) [17] is a large–scale face dataset with more than 200K celebrity images, each with 40 attribute annotations. Original images have size 178×218 px, and cover large pose variations and background clutter. In this work, we used all the images of the dataset, center–cropped at resolution 64×64 px. Examples are shown in Fig. 3b.

Large-scale Scene Understanding (LSUN) [24] is a dataset for large-scale scene classification and understanding with 10 scene categories (e.g. dining room, bedroom, kitchen), each one containing a number of images ranging from around 120K to 3 million. In this work, we used 126K 64×64 px resolution images of outdoor churches. Examples are shown in Fig. 3a.

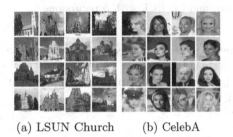

(a) LSUN Church   (b) CelebA

Fig. 3. Examples of real images from the two datasets

(a) WGAN–GP   (b) LoGAN_1   (c) LoGAN_3   (d) LoGAN_5

Fig. 4. Examples of generated images after training on CelebA dataset (epoch 100) with different configurations: (a) WGAN–GP without RCL, (b) feedforward RCL, (c) RCL with 3 recursions, and (d) RCL with 5 recursions

4.2 Experimental Setup

Our objective is to investigate whether the inclusion of RCL improves WGAN–GP. To this aim, RCLs with a different number of iterations (1, 2 and 5) are evaluated: experiments are referred to as LoGAN_1, LoGAN_3, and LoGAN_5. In all the experiments, we used WGAN–GP as the baseline, with $\beta = (0.5, 0.9)$, $lr = 10^{-4}$ and the gradient penalty set to 10 as in [8]. All the training were performed for 100 epochs.

| (a) WGAN–GP | (b) LoGAN_1 | (c) LoGAN_3 | (d) LoGAN_5 |

Fig. 5. Examples of generated images after training on LSUN Church dataset (epoch 100) with different configurations: (a) WGAN–GP without RCL, (b) feedforward RCL, (c) RCL with 3 recursions, and (d) RCL with 5 recursions

We measure the performance on 10K generated images using the Frechét Inception Distance (FID) [11].

Experiments were performed on a computer equipped with 128GB RAM and a 24 GB Nvidia Titan RTX GPU.

5 Results

In this section, we compare the WGAN–GP and the LoGAN with a single RCL iteration (LoGAN_1), we evaluate the effect of increasing the number of iterations in the RCL, and we make a comparison between LoGAN and the baseline WGAN–GP.

5.1 Feedforward Generator: WGAN–GP Vs. LoGAN_1

The WGAN–GP and the LoGAN_1 architectures are very similar in terms of both structure and number of trainable parameters. In fact, the RCL is unrolled for only one iteration, so the difference between the two architectures is only that the transposed convolution of WGAN–GP is replaced by the nearest neighbour upsampling followed by a standard convolution in LoGAN. The experimental results listed in Table 1 show that, although the two models give similar results, the WGAN–GP slightly outperforms LoGAN_1 in terms of FID. Nevertheless, we show below that the generation performance improves by increasing the number of RCL iterations and it is possible to improve the FID with respect to both the LoGAN_1 and WGAN–GP baselines.

Table 1. FID comparison between the baseline and our LoGAN with an RCL performing one iteration on 10K images generated from model at epoch 100 after training on CelebA and LSUN Church datasets

Dataset Name	Configuration	No. of parameters	FID ↓
CelebA	**WGAN–GP**	1,100,227	**88.133**
	LoGAN_1	1,095,107	92.033
LSUN Church	**WGAN–GP**	1,100,227	**27.640**
	LoGAN_1	1,095,107	30.293

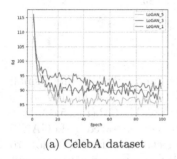

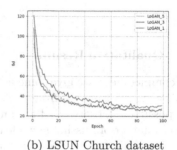

(a) CelebA dataset   (b) LSUN Church dataset

Fig. 6. Trend of FID evaluated for each epoch on 10K samples generated after training LoGAN_1, LoGAN_3 and LoGAN_5 on CelebA (a) and LSUN Church (b) datasets

5.2   Evaluating the Effect of a Different Number of Iterations

Figures 6a and 6b show the trend of FID score for LoGAN_1, LoGAN_3 and LoGAN_5, calculated for each training epoch on the CelebA and the LSUN Church datasets. It can be observed that, compared to LoGAN_1, there is a significant improvement in terms of FID as the number of RCL iterations increases. Interestingly, the trend of the FID differs between the two datasets: While the experiments on CelebA show a significant improvement from LoGAN_1 to LoGAN_5, the performance of LoGAN_3 and LoGAN_5 is similar in LSUN Church. This may suggest that (i) increasing the number of iterations can improve the performance of the model and (ii) the optimal number of iterations depends on the specific training dataset. It will be a matter of future research to better investigate on this phenomenon.

Significantly, LoGAN outperforms the baseline models in terms of FID for both the CelebA and LSUN Church datasets, as shown in Table 3. This preliminary result highlights the potential of back connections in improving the quality of GAN generation, opening up new research opportunities to study the impact of recursion on generative models (Table 2).

Table 2. FID comparison of LoGANs with RCL iterations (1, 3, and 5) on CelebA and LSUN Church datasets, evaluated on 10K images generated from the model at epoch 100 after training

Dataset	Configuration	FID ↓
CelebA	LoGAN_1	92.033
	LoGAN_3	89.996
	LoGAN_5	**85.602**
LSUN Church	LoGAN_1	30.293
	LoGAN_3	**26.107**
	LoGAN_5	27.785

5.3 Qualitative Results

For completeness, we give some qualitative results by randomly selecting a small set of generated images from each of the two datasets (see Fig. 4 and Fig. 5). It is possible to observe that the images generated by WGAN-GP (Fig. 5a) have a higher number of missing facial features than the images generated by LoGAN_5 (Fig. 5d). This may suggest that the feedback connections in LoGAN allow to correct errors in image generation. Nevertheless, this phenomenon is less evident in the lower resolution LSUN Church dataset (Fig. 5) so that in this case it is not possible draw significant conclusions.

Our hypothesis is that the optimal number of RCL iterations and their effect depend on the complexity of dataset in terms of both resolution and number of details.

The effectiveness of the number of recursions as a function of the resolution of the dataset will be further investigated in future works.

Table 3. FID comparison between LoGAN and the baseline on 10K images generated from the two models at epoch 100 after training on CelebA and LSUN Church datasets

Dataset	Configuration	No. of parameters	FID ↓
CelebA	WGAN–GP	1,100,227	88.133
	LoGAN	**1,095,107**	**85.602**
LSUN Church	WGAN–GP	1,100,227	27.640
	LoGAN	**1,095,107**	**26.107**

6   Conclusions

The preliminary study presented in this paper provides evidence for a postitive impact of incorporating a recursive layer into a generative architecture. This is demonstrated by introducing a novel model called LoGAN, which integrates an RCL into a WGAN–GP. It is shown that the presence of a recursive layer can significantly improve the performance when compared with the standard WGAN-GP.

This paper further investigated the impact of the number of recursions within the RCL on the generation performance. The results obtained by the presented study suggest that the number of recursions plays a crucial role in the generation performance of the model. Indeed, in our experiments we observe that, with more than one recursion, the quality of the generated samples is consistently improved. Moreover, we argue that the optimal number of recursions may vary depending on the complexity of the dataset, including factors such as the resolution and the depicted subject. These findings highlight promising avenues for further research on how back connections can enhance GAN performance. In particular, different datasets and models could be explored to delve deeply into the potential benefits of using back connections in generative models.

References

1. Alom, M.Z., Hasan, M., Yakopcic, C., Taha, T.M., Asari, V.K.: Recurrent residual convolutional neural network based on u-net (r2u-net) for medical image segmentation. arXiv preprint arXiv:1802.06955 (2018)
2. Andreini, P., Bonechi, S., Bianchini, M., Mecocci, A., Scarselli, F.: Image generation by GAN and style transfer for agar plate image segmentation. Comput. Methods Programs Biomed. **184**, 105268 (2020)
3. Andreini, P., et al.: A two-stage GAN for high-resolution retinal image generation and segmentation. Electronics **11**(1), 60 (2021)
4. Arjovsky, M., Chintala, S., Bottou, L.: Wasserstein generative adversarial networks. In: International Conference on Machine Learning, pp. 214–223. PMLR (2017)
5. Ciano, G., Andreini, P., Mazzierli, T., Bianchini, M., Scarselli, F.: A multi-stage GAN for multi-organ chest X-RAY image generation and segmentation. Mathematics **9**(22), 2896 (2021)
6. Curtó, J.D., Zarza, I.C., De La Torre, F., King, I., Lyu, M.R.: High-resolution deep convolutional generative adversarial networks. arXiv preprint arXiv:1711.06491 (2017)
7. Gilbert, C.D., Li, W.: Top-down influences on visual processing. Nat. Rev. Neurosci. **14**(5), 350–363 (2013)
8. Gulrajani, I., Ahmed, F., Arjovsky, M., Dumoulin, V., Courville, A.C.: Improved training of wasserstein GANs. In: Advances in Neural Information Processing Systems, vol. 30 (2017)
9. Hagenbuchner, M., Tsoi, A.C., Scarselli, F., Zhang, S.J.: A fully recursive perceptron network architecture. In: 2017 IEEE Symposium Series on Computational Intelligence (SSCI), pp. 1–8. IEEE (2017)
10. He, K., Zhang, X., Ren, S., Sun, J.: Deep residual learning for image recognition. 2016 IEEE Conference on Computer Vision and Pattern Recognition (CVPR), pp. 770–778 (2015)
11. Heusel, M., Ramsauer, H., Unterthiner, T., Nessler, B., Hochreiter, S.: GANs trained by a two time-scale update rule converge to a local nash equilibrium. In: Advances in Neural Information Processing Systems, vol. 30 (2017)

12. Ho, J., Jain, A., Abbeel, P.: Denoising diffusion probabilistic models (2020)
13. Huang, G., Liu, Z., van der Maaten, L., Weinberger, K.Q.: Densely connected convolutional networks. In: Proceedings of the IEEE Conference on Computer Vision and Pattern Recognition (2017)
14. Karras, T., Laine, S., Aila, T.: A style-based generator architecture for generative adversarial networks. In: 2019 IEEE/CVF Conference on Computer Vision and Pattern Recognition (CVPR), pp. 4396–4405 (2019)
15. Karras, T., Laine, S., Aila, T.: StyleGan: a style-based generator architecture for generative adversarial networks. In: Proceedings of the IEEE/CVF Conference on Computer Vision and Pattern Recognition (CVPR), pp. 4396–4405 (2019)
16. Karras, T., Laine, S., Aittala, M., Hellsten, J., Lehtinen, J., Aila, T.: Analyzing and improving the image quality of StyleGan. In: Proceedings of the IEEE/CVF Conference on Computer Vision and Pattern Recognition (CVPR), pp. 8110–8119 (2020)
17. Liu, Z., Luo, P., Wang, X., Tang, X.: Deep learning face attributes in the wild. In: Proceedings of International Conference on Computer Vision (ICCV), December (2015)
18. Lucic, M., Kurach, K., Michalski, M., Gelly, S., Bousquet, O.: Are GANs created equal? a large-scale study. In: Advances in Neural Information Processing Systems, vol. 31 (2018)
19. Nayebi, A., et al.: Task-driven convolutional recurrent models of the visual system. In: Advances in Neural Information Processing Systems, vol. 31 (2018)
20. Nayebi, A., et al.: Recurrent connections in the primate ventral visual stream mediate a tradeoff between task performance and network size during core object recognition. Neural Comput. **34**(18), 1652–1675 (2022)
21. Ronneberger, O., Fischer, P., Brox, T.: U-Net: convolutional networks for biomedical image segmentation. In: Navab, N., Hornegger, J., Wells, W.M., Frangi, A.F. (eds.) MICCAI 2015. LNCS, vol. 9351, pp. 234–241. Springer, Cham (2015). https://doi.org/10.1007/978-3-319-24574-4_28
22. Rossi, A., Hagenbuchner, M., Scarselli, F., Tsoi, A.C.: A study on the effects of recursive convolutional layers in convolutional neural networks. Neurocomputing **460**, 59–70 (2021)
23. Yang, L., et al.: A comprehensive survey of methods and applications, Diffusion models (2023)
24. Yu, F., Seff, A., Zhang, Y., Song, S., Funkhouser, T., Xiao, J.: LSUN: construction of a large-scale image dataset using deep learning with humans in the loop. arXiv preprint arXiv:1506.03365 (2015)
25. Zeiler, M.D., Krishnan, D., Taylor, G.W., Fergus, R.: Deconvolutional networks. In: 2010 IEEE Computer Society Conference on Computer Vision and Pattern Recognition, pp. 2528–2535. IEEE (2010)

GC-GAN: Photo Cartoonization Using Guided Cartoon Generative Adversarial Network

Jiachen Zhang[1], Huantong Hou[1], Jingjing Chen[2], and Donglong Chen[1](✉)

[1] Guangdong Provincial Key Laboratory IRADS, BNU-HKBU United International College, Zhuhai, China
franklinzjcc@gmail.com, huantonghou@gmail.com, donglongchen@uic.edu.cn
[2] Fudan University, Shanghai, China
chenjingjing@fudan.edu.cn

Abstract. Image cartoonization, a subfield of image translation, has gained increasing attention in recent years. However, the overall performance of existing methods is limited by shortcomings such as poorly fitting regions. To address these issues, our paper proposes the Guided Cartoon Generative Adversarial Network (GC-GAN). Our approach introduces a segmentation step before the training process, which splits and guides mixed training images into a human face set and a scenery set. This enables our model to extract features specifically from cartoon faces and generate more realistic results. Furthermore, we include a loss function called triplet loss in our framework, which drives the network to bring output closer to a referenced image and focus more on the detailed parts of the training images. This improves the overall quality of the generated images and addresses the issue of poorly fitting regions. Compared to the state-of-the-art White-box CartoonGAN, our work improves Fréchet Inception Distance by 18.7% and Kernel Inception Distance by 17.6%, respectively. Additionally, our work surpasses AnimeGAN in terms of Fréchet Inception Distance by 40.7% and Kernel Inception Distance by 47.4%.

Keywords: Generative adversarial network · Image cartoonization · Image translation

1 Introduction

Image cartoonization is a subfield of image translation that aims to transform real-world images into cartoon images. It has become an increasingly popular topic in the entertainment industry. However, the high cost of acquiring paired images makes supervised learning less feasible for practical applications. Therefore, unsupervised learning methods that use unpaired images for training are commonly employed in practical scenarios. Generative Adversarial Networks (GAN) [3] are one such method that utilizes unpaired images for training. They

L. Iliadis et al. (Eds.): ICANN 2023, LNCS 14258, pp. 65–77, 2023.
https://doi.org/10.1007/978-3-031-44192-9_6

enable tasks such as image translation and colorization. The working principle of a GAN model involves training two networks simultaneously and allowing them to compete with each other to improve their own performances. This ultimately results in high-quality outputs.

CycleGAN [13] is a well-known GAN framework that has made significant contributions to image translation. It utilizes two paired generators and discriminators, with each pair forming a mapping. Apart from cycle-based methods, there are other types of approaches for applying the GAN framework to image cartoonization tasks. For instance, White-box CartoonGAN [12] extracts different representations of an image and trains the generator based on the information contained in those representations.

While current methods are capable of cartoonizing images, there are still unresolved issues that need to be addressed. One issue is that the training data often contains a mixture of both human face images and scenery images, which can confuse the training of the generator. Additionally, the inability to effectively handle local features and properly fit them to detailed regions limits the effectiveness of these methods. Figure 1 provides some examples where it is apparent that the model is unable to properly balance the degree of detail preservation in the generated image, resulting in the presence of superfluous short lines in the main body of the output.

Fig. 1. Two failure cases of generated images, where the AnimeGANv2 [1] is applied.

To address the issues mentioned above, we propose an improved model called the Guided Cartoon Generative Adversarial Network (GC-GAN) to generate high-quality cartoon images. This work makes three major contributions:

- To improve the training accuracy of the generator model in generating human faces, which consist of intricate details compared to other scenery images, we incorporate a pre-processing phase at the beginning of the training process. This phase utilizes an instance segmentation network to split the input real-world images into two separate sets: one set containing images primarily featuring human faces, and another set containing images primarily featuring scenery. This strategy improves the training quality of the model in both domains.
- To improve the model's ability to handle local features of human faces, we integrate a loss function called triplet loss [10] into the architecture. This

function brings the output images and references closer together while simultaneously maximizing the distance between the output images and real-world photos. As a result, triplet loss helps the model to preserve more details in the generated images.

- The experimental results suggest that our proposed GC-GAN is capable of generating high-quality cartoonized images that outperform existing methods in terms of both qualitative and quantitative comparisons. Specifically, the Fréchet Inception Distance and Kernel Inception Distance are improved by 18.7% and 17.6%, respectively, when compared to White-box Cartoon-GAN [12]. Additionally, our work surpasses AnimeGAN by 40.7% on Fréchet Inception Distance and 47.4% on Kernel Inception Distance.

2 Related Work

Generative Adversarial Networks (GANs) have demonstrated impressive results in image cartoonization. As discussed in Sect. 1, training a GAN model involves simultaneously training a generator and discriminator to transfer an image to the target domain. In the context of image cartoonization, four different types of methods have been proposed to improve the quality of GAN models. The first type is cycle-based methods, exemplified by CycleGAN [13]. These methods leverage multiple generator-discriminator pairs and incorporate a cycle consistency loss into the training procedure to ensure that the generated image differs from the source image.

Furthermore, alternative methods that employ the GAN framework for image cartoonization tasks have been put forward. Conditional-based approaches [5] integrate supplementary information, such as class labels or data from other modalities, into the image generation process. This is accomplished by feeding the class labels into both the generator and discriminator. On the other hand, representation-based techniques [12] extract diverse representations of an image and train the generator based on the knowledge embedded in those representations.

Instance segmentation is a technique for segmenting images that identifies different objects and accurately delineates their boundaries. One of the most prominent frameworks for instance segmentation is the Mask Region-based Convolutional Neural Network (Mask R-CNN) [4], which has made significant contributions to the field. A key innovation of this approach is the introduction of RoIAlign, a novel layer that greatly improves the accuracy of mask prediction. Furthermore, Mask R-CNN has incorporated the backbones of other architectures, such as FPN [8], to enhance overall performance in instance segmentation. The method also offers the advantages of ease of inference and fast training time.

3 Methodology

In this work, we propose a novel GAN model called the Guided Cartoon Generative Adversarial Network (GC-GAN), the architecture of which is illustrated

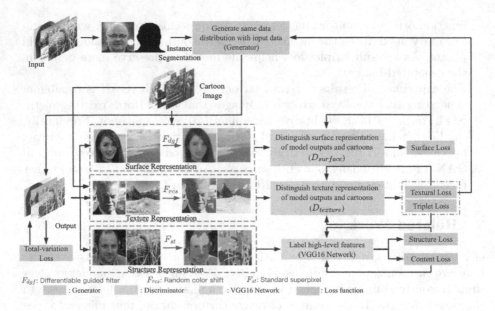

Fig. 2. Architecture of GC-GAN

in Fig. 2. The model is built upon the architecture of the White-box Cartoon-GAN [12] and consists of several components, as detailed below.

Compared to real-world images, cartoon images are characterized by sparse color blocks, smooth surfaces, clear boundaries, and high luminance. To generate better cartoon images, GC-GAN uses surface, textural, and structure representation. Discriminators then differentiate between the representation extracted from output images and cartoons. Surface and textural losses from two pairs of GANs aid the model in outlining smoother structures and effectively learning high-frequency features. For texture representation, a triplet loss works in conjunction with the textural loss to produce a more natural transformation of detailed edges. To constrain and achieve a desired structure, a structure loss is added to the structure representation. Furthermore, total variation loss is employed to address high-level noise that may significantly lower image quality, while content loss guarantees the cartoon images are semantically invariant. These two loss functions leverage a pre-trained VGG16 Network [11].

The experimental results demonstrate that the scenery images are more effectively transformed than human faces, particularly with respect to color information. As such, a pre-trained instance segmentation network is employed at the onset of training in order to separately refine these two sets of images and optimize performance accordingly. To this end, the Feature Pyramid Network (FPN) combined with Mask R-CNN is used to conduct instance segmentation of the training data, thus allowing the data to be partitioned into two distinct sets (i.e. human faces and scenery) and trained independently to adequately address the challenge of mixed training data.

3.1   Model Structure

Similar to White-box CartoonGAN, GC-GAN incorporates one generator, G, and two discriminators, $D_{surface}$ and $D_{texture}$ respectively, to generate surface and texture representations. The architecture of GC-GAN is depicted in Fig. 2, and it is capable of extracting three different representations from input images.

- **Surface representation**: In order to remove textures and details of instances while preserving the surface representation, a guided filter [12] is utilized, in which the input image serves as both a reference for the guided map and a filtering mechanism.
- **Structure representation**: To segment the color blocks of an image and enhance its contrast, we incorporate the Felzenszwalb algorithm [2] and an adaptive coloring algorithm. Moreover, a pre-trained VGG network is utilized to categorize high-level features and impose spatial constraints on global content.
- **Textural representation**. A random shifting algorithm [12] is proposed for the purpose of extracting single-channel texture representations of cartoon images, retaining only high-frequency textures.

The two discriminators $D_{surface}$ and $D_{texture}$ are instituted to guide G in learning the information from the extracted representations. Their purpose is to differentiate between extracted representations from model outputs and cartoons.

The significant differences between human faces and scenery may potentially affect the training of the generator when combining these two sets of images. To address this issue, a segmentation network is integrated at the beginning of the model to preprocess the training data and improve the efficacy of the training process.

3.2   Networks

The structure of our model comprises of three key components: an instance segmentation network utilized to separate the human faces in the training images; a generator which extracts three distinct representations; and two discriminators employed to guide the generator and direct its focus towards the information embodied by the extracted representations.

To be more specific, the pre-trained segmentation network produces binary masks of the instances in the input image and assigns corresponding labels. In each training image, the size of the face area relative to the overall image is used to determine whether it is classified as a human face image or a cartoon image. Only face areas that are sufficiently large within the image are considered as face images.

Therefore, after the network generates the mask for each instance in an input image, our model calculates the proportion of the number of pixels in the mask relative to its instance in the image. Only when the mask proportion exceeds a certain threshold is the image classified as a human face image. Based on the results of this calculation, the images are then assigned to one of two subsets of training images, either human faces or scenery.

The generator in GC-GAN is a fully convolutional U-Net-like network, which utilizes stride-2 convolutional layers as down-sampling layers and bilinear interpolation layers as up-sampling layers. This architecture effectively avoids checkerboard effects. The down-sampling part resizes the image to 64×64 pixels with 128 channels, from the original 256×256 pixels. The generator also contains four residual blocks. Spectral norm is included in the discriminator to generate stable results. The discriminator takes the generated images, which are 256×256 pixels with 3 channels, and outputs a 32×32 matrix.

3.3   Formulation

The GC-GAN proposed in this study incorporates six distinct loss functions, namely surface loss function $\mathcal{L}_{surface}(G, D_{surface})$, structure loss function $\mathcal{L}_{structure}$, triplet loss function $\mathcal{L}_{triplet}$, textural loss function $\mathcal{L}_{texture}$ $(G, D_{texture})$, total variation loss function $\mathcal{L}_{tv}$ and content loss function $\mathcal{L}_{content}$. Together, these loss functions function collaboratively within the model by

$$
\begin{aligned}
\mathcal{L}_{total} = \quad & \lambda_{st} \times (\mathcal{L}_{surface} + \mathcal{L}_{triplet}) \\
+ \;& \lambda_{tt} \times \mathcal{L}_{texture} + \lambda_{s} \times \mathcal{L}_{structure} \\
+ \;& \lambda_{c} \times \mathcal{L}_{content} + \lambda_{tv} \times \mathcal{L}_{tv}
\end{aligned} \tag{1}
$$

where $\lambda_{st}, \lambda_{tt}, \lambda_{s}, \lambda_{c}, \lambda_{tv}$ are weight parameters controlling the importance of different loss parts.

Surface Loss. Fig. 3(a) illustrates that the representation primarily preserves global semantic structures. Consequently, in surface representation, the surface loss function is primarily devoted to maintaining the structure. This function operates by utilizing a generator-discriminator pair trained on images that have undergone edge-preserving filtering named F_{dgf}.

The Discriminator $D_{surface}$ has the task of determining whether the referenced images have a similar surface to that of the mode outputs. It guides the Generator G to learn potential information from referenced cartoon images. The loss, denoted as I_p for input real-world images and I_c for target cartoon images, includes the surface loss, which is designed to be:

$$
\begin{aligned}
\mathcal{L}_{surface}(G, D_s) = \quad & \log D_S(F_{dgf}(I_c, I_c)) \\
& + \log(1 - D_S(F_{dgf}(G(I_p), G(I_p))))
\end{aligned} \tag{2}
$$

Structure Loss. To obtain color blocks, an adaptive coloring algorithm is applied to the structure representation (shown in Fig. 3(c)). During the pre-training phase, VGG extracts high-level features and labels them (shown in

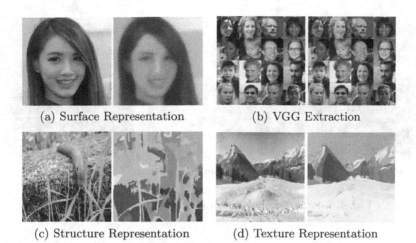

(a) Surface Representation   (b) VGG Extraction

(c) Structure Representation   (d) Texture Representation

Fig. 3. Three different representations and the extracted result of VGG in GC-GAN.

Fig. 3(b)). These features mainly have high luminance and may cause overexposure problems during the training procedure.

In order to ensure the output results are consistent with the extracted structure representation from the pre-trained VGG16 network, the loss function must impose constraints. The L_1 norm is specialized in features selection, and therefore, $L_{structure}$ is set as:

$$\mathcal{L}_{structure} = ||VGG_n(G(I_p)) - VGG_n(\mathcal{F}_{st}(G(I_p)))|| \tag{3}$$

where F_{st} is denoted as extracted structure representation.

Textural Loss. The objective of textural representation (shown in Fig. 3(d)) is to capture the color information of cartoons. Since luminance can have a negative impact on RGB images, the representation first utilizes a random color shift algorithm F_{rcs} to obtain a single channel by converting images from RGB to grayscale. This process helps to reduce the influence of luminance and color.

Similar to the surface loss, the textural loss function also incorporates ideas from GAN. The Discriminator $D_{texture}$ is responsible for differentiating between texture representations from model and target images. It also guides generator G to learn fine textures.

$$\mathcal{L}_{texture}(G, D_t) = \log D_t(\mathcal{F}_{rcs}(I_c)) + \log(1 - D_t(\mathcal{F}_{rcs}(G(I_p)))) \tag{4}$$

Triplet Loss. Clear edges are undoubtedly crucial for cartoon images. However, some objects, such as clouds in Fig. 4(b), have super sharp edges that could become distorted. The model must converge perfectly in a small area with many details and generate cartoon images with the true texture of objects (Fig. 4(c)).

(a) Real world image   (b) Without triplet   (c) With triplet

Fig. 4. Comparison between using triplet function or not.

To achieve this, a triplet loss function is introduced to help the model converge better in the textural representation only.

The triplet loss function plays a vital role in producing accurate results for detailed edges. It requires three instances, including anchor x_i^a, positive x_i^p, and negative x_i^n. In the context of cartoon images, the anchors are real cartoon images, the positive samples are generated cartoon images, and the negative samples are real-world images. The function aims to minimize distances between the anchor and positive and maximize distances between the anchor and negative under the constraint that the former distance must be smaller than the latter one.

$$||x_i^a - x_i^p||_2^2 + \alpha < ||x_i^a - x_i^n||_2^2, \ \forall (x_i^a, \ x_i^p, x_i^n) \in \mathcal{T} \qquad (5)$$

To achieve detailed convergence results, the model selects the output distances of two discriminators between real-world photos and cartoon images as the optimization targets.

Content Loss and Total-Variation Loss. To address overfitting during training, a regularization term is introduced in the form of total variation loss, which promotes spatial smoothness and reduces noise. In Eq. 6, the dimensions of the images are denoted by H, W, C, corresponding to height, width, and channels respectively.

$$\mathcal{L}_{tv} = \frac{1}{H * W * C} ||\nabla_x (G(I_p)) + \nabla_y (G(I_p))||. \qquad (6)$$

To ensure semantic consistency between the input photos and the resulting cartoonized images, a content loss is introduced. This loss computes weighted distances between local features and further improves the cartoonization process.

$$\mathcal{L}_{content} = ||VGG_n (G(I_p)) - VGG_n (I_p)||. \qquad (7)$$

4 Experimental Results and Comparisons

For model training, we use the same dataset as White-box CartoonGAN [12]. The training set comprises 10000 real-world images of human faces and 5000 images of landscapes, as well as 10,000 cartoon images of human faces and scenery, all of which have been resized to 256×256 pixels. The testing set includes 2006 human face images from FDDB database [6] and 5000 images of various scenarios images from Microsoft COCO Dataset [9].

The training process is divided into three stages. In the segmentation stage, all training images are fed into the pre-trained Mask R-CNN network to determine whether they are human faces. For the pre-training phase, the generator is fed with all training images for a total of 20 epochs (10 for face images and 10 for landscape images). Lastly, the training phase consists of 400 epochs, with 200 epochs for face images and 200 epochs for landscape images.

4.1 Evaluation Methods

The paper evaluates cartoon images from both quantitative and qualitative aspects. Experimental results show that GC-GAN improves in color hue, small object detection, and clear boundaries. For quantitative evaluation, three different indices are employed.

Fréchet Inception Distance (FID) measures the dissimilarity between two univariate Gaussian distributions. Generally, a lower FID suggests that the model is better suited for a wide range of images.

Kernel Inception Distance (KID) discerns the disparity between two clusters of samples by computing the square of the most significant mean discrepancy between Inception representations. Moreover, KID is more consistent with human perception compared to FID, as KID has a fair estimation of the cubic kernel.

4.2 Quantitative Evaluation

As evidenced in Table 1, the performance indicators of GC-GAN are superior to those of AnimeGANv2, U-GAT-IT, and White-box CartoonGAN in both indicators. FID measures the similarity between real-world images and cartoon images. When compared with the other two models, GC-GAN exhibits better outcomes, as the triplet function aids the model converge more effectively on transformed edges and preserve more details. Likewise, as KID gauges the maximum mean disparity between the extracted features from both real-world images and cartoon images, the KID value of GC-GAN implies that it could create better results. U-GAT-IT is specifically engineered for cartoonizing human faces, hence the generated substandard results of scenery images yield comparatively poorer FID and KID indices.

Given that the primary objective of the U-GAT-IT model is to transform faces into cartoons, we used faces exclusively as the test set and repeat the calculation for both the U-GAT-IT and GC-GAN models. The results are also presented in the Table 1. GC-GAN outperformed U-GAT-IT in both indicators.

Table 1. Performance comparison of AnimeGANv2 [1], White-box CartoonGAN [12], U-GAT-IT [7] and the proposed GC-GAN. Note that the test set used on the left contains both faces and scenery images, while the right contains only faces.

Index	Faces and Scenery				Faces	
	Anime	White-box	U-GAT-IT	GC-GAN	U-GAT-IT	**GC-GAN**
FID	40.6625	29.6287	119.4351	**24.0976**	170.2460	**132.1410**
KID	0.0196	0.0125	0.0836	**0.0103**	0.1590	**0.00031**

4.3 Qualitative Evaluation

Qualitative analysis of generated cartoon images is conducted as well. Specifically, as can be seen in Fig. 5 and Fig. 6, GC-GAN produces high-quality cartoon images with sparse coloring of major content and color hue.

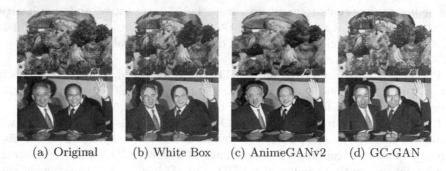

(a) Original   (b) White Box   (c) AnimeGANv2   (d) GC-GAN

Fig. 5. Other sceneries of GC-GAN have greater luminosity and more accurate colors compared to those of White-box CartoonGAN and AnimeGANv2.

In Fig. 7, our model is able to handle even the minutest of subjects better. For instance, the model recognizes and cartoonizes nets and lavender flowers. In Fig. 8, the model preserves more particulars and more distinct boundaries of the grass.

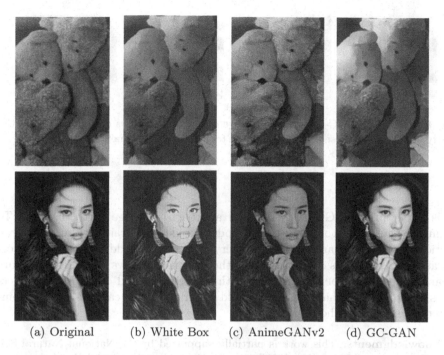

(a) Original   (b) White Box   (c) AnimeGANv2   (d) GC-GAN

Fig. 6. GC-GAN's human faces have greater luminosity and more accurate colors compared to those of White-box CartoonGAN and AnimeGANv2.

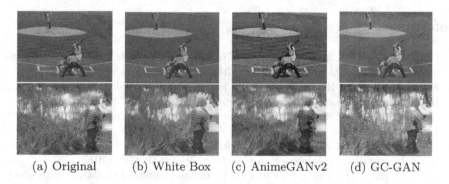

(a) Original   (b) White Box   (c) AnimeGANv2   (d) GC-GAN

Fig. 7. Examples of GC-GAN have more precise identification compared to those of White-box CartoonGAN and AnimeGANv2.

(a) Original   (b) White Box   (c) AnimeGANv2   (d) GC-GAN

Fig. 8. Examples of GC-GAN possess more distinct boundaries on animal fur particularly compared to those of White-box CartoonGAN and AnimeGANv2.

5   Conclusion

This paper presents GC-GAN, a novel approach to image cartoonization. To maintain the initial color hues, the model divides the training data into two sections to train human faces and scenery respectively. Additionally, the incorporation of triplet loss combined with other functions allows GC-GAN to secure clear boundaries. Experiments from both quantitative and qualitative perspectives demonstrated that GC-GAN could generate better cartoon images compared to existing methods.

Acknowledgments. This work is partially supported by the National Natural Science Foundation of China (No. 62002023), the Guangdong Provincial Key Laboratory IRADS (2022B1212010006, R0400001-22), and the UIC research grant (R202103).

References

1. Chen, J., Liu, G., Chen, X.: AnimeGAN: a novel lightweight GAN for photo animation. In: Artificial Intelligence Algorithms and Applications (2020)
2. Felzenszwalb, P.F., Huttenlocher, D.P.: Efficient graph-based image segmentation. Int. J. Comput. Vision **59**, 161–181 (2004)
3. Goodfellow, I.J., et al.: Generative adversarial networks. Commun. ACM **63**(11) 139–144 (2020)
4. He, K., Gkioxari, G., Dollar, P., Girshick, R.: Mask R-CNN. In: Proceedings of the IEEE International Conference on Computer Vision (ICCV) (2017)
5. Isola, P., Zhu, J.Y., Zhou, T., Efros, A.A.: Image-to-image translation with conditional adversarial networks. In: Proceedings of the IEEE Conference on Computer Vision and Pattern Recognition (CVPR) (2017)
6. Jain, V., Learned-Miller, E.: Fddb: A benchmark for face detection in unconstrained settings. Tech. Rep. UM-CS-2010-009, University of Massachusetts, Amherst (2010)
7. Kim, J., Kim, M., Kang, H., Lee, K.: U-GAT-IT: unsupervised generative attentional networks with adaptive layer-instance normalization for image-to-image translation. CoRR abs/1907.10830 (2019)
8. Lin, T.Y., Dollar, P., Girshick, R., He, K., Hariharan, B., Belongie, S.: Feature pyramid networks for object detection. In: Proceedings of the IEEE Conference on Computer Vision and Pattern Recognition (CVPR) (2017)

9. Lin, T.-Y., et al.: Microsoft COCO: common objects in context. In: Fleet, D., Pajdla, T., Schiele, B., Tuytelaars, T. (eds.) ECCV 2014. LNCS, vol. 8693, pp. 740–755. Springer, Cham (2014). https://doi.org/10.1007/978-3-319-10602-1_48
10. Schroff, F., Kalenichenko, D., Philbin, J.: FaceNet: A unified embedding for face recognition and clustering. In: Proceedings of the IEEE Conference on Computer Vision and Pattern Recognition (CVPR) (2015)
11. Simonyan, K., Zisserman, A.: Very deep convolutional networks for large-scale image recognition. CoRR abs/1409.1556 (2014)
12. Wang, X., Yu, J.: Learning to cartoonize using white-box cartoon representations. In: Proceedings of the IEEE/CVF Conference on Computer Vision and Pattern Recognition (CVPR) (2020)
13. Zhu, J.Y., Park, T., Isola, P., Efros, A.A.: Unpaired image-to-image translation using cycle-consistent adversarial networks. In: Proceedings of the IEEE International Conference on Computer Vision (ICCV) (2017)

Generating Distinctive Facial Images from Natural Language Descriptions via Spatial Map Fusion

Qi Guo ⓘ and Xiaodong Gu(✉) ⓘ

Department of Electronic Engineering, Fudan University, Shanghai 200438, China
xdgu@fudan.edu.cn

Abstract. Due to the abstract nature of language, creating accurate visual representations of faces using textual descriptions is a complex task. To overcome this challenge, we propose a novel approach called the Spatial-Text Semantic Fusion GAN (STSF-GAN) network that leverages multiple descriptions to generate distinct facial features. Our proposed method includes a new module called the Spatial Map Merge module, which predicts masks as the spatial condition to refine image feature maps based on textual semantics. Additionally, we introduce an attention mechanism called the Local Semantic Attention module that utilizes the potential distribution of each word in the description to compute local attention. Our experiments on Multi-Modal CelebA-HQ and CelebAText-HQ dataset demonstrate the effectiveness of our proposed approach.

Keywords: Text to Face · Attention Mechanism · Generative Adversarial Networks

1 Introduction

The task of text to face generation (T2F) has attracted significant attention in recent years, due to its potential applications in various fields such as virtual reality, entertainment, and law enforcement. The ability to generate realistic facial images from natural language descriptions can have a significant impact on improving human-computer interaction and can provide valuable tools for forensic investigators. However, this task presents significant challenges due to the inherent differences between textual and visual information.

T2F techniques have been developed due to rapid progress in deep learning, enabling the creation of powerful generative models capable of generating highly realistic images. One of the earliest and most influential works in this area is Generative Adversarial Networks (GANs) proposed by Goodfellow et al. [1]. Recently, numerous studies have been conducted to improve the performance of T2F by leveraging advanced deep learning techniques such as diffusion models [2]. However, GAN-based techniques, such as StyleGAN [3], have gained significant attention in the field of image generation. These models operate by training

L. Iliadis et al. (Eds.): ICANN 2023, LNCS 14258, pp. 78–89, 2023.
https://doi.org/10.1007/978-3-031-44192-9_7

a generator network to fabricate images with a high degree of realism, which can deceive a discriminator network into assuming them as genuine. GAN-based techniques have several advantages, such as producing high-quality images with natural-looking features and textures. Furthermore, they are flexible and can create various types of images ranging from realistic to stylized ones. Additionally, GAN-based methods offer rapid image generation, which makes them useful for real-time applications. Thus, we have optimized the GAN-based approach to enhance its suitability for T2F tasks. In summary, the contributions of this paper are as follows.

- We develop a novel system named Spatial-Text Semantic Fusion GAN (STSF-GAN), which can produce realistic facial images from various textual descriptions.
- We propose Spatial Map Merge module that allows more efficient combination of textual and visual data by predicting spatial mask maps, enabling the learning of text-adaptive affine transformation. To retain the intricacies of the text description while generating visually plausible human faces, we are also designing the Local Semantic Attention module to enhance the word-level semantic.
- The experimental outcomes demonstrate that the STSF-GAN system surpasses the prior models in terms of generating high-quality facial images from textual descriptions. Our research work is expected to foster more innovative and practical applications of T2F technologies.

2   Related Work

2.1   GAN

The fundamental principle behind Generative Adversarial Networks (GANs) is to train the generator and discriminator concurrently. The generator learns to simulate the true data distribution, while the discriminator distinguishes between real data and the generator's synthesized images. However, recent studies show that GANs still have scope for enhancement. In terms of the network architecture, there are generally two optimization techniques: optimizing the generator G or the discriminator D.

To optimize the generator, [4] focuses on enhancing the exact distribution of the input latent space, ultimately leading to a better fit of the true data distribution. [5] utilizes a Gaussian mixture model to shape the input latent space. Numerous other studies are dedicated to optimizing the discriminator's structure to enhance its performance on the generated data. For instance, multiple discriminators [6], multiresolution discrimination [7], or self-attention [8] are employed.

2.2   Text-To-Face

One of the most crucial visual cues is the human face, which comes in various shapes, colors, hairstyles, expressions, etc. Due to GAN's extraordinary ability to produce various images, an increasing amount of research is concentrating on utilizing GAN to produce faces. The task of generating face images from random textual descriptions is crucial since natural language is the most well-known form of human description.

Different methods, such as AttnGAN [9], ControlGAN [10], SEA-T2F [11], r-FACE [12], TediGAN [13], and AnyFace [14], are being developed to improve the accuracy and flexibility of face generation. These methods use attention mechanisms, example-guided attention modules, and tree-like structures to generate more realistic and controllable facial components. They also use mapping networks and latent spaces to improve learning efficiency and user autonomy.

However, a significant shortcoming in many current methods is their disregard of spatial information, which is critical. Without incorporating spatial information, the faces generated may lack coherence and exhibit unrealistic proportions, leading to a reduction in visual fidelity and believability.

3   Method

3.1   Spatial-Text Semantic Fusion GAN

In the T2F process using GANs, multiple stages typically occur, including an initial stage and a fine-tuning stage. The initial stage generates a low-resolution image based on text descriptions, while subsequent stages focus on refining this initial result. However, the quality of the final image is often heavily influenced by the fine-tuning stage, which might underplay the initial stage's contribution. Spatial information is integral to creating realistic and coherent faces, but many existing methodologies overlook this aspect. Moreover, certain datasets, as those used in [11,13], provide detailed text descriptions for face images. Unfortunately, current approaches often do not utilize this information effectively to generate high-quality, finely-detailed images.

To address these issues, we propose a new multi-stage network generation framework, named Spatial-Text Semantic Fusion GAN (STSF-GAN), as illustrated in Fig. 1. Our method employs semantic maps as an additional condition and merges multiple sentence descriptions into fusion information to augment the initial generation results. To enhance the authenticity of the generated facial features, we incorporate local attention into our model. This innovative approach results in the production of high-quality face images that are both semantically meaningful and visually compelling.

3.2   Spatial Map Merge Module

In order to make use of spatial information, it is better to generate good quality face images at the initial stage, our proposed STSF-GAN model utilizes a simple yet effective Spatial Map Merge module (SMM), as shown in Fig. 2, which is integrated only at the top of the initial stage. This module significantly enhances the quality of the final face image by improving the initial output.

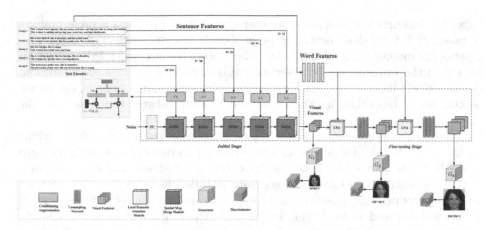

Fig. 1. The architecture of our proposed method, Spatial-Text Semantic Fusion GAN (STSF-GAN), involves utilizing a multi-stage generative network where every two sentence-level descriptions corresponding to the image are grouped together.

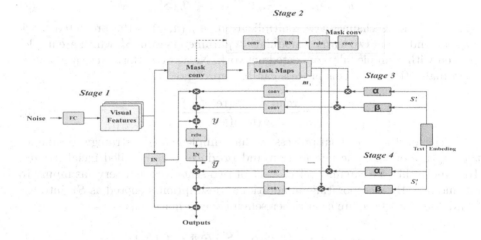

Fig. 2. Structure of the Spatial Map Merge Module

In the first stage, we handle the noise input by normalizing the input noise z to a zero mean and unit deviation using instance normalization, as

$$\bar{z} = \frac{z - \mu(z)}{\sigma(z)}, \tag{1}$$

Then we obtain the visual domain by projecting $\bar{z}$ onto it using a fully-connected layer. Then, we reshape the output to obtain the initial visual features

In the second stage, our approach adopts a mask map to fuse text and spatial semantic information, drawing inspiration from the work of Hu et al. [15]. Specifically, we generate the mask map, denoted as m_i, by utilizing a module that takes the intermediate visual feature map as input and predicts a value ranging between $[0, 1]$ for each element. The value of each element in the mask image represents the intensity of adding the text information to the corresponding position (h, w) on the feature map. By leveraging this mask map as a spatial condition, we selectively incorporate text information into particular regions of the image feature map, thus enhancing the semantic coherence between the image and the text.

In the third stage, we utilize the same grouping of ten-sentence descriptions as in the SEA-T2F [11] design, in which every two descriptions are input into a single SMM. For each image, we have ten descriptions and aim to utilize high-level textual information to generate detailed features that are relevant to corresponding subregions of the image. To preserve the intrinsic content of image features and avoid altering irrelevant textual information, we exclusively incorporate textual information into subregions that are pertinent to the text. The first description S_i incorporates the mask map m_i to obtain the semantic fusion information y of the text and spatial aspects, which is expressed as follows

$$y = m_i, (h, w)(\alpha_i \left(S_i'\right) \odot \bar{z} + \beta_i \left(S_i'\right)), \tag{2}$$

where $\odot$ denotes channel-wise multiplication, $m_i, (h, w)$ is the predicted mask map. α_i and β_i are two learned modulation parameters form S_i', which are implemented with a simple fully connected network. Next, we perform activation after denormalization to y. This process can be represented as

$$\bar{y} = \frac{\text{relu}(y) - \mu(\text{relu}(y))}{\sigma(\text{relu}(y))}, \tag{3}$$

In the fourth stage of our process, we have implemented a strategy to enhance the capture of semantic information and produce more detailed facial images. To achieve this, we carefully select a set of two sentences that serve as inputs to our module. By incorporating an additional description, denoted as S_j, into the SMM, we aim to acquire even richer semantic information as

$$outputs = m_i, (h, w(\alpha_j \left(S_j'\right) \odot \bar{y} + \beta_j \left(S_j'\right)). \tag{4}$$

where $outputs$ is the activation after the denormalization process.

3.3   Local Semantic Attention Module

Local level information can provide distinct facial features that are specific to each region of the face. By dividing face images into smaller regions, unique features can be identified for each region. Word level information in face descriptions can effectively capture these local features of the face. To this end, we propose the Local Semantic Attention module (LSA) illustrated in Fig. 3. By prioritizing local information, we can enhance the resolution of the facial feature representations, thus enabling them to be more suitable for T2F tasks.

The LSA module incorporates a Word Spatial Analysis (WSA) unit, which is designed to analyze word-level descriptions and extract local semantics. This

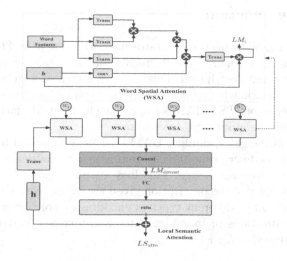

Fig. 3. Structure of Local Semantic Attention Module

process results in the production of semantically coherent images across modalities while maintaining both semantic diversity and depth-essential for generating fine-grained images. Furthermore, the LSA module tackles the challenge of capturing long-range interdependencies from multiple descriptions by employing an attention mechanism.

The WSA unit calculates attention weight by multiplying the visual feature h with the word feature w_i and normalizing the result with softmax.

$$\gamma_i = \text{softmax}\left(h^T w_i'\right), \tag{5}$$

here he γ_i element specifies the link between the sub-region of the visual feature and the matching i^{th} description word.

The modified local-attention map LM_i is obtained by multiplying the word feature w_i with the attention weight, resulting in a local-attention map as

$$LM_i = w_i'\left(\gamma_i\right)^T, \tag{6}$$

To combine all the local attention map, we concatenate each Local-attention LM_i to obtain a concatenated feature map $LM_{concat} = [LM_1, LM_2, ..., LM_N]$. We then apply a convolution operation with a kernel size of $1*1$ to LM_{concat} and a sigmoid activation function to generate the final attention map LS_{attn}. This attention map captures the salient information from all the textual descriptions and is used to selectively fuse the text information with the visual features.

$$LS_{attn} = \text{LayerNorm}\left(\text{relu}\left(\text{LM}_{concat}\ W\right) + h\right). \tag{7}$$

where $W \in \mathbb{R}^{(N*l) \times l}$ represents applying a linear transformation and a relu activation layer.

4   Objective Function

The STSF-GAN model trains the generator network using paired text and image data (I, T), aiming to generate facial images that are realistic and correspond well with the input text description. This network is trained adversarially against a discriminator network, which differentiates between real and generated images. The overall objective of STSF-GAN is to produce high-quality facial images that visually align with the input text descriptions.

In the realm of image captioning, DAMSM loss is employed to correlate the entire image with its description [9]. The goal here is to maximize the likelihood of the description given the image. This loss function, defined as the negative logarithmic probability of the description given the image, comprises four terms. These correspond to two different types of encodings - word-level and sentence-level - and two directions of matching: image-to-text and text-to-image. The final generator objective $\mathcal{L}_G$ is

$$\mathcal{L}_G = -\frac{1}{2}E_{I'\sim P_G}\left[\log\left(D\left(I'\right)\right)\right] - \frac{1}{2}E_{I'\sim P_G}\left[\log\left(D\left(I',T\right)\right)\right]$$
$$+ \lambda_1 \mathcal{L}_{\text{DAMSM}}\left(I',T\right) \tag{8}$$

The final discriminator objective $\mathcal{L}_D$ is

$$\mathcal{L}_D = -\frac{1}{2}E_{I'\sim P_{\text{data}}}\left[\log(D(I))\right] - \frac{1}{2}E_{I'\sim P_{\text{data}}}\left[\log\left(1 - D\left(I'\right)\right)\right]$$
$$- \frac{1}{2}E_{I'\sim P_{\text{data}}}\left[\log(D(I,T))\right] - \frac{1}{2}E_{I'\sim P_{\text{data}}}\left[\log\left(1 - D\left(I',T\right)\right)\right] \tag{9}$$

5   Experimental Results

Generating face images from text aims to learn the mapping from a semantic text space that describes facial attributes to the pixel space of images. In this study, we present the STSF-GAN model for the T2F task and evaluate its performance against state-of-the-art models through both qualitative and quantitative analyses using two datasets.

The Multi-Modal CelebA-HQ dataset consists of 30,000 high-resolution face images, while the CelebAText-HQ contains 30,000 high-fidelity images. We selected 15,010 frontal images from the CelebAMask-HQ dataset, as cited in [16]. Each image is annotated with ten text descriptions.

Furthermore, we conduct an ablation study to identify the individual contributions of the different components to the overall performance of the STSF-GAN model. The results demonstrate the superior performance of the STSF-GAN and emphasize the importance of its various components in achieving state-of-the-art T2F results

5.1   Qualitative Evaluation

For qualitative assessment, we compare the face images generated by our proposed STSF-GAN method with three state-of-the-art GAN models, namely AttnGAN [9], ControlGAN [17], and SEA-T2F [11]. The comparison is illustrated in Fig. 4. All the models were retrained with default settings on same datasets separately to ensure fair comparison.

Fig. 4. Qualitative results compared with other method

AttnGAN tends to generate face images of lower quality, lacking in facial details as seen in the 1st, 3rd, 4th, and 6th columns. ControlGAN, on the other hand, often produces cluttered results, showing a weak connection to word-level semantics as evident in the 4th, 5th, and 6th columns. Although SEA-T2F utilizes multiple sentence descriptions, it might result in blurry and artifact-laden outputs due to a lack of adequate understanding of word-level semantics, as shown in the 1st, 3rd, and 4th columns. Contrastingly, our STSF-GAN model surpasses existing state-of-the-art models in both visual quality and semantic coherence. It generates images with precise, fine-grained details and accurately captures word-level semantics. Demonstrating efficacy in creating face images with text descriptions, STSF-GAN holds promising potential for applications in sectors like entertainment, education, and healthcare

5.2   Quantitative Comparison

We evaluate the performance of different approaches using multiple metrics, including accuracy, realism, quality, and diversity, which were equally important. User research was conducted by selecting ten face images at random for each approach and distributing them to ten participants to choose the best image based on accuracy and realism.

Accuracy measures the degree to which the generated image aligns with the provided textual description, while realism measures the extent to which the generated images resemble real human faces. Overall performance evaluates the subjective quality judgment of the generated images.

Our proposed approach outperforms the other methods in all three categories, as shown in Table 1. Our method produces images with higher accuracy, more photorealistic details, and better overall quality. These results demonstrate the superiority of our method in generating high-quality face images that closely match the textual description while maintaining a high degree of realism.

Table 1. Results of user preferences.

Methods	Accuracy	Realism	Overall Performance
AttnGAN	59.37	0.511	0.215
ControlGAN	77.41	0.538	0.245
SEA-T2F	96.55	0.567	0.258
ours	**98.37**	**0.587**	**0.266**

To assess the quality and diversity of the generated images, we employ the Inception Score (IS) and Frechet Inception Distance (FID) metrics on the Multimodal CelebA-HQ and CelebAText-HQ datasets. The IS metric gauges the overall quality of the generated images, while the FID measures their visual diversity. A pre-trained Inception V3 network, originally trained on ImageNet, is used to classify the generated images. We statistically analyze its output values: a higher IS score indicates more diverse and unique images, while a lower FID score implies a greater similarity between the generated and actual images.

To evaluate the preservation of identity attributes in the generated images, we use the Relative Face Recognition Rate (RFRR) metric. ArcFace [18] is employed to extract features from the generated and real images, with the cosine similarity of these features then calculated. The method with the highest cosine similarity to the actual image is selected as the best match.

Our proposed approach for T2f has demonstrated exceptional performance in terms of quality, diversity, and identity preservation when compared to other state-of-the-art methodologies. The results, presented in Table 2 and Table 3, suggest that our method is an effective solution for generating high-quality, diverse facial images from textual descriptions, while effectively preserving the key identity attributes.

Table 2. IS, FID and RFRR of different methods evaluate on Multi-modal CelebA-HQ test set.

Methods	FID↓	IS↑	RFRR↑
AttnGAN	111.92	2.43	0.205
ControlGAN	98.41	2.53	0.269
SEA-T2F	90.55	2.77	**0.273**
ours	**88.55**	**2.82**	0.253

Table 3. IS, FID and RFRR of different methods evaluate on test CelebAText-HQ test set.

Methods	FID↓	IS↑	RFRR↑
AttnGAN	125.33	1.58	0.198
ControlGAN	112.21	1.67	0.231
SEA-T2F	96.55	**1.87**	**0.248**
ours	**93.37**	1.79	0.244

5.3   Ablation Study

The ablation study results, presented in Table 4, underscore the importance of both the Spatial Map Merge (SMM) and Local Semantic Attention (LSA) modules in our STSF-GAN model. Here, 'w/o SMM' indicates that the SMM module was not incorporated during training, while 'w/o LSA' signifies that the LSA module was not included. 'Full Model' refers to the fully proposed STSF-GAN.

Significantly, the SMM module appears to markedly enhance image quality, as evidenced by the noticeable increase in the inception score. Conversely, the LSA module, which learns the local-level attention map, plays a critical role in preserving identity information in the generated images-evident from the high RFRR score.

Our full STSF-GAN model, which incorporates both the SMM and LSA modules, outperforms in all aspects, further attesting to the effectiveness of our proposed approach. These findings reiterate the significance of incorporating both global and local information in generating realistic facial images from textual descriptions.

Table 4. Quantitative results of different variants of our method on CelebAText-HQ and Multi-modal CelebA-HQ dataset.

Methods	CelebAText-HQ		Multi-modal CelebA-HQ	
	RFRR↑	IS↑	RFRR↑	IS↑
w/o SMM	0.228	1.62	0.226	2.20
w/o LSA	0.201	1.76	0.212	2.41
Full Model	**0.244**	**1.79**	**0.253**	**2.82**

6   Conclusion

In conclusion, this paper introduces a new Text-to-Face (T2F) method, the STSF-GAN architecture, which leverages the Spatial Map Merge (SMM) and Local Semantic Attention (LSA) modules to generate high-quality, diverse facial images that seamlessly align with the provided textual input. By integrating an identity loss feature, this pioneering approach ensures that the generated images maintain semantic consistency with the input text. The comprehensive evaluation of the proposed method, using an array of metrics such as accuracy, realism, quality, diversity, and Relative Face Recognition Rate (RFRR), underscores its superiority over existing state-of-the-art techniques. The experimental results clearly demonstrate the effectiveness and advantages of our proposed methodology. Despite these advancements, there are areas for further refinement. Current limitations include an insufficiency in generating accessories like necklaces or earrings, especially when such items are mentioned in the input text. In the future, we aim to develop more lifelike T2F models that tackle these limitations.

Acknowledgments. This work is supported by National Natural Science Foundation of China under grant 62176062.

References

1. Goodfellow, I., et al.: Generative adversarial nets. Adv. Neural Inform. Process. Syst. **27** (2014)
2. Ho, J., Jain, A., Abbeel, P.: Denoising diffusion probabilistic models. Adv. Neural. Inf. Process. Syst. **33**, 6840–6851 (2020)
3. Karras, T., Laine, S., Aila, T.: A style-based generator architecture for generative adversarial networks. In: Proceedings of the IEEE/CVF Conference on Computer Vision and Pattern Recognition, pp. 4401–4410 (2019)
4. Brock, A., Donahue, J., Simonyan, K.: Large, scale gan training for high fidelity natural image. In: 7th International Conference on Learning Representations (ICLR), New Orleans, LA (2019)
5. Ben-Yosef, M., Weinshall, D.: Gaussian mixture generative adversarial networks for diverse datasets, and the unsupervised clustering of images. arXiv preprint arXiv:1808.10356 (2018)
6. Doan, T., et al.: On-line adaptative curriculum learning for gans. In: Proceedings of the AAAI Conference on Artificial Intelligence. vol. 33, pp. 3470–3477 (2019)
7. Sharma, R., Barratt, S., Ermon, S., Pande, V.: Improved training with curriculum gans. arXiv preprint arXiv:1807.09295 (2018)
8. Zhang, H., Goodfellow, I., Metaxas, D., Odena, A.: Self-attention generative adversarial networks. In: International Conference on Machine Learning, pp. 7354–7363. PMLR (2019)
9. Xu, T., et al.: Attngan: Fine-grained text to image generation with attentional generative adversarial networks. In: Proceedings of the IEEE Conference on Computer Vision and Pattern Recognition, pp. 1316–1324 (2018)
10. Li, B., Qi, X., Lukasiewicz, T., Torr, P.: Controllable text-to-image generation. Adv. Neural Inform. Process. Syst. **32** (2019)

11. Sun, J., Li, Q., Wang, W., Zhao, J., Sun, Z.: Multi-caption text-to-face synthesis: dataset and algorithm. In: Proceedings of the 29th ACM International Conference on Multimedia, pp. 2290–2298 (2021)
12. Deng, Q., Cao, J., Liu, Y., Chai, Z., Li, Q., Sun, Z.: Reference-guided face component editing. arXiv preprint arXiv:2006.02051 (2020)
13. Xia, W., Yang, Y., Xue, J.H., Wu, B.: Tedigan: Text-guided diverse face image generation and manipulation. In: Proceedings of the IEEE/CVF Conference on Computer Vision and Pattern Recognition, pp. 2256–2265 (2021)
14. Sun, J., Deng, Q., Li, Q., Sun, M., Ren, M., Sun, Z.: Anyface: Free-style text-to-face synthesis and manipulation. arXiv preprint arXiv:2203.15334 (2022)
15. Hu, K., Liao, W., Yang, M.Y., Rosenhahn, B.: Text to image generation with semantic-spatial aware gan. arXiv preprint arXiv:2104.00567 (2021)
16. Lee, C.H., Liu, Z., Wu, L., Luo, P.: Maskgan: Towards diverse and interactive facial image manipulation. In: Proceedings of the IEEE/CVF Conference on Computer Vision and Pattern Recognition, pp. 5549–5558 (2020)
17. Li, B., Qi, X., Lukasiewicz, T., Torr, P.: Controllable text-to-image generation. In: Wallach, H., Larochelle, H., Beygelzimer, A., d'Alché-Buc, F., Fox, E., Garnett, R. (eds.) Advances in Neural Information Processing Systems. vol. 32. Curran Associates, Inc. (2019). https://proceedings.neurips.cc/paper/2019/file/1d72310edc006dadf2190caad5802983-Paper.pdf
18. Deng, J., Guo, J., Xue, N., Zafeiriou, S.: Arcface: additive angular margin loss for deep face recognition. In: Proceedings of the IEEE/CVF Conference on Computer Vision and Pattern Recognition, pp. 4690–4699 (2019)

Generative Event Extraction via Internal Knowledge-Enhanced Prompt Learning

Hetian Song[1,2], Qingmeng Zhu[2], Zhipeng Yu[2], Jian Liang[2], and Hao He[2(✉)]

[1] University of Chinese Academy of Sciences, Beijing, China
songhetian20@mails.ucas.ac.cn
[2] Institute of Software, Chinese Academy of Sciences, Beijing, China
{hetian2020,qingmeng,yuzhipeng,liangjian,hehao21}@iscas.ac.cn

Abstract. Event extraction is a crucial research task in information extraction. In order to maximize the performances of the pre-trained language model (PLM), some works formulating event extraction as a conditional generation problem. However, most existing generative methods ignore the prior information between event entities, and are usually over-dependent on hand-crafted designed templates, which causing subjective intervention. In this paper, we propose a generative event extraction model named KEPGEE based on internal knowledge-enhanced prompt learning. We firstly use relational graph neural networks (RGCN) to encode the event triples entities and fuse them with the word embeddings to obtain the knowledge representation. Then the knowledge representation is concatenated with task-specific virtual tokens to compose knowledge-enhanced soft prompts, which can provide additional event information to adapt the sequence-to-sequence PLM for the generative event extraction task. Besides, in template design, we add the related topic words into the prompt templates to enhance the implicit event information. We evaluate our model on ACE2005 and ERE datasets, and the results show that our model achieves matched or better performances with several classification-based or generation-based event extraction models (including the state-of-the-art models).

Keywords: Event Extraction · Generative · Prompt · Knowledge

1 Introduction

Event extraction (EE) is a challenging task for natural language understanding and cognition in context, which aims to extract events for structured data from a piece of contexts. Each event is consists of triggers and arguments with their specific event roles [6].

The general event extraction work considers the identification of event triggers and event arguments as classification-based tasks, including in a pipeline

---

H. Song and Q. Zhu—Contributed equally to this work. This work is supported by the National Key R&D Program of China (2022YFC3103800) and National Natural Science Foundation of China (62101552).

L. Iliadis et al. (Eds.): ICANN 2023, LNCS 14258, pp. 90–102, 2023.
https://doi.org/10.1007/978-3-031-44192-9_8

paradigm that models the two sub-targets separately [3,7,26], or in a joint formulation which constructs an end-to-end model to extract triggers and arguments simultaneously [1,13,23].

Recently, to maximize the performances of the pre-trained language model, some works formulating event extraction as a conditional generation problem. These methods usually make a PLM output the conditional generation sequences by hand-crafted designed template [8,15]. In comparison with the classification-based methods, generative modeling methods could be more effective for low-resource, achieving competitive performances without complex structural modifications.

However, generation-based event extraction methods encounter two momentous obstacles to better performance. The one is **static event information**: Recent generation-based methods attempt to learn the event information by template, regardless of the prior information between event entities. The other is **over-dependence of predefined template**: The performances of generative methods are usually over-dependent on hand-crafted designed template, which is lack of internal information of the corresponding events [8,15].

In this paper, to address above challenges, we propose KEPGEE (**K**nowledge-**E**nhanced **P**rompt-based **G**enerative **E**vent **E**xtraction), a generation-based event extraction model with knowledge-enhanced soft prompts. Specifically, to capture the internal event knowledge into generative PLM, we firstly use relational graph neural networks (RGCN) to encode the event triples entities from given resources. Secondly, we design a semantic fusion module to align semantics association between words and event entities, using predefined prompt templates for the former and knowledge graphs for the latter. Then the fused knowledge representation (latent embeddings) is concatenated with task-specific virtual tokens (trainable embeddings) to compose knowledge-enhanced soft prompts. Finally we add them into the encoder of BART [10] to adapt the sequence-to-sequence PLM for generation-based event extraction task. Furthermore, following the prompt template design of previous works [8,15], we introduce a variant of Variational Auto-Encoders (VAE) model to get the topic words of event sentences as additional event priori information, and add them into the prompt templates. Our prompt templates leverages the implicit event knowledge effectively for conditional generation, and can be seen as an end-to-end method that solves event detection and event argument extraction simultaneously.

Contributions. The main contributions are as follows:

(1) We propose a novel generative event extraction model named KEPGEE, which is based on internal knowledge-enhanced prompt learning. This method is able to provide additional internal event entity information.
(2) Based on the original prompt templates, we add the related topic words into the prompt templates, and the topic words are generated by a neural topic model. This is an effective way to enhance the implicit event relating.
(3) We evaluate our model KEPGEE on ACE2005 and ERE datasets. The experimental results show that our model achieves matched or competitive performances with several classification-based model or generation-based

model for event extraction (including the state-of-the-art models). KEPGEE also performs well in low-resource settings.

2   Related Work

2.1   Classification-Based Event Extraction

Event extraction is an important task in the field of information extraction, and has been studied for a long time [2,6]. Traditionally, related works follow the sequence labeling classification modeling approach. DMCNN [3] is a classical model for event extraction by using two dynamic multi-pooling convolutional neural networks to classify trigger and argument words. PLMEE [26] is implemented for trigger extraction and argument extraction via double BERT [4]. Lin et al. [13] propose OneIE , which incorporates global features and employs beam search. Additionally, some works formulate EE as a machine reading comprehension problem, which constructs questions and query model to get triggers and arguments [7].

2.2   Generation-Based Event Extraction

There have recently been some works that formulate event extraction as a conditional generation problem. Lu et al. [18] encode the input context to a tree-like event structure, and parse the generation sentences to get corresponding structured events. Li et al. [12] attempt to mark the trigger words and design the event templates by using <arg> as a placeholder for argument extraction. DEGREE [8] is used for low-resource event extraction by predefined prompt templates, which incorporates explicit event knowledge. GTEE-DYNPREF [15] integrates context information via event-specific prefixes to establish links between different event type.

2.3   Prompt Tuning

Prompt-tuning is a new paradigm for adapting pre-trained language models, and has achieved outstanding performances in several downstream tasks with the help of textual prompts [14]. The method of designing hand-crafted prompt templates is called "hard prompts", which depends on mapping from class labels to answer tokens [17], and this method is effective in low-resource settings.

There are also some methods that optimize a series of embeddings into transformer, and can be seen as "soft prompts" [9,16], which focus on utilizing an abstract vector as the prompt template rather than label words. Besides, several works attempted to improve the performance of soft prompts by pre-training [22] or incorporating external knowledge [22,24].

2.4   Neural Topic Model

Topic model is a successful text analysis technology to mine the internal topics in the corpus, which is based on statistical methods. In recent years, variation auto-encoder (VAE) structure is the widely used in neural topic model (NTM), such as [19]. Additionally, Dieng et al. [5] propose an embedded topic model (ETM), which is a generative model of documents with word embeddings. [25] extract topic words by semantic correlation graphs. Recently, Li et al. [11] attempt to use a contrastive learning framework for topic mining.

3   Methods

In this section, we introduce our generative event extraction method KEPGEE, and the composition of prompt templates design. The model framework is shown in Fig. 1.

3.1   Overview of the Approach

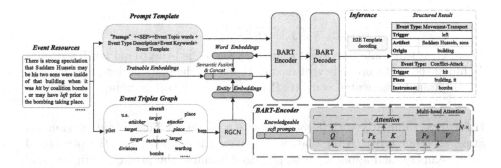

Fig. 1. The main structure of KEPGEE. We first encode known event triples entities by RGCN and generate the corresponding event prompt templates, then use a fusion module to align word-entity embeddings and concatenate with a series of trainable embeddings to construct soft prompts. Secondly, we integrate soft prompts into BART-Decoder. Finally, we decode the generative sentences to obtain event structure results.

Problem Statement. We conduct event extraction as a conditional generation task. We assume that we are given the event data sources $\mathcal{D}$ with an event type set $\varepsilon = \{e_i \mid i \in [1, |\varepsilon|]\}$. The inputs D_{gen} sent to model for event type e_i consists of context $\mathcal{C}$ and a specific predefined prompt template S_{e_i}. The generative output is A_{e_i}, which contains the event records in the original placeholder position.

The PLM. In our method, we take a pre-trained encoder-decoder language model BART [10] as our basic architecture. The text generation process models the conditional probability of selecting a new token given the previous tokens and the input to the encoder.

3.2 Training and Inference

Training. The Training objective of our model KEPGEE is to generate an output which is similar to event prompt templates. In this way, the position of original placeholders are replaced by generated words. As shown in Fig. 1, <Trigger> is expected to replaced by the trigger word *"left"*, and some-place is expected to replaced by the argument word *"building"* for role *"Origin"*, something is replaced by *"Saddam Hussein and sons"* for the same role *"Artifact"*. Specially, we assume that ϕ is trainable parameters. For event extraction task, we use prompt-augmented context D_{gen} which is generated in training set $\mathcal{D}$ to derive the prediction loss for learning ϕ , which is formally given as:

$$\mathcal{L}_\phi(\mathcal{D}) = -\sum_{j=1}^{|\mathcal{D}|}\sum_{i=1}^{|\varepsilon|} \log p\left(G_{e_i,C_j} \mid X_{e_i,C_j}\right)$$
$$X_{e_i,C_j} = [P_k; D_{gen,C_j}] \tag{1}$$
$$D_{gen,C_j} = [C_j; [SEP]; S_{e_i}]$$

where C_j is j-th context in event sources $\mathcal{D}$. G_{e_i,C_j} is j-th ground truth sequence by filling the gold words of event records replacing the placeholders, and D_{gen,C_j} is j-th prompt-augmented context. P_{kj} indicates j-th soft prompts.

Inference. Similarly with [8], we generate a corresponding output by enumerating all event types. After that, we compare the outputs with the predefined event template and apply slot mapping to determine the predicted triggers and arguments. We choose the closest one to the trigger span for argument predictions We set an acceptable sequence length and make our model generate the sequence by $BEAM = 4$.

3.3 Soft Prompts Components

Even if existing generative methods have achieved competitive performance for event extraction, they lack the internal prior information between event entities. Following previous works [24], we attempt to incorporate event-triples-KG from given event data sources $\mathcal{D}$, since it provides prior knowledge about event entities.

Knowledge Encoding. We first encode the entities to event-triples-KG. We use relational graph neural networks (RGCN) [20] to obtain the event entity embeddings, which can construct the event relational semantics by information aggregation and flow. The derived entity matrix is $E = [h_1^E, h_2^E, ..., h_{n_e}^E]$, where n_e is the number of event entities. Specially, we regard the output embeddings of BART-Encoder as word embeddings, which encoder the prompt-augmented sources $\mathcal{D}_{gen}$ to learn the particular format and information of corresponding event context. Similarity, the word embeddings matrix is denotes as $T = [h_1^T, h_2^T, ..., h_{n_w}^T]$, n_w is the length of input sequence.

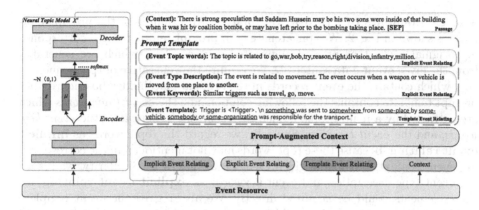

Fig. 2. The example of a prompt template for $MOVEMENT{:}TRANSPORT$ event.

Word-Entity Alignment. To align the semantic representation between words and entities, we use a cross interaction algorithm to associate with these two embeddings:

$$
\begin{aligned}
M &= T^\top W E \\
T' &= T + EM
\end{aligned}
\tag{2}
$$

where M is the correlation matrix between the two embeddings and T' denotes the fused word-entity representations. W is the transformation matrix. We establish the semantic association between words and entities via the simple transformation above.

The Soft Prompts Design. Specially, we concatenate the word-entity embeddings T' with task-specific soft prompts P_{ori} to construct the knowledge-enhanced soft prompts P_k. The task-specific soft prompts P_{ori} are series of trainable embeddings and can be considered as if they were virtual tokens. They are usually re-parameterized by a feed-forward network, which consists of two linear transformations with a $TANh$ activation function in between. The formal description of P_k is:

$$
P_k = [P_{ori}; T']
\tag{3}
$$

To limit the format of generating sequences in better, we then transfer P_k and concatenate it with the key-value pairs K and V respectively of the BART-Encoder attention layers rather than the BART-Decoder.

3.4 Prompt Template Design

The event templates we use are based on the design of [8], and we add the topic words of corresponding event sentences via a neural topic model. Our prompt template design method can relieve the problem of over-dependence, and make the model learn the implicit event information.

The Components of Prompt Templates. An example of the prompt template is shown in Fig. 2. We concatenate each prompt template with corresponding original context as prompt-augmented sources $\mathcal{D}_{gen}$, which are generated from the given event data sources $\mathcal{D}$. We acquire the generative output sequences A_{e_i}, which contain the event records in the original placeholder position. Every prompt template contains the following components: the *event topic words* which are extracted by a neural topic model, the *event type description*, the *event keywords*, and the *event template*. Specially, we regard the topic words as **implicit event relating**, because these topic words may not mentioned in the corresponding event context, but in the given event data sources $\mathcal{D}$. Similarity, we regard the event type description and event keywords as **explicit event relating**, for these elements could be acquired directly. We also regard the event template as **template event relating**, which guide the model to generate triggers and arguments at the locations of placeholders.

Implicit Event Relating. We introduce the topic words in prompt templates for providing related event information about corresponding context, because the hand-crafted designed prompts may cause the subjective intervention. We use a variant of classical topic model W-LDA [19] to obtain the topic words. The model is composed of an encoder and a decoder, working resembling the data reconstruction process. We assume that V is the vocabulary of given event data sources $\mathcal{D}$, and j-th context is represented as $C_j = (x_1, x_2, ..., x_n)$, where n is the length of this context. The expected topic type num is K which is predefined, and each topic $k = 1, ..., K$ is a probability distribution over the words in the vocabulary V. We also assume that every context has its related topics $\theta \in \Re^K, \sum_k \theta_k = 1, \theta_k \geq 0$. The flow path for getting topic words is as follows. We First get the intermediate embeddings μ and $\log \sigma$ via the encoder:

$$\mu = f_\mu (C_j) \tag{4}$$

$$\log \sigma = f_\sigma (C_j) \tag{5}$$

where μ and σ are the hyper-parameters of sampling topic-word distribution, and f_μ and σ are the two feed-forward networks which have the same structure. We use Gaussian distribution to generate topic words, and the the topic implicit variable of given context z is also subject to multi-dimensional Gaussian distribution.

$$z \sim N\left(\mu, \sigma^2\right) \tag{6}$$
$$\theta = softmax(z) \tag{7}$$
$$p_w = softmax\left(W_\varphi \theta\right) \tag{8}$$

where $W_\varphi \in R^{K \times V}$ represents the distribution matrix of topic words. We take given event data sources $\mathcal{D}$ as training data to reconstruct the predicted word probability. The model takes the Gaussian mixture distribution as priori distribution. We use above topic model to obtain the topic words of each context. Specially, we set the expected topic type num $K = 30$. We choose Top3 related topics and select Top3 words for each topic, amount of 9 words to add into the prompt template of corresponding context as implicit event relating. The topic words prompt is shown in Fig. 2.

Explicit Event Relating. We regard the event type description and event keywords as explicit event relating, because they are clearly prompted by the given event context. For each event type, we construct a unique event description which is annotated from given event data sources $\mathcal{D}$, and we treat some trigger words that are semantically related to the given event type as keywords.

Template Event Relating. We take the event template as template event relating, which defines the output format and slots for predicting. Firstly, we hope to detect the trigger word via replacing the placeholder "$< Trigger >$" of "$Trigger\ is\ < Trigger >$". Secondly, we hope to obtain the argument words related to events. In event template, we use some placeholders which are starting with "$some$" to represent argument roles, and make the model generate target arguments replacing these placeholders. Every event type has its own unique event template.

4 Experiments

In this section, we evaluate the performances of our model KEPGEE by conducting experiments on ACE2005 and ERE datasets.

4.1 Experiment Setup

Dataset. We conduct our experiments on two widely used datasets, ACE2005 [6] and ERE [21]. The former contains 33 event types and 22 argument roles, the latter contains 38 event types and 21 argument roles. Specifically,we choose English part and adopt the pre-process method in [13].

Experimental Details. We use the HuggingFace implementation of the pretrained encoder-decoder language model BART [10]. We set default prompt length to 20, input length to 250 on ACE2005 and 375 on ERE, max output length to 130. Epoch is 30, batchsize is 16 and the learning rate is set to 1e-5. We report average performance and the best methods are bold.

Evaluation Metircs. We use the same criteria in previous works [8,15]. We report the F1-scores of trigger classification (Trg-C) and argument classification (Arg-C) in major. We also report F1-scores of trigger identification (Trg-I) and argument identification (Arg-I) in sub-experiments. **Trg-I**: an trigger is identified correctly if its offset matches the ground truth. **Trg-C**: an trigger is classified correctly if its offset and event type both match the ground truth. **Arg-I**: an argument is identified correctly if its offset and event type both match the ground truth. **Arg-C**: an argument is classified correctly if its offset, event type and role all match the ground truth.

Compared Baselines. We compare our method KEPGEE with following classification-based models and generation-based models. **DYGIE++** [23]: a span-based method which introduces a graph structure to capture the interaction of span. **BERT_QA** [7]: a MRC-based method which uses QA pairs to classify the position of the predicted span. **OneIE** [13]: a joint-based method which employs global features to make decisions between instances and sub-tasks. **TEXT2EVENT** [18] : a generation-based method which converts the input sequences to the tree-like structure and generates target words. **DEGREE** [8]: a conditional generation method which uses prompt templates to obtain the triggers and arguments. **GTEE-DYNPREF** [15]: a conditional generation method which is also enhanced by static and dynamic prefixes.

4.2 Main Result

The main results on ACE2005 and ERE are shown in Table 1. We display the F1-scores of trigger classification (Trg-C) and argument classification (Arg-C). We take methods into two groups, the one is group of classification-based models, and the other is group of generation-based models. We implement our model in BART-large, which is similar with other generation-based methods. The model with * represents that the numbers are from previous paper.

Table 1. The Main results on ACE2005 and ERE datasets.

Model	Type	ACE2005-EN		ERE-EN	
		Trg-C	Arg-C	Trg-C	Arg-C
DyGIE++*	Cls	69.7	48.8	–	–
BERT_QA*	Cls	72.3	53.3	–	–
OneIE*	Cls	72.8	54.8	57.0	46.5
Text2Event*	Gen	71.8	54.4	59.1	50.5
DEGREE	Gen	73.5	55.3	57.2	49.8
GTEE-DYNPREF*	Gen	74.3	54.7	**66.9**	**55.1**
KEPGEE(ours)	Gen	**76.2**	**58.3**	64.9	54.6

Our proposed model KEPGEE achieves great performances for Trg-C and Arg-C compared with other baselines. KEPGEE outperforms OneIE, which is the state-of-the-art classification-based model, by 3.4/3.5% increase on ACE2005 and 7.4/8.1% increase on ERE for Trg-C/Arg-C. Although the test results of KEPGEE are not better than the SOTA generation-based method GTEE-DYNPREF on ERE, our model is competitive enough and outperforms the others. Compared with GTEE-DYNPREF, we attempt to use soft prompts in a knowledge-enhanced manner rather than aggregating information from various event types. And compared with DEGREE, we introduce the topic words in corresponding templates via a neural topic model instead of completely hand-crafted prompt templates.

4.3   Result for Low-Resource

We conduct a experiment for low-resource event extraction. We re-implement DEGREE and our model in BART-large. Following the pre-process method in [8], we split training data into different proportions (1%, 3%, 5%, 10%, 20%, 30%, 100%) and use the original test set.

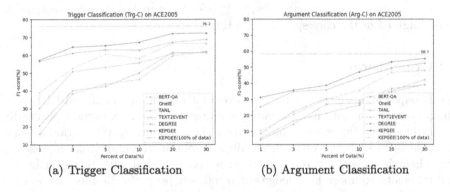

(a) Trigger Classification   (b) Argument Classification

Fig. 3. The F1-scores for low-resource event extraction.

As visualized in Fig. 3, our model KEPGEE outperforms DEGREE (the SOTA model for low-resource) and other models both trigger classification and argument classification in general. This benefits from the introduction of internal knowledge. Specifically, we discover that KEPGEE could improve more in event argument-classification with more data. This demonstrates the effectiveness of internal knowledge-enhanced soft prompts, making the model learn to recognize argument words more effectively by entity knowledge.

4.4   Ablation Study

We conduct an ablation study for the components of KEPGEE. We implement our model in BART-large and train in ACE2005. Table 2 demonstrates how different components of KEPGEE affect the performance.

Table 2. The ablation study for the components of KEPGEE.

Model	ACE2005-EN			
	Trg-I	Trg-C	Arg-I	Arg-C
Full KEPGEE	80.9	76.2	60.8	58.3
- w/o word-entity knowledge	80.2	75.8	60.4	57.8
- only task-specific soft prompts	79.1	75.5	60.2	57.6
- only topic words	77.5	74.1	59.7	56.4
- w/o extra components (original DEGREE)	76.8	73.5	58.3	55.3

We simply consider that there are three optimized components than DEGREE: word-entity knowledge, task-specific soft prompts and topic words. We discover that introducing topic words into the prompt templates is effective for event argument extraction particularly, this could demonstrate that the topic words contain the implicit event relating information. Task-specific soft prompts play an important role, which could greatly improve the performance via contributing the virtual tokens in the attention layers. The word-entity knowledge is also important to event extraction task, because it makes the event entities to be highlighted in the corresponding context.

5   Conclusion

In this paper, we propose a generative event extraction model named KEPGEE, which is based on internal knowledge-enhanced prompt learning. Specifically, we firstly encode the event triples entities via relational graph neural networks and fuse them with the word embeddings to obtain the knowledge representation, then the knowledge representation is concatenated with task-specific virtual tokens to compose knowledge-enhanced soft prompts. Besides, we add the topic words into corresponding prompt templates to enhance the implicit event information. Moreover, our experimental results show that KEPGEE achieves matched or better performances with several state-of-the-art classification-based or generation-based event extraction models.

References

1. Abdelaziz, I., Ravishankar, S., Kapanipathi, P., Roukos, S., Gray, A.G.: A semantic parsing and reasoning-based approach to knowledge base question answering. In: AAAI, pp. 15985–15987 (2021)
2. Ahn, D.: The stages of event extraction. In: Proceedings of the Workshop on Annotating and Reasoning about Time and Events, pp. 1–8 (2006)
3. Chen, Y., Xu, L., Liu, K., Zeng, D., Zhao, J.: Event extraction via dynamic multi-pooling convolutional neural networks. In: ACL, pp. 167–176 (2015)

4. Devlin, J., Chang, M.W., Lee, K., Toutanova, K.: BERT: Pre-training of deep bidirectional transformers for language understanding. In: NAACL, pp. 4171–4186 (2019)
5. Dieng, A.B., Ruiz, F.J., Blei, D.M.: Topic modeling in embedding spaces. Trans. Assoc. Comput. Linguist. **8**, 439–453 (2020)
6. Doddington, G.R., Mitchell, A., Przybocki, M.A., Ramshaw, L.A., Strassel, S.M., Weischedel, R.M.: The automatic content extraction (ACE) program - tasks, data, and evaluation. In: LREC (2004)
7. Du, X., Cardie, C.: Event extraction by answering (almost) natural questions. In: EMNLP, pp. 671–683 (2020)
8. Hsu, I., et al.: DEGREE: A data-efficient generation-based event extraction model. In: NAACL, pp. 1890–1908 (2022)
9. Lester, B., Al-Rfou, R., Constant, N.: The power of scale for parameter-efficient prompt tuning. In: EMNLP, pp. 3045–3059 (2021)
10. Lewis, M., et al.: BART: denoising sequence-to-sequence pre-training for natural language generation, translation, and comprehension. In: ACL, pp. 7871–7880 (2020)
11. Li, J., Shang, J., McAuley, J.J.: Uctopic: Unsupervised contrastive learning for phrase representations and topic mining. In: ACL, pp. 6159–6169 (2022)
12. Li, S., Ji, H., Han, J.: Document-level event argument extraction by conditional generation. In: NAACL-HLT, pp. 894–908 (2021)
13. Lin, Y., Ji, H., Huang, F., Wu, L.: A joint neural model for information extraction with global features. In: ACL, pp. 7999–8009 (2020)
14. Liu, P., et al.: Pre-train, prompt, and predict: a systematic survey of prompting methods in natural language processing. ACM Comput. Surv. **55**(9), 1–35 (2023)
15. Liu, X., Huang, H., Shi, G., Wang, B.: Dynamic prefix-tuning for generative template-based event extraction. In: ACL, pp. 5216–5228 (2022)
16. Liu, X., et al.: P-tuning: Prompt tuning can be comparable to fine-tuning across scales and tasks. In: ACL, pp. 61–68 (2022)
17. Lu, Y., Bartolo, M., Moore, A., Riedel, S., Stenetorp, P.: Fantastically ordered prompts and where to find them: overcoming few-shot prompt order sensitivity. In: ACL, pp. 8086–8098 (2022)
18. Lu, Y., et al.: Text2event: Controllable sequence-to-structure generation for end-to-end event extraction. In: ACL/IJCNLP, pp. 2795–2806 (2021)
19. Nan, F., Ding, R., Nallapati, R., Xiang, B.: Topic modeling with wasserstein autoencoders. In: ACL, pp. 6345–6381 (2019)
20. Schlichtkrull, M.S., Kipf, T.N., Bloem, P., van den Berg, R., Titov, I., Welling, M.: Modeling relational data with graph convolutional networks. In: ESWC. vol. 10843, pp. 593–607 (2018)
21. Song, Z., et al.: From light to rich ERE: annotation of entities, relations, and events. In: HLP-NAACL, pp. 89–98 (2015)
22. Vu, T., Lester, B., Constant, N., Al-Rfou', R., Cer, D.: Spot: Better frozen model adaptation through soft prompt transfer. In: ACL, pp. 5039–5059 (2022)
23. Wadden, D., Wennberg, U., Luan, Y., Hajishirzi, H.: Entity, relation, and event extraction with contextualized span representations. In: EMNLP-IJCNLP, pp. 5783–5788 (2019)
24. Wang, X., Zhou, K., Wen, J., Zhao, W.X.: Towards unified conversational recommender systems via knowledge-enhanced prompt learning. In: KDD, pp. 1929–1937 (2022)

25. Wang, Y., Li, X., Zhou, X., Ouyang, J.: Extracting topics with simultaneous word co-occurrence and semantic correlation graphs: neural topic modeling for short texts. In: EMNLP, pp. 18–27 (2021)
26. Yang, S., Feng, D., Qiao, L., Kan, Z., Li, D.: Exploring pre-trained language models for event extraction and generation. In: ACL, pp. 5284–5294 (2019)

Improved Attention Mechanism and Adversarial Training for Respiratory Infectious Disease Text Named Entity Recognition

Junhong Liu[1][ID], Wenxue Wei[1]([✉]), Yukun Zhang[1], and Lei Liang[2]

[1] Computer Science and Engineering, Shandong University of Science and Technology, 266590 Qingdao, Shandong, China
qfnu_ljh@163.com
[2] Shandong Zhengyuan Geophysical Information Technology, 250101 Jinan, Shandong, China

Abstract. Named entity recognition(NER) of biomedical texts is a meaningful task. It extracts medical entities from unstructured text data. With the development of deep learning, the combination of attention mechanism and deep learning has become the research trend of NER. However, calculating attention is quite expensive, especially for long sequences. And noise data will also have a negative impact on the robustness of NER model. This paper proposes a NER method AIANM based on adversarial training and improved attention to solve these problems. The improved attention mechanism approximates the attention matrix, which reduces the overall self-attention complexity from $O(n^2)$ to $O(n)$ in both time and space. And the attention mechanism greatly improves the recognition accuracy of the model by extracting information of interest. In addition, the applied adversarial training makes it keep steady performance even in face of micro disturbance. In this case, the correctness, robustness, and generalization ability are all improved on this new model. Experiments on respiratory infectious disease datasets show that, this method is featured with significantly improved accuracy, recall rate, and F1 score compared to previous entity recognition methods.

Keywords: Deep Learning · Named Entity Recognition · Adversarial Training · Attention Mechanism

1 Introduction

Respiratory infectious diseases refer to the infectious diseases caused by pathogens of respiratory tract infection such as nasal cavity, throat, trachea and bronchus. Common diseases include influenza, measles, chickenpox, rubella, meningitis, mumps, tuberculosis, etc. The novel coronavirus is one of the most representative severe respiratory infectious diseases caused by coronavirus. Due to its strong infectivity, various sectors around the world have been severely

L. Iliadis et al. (Eds.): ICANN 2023, LNCS 14258, pp. 103–114, 2023.
https://doi.org/10.1007/978-3-031-44192-9_9

affected by the novel coronavirus infection. During this period, the research literature on respiratory infectious diseases has been growing at an unprecedented rate, which also brings extremely rich data resources to the work in other research fields. It is a very meaningful work to study this data in the field of NLP (Natural Language Processing) to help researchers find effective drugs and have a clearer understanding of infectious diseases.

NER is actually a fundamental work in NLP. It has attracted a great deal of researches during the past decade, through which, lots of methods have also been proposed. Among the above, the LSTM+CRF [16] are the most representative methods. Though these technologies contribute greatly in NER, they still have certain shortages. First, attention mechanisms have achieved the most advanced results in many NLP tasks, showing remarkable success. However, for long sequences, the cost of training these models can be very high because the standard attention mechanism uses $O(n^2)$ time and space complexity, which is a very time consuming operation for long sequences. In addition, neural network models are susceptible to linear disturbances, and noisy data can significantly affect the robustness of NER models. In order to make deep NER models more widely useful, it is crucial to improve the robustness of our model.

To solve the above problems, an entity recognition model-AIANM (**A**dversarial Training and **I**mproved-**A**ttention **NER** Model) is proposed. Main research contributions of this paper include:

- This paper proposes a NER model based on attention mechanism. Compared with existing NER models, our method achieves SOTA performance on a series of medical datasets.
- This paper proposes an improved attention mechanism to reduce the time complexity of training and approximate the calculation of attention with a linear time complexity. AIANM uses multiple attention mechanisms to model context information, improving recognition accuracy.
- It adopts adversarial algorithms to create relative adversarial samples, imposing micro disturbance to the word vectors, which are then put into the neural network to accept adversarial training. This further improves the robustness and the recognition accuracy of the model.

2   Related Work

The research on the NER was firstly proposed and started by MUC-6 in 1995 [3]. Up to now, it has been greatly developed, and extended for more research fields. Reviewing the development history of NER in recent years, relative technologies can be divided into two types, including methods based on deep learning and methods that introduce attention mechanisms.

Recent years have witnessed a spurt of progress in deep learning, more and more automatic NER methods have been proposed. Xu et al. [17] design a simple but effective model based on supervised multi-head self-attention mechanism. Simultaneously, they introduce a multi-task framework to capture the dependencies between entity boundary detection and type classification, generating further improvement. Wang et al. [13] propose a neural network NER system called

ASTRAL. They add the Gate-CNN module to the network to help the model extract the spatial information between adjacent words. Su et al. [12] propose a global pointer (GP) solution for span-based NER task. Character Level Net [19] is a network model based on character level word embedding with BiLSTM-CRF as the backbone model. ROSE-NER [1] is a robust semi-supervised NER approach. A two-step semi-supervised model is introduced to expand a handful of labeled data with a large amount of predicted pseudo-labeled data.

Besides CNN and RNN networks, using Transformer in language model has become a research hotspot in NER field during recent years. And the architecture of Transformer is proposed based on the attention mechanism. The representatives of using Transformer in named entity recognition include the TENER model proposed by Yan [18] and the Transformer-CRF model proposed by Li Bo et al. [8] The former proposes a special Transformer structure for NER tasks, while the latter uses the Transformer to extract text features and introduce CRF for entity recognition. In addition, BERT-BiLSTM-CRF model proposed by Shen et al. [10], which combine the attention mechanism with RNN. Kong et al. [5] added an attention mechanism to deal with the information loss in long sentences based on the fact that the traditional CNN model cannot handle the loss of long-distance information.

3 Approach

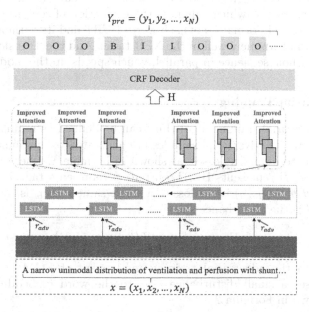

Fig. 1. The overall architecture of AIANM. x is the input sequence. r_{adv} is the adversarial disturbance added during the training. H is the output of the multi-head attention layer. y_{pre} is the prediction set of the model.

This section will demonstrate the architecture details of AIANM model, and then illustrate how the model fulfills the NER task in the respiratory infectious disease text domain.

The overall structure of AIANM is illustrated in Fig. 1. As shown in this figure, the goal of AIANM is to predict labels Y_{pre} with the same length of the input sentence x. $x = (x_1, x_2, \cdots, x_N)$ represents a sentence with N tokens and $Y_{pre} = (y_1, y_2, \cdots, y_N)$ represents the N predicted labels in x. In AIANM, BIO format (begin, inside and other) is used as the label standard. Since there are multiple types of named entities, suffixes are attached to represent their entity type after the B and I. So the label in Y_{pre} can be B-TYPE or I-TYPE, where TYPE is related to the specific named entity type, e.g., Chemical or Drug, Biological Process. For example, in Fig. 1, when recognizing the sentence "A narrow unimodal distribution of ventilation and perfusion with shunt", after the processing of the model, we can finally determine that "distribution" belongs to "B-PROC(Biological Process)", while "of ventilation" belongs to "I-PROC(Biological Process)".

3.1   BERT

BERT [2] is a bidirectional dynamic language model based on Transformer architecture proposed by Google AI Research, whose input $X = (x_1, x_2, \cdots, x_N)$ is a hybrid vector representation made by combining three embedding vectors, $B = (b_1, b_2, \cdots, b_N)$ is the output of BERT model, $B \in \mathbb{R}^{n \times d}$, and d denotes the vector dimension. The BERT model uses a bidirectional Transformer Encoder as the feature extractor, which enhances the extraction of semantic features by using the contextual information of each word. BERT and its variants have been shown to perform extremely well in the NER tasks. And the Transformer is able to process the whole sequence in parallel, which speeds up the model training.

3.2   Adversarial Training

In general, adversarial training algorithms can be defined as minmax optimization problems, where adversarial samples are generated to maximize losses and training models to minimize losses, as shown in Formula 1, where D represents the training set, B represents BERT output, y represents tag, θ is the model parameter, $L(\theta, b + r_{adv}, y)$ is the loss of a single sample, r_{adv} is the adversarial disturbance, S is the disturbance space.

$$\min_{\theta} E_{(B,y) \sim D} [\max_{r_{adv} \in S} L(\theta, b + r_{adv}, y)] \tag{1}$$

Referring to the adversarial training mechanism of FGM [9], the model directly imposes a small disturbance r_{adv} to the word embedding, which is defined as shown in Formula 2.

$$r_{adv} = \epsilon \frac{g}{||g||^2}, g = \nabla_B L(\theta, B, y) \tag{2}$$

During the training process, disturbance r_{adv} is injected into b, so as to enlarge the loss function. After the adversarial sample $b + r_{adv}$ are well constructed for all samples, the $(b + r_{adv}, y_{real})$ can be used as the data to lower the gradient of the loss function, so to update the model parameter θ, and achieve the purpose of improving model robustness and generalization ability.

3.3   BiLSTM Module

Long Short-Term Memory (LSTM) is an RNN variant. Due to the specific design features, it is quite suitable for the modeling of the time series data. It eases the vanishing gradient and exploding gradient problems and solves part of the long-term dependence problem. And the formulation of BiLSTM can be described as Formula 3.

$$h_t = |\overleftarrow{h^t_B}; \overrightarrow{h^t_F}|, \overrightarrow{h^t_F} = LSTM(b, \overrightarrow{h^{t-1}_F}), \overleftarrow{h^t_B} = LSTM(b, \overleftarrow{h^{t-1}_B}) \tag{3}$$

BiLSTM is composed by LSTM forward(F) and LSTM backward(B). Due to its two-way structure, it is often used in NLP tasks in order to extract semantic features of the context.

3.4   Improved Attention Module

Multi Head Self-Attention (MHA) is based on the idea of Self-Attention, which allows models to collectively focus on information from different locations in different representation subspaces. MHA is defined as Formula 4:

$$h_{MHA} = W_o(h^{atn}_{head_1}, h^{atn}_{head_2}, \cdots, h^{atn}_{head_n}),$$
$$h^{atn}_{head_i} = Attention(Q, K, V) = softmax(\frac{QK^T}{\sqrt{d_k}})V, \tag{4}$$

where $Q, K, V \in \mathbb{R}^{n \times d}$ are input mapping matrices, n is sequence length, d is the weighting matrices dimension, and $head_n$ is the number of heads. The word vector output from the BiLSTM layer is firstly mapped by three learnable weighting matrices W_q, W_k, W_v to obtain Q, K and V. Then they are fed into the attention function to calculate the correlation weights respectively to obtain the mixed vector representation. For the stability of the gradient, d_k is used to adjust the result of the activation function. AIANM calculates the contextual information based on the combination of all tokens in the BiLSTM output sequence, defining this information as the P matrix shown in Formula 5. However, computing P is expensive. It requires multiplying two $n \times d$ matrices, which is $O(n^2)$ in time and space complexity. This is a huge cost requirement for training.

$$P = softmax(\frac{QK^T}{\sqrt{d_k}}) = exp(A)D_A^{-1}, P \in \mathbb{R}^{n \times n}, A = \frac{QK^T}{\sqrt{d_k}} \tag{5}$$

Wang et al. [15] proved the property that the self-attention matrix is of low rank and proposed a probabilistic model based on this property as shown in Formula 6. This inequality illustrates that the result of doing projection on matrices A and V is similar to that of the original matrix.

$$Pr(||exp(A_i E_i^T)F_i V - exp(A_i)V|| \leq \epsilon ||exp(A_i)V||) > 1 - o(1) \qquad (6)$$

Since the Q, K and V matrices in the self-attention calculation are essentially from the same matrix, we make a projection on the Q matrix based on Wang et al. and also satisfy the above probability model. The main idea of improved self-attention is to add two linear projection matrices $E_i, F_i \in \mathbb{R}^{n \times k}$ when computing Q and V. According to the above probability model, the resulting $\widetilde{P} = softmax(\frac{EQK^T}{\sqrt{d_k}}), \widetilde{P} \in \mathbb{R}^{n \times k}$ matrix and P matrix are similar. Then $\widetilde{P}\Delta(FV)$ is used to calculate the attention of each head. Note the above operations only require $O(nk)$ time and space complexity. Thus, if we can choose a very small projected dimension k, such that $k << n$, then we can significantly reduce the memory and space consumption. The definition of the improved attention mechanism is shown in Formula 7, and its calculation process is shown in Fig. 2

$$Improved - Attention(Q, K, V) = softmax(\frac{EQK^T}{\sqrt{d_k}})FV \qquad (7)$$

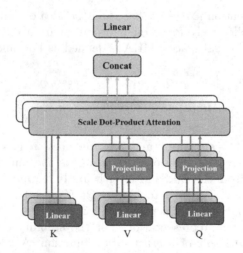

Fig. 2. The structure of improved Multi Head Attention Mechanism.

3.5   CRF Module

CRF(Conditional random fields) [6] is an undirected graphical model usually used for tagging or analyzing sequence. As shown in Fig. 1, the input variable of CRF is H generated by Improved Multi Head Self-Attention, and its output is predicted tags $Y_{pre} = (y_1, y_2, \cdots, y_N)$. CRF generates sequence tags Y_{pre} by status feature function $s_k(y_i, H, i)$ and the transition feature function $t_j(y_{i+1}, y_i, H, i)$. And the $s_k(y_i, H, i)$ indicates the influence of the input variable H on y_i. The $t_j(y_{i+1}, y_i, H, i)$ depicts the effect of H on the adjacent tag changes in Y_{pre}. The predicted tags Y_{pre} is generated by maximum the score. And the score of CRF can be described as Formula 8:

$$P(y|x) = \frac{1}{Z} exp(\sum_j \sum_{i=1}^{n-1} \lambda_i t_j(y_{i+1}, y_i, H, i)) + \sum_k \sum_{i=1}^{n} \mu_k s_k(y_i, H, i), \quad (8)$$

where λ_i and μ_k are hyperparameters, and Z is the normalization factor. The CRF module can learn the constraints of the sequence tags. For example, the beginning of a sentence should be "B-TYPE" or "O" instead of "I-TYPE" and named entity should start with "B-TYPE" instead of "I-TYPE".

Since model training usually aims to minimize the loss function, while *log* function is always greater than zero in the range of $P(y|x)$, the loss function of the model is defined as shown in Formula 9.

$$LossFunction = -logP(y|x) \quad (9)$$

4   Experiments and Results

4.1   Data Sets

This paper will compare AIANM model with existing methods on two respiratory infectious disease datasets. CORD19 [14] is a named entity recognition dataset in the field of diseases, which contains 11 types of entities. While MACROBBAT 2020 [4] consists of 200 source documents in plain text and 200 annotation documents, which also contains 11 types of entities. The statistics of the data sets are described in Table 1.

Table 1. Statistics of data sets CORD19 and MACROBBAT 2020.

	CORD19	MACROBBAT 2020
Train set	978451	86481
Dev set	38614	3148
Test set	68222	5185
Total Entities	87892	8159

4.2   Evaluation Metrics

In the experiment, mainly measure the F1 score of different models in the above two datasets. Precision (P), Recall(R), and F1 score are common indicators for measuring model performance Formula 10:

$$P = \frac{|A|}{|Y_{pre}|}, R = \frac{|A|}{|Y_{gt}|}, F1 = \frac{2PR}{P+R}, \tag{10}$$

where Y_{pre} represents the predicted answer collection, Y_{gt} denotes the ground truth answer collection, $A = Y_{pre} \cap Y_{gt}$ is the hit answers, and $|\cdot|$ is the number of elements in the collection. In detail, measure the performance of the system for each word. For example, as a named entity consisting of two words with labels "B-DISO I-DISO", it is considered to be two essential elements when evaluating.

4.3 Experimental Setup

During the training process, in order to obtain a domain pretraining model, we first use training sets to fine-tune the pre-training model, so as to obtain embedded domain knowledge of the words. After that, the training set is fed into the model for training and the model is placed on the GPU for acceleration.

We use random search to determine the values of network hyperparameters. This method finds the optimal hyperparameters by randomly sampling combinations of hyperparameters. In contrast to grid search, random search does not traverse all possible combinations of hyperparameters, but instead randomly samples a certain number of combinations in the hyperparameter space for evaluation. In this way, we can determine the optimal hyperparameter combinations as shown in Table 2.

Table 2. Hyperparameters of AIANM model.

Parameter	Value
Optimizer	Adam
Learning Rate	0.004
BiLSTM Hidden size	256
Number of BiLSTM layers	1
Batch size	64
Max Length	80
Attention heads	8
EPOCH	50

4.4 Comparison with Recent Research

To further verify the recognition effect of the model proposed in this paper, a couple of typical NER models are selected to conduct contrast experiment.

Among the machine learning methods, Dnorm [7] is a pipeline model applied to medical NER and NEN(Named Entity Normalization), which uses TF-IDF features to learn the bilinear mapping matrix for standardized tasks.

In order to reduce manual feature engineering, researchers began to apply deep learning to NER tasks. IDCNN [11] is an improved CNN model for the NER task. Character Level Net [19]is a network model based on character level word embedding with BiLSTM-CRF as the backbone model. Multi-level CNN [5] is a CNN model that CNN and attention mechanism are combined to complete the NER task, making up for the long-term memory problem of traditional CNN models. ROSE-NER [1] is a robust semi-supervised NER approach. And they introduce an adversarial training method to improve the robustness of the model by eliminating the impact of noise samples pseudo-labeled data.

Table 3 shows the evaluation results of the two datasets. The first model represent traditional machine learning method, and the rest are deep learning methods. In general, deep learning models are superior to machine learning model. Compared with IDCNN and Character Level Net, Multi-level CNN uses multi-head attention mechanism to model context semantics to improve recognition accuracy. ROSE-NER is a semi-supervised NER method, which reduces the dependence on feature data and improves the robustness of the model by means of adversarial training.

Compared with the baselines, AIANM achieves the best results on both data sets, which is 4.0% higher than ROSE-NER on the CORD19 dataset and 2.9% better on the MACROBBAT 2020 dataset. Because BERT architecture in AIANM can better represent medical texts through the domain pre-training model obtained by finetune. At the same time, the multi-head attention mechanism obtains the global context information by calculating the interaction between words, which improves the performance of the model in NER task. And the adversarial training used in the model reduces the impact of data noise and enhances the robustness of the model.

Table 3. F1 scores of each model on the CORD19 and MACROBBAT 2020 datasets.

	CORD19	MACROBBAT 2020
Dnorm [7]	0.561	0.651
IDCNN [11]	0.660	0.683
Character Level Net [19]	0.510	0.597
Multi-level CNN [5]	0.720	0.799
ROSE-NER [1]	0.879	0.891
AIANM	0.919	0.920

4.5   Ablation Study of AIANM Model

In order to further study the effects of components in the AIANM framework on the results, we conducted ablation experiments. The experimental results are shown in Table 4. As can be seen from the results, each component in our framework has a positive impact on the results. The word embedding generated by the adversarial training disturbance pretraining model can make the model more robust and improve the results. By using the attention mechanism, the model is trained to focus on relevant label of each word, and accurately and efficiently predict the label of each word using the similarity information.

Table 4. AIANM framework ablation experiment results.

Model	CORD19			MACROBBAT 2020		
	F1	Precision	Recall	F1	Precision	Recall
AIANM	0.919	0.927	0.913	0.920	0.916	0.924
w/o Adversarial training	0.881	0.879	0.883	0.849	0.842	0.856
w/o BERT	0.690	0.696	0.684	0.681	0.687	0.675
w/o Attention	0.789	0.782	0.796	0.778	0.787	0.771

4.6   Improved Attention Mechanism Performance

The improved attention mechanism proposed in this paper reduces the time complexity of training, so this paper study the impact of basic and improved attention mechanisms on training time, as shown in Fig. 3. The training time is counted on two data sets, CORD19 and MACROBBAT 2020. From the experimental results, it can be seen that the improved attention mechanism significantly shortens the training time, indicating that the improved model proposed in this paper achieves the expected effect and reduces the training cost of the model.

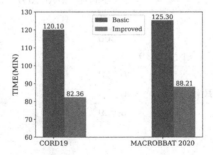

Fig. 3. Training time of our model on two datasets

We set max length to 268 and 512 for stress testing and counted the training time of the model at different max lengths, and the results are shown in Fig. 4. The reduction of training time by our proposed attention improvement algorithm is more obvious when the max length is longer. The training time is reduced by 164.09 min in CORD19 and 168.12 min in MACROBBAT 2020 when max length is 268, while the experimental time is reduced by 230.43 min in CORD19 and 224.03 min in MACROBBAT 2020 when max length is 512. The experimental results fully illustrate that our proposed algorithm is effective not only on short sentence datasets, but also plays a great role on long text datasets.

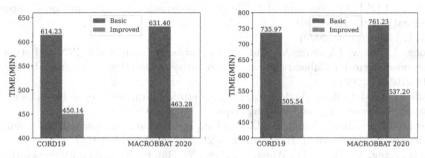

(a) Training time for Max Length=268   (b) Training time for Max Length=512

Fig. 4. Comparison of training time under different Max Length

5   Conclusion

For the task of named entity recognition, an efficient and adversarial training method called AIANM is proposed in this paper. On the one hand, we use adversarial training to solve the noise problem in the data. Therefore, the model can still maintain strong robustness and generalization in the face of micro disturbances of data. On the other hand, the attention mechanism improves the accuracy of recognition by locating the information of interest and suppressing the useless information. The most important point is that this paper approximates the attention score in a linear time complexity way, which reduces the cost of training. And our proposed model can be migrated to other domains for use. In this paper, we apply the model to the medical domain NER in order to prepare for future research on medical NLP downstream tasks. Finally, this paper verifies the effect of the model on many data sets. The experimental results show that the model proposed in this paper achieves state-of-the-art performance, the recognition accuracy is greatly improved, and the model training cost is significantly reduced.

References

1. Chen, H., Yuan, S., Zhang, X.: Rose-ner: robust semi-supervised named entity recognition on insufficient labeled data. In: The 10th International Joint Conference on Knowledge Graphs, pp. 38–44 (2021)
2. Devlin, J., Chang, M.W., Lee, K., Toutanova, K.: Bert: Pre-training of deep bidirectional transformers for language understanding. arXiv preprint arXiv:1810.04805 (2018)
3. Grishman, R., Sundheim, B.M.: Message understanding conference-6: A brief history. In: COLING 1996 Volume 1: The 16th International Conference on Computational Linguistics (1996)
4. JH, C.: Maccrobat (2020)
5. Kong, J., Zhang, L., Jiang, M., Liu, T.: Incorporating multi-level CNN and attention mechanism for Chinese clinical named entity recognition. J. Biomed. Inform. **116**, 103737 (2021)
6. Lafferty, J., McCallum, A., Pereira, F.C.: Conditional random fields: Probabilistic models for segmenting and labeling sequence data (2001)
7. Leaman, R., Islamaj Doğan, R., Lu, Z.: Dnorm: disease name normalization with pairwise learning to rank. Bioinformatics **29**(22), 2909–2917 (2013)
8. Li, B., Kang, X., Zhang, H., Wang, Y., Chen, Y., Bai, F.: Named entity recognition in Chinese electronic medical records using transformer-CRF. Comput. Eng. Appl. **56**(5), 153–159 (2020)
9. Miyato, T., Dai, A.M., Goodfellow, I.: Adversarial training methods for semi-supervised text classification. arXiv preprint arXiv:1605.07725 (2016)
10. Shen, T., Yu, L., Jin, L., et al.: Research on Chinese entity recognition based on BERT-BiLSTM-CRF model. J. Qiqihar Univ. (Natural Science Edition) **38**(01), 26–32 (2022)
11. Strubell, E., Verga, P., Belanger, D., McCallum, A.: Fast and accurate entity recognition with iterated dilated convolutions. arXiv preprint arXiv:1702.02098 (2017)
12. Su, J., et al.: Global pointer: Novel efficient span-based approach for named entity recognition. arXiv preprint arXiv:2208.03054 (2022)
13. Wang, J., Xu, W., Fu, X., Xu, G., Wu, Y.: Astral: adversarial trained LSTM-CNN for named entity recognition. Knowl.-Based Syst. **197**, 105842 (2020)
14. Wang, L.L., et al.: Cord-19: The Cdovid-19 open research dataset. ArXiv (2020)
15. Wang, S., Li, B.Z., Khabsa, M., Fang, H., Ma, H.: Linformer: Self-attention with linear complexity. arXiv preprint arXiv:2006.04768 (2020)
16. Xu, H., Hu, B., et al.: Legal text recognition using LSTM-CRF deep learning model. Comput. Intell. Neurosci. **2022** (2022)
17. Xu, Y., Huang, H., Feng, C., Hu, Y.: A supervised multi-head self-attention network for nested named entity recognition. In: Proceedings of the AAAI Conference on Artificial Intelligence, vol. 35, pp. 14185–14193 (2021)
18. Yan, H., Deng, B., Li, X., Qiu, X.: Tener: adapting transformer encoder for named entity recognition. arXiv preprint arXiv:1911.04474 (2019)
19. Zhai, Z., Nguyen, D.Q., Verspoor, K.: Comparing CNN and LSTM character-level embeddings in BiLSTM-CRF models for chemical and disease named entity recognition. arXiv preprint arXiv:1808.08450 (2018)

Low-Frequency Features Optimization for Transferability Enhancement in Radar Target Adversarial Attack

Bo Peng$^{(\boxtimes)}$, Bowen Peng, Jie Zhou, Xichen Huang, Lingxin Meng,
and Xunzhang Gao

College of Electronic Science, National University of Defense Technology, Changsha
410073, China
{ppbbo,pbow16,zhoujie_,huangxichen18,
menglingxin19,gaoxunzhang}@nudt.edu.cn

Abstract. Ensuring the transferability of adversarial examples between different recognition models is one of the keys to radar target adversarial attack technology. Analyzing the common transfer principles of different perturbations in various radar target recognition models is an important method to improve the transferability of adversarial examples. The features of radar targets can be divided in frequency domain. The high-frequency features are affected by the flicker phenomenon and have low stability, while the low-frequency features reflect the main structure of the target and have strong generalizations. Given the characteristic, this paper proposes a semantic-inspired synthetic aperture radar target adversarial attack algorithm based on low-frequency optimization and feature bias. By introducing low-frequency optimization in the process of perturbation generation, the generated adversarial examples focus on the low-frequency features of attacked targets, which are more generalized. The adversarial examples are guided to attack the high-level semantic features of the target, and the transferability of adversarial examples is improved. Experimental results on moving and stationary target acquisition and recognition (MSTAR) dataset show the effectiveness of the proposed method.

Keywords: Radar target recognition · Adversarial attack · Feature selection

1 Introduction

Despite radar target adversarial attacks has brought potential risks to radar target recognition based on deep learning models [22], the transferability of the adversarial examples has remained a key issue. Limited by tasks of both identification and attack in radar target adversarial attack situations, attackers usually neither know the structural parameters of the target model nor can they have access to the model predictions. Therefore, it is more necessary for the adversarial attack algorithm to generate perturbations on surrogate models that have good

L. Iliadis et al. (Eds.): ICANN 2023, LNCS 14258, pp. 115–129, 2023.
https://doi.org/10.1007/978-3-031-44192-9_10

transfer attack performance and can attack the black-box model with unknown structure and parameters. Adversarial examples with a high transferability are the basic requirement of radar target adversarial attacks and the foundation of attack effectiveness. Different from digital attacks in the optical community for the purpose of evaluation and testing, radar target adversarial examples mainly implant disturbance signals into the signal echoes received by the target system through various electronic jamming methods, which belongs to physical attacks and needs to be supported by corresponding physical implementation methods to improve the application potential.

Aiming at the above two requirements, this paper optimizes the existing adversarial attack algorithms. In terms of transferability, combined with the characteristics that human visual system (HVS) pays more attention to low-frequency semantic information and SAR data frequency domain distribution, we analyze the physical phenomenon of high-frequency features, and propose the empirical hypothesis that the generalization performance of low-frequency information is better than that of high-frequency information across different recognition models. A semantic heuristic attack based on low-frequency optimization and feature bias is designed. In terms of physical constraints, under the scenario jamming method of target scattering characteristics control, e.g., radar cross section enhancement and reduction, a region constrained attack method based on target segmentation is proposed. The pixel-level target-clutter labels of SAR images are obtained by target segmentation technique, and then the target mask is inserted into the iterative optimization process of perturbation generation. The algorithm only perturb the observable structure of the target to correctly guide the deployment of jamming techniques such as electromagnetic scattering characteristics manipulation.

The main contributions of this paper are summarized as follows.

- A hypothesis is proposed and verified to establish the relationship between the perturbation frequency component and the transfer attack performance based on empirical observation of existing algorithms.
- A new attack method based on low frequency optimization and feature bias is proposed based on the internal relationship between the high frequency components of perturbation and the performance of migration attack. The proposed method improves the transfer performance of the baseline method by 95.1% and achieves the best improvement compared with a variety of advanced transfer enhancement methods. The disturbance generated by the proposed method is mainly low-frequency distribution, which reduces the difficulty of the physical layout while having excellent visual characteristics.
- An attack method based on target segmentation is proposed, which reasonably inserts the region restriction into the optimization process against perturbations. Based on the proposed two methods, the attack performance of SAR target recognition model under regional constraints is discussed.

2   Related Works

Existing transferability boosting techniques could be roughly decomposed into three categories: 1) Input transformation-based methods, 2) update stabilizing-based methods, and 3) semantic attacking methods. The input transformation-based methods utilize differentiable transformations to alleviate the perturbation overfitting to surrogate model. For instance, Xie et al. [27] proposed to zoom the image when calculating gradients with a given probability. Lin et al. [18] allowed the input image to be divided by the power 2 for four times in the calculation of gradients. [6] updates the perturbation using the approximation of a set of translated images. The update stabilizing-based methods stabilizes the update direction using accumulation of the previous steps information, such as [5, 18]. Wang et al. suggested optimizing the update direction by tuning the gradient variation via dense samples in the neighborhood. Similarly, Huang et al. [12] aggregates the update direction from the neighborhood during the attack process. The last line of research adopts semantic and information with good generalization as extra attack objective to mount transferable adversarial examples. One of the auxiliaries these attacks capitalize on is the intermediate feature due to its high-level representation capability [28]. Another is the model attention as the strong generalizability over a variety of model architectures [3].

3   Methodology

3.1   Analyzing Adversarial Attack in a Frequency Perspective

There are many hypothesis trying to explain the transferability of adversarial examples, which are mainly related to features and optimization. Some research suggests that the the high-dimensional features extracted at the deep layer contain more semantic-level information and carry better generalization performance between different models. Therefore, the adversarial perturbations that attack high-dimensional features hold better transferability [15]. On this basis, researchers have also attacked the attention map activated by the model [3]. Some research has improved the attack process from the perspective of optimization, for example, using more advanced algorithms like momentum-based process [5, 18, 26], or performing small transformations on the input image [6, 27]. It is worth noting that some methods actually increase the computational burden by several times when calculating the aggregated gradient of multiple data points. This part of the research points out that poor transferability is the result of perturbation overfitting to the surrogate model, and the perturbation update biasing the optimal direction can alleviate the over-fitting and enhance the transferable attack performance of the example. An important experimental observation is that this kind of method often sacrifices the performance of white-box attack while enhancing the performance of transfer attack.

As a non-uniform and non-linear system [9], HVS is more sensitive to low-frequency signals. Recent research [14, 24] have pointed out that adversarial vulnerability may originate from non-robust features in data distribution, which

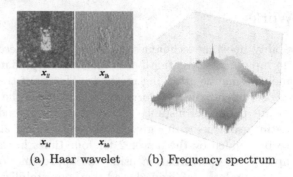

(a) Haar wavelet   (b) Frequency spectrum

Fig. 1. Frequency domain analysis of measured SAR data.

are highly predictable but difficult to understand by HVS. From the analysis of frequency response characteristics, HVS is sensitive to low-frequency features such as the contour and shape, but it is difficult to analyze its category through high-frequency features such as local texture, while the deep neural networks (DNN) model can well capture these local high-frequency features for classification. In [7], it also pointed out that the DNN model trained on optical images is more inclined to discriminate images by texture features. In addition to the low-frequency information such as local smooth target structure and shadow, there are also a lot of high-frequency information in synthetic aperture radar (SAR) target images. Previous research has also shown that some clutter information in the image that cannot be understood by HVS is also coupled with the target category [22], which makes HVS able to analyze the structure of the target (aspect ratio or equipment components, etc.) through the target or shadow information in the SAR image, but cannot capture the high-frequency clues emerged in the clutter. Figure 1 shows the wavelet components and Fourier spectrum of a SAR target slice. As one can observe, the measured SAR data have rich high-frequency information.

3.2   Transferability Enhancement Method Driven by Frequency Domain Distribution

Based on the above analysis, we assume that the generalization performance of low-frequency components is better, while the high-frequency information recognized by different models is quite different. In the process of adversarial perturbation to the surrogate model from under-fitting to over-fitting, the attack on the high-frequency features that the model focuses on gradually increased. Although the attack performance on the surrogate model is getting stronger, it cannot well transfer to other models. Therefore, this paper converts the transferability-enhanced target into low-frequency optimization of perturbation and attacks on robust features. This paper enhances the transferability of adversarial examples from the above two aspects, and Fig. 2 visualizes the framework of the proposed method. In the optimization iteration, the frequency distribution of the perturbation is optimized and the high-dimensional semantic features extracted from the middle layer are biased to improve the transferability performance. Note that the algorithm actually biases the features of all convolutional layers, which is simplified in the figure.

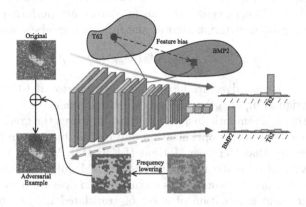

Fig. 2. Framework of the proposed method.

First, the goal of improving transferability can be transformed into optimizing the frequency domain distribution of perturbation. For instance, it can promote the attack process to pay more attention to the attack on the low-frequency information of the image. Another is to optimize the frequency domain distribution of perturbation in the attack iteration to reduce the proportion of high-frequency components of perturbation, so that the perturbation can be better perceived by various models, thereby improving the transferable attack performance. Considering the essential to take into account the sensitivity of the perturbation to HVS, this paper chooses the latter approach to enhance the adversarial transferability. While doing so, it will also give the perturbation's local pixels a certain continuity, reducing the difficulty of physical implementation. Specifically, the low-pass filtering operation $\mathcal{K}(\cdot)$ is performed on the perturbation in the sub-iteration, and the effects of various low-pass filtering schemes will be compared in the experiment. Second, from the perspective of high-dimensional semantic abstraction of images by DNN, attacking the high-dimensional semantic features of the middle layer of the network can further enhance the transferability. Referring to the perturbation to feature space proposed by Zhou et al. [28], the features extracted by the middle layers is biased. At this time, the optimization objective of adversarial examples are classification loss and feature bias measurement: $\mathcal{L} = \mathcal{L}_{CE} + \lambda\mathcal{L}_{FB}$, where $\mathcal{L}_{CE}$ is the cross-entropy loss function, $\mathcal{L}_{FB}$ is the feature manipulation term of the middle layer of the network, and λ plays the role of weight factor. In the experiment, $\lambda = 0.1$ is set to balance the influence of the two losses. $\mathcal{L}_{FB}$ is given by the following equation:

$$\mathcal{L}_{FB} = \sum_i \|l_i(x) - l_i(x + \delta)\|_2, \tag{1}$$

where l_i denotes the i-th feature extraction layer of the network, and the features of all convolutional layers are selected as target in the experiment. The purpose of $\mathcal{L}_{FB}$ is to increase the distance between the middle layer features extracted by the adversarial examples and those of the clean examples. Although the robust features extracted by the network cannot be accurately labeled, the overall feature bias will achieve better transferable attack performance. Overall, our optimization process is formulated as the following gradient ascent process

$$x_{i+1}^{\mathrm{adv}} = x_i^{\mathrm{adv}} + \epsilon_i \cdot \mathrm{Sign}\left(\mathcal{K}\left(\nabla_x \mathcal{L}\left(x_i^{\mathrm{adv}}, y^{\mathrm{gt}}\right)\right)\right), \tag{2}$$

where x_i^{adv} and ϵ_i is the adversarial example and step size at i-th iteration and thus x_0^{adv} the original input, y^{gt} is the ground-truth label.

Since the proposed semantic-inspired method improves the gradient direction based attack in low-frequency optimization and feature bias, we dub it Low Frequency and Feature Bias Iterative Method (LF^{2}B-IM). We also note that, the Translation-Invariant basic iterative method (TI-BIM) [6], based on the translation invariance of neural networks, uses a convolution operation to approximate the weighted gradient summation of a set of translated images in the k-pixel range. In the experiment, they found that the transferability improved best by using Gaussian kernel, which is similar to the low-pass filtering operation proposed in this paper based on the frequency domain distribution hypothesis. Meanwhile, Transferable Adversarial Perturbations (TAP) [28] directly proposes to punish the high-frequency components of the perturbation based on the low-frequency characteristics of the natural images. In specific, it increases the low-frequency components of the perturbation through a regularization term $\|\delta * w_s\|_1$, where w_s is a linear box convolution kernel. In the experiment, we will compare the proposed and the above competitors.

3.3 Target Segmentation-Based Attack Framework

SAR target segmentation is a key technique to obtain the contour and distribution of targets and shadows in SAR images. This chapter, SAR target segmentation technique is used to obtain the pixel-level label (a.k.a mask) of the target distribution in the image, i.e., a matrix of the same size as the image with elements of 0 or 1, where element 1 denotes the position index of the segmentation result in the original image as the target pixel. Then, the mask is inserted into the process of perturbation iteration to limit the coverage region of perturbation. Therefore, the framework is named Target Segmentation based Adversarial Attack (TSAA).

The most direct way to impose region limitation on the perturbation is to use the target mask to intercept the generated perturbation δ. Let m represents the target mask, which can be expressed as $m \odot \delta$, where $\odot$ is the Hadamard product. However, when the attack algorithm is an iterative process, interception in final stage will seriously degrade the attack performance due to the loss of gradient information in the intermediate steps. In addition, a regularization term can also be added to the optimization target to punish the perturbation of the non-target region, such as $\|(1-m) \odot \delta\|_2$, so that better optimization results can be obtained, but the perturbation may not be completely limited to the target region. Therefore, this paper directly inserts the mask into each iteration to intercept the perturbation:

$$x_{i+1}^{adv} = x_i^{adv} + \epsilon_i \cdot m \odot \text{Sign}\left(\nabla_x \mathcal{L}\left(x_i^{adv}, y^{gt}\right)\right). \tag{3}$$

In the above formula, the target mask becomes a hard constraint. Meanwhile, the information of sub-steps is also effectively utilized. ℓ_∞ norm sets the same upper and lower bounds for each element of the whole perturbation matrix. In the case of performing region constraint, taking the MSTAR data studied in this paper as an example, the perturbation occupies about 5% of the image on average, and the actual perturbation energy is expected to be reduced by more than 90%, which will have a great impact on the attack performance. If the attack performance is expected to be equivalent to the attack without region limitation, the ℓ_∞ amplitude of the perturbation needs to be greatly increased as the visual imperceptibility of the perturbation will be affected.

4 Experiments

4.1 Experimental Setup

MSTAR Dataset. Funded by DARPA (Defense Advanced Research Projects Agency) and the US Air Force Research Laboratory, the MSTAR (Moving and Stationary Target Recognition) research project released this dataset [1] to promote public research on SAR automatic target recognition (ATR). The measured data in the MSTAR dataset are collected using the Sandia National Laboratory SAR platform with 1-foot resolution X-band imaging capability. The generated dataset contains target images are of 128×128 pixel size with most azimuth angles, and several depression angles. The MSTAR dataset contains ten ground vehicle targets (Rocket launcher: 2S1; Armoured personnel carriers : BMP2, BRDM2, BTR70, BTR60 ; Bulldozer : D7 ; Tank : T62, T72 ; Truck : ZIL131 ; Air defense unit : ZSU234). The standard operating condition (SOC) subsets were selected for evaluation in experimental verification. In the SOC classification task, images of 17° depression angle are used for training, and images of 15° depression angle are used for testing, and there are 2747 and 2425 samples respectively for training and test. Following existing works in SAR ATR, we makes full use of training samples to train models.

Models. The experiments include AlexNet [16], VGG11 [23], ResNet50 [10], DenseNet121 [11], MobileNetV2 [21], AConvNet [4], ShuffleNetV2 [19] and SqueezeNet [13] for evaluation. The first four are typical architectures that are widely used as feature extraction backbone in various deep-learning applications. The latter four are lightweight designs, in which AConvNet is specialized for SAR ATR. These models are trained according to the procedure in [4]. Specifically, the random 88×88 patches are for training as data augmentation and center patches are for testing. The single-channel SAR image is processed as a gray-scale image and normalized to [0,1]. The SGD (88×88) optimizer [25] and multi-step learning rate adjustment strategy are used to train the model.

Measurements. Since we focus on the prediction label shift of the target classifier F after adding adversarial perturbation. Therefore, the following deception rate index is defined to evaluate the performance of attack algorithms:

$$\text{Deception rate} = \sum_i^{N_{\text{total}}} \mathbb{I}\left(F\left(x_i^{\text{adv}}\right) \neq y_i^{\text{gt}}\right) / N_{\text{total}}, \tag{4}$$

where $\mathbb{I}(\cdot)$ is the indicator function, N_{total} is the number of images for evaluation. It should be noted that in the experiment, in order to ensure that the prediction shift is caused by adversarial attacks, the evaluation samples of the test set samples correctly classified by all eight types of DNN models are used. At the same time, 100 samples that meet the above requirements are uniformly sampled in each category to reduce the impact of category imbalance. Therefore, the sample set to test the attack performance in the experiment is a subset of the SOC task test set has a sample size of $N_{\text{total}} = 1000$.

When examining the black box attack performance of the attack algorithm, the transfer ratio index is used. The transfer ratio is consistent with the form of Eq. (4), but the adversarial examples are mounted based on the gradient of surrogate model to attack target black-box models. The transfer attack performance of a surrogate model can be evaluated by the average transfer ratio of the generated adversarial examples in the remaining seven models. The transfer attack performance of an *algorithm* is indicated by the average transfer ratio over eight models as surrogate.

4.2   Analysis of Existing Algorithms

Firstly, we empirically evaluate our hypothesis with existing attack algorithms, including two gradient-based algorithms, Fast Gradient Sign Method (FGSM) [8] and Basic Iterative Method (BIM) [17], and two optimization-based algorithms (DeepFool [20] and C&W [2]), with results shown in Table 1. With a first glance, there is a gap between these two category attacks, that is, the optimization-based ones can achieve better deception-rate with smaller perturbations when adversary has access to the victim models. However, they show a far weaker transfer attack performance than gradient-based attacks. With a close into the gradient-based attacks, the multi-step method BIM holds higher deception rate than the single-step method FGSM while is harder to transfer the perturbation learned on surrogate model to other unknown victim models.

We then investigate the relationship between attack performance and frequency distribution, and to verify our hypothesis. Since the distribution of high and low frequency components in the frequency domain of the perturbation is mainly concerned, and the relative amplitude of the perturbation spectrum

Table 1. Attack performance summary of four attack algorithms.

Attack	FGSM	BIM	DeepFool	C&W
Average deception rate	93.1	97.9	96.1	99.8
Transfer ratio	36.4	26.4	5.1	3.1
Average ℓ_2 distance	2.12	1.45	0.27	0.25

of different algorithms needs to be further compared, thus we calculate average logarithmic spectrum as $lg\left|\sum_i^{1000} \mathcal{D}[\delta_i]/1000\right|$, where $\mathcal{D}[\cdot]$ denotes the two-dimensional discrete Fourier transform (2D-DFT). In addition, since the inverse gradient in the iteration will result multi-step method smaller perturbation than single-step one (see the average distance listed in Table 1), the BIM perturbation will be amplified during the calculation of the spectrum to make its perturbation equivalent to FGSM.

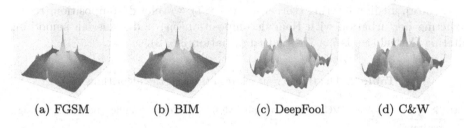

(a) FGSM   (b) BIM   (c) DeepFool   (d) C&W

Fig. 3. The spectrum of perturbation of each algorithm (VGG11 as surrogate).

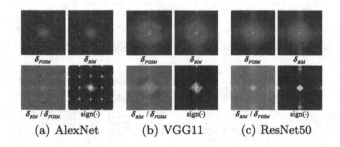

(a) AlexNet   (b) VGG11   (c) ResNet50

Fig. 4. The relative perturbation spectrum of BIM to FGSM.

As shown in Fig. 3, one can see the optimization-based methods which are short on transfer attack carry richer high-frequency components than gradient-based methods. And Fig. 4 further shows the relative frequency spectrum of

FGSM and BIM. From the figures we can capture the slight differences in frequency domain distribution of the multi-step and single-step method, and the results align with our hypothesis that, the more high-frequency components the perturbation carry on, the weaker transfer attack performance it can achieve.

4.3   Main Results

Comparative Experiments. We show the effectiveness of our method by comparing to other advanced transferability boosting techniques in optical community, including FGSM [8], BIM [17], Diverse Inputs Iterative FGSM (DI^2-FGSM), Momentum Iterative FGSM (MI-FGSM), Nesterov Iterative FGSM (NI-FGSM), TI-BIM [27] and TAP [28]. The above methods are all iterative methods except FGSM. In the experiment, the perturbation budget is set as $\|\delta\|_\infty = 8/255$, the number of iterations is 10 and the sub-step size $\epsilon_i = 0.8/255$. In addition to the above settings, the remaining hyper-parameters follow the settings in the original papers for fair comparison. For the method proposed in this paper, the influence of the low-frequency optimization is studied. We compare four methods, including ideal low-pass filtering in frequency domain (with a radius of $1/10$ image size), median filtering (kernel size is 7×7), wavelet decomposition (reconstructing perturbation with Haar decomposition δ_{ll}) and Gaussian smoothing filtering (kernel size is 7×7, standard deviation is $\sqrt{2}$).

Table 2. The transfer attack results of all the algorithms.

Attack	Alex.	VGG.	Res.	Dense.	Mobile.	AConv.	Shuffle.	Squeeze.	Average
Competitors									
FGSM	33.9	59.0	54.0	14.2	25.7	54.9	16.9	32.8	36.4
BIM	20.2	57.2	50.6	2.5	1.9	55.6	0.9	22.6	26.4
DI^2-FGSM	19.3	56.0	49.9	3.6	3.2	54.3	2.0	22.5	26.4
MI-FGSM	30.8	61.7	54.6	8.7	13.6	56.7	8.0	31.3	33.2
NI-FGSM	27.9	57.8	55.0	9.3	18.8	55.1	10.5	27.4	32.7
TI-BIM	59.5	64.0	61.6	26.1	10.2	**55.7**	18.9	**57.4**	44.2
TAP	49.8	49.5	49.6	20.2	24.6	45.3	22.4	50.9	39.0
LF^{2}B-IM									
Ideal filt.	52.1	68.5	56.4	24.1	27.0	50.5	28.0	47.9	44.3
Median filt.	57.6	70.0	61.3	22.6	27.7	54.8	23.5	55.1	46.6
Wavelet decomp.	40.2	65.8	56.9	21.3	20.6	54.3	16.7	47.0	40.3
Gaussian filt.	**60.0**	**71.8**	**63.1**	**37.9**	**36.0**	54.0	**33.8**	54.9	**51.5**

Table 2 shows the transfer ratio of all the competitors and our method. As aforementioned, each data below the model's name index (*column*) represents the transfer deception rate average on other seven models achieved by the attack algorithm (*row*), and the *Average* indicates the overall transfer attack performance of the algorithm. It can be observed that the proposed method obtains the best performance when using Gaussian smoothing as the low-frequency strategy. At this time, the overall transferability of the attack algorithm is 51.5%, which is 25.1% (95.1%×) higher than that of the baseline iterative method BIM, and also far exceeds the transferability of the single-step method FGSM. In addition, the proposed method, TI-BIM and TAP are all stronger than other methods without the frequency domain manipulation. On the other hand, the proposed LF^{2}B-IM shows better transferability than TI-BIM and TAP, which further its superiority. In Table 2, the VGG11 model is exhibited as the best surrogate model, that is, adversarial perturbations crafted on it are more likely to attack other models, and achieved 71.8% transfer ratio with the proposed method. Figure 5 visualizes the perturbation images of different algorithms. It can be seen that the perturbation values between the perturbation pixels generated by the above method have the advantage of small fluctuations and local smoothing, which further reduces the complexity of physical implementation.

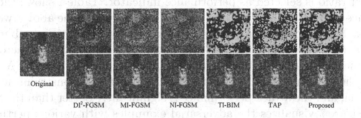

Fig. 5. Normalized perturbation and adversarial examples of each algorithm.

Ablative Analysis. Further ablation experiments were carried to verify the effectiveness of the proposed two-part improvements. The low-frequency optimization and feature bias were combined to obtain the following three settings: (1) applying low-frequency optimization, (2) applying feature bias, and (3) applying both strategies. Table 3 summarizes the attack performance of the above three settings with BIM as baseline. It can be seen that the proposed two strategies can both boost the transferability and can work together. Figure 6 shows the frequency spectrum of perturbation for the above three settings, and it can be seen that the feature bias has a detailed adjustment effect on the perturbation spectrum when only the low frequency is optimized.

Table 3. Two-part improvements ablation analysis of the proposed method.

Attack	BIM	Setting #1	Setting #2	Setting #3
Average deception rate	97.9	96.7	95.6	94.1
Transfer ratio	26.4	42.1	32.7	51.5

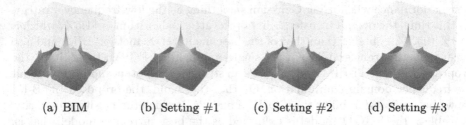

(a) BIM   (b) Setting #1   (c) Setting #2   (d) Setting #3

Fig. 6. The spectrum of perturbation of each setting (VGG11 as surrogate).

TSAA. After that, we investigated the effectiveness of TSAA. Firstly, the effectiveness of the proposed framework is analyzed. According to the results of the previous section, VGG11 was selected as the surrogate model. The target region is segmented across the iterations (TSAA) and after the iteration (baseline), and the transfer ratio is selected as performance indicator. Table 4 shows the attack performance of BIM and LF^{2}B-IM attack algorithms under the above two attack framework. The ℓ_∞ budget of the algorithm is set to 48/255, the number of iteration is set to 20, the step size of sub-step is 4.8/10, and the weight factor of the LF^{2}B-IM method is set to 0.01. It can be seen from the results that TSAA makes full use of the gradient update information with the region constraint across the sub-iteration, and the attack performance is significantly better than the baseline method. Figure 7 visualizes the adversarial examples with various perturbation budgets. As discussed in Sect. 3.3, restricting the perturbation within 5% region requires larger perturbation budget and will sacrifice its visual imperceptibility, while our TSAA was designed to find a better trade-off between at this dilemma.

Table 4. Impact of region constraint strategy on attack performance.

Attack	BIM		LF^{2}B-IM	
	Baseline	TSAA	Baseline	TSAA
Transfer ratio	20.1	43.3	21.4	52.2

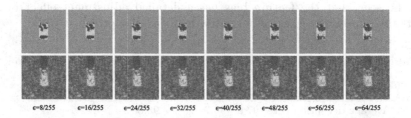

ϵ=8/255 ϵ=16/255 ϵ=24/255 ϵ=32/255 ϵ=40/255 ϵ=48/255 ϵ=56/255 ϵ=64/255

Fig. 7. Adversarial examples with various perturbation budgets.

5   Conclusion and Future Work

Transfer attack capability plays the key role in designing radar target adversarial example. This paper studied the transferable algorithms against DNN-based SAR ATR models. Based on the speciality of HVS and general distribution in frequency domain of SAR target images, we proposed the LF^2B-IM attack framework, which yields transferable adversarial examples. With the perturbation budget of $\|\delta\|_\infty = 8/255$, the proposed method achieved 71.8% transfer attack success rate against seven black-box models using the VGG11 model as surrogate, and outperformed other advanced algorithms. This paper also investigated the influence of restricting the perturbation only within the target area, ensuring the physical attack potentiality.

For future work, we plan to further exploit the frequency sensitivity of DNN trained on radar target data and the mechanism behind it. We would also like to model the existing electromagnetic jamming techniques into adversarial attack application for evaluation and defense purposes.

References

1. Air Force Research Laboratory: The MSTAR Database. https://www.sdms.afrl.af.mil/datasets/mstar
2. Carlini, N., Wagner, D.: Towards evaluating the robustness of neural networks. In: Proceedings of the IEEE Symposium on Security and Privacy, pp. 39–57. IEEE (2017)
3. Chen, S., He, Z., Sun, C., Yang, J., Huang, X.: Universal adversarial attack on attention and the resulting dataset DAmageNet. IEEE Trans. Pattern Anal. Mach. Intell. 44(4), 2188–2197 (2022)
4. Chen, S., Wang, H., Xu, F., Jin, Y.Q.: Target classification using the deep convolutional networks for SAR images. IEEE Trans. Geosci. Remote Sens. 54(8), 4806–4817 (2016)
5. Dong, Y., et al.: Boosting adversarial attacks with momentum. In: Proceedings of the IEEE Conference on Computer Vision and Pattern Recognition, pp. 9185–9193 (2018)
6. Dong, Y., Pang, T., Su, H., Zhu, J.: Evading defenses to transferable adversarial examples by translation-invariant attacks. In: Proceedings of the IEEE Conference on Computer Vision and Pattern Recognition, pp. 4312–4321 (2019)
7. Geirhos, R., Rubisch, P., Michaelis, C., Bethge, M., Wichmann, F.A., Brendel, W.: Imagenet-trained CNNs are biased towards texture; increasing shape bias improves accuracy and robustness. In: Proceedings of the International Conference on Learning Representations. Vancouver, BC, Canada (April 2018)
8. Goodfellow, I.J., Shlens, J., Szegedy, C.: Explaining and harnessing adversarial examples. In: Proceedings of the International Conference on Learning Representations. San Diego, USA (May 2015)
9. Hall, C.F., Hall, E.L.: A nonlinear model for the spatial characteristics of the human visual system. IEEE Trans. Syst. Man Cybern. 7(3), 161–170 (1977). https://doi.org/10.1109/TSMC.1977.4309680
10. He, K., Zhang, X., Ren, S., Sun, J.: Deep Residual Learning for Image Recognition. In: Proceedings of the IEEE Conference on Computer Vision and Pattern Recognition, pp. 770–778 (2016)

11. Huang, G., Liu, Z., Van Der Maaten, L., Weinberger, K.: Densely connected convolutional networks. In: Proceedings of the IEEE Conference on Computer Vision and Pattern Recognition, pp. 4700–4708 (2017)
12. Huang, T., Menkovski, V., Pei, Y., Wang, Y., Pechenizkiy, M.: Direction-aggregated attack for transferable adversarial examples. ACM J. Emerg. Technol. Comput. Syst. (JETC) **18**(3), 1–22 (2022)
13. Iandola, F.N., Han, S., Moskewicz, M.W., Ashraf, K., Dally, W.J., Keutzer, K.: SqueezeNet: AlexNet-Level Accuracy with 50x Fewer Parameters and < 0.5 MB Model Size. In: Proceedings of the International Conference on Learning Representations (2017)
14. Ilyas, A., Santurkar, S., Tsipras, D., Engstrom, L., Tran, B., Madry, A.: Adversarial examples are not bugs, they are features. In: Proceedings of the Advances in Neural Information Processing Systems, vol. 32 (2019)
15. Inkawhich, N., Wen, W., Li, H.H., Chen, Y.: Feature space perturbations yield more transferable adversarial examples. In: Proceedings of the IEEE Conference on Computer Vision and Pattern Recognition, pp. 7066–7074 (2019)
16. Krizhevsky, A., Sutskever, I., Hinton, G.E.: Imagenet classification with deep convolutional neural networks. In: Proceedings of the Advances in Neural Information Processing Systems, pp. 1097–1105 (2012)
17. Kurakin, A., Goodfellow, I., Bengio, S., et al.: Adversarial examples in the physical world. In: Proceedings of the International Conference on Learning Representations Workshops (2017)
18. Lin, J., Song, C., He, K., Wang, L., Hopcroft, J.E.: Nesterov accelerated gradient and scale invariance for adversarial attacks. In: Proceedings of the International Conference on Learning Representations. Addis Ababa, Ethiopia (April 2020)
19. Ma, N., Zhang, X., Zheng, H.T., Sun, J.: ShuffleNet V2: Practical guidelines for efficient CNN architecture design. In: Proceedings of the European Conference on Computer Vision (2018)
20. Moosavi-Dezfooli, S.M., Fawzi, A., Frossard, P.: Deepfool: A simple and accurate method to fool deep neural networks. In: Proceedings of the IEEE Conference on Computer Vision and Pattern Recognition, pp. 2574–2582 (2016)
21. Sandler, M., Howard, A., Zhu, M., Zhmoginov, A., Chen, L.C.: Mobilenetv 2: Inverted residuals and linear bottlenecks. In: Proceedings of the IEEE Conference on Computer Vision and Pattern Recognition, pp. 4510–4520 (2018)
22. Schumacher, R., Rosenbach, K.: ATR of Battlefield Targets by SAR Classification Results Using the Public MSTAR Dataset Compared with a Dataset by QinetiQ UK. In: Proceedings of the RTO SET Symposium on Target Identification and Recognition Using RF Systems. Citeseer (2004)
23. Simonyan, K., Zisserman, A.: Very deep convolutional networks for large-scale image recognition. In: Proceedings of the International Conference on Learning Representations (2015)
24. Springer, J.M., Mitchell, M., Kenyon, G.T.: Adversarial perturbations are not so weird: Entanglement of robust and non-robust features in neural network classifiers. https://arxiv.org/abs/2102.05110
25. Sutskever, I., Martens, J., Dahl, G., Hinton, G.: On the importance of initialization and momentum in deep learning. In: Proceedings of the International Conference on Machine Learning, pp. 1139–1147. PMLR (2013)
26. Wang, X., He, K.: Enhancing the transferability of adversarial attacks through variance tuning. In: Proceedings of the IEEE Conference on Computer Vision and Pattern Recognition, pp. 1924–1933 (2021)

27. Xie, C., et al.: Improving transferability of adversarial examples with input diversity. In: Proceedings of the IEEE Conference on Computer Vision and Pattern Recognition, pp. 2730–2739 (2019)
28. Zhou, W., et al.: Transferable adversarial perturbations. In: Proceedings of the European Conference on Computer Vision, pp. 452–467 (2018)

Multi-convolution and Adaptive-Stride Based Transferable Adversarial Attacks

Shuo Wang, Qingfu Huang, and Zhichao Lian$^{(\boxtimes)}$

Nanjing University of Science and Technology, Nanjing 210094, China
sharon_wang@njust.edu.cn

Abstract. Adversarial attacks pose a significant threat to deep neural networks, as they can be exploited to manipulate the models and cause incorrect predictions. One type of adversarial attack, known as black-box attacks based on transferability, seeks to generate adversarial examples that can be effective against multiple models. However, existing transferable attacks have a low success rate against deeply trained models, which limits their effectiveness. To address this issue, a novel method called Multi-Convolution Adaptive-stride Nesterov Fast Gradient Method (MCAN-FGM) has been proposed. This method incorporates Multi-Convolution and Adaptive-stride modules, which leverage Gaussian convolution and optimization algorithms to generate more transferable adversarial examples. The Multi-Convolution module designs multi-scale gradients to improve the forward-looking update direction, while the Adaptive-stride module adjusts the stride adaptively to control the change range of the stride. Experimental results have shown that MCAN-FGM has a higher attack success rate than state-of-the-art gradient-based attack methods.

Keywords: Black-box · transferable attacks · Gaussian filter · receptive field · optimization algorithm of gradient descent · attack success rate

1 Introduction

Deep neural networks have demonstrated superior image recognition performance compared to humans. However, they are vulnerable to adversarial examples [1], which are images with small perturbations that can cause the network to misclassify the image. This vulnerability has limited the application of deep neural networks in the field of security [2]. As a result, there has been extensive research conducted to investigate the shortcomings of deep neural networks with respect to adversarial examples, and to improve the robustness of these models.

Adversarial attacks can be categorized as black-box [3, 4] and white-box [5] attacks. In a black-box attack, the attacker is unable to access the parameters of the targeted model. Therefore, some attackers estimate model gradients or classification boundaries through multiple queries on the output of black-box models. However, the effectiveness of these query-based attack methods is limited by the number of queries, resulting in poor attack

This work was supported by the National Key R&D Program of China (2021YFF0602104-2).

performance. To address this limitation, transferable gradient attack methods [6] have been proposed, such as MI-FGSM [7], which applies cumulative momentum, TI-FGSM [8], which uses translation invariance, DI-FGSM [9], which leverages input transformation, and NI-FGSM [10], which adopts accelerated gradients. However, these methods have low attack success rates and poor transferability on deeply trained models.

Among the transferable methods, NI-FGSM has a high attack success rate but still has some shortcomings. Firstly, NI-FGSM uses the Nesterov accelerated gradient [11] method for forward-looking updates, which may introduce bias due to high-frequency noise in the gradient momentum. Secondly, NI-FGSM employs the gradient sign attack method to update adversarial examples. However, there is a deviation between the gradient sign direction and the gradient direction. Moreover, the fixed stride generates fixed disturbance, which may influence the accuracy of disturbance. To overcome these limitations, a new method needs to be designed to optimize NI-FGSM.

Therefore, we designed two optimization modules for NI-FGSM, namely the Multi-Convolution and Adaptive-stride. They can be easily integrated as a method named Multi-Convolution Adaptive-stride Nesterov Fast Gradient Method (MCAN-FGM) to achieve stronger attack effect.

Multi-convolution Module. Inspired by Gaussian filter, we introduce gradient convolution to filter high frequency noise. Additionally, multiple scales of receptive fields are used to convolve the gradient, and their average value is taken to reduce the negative impact of single-dimensional convolution. The resulting average gradient is used as the correction direction, which is combined with gradient momentum to form a new forward-looking update direction. This approach enhances the transferability of adversarial examples.

Adaptive-Stride Module. Inspired by the optimization algorithm of gradient descents, we apply the YOGI optimization method [12] to adversarial attacks. This method utilizes unsigned gradients to avoid errors caused by the sign direction of the gradient and adjusts the perturbation stride adaptively, stabilizing the change range of the stride and improving the accuracy of perturbation addition. The Adaptive-stride Module can optimize the convergence process effectively and increase the transferability of adversarial samples.

Extensive experiments conducted on the Imagenet database demonstrate that our method outperforms state-of-the-art gradient-based attack methods in terms of attack success rate and can also be applied to other transferable adversarial attack methods. Furthermore, our method can be integrated with other fast gradient attack methods to further improve the transferability of adversarial examples.

Our contributions are summarized as follows:

(1) We propose a new attack method MCAN-FGM to improve the transferability of adversarial examples.
(2) We design the Multi-Convolution in the MCAN-FGM, aiming at optimizing the forward-looking update direction by combining multi-scale gradients and gradient momentum.
(3) We introduce the Adaptive-stride in the MCAN-FGM, aiming at improve the accuracy of adding perturbation by adaptively adjusting the attack stride.

(4) We conduct experiments to verify the transferability of adversarial examples generated by the MCAN-FGM.

2 Related Work

In this work, we mainly focus on the transferability of adversarial examples generated by black-box attacks. There have been many works dedicated to improving the transferability of adversarial examples. However, these methods have a low attack success rate in deeply trained models. Dong et al. [7] adopted momentum idea that the previous momentum is used to update the current gradient to stabilize the update direction. Dong et al. [8] introduced a translation-invariant attack method to improve transferability of adversarial examples. Xie et al. [9] applied input transformation in images and saved the transformation result with probability p, which increases input diversity and reduces overfitting. Lin et al. [10] adopted Nesterov accelerate gradient to guide the forward-looking update of examples. Long et al. [13] adopted a spectrum transformation for the model augmentation to craft more transferable adversarial examples. Huang et al. [14] applied integrated gradients in transferable attack. Zhang et al. [15] conducted feature-level attacks with more accurate neuron importance estimations. Xiong et al. [16] proposed the stochastic variance reduced ensemble (SVRE) to enhance transferability.

The above methods are all based on fast gradient signed method. In order to avoid the error between the sign direction and the actual gradient direction, some unsigned transferable attack methods are proposed. Cheng et al. [17] proposed a fast gradient no-sign method, which sorted gradient and generated a scale factor to eliminate the bias of direction between real gradients and perturbations. Yang et al. [18] introduced an AdaBelief and Crop-invariance method to adjusted perturbations dynamically. Yuan et al. [19] utilized the exact gradient direction with adaptive scaling factor generator for generating adversarial perturbations.

3 Methodology

A classification model based DNN can be defined as $f(x, \theta): x \to y$, where x indicates the original input image, y represents the true label and θ indicate parameters of models. In transferable adversarial attacks, we need to generate adversarial example x^{adv}, that causes the target model to output an incorrect label. It is also desirable to keep the adversarial perturbation as small as possible to make the attack less noticeable. Thus, the generation of adversarial examples can be formulated as an optimization problem, which can be expressed as follows:

$$\arg\max_{x^{adv}} J\left(x^{adv}, y\right), s.t. ||x^{adv} - x||_\infty < \epsilon \tag{1}$$

where $J(\cdot)$ denote the loss function of classification model f (i.e. cross-entropy). The essence of adversarial attacks is to find a perturbation that maximizes the loss function while keeping the perturbation size under a certain threshold, typically denoted as ε. The goal is to generate adversarial examples that are perceptually similar to the original examples, but can fool the target model into making incorrect predictions.

Therefore, to enhance the transferability of adversarial examples, we propose a novel method that incorporates Multi-Convolution and Adaptive-stride modules. The Multi-Convolution module employs multi-scale convolution gradients to eliminate high-frequency noise from gradients and correct the forward-looking update direction of NI-FGSM. In the Adaptive-stride module, we introduce a YOGI gradient descent optimization method to adjust the magnitude and change rate of the stride. By combining these two modules, we generate a more robust method, MCAN-FGM, which can generate adversarial examples with higher transferability and lower perturbation size. The details of these modules and the proposed MCAN-FGM method can be found in the corresponding sections.

3.1 Multi-convolution Module

In transferable adversarial attacks, MI-FGSM is a typical attack method that uses gradient momentum to stabilize the update direction as shown in Fig. 1(a). Based on MI-FGSM, Lin et al. [10] proposed NI-FGSM as shown in Fig. 1(b). This is a transferable adversarial attack method that introduces a Nesterov accelerated gradient to perform a forward-looking update, as shown in Eqs. (2), (3) and (4):

$$x_t^{nes} = x_t^{adv} + \alpha \cdot u \cdot g_t \tag{2}$$

$$g_{t+1} = \mu \cdot g_t + \frac{\nabla_x J\left(x_t^{nes}, y; \theta\right)}{\left\|\nabla_x J\left(x_t^{nes}, y; \theta\right)\right\|_1} \tag{3}$$

$$x_{t+1}^{adv} = x_t^{adv} + \alpha \cdot sign(g_{t+1}) \tag{4}$$

where α denotes the stride, u indicates the decay factor, $\nabla_x J(\cdot)$ indicates the gradient, g_t denotes the gradient momentum, $sign(\cdot)$ is the sign function, and x_t^{nes} indicates the forward-looking adversarial example.

Before each calculation of the gradient, the adversarial sample x_t^{adv} needs to take a step forward along the direction of the gradient momentum g_t in Eq. (1), and then get the x_t^{nes} to calculate the gradient in Eq. (2). This makes the input image x_t^{nes} have more global information so that the result can get rid of the local maximum faster and have stronger transferability. However, the gradient momentum g_t may not be the best forward-looking direction because of the presence of high frequency noise. We try to find a better method to optimize the direction.

TI-FGSM [8] is a transferable attack based translation-invariant method. This method first translates each pixel of the image by x units, $x \in [-k, k]$ and k is integer. After that, the gradient calculation is performed on the $(2k + 1)^2$ translated pictures and the weighted sum is obtained. The author approximates this process as the Gaussian convolution on the image gradient as shown in Eq. (5):

$$x_{t+1}^{adv} = x_t^{adv} + \alpha \cdot sign\left(W * \nabla_x J\left(x_t^{adv}, y; \theta\right)\right) \tag{5}$$

where W denotes the Gaussian convolved kernel. The convolution kernel size is $2k + 1$. This method can generate more robust adversarial examples. We discover that the gradient $\nabla_x J\left(x_t^{adv}, y; \theta\right)$ eliminates the direction deviation caused by high-frequency noise after Gaussian convolution, which can make the update direction of the adversarial samples more accurate. So we combine Gaussian convolutional gradient g_t' with gradient momentum g_t and regard it as the forward-looking direction to optimize NI-FGSM, as shown in Fig. 2(a).

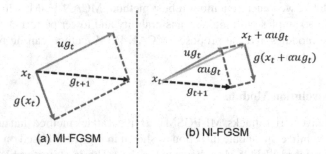

Fig. 1. Transferable adversarial attack methods. (a) denotes MI-FGSM, (b) denotes NI-FGSM.

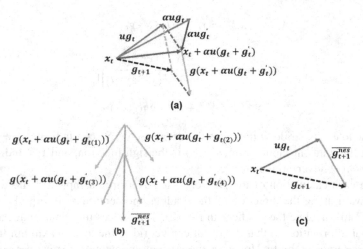

Fig. 2. Multi-Convolution module. (a) indicates single-scale convolution method. (b)(c) denotes the Multi-Convolution method based (a). (b) indicates we calculate the average gradient $\overline{g_{t+1}^{nes}}$ of different forward-looking adversarial examples. (c) denotes we use $\overline{g_{t+1}^{nes}}$ and current gradient momentum g_t to get new gradient momentum g_{t+1} to update adversarial example.

However, we find that single-scale convolution kernel has a defect. When the receptive field is too small, the degree of filtering high-frequency gradients is insufficient; When the receptive field is too large, the gradient is too smooth, and some useful information will be filtered out. From the perspective of the translation-invariant nature of TI, when the k is too large, the gradient information is over smoothed. If it is too small, the range of translation is small so that the obtained gradients contain more noise. Therefore, inspired by the receptive field, we define convolution kernels of different scales to obtain the Gaussian convolution results, and take the average to obtain the final gradient. This multi-dimensional convolution method can offset the negative impact of different sizes of receptive fields, which make gradient has stronger guidance for the forward-looking update of NI-FGSM.

The Multi-Convolution module is shown in Fig. 2(b) and (c).We first obtain the gradient $g'_{t(i)}$ after convolution of different dimensions, as shown in Eq. (6):

$$g'_{t(i)} = W_{2*i+1} * \overline{g_t^{nes}} \tag{6}$$

where W_{2*i+1} denotes the Gaussian convolution kernel whose size is $(2*i+1)*(2*i+1)$ and $\overline{g_t^{nes}}$ indicates the average of gradient of different forward-looking examples. Then, we combine gradient momentum g_t with convolutional gradient $g'_{t(i)}$ to generate forward-looking gradient, as shown in Eq. (7):

$$x_{t(i)}^{nes} = x_t^{adv} + \alpha \cdot u \cdot \left(g_t + g'_{t(i)}\right) \tag{7}$$

After that, we calculate gradient of different forward-looking examples $x_{t(i)}^{nes}$ and then get the average $\overline{g_{t+1}^{nes}}$, as shown in Eq. (8):

$$\overline{g_{t+1}^{nes}} = \frac{1}{N} \sum_{i=1}^{N} \frac{\nabla_x J\left(x_{t(i)}^{nes}, y; \theta\right)}{\left\|\nabla_x J\left(x_{t(i)}^{nes}, y; \theta\right)\right\|_1} \tag{8}$$

At last, we treat $\overline{g_{t+1}^{nes}}$ as the current gradient to obtain gradient momentum g_{t+1}, as shown in Eq. (9):

$$g_{t+1} = \mu \cdot g_t + \overline{g_{t+1}^{nes}} \tag{9}$$

We substitute g_{t+1} to Eq. (4) and get the adversarial examples x_{t+1}^{adv}.

Through this method, we can optimize the update direction of NI-FGSM's forward-looking adversarial examples and improve the transferability.

3.2 Adaptive-Stride Method

Observations from Eq. (4) of NI-FGSM reveal that the update of adversarial examples requires a fixed stride forward in the direction of the gradient sign. This creates two problems. Firstly, there is a deviation between the gradient sign direction and the gradient direction, which causes the updated direction to be inaccurate. Secondly, the fixed stride limits the size of the added perturbation, making the added perturbation imprecise and the adversarial samples oscillate. Inspired by the gradient descent optimization algorithm YOGI [12], we propose an adaptive stride method to solve the above problems.

In the gradient descent algorithm, Adam [20] is a very classic optimization method, as shown in Eqs. (10)–(13).

$$g_t = \nabla_\theta J(\theta) \tag{10}$$

$$m_t = \beta_1 m_{t-1} + (1 - \beta_1)g_t \tag{11}$$

$$v_t = v_{t-1} - (1 - \beta_2)\left(v_{t-1} - g_t^2\right) \tag{12}$$

$$\theta_t = \theta_{t-1} - \frac{\eta}{\sqrt{v_t} + \varepsilon}m_t \tag{13}$$

where θ_t denotes the model parameter and η indicates the learning rate. It is an optimization method that utilizes v_t, weighted average of the squares of historical gradients, to adjust learning rate adaptively. However, in this method, the magnitude of the change in the learning rate depends on the distance of $v_t - v_{t-1}$ (i.e. $v_{t-1} - g_t^2$). If v_{t-1} is much larger than g_t^2, the learning rate increase rapidly. This is not conducive to the convergence of the model. Compare to Adam, YOGI optimizes the v_t, as shown in Eq. (14):

$$v_t = v_{t-1} - (1 - \beta_2)sign\left(v_{t-1} - g_t^2\right)g_t^2 \tag{14}$$

The magnitude of the change in the learning rate depends on g_t^2 rather than $\left(v_{t-1} - g_t^2\right)$. When the value of $v_{t-1} - g_t^2$ is large, this method changes the learning rate in a controlled fashion and make the model converge faster.

The stride of the transferable adversarial attack is similar to the learning rate of gradient descent. Therefore, we apply YOGI to the transferable attack and design an Adaptive-stride module, as shown in Eqs. (15)–(18).

$$g_t^{cur} = \frac{\nabla_x J\left(x_t^{adv}, y; \theta\right)}{\left\|\nabla_x J\left(x_t^{adv}, y; \theta\right)\right\|_1} \tag{15}$$

$$g_{t+1} = \mu \cdot g_t + g_t^{cur} \tag{16}$$

$$v_{t+1} = v_t - (1 - \beta_2)sign\left(v_t - g_t^{cur2}\right)g_t^{cur2} \tag{17}$$

$$x_{t+1}^{adv} = x_t^{adv} + \frac{\alpha}{\sqrt{v_{t+1}} + \delta} \cdot g_{t+1} \tag{18}$$

where g_t^{cur} denotes the gradient of current iteration t and g_t^{cur} indicates the gradient of x_t^{adv}. There are two advantages of the method compared to NI-FGSM: (1) It use gradient momentum direction g_{t+1} rather than gradient sign $sign(g_{t+1})$ to update adversarial examples. It eliminates the deviation between the gradient sign direction and the gradient direction, and guarantees the accuracy of the update direction. (2) It adaptively adjusts the adversarial stride α and stabilizes the changing rate of the stride in the iterative process by adaptive sparse $\frac{1}{\sqrt{v_{t+1}} + \delta}$. It can help the adversarial examples get rid of the local optimum faster.

Algorithm 1 MCAN-FGM

Inputs: A white classifier f, loss function J, a clean image x and ground-truth label y, the max perturbation ϵ, number of iterations T, number of iterations I

Outputs: An adversarial image x_T^{adv}

1: $x_0^{adv} = x; \alpha = \epsilon/T; g_{0\,(i)}' = 0; v_0 = 0; \overline{g_t^{nes}} = 0; g_0 = 0$

2: **for** $t = 0$ to $T - 1$ **do**

3: **for** $i = 0$ to $I - 1$ **do**

4:    $g_{t\,(i)}' = W_{2*i+1} * \overline{g_t^{nes}}$

5:    $x_{t\,(i)}^{nes} = x_t^{adv} + \alpha \cdot u \cdot (g_t + g_{t\,(i)}')$

6: **end for**

7: $\overline{g_{t+1}^{nes}} = \frac{1}{I}\sum_{i=0}^{I-1} \frac{\nabla_x J(x_{t\,(i)}^{nes}, y; \theta)}{||\nabla_x J(x_{t\,(i)}^{nes}, y; \theta)||_1}$

8: $g_{t+1} = \mu \cdot g_t + \overline{g_{t+1}^{nes}}$

9: $v_{t+1} = v_t - (1 - \beta_2)sign(v_t - \overline{g_{t+1}^{nes}}^2)\overline{g_{t+1}^{nes}}^2$

10: $x_{t+1}^{adv} = x_t^{adv} + \frac{\alpha}{\sqrt{v_{t+1}}+\delta} \cdot g_{t+1}$

11:**end for**

12:**return** x_T^{adv}

In addition, we combine the Multi-Convolution method presented in Sect. 3.1 with the aforementioned Adaptive-stride method to optimize NI-FGSM, named the Multi-convolution adaptive stride Nesterov Fast Gradient Method(MCAN-FGM). By leveraging the advantages of these methods, we can significantly enhance the attack success rate of adversarial examples. The detailed implementation of MCAN-FGM is outlined in Algorithm 1.

4 Experiments

4.1 Experimental Settings

Dataset. We use ImageNet-compatible dataset including 1000 images to conduct experiments.

Metric. We define attack success rate (ASR) as follows:

$$ASR = \frac{N_{success}}{N_{total}} \qquad (19)$$

where $N_{success}$ is the number of adversarial examples which make models misclassify and N_{total} denotes the total number of samples.

Target Models. We select four trained models to attack, i.e. Vgg13_bn, InceptionV3(Inc-v3), ResNet101 (Res-101) and DenseNet169 (Dens-169) because their structures are quite different to verify the generalization of the attack method.

Hyper-parameters. For I-FGSM, We set the max perturbation $\varepsilon = 16$, the adversarial stride $\alpha = 1.6$ and number of iteration T = 10. In MI-FGSM, we set the decay factor u = 1. In DI-FGSM, we adjust transformation probability to 0.7. For TI-FGSM, we adopt the Gaussian kernel with kernel size 7×7. In FGNM_K [17], we define $K = 12000$. In ABI-FGM [18], β_1 is set as 0.9 and β_2 is set as 0.999. In our method MCAN-FGM, we set $\beta_2 = 0.9$. We also set the mean $u = 0$ and the standard deviation $\sigma = 1$ for Gaussian convolution in our method.

4.2 Attack Success Rate Comparison Among Transferable Fast Gradient Signed Method

In this section, we compared our proposed method, MCAN-FGM, with three other adversarial attacks based on the Fast Gradient Sign Method (FGSM) - I-FGSM, MI-FGSM, and NI-FGSM. Specifically, we used Vgg13_bn(Inc-v3/Res-101/Dens-169) as the source model and three other models as black-box networks to evaluate the performance of the attacks. We then used adversarial examples generated by these methods to attack the three black-box networks.

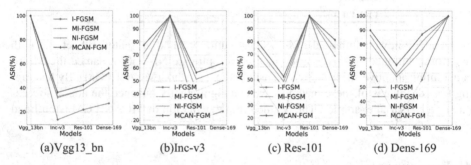

(a)Vgg13_bn   (b)Inc-v3   (c) Res-101   (d) Dens-169

Fig. 3. The attack success rate (ASR) of adversarial examples generated by I-FGSM, MI-FGSM, NI-FGSM, MACN-FGM. (a)(b)(c)(d) indicate four different source models.

The results are presented in Fig. 3, which demonstrates that MCAN-FGM achieves a higher attack success rate than the other three transferable methods and enhances the attack effect of NI-FGSM. This is because our method is more dependent on the gradient direction, which eliminates the bias caused by the gradient sign direction, resulting in a more accurate update direction of the disturbance.

4.3 Effect of the Fusion of MCAN-FGM and Other Transferable Attacks

To demonstrate the attack effect of the fusion MCAN-FGM and other transferable attacks. In this section, we first the introduce mixed approach DMI-FGSM\TMI-FGSM\DTMI-FGSM based DI-FGSM, TI-FGSM and MI-FGSM. Then We fuse MCAN-FGM with these three methods respectively to form new methods. We also set NI-FGSM as the control group of MACN-FGM. We choose Vgg13_bn as source model and other three models as black-box networks. The ASR is shown in Table 1.

Table 1. The attack success rate (ASR) of different fused methods against deeply trained models. The first column shows the attack methods and the first row lists target models.

Attack	Inc-v3	Res-101	Dens-169
DMI-FGSM	51.5	56.5	72.2
NI-DMI-FGSM	43.9	52.7	67.4
MCAN-DMI-FGM	**59.3**	**68.4**	**82.3**
TMI-FGSM	44.7	48.7	61.4
NI-TMI-FGSM	45.6	49.9	63.3
MCAN-TMI-FGM	**50.9**	**54.5**	**65.6**
DTMI-FGSM	60.8	63.1	74.0
NI-DTMI-FGSM	57.6	61.5	73.5
MCAN-DTMI-FGM	**67.5**	**72.9**	**83.4**

Our results show that both NI-FGSM and MCAN-FGM can be integrated with other adversarial attacks to obtain stronger transferability. Furthermore, the ASR of MCAN-FGM combined with the three adversarial attacks is better than that of NI-FGSM. In particular, MCAN-DTMI-FGM works best. Therefore, our proposed method, MCAN-FGM, can be integrated with other transferable attack methods to achieve a strong attack effect.

4.4 Attack Success Rate Comparison Among Transferable Fast Gradient Method

Since MCAN-FGM is essentially an unsigned-based fast gradient method (FGM), we select two other fast gradient methods based on transferable attacks, ABI-FGM and FGNM_K, to compare with MCAN-FGM and MCAN-DTMI-FGM in the attack success rate. We select Vgg13_bn(Inc-v3/Res-101/Dens-169) to attack, and use adversarial samples to attack the other three black-box models. The attack success rate (ASR) is shown in Fig. 4.

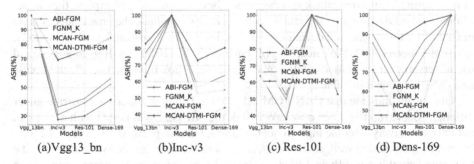

(a)Vgg13_bn   (b)Inc-v3   (c) Res-101   (d) Dens-169

Fig. 4. The attack success rate (ASR) of adversarial examples generated by ABI-FGM, FGNM_K, MACN-FGM, MACN-DIMI-FGM. (a)(b)(c)(d) indicate four different source models.

Table 2. The attack success rate (ASR) of CAN-FGM with different standard deviations. The first row lists a source models and other three black-box models. Each row represents the attack success rate (ASR) under different source model (Vgg13_bn/Inc-v3/Res-101/Dens-169).

σ	Vgg13_bn	Inc-v3	Res-101	Dens-169
0.5	100.0	33.7	38.1	52.2
1	100.0	**34.0**	**38.5**	**53.4**
10	100.0	33.1	38.4	52.4
0.5	74.1	100.0	51.3	60.1
1	**75.6**	100.0	**52.5**	**60.7**
10	71.8	100.0	52.0	59.0
0.5	78.3	48.9	100.0	79.2
1	**79.3**	**49.3**	100.0	**81.0**
10	76.2	49.1	100.0	77.6
0.5	88.7	62.9	83.9	100.0
1	**89.1**	**64.1**	**85.1**	100.0
10	87.9	62.8	83.5	100.0

We can observe that the attack success rate of MACN-FGM is higher than ABI-FGSM and FGNM_K. It can achieve better attack effect. And the ASR of the fused method MCAN-DTMI-FGM is the highest. The reason our method outperforms other unsigned methods is that it can add more precise perturbations to adversarial examples. Our method uses an adaptive stride optimization method, which can dynamically adjust the stride and stabilize the stride variation.

4.5   Effect of Standard Deviation in CAN-FGM

In this paper, we define CAN-FGM as the single-dimensional convolutional version of MCAN-FGM. We found that Gaussian kernels with different standard deviations have different filtering capabilities for high-frequency information during Gaussian convolution, resulting in different attack success rates. Therefore, in order to explore the impact of the standard deviation on the attack success rate, we evaluate the attack success rate of CAN-FGM with standard deviations σ of 0.5, 1 and 10 in Gaussian kernels separately, where the mean u is 0. We select Vgg13_bn(Inc-v3/Res-101/Dens-169) to attack, and use adversarial samples to attack the other three black-box models. The attack success rate (ASR) is shown in Table 2.

Our results indicate that CAN-FGM achieves the highest attack success rate under different source models when σ = 1. We think that the Gaussian kernel with σ = 1 can not only effectively filter the high-frequency noise, but also preserve the rest of the low-frequency information well, so the attack success rate is the highest. When σ = 0.5, the Gaussian kernel has insufficient filtering ability for high-frequency information. When σ = 10, the Gaussian kernel filters too much effective information. Therefore, they have a lower attack success rate.

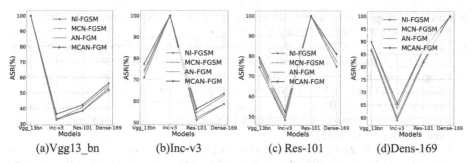

Fig. 5. The attack success rate (ASR) of adversarial examples generated by NI-FGSM, MCN-FGSM, AN-FGM MCAN-FGM. (a)(b)(c)(d) indicate four different source models.

4.6 Ablation Study

To demonstrate the effectiveness of each part of our method, we conduct ablation experiment on MACN-FGM. We divide MCAN-FGM into two parts MCN-FGSM and AN-FGM to observe their attack effects respectively. We select Vgg13_bn(Inc-v3/Res-101/Dens-169) to attack, and use adversarial samples to attack the other three black-box models. The ASR is shown in Fig. 5.

We can observe that both MCN-FGSM and AN-FGM can improve NI-FGSM. Because they optimize the update direction and stride of NI-FGSM. Meanwhile, the fused method MCAN-FGM can reach higher ASR than the two sub-methods. These experiments above can verify the effectiveness of each part of MCAN-FGM.

5 Conclusion

We propose the MCAN-FGM based on Multi-Convolution and Adaptive-stride modules. The Multi-Convolution aims to stabilize forward-looking direction of adversarial examples, and the Adaptive-stride pretends to adjust stride adaptively and stabilize the changing rate. Extensive experiments verify that this method can reach higher attack success rate and better attack effect than baseline methods.

References

1. Szegedy, C., Zaremba, W., Sutskever, I.: Intriguing properties of neural networks. In: 2nd International Conference on Learning Representations, pp. 1–10 (2014)
2. Athalye, A., Carlini, N., Wagner, D.: Obfuscated gradients give a false sense of security: circumventing defenses to adversarial examples. In: 35th International Conference on Machine Learning, pp. 274–283 (2018)
3. Brendel, W., Rauber, J., Bethge, M.: Decision-based adversarial attacks: Reliable attacks against black-box machine learning models. In: 6th International Conference on Learning Representations (2018)
4. Uesato, J., O'donoghue, B., Kohli, P., et al.: Adversarial risk and the dangers of evaluating against weak attacks. In: 35th International Conference on Machine Learning, pp. 5032–5041 (2018)

5. Carlini, N., Wagner, D.: Towards evaluating the robustness of neural networks. In: 2017 IEEE Symposium on Security and Privacy, pp. 39–57 (2017)
6. Liu, Y., Chen, X., Liu, C., et al.: Delving into transferable adversarial examples and black-box attacks. In: 5th International Conference on Learning Representations (2017)
7. Dong, Y., Liao, F., Pang, T., et al.: Boosting adversarial attacks with momentum. In: 2018 Conference on Computer Vision and Pattern Recognition, pp. 9185–9193 (2018)
8. Dong, Y., Pang, T., Su, H., et al.: Evading defenses to transferable adversarial examples by translation-invariant attacks. In: 2019 IEEE/CVF Conference on Computer Vision and Pattern Recognition, pp. 4312–4321 (2019)
9. Xie, C., Zhang, Z., Zhou, Y., et al.: Improving transferability of adversarial examples with input diversity. In: 2019 IEEE/CVF Conference on Computer Vision and Pattern Recognition, pp. 2730–2739 (2019)
10. Lin, J., Song, C., He, K., et al.: Nesterov accelerated gradient and scale invariance for adversarial attacks. In: 8th International Conference on Learning Representations (2020)
11. Nesterov, Y.: A method for unconstrained convex minimization problem with the rate of convergence O $(1/k^2)$. Doklady AN USSR **269**, 543–547 (1983)
12. Zaheer, M., Reddi, S., Sachan, D., et al.: Adaptive methods for nonconvex optimization. In: 2018 Neural Information Processing Systems, pp. 9815–9825 (2018)
13. Long, Y., Zhang, Q., Zeng, B., et al.: Frequency domain model augmentation for adversarial attack. In: Avidan, S., Brostow, G., Cissé, M., Farinella, G.M., Hassner, T. (eds.) Computer Vision – ECCV 2022. ECCV 2022. Lecture Notes in Computer Science, vol. 13664, pp. 549–566. Springer, Cham (2022). https://doi.org/10.1007/978-3-031-19772-7_32
14. Huang, Y., Kong, A.W.K.: Transferable adversarial attack based on integrated gradients. In: 10th International Conference on Learning Representations (2022)
15. Zhang, J., Wu, W., Huang, J.T., et al.: Improving adversarial transferability via neuron attribution-based attacks. In: 2022 IEEE/CVF Conference on Computer Vision and Pattern Recognition, pp. 14993–15002 (2022)
16. Xiong, Y., Lin, J., Zhang, M., et al.: Stochastic variance reduced ensemble adversarial attack for boosting the adversarial transferability. In: 2022 IEEE/CVF Conference on Computer Vision and Pattern Recognition, pp. 14983–14992 (2022)
17. Cheng, Y., Song, J., Zhu, X., et al.: Fast gradient non-sign methods. arXiv preprint arXiv (2021)
18. Yang, B., Zhang, H., Li, Z., et al.: Adversarial example generation with AdaBelief optimizer and crop invariance. In: 2022 Applied Intelligence, pp. 1–6 (2022)
19. Yuan, Z., Zhang, J., Shan, S., et al.: Adaptive perturbation for adversarial attack. arXiv preprint arXiv (2021)
20. Kingma, D.P., Ba, J.: Adam: a method for stochastic optimization. In: 3rd International Conference on Learning Representations (2015)

Multi-source Open-Set Image Classification Based on Deep Adversarial Domain Adaptation

Haitao Zhang, Xinran Liu⬤, Qilong Han$^{(\boxtimes)}$⬤, and Dan Lu

Harbin Engineering University, Harbin, China
hanqilong@hrbeu.edu.cn

Abstract. Existing unsupervised domain adaptation methods are often limited to specific settings, such as single-source open-set or multi-source closed-set scenarios. These limitations hinder the application of deep models in various domains. To address this issue, this study proposes a novel unsupervised adaptive learning method specifically designed for multi-source open-set scenarios to enhance the generalization performance of deep models. In particular, we incorporate a regularization term into the model to reduce the disparity in feature representations across different source domains, thus obtaining domain-invariant features. Additionally, an adversarial loss function is introduced to learn discriminative feature representations between known and unknown classes, and a weighted learning strategy is employed to dynamically adjust the distribution of known and unknown class samples in the feature space. Furthermore, to address the inadequate handling of unknown classes in existing methods, we further partition the unknown class samples in the target domain. The proposed model is evaluated on three datasets, and consistently outperforms baseline methods and benchmark single-source open-set unsupervised domain adaptation methods.

Keywords: Domain Adaptation · Open-Set · Multi-Source · Unsupervised Learning · Image Classification

1 Introduction

The excellent performance of neural networks largely depends on a large amount of labeled data. However, models trained on specific source domains face the challenge of distribution shift when deployed in new environments. To overcome this problem, unsupervised domain adaptation has emerged as an effective solution.

The purpose of unsupervised domain adaptation is to train a model on source domain data in order to demonstrate good generalization performance in the target domain, even in the absence of labeled target domain data. Excellent unsupervised domain adaptation methods improve the model's robustness and transferability, reducing the cost and workload of retraining the model in a new environment. Closed-set domain adaptation is one scenario where the source domain and target domain share the same set of classes. In closed-set adaptation,

L. Iliadis et al. (Eds.): ICANN 2023, LNCS 14258, pp. 143–156, 2023.
https://doi.org/10.1007/978-3-031-44192-9_12

the goal is to enable the model to correctly classify known shared categories in the target domain by learning the feature mapping between the source and target domains. Open-set adaptation is a more challenging scenario where the target domain may contain new categories that are unseen in the source domain. In open-set adaptation, the objective is not only to correctly classify known shared categories but also to identify and differentiate new categories in the target domain. This requires the model to robustly recognize and handle unknown categories to adapt to the variations in the target domain. A common approach is to identify non-shared classes, increase the distance between them and shared classes, and align the shared categories across the two domains. However, due to the lack of labeled samples and their diversity, this approach often treats all non-shared class samples in the target domain as a single large "unknown" class, overlooking the intrinsic structure and diversity within the "unknown" class. Furthermore, most unsupervised domain adaptation algorithms focus on single-source domain adaptation, whereas in practical scenarios, source domain data is often obtained from various sources. Therefore, single-source unsupervised closed-set domain adaptation algorithms exhibit suboptimal performance when dealing with such multi-source domain scenarios.

To address these issues, this paper proposes a new approach for multi-source open-set unsupervised domain adaptation, where there are multiple labeled source domains, each containing samples from the same semantic class, and an unlabeled target domain containing two types of data: known categories shared with the source domains and new categories from the unknown. In this case, our objective is to assign target domain samples to one of the shared categories with the source domains or assign them to a more explicit k^* new categories.

Our major contributions can be summarized as follows:

- This paper proposes a framework based on adversarial learning to solve the multi-source open-set domain adaptation problem.
- Firstly, a semantic-based regularization term is introduced to learn domain-invariant features for each source domain. Then, a fine-grained predictor is constructed to distinguish target domain samples into known and unknown classes in detail. Finally, an unsupervised clustering algorithm is designed to further divide unknown class samples in the target domain into k^* new categories instead of a single "unknown" class.
- We conducted extensive experiments on three benchmark datasets to determine the effectiveness of the network, and we conducted a comprehensive analysis in these experiments.

2   Related Work

Domain Adaptation: The main challenge of closed-set domain adaptation is how to handle the data distribution differences between the source domain and the target domain. One common strategy for addressing this problem is to use metric learning methods, which employ metrics such as Kullback-Leibler divergence [1], Jensen-Shannon divergence [2], Wasserstein distance [3], maximum mean discrepancy (MMD) [4,5], and correlation alignment (CORAL) [6] as loss functions to align the sample distributions across domains. These methods reduce the distribution differences between domains but come with high computational costs, thus increasing training time.

Another approach is adversarial domain adaptation, which aims to minimize the distribution differences between domains by confusing the source and target domain samples through adversarial learning. Ganin et al. [7] proposed domain adversarial neural networks to enforce feature invariance. Long et al. [8] introduced an adversarial domain adaptation model that utilizes class information to enhance feature discriminability and transferability. Shu et al. [9] employed a two-stage training process, first learning domain-invariant features and then fine-tuning the classifier on the target domain. Zhang et al. [10] incorporated domain discriminators into multiple CNN feature extraction modules in their collaborative adversarial network (CAN). Adversarial-based domain adaptation methods only require training a single domain discriminator to align the sample distributions across domains, significantly reducing computational and time costs in model training.

Domain adaptation has also been widely applied in tasks such as image reconstruction [11], image classification [12], and image recognition [13]. [13] proposed embedding attention modules into adversarial networks to distinguish the transferable parts.

Open-Set: The common open-set classification methods employ threshold-based approaches. Jain et al. [14] proposed using Support Vector Machines to compute the maximum probability for known class samples and select target domain samples based on a threshold. Bendale and Boult [15] introduced an OpenMax layer that matches each sample with prototypes of known classes to estimate the probability distribution of each class. In adversarial-based methods, Saito et al. [16] developed the OSBP model, which uses adversarial training between a classifier and feature extractor to classify samples into known and unknown classes. Fu et al. [17] enhanced the network performance of OSBP by incorporating symmetric KL loss. Liu et al. [18] proposed the STA model, which computes the similarity between target domain data and each source domain class using multiple binary classifiers and generates weights using fine-grained binary classifiers to identify unknown classes in the target domain.

Furthermore, Lian et al. [19] utilized teacher-student networks for domain transfer and achieved good results. Feng et al. [20] introduced a category-level alignment method and a semantic-based contrastive mapping approach. In multi-source open-set recognition, HyMOS [21] leveraged contrastive learning and the properties of hyperspherical feature space to separate known and unknown classes. [22] proposed an adversarial-based multi-source open-set unsupervised domain adaptation framework [23]. However, these existing multi-source open-set transfer learning methods often treat unknown classes in the target domain as a single large category, overlooking the diversity within unknown classes. To address this limitation, this paper proposes a multi-source open-set transfer learning network that not only distinguishes unknown classes in the target domain but further divides them to avoid confusion between unknown classes, thus increasing class diversity and interpretability.

3 Proposed Method

3.1 Problem Definition

Suppose we have L different source domains $DS = \{DS_1, DS_2, ..., DS_L\}$, each source domain has its own specific training set $X_L = \{x_l^i, y_l^i\}_{i=1}^{n_l}$, ($l \in \{1, 2, ...L\}$) and n_l defines the number of training samples of DS_l. Label space $Y_s = \{1, 2, 3, ...K\}$ is shared among all source domains. On the other hand, there is a target domain DT consisting of n_l unlabeled test samples $X_t = \{x_t^j\}_{j=1}^{n_t}$, with a total of Y_t categories, $Y_s \subset Y_t$, and $Y_{s/t}$ represents the open-set class that does not belong to DS. Suppose that the edge data distributions of all source and target domains are different from each other: $P_l(X_l) \neq P_m(X_m)$ and $P_l(X_l) \neq P_t(X_t), DS_l, DS_m \in DS$. For multi-source open-set unsupervised domain adaptation, the distribution of the known classes from DT differs from that of a given DS_l: $P_l(X_l) \neq P_t(X_t^{1:K})$ where $X_t^{1:K}$ represents the target domain sample with a known class label, and X_t^{1+K} is a sample from an unknown class in DT.

Under this setting, the task is to classify the data in X_t into $K + k^*$ categories, where the first K indexes correspond to the classes shared with the source domain, and the last $K + k^*$ indexes represent the newly discovered class labels in the target domain.

3.2 Training and Inference

Overview of the Training Process: Our network architecture comprises a shared feature extractor, independent multi-class classifiers for the source domain, and a fine-grained predictor. The classifiers are designed to accommodate $k + 1$ classes, where k represents the number of shared classes between the source and target domains, and the additional class represents the unknown class in the target domain. In our approach, we first leverage balanced batch construction and semantic regularization techniques to obtain domain-invariant features from multiple complementary source domains. This enables precise alignment of the source domain data, which in turn facilitates detailed discrimination of the target domain data. To achieve discriminative feature representations between shared classes and unknown classes, we introduce an adversarial learning framework. Additionally, in order to ensure fine-grained alignment between the source and target domains, we propose utilizing the output of the fine-grained predictor as soft weights to dynamically adjust the decision boundary between shared classes and unknown classes. Additionally, we employ an unsupervised clustering algorithm to partition the samples belonging to the unknown class into k^* new categories, enhancing the granularity of the adaptation process (Fig. 1).

I. Obtain domain invariant features in DS: We add a semantic-based contrast regularizer to train the model to reduce the difference in feature expression

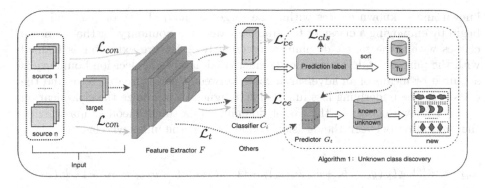

Fig. 1. A depiction of MOICA. It is mainly composed of shared feature encoder F, independent $K + 1$ class classifier C_i and fine-grained predictor. The figure also shows the losses that need to be evaluated.

between source domains. We will select an equal number of samples in L source domains to construct training batches containing all source domain categories; for the source domain samples in each batch, different transformation views are obtained by different data enhancement transformations such as grayscale, random cropping, and color jitter. Samples of the same category are regarded as positive samples, and samples of different categories are regarded as negative samples. Through training, the positive samples are closer in the feature space, while the different negative samples are farther apart:

$$\mathcal{L}_{con}\left(x_s\right) = -\log \frac{exp\left(D_{cos}\left(F\left(x_s\right), F\left(T\left(x_s\right)\right)\right)/\delta\right)}{\sum_{x_s' \in DS} 1_{\left[y_s \neq y_s'\right]} exp\left(D_{cos}\left(F\left(x_s\right), F\left(T\left(x_s'\right)\right)\right)/\delta\right)} \quad (1)$$

here, T denotes a geometric transformation, N represents the number of samples in a batch, D_{cos} represents the cosine similarity, and δ is a hyperparameter for balance.

By introducing this regularization term, the feature extractor not only retains the discriminative features of the data but also is more robust to data changes and improves the ability to express new domain data, which is particularly important in open- set transfer learning.

At the same time, we use cross entropy loss to classify known source samples:

$$\mathcal{L}_{ce}\left(x_s\right) = -y_s log\left(p_c\left(x_s\right)\right) \quad (2)$$

where $p_c\left(x_s\right) = p\left(y \mid x_s; \theta_f, \theta_c\right)$ represents the probability distribution of the prediction results of C_i on all known classes. The prediction label of the target domain is determined by the category corresponding to the highest score in the mean of the prediction probability of each source domain classifier for the target domain data.

II. Distinguish the known and unknown samples in DT: Our objective is to establish a discerning decision boundary that effectively distinguishes the known and unknown classes within the target domain. To accomplish this, we begin by employing a classifier to establish a decision boundary for the unknown classes within the target domain. Subsequently, a feature extractor is trained with the purpose of deceiving the classifier. Ultimately, the decision boundary is acquired by means of an adversarial game between the feature extractor and the classifier. The underlying loss function is designed to minimize the classification error of known classes in the target domain, while simultaneously maximizing the separation between the decision boundary and the unknown class.

$$\mathcal{L}_{cls} = \mathbb{E}\left[t \log\left(p\left(y_t = K + 1 \mid F\left(x_t\right)\right)\right) - (1 - t)\log\left(1 - p\left(y_t = K + 1 \mid F\left(x_t\right)\right)\right)\right] \tag{3}$$

III. Partition unknown class: When the similarity of sample features between unknown and known classes is substantial, the estimated class labels will be uncertain. Therefore, we propose a fine-grained predictor G_t, which predicts the probability that each sample belongs to an unknown class and dynamically adjusts the decision boundary t. For the target domain samples divided into unknown classes, we will use the unsupervised classification algorithm to calculate the best clustering results to assign pseudo labels to the newly discovered classes. This step has been summarized in Algorithm 1.

We use the known classes in the target domain to assist the further division of unknown classes. The prediction label is used to construct a high-confidence target domain known class sample candidate set T_k and an unknown class sample candidate set T_u, and the labels $d_i = 1$ and $d_i = 0$ are assigned to represent known classes and unknown classes, respectively. Specifically, for each sample in the target domain DT, the entropy H is calculated. Entropy is an index to measure the uncertainty of samples, and the lower entropy indicates that the samples have higher consistency. The calculation formula of entropy is as follows:

$$H\left(\boldsymbol{x}_t; F, C\right) = -\sum_{k=1}^{K} C^k\left(F\left(\boldsymbol{x}_t\right)\right) \log C^k\left(F\left(\boldsymbol{x}_t\right)\right) \tag{4}$$

where $C^k\left(F\left(\boldsymbol{x}_t\right)\right)$ represents the softmax value of the target domain sample belonging to the k-th class.

The feature extractor is used to extract the feature representation of the known class sample candidate set and the unknown class sample candidate set in the target domain. These features are input into a fine-grained predictor G_t for training, which is used to determine whether the sample belongs to a known class or an unknown class:

$$\mathcal{L}_t = \frac{1}{|X'|} \sum_{x_t \in X'} \mathcal{L}_{ce}\left(G_t\left(F\left(x_t\right)\right), d_i\right) \tag{5}$$

X' represents the samples from T_k and T_u in the target domain.

We use the softmax output of G_t as the weight of soft power level. When $G_t\left(F\left(x_t\right)\right)$ is closer to 0, the higher the probability of the sample from the

---

Algorithm 1: Unknown class discovery

Input: Target domain data set DT;   The range of radius r and neighborhood density domain value z;   pre-trained feature extractor F and classifiers C_i; fine-grained predict G_t

Output: The number of class estimation k^*;   The pseudo label $\tilde{y}_t$ of unknown classes in the target domain

1 Formula 4 is used to calculate the entropy H of each sample in DT. According to H, x_t is sorted and T_k and T_u are constructed.

2 Extract feature of T_k and T_u using F.

3 $(T_k, T_u) \longrightarrow G_t$(Formula 5).

4 **for** $x_i \in DT - (T_k \cup T_u)$ **do**

5 | **if** $C_t(x_i) < 0.5$ **then**

6 | | $x_i \longrightarrow T_{new}$

7 | **end**

8 **end**

9 Extract feature of T_{new} and T_u using F.

10 Take b values at equal intervals with a as the step distance, take all integer values in the z interval, and cross-combine to generate k_{max} group parameter pairs.

11 **for** $0 \leq k \leq k_{max}$ **do**

12 | Run DBSCAN on the extracted feature T_{new} and T_u.

13 | Calculate the contour coefficient .

14 | max = Max (max, η), and record z, r.

15 **end**

16 The recorded r and z are used to perform the DBSCAN algorithm on the data set T_{new} and T_u.

17 The optimal number of clusters is recorded, T_{new} and T_u is classified as $\{T_{new} \cup T_u\}_{i=1}^{k^*}$ by pseudo-labels.

---

unknown class, the lower the weight, and vice versa. We assume that the distance from the current sample to the decision boundary is linear with the output of the predictor, so the judgment formula of the decision boundary t is:

$$t = k * G_t (F (x_t)) + b \qquad (6)$$

where k is the adjustment factor and b is the deviation term. Therefore, t can be brought into formula (3) to adaptively quantify the importance of each target sample.

The unsupervised clustering algorithm DBSCAN is used to cluster the unknown class samples: due to the lack of real labels of unknown class samples, we evaluate the clustering results combined with cohesion and separation to evaluate the clustering results from the intra-cluster and inter-cluster perspectives.

I. Contour coefficient of sample individual: assuming that the unknown class sample x_t in the target domain is clustered into cluster U, its contour coefficient η_i is defined as where:

$$\eta_i = \frac{u_i - v_i}{\max (u_i, v_i)} \qquad (7)$$

u_i sample x_t the average distance from all other points in the same category, v_i is the average distance between the sample x_t and all other points in the next nearest cluster.

II. Clustering contour coefficient: the contour coefficient of the entire data set is the average of all sample contour coefficients. It is defined as:

$$\eta = \frac{1}{n} \sum_{i=1}^{n} \eta_i \tag{8}$$

Given the range of parameters: radius r and neighborhood density domain value z, the parameters r and z are adaptively determined by finding the maximum value of the contour coefficient to obtain the best clustering results.

3.3 Network Optimization

We iteratively train our network through the following steps until convergence:

Table 1. The classification accuracy of the model and related methods on office-Home, (s) = single best, (c) = source combine.

Method	Office-Home				
	ACP-R	ARP-C	PCR-A	ACR-P	AVG
	OS	OS	OS	OS	OS
OSVM(s)	67.1	59.7	59.3	75.1	65.3
OSVM(c)	60.2	46.3	48.6	50.7	53.0
DANN+OSVM(s)	54.5	31.6	40.9	53.8	45.2
STA(s)	72.3	53.9	64.4	65.8	64.1
OSBP(s)	73.0	57.0	58.1	70.4	64.6
OSBP(c)	53.6	38.0	46.9	54.9	48.3
IOSBP(s)	58.6	31.4	46.2	64.0	50.0
IOSBP(c)	64.5	46.2	54.9	66.4	58.1
baseline	**80.3**	67.5	60.6	80.2	72.1
MOICA	78.6	**70.7**	**65.2**	**82.5**	**74.25**

Stage 1: Fixed feature extractor, training source classifier to minimize the following losses:

$$\min_{\theta c} \frac{1}{L} \sum_{l=1}^{L} \mathcal{L}_{ce} + \mathcal{L}_{cls} \tag{9}$$

The first term of the equation indicates that the source domain samples have been correctly classified by optimizing the parameters of each classifier at the same time. The second term of the equation is to distinguish the known and unknown samples in the target domain.

Stage 2: By minimizing the equation-training feature extractor's ability to obtain domain-invariant features.

$$\min_{\theta f} \mathcal{L}_{con} + \mathcal{L}_{ce} - \mathcal{L}_{cls} \tag{10}$$

Stage 3: In order to further approximate the ideal performance, we use Algorithm 1 to train a fine-grained predictor to learn transferable features and further divide unknown class data.

4   Experimental Evaluations

4.1   Datasets

Office-Home is a data set with four domains, including art, sketch, painting, and decoration, and 65 categories each. The source and target domains share the first 25 categories alphabetically, while the remaining 40 are open-set classes. Office31 is a standard dataset with 4110 images of 31 categories across three domains: Amazon, Webcam, and DSLR. All possible combinations of two source domains and one target domain are adopted. The first 20 classes are shared alphabetically between the source and target domains, while the remaining 11 are open-set classes. Digit includes the USPS and MNIST datasets, containing 9298 and 60,000 grayscale handwritten digital images, respectively, and the SVHN dataset with 73,257 color real-world door number images. Three adaptive tasks are constructed: SVHN → MNIST, USPS → MNIST, and MNIST → USPS, with numbers 0–4 as known classes and numbers 5–9 as unknown classes in each task.

Table 2. The classification accuracy of the model and related methods on Office31, (s) = single best, (c) = source combine.

Method	AD-W		AW-D		WD-A		AVG	
	OS*	OS	OS*	OS	OS*	OS	OS*	OS
OSVM(s)	73.5	70.0	94.8	94.0	41.3	39.5	69.9±0.3	67.8±0.4
OSVM(c)	71.3	64.7	85.8	55.0	57.2	61.5	70.7±0.5	60.4±0.2
MMD+OSVM(s)	72.5	73.2	69.8	72.0	29.8	27.1	57.4±0.7	57.4±0.4
BP+OSVM(s)	70.6	72.5	71.1	73.2	31.2	27.9	57.6±0.3	57.9±0.2
STA(s)	86.1	88.1	82.9	84.3	65.2	64.8	78.1±0.6	79.1±0.5
OSBP(s)	95.7	92.8	98.2	90.3	82.0	51.9	92.0±0.3	78.3±0.5
OSBP(c)	90.8	88.6	92.2	88.3	79.0	75.9	87.3±0.6	84.3±0.4
IOSBP(s)	97.8	66.2	94.2	63.5	79.6	75.1	90.5±0.4	68.3±0.3
IOSBP(c)	89.8	83.2	87.2	83.5	76.6	75.1	84.5±0.3	80.6±0.2
baseline	**99.0**	**98.2**	**99.4**	98.3	81.0	79.3	**93.1±0.4**	91.9±0.2
MOICA	96.2	94.1	99.0	**98.5**	**82.9**	**83.3**	92.7±0.2	**92.0±0.2**

4.2   Model Framework and Experimental Methods

This chapter employs LeNet as the backbone network for Digit and ResNet for Office-31 and Office-Home. The network was trained for 200 rounds with random gradient descent, a batch size of 16 (64 for Digit), a learning rate of 0.0005, and a momentum coefficient of 0.9. Algorithm 1 defines the range of r as [0, 0.010] and takes 100 values at an equal interval of $0.0001.z$ is all integers in the interval [3, 12], totaling 10 values. The model's evaluation consists of three indicators: OS, OS^*, and UNK, with OS and OS^* representing the average accuracy of all classes and known classes at the category level, respectively, and UNK representing the accuracy of unknown classes.

Table 3. The classification accuracy of the model and related methods on Digits, (s) = single best, (c) = source combine.

Method	M+U-S			S+M-U			S+U-M			AVG OS
	OS	OS*	UNK	OS	OS*	UNK	OS	OS*	UNK	
OSVM(s)	65.3	59.8	75.2	79.4	77.9	84.2	43.1	30.6	64.2	62.6±0.3
OSVM(c)	66.1	69.8	65.4	75.3	72.5	80.3	51.4	57.9	46.2	64.3±0.4
MMD+OSVM(s)	55.4	59.8	42.6	78.9	77.9	84.2	63.2	58.9	69.3	65.8±0.3
DANN+OSVM(s)	62.3	70.8	39.2	33.6	42.1	19.3	84.4	89.3	70.8	60.1±0.8
STA(s)	76.9	68.2	78.8	93.0	92.8	88.3	92.2	91.5	90.9	87.4±0.4
OSBP(s)	66.0	58.4	71.8	92.1	93.7	81.3	92.3	90.2	93.7	83.5±0.4
OSBP(c)	60.4	62.2	69.5	83.0	82.8	79.3	86.5	89.7	90.6	76.6±0.3
IOSBP(s)	76.5	69.8	78.4	83.0	82.8	87.3	82.4	81.5	80.6	80.6±0.5
IOSBP(c)	78.9	73.7	88.6	83.4	79.2	89.1	82.1	81.6	90.4	80.6±0.6
baseline	79.1	88.2	93.8	86.6	**98.8**	**98.9**	95.2	98.2	**99.1**	87.1±0.3
MOICA	**82.7**	**88.6**	**94.8**	**89.6**	95.7	96.4	**96.2**	**98.9**	97.4	**89.5±0.5**

4.3   Comparison to the Literature and Baselines

We have introduced a new multi-source open-set transfer learning method MOS-DANET [22] as our baseline and compared it with several single-source methods, such as OSBP [16], IOSBP [17], and STA [18]. To evaluate the effectiveness of MOICA, we conducted three experiments: (1) Source domain combination: We combined all source domains and compared them with the single-source method. We allowed the OSVM [14] method to be combined with other feature extraction or similarity calculation methods. The model was trained on the source domain and evaluated on the target domain. (2) Single-source optimization, where we reported the best single-source transmission results in multiple source domains, such as A, D → W, by comparing the results between A → W and D → W. (3) Multi-source comparison: We compared MOICA with the latest multi-source method. Tables 1, 2 and 3 present the results of MOICA, showcasing its strong

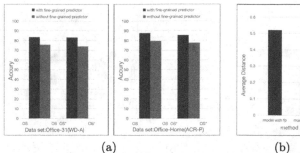 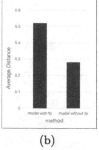 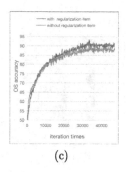

(a)   (b)   (c)

Fig. 2. (a) shows the effectiveness of the fine-grained predictor in Office-31 WD → A and Office-Home ACR → P. (b) and (c) show the performance of MOICA with and without fine-grained predictor and semantic-based regularizer, respectively (Office-31).

performance, particularly in datasets with a large number of samples (Digits) and complex class distributions (Office-Home). These experiments demonstrate the favorable performance of MOICA across different scenarios. The results highlight the effectiveness and versatility of MOICA in addressing multi-source open-set transfer learning tasks.

In this section, detailed ablation experiments were conducted to thoroughly evaluate the impact of various techniques on the experimental results. Figure 2(a) showcases the effectiveness of fine-grained predictors in two specific cases: WD → A (Office-31) and ACR → P (Office-Home). Furthermore, Fig. 2(b) illustrates that the complete model exhibits an average difference of approximately 0.52, while the model without the fine-grained predictor has an average difference of about 0.28. Additionally, Fig. 2(c) demonstrates the change in the OS value during model training when the loss term $\mathcal{L}_{con}$ is removed. This finding suggests that the complete model, with the inclusion of the semantic-based contrast regularization component, achieves approximately 4% points higher accuracy compared to the model without this component. These ablation experiments robustly demonstrate the effectiveness and importance of fine-grained predictors and the semantic-based contrast regularization component in enhancing the accuracy and overall performance of the model in the target domain.

In our evaluation, MOICA was compared with several modifications, including: (1) removing the unknown class classification module and setting the number of unknown class types, denoted as k, to 1; (2) utilizing the DBSCAN algorithm to distinguish unknown class types without additional iterations; and (3) employing the DBSCAN algorithm for iterative model training. Figure 3(a) presents the average OS and OS^* values for all transport tasks in the Office-31 dataset, supporting our hypothesis that identifying the structure of unknown classes contributes to improving the accuracy of open-set classification. Furthermore, Fig. 3(b) displays a t-SNE graph illustrating the discrimination achieved by MOICA in the shared feature space on the Office-31 dataset. It is evident that the known class samples appropriately overlap in all fields, while there is

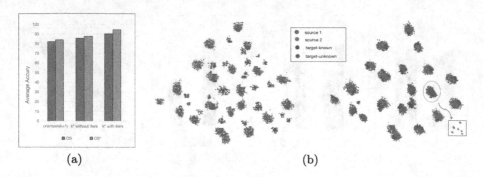

(a)   (b)

Fig. 3. (a) shows the influence of the number of iterations on the performance of the Algorithm 1 (Office-31). (b) t-SNE plot for the case A, D-W (Office-31) before and after adaptation.

clear distinction between different categories. These comparisons and visualizations demonstrate the effectiveness of MOICA in addressing the challenges of open-set classification tasks.

5   Conclusions

MOICA method enhances the exploration and utilization of target domain data by effectively reducing domain differences. It achieves this through an advanced adversarial learning strategy that aligns category data from different domains and dynamically adjusts decision boundaries for known and unknown category data. Additionally, an unsupervised classification algorithm is utilized to further differentiate the unknown class data. The effectiveness of MOICA has been demonstrated through extensive testing on multiple datasets, yielding favorable results. While the proposed method shows promising performance, further research and enhancements are necessary to address the challenges posed by unknown class classification. Future work will be dedicated to refining the classification algorithm, exploring innovative techniques to improve the accuracy and robustness of handling unknown classes.

Acknowledgements. This work was supported by the National Key R&D Program of China under Grant No. 2020YFB1710200, and the National Natural Science Foundation of China under Grant No. 62072136.

References

1. Van Erven, T., Harremos, P.: Rényi divergence and Kullback-Leibler divergence. IEEE Trans. Inf. Theory **60**(7), 3797–3820 (2014)
2. Fuglede, B., Topsoe, F.: Jensen-Shannon divergence and Hilbert space embedding. In: International Symposium on Information Theory, p. 31 (2004)

3. Vallender, S.: Calculation of the Wasserstein distance between probability distributions on the line. Theory Probab. Appl. **18**(4), 784–786 (1974)
4. Pan, S.J., Tsang, I.W., Kwok, J.T., Yang, Q.: Domain adaptation via transfer component analysis. IEEE Trans. Neural Netw. **22**(2), 199–210 (2010)
5. Dorri, F., Ghodsi, A.: Adapting component analysis. In: IEEE International Conference on Data Mining, pp. 846–851 (2012)
6. Sun, B., Saenko, K.: Deep CORAL: correlation alignment for deep domain adaptation. In: Hua, G., Jégou, H. (eds.) ECCV 2016. LNCS, vol. 9915, pp. 443–450. Springer, Cham (2016). https://doi.org/10.1007/978-3-319-49409-8_35
7. Ganin, Y., et al.: Domain adversarial training of neural networks. J. Mach. Learn. Res. **17**(1), 2096–2030 (2016)
8. Long, M., Cao, Z., Wang, J., et al.: Conditional adversarial domain adaptation. In: Proceedings of Advances in Neural Information Processing Systems, pp. 1647–1657 (2018)
9. Shu, R., Bui, H.H., Narui, H., et al.: A DIRT-T approach to unsupervised domain adaptation. In: Proceedings of International Conference on Learning Representations (2018)
10. Zhang, W., Ouyang, W., Li, W., Xu, D.: Collaborative and adversarial network for unsupervised domain adaptation. In: IEEE Conference on Computer Vision and Pattern Recognition, pp. 3801–3809 (2018)
11. Wang, Chao, Cheng: Image super-resolution reconstruction based on self-attention generative adversarial networks. Control Decis. **36**(6), 1324–1332 (2021)
12. Nian, F., Sheng, Y., Wang, J., et al.: Zero-shot visual recognition via semantic attention-based compare network. IEEE Access **8**, 26002–26011 (2020)
13. Chen, W., Hu, H.: Generative attention adversarial classification network for unsupervised domain adaptation. Pattern Recogn. **107**, 107440 (2020)
14. Jain, L.P., Scheirer, W.J., Boult, T.E.: Multi-class open set recognition using probability of inclusion. In: Fleet, D., Pajdla, T., Schiele, B., Tuytelaars, T. (eds.) ECCV 2014. LNCS, vol. 8691, pp. 393–409. Springer, Cham (2014). https://doi.org/10.1007/978-3-319-10578-9_26
15. Bendale, A., Boult, T.E.: Towards open set deep networks. In: IEEE Conference on Computer Vision and Pattern Recognition, pp. 1563–1572 (2016)
16. Saito, K., Yamamoto, S., Ushiku, Y., Harada, T.: Open set domain adaptation by backpropagation. In: Ferrari, V., Hebert, M., Sminchisescu, C., Weiss, Y. (eds.) ECCV 2018. LNCS, vol. 11209, pp. 156–171. Springer, Cham (2018). https://doi.org/10.1007/978-3-030-01228-1_10
17. Fu, J.H., Wu, X.F., Zhang, S.F., et al.: Improved open set domain adaptation with backpropagation. In: IEEE International Conference on Image Processing, pp. 2506–2510 (2019)
18. Liu, H., Cao, Z.J., Long, M.S., et al.: Separate to adapt: open set domain adaptation via progressive separation. In: IEEE Conference on Computer Vision and Pattern Recognition, pp. 2927–2936 (2019)
19. Lian, Q., Li, W., Chen, L., et al.: Known-class aware self-ensemble for open set domain adaptation. arXiv preprint arXiv:1905.01068 (2019)
20. Feng, Q., Kang, G., Fan, H., et al.: Attract or distract: exploit the margin of open set. In: Proceedings of IEEE International Conference on Computer Vision, pp. 7990–7999 (2019)
21. Bucci, S., Borlino, F.C., Caputo, B., et al.: Distance-based hyperspherical classification for multi-source open-set domain adaptation. In: Proceedings of the IEEE/CVF Winter Conference on Applications of Computer Vision, pp. 1119–1128 (2022)

22. Rakshit, S., Tamboli, D., Meshram, P.S., Banerjee, B., Roig, G., Chaudhuri, S.: Multi-source open-set deep adversarial domain adaptation. In: Vedaldi, A., Bischof, H., Brox, T., Frahm, J.-M. (eds.) ECCV 2020. LNCS, vol. 12371, pp. 735–750. Springer, Cham (2020). https://doi.org/10.1007/978-3-030-58574-7_44
23. Long, M., Cao, Y., Wang, J., Jordan, M.I.: Learning transferable features with deep adaptation networks. arXiv preprint arXiv:1502.02791 (2015)

SAL: Salient Adversarial Attack with LRP Refinement

Xinlei Gao and Jing Liu[✉]

Inner Mongolia University, Hohhot, China
liujing@imu.edu.cn

Abstract. Deep Neural Networks (DNNs) are susceptible to attacks by adversarial examples, which could cause serious consequences in safety-critical systems. Towards recent studies on generating efficient adversarial examples, how to enhance the imperceptibility of adversarial examples has been an issue worth more investigating. In this paper, we propose a novel salient adversarial attack method based on Layer-Wise Relevance Propagation (LRP), named SAL, which restricts perturbations to salient regions and subsequently refines them using the LRP interpretation algorithm, reducing perturbations to some pixel points. We conduct sufficient experiments on the ImageNet-Compatible dataset. Experiment results demonstrate that our method is capable of generating higher imperceptibility adversarial examples in quite less time, compared to the representative PerC-AL method. Besides, the robustness and transferability of our method are validated to perform better than the baseline methods.

Keywords: Adversarial examples · Imperceptibility · Robustness · Transferability

1 Introduction

Deep Neural Networks (DNNs) have found widespread applications in image classification [1], face recognition [2], object detection [3], speech recognition [4], and machine translation [5]. However, despite their success, DNNs exhibit vulnerabilities [6], including susceptibility to adversarial examples attacks that can cause them to misclassify, posing significant risks in real-world applications like self-driving. Researchers have proposed several approaches to address this issue, including adversarial attacks, categorized as white-box or black-box attacks based on whether attackers have access to the internal parameters and structure of the model. White-box attacks are usually more powerful, as attackers can use knowledge of the internal structure of the model to generate more effective attacks. In the past, both black-box and white-box attacks mainly focused on achieving high success rates with adversarial examples, which is certainly important. However, some of the generated adversarial examples produced noise that was visible to the naked eye. Subsequent research directions have therefore shifted toward generating high-quality adversarial examples. Recent research has

© The Author(s), under exclusive license to Springer Nature Switzerland AG 2023
L. Iliadis et al. (Eds.): ICANN 2023, LNCS 14258, pp. 157–168, 2023.
https://doi.org/10.1007/978-3-031-44192-9_13

mostly focused on ensuring the success of the attacks while also making the generated adversarial examples as imperceptible as possible to the human eye. This emphasis on imperceptibility has become a major focus of recent research.

The imperceptibility of adversarial examples has been extensively researched. Guo et al. [8] utilized low-frequency perturbations to search for adversarial examples in the frequency domain, while Zhang et al. [9] combined Laplace smoothing with optimization. Despite these efforts, most approaches still rely on L_p norms to improve the imperceptibility of adversarial examples. Recent studies, however, have shown that L_p norms do not perfectly match the human visual perception [10]. In other words, the magnitude of the L_p norm value does not fully indicate the strength of imperceptibility in adversarial examples. Instead, experiments have shown that CIEDE2000 [11], a color perception distance, is a better metric to match human visual perception. This means that the smaller the CIEDE2000 metric of perceived distance, the greater the imperceptibility of the adversarial examples. PerC-AL [12] is a method that generates adversarial examples around this color perception distance, making them more imperceptible than most other algorithms. However, this method has a high number of iterations and a long running time, which may not be suitable for real-world online Application Programming Interfaces (APIs) that have mandatory time or money limits on user queries [13]. Hence, it is important to explore methods for generating adversarial examples with smaller CIEDE2000 values and in a more time-efficient manner.

In this paper, we propose a novel salient adversarial attack method based on Layer-Wise Relevance Propagation (LRP), named SAL, which restricts perturbations to salient regions and subsequently refines them using the LRP interpretation algorithm, reducing perturbations to some pixel points. To achieve this, we use the Pyramid Feature Attention (PFA) network method to extract salient regions, and then refine them by reducing the image from the overall region to the salient region, the area for subsequent refinement and perturbation is significantly reduced, thus enhancing the generation speed. Additionally, the reduction in the computational region further improves the imperceptibility of the image. We conduct sufficient experiments on the ImageNet-Compatible dataset. Our experimental results demonstrate that our method generates adversarial examples with higher imperceptibility compared to the representative PerC-AL method and in a shorter time across various models. Additionally, our approach outperforms the baseline methods in terms of robustness and transferability.

The contributions of this paper are as follows:

- Our SAL method takes about 20% of the time of the PerC-AL method while generating smaller adversarial examples in the CIEDE2000 metric.
- The performance of our method in terms of robustness and transferability is about 1.5 times better than existing the baseline methods.

The rest of this paper is organized as follows: Sect. 2 describes the PerC-AL method and the extraction of imperceptibility and salient regions. Next, in Sect. 3, we define the problem of untargeted attacks and present the proposed SAL method in detail. Experimental results and analysis are given in Sect. 4, and conclusions are given in Sect. 5.

2   Preliminaries

This section will first introduce the PerC-AL algorithm and its principles. Next, we will review related work that aims to improve the imperceptibility of adversarial attacks. Finally, we will discuss various methods for extracting significant regions of images.

2.1   Imperceptible Attack

To generate high-quality adversarial examples that are difficult for humans to recognize, researchers have designed perceptual similarity metrics to limit perturbations during generation [15,16]. Typically, these metrics use L_p norms to measure perturbations. However, recent studies have shown that L_p norms do not align with human perception. To address this, researchers have proposed other perceptual distance metrics, such as object structure similarity [15] and edge similarity [16], to improve perturbation imperceptibility. Experimental results [11] show that CIEDE2000 is a metric that is more consistent with the human visual system. Therefore, our method continues to use CIEDE2000 to evaluate the imperceptibility of the adversarial final examples. The mathematical definition is as follows:

$$\Delta E = \sqrt{\frac{(\Delta L')^2}{k_L^2 \cdot S_L^2} + \frac{(\Delta C')^2}{k_C^2 \cdot S_C^2} + \frac{(\Delta H')^2}{k_H^2 \cdot S_H^2} + \Delta R}, \Delta R = R_T \cdot \frac{\Delta C'}{k_C \cdot S_C} \cdot \frac{\Delta H'}{k_H \cdot S_H} \quad (1)$$

where ΔE stands for the overall color difference value. It is calculated by the open square of the weighted sum of squares of the luminance difference $\Delta L'$, chromaticity difference $\Delta C'$, and chromaticity difference $\Delta H'$. Where k_L, k_C, and k_H are correction factors and S_L, S_C, and S_H are standard deviation values. ΔR represents the effect of the luminance difference of the color on the overall color difference value. It is calculated by applying the correction factor and standard deviation value to the product of the chromaticity difference value $\Delta C'$ and the hue difference value $\Delta H'$ and multiplying by the temperature-dependent factor R_t.

2.2   PerC-AL Algorithm

Zhao [12] suggested that the human eye perceives changes in Red, Green, and Blue (RGB) colors differently, making noise noticeable in some sensitive color gamuts but not in non-sensitive ones. To address this, it proposed an improved algorithm for creating color image adversarial examples. This approach involves processing images in the CIELAB color space, adding a limit term for CIEDE2000 color distance to the loss function, and using Projected Gradient Descent (PGD) [27]: PerC-AL to update interference noise by calculating category loss and gradient descent of perceived color difference alternately. By considering human color perception, PerC-AL can generate visually imperceptible adversarial examples even with increased interference noise intensity,

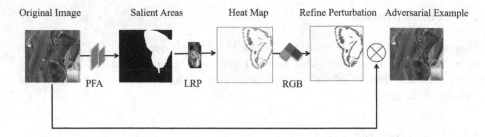

Fig. 1. The overall flowchart of the proposed SAL

achieving higher robustness than traditional algorithms within the same color distance. The algorithm also shows better immunity in JPEG conversion, color compression, and other anti-defense processing experiments. However, the algorithm uses a high number of iterations to continuously reduce CIEDE2000, an imperceptibility metric, making it time-consuming for practical applications.

2.3   Extracting Salient Region

There are several techniques available for working with feature regions, including the BP-saliency map of JSMA [17] and the heat map of the LRP [14] extraction method for edge region extraction. Our approach for identifying high-feature regions involves using the PFA [20] network to extract significant regions. We then extract the corresponding regions from the heat map obtained through LRP and refine the perturbed regions by placing them in the channels. Using the channel approach is preferred because it has strong generalization capabilities and does not require access to network parameters or target model structure.

3   Method

In this section, we will first introduce the concept of CIEDE2000-based adversarial examples. Then, we will explain how we determine the significant regions of the image using the PFA network. Finally, we will provide a detailed description of our method. The general flowchart of SAL is illustrated in Fig. 1. Firstly, we extract the significant regions using the PFA method. Next, we obtain the heat map corresponding to the significant regions using LRP. To refine the perturbed regions, we apply them through the channels and add perturbations to the resulting areas. Finally, these perturbations are then superimposed on the original image to complete the process.

3.1   Problem Model

Set the input to the adversarial examples as x. Given a DNN classifier, denoted as $h : [0,1]^d \rightarrow R^K$, where d is the input's dimensionality x, and K is the

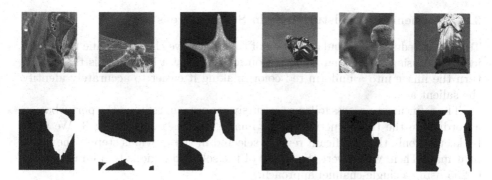

Fig. 2. Identify salient areas

number of classes. The predicted score $h_k(x)$ is associated with the probability of x belonging to class k. The classifier assigns the class that maximizes $h(x)$ to the input x. Previously, the goal of the untargeted attack is to find an x_{adv} that causes the model to misclassification with the true class l_{ori} and at the same time keep the distance between the x_{adv} and the benign input x less than the threshold ε.

$$\underset{k=1,\dots,K}{argmax}\, h_k(x) \neq l_{ori}, \text{s.t.}\, \|x_{adv} - x\|_p \leq \varepsilon, x_{adv} \in [0,1]^d \qquad (2)$$

Note the last constraint indicates that x_{adv} is a valid image. In this study, we focus on ΔE. Conventionally, the task of finding x_{adv} can be rephrased as solving a constrained continuous problem:

$$max\ f(x_{adv}), min\, \|\Delta E\, (x_{adv}, x)\|_2\,, \text{s.t.} x_{adv} \in [0,1]^d \qquad (3)$$

where $f(x) = L(x, l_{ori})$ is the loss function and ΔE is CIEDE2000 color distance.

3.2 Identify Salient Areas

The purpose of identifying salient areas in an image is to automatically and accurately extract salient objects, as illustrated in Fig. 2. Various methods are available for highlighting areas for extraction, such as BP-saliency map [13,18] and gradient CAM [19]. These models do not require any information beyond the input image and are suitable for black-box attacks. In this work, we utilized the PFA network to identify salient regions, which achieves advanced performance on multiple datasets by capturing both high-level contextual features and low-level spatial structure features. Given an input image, PFA generates a saliency score between 0 and 1 for each pixel, where higher values indicate higher visual saliency. We then use a threshold *epsilon* to convert the saliency score into a binary saliency mask, which determines the salient region. By reducing the image from the overall region to the salient region, the area for subsequent refinement and perturbation is significantly reduced, thus enhancing the generation speed. Additionally, the reduction in the computational region further improves the imperceptibility of the image.

3.3   Refinement of Disturbance in Salient Areas

To further reduce the calculation area of the image, we chose to refine the significant area using a heat map. The reason for selecting a heat map is that it can turn the image into a uniform red color, making it easier to accurately identify the salient area.

The refinement process follows a recursive approach, refining the perturbation according to the tree structure of the image, as illustrated in Fig. 3. We start by keeping only the significant regions selected in the previous step in the input heat map. Then, we convert the values of the selected regions to a number from 0–255 using a single-channel approach.

After that, we set a threshold value and attempt to perturb the regions with values less than the threshold while observing the impact on the output of the model. If the output results in misclassification, we continue to decrease the threshold until the model can correctly classify the image. This approach allows us to minimize the number of perturbed pixel points. We present the algorithm for refining the heat map in Algorithm 1.

Algorithm 1. Refined Heat Map

1: Let H be the input heat map.
2: Select the significant regions S from H.
3: Set $H' = H \cdot S$.
4: Let f be a function that maps the values of the selected regions to a 0-255 scale.
5: Set $H' = f(H')$.
6: Set the initial threshold value T.
7: Set the small step size ΔT for reducing T.
8: Let P be the perturbation function.
9: **while** $P(H', T)$ results in misclassification **do**
10:     Set $T = T - \Delta T$.
11:     Set $H' = H' + P(H', T)$.
12: **end while**
13: **return** Refined heat map H'.

In this algorithm, we first define the input heat map H and select the significant region S (line 2). Next, we initialize a heat map H' and assign it the part of H that contains only the S region (line 3). We then define a function f that maps the values of H' to the $0 - 255$ range and apply it to H' (lines 4–5). After setting the initial threshold T and the threshold reduction step ΔT (lines 6–7), we define the perturbation function P (line 8). We use a loop to gradually decrease the threshold T, perturb the region below the threshold, and continue computing the model output until it no longer leads to misclassification (lines 9–12). Finally, we return the refined heat map H' (line 13).

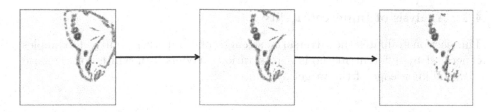

Fig. 3. Refine the disturbance area

4   Experiments

We have evaluated the following three aspects: (1) whether SAL can generate adversarial examples more efficiently with higher **Imperceptibility** under various models; (2) the **Robustness** of the bit depth of the adversarial examples generated by SAL in JPEG compression; (3) the **Transferability** of the adversarial examples generated by SAL between different network architectures and between different depths of the same network architecture.

4.1   Experimental Setup

Dataset and Networks. Our experiments were conducted on the ImageNet-Compatible dataset, which contains 1000 RGB natural images sized at 299 × 299 and was introduced in the NIPS 2017 Competition on Adversarial Attacks and Defenses [22]. The dataset is labeled with 1000 ImageNet classes and includes 6000 images. We chose this dataset because it provides a real-world scenario to investigate imperceptibility, as opposed to previous works that focused on small images from MNIST [23] and CIFAR-10 [24]. We selected 1000 images from the ImageNet-Compatible dataset for testing. This selection of dataset allows us to better understand the imperceptibility of adversarial attacks in practical scenarios. To provide a thorough evaluation of my approach, we tested five models individually. These models included the commonly used ResNet-50 and its deeper version ResNet-152, which can achieve higher accuracy on image recognition tasks but has more parameters. Additionally, we tested three models known for their high performance: DenseNet-121, Vgg-19, and Efficientnet-b0.

Baselines. We compared our method with three well-known baselines: PerC-AL [12], C&W [7], and SSAH [25]. PerC-AL aims to minimize the CIEDE2000 distance, while C&W aims to minimize the L_2 norm. SSAH is another recently proposed method that effectively increases image imperceptibility.

Evaluation metrics. To evaluate and compare the performance of different methods, we use the attack success rate (ASR) as well as three different metrics. These include the traditional average L_2 distortion, the runtime (RunTime), and the CIEDE2000 distance (C_2).

4.2   Analysis of Imperceptibility

This section evaluates the adversarial strength and imperceptibility of examples generated by different methods across various models in a white-box scenario with full knowledge of the target system.

Table 1. Attack performance comparison on different models.

Models	Attack	Iteration	RunTime (s)↓	ASR (%)↑	L_2 ↓	C_2 ↓
ResNet-50	C&W	1000	3154	99.36	3.63	174.36
	SSAH	150	906	**99.89**	5.73	190.50
	PerC-AL	1000	3785	99.25	4.04	83.15
	SAL	100	**608**	99.68	**3.40**	**79.81**
ResNet-152	C&W	1000	6599	99.26	3.87	174.82
	SSAH	150	1871	**99.58**	5.82	189.64
	PerC-AL	1000	7920	99.15	4.31	83.37
	SAL	100	**1328**	99.47	**3.64**	**82.32**
Vgg-19	C&W	1000	3479	91.93	4.05	184.05
	SSAH	150	983	92.38	4.30	175.61
	PerC-AL	1000	4176	**100**	4.51	87.25
	SAL	100	**696**	**100**	**3.28**	**78.50**
DenseNet-121	C&W	1000	3522	86.22	4.62	195.22
	SSAH	150	1076	76.85	4.05	181.50
	PerC-AL	1000	4227	99.89	5.15	93.10
	SAL	100	**723**	**100**	**3.95**	**86.72**
Efficientnet-b0	C&W	1000	2763	95.43	10.04	204.05
	SSAH	150	728	74.47	**4.91**	185.97
	PerC-AL	1000	3316	99.89	11.62	145.50
	SAL	100	**503**	**100**	9.70	**139.04**

As mentioned earlier, the L_p norms do not perfectly match the human visual perception. Therefore, we only included the L_2 norm as one of the evaluation metrics since it is more widely evaluated. The iteration counts of the other three methods in the table, which use iteration counts from their original papers, are noticeably higher than our iteration counts. This is because they aim to improve the imperceptibility of the generated images. Thus, our research focuses on generating adversarial examples with higher imperceptibility in fewer iterations.

Table 1 demonstrates that we have successfully achieved our goal. First, our SAL approach generates adversarial examples the fastest while obtaining high attack success rates on all models. We also achieved 100% attack accuracy on more powerful models such as Vgg-19, DenseNet-121, and EfficientNet-b0 models. Second, our CIEDE2000 distance, which is our main imperceptibility metric, is the smallest, indicating superior imperceptibility. While generating adversarial examples, we do not strictly restrict the L_2 to be smaller than ε, but except for the EfficientNet-b0 model, the SAL method still has the lowest L_2 among the four methods.

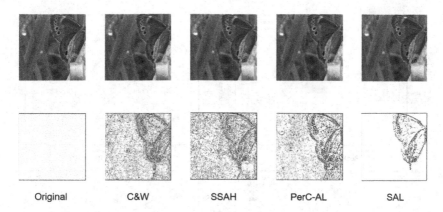

| Original | C&W | SSAH | PerC-AL | SAL |

Fig. 4. The figure displays various examples of generated attacks. The top row of each example shows the original image and its corresponding adversarial example, while the next row shows the pixel points of the perturbed image.

Some examples are shown in Fig. 4. We can easily find that C&W, PerC-AL, and SSAH attack methods perturb at the global level. However, the target identified by the model is only the butterfly location shown in the figure, but perturbations in other regions cause a reduction in imperceptibility. Thus, our SAL approach, by using PFA can undoubtedly keep our perturbations within the region identified by the model, which will improve the accuracy of the perturbations, and the heat map, which further reduces the region to points and then a portion of the pixel points are perturbed, will further improve the imperceptibility of the adversarial examples.

4.3 Analysis of Robustness

Several studies have demonstrated that JPEG compression [21,26] and bit-depth compression [26] are robust against attacks with a maximum resistance rate of

Table 2. The results of transferability between different models for various methods.

Models	Attack	Model-1	Model-2	Model-3
		ResNet-18	ResNet-101	ResNet-152
ResNet-50	C&W	0.1019	0.1094	0.0943
	SSAH	0.0453	0.0289	0.0226
	PerC-AL	0.1308	0.1371	0.0981
	SAL	**0.2101**	**0.2214**	**0.1409**
		Efficientnet-b0	VGG-19	ResNet-152
DenseNet-121	C&W	0.0360	0.0720	0.0682
	SSAH	0.0062	0.0285	0.0149
	PerC-AL	0.0471	0.1141	0.1079
	SAL	**0.1042**	**0.1725**	**0.1824**

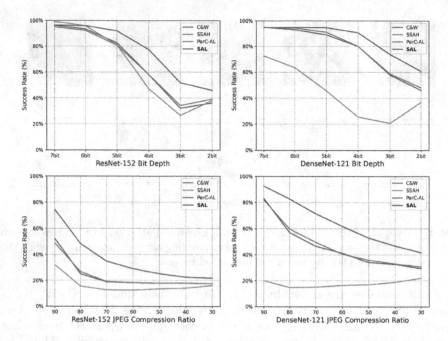

Fig. 5. The robustness of the adversarial example is evaluated for two types of image transformations under two models: bit depth reduction (top row) and JPEG compression (next row).

80%–90%. From the five models mentioned above, we selected the deeper ResNet-152 and the better-performing DenseNet-121 models for our robustness testing. We tested the robustness of the adversarial examples against two commonly used image transformation-based defense methods, namely JPEG compression and bit-depth reduction.

The results are presented in Fig. 5. Our method outperforms several other methods in terms of total JPEG compression and bit depth reduction. Specifically, it is twice as successful as the SSAH method in several metrics of JPEG compression and more successful than several other methods in terms of bit depth compression. In all cases, the SAL method consistently outperforms the other three methods and achieves the best results.

4.4 Analysis of Transferability

To test the transferability of adversarial examples generated by our method, we evaluated it from two perspectives. Firstly, we conducted a transferability study between different depths of the same network architecture. We tested the transferability from the initial ResNet-50 to three other pre-trained identical networks of different depths, namely ResNet-18, ResNet-101, and ResNet-152. Secondly, we performed a transferability study between different network architectures. We conducted another aspect of the transferability study by testing the migration from the original DenseNet-121 to three other different networks, namely Efficientnet-b0, VGG-19, and ResNet152. As shown in Table 2, our method demonstrated the best transferability regardless of the perspective judged.

5   Conclusion

In this paper, we propose a method called SAL, which restricts adversarial attacks to salient regions to improve imperceptibility and reduce running time. Our algorithm restricts perturbations to the target region using the PFA method and refines the perturbed pixel points using the LRP heat map. Our experiments show that our method performs well in terms of runtimes, imperceptibility, robustness, and transferability. In the future, we will continue to explore new ways to further improve imperceptibility and runtime.

Acknowledgement. This work was supported in part by the Inner Mongolia Science and Technology Plan Project (No. 2020GG0187), and the Engineering Research Center of Ecological Big Data, Ministry of Education, Inner Mongolia Engineering Laboratory for Cloud Computing and Service Software, Inner Mongolia Key Laboratory of Social Computing and Data Processing.

References

1. Deng, J., Dong, W., Socher, R., et al.: ImageNet: a large-scale hierarchical image database. In: Proceedings of the IEEE/CVF Conference on Computer Vision and Pattern Recognition (CVPR), pp. 248–255 (2009)
2. Parkhi, O.M., Vedaldi, A., Zisserman, A.: Deep face recognition. In: Proceedings of the 26th British Machine Vision Conference (BMVC), pp. 41.1-41.12 (2015)
3. Redmon, J., Divvala, S., Girshick, R., et al.: You only look once: unified, real-time object detection. In: Proceedings of the IEEE/CVF Conference on Computer Vision and Pattern Recognition (CVPR), pp. 779–788 (2016)
4. Hinton, G., Deng, L., Yu, D., et al.: Deep neural networks for acoustic modeling in speech recognition: the shared views of four research groups. Proc. IEEE Signal Process. Mag. **29**(6), 82–97 (2012)
5. Bahdanau, D., Cho, K., Bengio, Y.: Neural machine translation by jointly learning to align and translate. arXiv preprint arXiv:1409.0473 (2014)
6. Goodfellow, I.J., Shlens, J., Szegedy, C.: Explaining and harnessing adversarial examples. arXiv preprint arXiv:1412.6572 (2014)
7. Carlini, N., Wagner, D.: Towards evaluating the robustness of neural networks. In: Proceedings of the IEEE Symposium on Security and Privacy (S&P), pp. 39–57 (2017)
8. Guo, C., Frank, J.S., Weinberger, K.Q.: Low frequency adversarial perturbation. arXiv preprint arXiv:1809.08758 (2018)
9. Zhang, H., Avrithis, Y., Furon, T., et al.: Smooth adversarial examples. EURASIP J. Inf. Secur. **1**, 1–12 (2020)
10. Sharif, M., Bauer, L., Reiter, M.K.: On the suitability of LP-norms for creating and preventing adversarial examples. In: Proceedings of the IEEE/CVF Conference on Computer Vision and Pattern Recognition (CVPR), pp. 1605–1613 (2018)

11. Luo, M.R., Cui, G., Rigg, B.: The development of the CIE 2000 colour-difference formula: CIEDE2000. Color Res. Appl. **26**(5), 340–350 (2001)

12. Zhao, Z., Liu, Z., Larson, M.: Towards large yet imperceptible adversarial image perturbations with perceptual color distance. In: Proceedings of the IEEE/CVF Conference on Computer Vision and Pattern Recognition (CVPR), pp. 1039–1048 (2020)

13. Simonyan, K., Vedaldi, A., Zisserman, A.: Deep inside convolutional networks: visualising image classification models and saliency maps. arXiv preprint arXiv:1312.6034 (2013)

14. Binder, A., Montavon, G., Lapuschkin, S., et al.: Layer-wise relevance propagation for neural networks with local renormalization layers. In: Proceedings of the International Conference on Artificial Neural Networks (ICANN), pp. 63–71 (2016)

15. Hameed, M.Z., Gyorgy, A.: Perceptually constrained adversarial attacks. arXiv preprint arXiv:2102.07140 (2021)

16. Jang, U., Wu, X., Jha, S.: Objective metrics and gradient descent algorithms for adversarial examples in machine learning. In: Proceedings of the IEEE/CVF Conference on Computer Vision and Pattern Recognition (CVPR), pp. 262–277 (2017)

17. Papernot, N., McDaniel, P., Jha, S., et al.: The limitations of deep learning in adversarial settings. In: Proceedings of the IEEE European Symposium on Security and Privacy (EuroS&P), pp. 372–387. IEEE (2016)

18. Zhou, B., Khosla, A., Lapedriza, A., et al.: Learning deep features for discriminative localization. In: Proceedings of the IEEE/CVF Conference on Computer Vision and Pattern Recognition (CVPR), pp. 2921–2929 (2016)

19. Selvaraju, R.R., Cogswell, M., Das, A., et al.: Grad-CAM: visual explanations from deep networks via gradient-based localization. In: Proceedings of the IEEE/CVF Conference on Computer Vision and Pattern Recognition (CVPR), pp. 618–626 (2017)

20. Zhao, T., Wu, X.: Pyramid feature attention network for saliency detection. In: Proceedings of the IEEE/CVF Conference on Computer Vision and Pattern Recognition (CVPR), pp. 3085–3094 (2019)

21. Liu, Z., Liu, Q., Liu, T., et al.: Feature distillation: DNN-oriented JPEG compression against adversarial examples. In: Proceedings of the IEEE/CVF Conference on Computer Vision and Pattern Recognition (CVPR), pp. 860–868 (2019)

22. Kurakin, A., Goodfellow, I., Bengio, S., et al.: Adversarial attacks and defences competition. In: Proceedings of the Conference on Neural Information Processing Systems (NIPS), pp. 195–231 (2018)

23. LeCun, Y., Bottou, L., Bengio, Y., et al.: Gradient-based learning applied to document recognition. Proc. IEEE **86**(11), 2278–2324 (1998)

24. Krizhevsky, A., Hinton, G.: Learning multiple layers of features from tiny images (2009)

25. Luo, C., Lin, Q., Xie, W., et al.: Frequency-driven imperceptible adversarial attack on semantic similarity. In: Proceedings of the IEEE/CVF Conference on Computer Vision and Pattern Recognition (CVPR), pp. 15315–15324 (2022)

26. Guo, C., Rana, M., Cisse, M., et al.: Countering adversarial images using input transformations. arXiv preprint arXiv:1711.00117 (2017)

27. Madry, A., Makelov, A., Schmidt, L., et al.: Towards deep learning models resistant to adversarial attacks. arXiv preprint arXiv:1706.06083 (2017)

Towards Background and Foreground Color Robustness with Adversarial Right for the Right Reasons

Flávio Arthur O. Santos[(✉)], Maynara Donato de Souza,
and Cleber Zanchettin

Centro de Informática, Universidade Federal de Pernambuco,
Recife, Pernambuco 52061080, Brazil
{faos,mds3,cz}@cin.ufpe.br

Abstract. Deep learning models are robust to classify complex inputs with high accuracy. However, as these models automatically select the important input features based on the training data, there is no assurance that the right input information drives the model inference process. Different techniques guide the training model process to focus on the right features for the problem. These methods usually minimize the input gradients of the non-important features dimension, forcing the model to use signal features and be right for the right reasons. However, some tasks have a bias in their signal features, so if the model learns to focus on it, the model will be biased by the signal bias. In addition, these strategies expose the important features to attacks because the input gradients of the important features have a high norm. In this work, we propose a new loss function that jointly teaches the model to be right for the right reasons and be adversarial robust. We evaluate the proposed approach with two categories of problems: texture-based and structure-based. The proposed method presented SOTA results in the structure-based problems and competitive results in the texture-based ones.

1 Introduction

Deep learning (DL) models have achieved SOTA results in several domains, such as computer vision [6] and natural language understanding [4]. Besides, some authors indicate that their models perform better than humans for some tasks [9]. This success has made them more common in our daily life, and today we have contact with them in several applications, for example, the search engines, personal assistants, and the various recommender systems[1] that we use directly or indirectly. Concomitantly with the growth in social impact, the DL scientific community has grown dissatisfied with the lack of a detailed and in-depth understanding of the limitations of these models. Questions like "Why does DL work?" and "When and why does DL fail?" remain open.

---

[1] https://ai.facebook.com/blog/powered-by-ai-instagrams-explore-recommender-system/.

L. Iliadis et al. (Eds.): ICANN 2023, LNCS 14258, pp. 169–180, 2023.
https://doi.org/10.1007/978-3-031-44192-9_14

Moving toward investigating the behavior of deep learning models, the scientific community has discovered several situations in which those models fail. For example, Szegedy et al. (2014) [22] discovered counter-intuitive and intriguing properties in deep learning models, which showed that making minor changes to the model's input images causes significant changes to its inference. Another direction of analysis tries to answer why the models are making their decisions, whether it is Right for the right reasons (RRR) or whether the model uses unrelated or noisy information that does not directly connect to the treated problem (Shortcut Learning). For example, [10] showed that CNNs trained in a standard way on the ImageNet dataset [3] are biased by the texture of the images instead of learning the spatial structure of the objects. In addition, the models may also are learning information from the context. For example, the authors of [1] showed that the model could not identify a cow in an image because it is on the beach, as the beach is not a common scenario for a cow in training images.

Some methods have been proposed to solve the shortcut learning issue, for example, Right for the right reasons [17], Contextual decomposition explanation penalization [16], and Expected gradient [8]. Generally, these methods comprise a custom loss function that minimizes the prediction error loss and a loss that quantifies if the model uses the correct information. This second loss is based on model interpretability. As the model interpretability methods generally are based on the gradient of the model output with relation to the input, and the models trained using adversarial can be unbiased by texture and learning spatial information [23], we hypothesize that introducing adversarial training in the RRR methods can help the models to avoid shortcut learning during the training step.

1.1 Toy Problem Motivation

To evaluate our assumption, we first compared the decision boundary learning of models trained using standard, adversarial, and RRR approaches. This first setup uses a toy problem described in [17]. It comprises a two-class color dataset, as in Fig. 1. The first class is composed of images whose corners have the same color, and the three top-middle blocks have different colors. The images from class 2 are the ones in which none of the two class-1 conditions are satisfied.

The evaluation setup consists in training a multilayer-perceptron (MLP) architecture with three different approaches: (i) standard, (ii) adversarial training, and (iii) right for the right reasons. The MLP model comprises two hidden layers, the first with 50 units and the last with 30 units. Both layers use the ReLU activation function. After training, we compute the test accuracy, adversarial robustness accuracy and perform a qualitative analysis of the interpretability of each model decision. Thus, we can compare how the models give importance to each input.

Table 1 present the results obtained from this analysis. All models have competitive accuracy on the test set, and the model trained using the adversarial approach has better accuracy on the adversarial evaluation scenario, as expected.

Class 1   Class 2

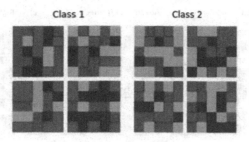

Fig. 1. Input examples of the Toy problem dataset. The toy problem has two different classes defined by two well-defined rules. Thus we can use it to evaluate if the model inference uses features related to the rules.

Table 1. Results of the toy problem analysis.

Model	Test Accuracy	Adversarial Accuracy
Standard Training	99.0	45.0
Adv. Training	99.0	92.0
RRR	100.0	87.0

From Fig. 2, we can see the qualitative analysis of the interpretability obtained from each trained model. This analysis shows that the model trained with the standard approach uses many unimportant features, while the models trained with adversarial and RRR approaches use the important ones. These results strengthen our claim and indicate that adversarial training can help the model to be right for the right reasons. Therefore, we propose a new method incorporating adversarial samples in the RRR methods called Adversarial Right for the Right Reasons (ARRR).

In the following, we describe the related works in Sect. 2 and discuss the proposed method in Sect. 3. Finally, Sect. 4 presents the experiments and analyses of the results, concluding our findings.

2   Related Works

2.1   Adversarial Robustness

Although deep learning models have achieved expressive results in the most varied domains [5], even achieving super-human performance in certain tasks [9], the work of [22] has shown that these models have intriguing properties that go against our intuition. For example, they showed that if we add an amount of barely perceptible noise to the human eye in an image, the models fail drastically. This work started an area of research called Adversarial Attacks, which represent examples built by an attacker whose intent is to cause models to fail (when they should not). With the emergence of adversarial attacks, the scientific community

a)   **Standard Model**   b)   **Adversarial Trained**   c)   **Right for the right Reasons**

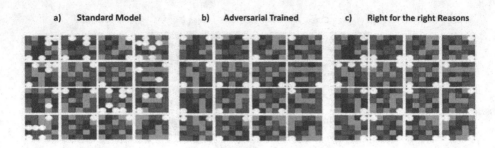

Fig. 2. Qualitative analysis of the input interpretability of all trained models. Figures a, b, and c represent the interpretability obtained from the standard training, adversarial training, and RRR model, respectively. The white dot highlight which features are the most important to each model inference.

also began investigating ways to make models robust to these types of inputs, which we call Adversarial Robustness.

Next, we will discuss the most common methods to generate adversarial attacks and mitigate this problem. Initially, the training approaches to make the model robust to adversarial attacks are presented, and then we will discuss the new implications that this training can lead to.

Goodfellow et al. (2014) [11] proposed the method *Fast gradient sign method* (FGSM) to generate adversarial attacks. FGSM consists of calculating the gradient of the error function concerning the input vector and obtaining the signs (direction) of each dimension of the gradient vector. The authors argue that the direction of the gradient is more important than the specific point of the gradient because the space in which the input vector is contained is not composed of subregions of adversarial attacks. Other variations of FGSM are also present in the literature, such as R-FGSM and Step-LL [12]. The Eq. 1 presents a cost function for adversarial training based on the FGSM. Given a standard error function (J) and the input vector x, it obtains the final error based on the sum of two steps: (1) Calculates the error based on the original input vector ($J(\theta, x, y)$) and (2) Error based on FGSM opponent attack ($J(\theta, x + \epsilon sign(\nabla_x J(\theta, x, y)))$).

$$J'(\theta, x, y) = \alpha J(\theta, x, y)(1 - \alpha)J(\theta, x + \epsilon sign(\nabla_x J(\theta, x, y))) \qquad (1)$$

Madry et al. (2018) [14] studied adversarial attacks from a $min - max$ perspective to be precise about which attack class they try to recognize and defend. The Eq. 2 presents the $min - max$ formulation. The max part of this equation aims to find an adversarial noise that produces a high error function value L when added to the input vector. The min term, on the other hand, aims to find the model parameters that minimize the error function L, thus making the model robust to the $max - attack$. From this analysis, the authors proposed the *Projected Gradient Descent* (PGD) method, which they call the universal first-order attack, the most difficult attack using only first-order information.

$$\min_{\theta} \ p(\theta), \ \text{where} \ p(\theta) = \mathop{\mathbb{E}}_{(x,y)\in D}[\max_{\delta\in S} L(\theta, x+\delta, y)] \tag{2}$$

2.2 Right for the Right Reasons

The interpretability methods such as GradCam [19], Integrated Gradients [21], and Vanilla Gradient [20] only return the importance degree of each *feature* for model output. Therefore, they must keep how the models give importance to each feature. In order to address this issue, a class of methods has been proposed to make the model able to infer correctly for the right reasons (based on the important information for the problem in inference). As far as we know, the first method proposed to train the models to be right for the right reasons (RRR) was presented in [17]. They introduced the *Vanilla Gradient* during the model training and regularized it so that it only uses the *features* that are important to the problem according to the domain expert's view. This regularization is performed by penalizing the gradients of *features* that are considered unimportant by the domain expert, forcing them to have the value zero. The Eq. 3 represents the method RRR. As we can see, it is composed of three-loss functions: the first forces the model to return the right answers, the second forces the model interpretability to match the domain expert knowledge (mask A), and the last one is the well-known regularization factor.

$$L(\theta, X, y, A) = \underbrace{\sum_{n=1}^{N}\sum_{k=1}^{K} -y_{nk}log(\hat{y}_{nk})}_{Right \ Answer} + \lambda_1 \underbrace{\sum_{n=1}^{N}\sum_{d=1}^{D}(A_{nd}\frac{\partial}{\partial x_{nd}}\sum_{k=1}^{K}log(\hat{y}_{nk}))^2}_{Right \ for \ right \ reasons} \tag{3}$$

Following the direction of making the model coherent with a domain expert, Liu et al. (2019) [8] proposes a new and flexible method of interpretation called *Expected Gradient* (EG) that can be used in several applications. Furthermore, as in [13], they incorporated a priori information into the model using EG as an interpretation method. Their experiments show that to find the *features* that the model uses to perform the inference, the EG method has more reliable results than its predecessor *Integrated Gradients*.

Another method in this context, Du et al. (2019) [7] proposed the CREX. This approach forces the interpretation of the model to be equal to the interpretability obtained by a domain expert. Furthermore, it also forces the model interpretability to be sparse. This second point is important when the model does not have the domain expert's annotations during training or when it has them partially. Rieger et al. (2020) [16] proposed the method *Contextual Decomposition Explanation Penalization* (CDEP), whose objective is to add domain knowledge to models so that they can penalize unimportant *features* and prioritize the important ones. To achieve this goal, CDEP uses the *Contextual Decomposition* (CD) [15] method as a base. CD decomposes the input vector into subregions of interest and obtains an output score from the network for each region. Therefore, the CDEP uses the scores obtained by the CD and forces the region's score with *unimportant features* to be zero, consequently making the region of *important features* by the domain expert responsible for the model inference. The Eq. 4 represents the modeling by the authors of the CDEP, in which the function L_{expl} is responsible for obtaining the interpretation of the model and forcing it to be equal to an interpretation $expl_X$.

$$\hat{\theta} = \underset{\theta}{argmin} \underbrace{L(f_\theta(X), y)}_{Prediction\ error} + \lambda \underbrace{L_{expl}(expl_\theta(X), expl_X)}_{Interpretability\ error} \tag{4}$$

Unlike the methods already discussed, [18] proposed the method *Explanatory Interactive Learning* (XIL) to introduce domain experts in the model training process. The XIL expert's role is to provide *feedbacks* of the model's interpretations so that from these *feedbacks*, the model adjusts itself to use the *features* considered relevant by the expert. In addition to the interactive use of domain experts, XIL also uses the RRR method during model training.

3   Adversarial Right for the Right Reasons

Deep neural networks are robust to classify complex and high-dimensional data accurately. These models automatically select important *features* based on what was learned during the training step. Thus, there is no guarantee that the input vectors with correct (discriminatory) information guide the decision-making process. The *Right for the right reasons* (RRR) methods try to mitigate this problem by directing the models during training and making them use important information on performing the inference.

We propose introducing adversarial training in the right for the right reasons methods, generating a new approach we named Adversarial Right for Right Reasons (ARRR). Figure 3 present the ARRR method. Our motivation to add adversarial attack in the right for right reasons methods is due to two main points: (i) both adversarial attacks and right for right reasons methods use the gradient of the output with relation to the input, so this gradient vector is a connection between them, and (ii) models trained with adversarial attacks demonstrated to learn features related to the structure of objects, thus being less biased by the texture of image data [23], so can be an indication that it can help the model be right for the right reasons.

$$Loss(X, y, I, rr) = \lambda_1 \underbrace{L_{pe}(f_\theta(X), y)}_{Prediction\ error} + \lambda_2 \underbrace{L_{rrr}(I(f_\theta(X)), rr)}_{RRR\ error} \tag{5}$$

The Eq. 5 represents the general structure of the right for the right reasons loss functions. The vector X represents the input vector, y the input target, I the interpretability method, and rr the right reasons. It is composed of two-loss functions, the first one (L_{pe}) to compute the prediction error and the second one (L_{rrr}) to calculate how the model is giving importance to the right reasons features.

In order to introduce adversarial training in this loss function, we propose to replace the input vector X with its adversarial attack, named X_{atk}. Thus, the adversarial right for the right reasons loss equations results in the Eq. 6.

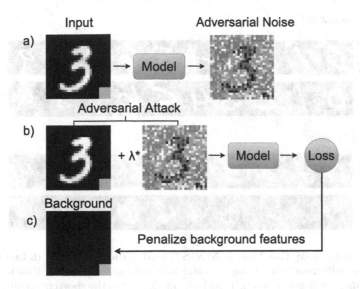

Fig. 3. Steps of adversarial right for the right reasons method. The ARRR method comprises three stages, presented in parts a), b), and c), respectively. Given an input image, first, it computes an adversarial noise using some adversarial attack approach. Second, it uses this adversarial noise to generate an adversarial attack and feed the model to compute the inference loss. From the loss, ARRR uses RRR methods to penalize the importance of background pixels, thus learning to focus on signal information.

$$Loss(X_{atk}, y, I, rr) = \lambda_1 \underbrace{L_{pe}(f_\theta(X_{atk}), y)}_{Prediction\ error} + \lambda_2 \underbrace{L_{rrr}(I(f_\theta(X_{atk})), rr)}_{RRR\ error} \quad (6)$$

4   Experiments and Results

We rely on the experiments suggested by [16] to evaluate the proposed method. In this section, they have been grouped into two categories of problems: (i) Structure-based problems, in which the model must be able to learn the structure of objects, and (ii) Texture-based problems, in which the extraction of features related to textures is critical for accurate classification. As we want to analyze whether the model extracts the *features* that are important to solve the problem, all the data sets used have information that is not important for the problem in question and is biased. Thus, they must learn to ignore those unimportant and biased features to have good results on the test set.

4.1   Structure-Based

We have used two toy datasets based on MNIST to perform this analysis, (1) Color MNIST and (2) Decoy MNIST. Like MNIST, both databases comprise ten

DecoyMNIST

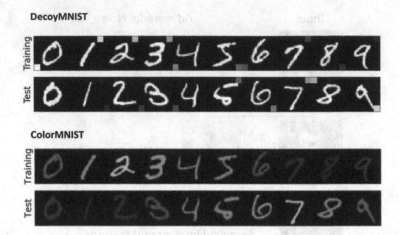

ColorMNIST

Fig. 4. Examples of the Decoy MNIST and Color MNIST datasets. Both datasets are built from MNIST samples and have ten classes. Besides, they have a bias in the training input information. Thus if the model learns the shortcut to minimize the training loss, it will have low accuracy in the test set. Decoy MNIST has a gray patch class-indicative in the training samples, while the Color MNIST has a color indicative. However, these biases are different in the test set.

classes, 60,000 training, and 10,000 test images. The difference between them and the original MNIST lies in the information contained in each one. The first dataset has a color-class indicative in the training set, but the colors-class is different in the test set; thus, if the model learns to identify the color instead of the shape, it will have poor results in the test set. The second dataset, Decoy MNIST, has a gray-scale patch in a random image position, indicating the class. Thus, if the model learns to identify the patch instead of the object to classify shape (in this dataset, the object is a number from 0–9), it will achieve poor results. To evaluate the impact of the adversarial training in these models, we trained a simple CNN model with the FGSM attack and used it in combination with RRR, CDEP, and EG approach. It is important to highlight that image processing functions can solve both datasets' biases. However, it can be used to evaluate if the deep learning models can ignore such biases easily identified by humans (Fig. 4).

From the results presented in Table 2, we can see that the adversarial training helps to improve the accuracy of all models, and even when we train the model only with the FGSM, it achieves better accuracy than Vanilla, RRR, and EG training. In both tasks, Decoy Mnist and Color Mnist, the model should be capable of identifying the number structure (class information) to classify it correctly, so these results confirm the findings in [23] and indicate that adversarial training can help the model to be right for the right reasons in structure-based problems.

Table 2. Results of the structure-based problem.

Model	ColorMNIST	DecoyMNIST
Vanilla	0.2	60.1
CDEP	31.0	97.2
RRR	0.2	99.0
EG	10.0	97.8
FGSM	20.51	**99.70**
RRR + FGSM	19.90	**99.70**
EG + FGSM	11.35	98.90
CDEP + FGSM	**46.27**	99.55

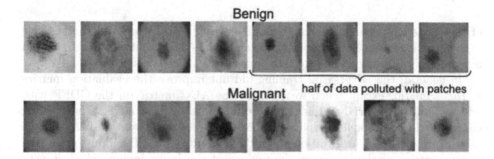

Fig. 5. Examples of the ISIC dataset.

4.2 Texture-Based

In image classification problems, texture is an important signal information, and some tasks can be categorized as texture-based because the pattern to be extracted and identified is texture. This section evaluates the connection between adversarial training and the right for the right reasons considering a texture-based task. We use the ISIC Skin Cancer dataset [2], a benchmark comprising 21,654 images. Its task is to classify skin lesions as benign or malignant. However, the dataset has a bias in half of the benign images. The bias is a color patch present only in benign images; thus, if the model identifies that color patch, it can classify half of the benign lesions without knowing any pattern about the malignant or benign lesion. Therefore, it is an important benchmark to evaluate whether the model learns to identify the right or biased pattern. Figure 5 presents some samples from the ISIC dataset.

Table 3 presents the results obtained from this analysis. We disagreed with the experiments performed in [16] on this task. Since the dataset is unbalanced, the batch size parameter is important. Due to computational constraints, they used different batch sizes for each right for the right reasons. In this work, we re-implemented the RRR and the CDEP model with a ResNet-18 instead of a VGG to keep the batch size equal for every experiment. So, the first three rows

Table 3. Results of the texture-based problem.

Model	AUC (NO PATCHES)	F1 (NO PATCHES)	AUC (ALL)	F1 (ALL)
Vanilla [16]	0.87	0.56	0.93	0.56
RRR [16]	0.75	0.46	0.86	0.44
CDEP [16]	0.89	0.61	0.94	0.60
Vanilla	0.91	0.69	0.94	0.69
RRR	0.91	0.67	0.95	0.67
CDEP	0.88	0.62	0.91	0.62
FGSM	0.82	0.52	0.90	0.52
RRR + FGSM	0.89	0.67	0.94	0.67
CDEP + FGSM	0.89	0.64	0.94	0.64

of the Table 3 represent the results obtained in the [16] work and the last one is from our execution. Our implementation of the CDEP and RRR methods did not present any weakness because their results are better than those in [16].

In general, the adversarial training did not improve the evaluation metrics in this scenario, except when we compare the AUC metric on the CDEP with and without adversarial training. This result indicates that adversarial training can not help the model be right for the right reasons on texture-based image classification tasks. Our intuition about these results is that the inputs generated by adversarial methods change the texture of the input image, which is very important for this task. Thus, this can change the class texture pattern, making it challenging for the model to learn this information.

5   Conclusion

In this paper, we proposed the adversarial rights for the right reasons method (ARRR) to combine two important properties that deep neural networks must have: 1) adversarial robustness and 2) right for the right reasons. Our assumption is combining adversarial samples and right for the right reasons constraints can boost the model's robustness. We evaluate the proposed approach with two categories of image classification problems: structure-based and texture-based. The findings indicate that introducing adversarial training on the RRR loss helps the model robustness on the structure-based problem and achieves competitive results on texture-based problems.

In future work, we intend to extend the experiments to other domains, such as natural language processing problems, and use other adversarial attack methods.

References

1. Beery, S., Van Horn, G., Perona, P.: Recognition in terra incognita. In: Proceedings of the European Conference on Computer Vision (ECCV), pp. 456–473 (2018)

2. Codella, N.C., et al.: Skin lesion analysis toward melanoma detection: a challenge at the 2017 international symposium on biomedical imaging (ISBI), hosted by the international skin imaging collaboration (ISIC). In: 2018 IEEE 15th International Symposium on Biomedical Imaging (ISBI 2018), pp. 168–172. IEEE (2018)

3. Deng, J., Dong, W., Socher, R., Li, L.J., Li, K., Fei-Fei, L.: ImageNet: a large-scale hierarchical image database. In: CVPR 2009 (2009)

4. Devlin, J., Chang, M., Lee, K., Toutanova, K.: BERT: pre-training of deep bidirectional transformers for language understanding. In: Burstein, J., Doran, C., Solorio, T. (eds.) Proceedings of the 2019 Conference of the North American Chapter of the Association for Computational Linguistics: Human Language Technologies, NAACL-HLT 2019, Minneapolis, MN, USA, 2–7, June 2019 (Volume 1: Long and Short Papers), pp. 4171–4186. Association for Computational Linguistics (2019). https://doi.org/10.18653/v1/n19-1423

5. Dong, S., Wang, P., Abbas, K.: A survey on deep learning and its applications. Comput. Sci. Rev. **40**, 100379 (2021)

6. Dosovitskiy, A., et al.: An image is worth 16×16 words: transformers for image recognition at scale. In: 9th International Conference on Learning Representations, ICLR 2021, Virtual Event, Austria, 3–7 May 2021. OpenReview.net (2021). https://openreview.net/forum?id=YicbFdNTTy

7. Du, M., Liu, N., Yang, F., Hu, X.: Learning credible deep neural networks with rationale regularization. In: Wang, J., Shim, K., Wu, X. (eds.) 2019 IEEE International Conference on Data Mining, ICDM 2019, Beijing, China, 8–11 November 2019, pp. 150–159. IEEE (2019). https://doi.org/10.1109/ICDM.2019.00025

8. Erion, G.G., Janizek, J.D., Sturmfels, P., Lundberg, S., Lee, S.: Learning explainable models using attribution priors. CoRR abs/1906.10670 (2019). http://arxiv.org/abs/1906.10670

9. Fuchs, F., Song, Y., Kaufmann, E., Scaramuzza, D., Dürr, P.: Super-human performance in gran Turismo sport using deep reinforcement learning. IEEE Robot. Autom. Lett. **6**(3), 4257–4264 (2021). https://doi.org/10.1109/LRA.2021.3064284

10. Geirhos, R., Rubisch, P., Michaelis, C., Bethge, M., Wichmann, F.A., Brendel, W.: ImageNet-trained CNNs are biased towards texture; increasing shape bias improves accuracy and robustness. In: International Conference on Learning Representations (2018)

11. Goodfellow, I.J., Shlens, J., Szegedy, C.: Explaining and harnessing adversarial examples. In: Bengio, Y., LeCun, Y. (eds.) 3rd International Conference on Learning Representations, ICLR 2015, San Diego, CA, USA, 7–9 May 2015, Conference Track Proceedings (2015). http://arxiv.org/abs/1412.6572

12. Kurakin, A., Goodfellow, I.J., Bengio, S.: Adversarial machine learning at scale. In: 5th International Conference on Learning Representations, ICLR 2017, Toulon, France, 24–26 April 2017, Conference Track Proceedings. OpenReview.net (2017). https://openreview.net/forum?id=BJm4T4Kgx

13. Liu, F., Avci, B.: Incorporating priors with feature attribution on text classification. In: Korhonen, A., Traum, D.R., Màrquez, L. (eds.) Proceedings of the 57th Conference of the Association for Computational Linguistics, ACL 2019, Florence, Italy, 28 July–12 August 2019, Volume 1: Long Papers, pp. 6274–6283. Association for Computational Linguistics (2019). https://doi.org/10.18653/v1/p19-1631

14. Madry, A., Makelov, A., Schmidt, L., Tsipras, D., Vladu, A.: Towards deep learning models resistant to adversarial attacks. In: International Conference on Learning Representations (2018)

15. Murdoch, W.J., Liu, P.J., Yu, B.: Beyond word importance: contextual decomposition to extract interactions from LSTMs. In: 6th International Conference on Learning Representations, ICLR 2018, Vancouver, BC, Canada, 30 April–3 May 2018, Conference Track Proceedings. OpenReview.net (2018). https://openreview.net/forum?id=rkRwGg-0Z

16. Rieger, L., Singh, C., Murdoch, W., Yu, B.: Interpretations are useful: penalizing explanations to align neural networks with prior knowledge. In: International Conference on Machine Learning, pp. 8116–8126. PMLR (2020)

17. Ross, A.S., Hughes, M.C., Doshi-Velez, F.: Right for the right reasons: training differentiable models by constraining their explanations. In: Sierra, C. (ed.) Proceedings of the Twenty-Sixth International Joint Conference on Artificial Intelligence, IJCAI 2017, Melbourne, Australia, 19–25 August 2017, pp. 2662–2670. ijcai.org (2017). https://doi.org/10.24963/ijcai.2017/371

18. Schramowski, P., et al.: Making deep neural networks right for the right scientific reasons by interacting with their explanations. Nat. Mach. Intell. **2**(8), 476–486 (2020)

19. Selvaraju, R.R., Cogswell, M., Das, A., Vedantam, R., Parikh, D., Batra, D.: Grad-CAM: visual explanations from deep networks via gradient-based localization. In: Proceedings of the IEEE International Conference on Computer Vision, pp. 618–626 (2017)

20. Simon, M., Rodner, E., Denzler, J.: Part detector discovery in deep convolutional neural networks. In: Cremers, D., Reid, I., Saito, H., Yang, M.-H. (eds.) ACCV 2014. LNCS, vol. 9004, pp. 162–177. Springer, Cham (2015). https://doi.org/10.1007/978-3-319-16808-1_12

21. Sundararajan, M., Taly, A., Yan, Q.: Axiomatic attribution for deep networks. In: Precup, D., Teh, Y.W. (eds.) Proceedings of the 34th International Conference on Machine Learning, ICML 2017, Sydney, NSW, Australia, 6–11 August 2017. Proceedings of Machine Learning Research, vol. 70, pp. 3319–3328. PMLR (2017). http://proceedings.mlr.press/v70/sundararajan17a.html

22. Szegedy, C., et al.: Intriguing properties of neural networks. In: Bengio, Y., LeCun, Y. (eds.) 2nd International Conference on Learning Representations, ICLR 2014, Banff, AB, Canada, 14–16 April 2014, Conference Track Proceedings (2014). http://arxiv.org/abs/1312.6199

23. Zhang, T., Zhu, Z.: Interpreting adversarially trained convolutional neural networks. In: International Conference on Machine Learning, pp. 7502–7511. PMLR (2019)

Towards Robustness of Large Language Models on Text-to-SQL Task: An Adversarial and Cross-Domain Investigation

Weixu Zhang, Yu Wang, and Ming Fan[(⊠)]

Xi'an Jiaotong University, Xi'an 710049, China
{weixu_zhang,uyleewang}@stu.xjtu.edu.cn, mingfan@mail.xjtu.edu.cn

Abstract. Recent advances in large language models (LLMs) like Chat-GPT have led to impressive results on various natural language processing (NLP) challenges including text-to-SQL task, which aims to automatically generate SQL queries from natural language questions. However, these language models are still subject to vulnerabilities such as adversarial attacks, domain shift and lack of robustness, which can greatly affect their performance and reliability. In this paper, we conduct a comprehensive evaluation of large language models, such as ChatGPT, on their robustness in text-to-SQL tasks. We assess the impact of adversarial and domain generalization perturbations on LLMs using seven datasets, five of which are popular robustness evaluation benchmarks for text-to-SQL tasks and two are synthetic adversarial datasets generated by ChatGPT. Our experiments show that while LLMs exhibit promise as zero-shot text-to-SQL parsers, their performances degrade under adversarial and domain generalization perturbations, with varying degrees of robustness depending on the type and level of perturbations applied. We also explore the impact of usage-related factors such as prompt design on the performance and robustness of LLMs. Our study provides insights into the limitations and potential directions for future research to enhance the performance and robustness of LLMs on text-to-SQL and other NLP tasks.

Keywords: Large language model · ChatGPT · text-to-SQL · Robustness · Adversarial attacks

1 Introduction

Text-to-SQL is a natural language processing task that aims to automatically generate structured SQL queries from natural language questions [4]. This task has been an active research area in natural language processing field with a wide range of applications, including database querying, question answering, and data retrieval. Although existing models have achieved impressive performance on many public benchmarks [11,20], research work has found that text-to-SQL models exhibit a lack of robustness under various conditions including adversarial

L. Iliadis et al. (Eds.): ICANN 2023, LNCS 14258, pp. 181–192, 2023.
https://doi.org/10.1007/978-3-031-44192-9_15

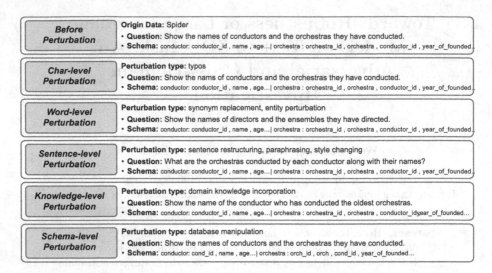

Fig. 1. An example in Spider dataset with different levels of perturbations.

attacks and domain shifts [6,7], where small perturbations added to the input text can severely deteriorate the performance of the victim model.

Figure 1 provides examples that showcase how state-of-the-art text-to-SQL models can be vulnerable to perturbations, which can come in a variety of forms and levels. These perspectives of perturbation include adversarial and domain generalization. Adversarial perturbations can be introduced into input data at different levels (character, word, or sentence) by creating typos, synonym replacement, entity perturbation, or sentence restructuring [3]. Additionally, adversarial examples can be generated by modifying the database, such as synonym or abbreviation replacement [13] on the database schema. On the other hand, the cross-domain perspective evaluates the model's ability to generalize to significantly different domains, and knowledge-level perturbations can be introduced by incorporating domain-specific knowledge [7].

Large language models (LLMs), such as ChatGPT, have received increasing attention in recent months due to their impressive performance on wide range of natural language processing tasks [16]. However, the robustness of these models against adversarial attacks and cross-domain data remains a challenge. While previous studies have evaluated the robustness of LLMs on other NLP tasks, such as text classification and sentiment analysis [19], their robustness on text-to-SQL tasks has not been thoroughly investigated. Given the ever-increasing use of LLMs in real-world applications, it is essential to evaluate the robustness of these models on this task and understand their limitations to identify potential areas for improvement.

In this work, we conduct a comprehensive evaluation of LLMs on its adversarial and domain generalization robustness on text-to-SQL tasks. We aim to explore the extent to which the performances of LLMs are affected when tested on adversarial and domain generalization data. We used 7 datasets including 5 popular robustness evaluation benchmark of text-to-SQL task and 2 dataset generated by ChatGPT to cover all levels of perturbations (character, word, sentence, schema, etc.) and overall 20k+ test examples. We also selected several SOTA text-to-SQL models to compare with LLMs.

Moreover, the performance of LLMs is known to depend heavily on its usage, including prompt design, input formatting, parameter setting and fine-tuning [12,21]. In this paper, we investigate the impact of usage-related factors such as prompt designs and temperature setting on the performance and robustness of LLMs in the text-to-SQL task. Our study aims to provide insights into the limitations of current LLMs and potential directions for future research to enhance their performance and robustness on text-to-SQL and other NLP tasks. Our key findings and insights are:

- LLMs like ChatGPT show promise as zero-shot text2sql parsers, but they are not yet expert compared to carefully designed and fine-tuned models. However, their performance has been improving with version updates.
- The performance of LLMs degrades in the face of perturbations of adversarial and domain generalization. However, LLMs are also more robust to adversarial examples than domain generalization examples.
- LLMs exhibit varying degrees of robustness depending on the type and level of perturbations applied, with NLP perturbations being easier to handle than DB perturbations.
- LLMs perform better on examples generated by LLMs themselves than on human-created datasets, showing the potential benefits of these models in generating synthetic data for training.
- Usage-related factors such as prompt design and temperature settings influence the performance of LLMs on text2sql tasks. Providing additional information in prompts such as CREATE TABLE commands and more examples improves the performance of LLMs on text-to-SQL tasks.

2 Background

2.1 Text-to-SQL Problem

The task of converting natural language into structured query language (SQL), which is commonly referred to as text-to-SQL problem, has been studied extensively in the NLP community [4]. Approaches based on rule, pattern or grammar have been proposed during early years. With the advent of machine learning techniques, researchers have explored statistical models to learn the mapping between natural language and SQL. The release of Spider leaderboard in 2018 [22] has sparked a strong interest in approaches using advanced neural networks [18]. With the prevalence of pretrained language models, most recent works tend to build transformer-based parsers with pretrained models like T5 [15] and Bart [10]. The use of LLMs, such as GPT-3 [1] and ChatGPT, has also shown impressive results on text-to-SQL task in recent months.

2.2 Large Language Models and Prompting

Large Language Models (LLMs) have garnered significant attention in recent research for their ability on various downstream NLP tasks [9]. These models generate high-quality responses by training on massive amounts of text data [10,15]. Improved prompting has been identified as a key factor in effectively applying the information contained in LLMs to target tasks. Carefully designed prompts can provide contextual information that guides the LLMs to generate intermediate reasoning steps and high-quality responses through the establishment of a Chain-of-Thought. One most notable example is ChatGPT, a variant of the GPT (Generative Pre-trained Transformer) [1] model family specifically designed to generate human-like text, which has shown impressive performances on various NLP tasks, making it an attractive candidate for text2sql task.

2.3 Robustness

The robustness of natural language processing models, including those for text-to-SQL, is a critical concern for their practical deployment. Although existing Text-to-SQL parsers have achieved good performance on many public datasets, they were recently found to be vulnerable to adversarial attacks and domain generalization [6,13]. Perturbations can come in a variety of forms sides, including perturbations on natural language question and database schema [5]. Adversarial examples can also be generated at different levels(character, word, or sentence) by creating typos, synonym replacement, or sentence restructuring. In addition to adversarial attacks, domain generalization is another challenge that can affect the performance of parsers. This problem arises when models encounter rarely observed domain-specific knowledge, which can lead to incorrect SQL queries in real-world applications [7].

Table 1. Statistics of robustness evaluation datasets in this paper. ADV_T and ADV_S are adversarial datasets curated from Spider with gpt-3.5-turbo on perturbations of typo creating and style changing. Level C, W, S, D, K represents perturbations in the levels of character, word, sentence, database, knowledge, respectively.

Type	Dataset	Size	Data manipulation	Level
Standard	Spider	1034	no manipulation	–
Adversarial	ADV_T	1034	typo creating	C
	Spider-Syn	1034	synonym replacement	W
	Spider-Realistic	508	paraphrasing	S
	ADV_S	1034	style changing	S
	Dr. Spider	15k	multitype perturbation	W, S, D
Cross-domain	Spider-DK	535	knowledge incorporation	K

3   Datasets and Tasks

In this work, we utilize the widely used Spider dataset [22] as our baseline. To assess robustness of text-to-SQL models against a range of challenging inputs, we incorporate several evaluation benchmarks curated from the Spider development dataset that encompass both adversarial and domain-generalization perspectives. Table 1 presents statistics of evaluation datasets we use.

Adversarial Dataset. We evaluate the robustness of LLMs on text-to-SQL tasks against adversarial inputs using a combination of publicly available datasets and synthetic adversarial examples generated by the gpt-3.5-turbo (ChatGPT) model. The three publicly available datasets that we use are Spider-Syn, Spider-Realistic, and Dr. Spider. **Spider-Syn** [6] includes questions that have been perturbed on a word level using synonym replacement to test the model's ability to handle variations in expressions for the same meaning. **Spider-Realistic** [5] includes sentence-level perturbations of removing explicitly mentioned column names in natural language questions. **Dr. Spider** [3] is a comprehensive diagnostic benchmark containing 15,000 perturbed examples covering multiple types of perturbations from three perspectives: database, natural language questions, and SQL.

In addition to these three datasets, we use synthetic adversarial examples generated by ChatGPT to evaluate the robustness of LLMs against two specific types of perturbations not covered by the aforementioned benchmarks. The first type, ADV_T, includes typo-creating perturbations such as adding, deleting, or altering a character in a word, designed to test the model's robustness against character-level changes. The other type, ADV_S, includes perturbations where the writing style of the question is altered, such as changing the tone or language register, to test the model's robustness against stylistic changes.

Domain Generalization Dataset. To evaluate the robustness of LLMs on text-to-SQL under cross-domain conditions, we incorporate the **Spider-DK** dataset [7]. Spider-DK is a human-curated dataset based on Spider for evaluating the generalization ability of text-to-SQL models across different domains. It contains 535 samples incorporating domain information to paraphrase questions to assess performances of LLMs where domain-specific knowledge is essential for accurate translations.

4   Experiments

4.1   Experiment Setup

Baselines. To evaluate the robustness of the LLMs on text2sql tasks, we compared their performance against several state-of-the-art baseline models. We tested the LLMs accessible via the OpenAI API, including **ChatGPT** (gpt-3.5-turbo), **GPT-3** (text-davinci-002, text-davinci-003) [1], and **Codex**.

Table 2. Exact match accuracy (EM) and execution accuracy (EX) (%) results on Spider, Spider-DK, Spider-Syn, and Spider-Realistic.

Model	Spider		Spider-DK		Spider-Syn		Spider-Realistic	
	EM	EX	EM	EX	EM	EX	EM	EX
Finetuned								
RAT-SQL + BERT	–	–	40.9	–	48.2	–	58.1	62.1
RAT-SQL + GRAPPA	73.4	–	38.5	–	49.1	–	59.3	–
LGESQL + ELECTRA	75.1	–	48.4	–	64.6	–	69.2	–
LGESQL + ELECTRA + SUN	–	–	52.7	–	66.9	–	70.9	–
TKK-3B	–	–	–	–	63.0	68.2	68.5	71.1
T5-3B	71.5	74.4	–	–	59.4	65.3	63.2	65.0
T5-3B + PICARD	75.5	79.3	–	–	–	–	68.7	71.4
RASAT + PICARD	75.3	80.5	–	–	–	–	69.7	71.9
RESDSQL-3B + NatSQL	**80.5**	**84.1**	**53.3**	**66**	**69.1**	**76.9**	**77.4**	**81.9**
Inference − only								
text-davinci-002	6.0	12.5	5.5	11.4	4.2	10.5	5.8	11.6
text-davinci-003	31.9	55.6	30.7	53.8	22.8	43.3	30.7	52.0
gpt-3.5-turbo	**46.6**	**71.4**	**41.5**	**59.1**	**38.9**	**61.7**	**41.1**	**64.6**

GPT-3 is trained on diverse sources of text from the internet, Codex is further fine-tuned on code from GitHub, while ChatGPT gained further performance boosts from RLHF (reinforcement learning from human feedback). We conducted zero-shot evaluations of these models on the previously mentioned text2sql benchmarks. We also compared their performances with several state-of-the-art text2sql baseline models fine-tuned from the Spider training set. They have been previously reported as SOTA on Spider benchmark which use various techniques including attention mechanisms (**RATSQL** [18], **RASAT** [14]), graph-based approaches (**LGESQL** [2]), pretained language models (**T5-family** [20]), process decoupling (**TKK** [8]), carefully designed encoders and decoders (**RESDSQL** [11],**PICARD** [17]) to address generalization and robustness challenges.

Evaluation Metric. To evaluate the performance of the Text-to-SQL parser, we used two metrics: Exact set match accuracy (EM) and Execution accuracy (EX) [22]. EM measures the percentage of queries for which the generated SQL query exactly matches the gold SQL query, while EX compares the execution results of the predicted and gold SQL queries on databases, with the percentage of queries that produce correct results.

EM and EX are essential in measuring the parser's ability to generate semantically complete and accurate SQL queries, and produce expected results. However, EM lacks flexibility and can produce false-negative examples, whereas the EX metric is more sensitive to the generated values.

Table 3. Data statistics and the execution (EX) accuracy of SOTA text-to-SQL models on the original Spider development set (Spider-dev) and Dr. Spider (%).

	Perturbation	sample	RATSQL	T5-3B	PICARD	RESDSQL	CodeX	GPT-3.5-turbo
	Spider-dev	1,034	72.8	71.7	79.3	**84.1**	67	71.4
DB	Schema-synonym	2,619	45.4	41.6	56.5	**68.3**	62	53.7
	Schema-abbreviation	2,853	44.2	50.7	64.7	**70**	68.6	64
	DBcontent-equivalence	382	12	36.4	43.7	40.1	**51.6**	41.9
	Average	–	33.9	42.9	55	59.5	**60.7**	53.2
NLQ	Keyword-synonym	953	53.7	60.3	66.3	**72.4**	55.5	57.6
	Keyword-carrier	399	81	76.9	82.7	83.5	**85.2**	78.4
	Column-synonym	563	42.6	46.5	57.2	**63.1**	54.7	47.4
	Column-carrier	579	58	59.6	64.9	63.9	51.1	**67.4**
	Column-attribute	119	42.9	52.1	56.3	**71.4**	46.2	61.3
	Column-value	304	52.6	50	69.4	**76.6**	71.4	56.3
	Value-synonym	506	18.6	35.8	53	53.2	**59.9**	46.2
	Multitype	1,351	39.7	47	57.1	**60.7**	53.7	52.9
	Others	2,819	67.2	66	78.3	**79**	69.7	65.1
	Average	–	50.7	54.9	65	**69.3**	60.8	59.2
SQL	Comparison	178	59.6	60.1	68	**82**	66.9	69.1
	Sort-order	192	68.2	73.4	74.5	**85.4**	57.8	60.9
	NonDB-number	131	58.8	82.4	77.1	85.5	**89.3**	89.3
	DB-text	911	51.2	52.1	65.1	**74.3**	72.4	65.5
	DB-number	410	74.4	79.3	85.1	**88.8**	79.3	77.1
	Average	–	62.4	69.5	74	**83.2**	73.1	72.4
All		–	51.2	57.1	65.9	**71.7**	64.4	61.6

4.2   Results

RQ1: How effective and robust are LLMs in zero-shot text2sql parsing compared to fine-tuned text2sql models?

Table 2 presents EM and EX results on Spider, Spider-DK, Spider-Syn, and Spider-Realistic. Overall, our experiments demonstrate that large language models (LLMs) like ChatGPT show promise as zero-shot text2sql parsers, but are not yet expert compared to carefully designed and fine-tuned text2sql models. However, performances of LLMs have been improving with version updates, suggesting that they have potential to gain expert-level performance in future.

Additionally, we found that LLMs achieved higher results on EX accuracy than EM accuracy. This suggests that LLMs are better at producing SQL queries that produce the expected results rather than generating the SQL queries that match the exact components of the gold SQL. Furthermore, our experiments showed that LLMs are more robust to adversarial examples (Spider-Syn, Spider-Realistic) than domain generalization (Spider-DK) examples, but their performance degrades in the face of perturbations of both types.

RQ2: What is the impact of adversarial attacks with different levels of perturbation on the performance of LLMs?

Table 4. Statistics and evaluation results on adversarial test data generated by gpt-3.5-turbo

Data	Size	EM	EX	Example utterance
Spider	1034	46.6	71.4	*What is the total number of **singers**?*
Spider-Syn	1034	38.9	61.7	*What is the total number of musicians?*
ADV$_T$	1034	46.5	64.9	*What is teh total number of sngers?*
ADV$_S$	2068	40.0	64.5	*Show me the count of all the singers.*

Table 3 presents more detailed results of models on the Dr. Spider benchmark under different levels and sides of perturbations. Our findings indicate that LLMs exhibit varying degrees of robustness depending on the type and level of perturbations applied.

Specifically, we found that LLMs are generally more robust to natural language processing (NLP) perturbations, such as synonym replacements and paraphrasing, than database (DB) perturbations, such as schema synonym and table content equivalence. They are found more robust to low-level perturbations, such as a small number of surface-level word changes, and show lower robustness when facing high-level perturbations, such as significant changes in data structure.

We also evaluated the performance of large language models (LLMs) on additional test examples generated by ChatGPT using two types of perturbations: typo and style changing. These additional test examples were used to investigate the ability of LLMs to handle character-level and style-level perturbations as well as synthetic data generated by LLMs. Statistics of test data and evaluation results are presented in Table 4.

RQ3: What is the role of LLMs in generating synthetic data for text2sql tasks?

Our results in Table 4 indicate that LLMs perform better on the examples generated by LLMs themselves than on human-created datasets, showing the potential benefits of these models in generating synthetic data for training. Specifically, we observed that LLMs could better handle and correct typos introduced by ChatGPT, suggesting that they have the potential to improve their own generated data quality.

4.3 Case Study

Table 5 presents a case study using an original example fetched from the Spider benchmark to further illustrate the performance of large language models on the text2sql task under different levels of perturbations including typos, synonym replacement and sentence restructuring.

This example indicates that the large language models like ChatGPT can produce reasonably accurate SQL queries under low-level perturbations such as typos, but struggle to handle high-level perturbations that involve synonym replacement or sentence paraphrasing of the original question. Specifically, we

Table 5. Examples of different types of perturbations applied to a natural language question (NL) from the Spider benchmark, along with the associated ground truth SQL (Gold) and predicted SQL queries (Pred) made by the GPT-3.5-turbo model using question and schema prompts.

NL	**How many different series and contents are listed in the TV Channel table?**
Gold	SELECT count(DISTINCT series_name), count(DISTINCT content) FROM TV_Channel
Pred	SELECT COUNT(DISTINCT series_name), COUNT(DISTINCT content) FROM tv_channel
NL	How many different serias and contents are listed in the TV Channel table?
Gold	SELECT count(DISTINCT series_name), count(DISTINCT content) FROM TV_Channel
Pred	SELECT COUNT(DISTINCT series_name), COUNT(DISTINCT content) FROM tv_channel
NL	How many different serial and contents are listed in the TV Channel table?
Gold	SELECT count(DISTINCT series_name), count(DISTINCT content) FROM TV_Channel
Pred	SELECT COUNT(DISTINCT content) FROM tv_channel
NL	Count the different series and contents listed in the TV Channel table.
Gold	SELECT count(DISTINCT series_name), count(DISTINCT content) FROM TV_Channel
Pred	SELECT COUNT(*) FROM tv_channel

observed that the large language models could omit perturbed entities or misunderstand the intent of the perturbed question, leading to inaccurate or partial SQL queries. However, it is still noteworthy that the large language models are able to generate readable and partially correct SQL queries in the presence of the high-level perturbation, which suggests their potential for handling diverse types of inputs.

5 Discussion

5.1 The Effect of Temperature

The temperature setting is a crucial hyperparameter for LLMs. It controls the degree of randomness in the generated output and affects the trade-off between accuracy and diversity of the generated text. Figure 2 shows the performance of LLMs on text2sql task under different temperature settings.

Specifically, the result suggests that for both ChatGPT and Text-Davinci-003, higher temperature settings tend to degrade the model's performance on the text2sql task. This can be attributed to the increased level of randomness in the generated output, which can lead to a higher likelihood of generating incorrect or nonsensical queries. According to our findings, controlling the temperature between 0 and 0.4 can lead to a better balance between accuracy and diversity. We also found that gpt-3.5-turbo is more robust and less affected by temperature settings compared to Text-Davinci-003.

5.2 The Effect of Prompt Design

The design of the prompts plays a critical role in the performance of LLMs on text2sql tasks. In our study, we explored five prompt structures: (1) question

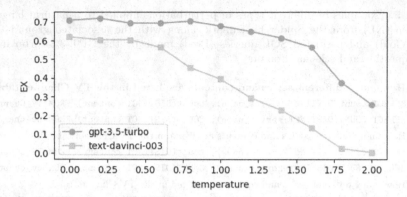

Fig. 2. The relationship between temperature and performance of LLMs on text2sql task evaluated by EX on Spider development set.

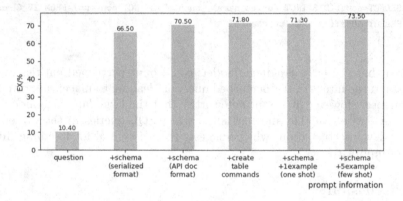

Fig. 3. Performance of LLMs with different prompt information evaluated by EX on Spider development set.

only, providing no information about the database, (2) question and serialized schema as in T5 inputs, (3) question and schema formatted as API documentation, (4) question and CREATE TABLE commands for the related database, including column types and foreign key declarations, (5) "one-shot" and "five-shot" prompts that included the question, serialized schema, and one or five random examples from the Spider training set.

The results are shown in Fig. 3. Our analysis reveals that providing additional information in prompts can significantly improve the performance of LLMs on text-to-SQL tasks. We found that using a more comprehensive schema prompt, such as providing CREATE TABLE commands, can enhance the model's ability to generate accurate SQL queries. Moreover, using additional examples from the training set as part of the prompt, as in the "one-shot" and "five-shot" prompts, can also help the model better understand the structure and relationships of the database and generate more accurate queries.

6 Conclusion

In this study, we investigated the robustness of large language models on Text-to-SQL tasks. Our findings suggest that while LLMs can be good zero-shot text2SQL parsers, but they face challenges in handling adversarial and domain generalization examples with varying degrees of robustness depending on the type and level of perturbations applied. Moreover, the performance of LLMs is influenced by usage-related factors, such as prompt design and temperature settings. Our study provides insights into the strengths and weaknesses of LLMs on Text-to-SQL tasks and suggests future research directions for improving their performance and robustness.

Acknowledgements. This work was supported by National Key R&D Program of China (2022YFB2703500), National Natural Science Foundation of China (62232014, 62293501, 62272377, 62293502, 72241433, 61721002, 62032010, 62002280), the Fundamental Research Funds for the Central Universities, CCF-AFSG Research Fund, China Postdoctoral Science Foundation (2020M683507, 2019TQ0251, 2020M673439), and Young Talent Fund of Association for Science and Technology in Shaanxi, China.

References

1. Brown, T., et al.: Language models are few-shot learners. In: Advances in Neural Information Processing Systems, vol. 33, pp. 1877–1901 (2020)
2. Cao, R., Chen, L., Chen, Z., Zhao, Y., Zhu, S., Yu, K.: LGESQL: line graph enhanced text-to-SQL model with mixed local and non-local relations. In: Proceedings of the 59th Annual Meeting of the Association for Computational Linguistics and the 11th International Joint Conference on Natural Language Processing (Volume 1: Long Papers), pp. 2541–2555 (2021)
3. Chang, S., et al.: Dr. Spider: a diagnostic evaluation benchmark towards text-to-SQL robustness (2023)
4. Deng, N., Chen, Y., Zhang, Y.: Recent advances in text-to-SQL: a survey of what we have and what we expect. In: Proceedings of the 29th International Conference on Computational Linguistics, pp. 2166–2187 (2022)
5. Deng, X., Hassan, A., Meek, C., Polozov, O., Sun, H., Richardson, M.: Structure-grounded pretraining for text-to-SQL. In: Proceedings of the 2021 Conference of the North American Chapter of the Association for Computational Linguistics: Human Language Technologies, pp. 1337–1350 (2021)
6. Gan, Y., et al.: Towards robustness of text-to-SQL models against synonym substitution. In: Proceedings of the 59th Annual Meeting of the Association for Computational Linguistics and the 11th International Joint Conference on Natural Language Processing (Volume 1: Long Papers), pp. 2505–2515 (2021)
7. Gan, Y., Chen, X., Purver, M.: Exploring underexplored limitations of cross-domain text-to-SQL generalization. In: Proceedings of the 2021 Conference on Empirical Methods in Natural Language Processing, pp. 8926–8931 (2021)
8. Gao, C., Li, B., Zhang, W., et al.: Towards generalizable and robust text-to-SQL parsing. arXiv preprint arXiv:2210.12674 (2022)
9. Jiang, Z., Xu, F.F., et al.: How can we know what language models know? Trans. Assoc. Comput. Linguist. **8**, 423–438 (2020)

10. Lewis, M., et al.: BART: denoising sequence-to-sequence pre-training for natural language generation, translation, and comprehension. In: Proceedings of the 58th Annual Meeting of the Association for Computational Linguistics, pp. 7871–7880 (2020)
11. Li, H., Zhang, J., Li, C., Chen, H.: RESDSQL: decoupling schema linking and skeleton parsing for text-to-SQL (2023)
12. Peng, K., et al.: Towards making the most of ChatGPT for machine translation (2023)
13. Pi, X., Wang, B., Gao, Y., Guo, J., Li, Z., Lou, J.G.: Towards robustness of text-to-SQL models against natural and realistic adversarial table perturbation. In: Proceedings of the 60th Annual Meeting of the Association for Computational Linguistics (Volume 1: Long Papers), pp. 2007–2022 (2022)
14. Qi, J., et al.: RASAT: integrating relational structures into pretrained Seq2Seq model for text-to-SQL. arXiv preprint arXiv:2205.06983 (2022)
15. Raffel, C., et al.: Exploring the limits of transfer learning with a unified text-to-text transformer. J. Mach. Learn. Res. **21**, 140:1–140:67 (2020). http://jmlr.org/papers/v21/20-074.html
16. Rajkumar, N., Li, R., Bahdanau, D.: Evaluating the text-to-SQL capabilities of large language models (2022)
17. Scholak, T., Schucher, N., Bahdanau, D.: PICARD: parsing incrementally for constrained auto-regressive decoding from language models. In: Proceedings of the 2021 Conference on Empirical Methods in Natural Language Processing, pp. 9895–9901 (2021)
18. Wang, B., Shin, R., Liu, X., et al.: RAT-SQL: relation-aware schema encoding and linking for text-to-SQL parsers. In: Proceedings of the 58th Annual Meeting of the Association for Computational Linguistics, pp. 7567–7578 (2020)
19. Wang, J., et al.: On the robustness of ChatGPT: an adversarial and out-of-distribution perspective (2023)
20. Xie, T., et al.: UnifiedSKG: unifying and multi-tasking structured knowledge grounding with text-to-text language models. arXiv preprint arXiv:2201.05966 (2022)
21. Yang, Z., et al.: MM-ReAct: prompting ChatGPT for multimodal reasoning and action (2023)
22. Yu, T., et al.: Spider: a large-scale human-labeled dataset for complex and cross-domain semantic parsing and text-to-SQL task. In: Proceedings of the 2018 Conference on Empirical Methods in Natural Language Processing, pp. 3911–3921 (2018)

TransNoise: Transferable Universal Adversarial Noise for Adversarial Attack

Yier Wei[1], Haichang Gao[1(✉)], Yufei Wang[1], Huan Liu[1], Yipeng Gao[1], Sainan Luo[1], and Qianwen Guo[2]

[1] School of Computer Science and Technology, Xidian University, Xi'an 710071, China
hchgao@xidian.edu.cn

[2] SongShan Laboratory, Zhengzhou 452470, China

Abstract. Deep neural networks have been proven to be vulnerable to adversarial attacks. The early attacks mostly involved image-specific approaches that generated specific adversarial noises for each individual image. More recent studies have further demonstrated that neural networks can also be fooled by image-agnostic noises, called "universal adversarial perturbation". However, the current universal adversarial attacks mainly focus on untargeted attacks and exhibit poor transferability. In this paper, we propose TransNoise, a new approach for implementing a transferable universal adversarial attack that involves modifying only a few pixels of the image. Our approach achieves state-of-art success rates in the universal adversarial attack domain for both targeted and non-target settings. The experimental results demonstrate that our method outperforms the current methods from three aspects of universality: 1) by adding our universal adversarial noises to different images, the fooling rates of our method on the target model are almost all above 95%; 2) when no training data are available for the targeted model, our method is still able to implement targeted attacks; 3) the method transfers well across different models in the untargeted setting.

Keywords: Adversarial attack · Universal adversarial noise · Deep neural networks

1 Introduction

Deep neural networks can easily be fooled by imperceptible perturbations, causing them to output incorrect predictions. This property has raised security concerns about the applicability of deep networks in security-critical domains such as computer vision, autonomous driving, speech recognition, etc. Researchers call such quasi-imperceptible perturbations "adversarial perturbations" and call inputs with adversarial perturbations "adversarial examples". Szegedy et al. [1] first revealed this type of neural network vulnerability; subsequently, several other studies [2–5] have also investigated this interesting property. Most

Supported by organization Natural Science Foundation of China and SongShan Laboratory.

adversarial perturbations [1–3, 6–9] are image-dependent, which means that the applied perturbations vary with the input images. Moosavi-Dezfooli et al. [4] indicated that a universal adversarial perturbation may exist; this type of perturbation is a fixed pattern that causes natural images to be misclassified with high probability. However, the perturbations in [4] were aimed only at untargeted attacks and they required changing nearly every pixel in the image.

In this study, a transferable method is developed that generates universal adversarial noises that can be used to implement both targeted and untargeted attacks. The modified pixels occupy only a small proportion of the natural image. Our main contributions are summarized as follows:

– We propose an attack strategy based on reverse engineering to generate visible universal adversarial noise. In experiments with both targeted and untargeted attacks, almost all the attack success rates exceed 95%.
– Our method has good transferability across multiple deep neural networks, which means that we can successfully launch black-box attacks. This is because we find the common features of the target class and use them to fool the target models.
– Our method has good transferability across different data domains, which makes our attack easier to implement. In fact, even when our method has no access to the data used to train the target network, using data from other task domains to train the adversarial noises also achieves a high fooling rate.

2   Related Work

2.1   Untargeted Universal Attack

Moosavi-Dezfooli et al. [4] were the first to report the existence of universal adversarial perturbations (UAP). They applied an iterative method, DeepFool [3], for each training example to get non-targeted universal perturbation, which was time-consuming. Besides, this method has a strict requirement regarding the original training samples of the target model and their amounts. Konda et al. [10] first used a generative model to establish an adversarial perturbation distribution that ensures the generated perturbations different from each other. They also introduced Fast Feature Fool [5], an image-agnostic perturbation generation method that did not require training data that maximizes the product of the average activations of multiple layers of the network to generate adversarial perturbations. An extended version [11] improves performance by using l_2 norm of activations instead of the mean activations. However, the lack of training data leads to poor performance compared with the UAP approach in [4]. Konda et al. [12] further proposed a two-stage process to generate the adversarial perturbation that first simulate the real data samples with class impression and then use generative models to obtain perturbations by using randomly sampled vectors in latent space, which performs better than UAP. Shafahi et al. [13] proposed an improved optimization algorithm based on UAP that maximized the cross-entropy loss through parameter limitations using stochastic gradient methods.

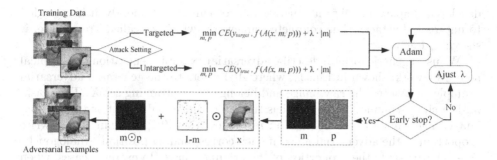

Fig. 1. Transferable universal adversarial example generation framework.

This method reduced the time consumption under the premise of achieving the same effect as UAP.

2.2 Targeted Universal Attack

Omid et al. [14] first focused on targeted universal adversarial attacks and presented a unifying framework called GAP to create both untargeted and targeted approaches in universal and dependent situations. They parameterized an end-to-end trained model to seek a mapping from a random pattern to a universal perturbation. Zhang et al. [15] proposed MIIP, a method for generating targeted universal adversarial perturbations using random source images. It completes targeted universal attacks without using original training data and achieves a performance equivalent to the state-of-the-art baseline using the original training dataset. Karmon D et al. [16] proposed LaVAN, which implements a targeted universal adversarial attack by adding a visible local patch to the natural image. This method has achieved high success rates. The local noise occupies only 2% of the original image area, and it is translation invariant. Nevertheless, due to the locality and the marginality of the noise's position, this visible perturbation is easily detected by anomalies and masked or partially removed. Targeted universal adversarial attacks are more challenging than untargeted attacks because finding a single pattern that can mislead the target model to output a specific target label is a more restrictive problem. The results of these targeted attacks still have room for improvement.

Our work focuses more on universal adversarial attacks in the digital domain than in the physical domain [17–21]. Our main goals are to improve the fooling rate of attacks in both targeted and untargeted situations and to lower the data requirement needed to train the adversarial noises.

3 Transferable Universal Adversarial Noise

Starting with targeted attacks, we discuss the generation process of universal adversarial noises, establish the connection between target labels and noises, and develop a simple and efficient generation algorithm. Subsequently, it is extended to untargeted attacks. The complete framework, which we called TransNoise, is shown in Fig. 1.

We use a generic form to describe adversarial example generation for a typical neural network, shown in Eq. (1), where $A(\cdot)$ refers to the generated adversarial example, x denotes the raw image and belongs to the training set X. The mask, m, is a single-channel image that has the same width and height as the original image. The value of each element in m ranges from [0,1], meaning the rewrite proportion of the adversarial noise at each corresponding position. Analogously, $(1-m)$ represents the proportion of the original image. In extreme cases, when the mask value is 0, the corresponding value is the original pixel intensity. Similarly, when the mask value is 1, the pixel intensity of the pattern p completely overwrites the original image pixel. The pattern, p, is an RGB image with the same size as x. In short, we generate adversarial samples by overlapping the original image with a masked adversarial pattern.

$$A(x, m, p) = m \odot p + (1 - m) \odot x \tag{1}$$

For the targeted attacks, a universal adversarial noises is designed to move each original sample from its original category across the decision boundary to the target category. In other words, the universal adversarial noises can be regarded as a "shortcut" for feature transformation between different categories in the multidimensional space. It is difficult to search for the minimum perturbation for each sample in pixel space and perform perturbation superposition to achieve generalization. We find the common characteristics of each specific category related to the model, that is, to build the relationship between the noises and the target label. On this basis, we develop a simple generation method to find universal adversarial perturbations. The optimization process mainly follows the work of [22].

$$\min_{m,p} CE(y_{target}, f(A(x, m, p))) + \lambda \cdot |m| \tag{2}$$

The optimization function of the targeted attack is shown in Eq. (2), where y_{target} is a one-hot vector of the target category, $f(\cdot)$ denotes the target neural network's prediction under our attack, $CE(\cdot)$ describes the cross-entropy loss. $|m|$ means the L_1 norm of the mask. The hyperparameter λ balances the cross-entropy loss and the L_1 norm loss of m dynamically, which is controlled by a scaling factor. It is initialized to 1×10^{-3}. When the attack success rate of the perturbations is consistently lower than the threshold ε within a few epochs, λ is reduced to relax the restriction on m. Conversely, lambda is increased to enhance the restriction on m to obtain the smallest possible perturbed area. If λ has undergone an increased stage and a decreased stage, we have both the attack success rate and the mask throughout the optimization process. If the loss is no longer falling, it means that there is no more room for further optimization of the attack, and then the optimization is stopped. When the optimization stops, the final m and p will be the optimal mask and pattern in the whole iteration process.

$$\min_{m,p} -CE(y_{true}, f(A(x, m, p))) + \lambda \cdot |m| \tag{3}$$

For an untargeted attack, we only need the neural networks to output an incorrect answer. In this case, the goal is to maximize the distance between the predicted probability and the true label while constraining the size of the noises. The objective function is shown in Eq. (3), where y_{true} means the one-hot vector of the correct category.

Algorithm 1. TransNoise.

Input: image $x \in X$, y_{target}, y_{true}, threshold ε
  Random initialize mask m and pattern p; $|m_{best}| \leftarrow$ INF
  for $Epoch = 1$ to N **do**
    for minibatch $B \subset X$ **do**
      Compute loss function as Eq. (2) or Eq. (3).
      Update m, p through Adam Optimizer.
      $A(B, m, p) = m \odot p + (1 - m) \odot B$
    end for
    if average_attack_acc $\geq \varepsilon$ and $|m| < |m_{best}|$ **then**
      $m_{best} = m$, $p_{best} = p$
    end if
    Ajust λ and use the early stop scheme to break.
  end for
  return m_{best}, p_{best}

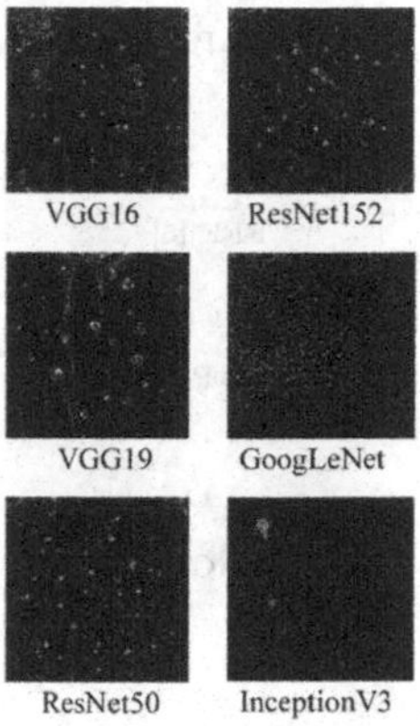

Fig. 2. Visualized untargeted universal adversarial noises for different models.

We used the Adam [23] optimizer to solve this multiobjective optimization task. The pattern p and mask m were initialized randomly. The optimization process terminated when the average attack success rates over the expected threshold ε and the L_1 norm of the mask no longer decreased. To reduce the time consumption, the early stopping scheme was used. When the average attack success rate of the perturbation in an iteration for n consecutive batch data reaches the threshold ε and the hyperparameter λ obtains a balance between the cross-entropy loss and the norm loss of m, the optimization stops. The transferable universal adversarial noises algorithm is shown in Algorithm 1. Specifically, the maximum iteration step for the experiment is 1000 times. The initial value of λ is set to 0.001 and ε is set to 0.99. We conducted all experiments using the Keras framework on an NVIDIA GTX 3090 GPU.

4   Evaluation

4.1   Untargeted Attacks

We selected a group of mainstream deep neural networks as our untargeted attack models, including VGG-16,19, ResNet152,50, GoogLeNet, and Inception-V3. These models were pretrained on the ImageNet dataset using the weight settings published by Keras, except ResNet-152 and GoogLeNet. For the 1,000

ImageNet classes, we selected 10 images for each class as a training set X and used all 50,000 validation images as testing samples. Table 1 shows the untargeted attack results for each model.

Table 1. Fooling rates of untargeted attacks and the transferability.

		VGG16	VGG19	GoogLeNet	ResNet152
UAP [4]	VGG16	**78.30%**	73.10%	56.50%	63.40%
	VGG19	73.50%	**77.80%**	53.60%	58.00%
	GoogLeNet	39.20%	39.80%	**78.90%**	45.50%
	ResNet152	47.00%	45.50%	50.50%	**84.00%**
FFF [5]	VGG16	**47.10%**	41.98%	34.33%	–
	VGG19	38.19%	**43.62%**	30.71%	–
	GoogLeNet	40.91%	40.17%	**56.44%**	–
GAP [14]	VGG16	**93.90%**	89.60%	–	52.20%
	VGG19	88.00%	**94.90%**	–	49.00%
	VGG16+VGG19	90.50%	90.10%	–	54.10%
	ResNet152	31.90%	30.60%	–	**79.50%**
NAG [10]	VGG16	**77.57%**	73.25%	67.38%	54.38%
	VGG19	80.56%	**83.78%**	74.48%	65.43%
	GoogLeNet	56.40%	59.14%	**90.37%**	59.22%
	ResNet152	52.17%	53.18%	62.33%	**87.24%**
AAA [12]	VGG16	**71.59%**	65.64%	60.74%	45.33%
	VGG19	69.45%	**72.84%**	68.79%	51.74%
	GoogLeNet	59.12%	48.61%	**75.28%**	47.81%
	ResNet152	47.21%	48.78%	56.41%	**60.72%**
GD-UAP [11]	VGG16	**63.08%**	56.04%	46.59%	36.84%
	VGG19	55.73%	**64.67%**	40.90%	35.81%
	GoogLeNet	37.95%	37.90%	**71.44%**	34.56%
	ResNet152	27.76%	26.52%	33.22%	**37.30%**
Cosine-UAP [24]	VGG16	**89.48%**	76.84%	48.97%	38.37%
	VGG19	–	**86.81%**	–	–
	GoogLeNet	–	–	**87.57%**	–
	ResNet152	–	–	–	**65.35%**
TransNoise(Ours)	VGG16	**98.41%**	93.43%	80.59%	85.76%
	VGG19	95.42%	**98.10%**	81.19%	82.87%
	GoogLeNet	72.08%	70.51%	**93.62%**	74.21%
	ResNet152	71.89%	71.30%	75.11%	**98.87%**

4.2   Transferability Across Models

Table 1 also shows the tranferability of different untargeted attacks. Transferability across models means that the adversarial perturbation generated for a specific network will fool other models as well. The first column lists the different adversarial attack approaches, the second column lists the models on which the adversarial perturbations are trained, and the first row lists the names of the models that are victims of the untargeted attack. The experimental results demonstrate that a similar model structure leads to higher transferability. The transferability of all approaches achieve higher scores across models with similar architectures; for example, the fooling rates of our TransNoise reach 93.43% and 95.42% for an adversarial attack transferred between VGG16 and VGG19. When transferring from VGG16 or VGG19 to other model structures, the attack success rate decreased by more than 10%. For the untargeted attacks against ResNet50 and InceptionV3 that are not listed in Table 1, our TransNoise method reached success rates of 98.59% and 98.60%, respectively. These results show that our method's performance is not limited to any specific model architecture. But the noise we generate is also relatively obvious. We visualized the generated perturbation noise for the six attacked models, as shown in Fig. 2. The generated universal adversarial noises vary depending on the structure of the target model. This phenomenon was also reported in [4] and [5] and also explains why the noises are similar for the VGG16 and VGG19 networks, i.e., dot-line patterns and dot-circle patterns. The noises in ResNet50 and ResNet152 are also similar.

4.3 Targeted Attack

We used the CIFAR-10, GTSRB, and ImageNet datasets to generate universal adversarial noises for targeted attacks. To further explore the transferability across different data domains, we consider an even tougher condition to implement our attack in which the original data are entirely absent. Finally, the performance of our TransNoise targeted attack is compared with the first and the state-of-the-art targeted universal adversarial perturbation methods in the digital domain, GAP [14] and LaVAN [16], respectively.

Attack on the CIFAR-10 Task. The CIFAR-10 dataset includes 10 total classes, and each class contains 5,000 training images and 1,000 test images. The image size is 32×32. We trained a VGG-16 model on CIFAR-10 and achieved a recognition accuracy of 88% on the test dataset. To implement a targeted attack, we treated each class in turn as the target. The lowest attack success rate for the 10 target categories was 97.79%, the highest attack result was 99.28%, and the modified pixel proportion was less than 8%. The first two rows of Fig. 3(a) shows universal adversarial noises(UAN) generated for different target classes on the CIFAR-10 dataset.

Attack on the German Traffic Sign Benchmarks (GTSRB) Task. GTSRB includes 43 categories, 39,209 training images and 12,630 test images in total. However, the number of samples in each category is extremely unbalanced; the minimum number is approximately 200 and the maximum number exceeds 2,000. The image sizes are also diverse. We resized every image to 32×32 before inputting them to the model. The target network for this task is a CNN that consists of six convolutional layers, three max-pooling layers, and two fully connected layers. The baseline CNN achieves a classification accuracy of 96.50% on the GTSRB dataset. We generated targeted universal adversarial noises for each class. The targeted attack success rates on the 43 categories range from 96.13% to 99.18%. The last row of Fig. 3(a) shows the pattern, mask, and combined universal adversarial noises for the target class 'stop'. After adding noise to the 'speed limit 20' sign, it was recognized as a 'stop' class.

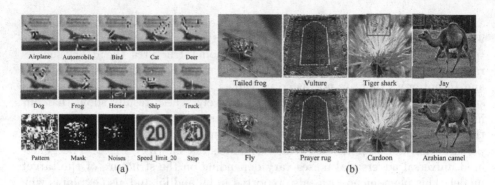

Fig. 3. Examples of samples with targeted universal adversarial noises. (a) The first two rows show the targeted universal adversarial noises on the CIFAR-10 task and the last row shows universal adversarial noises for GTSRB task. (b) Examples of ImageNet samples with different targeted universal adversarial noises where the first row shows the adversarial images and the second row shows the clean images.

Attack on the ImageNet Task. We performed our attack on the standard Inception-v3 network. To construct the targeted attack, we chose 100 random classes as the target categories and attacked them sequentially. Figure 3(b) shows some examples of the generated universal adversarial noises. Based on the perturbation noise images, we found that the generated noises are mostly concentrated primarily in a certain area of the image, while others are distributed over the image in blocks. It is worth mentioning that our perturbations involve only small areas, which ensures that they do not mislead human beings. The noise-to-image ratio is less than 2%, which is comparable to LaVAN [16]. Our attack achieved good results on all 100 classes; the highest result was 99.17% and the lowest was 97.73%. The average fooling rates of the GAP [14] and LaVAN are 52.0% and 74.1%, respectively, both of which are much lower than those of our TransNoise method 99.23%. Compared with the existing methods, our algorithm achieves state-of-the-art performance.

Table 2. Targeted attack results.

	Baseline Error	Categories	Highest	Lowest
CIFAR-10	11.98%	10	99.28%	97.79%
GTSRB	3.50%	43	99.18%	96.13%
ImageNet	23.72%	100	99.17%	97.73%

The results of the three groups of attack experiments are summarized in Table 2. Regardless of the size of the data or the scale of the model, our attack method performs well, which confirms its capability.

4.4 Transferability Across Data

We considers a more realistic situation in which the attackers do not have access to the original training dataset for the target model. To evaluate TransNoise's transferability across different data domains, we conducted four groups of experiments using the MNIST, CIFAR-10, and GTSRB datasets. In each of the first three groups of experiments, only one of these datasets is adopted to generate adversarial perturbations, while in the fourth experiment, a mixture of the three datasets is utilized to generate targeted universal adversarial noises. The trained baseline CNN architecture described in the GTSRB task was adopted as the target model. The four sets of experimental results are shown in Table 3. The rows show the data used for generating universal noises, and the columns shows the dataset to which the noises were added. We found that regardless of which dataset we used to generate the noise, when testing on the same type of dataset, the success rate of targeted attacks is above 95%, as shown by the results on the diagonal of Table 3. And the mixed dataset has better performance. In addition, the attack transfers well across the GTSRB and CIFAR10 datasets but poorly to the MNIST dataset. The average fooling rate is only approximately 50% when the noises generated by CIFAR-10 and GTSRB are added to the MNIST dataset during the testing stage. In contrast, universal adversarial noises generated on the MNIST dataset have good transferability to CIFAR-10 and GTSRB.

Table 3. The fooling rate (FR) for the GTSRB classification task across data.

	MNIST		CIFAR10		GTSRB	
	Max FR	Min FR	Max FR	Min FR	Max FR	Min FR
MNIST	99.58%	**97.54%**	99.89%	73.23%	99.55%	79.74%
CIFAR-10	90.34%	23.06%	99.26%	97.47%	97.14%	83.43%
GTSRB	99.60%	14.80%	99.50%	95.56%	99.07%	96.70%
Mixture	**99.80%**	94.45%	**100.00%**	**99.00%**	**99.65%**	**96.80%**

For the ImageNet dataset, we performed similar transferability experiments but took the training images from the COCO dataset. We used 50,000 COCO images as training samples to generate noises for 20 different classes in ImageNet and added the generated noises to 50,000 images in the original dataset. The average attack success rate ranged up to 94.71%. When the noises generated by the ImageNet dataset were added to the COCO dataset, the fooling rates were better than those in the other set of experiments. Attacks on all 20 categories achieved high success rates (above 99%). Figure 4 shows the generated noises for the object classes 'stingray' and 'chickadee' in the ImageNet and COCO datasets, which are similar in shape, size, and location.

4.5 Time Consumption

We compared the expenses of our algorithm with that of UAP [4] method (in seconds) when generating the untargeted perturbation. UAP and our TransNoise both use 10,000 images as the training set. The average time cost of using

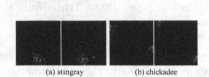

(a) stingray   (b) chickadee

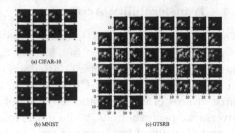

(a) CIFAR-10

(b) MNIST   (c) GTSRB

Fig. 4. Adversarial noises of two classes generated by the ImageNet(Left) and COCO(Right) datasets.

Fig. 5. The combined feature map of universal adversarial noises for the 'speed_limit_20' class when using the CIFAR-10, MNIST and GTSRB datasets separately as training data.

TransNoise to generate one universal noise is 1773.27 s, while that of UAP is 7078.47 s, which is nearly four times as long. Moreover, the time consumption of UAP varies substantially for different models, but TransNoise maintains the same order of magnitude for multiple models. Although the FFF [5] method requires less time to generate perturbations, its attack success rate is relatively poor. Our method reduces the convergence time based on mini-batch data rather than individual data.

5   Discussion

We discuss the robustness of TransNoise and the relationship between the universal adversarial noise itself and the target category.

Robustness to Samples. We analyse the influence of samples on the performance of TransNoise. We tested two situations. 1) The data distribution is extremely unbalanced, that is, the data used to generate universal adversarial noises includes only one image category; and 2) The data distribution is balanced, but the category representations are limited to one image per class. In the first situation, for the CIFAR-10 task, we used only 5,000 'plane' images to generate adversarial noises and fool the VGG-16 model to output specific category labels. More than three-quarters noises completed the attack at a rate above 80%. This results reveals that we successfully fooled a large set of unseen images even when starting with an extremely limited data distribution. In the second situation, we focus on the ImageNet task. From a set X containing only one image per class, we randomly selected two target categories, 'goldfish' and 'great white shark'. By adding universal adversarial noises to the 50,000 validation images, we achieved a fooling rate of 95.21% for 'goldfish' images and 97.01% for the 'great white shark' images, which demonstrates the high robustness of our method.

Classify the Universal Adversarial Noises. We believe that each targeted universal adversarial noise generated by our TransNoise reflects characteristics of the target category itself. Therefore, for each classification task, we input the generated universal adversarial noise directly to the classification model and found that the model output matched the target category 100% of the time. This result strongly supports our hypothesis.

Feature Analysis of the Noises. For the extended dataset experiment on the GTSRB task, we extracted the feature maps after the fourth convolution layer and combined them into one composite image. The universal adversarial noises generated by different datasets for the same target category have similar combined feature maps. Figure 5 shows the combined feature maps of universal adversarial noises for the target class 'speed_limit_20' when using different datasets as training data. Each small black block represents one combined feature map using only one category as training data. Although the noises were generated by different data, they activated the same area. This also explains why our universal adversarial noises are transferable across different datasets from another aspect.

6   Conclusion

In this paper, we introduced TransNoise, a novel optimization algorithm for generating universal adversarial perturbations and fooling deep neural networks by modifying only a few pixels. We consider both untargeted and targeted attacks, and almost all the main experiments achieve state-of-the-art fooling rates exceeding 95%. Even when our method has only a fraction (or even no) knowledge of the training data, the perturbations generated by other external data also achieve fairly high attack success rates. Moreover, the perturbations can be successfully transferred across different model architectures. Our approach considers several aspects of the universal adversarial attack and performs extremely well. In future work, we intend to extend the algorithm to other fields based on deep neural networks.

Acknowledgements. This work was supported in part by the Natural Science Foundation of China under Grant 61972306, in part by SongShan Laboratory under Grant YYJC012022005.

References

1. Szegedy, C., et al.: Intriguing properties of neural networks. In: ICLR (Poster) (2014)
2. Kurakin, A., Goodfellow, I.J., Bengio, S.: Adversarial examples in the physical world. In: ICLR (Workshop). OpenReview.net (2017)
3. Moosavi-Dezfooli, S., Fawzi, A., Frossard, P.: DeepFool: a simple and accurate method to fool deep neural networks. In: CVPR, pp. 2574–2582. IEEE Computer Society (2016)

4. Moosavi-Dezfooli, S., Fawzi, A., Fawzi, O., Frossard, P.: Universal adversarial perturbations. In: CVPR, pp. 86–94. IEEE Computer Society (2017)
5. Mopuri, K.R., Garg, U., Radhakrishnan, V.B.: Fast feature fool: a data independent approach to universal adversarial perturbations. In: BMVC. BMVA Press (2017)
6. Goodfellow, I.J., Shlens, J., Szegedy, C.: Explaining and harnessing adversarial examples. In: ICLR (Poster) (2015)
7. Su, J., Vargas, D.V., Sakurai, K.: One pixel attack for fooling deep neural networks. IEEE Trans. Evol. Comput. **23**(5), 828–841 (2019)
8. Carlini, N., Wagner, D.A.: Towards evaluating the robustness of neural networks. In: IEEE Symposium on Security and Privacy, pp. 39–57. IEEE Computer Society (2017)
9. Chen, J., Wu, X., Guo, Y., Liang, Y., Jha, S.: Towards evaluating the robustness of neural networks learned by transduction. In: ICLR. OpenReview.net (2022)
10. Mopuri, K.R., Ojha, U., Garg, U., Babu, R.V.: NAG: network for adversary generation. In: CVPR, pp. 742–751. Computer Vision Foundation/IEEE Computer Society (2018)
11. Mopuri, K.R., Ganeshan, A., Babu, R.V.: Generalizable data-free objective for crafting universal adversarial perturbations. IEEE Trans. Pattern Anal. Mach. Intell. **41**(10), 2452–2465 (2019)
12. Mopuri, K.R., Uppala, P.K., Babu, R.V.: Ask, acquire, and attack: data-free UAP generation using class impressions. In: Ferrari, V., Hebert, M., Sminchisescu, C., Weiss, Y. (eds.) ECCV 2018. LNCS, vol. 11213, pp. 20–35. Springer, Cham (2018). https://doi.org/10.1007/978-3-030-01240-3_2
13. Shafahi, A., Najibi, M., Xu, Z., Dickerson, J.P., Davis, L.S., Goldstein, T.: Universal adversarial training. In: AAAI, pp. 5636–5643. AAAI Press (2020)
14. Poursaeed, O., Katsman, I., Gao, B., Belongie, S.J.: Generative adversarial perturbations. In: CVPR, pp. 4422–4431. Computer Vision Foundation/IEEE Computer Society (2018)
15. Zhang, C., Benz, P., Imtiaz, T., Kweon, I.S.: Understanding adversarial examples from the mutual influence of images and perturbations. In: CVPR, pp. 14 509–14 518. Computer Vision Foundation/IEEE (2020)
16. Karmon, D., Zoran, D., Goldberg, Y.: LaVAN: localized and visible adversarial noise. In: ICML. Proceedings of Machine Learning Research, vol. 80, pp. 2512–2520. PMLR (2018)
17. Hwang, R., Lin, J., Hsieh, S., Lin, H., Lin, C.: Adversarial patch attacks on deep-learning-based face recognition systems using generative adversarial networks. Sensors **23**(2), 853 (2023)
18. Cheng, Z., et al.: Physical attack on monocular depth estimation with optimal adversarial patches. In: Avidan, S., Brostow, G., Cissé, M., Farinella, G.M., Hassner, T. (eds.) ECCV 2022. LNCS, vol. 13698, pp. 514–532. Springer, Cham (2022). https://doi.org/10.1007/978-3-031-19839-7_30
19. Wang, J., Cui, C., Wen, X., Shi, J.: TransPatch: a transformer-based generator for accelerating transferable patch generation in adversarial attacks against object detection models. In: Karlinsky, L., Michaeli, T., Nishino, K. (eds.) ECCV 2022. LNCS, vol. 13801, pp. 317–331. Springer, Cham (2023). https://doi.org/10.1007/978-3-031-25056-9_21
20. Brown, T.B., Mané, D., Roy, A., Abadi, M., Gilmer, J.: Adversarial patch. CoRR, vol. abs/1712.09665 (2017)
21. Liu, A., et al.: Perceptual-sensitive GAN for generating adversarial patches. In: AAAI, pp. 1028–1035. AAAI Press (2019)

22. Wang, B., et al.: Neural cleanse: identifying and mitigating backdoor attacks in neural networks. In: IEEE Symposium on Security and Privacy, pp. 707–723. IEEE (2019)
23. Kingma, D.P., Ba, J.: Adam: a method for stochastic optimization. In: ICLR (Poster) (2015)
24. Zhang, C., Benz, P., Karjauv, A., Kweon, I.S.: Data-free universal adversarial perturbation and black-box attack. In: ICCV, pp. 7848–7857. IEEE (2021)

A Spatial Interpolation Method Based on Meta-learning with Spatial Weighted Neural Networks

Liang Zhu, Shijie Jiao, Xin Song, Yonggang Wei, and Yu Wang$^{(\boxtimes)}$

Hebei University, Baoding 071002, Hebei, China
wy@hbu.edu.cn

Abstract. Most of traditional spatial interpolation methods such as the family of Kriging or Inverse Distance Weighted (IDW) methods are based on spatial auto-correlation weight coefficients by using spatial distances and some assumptions to simplify the complexity of geospatial data and computation. Due to the complex non-linear relationship between spatial distance and autocorrelation weight, those traditional methods have limitations for obtaining highly accurate estimates. To address this problem, in this paper, we propose a meta-learning based spatial interpolation method, namely MetaSWNN, using a BP neural network to learn information from a sample dataset. Firstly, the MetaSWNN eliminates abnormal data by using a clustering algorithm for cleaning the sample set. Secondly, designing the spatial weighted neural network (SWNN) to calculate the spatial correlation weight coefficients, a predicted property value is estimated by the coefficients and the property values of the corresponding samples. Finally, MetaSWNN optimizes the network weights to obtain the accurate estimated values of predicted points by integrating with the mechanism of model-agnostic meta-learning. Our MetaSWNN method is utilized for a system of soil testing and formulated fertilization for intelligent agriculture. We compared MetaSWNN with eight state-of-the-art interpolation methods, and the results show that our MetaSWNN method outperforms the eight methods significantly.

Keywords: Spatial Interpolation · Neural Networks · Meta Learning · K Nearest Neighbors · Spatial Weight

1 Introduction

Continuous spatial data (e.g., geological data, meteorological data, etc.) is the foundation for a variety of scientific modeling studies [1], and accurate spatial data can be obtained by high-density sampling. In many scenarios, however, high-density sampling cannot be performed due to time and capital costs, technical means, terrain conditions, and other factors. To address this problem, according to the first law of geography "everything is related to everything else, but near things are more related than distant things" [2], spatial interpolation methods can be used to estimate the values of specific locations based on some observation values of samples, including Moving Average Method [3], Inverse Distance Weighted (IDW) [4], Spline Function Method [5], Trend Surface Analysis Method

L. Iliadis et al. (Eds.): ICANN 2023, LNCS 14258, pp. 206–218, 2023.
https://doi.org/10.1007/978-3-031-44192-9_17

[6], Ordinary Kriging (OK) [7], and their variations. Those methods are mainly based on geometric features or linear weighting. To prevent models from becoming overly complex, moreover, they typically make some priori assumptions, such as assuming that the geographic space is stationary and spatially homogeneous. However, those assumptions are contrary to the complexity of geographic systems [8], and result in numerous defects in practical applications [9].

Due to the excellent nonlinear computing ability of the artificial neural network method, it has become a powerful tool for exploring the nonlinear problems in complex systems; therefore, it has been gradually introduced into the research of spatial interpolation [10]. However, those studies have some shortcomings including: (1) they have not considered how to handle the outliers in a sample dataset; (2) they only considered the influence of known data on the network during training and neglected its impact during prediction, but did not make good use of the information contained in the known data; (3) most of them only utilize neural networks to directly fit the nonlinear relationship between spatial coordinates and property values, which lead to the complexity of models and inaccurateness of spatial correlation weights.

To address the above problems, we discuss a new kind of spatial interpolation method. The contributions of this paper are summarized below: (1) We employ a clustering algorithm to eliminate outliers from a sample dataset. (2) Inspired by the main idea of K Nearest Neighbor (KNN, or top-K) query mechanism in [11], we construct a Spatial Weighted Neural Network (SWNN) with the mechanism of Model-Agnostic Meta-Learning (MAML) method [12] to dynamically optimize the parameters of the SWNN during the prediction process. (3) We propose a new spatial interpolation method, namely MetaSWNN (Meta-learning on Spatial Weighted Neural Networks), which try to overcome the shortcomings of the neural networks mentioned above. (4) Our MetaSWNN method is applied to a system of soil testing and formulated fertilization for intelligent agriculture; moreover, extensive experiments were conducted to compare MetaSWNN with eight methods over three datasets of soil samples.

The rest of this paper is organized as follows. In Sect. 2, we briefly review some related work. In Sect. 3, our method MetaSWNN is proposed. In Sect. 4, we present the experimental results. Finally, we conclude the paper in Sect. 5.

2 Related Work

Many researchers have been exploring how to apply neural networks to spatial interpolation. In this section, we review briefly some related work on neural network research in the field of spatial interpolation.

Rigol et al. [14] studied the daily minimum temperature of the interpolation point as the network output, and observed the impact on the interpolation result by setting different network inputs. For the rainfall of an interpolation point, by employing the mechanism of OK method, and replacing the activation function in the radial basis function network (RBFN) with the semivariogram that contains spatial correlation information, Lin and Chen [15] proposed an improved RBFN (i.e., IRBFN). Zhang and Wang [17] combined BP neural network with a genetic algorithm (GA), and improved the efficiency, accuracy and stability of BP neural network in predicting rainfall. Sivapragasam et al. [18] built a BP neural network to observe the impact on the prediction results by adjusting the number of neurons in the input layer. Liu et al. [19] combined RBF neural network with bagging technology to improve the accuracy of RBF neural network in spatial interpolation. Zeng et al. [10] proposed a spatial auto-regressive neural network (SARNN) model, in which the input is the distance from the interpolation point to the observation point, the output is the corresponding observation point weight, and the predicted value is the weighted sum of the observation point and its properties. Jesus et al. [20] combined particle swarm optimization (PSO) algorithm and BP neural network, which improved the accuracy and efficiency of water quality monitoring.

Most of neural network based spatial interpolation models (including the above ones) fit the nonlinear relationship between known and unknown data directly, without considering in-depthly the internal relationship of values in a sample dataset. As a result, these models are complex. We will propose a new method, namely MetaSWNN, which simplifies the complexity of the model and improves the interpolation accuracy.

3   MetaSWNN Method

The model SARNN [10] does not take into account the first law of geography, thus it uses all observation points in its input layer, and its costs in terms of both space and time grow significantly with the number of observation points becoming larger. Based on KNN mechanism, we will construct a Spatial Weighted Neural Network (SWNN) with a smaller size and cost than SARNN. The model MetaSWNN proposed in this paper will integrate our SWNN with the mechanisms of a clustering algorithm and the model MAML (i.e., Model-Agnostic Meta-Learning) [12].

3.1   Cluster of Spatial Data

The data used in spatial interpolation is usually measured data with noise, which can seriously affect the accuracy of prediction. To make accurate estimates about the predicted points, we use the mechanism of the clustering method DBSCAN in [22] to eliminate abnormal observation points in a sample set.

Generally, the values of geographical locations (e.g., latitude, longitude, etc.) and values of spatial properties (say, nitrogen, phosphorus, or potassium, etc.) are related to each other. However, the distances used in most of traditional spatial clustering algorithms are calculated by using either location values or property values, which implies the limitations on spatial clustering. We will use the distances with the values of both location and property in the spatial clustering and our model.

We will discuss the dataset of samples in a metric space. Let $(\Re^n, d(\cdot, \cdot))$ be the n-dimensional real vector space with the distance function $d(\cdot, \cdot)$ that is derived by the ℓ_p norm $\| \cdot \|_p (1 \leq p \leq \infty)$. For $x = (x_1, x_2, \cdots, x_n)$ and $y = (y_1, y_2, \cdots, y_n)$ in $\Re^n$, $d_p(x, y)$ is defined as follows.

$$d_p(x, y) = \|x - y\|_p = \left(\sum\nolimits_{i=1}^{n} |x_i - y_i|^p\right)^{1/p} \text{ for } 1 \leq p < \infty \tag{1}$$

$$d_\infty(x, y) = \|x - y\|_\infty = \max_{1 \leq i \leq n}(|x_i - y_i|) \text{ for } p = \infty \tag{2}$$

Moreover, when $p \to \infty$, $\|x\|_p \to \|x\|_\infty$. When $p = 1, 2$ and ∞, $d_p(x, y)$ will be the *Manhattan* distance $d_1(x, y)$, *Euclidean* distance $d_2(x, y)$ and *Maximum* distance $d_\infty(x, y)$ respectively, which are useful in many applications. We only use the Euclidean distance denoted by $d(x, y)$ in the following discussion. We define the spatial distance

$$D\big((x_i, x_j), (a_i, a_j)\big) = wd(x_i, x_j) + (1 - w)d(a_i, a_j) \tag{3}$$

which is an integration of the location-distance $d_p(x_i, x_j)$ and the property-distance $d_p(a_i, a_j)$, where $x_i = (x_{i1}, x_{i2}, \cdots, x_{im})$ is a location (vector) with m coordinates, $a_i = (a_{i1}, a_{i2}, \cdots, a_{in})$ is a vector of n property values at the location x_i, w is the weight of the location-distance, $(1 - w)$ is the weight of the property-distance. In our experiments, $x_i = (x_{i1}, x_{i2})$ means the latitude and longitude, and the location-distance weight w is 0.5. Due to the different units of the spatial coordinates and property values, the specific values may vary greatly. To eliminate the influence of the value units on clusters, the data will be normalized by

$$u_i = (z_i - z_{min})/(z_{max} - z_{min}) \tag{4}$$

where z_{max} and z_{min} are the maximum and minimum values of each dimension value z_i, (e.g., z_i may be the value of latitude or nitrogen) for a sample point.

3.2 Spatial Weighted Neural Network

Traditional spatial interpolation methods (e.g., Kriging and IDW) transform geographic location information into spatial correlation weights in various ways, and the predicted property value is the weighted sum of the spatial correlation weights and the corresponding property values of observation points. However, most traditional interpolation methods calculate spatial weights based on some priori assumption(s), which do not account for the complexity of the geographic system.

Most of neural network-based spatial interpolation methods use a geographic location as the network input and a property value as the output without calculating the spatial correlation weights explicitly. Thus, those approaches lack physical meaning and cannot make good use of the property information of sample/observation points. On the other hand, neural networks have the ability to simulate such complex systems. Therefore, we constructed the spatial weighted neural network (SWNN) with the structure shown in Fig. 1 to simulate the complex nonlinear relationship between geographic location and spatial correlation weights. At the same time, integrating with the weighted summation method of traditional interpolation methods, our SWNN can optimize and utilize well the information in the dataset.

The network SWNN in Fig. 1 is a BP neural network that includes an input layer, an output layer, and a hidden layer. The hidden layer is divided into two parts named SWNN-H and SWNN-W. SWNN-H contains three layers of neurons with the number of neurons being X, $2X$, and X respectively. SWNN-W calculates the predicted value by weighting the output of SWNN-H with the corresponding property values. In Fig. 1 (and Fig. 2), there are arrows from the training set or test set to the interpolation point x_i. For training the model, the x_i is obtained from training set, while if testing the model, the

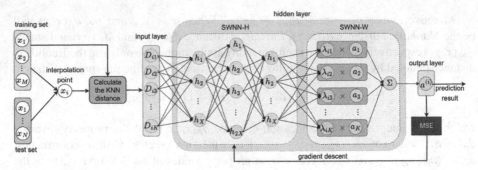

Fig. 1. Diagram of SWNN Network Structure

x_i is obtained from test set. The unit "Calculate the KNN distance" calculates distances between x_i and all points in the training set to obtain the KNN distances of x_i.

According to the first law of geography and the experience gained from using traditional spatial interpolation methods, when the distance between two points is large, their influence on each other is small, and can be ignored. Thus, using the KNN mechanism, only the distances of the K observation points closest to the interpolation point are selected as the network input. The input of SWNN is defined as follows.

$$D_i = (D_{i1}, D_{i2}, D_{i3}, \cdots, D_{iK})^T \text{ s.t. } D_{i1} \le D_{i2} \le D_{i3} \le \cdots \le D_{iK} \tag{5}$$

$$D_{ij} = d(x_i, x_j) = \left(\sum_{l=1}^{m} |x_{il} - x_{jl}|^2\right)^{1/2} \tag{6}$$

where column vector D_i is the input of the SWNN for the i-th interpolation point, D_{ij} is obtained by Eq. (6) that is the Euclidean distance between the i-th interpolation point and the j-th observation point, x_i is the location vector (i.e., longitude, latitude, etc.) of the i-th interpolation point, x_j is the location vector of the observation point, x_{il} and x_{jl} represent the l-th coordinate value of x_i and x_j, respectively, $l = 1, 2, ..., m$.

Let X be an appropriate value (usually X should be smaller than the number of neurons in the input layer, i.e., $X < K$). The spatial correlation weight vector λ_i is the output of the SWNN-H layer, which is defined by Eq. (7).

$$\lambda_i = \text{SWNN-H}(D_i) = (\lambda_{i1}, \lambda_{i2}, \lambda_{i3}, \cdots, \lambda_{iK})^T \tag{7}$$

The SWNN-W layer calculates the inner product of vectors λ_i^T and a, where $a = (a_1, a_2, a_3, \cdots, a_K)^T$ is the column vector of corresponding property values of observation points that are the K nearest neighbors of the i-th interpolation point. Thus, we obtain a predicted property value $a^{(i)}$ of the i-th interpolation point by Eq. (8).

$$a^{(i)} = \lambda_i^T a = (\lambda_{i1}, \lambda_{i2}, \lambda_{i3}, \cdots, \lambda_{iK})(a_1, a_2, a_3, \cdots, a_K)^T = \sum_{l=1}^{K} \lambda_{il} a_l \tag{8}$$

In addition, since observation points are used as interpolation points during training, the distance between an observation point and itself is always zero. Therefore, to prevent the self-fitting of the SWNN, we adjust its input vector D_i by $K := K + 1$ during training.

The optimization algorithm used in training is the Adaptive Moment Estimation (Adam) algorithm.

The activation function used in the SWNN network is the PreLU function, which is given by Eq. (9) with an adjustable network weight b.

$$f(x) = \begin{cases} x, x > 0 \\ bx, x \le 0 \end{cases} \tag{9}$$

The loss function used during training is the mean squared error (MSE) function, which is given by Eq. (10).

$$\text{MSE}(\boldsymbol{p}, \boldsymbol{t}) = \left(\sum\nolimits_{i=1}^{n} (p_i - t_i)^2 \right) / n \tag{10}$$

where $\boldsymbol{p} = (p_1, p_2, \cdots, p_r)^{\text{T}}$ is the predicted output vector of the neural network, $\boldsymbol{t} = (t_1, t_2, \cdots, t_r)^{\text{T}}$ is the corresponding target vector of $\boldsymbol{p}$, and n is the number of neurons in the output layer.

3.3 Meta-learning on SWNN

Let θ be all the weights of the network SWNN above. By training, SWNN updates θ and ultimately obtains one θ with better generalization performance for an entire interpolation region. For a certain interpolation point, there must be an optimal weight θ'' such that SWNN utilizes this θ'' to predict accurately the property value of this certain interpolation point (almost) without error. However, the weight θ'' may not perform as well as the θ for other interpolation points; meanwhile, it is difficult and expensive to find this θ''. Using smaller costs, according to the first law of geography, it is possible to obtain a sub-optimal weight θ' which is calculated by the c nearest observation points of the interpolation point. Comparing with θ, SWNN can use this θ' to predict the values of the certain interpolation point more accurately. To obtain better prediction performance, in this subsection, we integrate the SWNN with the mechanism of the MAML [12] to construct the model MetaSWNN that can find a sub-optimal θ' by adjusting the pre-trained network weight θ dynamically.

MetaSWNN (see Fig. 2 and Algorithm 1) uses the same training set and test set as the SWNN above, but its input has been changed to a set of tasks $\boldsymbol{T} = \{T_1, T_2, \cdots, T_N\}$, where T_i for the i-th interpolation point is defined by Eqs. (11), (12) and (13).

$$T_i = \{\mathcal{L}(t_i, a_i), \mathcal{S}_i, \mathcal{Q}_i\} \tag{11}$$

$$\mathcal{Q}_i = (D_{i1}, D_{i2}, \cdots, D_{iK})^{\text{T}} \text{ s.t. } D_{i1} \le D_{i2} \le \cdots \le D_{iK} \tag{12}$$

$$\mathcal{S}_i = \left\{ (D_{11}, D_{12}, \cdots, D_{1K}, a_1)^{\text{T}}, (D_{21}, D_{22}, \cdots, D_{2K}, a_2)^{\text{T}}, \cdots, (D_{c1}, D_{c2}, \cdots, D_{cK}, a_c)^{\text{T}} \right\} \tag{13}$$

where $\mathcal{L}(t_i, a_i)$ is the loss function using Eq. (10) by default, t_i is the predicted vector, a_i is the target vector that contains the corresponding actual values of a_i; $\mathcal{Q}_i$ is the query set of T_i, which is obtained by Eq. (6) with the KNN distances between the interpolation point and its K nearest observation points; $\boldsymbol{S}_i$ is the support set of T_i, in fact $\boldsymbol{S}_i$ is a $((K+1) \times c)$ matrix with the submatrix $\boldsymbol{S}_i[\boldsymbol{D}] = (D_{hl})_{cK}^{\mathrm{T}}$ and the $(K+1)$-th row $\boldsymbol{S}_i[r_{K+1}]$ $= (a_1, a_2, ..., a_c)$. To obtain $\boldsymbol{S}_i$, firstly, we use Eq. (6) to identify c $(c < K)$ observation points closest to the i-th interpolation point; secondly, for each one of the c points, we apply Eq. (6) again to find its the K nearest observation points from the sample set; finally, we combine the distances and the property values for the c points and their K nearest observation points to make $\boldsymbol{S}_i$ as shown in Eq. (13).

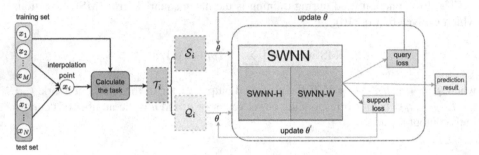

Fig. 2. Diagram of MetaSWNN training process

Algorithm 1 // Meta-learning-based SWNN, i.e., MetaSWNN
Input: $\mathcal{T}, \alpha, \beta$ // $\mathcal{T}$ is the set of all tasks, α and β are step size hyperparameters
Output: θ // The trained MetaSWNN network weights θ

---

1   randomly initialize θ // θ is the network weights of MetaSWNN
2   **While** not done
3   **For** each $\mathcal{T}_i$ in $\mathcal{T}$
4   Let $\theta' = \theta$, $u = 0$;
5   **While** $u < U$ //U is the number of times updating θ' for each task
6   evaluate $\nabla_{\theta'}\mathcal{L}_{\mathcal{T}i}(\mathrm{SWNN}(\boldsymbol{S}_i[\boldsymbol{D}]), \boldsymbol{S}_i[r_{K+1}]^{\mathrm{T}})$ using $\boldsymbol{S}_i$ and $\mathcal{L}_{\mathcal{T}i}$ in Equation(10);
7         $\theta' = \theta' - \alpha\nabla_{\theta'}\mathcal{L}_{\mathcal{T}i}(\mathrm{SWNN}(\boldsymbol{S}_i[\boldsymbol{D}]), \boldsymbol{S}_i[r_{K+1}]^{\mathrm{T}})$; // compute adapted parameters
8   u++;
9   **End While**
10      $\theta = \theta - \beta\nabla_{\theta'}\mathcal{L}_{\mathcal{T}i}(\mathrm{SWNN}(\boldsymbol{Q}_i), \boldsymbol{a}_i)$; // Update θ using $\boldsymbol{Q}_i$ and $\mathcal{L}_{\mathcal{T}i}$ in Equation(10)
11   **End For**
12 **End While**
13 **Return** θ;

The training process of MetaSWNN is shown in Fig. 2. The unit "Calculate the task" calculates the task T_i of x_i using x_i and all points in the training set. For a given input task T_i, we first set $\theta' = \theta$, and then use the support set $\boldsymbol{S}_i$ of T_i to train the MetaSWNN and obtain the support loss, which is defined by Eq. (14).

$$\text{support loss} = \nabla_{\theta'}\mathcal{L}_{T_i}\left(t_i, \boldsymbol{S}_i[r_{K+1}]^{\mathrm{T}}\right) \tag{14}$$

where $\nabla_{\theta'}\mathcal{L}_{\mathcal{T}_i}(\cdot, \cdot)$ computes the gradient of $\mathcal{L}_{\mathcal{T}_i}$ at the predicted vector t_i obtained by MetaSWNN with θ' and the vector $\mathcal{S}_i[r_{K+1}]^{\mathrm{T}}$ with the corresponding actual values of a_i.

Performing backpropagation, θ' is updated (one or more times) by Eq. (15).

$$\theta' = \theta' - \alpha\nabla_{\theta'}\mathcal{L}_{\mathcal{T}_i}\left(t_i, \mathcal{S}_i[r_{K+1}]^{\mathrm{T}}\right) \tag{15}$$

where α is the inner learning rate.

After evaluating θ', it can be used to directly make predictions on $\mathcal{Q}_i$ and to get the query loss using t_i and a_i when training MetaSWNN, which is defined by Eq. (16).

$$\text{query loss} = \nabla_{\theta'}\mathcal{L}_{\mathcal{T}_i}(t_i, a_i) \tag{16}$$

where a_i is a vector with the corresponding actual values of the predicted vector t_i.

Performing backpropagation, θ is updated by Eq. (17).

$$\theta = \theta - \beta\nabla_{\theta'}\mathcal{L}_{\mathcal{T}_i}(t_i, a_i) \tag{17}$$

where β represents the outer learning rate.

The optimization algorithm used to update θ' during training is the Gradient Descent (GD) algorithm, and the optimization algorithm used to update θ is the Adam algorithm.

4 Experimental Results

The program is written using Python 3.11 and PyTorch 1.13.1 CPU version, and the experiments are conducted on a PC with an Intel(R) Core(TM) i5-10505 CPU @ 3.20 GHz 3.19 GHz and 16 GB of RAM.

We will compare our MetaSWNN method with eight representative or state-of-the-art interpolation methods coming from three families of OK, IDW and Neural Network. Three OK-like methods are: (1) Ordinary Kriging (OK), (2) Universal Kriging (UK), and (3) Regression Kriging (RK). Four IDW-like methods ones are: (4) the classic IDW (IDW), (5) IDW regression (IDWR), (6) density-based adaptive inverse distance weighting (AIDW), and (7) cluster-based inverse distance weighting (CIDW). A Neural Network method is: (8) spatial auto-regressive neural network (SARNN). IDW, CIDW and IDWR methods use the most commonly used distance-decay parameter 2. Clustering algorithms used in CIDW are the classic k-Means algorithm and the DBSCAN algorithm. These settings can ensure IDW-like methods achieve the best results. Moreover, the SARNN method has the same number of neurons in the input layer and output layer, with 320 in the Tangshan dataset, 325 in the Xinjin dataset, and 542 in the Sanyuan dataset, and three hidden layers with 256, 512, and 256 neurons respectively for all datasets. Meanwhile, all other parameters of SARNN are the same as those of MetaSWNN to ensure that SARNN achieves the best results. We also adjust the parameters of Kriging-like methods to let them achieve the best results.

Cross-validation is adopted for the comparative analyses in our experiments. Randomly selected 80% of all data for the spatial interpolation process and reserved the remaining 20% for validation. The Root Mean Square Error (RMSE) will be used to measure the accuracy of each interpolation method, which is given below.

$$\text{RMSE} = \left(\left(\sum_{i=1}^{N} (p_i - t_i)^2 \right) / n \right)^{1/2} \tag{18}$$

where n is the number of interpolation points participated in the validation, p_i and t_i are the predicted value and actual value for the i-th interpolation point, respectively.

We use the abbreviations of property names in this section, i.e., *om* stands for *organic-matter*, *aph* is *available-phosphorus*, *sap* means *slowly-available-potassium*, *ap* indicates *available-potassium*, and *tn* represents *total-nitrogen*.

Three datasets are used in our experiments. (1) Tangshan(*county-name, longitude, latitude, om, aph, sap, ap, tn*) with 400 soil nutrient sample points in Luanzhou and Luannan counties of Tangshan City, Hebei Province, China. (2) Xinjin(*longitude, latitude, aph, ap, tn*) with 406 soil nutrient sample points in Xinjin District, Chengdu City, Sichuan Province, China. (3) Sanyuan(*longitude, latitude, aph, ap, tn*) with 677 soil nutrient sample points in Sanyuan County, Xianyang City, Shaanxi Province, China. As an example, we only give the distribution map of sample points in Tangshan dataset as shown in Fig. 3. The Xinjin and Sanyuan datasets can be obtained from the National Earth System Science Data Center, National Science & Technology Infrastructure of China [23], and the values were extracted using ArcGIS software.

The parameters used in our model MetaSWNN (or others) over three soil datasets includes: the specified radius ε, and the density threshold *minPts* in the DBSCAN algorithm; the number of neurons X in the SWNN-H component of the SWNN method, the number of neurons K in the input layer, and the inner learning rate α during gradient descent of MetaSWNN. Some parameters of the MetaSWNN method on the three soil datasets are the same, including the outer learning rate β during gradient descent of MetaSWNN is 0.001, the number of observation points c used by support set for each task is 5, and the number of times that MetaSWNN uses support set to update θ' for each task is 1. The parts of these parameters are illustrated in Table 1. Because the property value in our datasets is large, the rate α should be very small to make MetaSWNN converge. Moreover, the average time to run an epoch is 0.5 s.

Table 2 shows the results of our experiments. The values of RMSE with our MetaSWNN are smaller than those with all eight other methods over three datasets except for the value of *ap* with OK over Sanyuan datasets (i.e., 38.7002 vs 37.8340). As an example, we only give the visualization of interpolation results on available phosphorus property for Tangshan dataset as shown in Fig. 4.

For Tangshan dataset in Table 2, our MetaSWNN is better than CIDW, meanwhile CIDW significantly outperforms the other seven methods with regard to the four properties *om, aph, ap* and *tn*, because MetaSWNN and CIDW effectively filter out the outliers in these properties. Moreover, the MetaSWNN is significantly better than SARNN, which outperforms the other methods for the property *sap*. The primary reasons are that MetaSWNN uses the K nearest observation points and integrates with MAML mechanism that can significantly simplify the network model, speed up the training process and improve the prediction accuracy, while SARNN uses all observation points as network input.

For Xinjin dataset with the three properties *aph*, *ap* and *tn* in Table 2, our MetaSWNN had a significantly better performance than the other eight methods. Moreover, the other eight ones perform similarly well, because this dataset is smoother and more regular compared to the Tangshan dataset.

For Sanyuan dataset in Table 2, our MetaSWNN significantly outperforms all the other methods for the three properties, except for the OK method, which slightly outperforms MetaSWNN for the property *ap*. The reason for this exception is that the high correlation between the values for this property and the spherical variogram function leads to a good performance of the OK method.

Table 1. Parameter values used in the MetaSWNN method for three soil datasets

dataset	property	ε	*minPts*	X	K	α
Tangshan	om	0.12	3	4	40	10^{-8}
	aph	0.12	5	4	30	10^{-9}
	sap	0.10	3	8	30	10^{-11}
	ap	0.11	3	8	30	10^{-10}
	tn	0.12	3	4	20	10^{-6}
Xinjin	aph	0.12	3	4	20	10^{-11}
	ap	0.11	5	4	30	10^{-9}
	tn	0.12	3	4	20	10^{-11}
Sanyuan	aph	0.10	5	8	20	10^{-10}
	ap	0.10	5	8	20	10^{-10}
	tn	0.10	5	8	30	10^{-10}

Table 2. The Root Mean Square Error (RMSE) of nine spatial interpolation methods

dataset	methods	om	aph	sap	ap	tn
Tangshan	OK	3.761	20.962	113.742	65.011	0.205
	UK	3.752	20.754	113.068	66.135	0.182
	RK	3.753	21.316	116.034	63.732	0.181
	IDW	3.889	20.792	115.506	63.968	0.186
	IDWR	3.874	22.913	117.761	73.498	0.192
	AIDW	3.785	21.665	113.701	67.888	0.184
	CIDW	3.737	18.258	120.874	54.818	0.155
	SARNN	3.747	18.537	110.030	65.355	0.179

(continued)

Table 2. (*continued*)

dataset	methods	*om*	*aph*	*sap*	*ap*	*tn*
	MetaSWNN	**3.337**	**15.860**	**93.142**	**50.436**	**0.143**
Xinjin	OK	–	2.9289	–	45.9950	4.7551
	UK	–	2.7751	–	45.7944	4.8265
	RK	–	2.8295	–	46.0680	4.5449
	IDW	–	3.3054	–	47.1201	5.0349
	IDWR	–	2.9283	–	44.8884	4.7301
	AIDW	–	2.8278	–	43.9506	4.6209
	CIDW	–	3.0082	–	44.1023	4.7766
	SARNN	–	2.9435	–	45.6382	4.7973
	MetaSWNN	–	**2.7028**	–	**41.7425**	**4.2712**
Sanyuan	OK	–	2.8619	–	**37.8340**	4.0921
	UK	–	5.0093	–	48.0508	5.5076
	RK	–	2.8421	–	44.0787	4.0893
	IDW	–	3.0842	–	48.4151	4.0185
	IDWR	–	2.9954	–	39.8354	4.1123
	AIDW	–	2.9372	–	41.0085	3.9508
	CIDW	–	3.0045	–	40.1168	4.0832
	SARNN	–	3.1995	–	46.3869	4.3016
	MetaSWNN	–	**2.8003**	–	38.7002	**3.7278**

Fig. 3. Distribution map of soil nutrient sample points

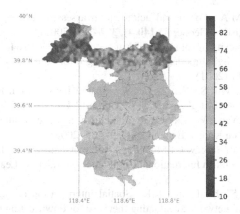

Fig. 4. Visualization of interpolation results of the MetaSWNN method

5 Conclusion

To improve the accuracy of spatial interpolation, in this paper, we proposed the model MetaSWNN (Meta-learning on Spatial Weighted Neural Networks), which integrates with the mechanisms of the clustering algorithm, KNN (K Nearest Neighbor), SWNN (Spatial Weighted Neural Network) and MAML (Model-Agnostic Meta-Learning) for removing abnormal values from a sample dataset, simplifying the complexity of neural networks, calculating the spatial weights, and optimizing the information in the dataset. Our model MetaSWNN was applied to a system of soil testing and formulated fertilization for intelligent agriculture. Moreover, extensive experiments were conducted to measure the performance of MetaSWNN on three datasets of soil samples and compare it with eight state-of-the-art interpolation methods. The experimental results demonstrated that our MetaSWNN significantly outperforms the eight methods.

References

1. Li, J., Heap, A.D.: A review of comparative studies of spatial interpolation methods in environmental sciences: performance and impact factors. Eco. Inform. **6**(3–4), 228–241 (2011)
2. Tobler, W.R.: A computer movie simulating urban growth in the Detroit region. Econ. Geogr. **46**(2), 234–240 (1970)
3. Wang, K., Xu, H., Shi, Z., Balley, J.S., Crawford, J.: Soil potassium spatial variability and comparison of several interpolation methods. Plant Nutr. Fertilizer Sci. **6**(3), 318–322 (2000)
4. Brodsky, L., Vanek, V., Bazalova, M., Balik, J.: The differences in the interpolation methods for mapping spatial variability of soil property. Rostlinna-Vyroba **47**(12), 529–535 (2001)
5. Shi, X., Yang, L., Zhang, L.: Comparison of spatial interpolation methods for soil available kalium. J. Soil Water Conserv. **20**(2), 68–72 (2006)
6. Li, Y., Tian, J., Liu, P.: A study on laws of regional variance of soil element content in loess plateau through trend surface analysis method. Acta Agriculturae Boreali-occidentalis Sinica **9**(3), 63–66 (2000)

7. Kerry, R., Oliver, M.A.: Forest soil acidification assessment using principal component analysis and geostatistics. Geoderma **140**(4), 374–382 (2007)
8. Werner, B.T.: Complexity in natural landform patterns. Science **284**(5411), 102–104 (1999)
9. Yue, T., Liu, J.: The digital model for transforming information at various scales. J. Image Graph. **6**(9), 907–911 (2001)
10. Zeng, J., Zhang, F., Wu, S., Du, Z, Liu, R.: Spatial interpolation based on spatial auto-regressive neural network. J. Zhejiang Univ. (Sci. Ed.) **47**(5), 572–581 (2020)
11. Zhu, L., Meng, W., Yang, W., Liu, C.: Region clustering based evaluation of multiple topN selection queries. Data Knowl. Eng. **64**(2), 439–461 (2008)
12. Chelsea, F., Pieter, A., Sergey, L.: Model-agnostic metalearning for fast adaptation of deep networks. In: Thirty-Fourth International Conference on Machine Learning, pp. 1126–1135. ACM (2017)
13. Snell, S.E., Gopal, S., Kaufmann, R.K.: Spatial interpolation of surface air temperatures using artificial neural networks: evaluating their use for downscaling GCMs. J. Clim. **13**(5), 886–895 (2000)
14. Rigol, J.P., Jarvis, C.H., Stuart, N.: Artificial neural networks as a tool for spatial interpolation. Int. J. Geogr. Inf. Sci. **15**(4), 323–343 (2001)
15. Lin, G.F., Chen, L.H.: A spatial interpolation method based on radial basis function networks incorporating a semivariogram model. J. Hydrol. **288**(3–4), 288–298 (2004)
16. Li, B., McClendon, R.W., Hoogenboom, G.: Spatial interpolation of weather variables for single locations using artificial neural networks. Trans. ASAE **47**(2), 629–637 (2004)
17. Zhang, Q., Wang, C.: Integrated application of artificial neural network and genetic algorithm to the spatial interpolation of rainfall. In: 2008 Fourth International Conference on Natural Computation, vol. 4, pp. 516–520. IEEE (2008)
18. Sivapragasam, C., Arun, V.M., Giridhar, D.: A simple approach for improving spatial inter-polation of rainfall using ANN. In: Meteorology and Atmospheric Physics, vol. 109, pp. 1–7. Springer, Cham (2010)
19. Liu, S., Zhang, Y., Ma, P., Lu, B., Su, H.: A novel spatial interpolation method based on the integrated RBF neural network. Procedia Environ. Sci. **10**, 568–575 (2011)
20. De Jesus, K.L.M., Senoro, D.B., Dela Cruz, J.C., Chan, E.B.: A hybrid neural network-particle swarm optimization informed spatial interpolation technique for groundwater quality mapping in a Small Island Province of the Philippines. Toxics **9**(11), 273 (2021)
21. Hagenauer, J., Helbich, M.: A geographically weighted artificial neural network. Int. J. Geogr. Inf. Sci. **36**(2), 215–235 (2022)
22. Ester, M., Kriegel, H., Sander, J., Xu, X.: A density-based algorithm for discovering clusters in large spatial databases with noise. In: KDD, pp. 226–231 (1996)
23. Liu, F., et al.: Mapping high resolution National Soil Information Grids of China. Sci. Bull. **67**(3), 328–340 (2022). https://doi.org/10.1016/j.scib.2021.10.013

Adapted Methods for GAN Vocoders via Skip-Connections ISTFT and Cooperative Structure

Shaoqi Xiao, Jian Yang[✉], and Zhan Wang

School of Information Science and Engineering, Yunnan University, Kunming 650504, China
bai-li@mail.ynu.edu.cn, {jianyang,wangzhan000}@ynu.edu.cn

Abstract. Although recent works on GAN vocoders have improved the quality of synthesized speech by replacing current network design modules with various new modules, they often neglect to fully exploit the potential of the existing network architecture. Aside from exploring new network modules, exploiting the potential of existing network architectures is another effective strategy to enhance GAN vocoders. We thus propose two improvement methods that can further exploit the information contained in the network and apply them to HiFi-GAN. The first method is to introduce the skip-connections inverse short-time Fourier transform (skip-connections iSTFT) in the generator, and the second method is to introduce the cooperative structure in the discriminator. Experimental results show both methods synthesize speech with better quality compared to HiFi-GAN, with MOS improvement of 0.04 for the first method and 0.06 for the second method, and both methods also outperform HiFi-GAN in objective evaluation of MCD and PESQ. In addition, we also perform joint training of these two methods.

Keywords: GAN vocoders · HiFi-GAN · Inverse short-time Fourier transform · Cooperative structure

1 Introduction

Traditional text-to-speech (TTS) consists of two stages [1,2]: (1) In the first stage, the speech intermediate representation corresponding to the input text is generated, the most commonly used intermediate representation of speech is the mel-spectrogram, and this stage is known as the synthesizer module. (2) Then, another module, the vocoder module, generates the required raw scale speech using the representation created in the previous stage as input. As indicated in Fig. 1. So vocoders have become an essential component of TTS.

With the application of neural networks in the field of speech, neural vocoders have gradually replaced traditional vocoders [3,4] whose synthesis quality and naturalness are unsatisfactory. Many breakthroughs have been made in neural vocoders so far. Autoregressive models [5,6] enable models to synthesize high-quality speech due to their sample-by-sample estimation property, but this

L. Iliadis et al. (Eds.): ICANN 2023, LNCS 14258, pp. 219–229, 2023.
https://doi.org/10.1007/978-3-031-44192-9_18

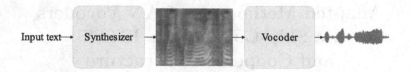

Fig. 1. TTS and VC commonly adopt a two-stage method.

also leads to slow inference speed. To address the issue caused by autoregressive models, non-autoregressive models have attracted researchers' attention. Non-autoregressive models are further classified into four categories. They are knowledge distillation models [7,8], diffusion probability models [9,10], flow-based models [11,12] and generative adversarial networks (GAN) based models [13,14]. In comparison to other types of neural vocoders, GAN-based models have won widespread attention due to their complete parallelism and constraints-free architectures.

Recent research on GAN-based neural vocoders focuses on proposing new modules to replace the original modules in the network architecture. For instance, WOLONet [15] uses the WOLO Block to replace the MRF Block in HiFi-GAN [13] to improve its synthesis quality, BigVGAN [16] replaces the MRF Block with the AMP Block, and it uses MRD to replace MSD in HiFi-GAN to improve the synthesis quality and universality of the vocoder. Although this approach improves the performance of the vocoder, it ignores whether the information contained in the network architecture is fully exploited and utilized. So we propose two improvement methods and take HiFi-GAN as the baseline model without modifying its original architecture. The first method is to introduce the skip-connections inverse short-time Fourier transform (skip-connections iSTFT) in the generator to exploit the information in the mel-spectrogram, and the second one is to introduce the cooperative structure in the discriminator to utilize the intermediate quantities of the generator. As a result, the information in the HiFi-GAN architecture is further exploited and utilized to improve the synthesis quality of the vocoder.

The rest of this paper is organized as follows. In Sect. 2, we discuss related work. In Sect. 3, two improvement methods are introduced. In Sect. 4, the experimental setup and results are presented. In Sect. 5, we summarize the whole paper and propose future research directions.

2   Related Work

HiFi-GAN is a classical model of GAN-based neural vocoders with three variants: high-quality (V1), light (V2) and carefully tuned (V3). We select HiFi-GAN V1 as the baseline system in this study to reflect the effectiveness of both improvement methods. The model consists of two parts, the generator and the discriminator. The generator takes the mel-spectrogram as input and gradually upsamples it to the raw scale speech waveform through four transposed convolutions. The discriminator employs the multi-period discriminator (MPD) and

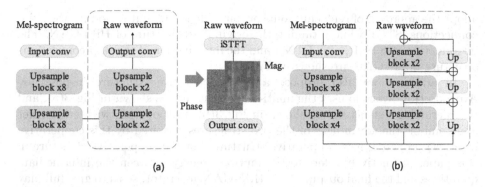

Fig. 2. ISTFT of iSTFTNet and the skip-connections structure of Fre-GAN. (a) denotes the introduction of iSTFT in iSTFTNet. (b) denotes the introduction of skip-connections in Fre-GAN.

the multi-scale discriminator (MSD) to capture the periodicity in speech and the continuous pattern and long-term dependencies in speech.

Inspired by iSTFTNet [17] and Fre-GAN [18], we introduce the combination of skip-connections structure and inverse short-time Fourier transform (iSTFT) into the generator to further exploit the information existing in the generator, where the skip-connections structure makes the model utilize the intermediate quantities of the generator and the iSTFT makes the model no longer directly generate the raw scale speech waveform, but rather the magnitude and phase. The generated magnitude and phase are then synthesized into the raw scale speech waveform by iSTFT, so as to utilize the information contained in the mel-spectrogram in a white box modeling way. Unlike iSTFTNet, we don't

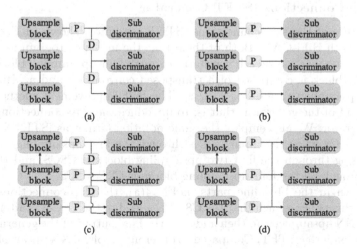

Fig. 3. Comparison on various structure of discriminators. (a) Multi-scale structure. (b) Hierarchical structure. (c) Cooperative structure of Avocodo. (d) Our cooperative structure.

adopt the approach of replacing some output-side layers, but introduce the skip-connections iSTFT while retaining the original architecture of HiFi-GAN. The introduction of iSTFT in iSTFTNet and the introduction of the skip-connections structure in Fre-GAN are shown in Fig. 2.

In addition, we also propose a new cooperative structure inspired by Avocodo [19]. Avocodo uses the multi-scale structure, as shown in Fig. 3(a), and the hierarchical structure, as shown in Fig. 3(b), to cooperate with each other and combine the advantages of the two structures. Inspired by this cooperative form, we propose a new cooperative structure, but the cooperative structure in this paper distinctively refers to the mutual synergy between the intermediate quantities and the final output of the HiFi-GAN generator, so as to give full play to the advantages of each intermediate quantity and the final output. It can also be considered that the cooperative structure in Avocodo is the synergy among sub-discriminators, while the cooperative structure in this paper is the synergy within sub-discriminators.

3   Methodology

Although proposing new modules to replace the original modules can improve various aspects of the vocoder such as high fidelity, universality and inference speed, it ignores whether the information in the architecture is completely exploited and utilized. Therefore, we propose two improvement methods. On the basis of unchanging the original architecture of HiFi-GAN, we exploit the information in the architecture to improve the synthesis quality by introducing skip-connections iSTFT and cooperative structure. The two methods are named skip-connections iSTFT generator and cooperative multi-period discriminator.

3.1   Skip-Connections ISTFT Generator

The structure of the skip-connections iSTFT generator, shown in Fig. 4(a), is consistent with HiFi-GAN. Both of them take the mel-spectrogram as input to synthesize the raw scale speech waveform through four upsampling blocks. Each upsampling block is composed of a transposed convolution and a MRF block, and the upsampling rate is [8, 8, 2, 2]. The first improvement method is the improvement of the generator, that is, to introduce the skip-connections iSTFT in the generator. We also employ the same notation format as iSTFTNet: Cx..., the result is C8 when the input passes through the first upsampling block, the result passing through the first two upsampling blocks is C8C8, and the result passing through all the four upsampling blocks is C8C8C2C2.

As shown in the blue line parts in Fig. 4(a), the skip-connections iSTFT applied in this paper is such that the C8C8 is added to the C8C8C2 after passing through a NN upsampler and then added to the final output of the generator after passing through the iSTFT. Compared to other upsamplers, NN upsamplers have been proven to alleviate tonal artifacts caused by transposed convolutions [20].

We use C8C8 and C8C8C2, because iSTFTNet experiments demonstrate that they are richer in information.

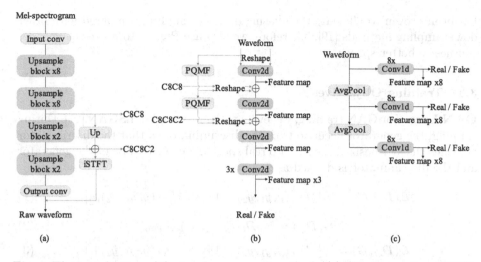

Fig. 4. The introduction of the two improvement methods. (a) Skip-connections iSTFT generator. (b) Cooperative multi-period discriminator. (c) Multi-scale discriminator of HiFi-GAN.

3.2 Cooperative Multi-period Discriminator

Cooperative Multi-Period Discriminator (CoMPD) is a new discriminator proposed in our work. The second improvement method is for the discriminator, that is, to introduce a new cooperative structure in MPD. Figure 4(b) shows the structure of CoMPD. From the previous subsection, we know C8C8 and C8C8C2 contain rich information, while previous discriminators tend to evaluate only the final output of the generator, but the utilization of the intermediate quantities of the generator is insufficient. Thus, we collaboratively input C8C8, C8C8C2 and the final output of the generator into CoMPD for evaluation, so that the discriminator can compare the generated speech with the real speech more finely to improve the quality of the synthesized speech.

Like MPD, CoMPD also owns five sub-discriminators with periods set to [2, 3, 5, 7, 11]. The cooperative structure employed in CoMPD is for each sub-discriminator, so the introduction is to use the final output of the generator as the input of each sub-discriminator, use C8C8 after the first convolution layer of each sub-discriminator, and use C8C8C2 after the second convolution layer of each sub-discriminator.

CoMPD also differs from traditional MPD during training. The evaluation of the generated speech is based on the orange line and black line parts in Fig. 4(b), that is, the final output, C8C8 and C8C8C2 are evaluated in concert. And the evaluation of the corresponding real speech is based on the blue line and black line parts in Fig. 4(b), that is, real speech, real speech x2 downsampling and real speech x4 downsampling are evaluated in concert. We utilize a pseudo quadrature mirror filter bank (PQMF) as the downsampling method. PQMF has been successfully and widely used in the field of speech. In addition, PQMF also has been proven to alleviate the aliasing in downsampling compared with other downsampling methods [19]. Therefore, we also use PQMF to make the vocoder synthesize better speech.

3.3 Training Objectives

GAN Loss. For GAN training, we leverage the loss used in LSGAN [21]. During training, the generator needs to trick the discriminator so that the discriminator classifies the synthesized speech into real speech. The GAN loss of the generator and the discriminator is defined as :

$$\mathcal{L}\left(D_C; G\right) = \mathbb{E}\left[\|D_C\left(y, y_1, y_2\right) - 1\|_2 + \|D_C\left(\tilde{y}, \tilde{y}_1, \tilde{y}_2\right)\|_2\right] \tag{1}$$

$$\mathcal{L}\left(G; D_C\right) = \mathbb{E}\,\|D_C\left(\tilde{y}, \tilde{y}_1, \tilde{y}_2\right) - 1\|_2 \tag{2}$$

$$\mathcal{L}\left(D_O; G\right) = \mathbb{E}\left[\|D_O\left(y, y_1, y_2\right) - 1\|_2 + \|D_O\left(\tilde{y}, \tilde{y}_1, \tilde{y}_2\right)\|_2\right] \tag{3}$$

$$\mathcal{L}\left(G; D_O\right) = \mathbb{E}\,\|D_O\left(\tilde{y}, \tilde{y}_1, \tilde{y}_2\right) - 1\|_2 \tag{4}$$

For simplicity, we describe MPD and MSD as one discriminator D_O. D_C denotes the CoMPD, G denotes the generator. y is real speech, y_1 is the result of real speech downsampled by PQMFx2, y_2 is the result of real speech downsampled by PQMFx4, $\tilde{y}$ represents the generated speech, $\tilde{y}_1$ represents the result of C8C8C2, $\tilde{y}_2$ represents the result of C8C8.

Feature Matching Loss. Feature matching loss has been successfully used as a perceptual loss in the training of GAN vocoders, so we also employ it as an auxiliary loss. The loss is to extract each intermediate feature of the discriminator and calculate the L1 distance between the real speech and the generated speech in each feature space [22]. The loss can be defined as follows:

$$\mathcal{L}_{fm}\left(G; D_C\right) = \mathbb{E}\left[\sum_{i=1}^{T}\frac{1}{N_i}\left\|D_C^i\left(y, y_1, y_2\right) - D_C^i\left(\tilde{y}, \tilde{y}_1, \tilde{y}_2\right)\right\|_1\right] \tag{5}$$

$$\mathcal{L}_{fm}\left(G; D_O\right) = \mathbb{E}\left[\sum_{i=1}^{T}\frac{1}{N_i}\left\|D_O^i(y) - D_O^i(\tilde{y})\right\|_1\right] \tag{6}$$

where T denotes the number of layers in the discriminator, D^i and N_i denote the feature map and the number of features in the ith layer of the discriminator, respectively.

Reconstruction Loss. We employ reconstruction loss to assist network training. Reconstruction loss helps the generator to synthesize the real waveform corresponding to the input condition and stabilize the training from an early stage [23]. The loss calculates the L1 distance between the mel-spectrogram of the generated speech and the mel-spectrogram of the real speech, the definition is as follows:

$$\mathcal{L}_{mel}(G) = \mathbb{E}\left[\|\phi(y) - \phi(\tilde{y})\|_1\right] \tag{7}$$

where ϕ is the function of converting the waveform into the corresponding mel-spectrogram.

Final Loss. For the training of method 1, we use the skip-connections iSTFT generator, MPD and MSD, the final loss can be defined as follows:

$$
\begin{aligned}
\mathcal{L}_D &= \sum_{p=1}^{5} \mathcal{L}\left(D_{O_p}; G\right) + \sum_{s=1}^{3} \mathcal{L}\left(D_{O_s}; G\right) \\
\mathcal{L}_G &= \sum_{p=1}^{5} \left[\mathcal{L}\left(G; D_{O_p}\right) + \lambda_{fm}\mathcal{L}_{fm}\left(G; D_{O_p}\right)\right] \\
&\quad + \sum_{s=1}^{3} \left[\mathcal{L}\left(G; D_{O_s}\right) + \lambda_{fm}\mathcal{L}_{fm}\left(G; D_{O_s}\right)\right] \\
&\quad + \lambda_{mel}\mathcal{L}_{mel}\left(G\right)
\end{aligned}
\tag{8}
$$

For the training of method 2, we use the generator of HiFi-GAN, CoMPD and MSD, the final loss is:

$$
\begin{aligned}
\mathcal{L}_D &= \sum_{k=1}^{5} \mathcal{L}\left(D_{C_k}; G\right) + \sum_{s=1}^{3} \mathcal{L}\left(D_{O_s}; G\right) \\
\mathcal{L}_G &= \sum_{k=1}^{5} \left[\mathcal{L}\left(G; D_{C_k}\right) + \lambda_{fm}\mathcal{L}_{fm}\left(G; D_{C_k}\right)\right] \\
&\quad + \sum_{s=1}^{3} \left[\mathcal{L}\left(G; D_{O_s}\right) + \lambda_{fm}\mathcal{L}_{fm}\left(G; D_{O_s}\right)\right] \\
&\quad + \lambda_{mel}\mathcal{L}_{mel}\left(G\right)
\end{aligned}
\tag{9}
$$

For the joint training of method 1 and 2, we use the skip-connections iSTFT generator, CoMPD and MSD, and the final loss is the same as Eq. 9. λ_{fm} and λ_{mel} in Eq. 8, 9 denote the loss scales of feature matching loss and reconstruction loss, respectively. We set λ_{fm} to 2, and λ_{mel} to 45. p represents the pth sub-discriminator of MPD, s represents the sth sub-discriminator of MSD, k represents the kth sub-discriminator of CoMPD.

4   Experiments

4.1   Experiments Setup

All experiments are evaluated on the LJSpeech dataset, which contains 13,100 audio samples recorded by the same female speaker with a total duration of 24 h. The audio format is 16-bit PCM encoding with a sampling rate of 22.05 kHz. The training set, validation set and test set are configured using the same configuration as in the original HiFi-GAN article. And the mel-spectrogram was extracted with FFT size of 1024, hop length of 256 and window length of 1024.

For HiFi-GAN, we use the open-source code, and both improvement methods are added on its basis. For the training configuration, we use the HiFi-GAN (V1) configuration file provided in the open-source code to train all models. We train all models for 500K iterations using the AdamW optimizer with an initial learning rate of 0.0002, and momentum terms β_1 and β_2 of 0.5 and 0.9, respectively.

4.2   Evaluation Metrics

Experiments are assessed on both subjective evaluation and objective evaluation. As a subjective test, we perform 5-scale MOS [24] tests by asking 15 raters to rate the naturalness of speech with 95% confidence interval. As an objective evaluation, we use MCD [25] and PESQ [26]. MCD evaluates the gap between the real speech and the synthesized speech from the mel cepstral sequence level, while PESQ assesses the gap between the real speech and the synthesized speech based on the psychological auditory characteristics of human perception of speech signals. 20 and 150 utterances are used for subjective evaluation and objective evaluation, respectively.

4.3   Experiments Results

All experiments are conducted on the LJSpeech dataset, and each model and its effects are evaluated from five aspects: MOS, PESQ, MCD, generator parameters, and period discriminator parameters, where smaller MCD values indicate better speech quality and larger PESQ and MOS values indicate better speech quality. The experimental results of the two improvement methods compared with the baseline are shown in Table 1, where the first improvement method, i.e., the skip-connections iSTFT generator, is described as method 1 in the table, the second improvement method, i.e., the cooperative multi-period discriminator, is described as method 2 in the table.

The evaluation results for method 1 are shown in Table 1 (Nos. 2 and 3). We find that the model after the introduction of the skip-connections iSTFT increases the parameters of the generator part by 0.02M, while the parameters of the discriminator part remain unchanged. Compared with HiFi-GAN, method 1 improves the system significantly in both MCD and PESQ, with MCD improved by 0.15 and PESQ improved by 0.05. Method 1 also results in a MOS improvement of 0.04.

Table 1 (Nos. 2 and 4) presents the evaluation results for method 2. Method 2 is an improvement for the multi-period discriminator, so the parameters of the period discriminator increased by 0.01M, but these small parameter changes improve the model in MOS, MCD and PESQ. Among them, MOS increased by 0.06, MCD improved by 0.27, and PESQ increased by 0.07. Method 2 also makes the model achieve the best results in MOS, MCD and PESQ in all the experiments in this paper.

The joint training results for method 1 and method 2 are shown in Table 1 (Nos. 2, 3, 4 and 5). Joint training achieves an optimal MOS score of 4.40 for all experiments, but compared to the separate training of method 1 and method 2, the joint training doesn't achieve further improvement. We speculate this is because the two improvement methods are aimed at C8C8 and C8C8C2 for exploiting and utilizing. Therefore, the optimal joint training results of method 1 and method 2 can only achieve the optimal results of the two methods in separate training.

Table 1. Evaluation results. CI denotes the confidence intervals. ↑ denotes higher is better. ↓ denotes lower is better. Param_G denotes the parameters of the generator. Param_D_P denotes the parameters of the multi-period discriminator. M denotes million. Values in bold represent the best results for each metric.

Model	MOS (CI)	PESQ (↑)	MCD (↓)	Param_G (M)	Param_D_P (M)
1. Ground Truth	4.57 ± 0.05	4.50	–	–	–
2. HiFi-GAN	4.34 ± 0.06	3.53	4.53	**13.93**	**41.10**
3. HiFi-GAN+method1	4.38 ± 0.08	3.58	4.38	13.95	**41.10**
4. HiFi-GAN+method2	**4.40 ± 0.07**	**3.60**	**4.26**	13.94	41.11
5. HiFi-GAN+method1, 2	**4.40 ± 0.07**	3.59	4.28	13.95	41.11

Ablation Study. Since method 1 is a new structure that combines the skip-connections structure with the iSTFT, so we further conduct ablation experiments to verify the performance of the combined skip-connections iSTFT.

Table 2. Ablation study of the skip-connections iSTFT. The average MOS score of method 1 is used as the reference and is recorded as 0. Other experiments' results are shown in the form of improvement or decrease compared to the reference score.

Model	MOS
1. HiFi-GAN+method1	0
2. w/o skip-connections	−0.03
3. w/o iSTFT	−0.01

From the experimental results of the ablation experiments, we find both separate structures decreased in MOS. The MOS score of the model decreased by 0.03 after removing the skip-connections structure alone for method 1 and by 0.01 after removing the iSTFT alone for method 1. Results show the combination of skip-connections structure and iSTFT can further exploit the information contained in the network architecture. The ablation results are shown in Table 2.

5   Conclusions

In this paper, we propose two improvement methods to further exploit the information contained in the network without changing the original architecture of the network and verify the effectiveness of the two improvement methods through experiments based on HiFi-GAN. In addition, the two improvement methods proposed in this paper are for the improvement of the generator and the improvement of the discriminator, so the ideas of these two improvement methods can also be applied to other GAN vocoders, and we plan to verify the effectiveness of these two improvement methods in other GAN vocoders in future research.

Acknowledgements. This work is supported by the National Key R&D Program of China (2020AAA0107901).

References

1. Shen, J., et al.: Natural TTS synthesis by conditioning WaveNet on Mel spectrogram predictions. In: 2018 IEEE International Conference on Acoustics, Speech and Signal Processing (ICASSP), pp. 4779–4783. IEEE (2018)
2. Ren, Y., et al.: FastSpeech 2: fast and high-quality end-to-end text to speech. In: International Conference on Learning Representations (2020)
3. Kawahara, H., Masuda-Katsuse, I., De Cheveigne, A.: Restructuring speech representations using a pitch-adaptive time-frequency smoothing and an instantaneous-frequency-based F0 extraction: possible role of a repetitive structure in sounds. Speech Commun. **27**(3–4), 187–207 (1999)
4. Morise, M., Yokomori, F., Ozawa, K.: WORLD: a vocoder-based high-quality speech synthesis system for real-time applications. IEICE Trans. Inf. Syst. **99**(7), 1877–1884 (2016)
5. van den Oord, A., et al.: WaveNet: a generative model for raw audio. In: 9th ISCA Speech Synthesis Workshop, p. 125 (2016)
6. Kalchbrenner, N., et al.: Efficient neural audio synthesis. In: International Conference on Machine Learning, pp. 2410–2419. PMLR (2018)
7. Oord, A., et al.: Parallel WaveNet: fast high-fidelity speech synthesis. In: International conference on machine learning, pp. 3918–3926. PMLR (2018)
8. Ping, W., Peng, K., Chen, J.: ClariNet: parallel wave generation in end-to-end text-to-speech. In: International Conference on Learning Representations (2018)
9. Chen, N., Zhang, Y., Zen, H., Weiss, R.J., Norouzi, M., Chan, W.: WaveGrad: estimating gradients for waveform generation. In: International Conference on Learning Representations (2020)

10. Kong, Z., Ping, W., Huang, J., Zhao, K., Catanzaro, B.: DiffWave: a versatile diffusion model for audio synthesis. In: International Conference on Learning Representations (2020)
11. Prenger, R., Valle, R., Catanzaro, B.: WaveGlow: a flow-based generative network for speech synthesis. In: ICASSP 2019–2019 IEEE International Conference on Acoustics, Speech and Signal Processing (ICASSP), pp. 3617–3621. IEEE (2019)
12. Ping, W., Peng, K., Zhao, K., Song, Z.: WaveFlow: a compact flow-based model for raw audio. In: International Conference on Machine Learning, pp. 7706–7716. PMLR (2020)
13. Kong, J., Kim, J., Bae, J.: HiFi-GAN: generative adversarial networks for efficient and high fidelity speech synthesis. Adv. Neural. Inf. Process. Syst. **33**, 17022–17033 (2020)
14. Kumar, K., et al.: MelGAN: generative adversarial networks for conditional waveform synthesis. Adv. Neural. Inf. Process. Syst. **32** (2019)
15. Wang, Y., Si, Y.: WoloNet: wave outlooker for efficient and high fidelity speech synthesis. arXiv preprint arXiv:2206.09920 (2022)
16. Lee, S.G., Ping, W., Ginsburg, B., Catanzaro, B., Yoon, S.: BigVGAN: a universal neural vocoder with large-scale training. arXiv preprint arXiv:2206.04658 (2022)
17. Kaneko, T., Tanaka, K., Kameoka, H., Seki, S.: iSTFTNet: fast and lightweight Mel-spectrogram vocoder incorporating inverse short-time Fourier transform. In: ICASSP 2022–2022 IEEE International Conference on Acoustics, Speech and Signal Processing (ICASSP), pp. 6207–6211. IEEE (2022)
18. Kim, J.H., Lee, S.H., Lee, J.H., Lee, S.W.: Fre-GAN: adversarial frequency-consistent audio synthesis. In: 22nd Annual Conference of the International Speech Communication Association, INTERSPEECH 2021, pp. 3246–3250. International Speech Communication Association (2021)
19. Bak, T., Lee, J., Bae, H., Yang, J., Bae, J.S., Joo, Y.S.: Avocodo: generative adversarial network for artifact-free vocoder. arXiv preprint arXiv:2206.13404 (2022)
20. Odena, A., Dumoulin, V., Olah, C.: Deconvolution and checkerboard artifacts. Distill **1**(10), e3 (2016)
21. Mao, X., Li, Q., Xie, H., Lau, R.Y., Wang, Z., Paul Smolley, S.: Least squares generative adversarial networks. In: Proceedings of the IEEE International Conference on Computer Vision, pp. 2794–2802 (2017)
22. Larsen, A.B.L., Sønderby, S.K., Larochelle, H., Winther, O.: Autoencoding beyond pixels using a learned similarity metric. In: International Conference on Machine Learning, pp. 1558–1566. PMLR (2016)
23. Isola, P., Zhu, J.Y., Zhou, T., Efros, A.A.: Image-to-image translation with conditional adversarial networks. In: Proceedings of the IEEE Conference on Computer Vision and Pattern Recognition, pp. 1125–1134 (2017)
24. Wester, M., Wu, Z., Yamagishi, J.: Analysis of the voice conversion challenge 2016 evaluation results. In: Interspeech, pp. 1637–1641 (2016)
25. Kubichek, R.: Mel-cepstral distance measure for objective speech quality assessment. In: Proceedings of IEEE Pacific Rim Conference on Communications Computers and Signal Processing, vol. 1, pp. 125–128. IEEE (1993)
26. Rix, A.W., Beerends, J.G., Hollier, M.P., Hekstra, A.P.: Perceptual evaluation of speech quality (PESQ)-a new method for speech quality assessment of telephone networks and codecs. In: Proceedings of the 2001 IEEE International Conference on Acoustics, Speech, and Signal Processing (Cat. No. 01CH37221), vol. 2, pp. 749–752. IEEE (2001)

An Efficient Approximation Method Based on Enhanced Physics-Informed Neural Networks for Solving Localized Wave Solutions of PDEs

Yanan Guo[1,2,3](✉)(iD), Xiaoqun Cao[2,3](iD), Kecheng Peng[2,3], Wei Dong[2](iD),
Wenlong Tian[2,3], and Mengge Zhou[3]

[1] Naval Aviation University, Huludao, Liaoning, China
guoyn14@lzu.edu.cn
[2] College of Computer, National University of Defense Technology, Changsha,
Hunan, China
[3] College of Meteorology and Oceanography, National University of Defense
Technology, Changsha, Hunan, China

Abstract. Partial Differential Equations (PDEs) are an important branch of mathematics and are of great value in describing and solving natural phenomena and engineering problems. In recent years, with the rapid development of deep learning techniques, physics-informed neural networks (PINNs) have been successfully applied to solve partial differential equations and physical field simulations. Based on physical constraints, PINNs have received a lot of attention from researchers as they can quickly obtain highly accurate data-driven solutions with a small amount of data. In the realm of nonlinear science, the investigation of localized waves holds significant research significance and has found applications across various domains. In the present study, we have employed an enhanced version of physics-informed neural networks to conduct numerical simulations of localized waves governed by nonlinear partial differential equations. The improved PINNs not only incorporate the inherent constraints of the equations but also integrate constraints derived from gradient information. Moreover, we have employed an adaptive learning approach to dynamically update the weight coefficients of the loss function, thereby enhancing the training efficiency. In our experiments, we have chosen the nonlinear Schrödinger equation for the study and evaluated the accuracy of the localized wave simulation results by error analysis. The experimental results show that the improved PINNs significantly outperform the traditional PINNs with shorter training time and more accurate prediction results.

Supported by the National Natural Science Foundation of China (Grant No. 42005003, No. 41475094 and No. 62032024) and the National Key R&D Program of China (Grant No. 2018YFC1506704).

Keywords: Physics-informed neural networks · Partial differential equations · Localized waves · Gradient-enhanced constraints · Self-adaptive loss function

1   Introduction

In recent years, deep learning methods have emerged as a new paradigm in scientific research, rapidly and profoundly impacting various scientific fields such as physics, chemistry, materials science, and biology [2,5,7], and thus are receiving increasing attention from researchers. There have been numerous exciting achievements in this emerging cross-disciplinary research area. One notable example is the application of deep learning in weather and climate prediction, which has significantly enhanced the accuracy of forecasting catastrophic weather events such as super hurricanes and rainstorms [3]. Another hot work in this area is the application of deep neural networks to solve partial differential equations (PDEs) [6,11]. Raissi et al. conducted a comprehensive investigation and advancement of preceding neural network methodologies for solving differential equations. Their seminal contribution involved the introduction of physics-informed neural networks (PINNs), which are founded upon the incorporation of physics constraints [10]. As a framework for modeling physical phenomena governed by both empirical data and fundamental laws of physics, physics-informed neural networks introduce a novel paradigm by incorporating physical constraints as regularization terms into neural networks. This innovative approach effectively reduces the reliance on extensive training data and enhances the interpretability of the neural network models. A key aspect of PINNs lies in their versatile loss function, which comprises four fundamental components: constraints derived from observed data, partial differential equations, boundary conditions, and initial conditions. Since the inception of PINNs, numerous researchers have dedicated significant efforts towards their exploration and refinement in recent years. Consequently, a large number of novel PINN variants have emerged, finding applications in diverse domains such as fluid mechanics, solid mechanics, thermodynamics, and materials science [1,4,8].

Nonlinear localized waves are fluctuating phenomena with specific dynamical properties generated by nonlinear physical systems, often with complex distribution and evolutionary properties. Localized waves mainly include solitons, rogue waves, breathers, etc. They are widely found in various nonlinear physical systems such as nonlinear optics and plasma physics [13]. As a unique fluctuation phenomenon existing in nature, localized waves have become an important research topic in the field of nonlinear science [12]. In recent years, a large number of researchers have carried out high-precision simulations of localized waves [9], hoping to deepen the understanding of the law of localized waves. However, the traditional numerical computational methods have problems such as low computational efficiency and truncation errors, so researchers have started to search for new numerical simulation methods. In view of the above difficulties, the simulation of localized waves phenomenon is deeply studied in this paper.

Based on the traditional PINNs method, a new PINNs structure and loss function applicable to the simulation of the localized waves phenomenon are designed and verified by numerical experiments.

2   Method

This section is dedicated to the enhancement of Physics-Informed Neural Networks (PINNs), with a particular emphasis on the refinement of loss functions through the utilization of gradient information and adaptive techniques. Subsequently, a comprehensive exposition is provided on both the conventional PINNs and the refined PINNs methodologies.

2.1   Physics-Informed Neural Networks

From the perspective of mathematical function approximation theory, neural networks are recognized as versatile tools for approximating general nonlinear functions. Consequently, the task of solving partial differential equations can be reformulated as the search for nonlinear functions that adhere to the given constraints. Raissi et al. employed a limited number of observations, control equations, as well as initial and boundary conditions, to construct residual terms, which were subsequently aggregated to form the loss function. By utilizing this composite loss function, the neural network not only approximates the observed data but also inherently satisfies the physical properties of symmetry, invariance, and conservation dictated by the underlying partial differential equations. In summary, the underlying concept of physics-informed neural networks lies in the integration of data-driven and physical constraints, offering a novel approach to tackling partial differential equations. Next, partial differential equations of the following type are analyzed.

$$
\begin{aligned}
u_t + \mathcal{N}_x[u] &= 0, \quad x \in \Omega, t \in [T_0, T] \\
u(x, T_0) &= h(x), \quad x \in \Omega \\
u(x, t) &= g(x, t), \quad x \in \partial\Omega, t \in [T_0, T]
\end{aligned}
\tag{1}
$$

In the above formula, t and x represent time variable and space variable respectively, T and Ω represent their value ranges respectively, and $\partial\Omega$ is the boundary of the space domain Ω. $\mathcal{N}_x$ is a combination of linear and nonlinear operators, $h(x)$ is the initial condition, and $g(x, t)$ is the boundary condition.

To begin, we construct a neural network denoted as $\widehat{u}(x, t; \theta)$ to serve as an approximation of the solution to the given partial differential equation, where θ represents the network's parameters. The trained neural network, $\widehat{u}(x, t; \theta)$, should satisfy two essential criteria. Firstly, it should generate predicted values that adhere to the prescribed initial and boundary conditions. Secondly, the neural network must adhere to the physical constraints inherent in the partial differential equation. To achieve this, automatic differentiation techniques are employed to incorporate the differential constraints of the partial differential equation directly into the neural network. This integration facilitates the construction of a residual network that ensures compliance with the aforementioned physical constraints. Mathematically, the residual network is defined as depicted in Eq. (2).

$$f(x, t; \theta) := \frac{\partial}{\partial t} \widehat{u}(x, t; \theta) + \mathcal{N}_x[\widehat{u}(x, t; \theta)] \tag{2}$$

The subsequent crucial task entails the formulation of the loss function for physics-informed neural networks, encompassing four distinct components: the loss function for observed data constraints, the loss function for governing equation constraints, the loss function for initial condition constraints, and the loss function for boundary condition constraints. Mathematically, the definitions of these four loss functions are presented below.

$$L_o\left(\theta; N_o\right) = \frac{1}{2\left|N_o\right|} \sum_{j=1}^{N_o} \left\| \widehat{u}\left(x_o^j, t_o^j; \theta\right) - u_o^j \right\|_2^2, \tag{3}$$

$$L_{PDE}\left(\theta; N_f\right) = \frac{1}{2\left|N_f\right|} \sum_{j=1}^{N_f} \left\| f\left(x_f^j, t_f^j; \theta\right) \right\|^2 \tag{4}$$

$$L_{IC}\left(\theta; N_i\right) = \frac{1}{2\left|N_i\right|} \sum_{j=1}^{N_i} \left\| \widehat{u}\left(x_i^j, 0; \theta\right) - h_i^j \right\|_2^2 \tag{5}$$

$$L_{BC}\left(\theta; N_b\right) = \frac{1}{2\left|N_b\right|} \sum_{j=1}^{N_b} \left\| \widehat{u}\left(x_b^j, t_b^j; \theta\right) - g_b^j \right\|_2^2 \tag{6}$$

The loss function term under the observed data constraint is expressed in Eq. (3), signifying that the efficacy of the observed data significantly impacts the training results. On the other hand, Eq. (4) characterizes the loss function term under the constraint of the differential equation. This term is formulated by evaluating the residual values of the partial differential equations using the sample points within the defined domain. All the residuals are in the time and space domains and can be selected randomly, or a suitable selection method can be designed according to the specific questions, and N_f is the number of selected points. Equation (4) necessitates the neural network to conform to the constraints imposed by the partial differential equation, denoted as the regularization term for incorporating physical information. By extension, Eq. (5) characterizes the loss term computed based on the initial conditions, thereby demanding the neural network to adhere to the constraints dictated by these initial conditions. Similarly, Eq. (6) denotes the loss function term derived from the boundary conditions, necessitating the neural network to satisfy the constraints originating from the boundary conditions. Ultimately, the mathematical formulation of the loss function to be optimized can be expressed as follows.

$$L(\theta; N) = \lambda_o L_o\left(\theta; N_o\right) + \lambda_f L_{PDE}\left(\theta; N_f\right) + \lambda_b L_{BC}\left(\theta; N_b\right) + \lambda_i L_{IC}\left(\theta; N_i\right) \tag{7}$$

where $\lambda = \{\lambda_o, \lambda_f, \lambda_b, \lambda_i\}$ are the weight coefficients of each term of the loss function. Next, gradient descent algorithms, such as Adam, stochastic gradient descent (SGD) or L-BFGS, are generally used to optimize the loss function and find the minimum value of the loss function. Through iterative parameter optimization, the neural network's loss function is systematically minimized, thereby driving the network's output toward a close approximation of the genuine solution to the partial differential equation. The framework of the physics-informed neural network is shown in Fig. 1.

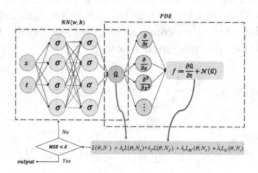

Fig. 1. Schematic of physics-informed neural networks for solving partial differential equation

2.2   The Gradient-Enhanced Physics-Informed Neural Networks with Self-adaptive Loss Function

In the original physics-informed neural networks, only PDE residuals f are forced to be zero. But further analysis shows that since $f(x)$ is zero for any x, then the derivative of $f(x)$ is also zero. Therefore, we can assume that the exact solution of PDE is smooth enough so that the gradient of PDE residuals $\nabla f(x)$ exists, and propose gradient-enhanced PINNs so that the derivative of PDE residuals is also zero [15], which can be expressed in mathematical form by the following formula:

$$\nabla f(\mathbf{x}) = \left(\frac{\partial f}{\partial x_1}, \frac{\partial f}{\partial x_2}, \dots, \frac{\partial f}{\partial x_d}\right) = \mathbf{0}, \quad \mathbf{x} \in \Omega \tag{8}$$

Based on the aforementioned definition, it is inherent to derive the loss function for the gradient-enhanced PINNs:

$$L(\theta; N) = w_o L_o(\theta; N_o) + w_f L_f(\theta; N_f) + w_b L_b(\theta; N_b)$$
$$+ w_i L_i(\theta; N_i) + \sum_{i=1}^{d} w_{gi} L_{g_i}(\theta; \mathcal{T}_{g_i}) \tag{9}$$

where the loss of the derivative with respect to x_i is:

$$L_{g_i}(\theta; \mathcal{T}_{g_i}) = \frac{1}{|\mathcal{T}_{g_i}|} \sum_{\mathbf{x} \in \mathcal{T}_{g_i}} \left|\frac{\partial f}{\partial x_i}\right|^2 \tag{10}$$

where $\mathcal{T}_{g_i}$ is the set of residual points for the derivative $\frac{\partial f}{\partial x_i}$. It should be noted that $\mathcal{T}_{gi}(i = 1, 2, \cdots, d)$ may be different for different equations. Extensive research has demonstrated that the utilization of neural networks for solving PDEs necessitates the careful determination of weight coefficients within the loss function. These coefficients significantly influence the performance of PINNs. Consequently, the effective selection of optimal weight coefficients for the loss function is a crucial aspect to be taken into account during the design of PINNs [14]. To improve the accuracy and robustness of the localized waves simulation, We have conducted an in-depth study of the loss function of PINNs and its weight coefficients. Next, the adaptive learning method for optimizing the loss function weight coefficients is presented.

Initially, a Gaussian probability model is constructed utilizing the neural network model's output. In this context, the mean value of the Gaussian probability model represents the predicted value of gradient-enhanced physics-informed neural networks, while the uncertainty parameter is postulated as ε_d^2.

$$p(u \mid \hat{u}(x, t; \theta)) = N\left(\hat{u}(x, t; \theta), \varepsilon_d^2\right) \tag{11}$$

In the process of optimizing the neural network parameters, the uncertainty parameter ε_d^2 is also continuously adjusted to maximize the likelihood estimate so as to satisfy the following formula:

$$
\begin{aligned}
-\log p(u \mid \hat{u}(x, t; \theta)) \quad &\propto \frac{1}{2\varepsilon_d^2}\|u - \hat{u}(x, t; \theta)\|^2 + \log \varepsilon_d \\
&= \frac{1}{2\varepsilon_d^2} L_{\text{data}}(\theta) + \log \varepsilon_d
\end{aligned}
\tag{12}
$$

The aforementioned equation denotes the term of the loss function formulated using the observed data within the framework of the Gaussian probability model. Employing a similar approach, the loss functions incorporating constraints of the partial differential equation, initial condition, boundary condition, and gradient condition can be derived within the Gaussian probability model. Subsequently, leveraging the principles of probability calculation, a composite loss function with adaptive learning capability is constructed for the multi-output neural network model. The mathematical expression of this enhanced loss function is presented as follows:

$$
\begin{aligned}
L(\varepsilon; \theta; N) =& \frac{1}{2\varepsilon_f^2} L_{PDE}(\theta; N_f) + \frac{1}{2\varepsilon_b^2} L_{BC}(\theta; N_b) + \frac{1}{2\varepsilon_i^2} L_{IC}(\theta; N_i) \\
&+ \frac{1}{2\varepsilon_d^2} L_{\text{data}}(\theta; N_{\text{data}}) + \frac{1}{2\varepsilon_g^2} L_{\text{gradient}}(\theta; N_{\text{gradient}}) + \log \varepsilon_f \varepsilon_b \varepsilon_i \varepsilon_d \varepsilon_g,
\end{aligned}
\tag{13}
$$

where $\varepsilon = \{\varepsilon_f, \varepsilon_b, \varepsilon_i, \varepsilon_d, \varepsilon_g\}$ is the adaptive weight coefficient of the loss function. Based on the above loss function, the problem of solving the partial differential equation is transformed into the optimization problem of the loss function $L(\varepsilon; \theta; N)$. The next main task is to find the optimal adaptive weight ε and the optimal parameter θ of the neural network model, so as to obtain the optimal neural network model to achieve the goal of solving the partial differential equation. In the optimization process, stochastic gradient descent (SGD),

Adam and L-BFGS are often chosen to update the parameters of the neural network. The last term of the above Eq. (13) is a regularization term, which prevents the adaptive weight coefficients falling too much. To prevent the adaptive weight coefficients from converging to zero quickly and to facilitate the computation, we further improve the loss function of PINNs by using the log variance $s = \{s_f, s_b, s_i, s_d, s_g\}, s := \log \varepsilon^2$, as follows:

$$
\begin{aligned}
L(s; \theta; N) = & \frac{1}{2} \exp\left(-s_f\right) L_{PDE}\left(\theta; N_f\right) + \frac{1}{2} \exp\left(-s_b\right) L_{BC}\left(\theta; N_b\right) \\
& + \frac{1}{2} \exp\left(-s_i\right) L_{IC}\left(\theta; N_i\right) + \frac{1}{2} \exp\left(-s_d\right) L_{\text{data}}\left(\theta; N_{\text{data}}\right) \\
& + \frac{1}{2} \exp\left(-s_g\right) L_{\text{gradient}}\left(\theta; N_{\text{gradient}}\right) + s_f + s_b + s_i + s_d + s_g.
\end{aligned}
$$

(14)

The training and optimization process for the above loss function will be more stable because $\exp(-s_j)$ resolves to a positive domain. Likewise, in the training process, it becomes essential to adaptively learn the weight coefficients associated with each term of the loss function, aiming to achieve the optimal coefficients and neural network parameters. Leveraging a range of optimization algorithms, the parameters of gradient-enhanced PINNs, equipped with adaptive learning capability, undergo continuous updates, thereby diminishing the value of the loss function. Consequently, the output of the neural network progressively approximates the exact solution of the nonlinear partial differential equations.

3   Experiments and Results

In this section, we conduct simulations on the phenomenon of localized waves by employing gradient-enhanced PINNs with adaptive learning capability. Localized waves hold significant importance in the realm of nonlinear science, finding applications in various fields such as fluid mechanics, quantum mechanics, and nonlinear fiber optic communication. Consequently, the high-precision simulation of localized wave phenomena has garnered considerable attention from researchers in recent years. In our experimental study, we utilize the improved PINNs to simulate localized waves governed by nonlinear partial differential equations, subsequently analyzing the convergence rate and accuracy of the proposed approach. The accuracy of the neural network model's approximate solution is assessed through the relative L2 norm error, which is defined as follows:

$$
\text{L2 error} = \frac{\sqrt{\sum_{i=1}^{N} |\hat{u}\left(x_i, t_i\right) - u\left(x_i, t_i\right)|^2}}{\sqrt{\sum_{i=1}^{N} |u\left(x_i, t_i\right)|^2}}.
$$

(15)

where $u\left(x_i, t_i\right)$ represents the exact solution and $\hat{u}\left(x_i, t_i\right)$ represents the approximate solution.

3.1 The Single Soliton Solution of the Derivative Nonlinear Schrödinger Equation (DNLS)

In this study, the single soliton solution of the derivative nonlinear Schrödinger equation (DNLS) has been studied based on the improved PINNs. The mathematical form of the DNLS is defined as follows:

$$iq_t + q_{xx} + i\left(q^2 q^*\right)_x = 0 \tag{16}$$

In this experiment, we consider DNLS with Dirichlet boundary conditions, and the detailed mathematical formulation is given as follows:

$$
\begin{aligned}
&iq_t + q_{xx} + i\left(q^2 q^*\right)_x = 0, x \in [x_0, x_1], t \in [t_0, t_1] \\
&q(x, t_0) = q_0(x) \\
&q(x_0, t) = q(x_1, t)
\end{aligned}
\tag{17}
$$

We consider the following initial condition:

$$q_0(x) = \frac{4[4i(1.4 + x) - 1]e^{2i(1.2+x)}}{[4i(1.4 + x) + 1]^2} \tag{18}$$

In the above formula, the spatial range is $[-2.0, 0]$, and the time range is $[-0.1, 0.1]$. Under the above conditions, the single soliton solution of the DNLS is given as follows:

$$q(x, t) = \frac{4[4i(1 - 4t + x) - 1]e^{2i(1-2t+x)}}{[4i(1 - 4t + x) + 1]^2} \tag{19}$$

We build a neural network with five hidden layers, and the number of neurons in each hidden layer is 64. The initial weight coefficients of each loss function are set to 0.2, and they are continuously optimized and updated during the subsequent training. We consider the initial condition as a specialized form of Dirichlet boundary condition within the spatiotemporal domain. To obtain training data for the initial and boundary conditions, we employ random sampling with a sample size of 500. Furthermore, we randomly select sample points within the spatiotemporal domain to compute the residuals and establish physical constraints. The total amount of data sampled in this experiment amounts to 8,000. Additionally, a small number of observations are utilized for training with the number of 600. Throughout the training process, a learning rate of 0.001 is employed. To speed up the training process, we initially perform 5,000 iterations using L-BFGS, followed by continued optimization using Adam until convergence is achieved. Figure 2 shows the exact solution and the prediction results using the trained model. From Fig. 2, it can be seen that the neural network can simulate the exact solution of DNLS with high accuracy. In addition, we choose the prediction results at different times to compare with the exact solution. Figure 3 shows the comparison of the true and approximate solutions of the single soliton solution of DNLS at different times. It can be found that the predicted values are very close to the true solutions. We counted the errors between the approximate solution and exact solution, and the relative L2 error between the predicted solutions and true solutions is about $1.73 * 10^{-3}$. With the same training data and parameter settings, the L2 norm relative error of the original PINNs is about $5.85 * 10^{-3}$. Figure 4 shows the error statistics of the improved PINNs and the original PINNs. Finally, the training time of the model before and after the improvement is analyzed, and it is found that the average time of the improved PINNs to complete the training task is about 56.9% of the training time of the original PINNs. The experimental results demonstrate that the improved PINNs exhibit superior training efficiency and yield more precise prediction outcomes compared to the original PINNs when applied to the simulation problem involving the single soliton solution of DNLS.

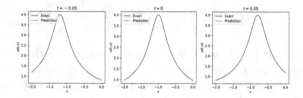

Fig. 2. The exact single soliton solution (left) and learned solution (right) of the DNLS equation

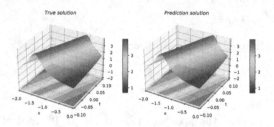

Fig. 3. Comparison of the exact single soliton solution of the DNLS equation and the approximate solution of the neural network at different times.

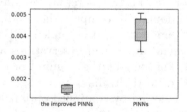

Fig. 4. Error statistics for the improved PINNs and the original PINNs for solving single soliton solutions of the DNLS equation.

3.2   The Akhmediev Breather of Nonlinear Schrödinger Equation

In this section, the initial value problem of nonlinear Schrödinger equation (NLSE) is given as follows:

$$iu_t + 0.5u_{xx} + |u|^2 u = 0, \quad t \in [-5, 15], \quad x \in [-L/2, L/2]$$

$$u(x, -5) = \left[1 - \frac{k^2 \cosh(-5\delta) + 2ikv \sinh(-5\delta)}{2(\cosh(-5\delta) - v\cos(kx))}\right] e^{i(-5+\pi)} \tag{20}$$

where $L = 8\pi/k$, $\delta = vk$ and $k = 2\sqrt{1 - v^2}$. The value of v is 0.9, the value of L is 1.0, the spatial domain range is $[-L/2, L/2]$, and the time range is $[-5, 15]$. Under the above conditions, the Akhmediev breather of the nonlinear Schrödinger equation is given as follows:

$$u_{AB}(x, t) = \left[1 - \frac{k^2 \cosh \delta t + 2ikv \sinh \delta t}{2(\cosh \delta t - v\cos kx)}\right] e^{i(t+\pi)} \tag{21}$$

We constructed a neural network with 6 hidden layers and the number of neurons in each hidden layer is 64. The initial weight coefficients of the loss function were also set to 0.2, and the values of the weight coefficients were continuously optimized during the later training process based on the adaptive learning method. Similar to the previous experiments, the initial conditions are considered as special types of Dirichlet boundary conditions in the spatio-temporal domain. The training data about the initial and boundary conditions were obtained by random sampling with a sample size of 800. The selected points for calculating the residuals were chosen randomly in the spatio-temporal domain with a number of 15,000. A small number of observations were used in the training process with the number of 800. The learning rate was set to 0.001 during the training process. In this experiment, different gradient descent algorithms were chosen to accomplish the training optimization task by first completing 5000 epoch iterations with L-BFGS, and then continuing the optimization with Adam until convergence. After training, the trained model is used to approximate the Akhmediev breather for the nonlinear Schrödinger equation. Figure 5 shows the exact solution and prediction results of the neural network. From Fig. 5, it can be seen that the neural network successfully simulates the Akhmediev breather for the nonlinear Schrödinger equation. In addition, Fig. 6 shows the true solutions and approximate solutions at different times, and it can be seen that the two are very close to each other. Further, we statistically calculated the error between the approximate solutions and exact solutions and found that the L2 norm relative error between the prediction result and the true solution is about $1.94 * 10^{-3}$. With the same training data and parameter settings, the L2 norm relative error of the results calculated by the original PINNs is about $6.63 * 10^{-3}$. Figure 7 shows the error statistics of the improved PINNs and the original PINNs. Finally, the training time of the neural network models before and after the improvement is analyzed, and it is found that the average time of the improved PINNs to complete the training task is about 62.5% of the training time of the original

PINNs. The experiments show that for the Akhmediev breather simulation problem of nonlinear Schrödinger equation, the improved PINNs have more accurate prediction results, higher training efficiency and shorter training time than the original PINNs.

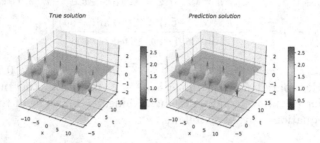

Fig. 5. The exact Akhmediev breather solution (left) and learned solution (right) of the nonlinear Schrödinger equation

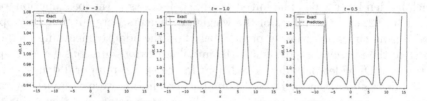

Fig. 6. Comparison of the exact Akhmediev breather solution of the NLSE and the approximate solution of the neural network at different times.

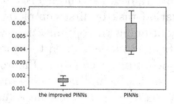

Fig. 7. Error statistics for the improved PINNs and the original PINNs for solving Akhmediev breather solution of the nonlinear Schrödinger equation.

4   Conclusion

This paper presents numerical simulations of localized waves using gradient-enhanced PINNs with adaptive learning capability. The enhanced PINNs not only incorporate the constraints of the partial differential equation to ensure the interpretability of prediction results but also introduce gradient information and employ an adaptive learning method to dynamically update the weight coefficients of each term in the loss function during the training process. This improved PINNs model encompasses richer physical information and allows for dynamic adjustment of constraint weights. For the experiments, we specifically selected the nonlinear Schrödinger equation as the focus of study and analyzed the simulation errors to evaluate the model's accuracy. The experimental results demonstrate a significant improvement in the training speed of the enhanced PINNs, accompanied by a substantial reduction in prediction errors. This notable enhancement greatly improves the simulation accuracy and efficiency of solitary waves. Given the successful simulation of localized wave phenomena achieved by the improved PINNs, our future endeavors will involve extending and applying this methodology to other complex system simulation problems, such as ocean wave simulation and atmospheric pollutant dispersion process simulation. Furthermore, there remain several intriguing aspects to explore in PINNs, including effective handling of noisy data interference and successful integration with traditional numerical methods. These aspects will be thoroughly investigated and analyzed in our forthcoming research.

References

1. Bai, J., Rabczuk, T., Gupta, A., Alzubaidi, L., Gu, Y.: A physics-informed neural network technique based on a modified loss function for computational 2D and 3D solid mechanics. Comput. Mech. **71**(3), 543–562 (2023)
2. Bourilkov, D.: Machine and deep learning applications in particle physics. Int. J. Mod. Phys. A **34**(35), 1930019 (2019)
3. Boussioux, L., Zeng, C., Guénais, T., Bertsimas, D.: Hurricane forecasting: a novel multimodal machine learning framework. Weather Forecast. **37**(6), 817–831 (2022)
4. Cai, S., Mao, Z., Wang, Z., Yin, M., Karniadakis, G.E.: Physics-informed neural networks (PINNs) for fluid mechanics: a review. Acta. Mech. Sin. **37**(12), 1727–1738 (2021)
5. Goh, G.B., Hodas, N.O., Vishnu, A.: Deep learning for computational chemistry. J. Comput. Chem. **38**(16), 1291–1307 (2017)
6. Guo, Y., Cao, X., Liu, B., Gao, M.: Solving partial differential equations using deep learning and physical constraints. Appl. Sci. **10**(17), 5917 (2020)
7. Guo, Y., Cao, X., Liu, B., Peng, K.: El niño index prediction using deep learning with ensemble empirical mode decomposition. Symmetry **12**(6), 893 (2020)
8. Guo, Y., Cao, X., Peng, K.: Solving nonlinear soliton equations using improved physics-informed neural networks with adaptive mechanisms. Commun. Theor. Phys. (2023)
9. Lamb, K., Warn-Varnas, A.: Two-dimensional numerical simulations of shoaling internal solitary waves at the ASIAEX site in the South China Sea. Nonlinear Process. Geophys. **22**(3), 289–312 (2015)
10. Raissi, M., Perdikaris, P., Karniadakis, G.E.: Physics-informed neural networks: a deep learning framework for solving forward and inverse problems involving nonlinear partial differential equations. J. Comput. Phys. **378**, 686–707 (2019)
11. Sirignano, J., Spiliopoulos, K.: DGM: a deep learning algorithm for solving partial differential equations. J. Comput. Phys. **375**, 1339–1364 (2018)
12. Skipetrov, S., Van Tiggelen, B.: Dynamics of weakly localized waves. Phys. Rev. Lett. **92**(11), 113901 (2004)

13. Sukhorukov, A.A., Kivshar, Y.S.: Nonlinear localized waves in a periodic medium. Phys. Rev. Lett. **87**(8), 083901 (2001)
14. Xiang, Z., Peng, W., Liu, X., Yao, W.: Self-adaptive loss balanced physics-informed neural networks. Neurocomputing **496**, 11–34 (2022)
15. Yu, J., Lu, L., Meng, X., Karniadakis, G.E.: Gradient-enhanced physics-informed neural networks for forward and inverse PDE problems. Comput. Methods Appl. Mech. Eng. **393**, 114823 (2022)

Causal Interpretability and Uncertainty Estimation in Mixture Density Networks

Gokul Swamy⊙, Arunita Das(✉)⊙, and Shobhit Niranjan

Amazon, Seattle, WA 98170, USA
{swagokul,arunita,shobhnir}@amazon.com

Abstract. Neural network implementations have predominantly been a black box lacking both in interpretability and estimation of uncertainty. In this study, we propose a novel causal attribution methodology for mixture density networks wherein we outline a framework to compute the causal effect of each feature on the target variable along with the associated uncertainty in the attribution. Our approach allows for the prediction and causal estimation tasks, along with the uncertainty estimation, to be integrated within the same architecture thus obviating the need to train a separate causal model. We report experimental results on two real-world problems comprising of studying the causal impact of bio markers on diabetes progression and the causal impact of certain key features on ecommerce sales. We also evaluate our approach on an open source simulated dataset and compare our results against multiple state-of-the-art baselines.

Keywords: Causality · Neural Network · Mixture Density Network

1 Introduction

Most (deep) neural network implementations in practice continue to be black-boxes with scant regard for model interpretability and output stochasticity. This has led to low adoption of these techniques in sensitive arenas such as banking and finance etc. In other instances, deep learning models have fallen foul of fairness standards which could have been thwarted had model interpretability been incorporated into the architecture [8]. Furthermore, traditional neural network models are trained to yield conditional mean estimates (especially in the regression setting) without estimating associated confidence bounds. It is pertinent to estimate the uncertainty in the target predictions as these estimates can help the practitioner implement a robust decisioning system that can for example preclude a treatment being applied to an instance where the uncertainty in the estimate is high. Several works have focused on uncertainty estimation in neural networks through either learning probability distributions [4] of the target variable or through sampling based approaches [16]. Interpretability has also

---

Supported by Amazon.

L. Iliadis et al. (Eds.): ICANN 2023, LNCS 14258, pp. 243–254, 2023.
https://doi.org/10.1007/978-3-031-44192-9_20

received a lot of attention in the recent past with a slew of methods proposed to solve this problem [12,19]. While these methodologies work well for a large number of scenarios, the feature importance doled out by these algorithms do not constitute a "causal estimate". Further, Sundararajan et al., [21] presented a set of two axiomatic properties, sensitivity and implementation invariance, that are desirable for any attribution framework and showed that gradient based attribution methods violate the sensitivity criterion while surrogate methods suffer from not being implementation invariant. In causal estimation, we seek to understand the influence of a particular feature on the target variable when adjusted for the confounders [13]. In the absence of a causal estimate, the feature attributions generated by these algorithms could sometimes lead to grossly erroneous conclusions. There are multiple algorithms for causal estimation which involve training a separate causal model such as propensity score matching [15], doubly robust regression [14], double ML [6] and more recently the causal forest [2] and generalized random forest [1] algorithms. In the context of neural networks, a few approaches have been proposed such as DragonNet [18], TarNet [17], NedNet [17], etc. that aim to combine the prediction and causal estimation within the same architecture. However, these methods are only suitable for binary treatment regimes and are also somewhat more optimized for the causal estimation task as opposed to the prediction task.

In this study, we present an approach towards estimating the causal impact of each feature in a neural network on a target variable basis a pre-trained prediction model. Our main contributions in this work include:

- We propose a unified model using a mixture density network towards combining the prediction task, output uncertainty prediction and the causal attribution of each feature on the target variable without the need for training a separate causal model.
- The model can generate the causal impact of a feature on the target variable with very little computational overhead.
- Our methodology estimates the associated uncertainty bounds around the causal estimates. The uncertainty bounds are especially pertinent when training in a few-shot setting i.e., low data domains.

The rest of this paper is organized as follows: In Sect. 2, we outline our proposed methodology for causal impact estimation from mixture density networks and in Sect. 3, we highlight the performance of our methodology on two real-world datasets and a benchmark simulated dataset from the public domain. Finally in Sect. 4, we conclude our work and outline scope for future research.

2   Methodology

2.1   Task Definition

Let us denote the problem domain to consist of a set of n features X as $\{x_1, ..., x_n\}$, where the problem involves mapping the function $y = f(X)$. Given this setting, our goal is to develop the causal relationship between x_i and y $\forall i \in \{1, .., n\}$ along with the associated uncertainty in the estimates. In order to characterize this uncertainty we model the regression problem using a mixture density network (MDN). For the sake of completeness we briefly elaborate on the MDN in the next subsection and detail our causal estimation framework using MDN as the base architecture in subsequent subsections.

2.2   Mixture Density Network

Mixture density networks are trained to output the parameters of a mixture density for every model input. For example, in the case of Gaussian mixtures (GMM), the model would output the mixing coefficients (π), the variances (σ) and the means (μ) of each of the constituents in the GMM. The loss function for the MDN is usually the likelihood of the data under the predicted distribution and is given by:

$$\arg_{\theta^*} \min l(\theta^*) = -\frac{1}{|\mathbb{D}|} \sum_{(x,y) \in \mathbb{D}} \log p(h(x)|x) \tag{1}$$

In the remainder of this text we will reference the Gaussian mixture density model using the functional form f_{s_i} with the subscript s_i indicating the ith mixture component of either the mean (μ_i), the variance (σ_i) or the mixing coefficient (π_i). In the simplest case, the mixture density network can be trained to output the mean (f_μ) and standard deviation (f_σ) of a uni-modal Gaussian distribution of the target variable. We derive the causal framework for this simple case and subsequently extend it for multi-modal Gaussian mixtures.

Causal Attribution Uni-Modal Gaussian MDN. We define the average causal attribution of an input feature x_i on the output y as (see [5]):

$$G^y_{x_i=\alpha} = \mathbb{E}[y|do(x_i = \alpha)] - b_{x_i} \tag{2}$$

here the $do(.)$ operator [13] indicates the causal dependence wherein x_i is an intervened variable forced to take on the value α, as opposed to the Bayesian dependence given by $\mathbb{E}[y|x_i = \alpha]$, where x_i is observed and takes on the value α in accordance with the data distribution. b_{x_i} is some chosen baseline against which the intervention is measured. In the case of a GMM with a single mixture component we can define the average causal estimate to be the expectation of the mean given by:

$$CE^{ATE}_{x_i=\alpha} = \mathbb{E}[\mu_y|do(x_i = \alpha)] - b_{x_i} \tag{3}$$

One possible approach to estimate $G^{\mu_y}_{x_i=\alpha}$ would be to perform a summation over μ_y while sampling all possible states of the input features $\{x_1, ..., x_{i-1}, x_{i+1}, ..., x_n\}$ keeping $x_i = \alpha$. This of course is not computationally feasible even for modestly sized datasets when multiple such computations are desired. To overcome this limitation, we can perform a Taylor expansion of the mixture density network around $\mu_x = \{\mu_{x1}, ..., \mu_{xn}\}$, with μ_{xj} being given as: $\mu_{xj} = \mathbb{E}[x_j|x_i = \alpha]$, to yield:

$$f_\mu(z) = f_\mu(\mu_x) + \nabla^T f_\mu(\mu_x)(z - \mu_x) + \frac{1}{2}(z - \mu_x)^T \nabla^2 f_\mu(\mu_x)(z - \mu_x) + ... \quad (4)$$

Ignoring the higher order terms, marginalising the input features (except for x_i) and computing the expectation we get:

$$CE_{x_i=\alpha}^{ATE} = \mathbb{E}[f_\mu(z)|do(x_i = \alpha)] \quad (5)$$

$$\approx f_\mu(\mu_x) + \frac{1}{2}Tr(\nabla^2 f_\mu(\mu_x)\mathbb{E}[(z - \mu_x)(z - \mu_x)^T|do(x_i = \alpha)]$$

If we make the assumption that none of the inputs are causally related to each other (they could still be correlated) then the causal dependence $\mu_{xj} = \mathbb{E}[x_j|do(x_i = \alpha)]$ boils down to $\mu_{xj} = \mathbb{E}[x_j]$. This causal independence allows for the means and the covariance matrices in Eq. (5) to be precomputed resulting in fast computations of the average causal effect of all the features taking on any continuous value within the allowable range. In several instances, the average causal estimate does not suffice to completely characterize the impact of a feature value/treatment on a target variable. As an example, while a drug may exhibit a good average treatment effect, it might so happen that the drug does not result in any treatment effect being observed in 20% of the population. While it is possible to infer such findings using methodologies aimed at estimating individual causal effects (ICE), such approaches have several pitfalls including the requirement for a separate model to be learnt to infer the ICE and also the inability to use a single model to estimate the causal impact from a large set of features. In order to overcome these limitations and estimate the uncertainty bounds around the average causal estimate of any of the desired features we make note of the Quantile function of the Gaussian distribution given by:

$$l_p = inf\{x \in \mathbb{R} : F(x) \geq p\} = \mu + \sigma(\sqrt{2} * erf^{-1}(2p - 1)) \quad (6)$$

where $F(x)$ is the cumulative distribution function of the Gaussian distribution and $erf^{-1}(.)$ is the inverse error function. By performing an interventional expectation on the pth percentile we can estimate the causal uncertainty bounds as:

$$CE_{x_i=\alpha}^{lb} = \mathbb{E}[l_{p_{low}}|do(x_i = \alpha)] - b_{x_i} \quad (7)$$

$$CE_{x_i=\alpha}^{ub} = \mathbb{E}[l_{p_{high}}|do(x_i = \alpha)] - b_{x_i}$$

Once again, we can approximate the function for the pth percentile using a Taylor expansion around μ_x and take the interventional expectation to obtain:

$$CE_{x_i=\alpha}^{lb} \approx f_{lb}(\mu_x) + \frac{1}{2}Tr(\nabla^2 f_{lb}(\mu_x)\mathbb{E}[(z - \mu_x)(z - \mu_x)^T|do(x_i = \alpha)] \quad (8)$$

$$CE_{x_i=\alpha}^{ub} \approx f_{ub}(\mu_x) + \frac{1}{2}Tr(\nabla^2 f_{ub}(\mu_x)\mathbb{E}[(z - \mu_x)(z - \mu_x)^T|do(x_i = \alpha)]$$

with

$$f_{lb/ub}(x) = f_\mu(x) + f_\sigma(x) * (\sqrt{2} * erf^{-1}(2p_{low/high} - 1)) \qquad (9)$$

It is straightforward to compute (8) as the data covariance remains invariant under μ_x and the terms $f_{lb/ub}(\mu_x)$ and $\nabla^2 f_{lb/ub}(\mu_x)$ can be easily computed using Eq. (9) through plugging in the appropriate input and employing gradient back propagation for computing the Hessian. While we have discussed the estimation of the average causal effect so far, it is also possible to compute the conditional average treatment effect (CATE) given by:

$$CE^{CATE}_{x_i=\alpha} = \mathbb{E}[\mu_y|X = x, do(x_i = \alpha)] - b_{x_i} \qquad (10)$$

by setting $\mu_x = X$ in Eq. (5) and performing a Taylor expansion of the neural network around the conditional mean of the input features. The uncertainity bounds for the CATE can be estimated in a similar manner using Eqs. (6) to (9).

Causal Attribution for the Multi-modal Gaussian MDN. In several instances a unimodal distribution is insufficient to characterize the target distribution and it is required to have more than one mixture component to better characterize the output stochasticity. The output of a MDN employing a GMM, with multiple mixture components, comprises of the set $[\pi_i, \mu_i, \sigma_i] \; \forall \; i \in \{1, 2...M\}$ where M is the number of mixtures in the GMM. For a multi-modal Gaussian mixture model we define the average causal estimate to be the interventional expectation of the target mean given by:

$$CE^{ATE}_{x_i=\alpha} = \mathbb{E}[\mu_y|do(x_i = \alpha)] - b_{x_i} \qquad (11)$$

where, $\mu_y = \sum_{i=1}^{M} \pi_i \mu_i$, is the mean of the Gaussian Mixture. As before, μ_y can be approximated using a Taylor expansion and the interventional expectation can be computed similar to Eq. (5). In order to estimate the uncertainty around the average causal estimate it is required to obtain the Quantile function (l_p) for the Gaussian Mixture. Unlike the uni-modal case the Quantile function for the GMM does not have a closed form analytic expression. In order to overcome this impediment, we model l_p as a feed forward neural network (f_p) with the input to this network being the outputs of the MDN and the percentile p. A permutation of the mixture components has no bearing on the underlying distribution and therefore the proposed feed forward network must be invariant to the permutations of the input space. In order to incorporate this property into our network, we make use of the deep set architecture defined in [23] wherein the feed forward neural network is constrained to have the following form:

$$h(.) = \rho(\sum_{i=1}^{M} \phi(\beta_i)) \qquad (12)$$

where β_i is the vector $[\pi_i, \mu_i, \sigma_i, p]$ and $\beta = \cup_{i=1}^{M}\{\beta_i\}$. The function $\phi : \mathbb{R}^{4\times1} \to \mathbb{R}^{n_h \times 1}$ can be thought of as a distinct neural network with a 4×1 input and

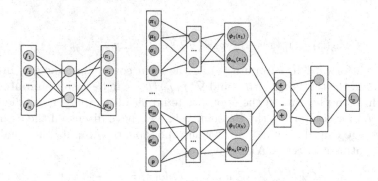

Fig. 1. Left (pink): Representation of a mixture density network (MDN) with M-mixtures. Right (orange): A permutation invariant Quantile prediction network with the distribution parameters as the input. (Color figure online)

a $n_h \times 1$ output. ϕ is applied to each individual element in the set β and the results are aggregated before passing it through additional layers of a neural network defined by ρ. The overall architecture of the MDN and its extension towards predicting the value of the pth GMM quantile is depicted in Fig. 1. Given the approximation for the quantile function, we can easily compute the uncertainty bounds around the average causal estimate using Eq. (8) while replacing $f_{lb/ub}$ with the feed forward network f_p and using gradient back propagation to compute the hessian $\nabla^2 f_p(\mu_x)$. In the next section we highlight the results of our approach on two real-world datasets from the e-commerce and healthcare domains and subsequently compare our results against multiple state-of-the-art baselines using the benchmark IHDP causal inferencing dataset.

3   Results

3.1   Baselines

We compare the proposed approach (Causal MDN) against multiple baselines including causal forest double machine learning (DML) [1], DragonNet [18], TarNet [17] and NedNet [18] causal inferencing architectures. DragonNet, TarNet and NedNet are neural network based causal estimation architectures that combine the outcome prediction and the causal estimation within the same architecture while the causal forest DML algorithm requires training a separate model for estimating the causal attribution of each feature. However, since the DragonNet, TarNet and NedNet baselines are only suitable for a binary treatment regime, we use the causal forest DML algorithm as a baseline for the two real-world problems and do a full comparison of all the baselines on the benchmark synthetic IHDP dataset [11].

3.2   Causal Impact of Bio-Markers in Diabetes Progression

In this section, we test the robustness of our approach on an external diabetes dataset [9] consisting of 442 data samples. The feature set comprises of ten features and one target variable indicative of disease progression after one year. The input features and the target variable are all normalized to lie in the range of [0, 1] and the baseline is set to 0.5 for all the features. We train a MDN model on this dataset with two hidden layers of size 64 and 32 followed by ReLU activation. The final layer is an MDN layer outputting the parameters of a uni-modal Gaussian distribution ($M = 1$). We employ the proposed methodology to ascertain the average causal estimate and the associated uncertainty for each of the features as in the previous section. We compare our method against the state-of-the-art double machine learning (DML) based causal forest estimator [1] by measuring the average treatment effect (ATE) for each feature taking on values in the range [0, 1] against a baseline of 0.5. The data generating process for a DML estimator is given by:

$$y = \theta(x) * T + g(x) + \epsilon, \ T = m(x) + \eta$$

where T is the treatment variable set to the feature of interest and g(.) and m(.) are chosen to be random forest regressors. The ATE can then be estimated by computing the expectation:

$$ATE(t) = E[y(T = t) - y(T = baseline)] \forall t \in [0, 1] \tag{13}$$

It must be noted that in DML, the effect model between the outcome and treatment is linear. The Microsoft EconML [3] package was used for training the DML causal forest estimator and required training of ten separate models to characterize the causal impact of each of the ten features with the remaining features comprising of the confounder set.

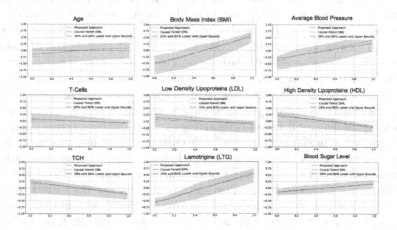

Fig. 2. Average Causal Estimate along with the uncertainty for different interventions of the features in the Diabetes progression prediction problem

The plots in Fig. 2 depict the average causal estimate and the 20% and 80% uncertainty bounds for each of the features along with the causal estimates from the causal forest DML algorithm (red line). The causal estimates from the pretrained MDN network closely mirror the causal estimates from the dedicated causal models. Table 1 captures the root-mean-squared errors between the causal estimates from the proposed method and the Causal Forest DML methodology.

It is also apparent from the plot that BMI has the highest causal impact with an increasing BMI being suggestive of more rapid disease progression. This correlates well with clinical literature as detailed in [10]. The variance in the causal estimate, with BMI as the intervened feature, is higher for lower BMI's and decreases with increasing BMI. This finding is corroborated by clinical studies [7] which found a strong correlation between variance of glucose increase with decreasing BMI ($p - value \approx 0.02$). Clinical literature studies also indicate a higher risk of diabetes progression with increasing arterial blood pressures [22], increasing LTG and decreasing levels of LDL and HDL proteins [7]. A mild increase in risk has also been observed with increasing age [10]. These trends are evident in our causal estimates as can be visualized from Fig. 2.

Table 1. RMSE of Causal MDN against Causal Forest DML

Feature Name	Age	BMI	BP	T-cells	LDL	HDL	TCH	LTG	Blood Sugar Level
RMSE	0.063	0.035	0.058	0.011	0.084	0.057	0.024	0.036	0.021

3.3 Causal Impact of a Key Feature on Downstream Customer Spends

In most instances ecommerce deliveries are unattended wherein the package is left outside the customers door without the customer being physically present to receive the shipment. However, in certain instances where there is a high propensity of a shipment being lost or a shipment containing high-value contents it is required of the customer to physically receive the shipment (attended delivery). This requirement adds friction to the delivery process and in this study we are primarily concerned with estimating the causal impact of the percentage of attended deliveries on a customers one-month downstream spend. The base model for predicting a customers downstream spend comprises of the transformer architecture for tabular data proposed in [20] with the final layer being replaced with a mixture density network comprising of a uni-modal mixture component. The input to the model comprises of 180 customer level features involving the customers past spends, frequently shopped categories, percentage of attended deliveries, payment means adopted, etc. The layer wise details of the model architecture are shown in Fig. 3. The plots in Fig. 4 show the causal trends for two selected features (past spends and attended delivery percentage) along with the associated uncertainties. The red lines are the estimates from the doubly debiased causal forest methodology wherein a causal model was trained separately for each feature as in the previous example. While the causal estimates

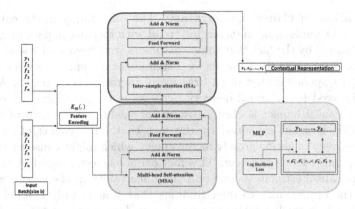

Fig. 3. The transformer architecture adapted from [20] for predicting downstream spend

for the attended delivery treatment are very close, there is a significant deviation for the past spends feature primarily on account of the causal forest DML algorithm mapping the estimates to a linear trend. We compare the computation time of two approaches on a d2.8xlarge AWS cloud instance. Our method while directly operating on the pre-trained MDN architecture was 71x faster than having to train a causal forest DML algorithm from scratch thus offering a significant benefit for practical applications with stringent computational and latency constraints.

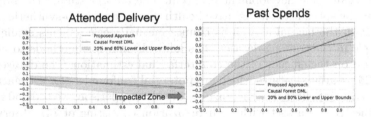

Fig. 4. Average Causal Estimate along with the uncertainty for two key features. The impacted zone in the lower bound of the causal uncertainty arises from customers who are more negatively impacted by the proposed treatment

A look at the causal attribution graph for the past spends indicates that past spends are highly causative of future spends which is to be expected. Causal attribution from the attended delivery feature is indicative of the fact that a majority of the customers are largely agnostic of how they receive their packages. However, the small negative slope might imply some customers tend to reduce their spends when faced with repeated attended deliveries as they may find the experience inconvenient.

Interpretation of Causal Uncertainty. The uncertainty in the causal estimates for past spends show an increasing trend with increase in past spends. This can be explained by the fact that some customers with high past spends tend to either lower or increase their spends by a significant amount whereas customers with low past spends do not often drastically increase their spends. A similar trend is observed for attended delivery percentage feature where a larger variance in the causal impact is observed with increasing percentages of attended delivery. This is again explained by the fact that for a cohort of customers, attended delivery might be grossly inconvenient which might cause them to curtail their spends to a large extent. This fact cannot be established by looking at the average causal estimates alone and the uncertainty in the causal estimates allows us the opportunity to infer findings that impact only a much smaller cohort and take remedial actions to prevent a detrimental outcome. We used the CATE estimation proposed in Eq. (10) to identify this customer cohort and adjusted our policies to minimize the attended delivery percentage for this customer cohort while simultaneously optimizing for the costs incurred on account of lost packages. Basis a randomized trial we were able to measure a 10 basis points improvement (p value ≤ 0.005) in customer downstream spends leading to a significant increase in sales revenue (not disclosed) basis the proposed intervention.

3.4 ATE Estimation for the Benchmark IHDP Dataset

In order to evaluate our algorithm on a public benchmark, we make use of the popular IHDP dataset [11]. IHDP is a semi-syntehtic dataset constructed from the infant health and development program. The dataset studies the impact of home visits by specialists on cognitive health. Given its a semi-synthetic dataset we have both the factual as well as counterfactual measurements available for each sample in the training dataset thus allowing multiple methods to be compared based on the efficacy of the counterfactual estimation. The dataset comprises of 26 covariate features which are potential confounders for estimating the average treatment effect. For the purpose of this comparison, we took 50 realizations of the IHDP dataset with each realization consisting of 747 observations and compute the ATE for each of these realizations basis the proposed method, DragonNet, TarNet, NedNet and causal forest DML architectures. The results of our experiment are summarized in Fig. 5 and in Table 2 where it is evident that the Causal MDN is able to outperform the other baselines by a significant margin. The blue shaded area in Fig. 5 represents the uncertainty bounds in the ATE estimate and interestingly the uncertainty bounds are larger when the error between the actual and predicted ATE (from the proposed approach) is higher (e.g., DATASET ID# 2, 5, 14, 21, 28) thus indicating that the proposed model is able to accurately characterize the uncertainty in the causal estimate which can be used to guide the final decisioning.

Table 2. RMSE of Causal MDN Vs Baselines for IHDP Dataset

Model	Causal MDN	Dragonnet	Tarnet	Nednet	Causal Forest DML
Overall RMSE	**0.22**	0.45	0.58	0.71	0.86

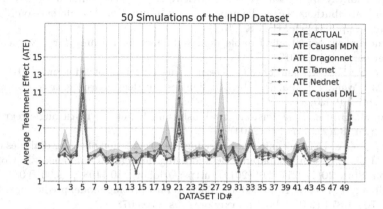

Fig. 5. ATE plot for 50 Simulations of the IHDP Dataset

4   Conclusion

In this study we have presented a novel causal estimation algorithm enabling the twin pillars of causal interpretability and uncertainty prediction for a host of applications. The proposed model works by approximating the neural network using a second order Taylor expansion and employing a mixture density network architecture to model the underlying uncertainty in the causal estimates. The proposed architecture does not require a separate causal model to be learnt for every feature and is capable of generating the causal estimates for the entire set of features (or any desired set of features) with minimal computational overload thus making it highly suited for many practical applications with computational and latency constraints. Also, while other contemporary models are able to generate uncertainty estimates using bootstrap aggregation or Monte Carlo sampling, our approach elegantly blends the uncertainty estimation within the proposed network architecture. We have compared our method against multiple state-of-the-art baselines and show that our method is superior both in terms of predictive performance as well as computational efficiency. Finally, our methodology is not limited to the mixture density network alone and can be adapted to other architectures where the prediction function is continuous and differentiable.

References

1. Athey, S., Tibshirani, J., Wager, S.: Generalized random forests. Ann. Stat. **47**(2), 1148–1178 (2019). https://doi.org/10.1214/18-AOS1709
2. Athey, S., Wager, S.: Estimating treatment effects with causal forests: an application (2019)

3. Battocchi, K., et al.: EconML: a python package for ml-based heterogeneous treatment effects estimation (2019). https://github.com/microsoft/EconML. Version 0.x
4. Bishop, C.M.: Mixture density networks. Technical report (1994)
5. Chattopadhyay, A., Manupriya, P., Sarkar, A., Balasubramanian, V.N.: Neural network attributions: a causal perspective. In: International Conference on Machine Learning, pp. 981–990. PMLR (2019)
6. Chernozhukov, V., et al.: Double/debiased machine learning for treatment and causal parameters (2017)
7. Das, R.N.: Diabetes and obesity determinants based on blood serum (2018)
8. Du, M., Yang, F., Zou, N., Hu, X.: Fairness in deep learning: a computational perspective (2020)
9. Efron, B., Hastie, T., Johnstone, I., Tibshirani, R., et al.: Least angle regression. Ann. Stat. 32(2), 407–499 (2004)
10. Fonseca, V.A.: Defining and characterizing the progression of type 2 diabetes (2009)
11. Hill, J.L.: Bayesian nonparametric modeling for causal inference. J. Comput. Graph. Stat. 20(1), 217–240 (2011). https://doi.org/10.1198/jcgs.2010.08162
12. Lundberg, S., Lee, S.: A unified approach to interpreting model predictions. CoRR abs/1705.07874 (2017). http://arxiv.org/abs/1705.07874
13. Pearl, J.: Causality. Cambridge University Press, Cambridge (2009)
14. Robins, J., Sued, M., Lei-Gomez, Q., Rotnitzky, A.: Double-robust and efficient methods for estimating the causal effects of a binary treatment (2020)
15. Rubin, D.B., Thomas, N.: Combining propensity score matching with additional adjustments for prognostic covariates. J. Am. Stat. Assoc. 95(450), 573–585 (2000)
16. Schupbach, J., Sheppard, J.W., Forrester, T.: Quantifying uncertainty in neural network ensembles using U-statistics. In: 2020 International Joint Conference on Neural Networks (IJCNN), pp. 1–8 (2020). https://doi.org/10.1109/IJCNN48605.2020.9206810
17. Shalit, U., Johansson, F.D., Sontag, D.: Estimating individual treatment effect: generalization bounds and algorithms (2016). https://doi.org/10.48550/ARXIV.1606.03976, https://arxiv.org/abs/1606.03976
18. Shi, C., Blei, D.M., Veitch, V.: Adapting neural networks for the estimation of treatment effects (2019). https://doi.org/10.48550/ARXIV.1906.02120, https://arxiv.org/abs/1906.02120
19. Shrikumar, A., Greenside, P., Kundaje, A.: Learning important features through propagating activation differences. CoRR abs/1704.02685 (2017). http://arxiv.org/abs/1704.02685
20. Somepalli, G., Goldblum, M., Schwarzschild, A., Bruss, C.B., Goldstein, T.: SAINT: improved neural networks for tabular data via row attention and contrastive pre-training. CoRR abs/2106.01342 (2021). https://arxiv.org/abs/2106.01342
21. Sundararajan, M., Taly, A., Yan, Q.: Axiomatic attribution for deep networks (2017)
22. Tsimihodimos, V., Gonzalez-Villalpando, C., Meigs, J.B., Ferrannini, E.: Hypertension and diabetes mellitus (2003)
23. Zaheer, M., Kottur, S., Ravanbakhsh, S., Poczos, B., Salakhutdinov, R., Smola, A.: Deep sets (2018)

Connectionist Temporal Sequence Decoding: M-ary Hopfield Neural-Network with Multi-limit Cycle Formulation

Vandana M. Ladwani[1,2]([✉])[iD] and V. Ramasubramanian[1][iD]

[1] International Institute of Information Technology Bangalore (IIIT-B),
Bangalore, India
{vandana.ladwani,v.ramasubramanian}@iiitb.ac.in
[2] PES University, Bangalore, India

Abstract. Recently, we have proposed a novel M-ary (multi-level) Hopfield neural-network (MHNN) based auto-associative memory formulation for storage and retrieval of variable length sequences. This formulation modeled variable length sequences in a M-ary Hopfield network in the form of multiple variable length limit cycles. In the current paper, we extend this limit cycle formulation and propose a novel 'connectionist temporal sequence decoding' algorithm to solve the generic 'temporal sequence decoding' problem (which is the central decoding process in sequence-to-sequence learning tasks such as automatic speech recognition (ASR), movie scene recognition (MSR) etc.). Here, we model multiple prototype movie sub-sequences (scenes) of variable lengths from a given vocabulary as multiple limit cycles of a single MHNN of size 10000 neurons (and 100 million interconnection weights) and apply the proposed decoding algorithm. The proposed algorithm, uses the trained MHNN model along with Hopfield energy based End-of-Sequence markers to decode a very long noisy movie scene (comprising sub-sequence scenes with non-linear temporal and statistical variability). The proposed method solves the movie scene segmentation and labelling task with zero error. We note that this is a first of its kind solution in associative-memory based formulation using multi-level multi-limit cycle Hopfield networks for realization of such a 'connectionist temporal sequence decoding', representing a pleasing solution with biological-realism for such sequence decoding problems, which are conventionally solved by dynamic programming frameworks such as Viterbi decoding and finite-state networks in ASR kind of problems.

Keywords: M-ary Hopfield neural-network · Multi-limit cycle · Connectionist temporal sequence decoding · Dual-Weight learning · Two-Stage firing

L. Iliadis et al. (Eds.): ICANN 2023, LNCS 14258, pp. 255–268, 2023.
https://doi.org/10.1007/978-3-031-44192-9_21

1   Introduction

We propose a biologically plausible solution for the 'temporal sequence decoding' problem using multi-limit cycle M-ary Hopfield neural network (MHNN) trained on K variable length subsequences. We first introduce our work on multi-limit cycle MHNN formulation in Sect. 1.1, define connectionist temporal sequence decoding in Sect. 1.2, briefly describe in Sect. 1.3 conventional temporal sequence decoding approaches and in Sect. 1.4, we outline our contribution to solve the problem of 'temporal sequence decoding' on a long test sequence using multi-limit cycle MHNN, in what we term as the 'connectionist temporal sequence decoding' framework.

1.1   Multi-limit Cycle MHNN

In our recent work in [6], we proposed a basic formulation required to store and retrieve K variable-length prototypical sub-sequences of vectors in MHNN using a coupled weight learning procedure involving two kind of weights: i) Transition weights that allow the MHNN to switch synchronously from one state of the limit cycle to the next, and ii) Static weights that allow the MHNN to converge and stabilize into an attractor well (basin) corresponding to the state mapping to the input vector at a specific time-instant of the input vector sequence being retrieved. In order to retrieve the stored sequences we used a Two-Stage retrieval 'firing' procedure comprising a i) Synchronous firing rule governed by the transition weights to respond to an input vector to transit to a new attractor well, and ii) Asynchronous firing rule governed by the static weights to let the MHNN roll down the attractor well to stabilize to a stored vector as the retrieved state corresponding to the input vector cue. The weight learning and retrieval dynamics proposed by us in [6] allow handling of input vector sequences for retrieval under non-linear temporal variability and vector errors. In the present paper, we extend this framework further for generic temporal sequence decoding (optimal segmentation and labeling problem) and validate this in a movie scene segmentation and labeling setting (and potentially applicable to other sequence decoding settings such as automatic speech recognition etc.).

1.2   Temporal Sequence Decoding

This is a joint segmentation/labeling problem involving

- Finding an 'optimal' segmentation of a long input test sequence into P contiguous segments with segment boundaries that define each segment and
- Finding an 'optimal' labeling of each segment from a vocabulary of K subsequences. (The input test sequence is made of variants of these prototypical sub-sequences under non-linear temporal variability and vector-errors (statistical variability).

Figure 1(a) illustrates this temporal sequence decoding problem. We are given a vocabulary of stored original (prototypical) sub-sequences $V = (\Xi^1, \Xi^2, \ldots, \Xi^k \ldots, \Xi^K)$, where the kth vocabulary entry in V is a sub-sequence Ξ^k of length L_k. An input 'test' vector sequence denoted as $T = (\xi_1, \ldots \xi_L)$ is made of P^* (with $P^* << L$) 'variants' of these prototypical sub-sequences arranged in some arbitrary order. The notion of 'variants' corresponds to the scenario where the prototypical sub-sequence used in the input test sequence are subject to non-linear temporal variability and vector-errors (statistical variability) when occurring in the test sequence.

The temporal sequence decoding problem involves segmenting the input test vector sequence $T = (\xi_1, \ldots \xi_L)$ into hypothesized P sub-sequences, indexed as $Q = (q_1, q_2, \ldots, q_p, \ldots, q_P)$; the segment boundaries of the P resulting hypothesized segments are defined as $B = [(b_1, e_1), \ldots, (b_p, e_p), \ldots (b_P, e_P)]$ with the segment length of the pth segment $l_p = e_p - b_p + 1$ and boundary conditions $b_1 = 1$ and $b_p = e_{p-1} + 1$ and $e_P = L$. The decoding (or the joint segmentation and labeling) has to obtain the optimal solution (P^*, B^*, Q^*) under some criterion from a combinatorially large hypothesis space of (P, B, Q). Note that the segment p in the decoding solution is mapped to stored sub-sequence q_p, i.e., Ξ^{q_p} and the length l_p of the segment p is in general different from the length L_{q_p} of its stored counterpart Ξ^{q_p}, due to non-linear temporal variability (characterized by I/D errors here).

1.3   Conventional Approaches to Temporal Sequence Decoding

There have been a class of conventional solutions for solving the temporal sequence decoding as defined above, all typically based on dynamic-programming (DP) principles; for example, most of these solutions evolved from the classic 'automatic speech recognition' (ASR) problem of decoding input speech in the form of a long sequence of feature vectors into a sequence of words or linguistic-units (such as phones, sub-words, words etc.) that comprise the vocabulary V of the ASR system. This vocabulary V can typically comprise a set of words (typically large), in a Large Vocabulary Continuous Speech Recognition (or LVCSR system) each modeled by DTW (dynamic-time-warping) templates or stochastic generative models such as HMMs (hidden Markov models). An input speech feature vector sequence T (as defined above) is made of some arbitrary word-sequences (e.g. 'John is good'). Here, the ASR decoding problems recovers $P^* = 3$, $Q^* = ($'John', 'is', 'good'$)$ and $B^* = (b_1, e_1), (b_2, e_2), (b_3, e_3)$, while optimizing a DP matching error or HMM log-likelihood. There is a large body of work [8] for these ASR acoustic modeling and decoding techniques, such as for example, model-based techniques based on DTW, HMM, 2-pass DP, Level Building, 1-pass DP, Viterbi decoding, finite-state networks as well as model-free segmentation/labeling techniques, and more recently, techniques such as CTC (connectionist temporal classification) prefix-decoding in deep-learning end-to-end (E2E) ASR frameworks [3].

1.4 Connectionist Temporal Sequence Decoding Using Multi-limit Cycle MHNN

We adapt the MHNN with K variable length limit cycles as described in Sect. 1.1 and propose a decoding algorithm to perform 'connectionist temporal sequence decoding' on a long test sequence. A 'test sequence' is defined as a concatenation of the prototypical sub-sequences in arbitrary order, with each sub-sequence subject to non-linear temporal variability and vector errors - e.g. characterized in the present work by Insertion/Deletion/Substitution (or I/D/S for short) errors with respect to the original stored sub-sequence. In our work, we create 'models' of the K entries (sub-sequences) in vocabulary V as variable length limit cycles in a single MHNN as shown in Fig. 1(c) and use it to 'decode' T to recover (P^*, B^*, Q^*) as close as possible to the ground truth, under non-linear temporal variability and statistical variability (vector errors), together modeled as I/D/S errors here. The proposed decoding algorithm is formulated to use the 'energy' associated with 'End-of-Sequence marker' states to determine the labels for the segments.

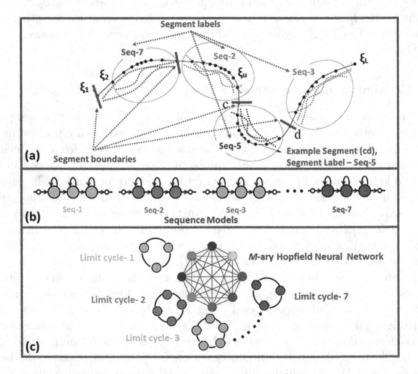

Fig. 1. Connectionist Temporal Sequence Decoding Process: (a) General decoding process (b) Conventional decoding approach based on sequence models (c) Multi-limit cycle M-ary Hopfield neural-network based decoding system (Proposed Approach)

We wish to note that our work here is a first of its kind attempt in proposing and realizing a biologically realistic decoding framework using an auto-associative M-ary Hopfield neural network. The proposed solutions can be qualitatively viewed as the input test sequence $\mathcal{T}$ being 'listened' to by a single MHNN which detects each sub-sequence by 'triggering' the corresponding limit cycle (among the multi-limit cycles stored in it) and switching from one limit cycle to the next as dictated by the input test vector sequence.

2 Hopfield Network Based Auto-associative Memory Formulations

An auto-associative network, when presented with partial/noisy input, possesses the capability to retrieve the complete information. The Hopfield network was first proposed by Hopfield [4,5] as an 'auto-associative memory' formalism and belongs to the class of neuro-dynamical systems which possesses 'attractors' which represent stable states of the network and which can be made to correspond to a set of patterns in what is called the 'storage' phase, and each of which can be subsequently retrieved by giving a partial or noisy pattern as input, in what is called the 'retrieval' phase. Hopfield network possesses two kinds of attractors, point attractors and limit cycles [2].

2.1 M-ary Hopfield Neural Network

Bijjani and Das [1] proposed M-ary Hopfield Neural Network model which is an extension of original bipolar hopfield network, it consists of neurons which can be in any of the M permissible states at a particular instant of time. They used hebbian learning rule to demonstrate storage of multivalued patterns (point attractors) and asynchronous firing to retrieve stored patterns with noisy queries. Hebbian learning limits the storage capacity of the network to $0.14N$ (where, N is the network size). In the present work, we explore limit cycles as opposed to point attractors and pseudo-inverse based high capacity learning rule to get scaled performance for sequence data [7].

2.2 Limit Cycles of Hopfield Network

Limit cycle is a closed trajectory of sequence of states. Limit cycles can be used to model sequence data such as for example i) a movie clip, where each frame in the movie clip represents a state of the limit cycle or ii) speech utterances as a sequence of feature vectors, where each feature vector (in some spectral representation of suitable dimensionality) represents a state of the limit cycle. Zhang et al. [9] proposed a Hopfield network for storing sequence data as limit cycles of the network. They demonstrated storage of 'very short synthetic bipolar' sequence in the limit cycle of the network using psuedo-inverse based learning rule given in Eq. (1). Synchronous firing mechanism was used to retrieve the stored sequence.

$$J = \frac{\beta_k}{2}(C_0 \varXi \varXi^+ + C_1 \varXi_1 \varXi^+) \tag{1}$$

where, $\Xi_1 = (\xi_2, \xi_3, \ldots, \xi_u, \ldots, \xi_L, \xi_1)$ and Ξ^+ represents the pseudo-inverse of Ξ; β_k, C_0 and C_1 are constants

3 Multi-limit Cycle M-ary HNN for Variable Length Sequences

In our recent work [6], we proposed multi-limit cycle M-ary Hopfield network for storage and retrieval of multiple sequences of variable lengths in limit cycles of a single network. The proposed system uses a Dual-Weight learning to train the network and a Two-Stage firing procedure to retrieve the stored sequence with partial or noisy query. During retrieval phase, we noted that the network cannot be fired for a fixed number (not known a priori) steps, for the case when the stored sequences are of variable length. In order to control the firing procedure, we therefore associated with each sequence a unique End-of-Sequence (EOS) marker state. The energy associated with this state is determined during the learning phase and is used during the retrieval phase to control the firing process and determine a 'stopping' criterion for detecting when the firing process can be terminated and obtain the retrieved sequence from the corresponding limit cycle.

3.1 Dual Coupling Strengths

In order to model the prototype sequences of variable lengths in limit cycles of a single network, the network needs to memorise information about

1. Task-1: Given a corrupted state, how to settle down to stable state for the correct limit cycle
2. Task-2: Given a stable state, how to transit to next state of the correct limit cycle

Consider K sequences $\Xi^1, \Xi^2, \ldots, \Xi^k, \ldots, \Xi^K$ of length $L_1, L_2, \ldots, L_k, \ldots, L_K$. A sequence Ξ^k is a sequence of vectors denoted as $\xi_1^k, \xi_2^k, \ldots, \xi_u^k, \ldots, \xi_v^k, \ldots, \xi_{L_k}^k$ where, ξ_u^k is a M-valued pattern vector of N elements (same as size of MHNN) which represents u^{th} vector of the kth sequence; i.e., ξ_{ui}^k represents the ith component of the uth vector of the kth sequence. We use Pseudo-Inverse based learning rule [7] to determine static and transition weights as it imparts high storage capacity($O(N)$) to the network. We thus maintain two different types of coupling strengths as opposed to single weight matrix used in Zhang's work [9].

Static Weight Learning. Static Weight matrix is used by the system during 'Task-1' above to converge to stable state by using asynchronous update. Static weight matrix is determined using pseudo-inverse based learning rule given by Eq. (2)

$$S_{ij} = \frac{1}{N} \sum_{k=1}^{K} \sum_{v=1}^{L_k} \sum_{u=1}^{L_k} \xi_{ui}^k (C^{-1})_{uv}^k \xi_{vj}^k \tag{2}$$

Transition Weight Learning. Transition weight matrix is used to accomplish 'Task2' to drive the network to the next state via synchronous update. Transition Weight matrix is determined by Eq. (3)

$$T_{ij} = \frac{1}{N} \sum_{k=1}^{K} \sum_{v=1}^{L_k} \sum_{u=1}^{L_k} \xi_{u'i}^{k} (C^{-1})_{uv}^{k} \xi_{vj}^{k} \qquad u' = (u+1) \mod L_k \qquad (3)$$

C^k is the co-variance matrix of Ξ^k.

3.2 Two-Stage Firing Mechanism

During weight learning procedure system memorizes information in the form of energy landscape. Two-Stage firing mechanism uses combination of synchronous and asynchronous firing which drive system state on the energy landscape to retrieve the stored sequence.

Asynchronous Firing. Asynchronous firing is an iterative procedure which drives the current state of the network to stable state configuration (point attractor) in the current basin of attraction. Given current state of the network, asynchronous firing changes network state by updating all the neurons but by selecting one at a time randomly. Asynchronous firing repeatedly performs the operations specified by Eq. (4) till it stabilises (no change in state with further firing). Equation (5) represents the updated state of the network.

$$h_i(t) = \sum_{j=1}^{N} S_{ij} x_j(t); \qquad x_i(t) = f(h_i(t)) \qquad (4)$$

At convergence

$$x_i(t+1) = x_i(t) \qquad (5)$$

Synchronous Firing. Synchronous-firing is used to drive the system from one basin of attraction to the next which marks inception of the transition in to next state from the current state. Synchronous-firing is given by Eq. (6)

$$h_i(t) = \sum_{j=1}^{N} T_{ij} x_j(t); \qquad x_i(t+1) = f(h_i(t)) \qquad (6)$$

where, $h_i(t)$ represents input potential to the ith neuron, $x_i(t+1)$ is the updated state of ith neuron and $f()$ is a staircase activation function. This is again followed by asynchronous firing to stabilize the network.

A sequence of synchronous and asynchronous firings enables the MHNN to retrieve a memorized sequence from minimal cue (e.g. a start state or intermediate state of the stored sub-sequence) constituting a limit cycle generalization to content-addressable memory formulation of the original Hopfield network on vector states.

3.3 End-of-Sequence (EOS) Marker Energies

Hopfield network associates a unique metric with each memorised state termed as energy which is given by Eq. (7)

$$E_u = -\frac{1}{2} \sum_{i=1}^{N} \sum_{j=1}^{N} S_{ij} x_i x_j \tag{7}$$

For each stored sub-sequence, the last state is marked with End-of-Sequence (EOS) marker. Energy for these markers is determined as per Eq. (7) using static weight matrix learnt during the weight learning phase. Sequence-id is assigned to these markers based on the sequence it belongs to. End-of-Sequence marker energies and their associated sequence ids are used to support retrieval of variable length sequences which are stored in a multi-limit cycle MHNN and this is extended to achieve connectionist temporal sequence decoding. Figure 2(a) shows 4 sub-sequences with EOS marker states, MHNN unit and associated energies.

3.4 Isolated Sequence Retrieval

Retrieval and identification of stored sequence from a particular state is depicted in Fig. 2(b). Given a particular state, in order to determine the sequence id to which the state belongs to, state is clamped on to neurons of multi-limit cycle MHNN sequence model and this MHNN is fired using a Two-Stage firing procedure to retrieve the next state. Energy associated with the state is determined using Eq. (7). This energy value is compared with End-of-Sequence marker energies to find best match within specified threshold, system repeats this process till a match is found (which represents reaching an EOS marker), trigger state is marked with the sequence-id associated with the matching End-of-Sequence marker.

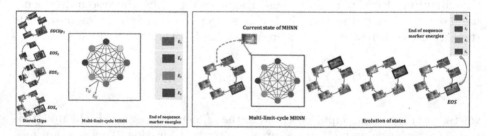

Fig. 2. (a) End-of-Sequence marker energies for variable length sequences stored in multi-limit cycle MHNN (b) Sequence identification using trained multi-limit cycle MHNN

4 Connectionist Temporal Sequence Decoding

In this section, we discuss decoding of a long connected temporal sequence. Examples of such sequence include a long movie sequence made of multiple scenes (clips), speech utterances (made of a sequence of phonemes or words, as in the ASR problem) etc. We first train multi-limit cycle MHNN to store variable length prototype sub-sequences using Dual-Weight learning procedure described in Sect. 3.1. Figure 3(b) shows a single multi-limit cycle MHNN trained on 4 variable length sub-sequences. Energies of End-of-Sequence (EOS) marker states are derived during the learning phase as per the formulation in Sect. 3.3 and these energies are depicted as color coded values. We then clamp each state of the 'input unsegmented noisy connected sequence' to be decoded to the trained network. Figure 3(a) shows such a sequence. The network starts switching its state using Two-Stage firing to retrieve a sub-sequence in response to the trigger state and this retrieval terminates once End-of-Sequence marker state is reached as shown in Fig. 3(c). In the worst case, the network fires for the duration equal to the length of the longest sub-sequence it has memorised and fails to get End-of-Sequence marker state; this represents detection of an 'out-of-vocabulary' (OOV) sub-sequence in the input test sequence. In this case, we mark the trigger state with 'OOV' sequence-id, indicating that this particular state does not belong to any of the memorised prototypes (Alien sequence). Energy transitions during the decoding process can be depicted by the following matrix.

$$
E =
\begin{pmatrix}
E_{11} & E_{12} & \cdots & E_{1t} & \cdots & E_{1t_1} & & & E_1 \\
E_{21} & E_{22} & \cdots & E_{2t} & \cdots & \cdots & \cdots & E_{2t_2} & E_2 \\
\vdots & \vdots & \ddots & \vdots & \ddots & \vdots & \ddots & \vdots & \\
E_{u1} & E_{u2} & \cdots & E_{ut} & \cdots & \cdots & \cdots & \cdots & E_{ut_u} & E_u \\
\vdots & \vdots & \ddots & \vdots & \ddots & \vdots & \ddots & \\
E_{L1} & E_{L2} & \cdots & E_{Lt} & \cdots & \cdots & E_{Lt_L} & & E_L
\end{pmatrix},
$$

This matrix consists of jagged rows with the uth row representing energy transitions for the sub-sequence retrieved in response to u^{th} trigger state of the input test sequence; column 't' representing the tth firing instant of MHNN and the last column represents the energy of the terminating state. This is depicted as color coded values in Fig. 3(d); each of these (last column energies) is compared with End-of-Sequence marker energies to find the closest match within a threshold to label the trigger state (in the given test sequence). Run-length encoding on the retrieved label sequence determines the segmentation boundaries. We now present Algorithm 1 which gives the details of the decoding procedure as outlined above.

5 Dataset and Experiments

We synthesized multiple temporal sequences (prototype sequences) of variable lengths from movie clips of different durations extracted from the movies 'Lord

---

Algorithm 1. Connectionist Temporal Sequence Decoding using Multi-limit cycle M-ary Hopfield Neural Network

---

Input: $\xi_1, \xi_2, \xi_3, \ldots, \xi_u, \ldots, \xi_L$ ▷ Temporal sequence of length L to be decoded

    $\theta = N, M, K, S, T, Max, \epsilon, f(.)$ ▷ Model Parameters

    (N: Network size, M: Neuron states, K: Prototypes stored, S: Static Weight Matrix, T: Transition Weight Matrix, $Max : Max(L_k), k \in 1, K$, ϵ: threshold, $f(.)$: staircase activation function)

Output: $(b_1, e_1, label_1), \ldots, (b_p, e_p, label_p), \ldots, (b_P, e_P, label_P)$ ▷ (labelled segments)

1:   $u \leftarrow 1$

2:   **while** $u \leq L$ **do**   ▷ each state in temporal sequence

       $\xi_u = (\xi_{u1}, \xi_{u2}, \ldots, \xi_{ui}, \ldots, \xi_{uN}), \xi_{ui} \in R^M, M = 256$

3:     $x_i \leftarrow \xi_{ui}, \forall i \in [1, N]$ ▷ Network Initialization

4:     $t \leftarrow 1$

5:     **while** $t \leq Max$ **do**

6:        Fire the network using Two-Stage firing procedure

7:        Synchronous Firing

8:        $x_i' \leftarrow f(\sum_{j=1}^{N} T_{ij} x_j), \forall i \in [1, N]$

9:        Asynchronous Firing

10:       **repeat**

11:          $x_i' \leftarrow f(\sum_{j=1}^{N} S_{ij} x_j'), \forall i \in Random[1, N]$

12:         **until** Convergence(no change in x_i')

13:         $x_i \leftarrow x_i', \forall i \in [1, N]$ ▷ Updated State

14:         $E_{u,t} \leftarrow -\frac{1}{2} \sum_{i=1}^{N} \sum_{j=1}^{N} S_{ij} x_i x_j$

15:         $k^* \leftarrow \arg\min_{k}(E_{u,t} - E_{EOS_k})$

16:         **if** $(E_{u,t} - E_{EOS_{k^*}}) < \epsilon$ **then**

17:           $label_u \leftarrow k; E_u \leftarrow E(u,t)$

18:           break

19:         **end if**

20:         $t \leftarrow t + 1$

21:       **end while**

22:       **if** $(t > Max)$ **then**

23:         $label_u \leftarrow -1$ ▷ Alien (OOV) Pattern

24:       **end if**

25:       $u \leftarrow u + 1$

26: **end while**

27: Perform run-length encoding of label sequence $label_1$, $label_2$, $\ldots, label_u, \ldots, label_U$ to determine segmentation boundaries

28: **return**

    $(b_1, e_1, label_1)), \ldots, (b_p, e_p, label_p), \ldots, (b_P, e_P, label_P)$

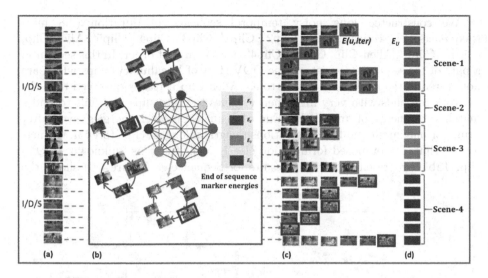

Fig. 3. Sequence identification using multi-limit cycle sequence model: (a) connected sequence to be decoded (b) multi-limit cycle M-ary HNN (c) retrieved sequence of frames(coloured frames are EOS markers) for each trigger state (d) color coded energy values and labels

of the Rings' (LOR), 'Gone with the Wind' (GWW), 'The Departed' (DEP), 'No Country for Old Men' (NCO), 'Shakespeare In Love' (SIL) [10] and Rhyme Videos. RGB frames are extracted at the rate of 25 frames/sec and are converted to gray frames (pixel value 0–255) with resolution set to 100×100 using nearest neighbor interpolation. Each rasterized frame represents a specific state in the sequence Ξ_k. We have considered a single M-ary Hopfield neural network of size=10000 neurons. Parameter M is set to 256 so that each neuron can assume any value from a set of 256 values at a particular instant of time. We trained the network using our proposed 'Dual Weight Learning' procedure with different number of sequences of variable lengths to examine its storage capacity. We observed that the network has an upper bound of $O(N)$ on total number of state transitions across all the stored sequences $\sum_{k=1}^{K} L_k$.

For the decoding experiment, we stored 18 such cycles with total state transitions 5564 in a single MHNN using Dual-Weight learning. Figure 4(a) shows sorted energies of end of sequence markers of all the sequences. Out of these 18 movie clips (prototype sequences), 5 clips were chosen randomly (marked in Fig. 4(a) and corrupted using 30% insertion, deletion and substitution (I/D/S) errors randomly injected into the sequences to get corrupted clips Clip1', Clip2', Clip3', Clip4' and Clip5'. Likewise, 40% error was inserted into the same prototype sequences to generate Clip1'', Clip2'', Clip3'', Clip4'' and Clip5''. We performed decoding tasks for multiple test sequences constructed by connecting the corrupted clips in random order. We present here results for decoding one such long sequence (sequence-A).

We constructed long noisy temporal sequence of duration (2.8 min) (Sequence-A) by concatenating Clip2′, Clip1′, Clip3′, Clip4′, Clip5′, Alien-Clip, Clip1″, Clip2″, Alien-Clip, Clip3″, Clip4″, Clip5″ in that order. In this sequence, a part of the sequence consists of the OOV (Out of Vocabulary) clips which are not stored in the network (referred to as 'Alien-Clip'). It was observed that the network responds with very high energy values to these clips and fails to find a match with energy of any of the 'End of Sequence marker energies' even after firing for maximum number of iterations (length of longest clip stored in the network); thus, the proposed formulation clearly identifies it as 'unknown' (OOV) clip. Table 1 represents decoding results for Sequence-A. Figure 4(b) shows the

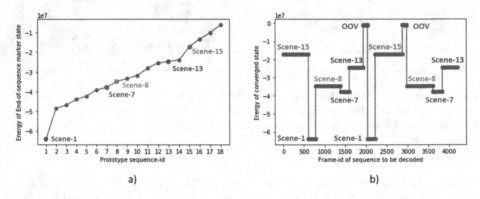

a)

b)

Fig. 4. (a) End of sequence marker energies of isolated prototype sequences stored in the M-ary HNN (b) Decoding of long noisy connected temporal sequence (sequence-A)

Table 1. Decoding Results for Sequence-A (I/D/S: 30% (Clip′), 40% (Clip″))

Ground Truth				Decoder output	
I/P Seq	start	end	id	(start, end, id)	Energy
Clip2′	0	610	Scene-15	(0, 610, Scene-15)	−1.7E+07
Clip1′	611	779	Scene-1	(611, 779, Scene-1)	−6.3+07
Clip3′	780	1386	Scene-8	(780, 1386, Scene-8)	−3.4E+07
Clip4′	1387	1597	Scene-7	(1387, 1597, Scene-7)	−3.7E+07
Clip5′	1598	1937	Scene-13	(1598,1937, 13)	−2.4E+07
Alien-Clip	1938	2041	Alien-clip	(1938, 2041, OOV)	−0.1E+07
Clip1″	2042	2217	Scene-1	(2042, 2217, Scene-1)	−6.3E+07
Clip2″	2218	2870	Scene-15	(2218, 2870, Scene-15)	−1.7E+07
Alien-Clip	2871	2974	Alien-Clip	(2871, 2974, OOV)	−0.1E+07
Clip3″	2975	3620	Scene-8	(2975, 3620, Scene-8)	−3.4E+07
Clip4″	3621	3845	Scene-7	(3621, 3845, Scene-7)	−3.7E+07
Clip5″	3846	4205	Scene-13	(3846, 4205, Scene-13)	−2.4E+07

energy of the profile of the network during decoding process, where energy corresponds to the last column of the matrix 'E' in Sect. 4. Proposed system solves segmentation and labelling task with '0' error.

The above experimental results demonstrate the effectiveness of the proposed algorithm to deal with the 'alignment problem' and 'alien patterns' (OOVs) which are very important aspects of connectionist temporal sequence decoding in practical settings such as ASR or movie-scene segmentation and labeling.

6   Conclusion

We have proposed a multi-limit cycle M-ary HNN (MHNN) based formulation and a connectionist algorithm to solve the temporal sequence decoding problem. Multi-limit cycle MHNN stores multiple variable length multi-valued sequences in a single network and has storage capacity of $O(N)$ which makes it easily adaptable for modelling prototype sub-sequences. Due to the M-ary nature of the neurons, there is no loss of information being modelled. It supports retrieval of the correct prototype sub-sequence stored in its limit cycle with a minimal cue (partial/corrupted). The proposed decoding algorithm uses the trained multi-limit cycle MHNN and End-of-Sequence marker energies to realize a connectionist temporal sequence decoding solution. Robustness of the proposed formulation and algorithm to temporal errors and its capability to handle unknown sequences with very high energy response makes it a biologically plausible alternative to existing decoding frameworks for various sequence alignment and decoding tasks. This is a first of its kind approach to solve temporal sequence decoding using M-ary HNN within the framework of attractor neural networks in a fully connectionist paradigm.

References

1. Bijjani, R., Das, P.: An M-ary neural network model. Neural Comput. **2**(4), 536–551 (1990). https://doi.org/10.1162/neco.1990.2.4.536
2. Denizdurduran, B.: In: Attractor Neural Network Approaches in the Memory Modeling (2012)
3. Graves, A., Fernandez, S., Gomez, F., Schmidhuber, J.: Connectionist temporal classification: labelling unsegmented sequence data with recurrent neural networks. In: ICML (2006)
4. Hopfield, J.J.: Neural networks and physical systems with emergent collective computational abilities. Proc. Natl. Acad. Sci. **79**(8), 2554–2558 (1982). https://doi.org/10.1073/pnas.79.8.2554
5. Hopfield, J.J.: Neurons with graded response have collective computational properties like those of two-state neurons. Proc. Natl. Acad. Sci. **81**(10), 3088–3092 (1984). https://doi.org/10.1073/pnas.81.10.3088
6. Ladwani, V.M., Ramasubramanian, V.: M-ary hopfield neural network for storage and retrieval of variable length sequences: multi-limit cycle approach. In: IEEE Symposium Series on Computational Intelligence, SSCI 2022, Singapore, 4–7 December 2022, pp. 436–441. IEEE (2022). https://doi.org/10.1109/SSCI51031.2022.10022082

7. Personnaz, L., Guyon, I., Dreyfus, G.: Collective computational properties of neural networks: new learning mechanisms. Phys. Rev. A **34**(5), 4217 (1986)
8. Vidal, E., Marzal, A.: A review and new approaches for automatic segmentation of speech signals. Signal Process. V: Theories Appl. **1**, 43–53 (1990)
9. Zhang, C., Dangelmayr, G., Oprea, I.: Storing cycles in Hopfield-type networks with pseudoinverse learning rule: admissibility and network topology. Neural Netw. **46**, 283–298 (2013). https://doi.org/10.1016/j.neunet.2013.06.008
10. Zlatintsi, A., et al.: COGNIMUSE: a multimodal video database annotated with saliency, events, semantics and emotion with application to summarization. EURASIP J. Image Video Process. **2017**(1), 1–24 (2017). https://doi.org/10.1186/s13640-017-0194-1

Explaining, Evaluating and Enhancing Neural Networks' Learned Representations

Marco Bertolini[✉], Djork-Arnè Clevert, and Floriane Montanari

Bayer AG, Machine Learning Research, Berlin, Germany
{marco.bertolini,djork-arne.clevert}@pfizer.com,
floriane.montanari@owkin.com

Abstract. Most efforts in interpretability in deep learning have focused on (1) extracting explanations of a specific downstream task in relation to the input features and (2) imposing constraints on the model, often at the expense of predictive performance. New advances in (unsupervised) representation learning and transfer learning, however, raise the need for an explanatory framework for networks that are trained without a specific downstream task. We address these challenges by showing how explainability can be an aid, rather than an obstacle, towards better and more efficient representations. Specifically, we propose a natural aggregation method generalizing attribution maps between any two (convolutional) layers of a neural network. Additionally, we employ such attributions to define two novel scores for evaluating the informativeness and the disentanglement of latent embeddings. Extensive experiments show that the proposed scores do correlate with the desired properties. We also confirm and extend previously known results concerning the independence of some common saliency strategies from the model parameters. Finally, we show that adopting our proposed scores as constraints during the training of a representation learning task improves the downstream performance of the model.

Keywords: Explainable AI · Representation Learning · Convolutional Neural Networks

1 Introduction

The steadily growing field of representation learning [1,18] has been investigating possible answers to the question "how can we learn good representations?". This has led to the rise of self-supervised learning and transfer learning [48]. In practice, the quality of a representation is measured by the performance on the downstream task of interest. This can lead to a proliferation of models that potentially overfit the few benchmark datasets typically used as downstream tasks.

In this work, we would like to step away from such traditional evaluations and instead come back to the seminal work by [7], questioning "what makes

© The Author(s), under exclusive license to Springer Nature Switzerland AG 2023
L. Iliadis et al. (Eds.): ICANN 2023, LNCS 14258, pp. 269–287, 2023.
https://doi.org/10.1007/978-3-031-44192-9_22

one representation better than another?". Our proposal arises from the field of explainable AI (XAI) [5,12,17,35]. In XAI, the primary goal is usually to provide an interpretation of a model's predictions either in terms of the input features or in terms of some user-defined high-level concepts [21]. Here as well, the field has suffered from the same endpoint-bias propelling model development, as XAI methods are in most cases designed to extract explanations for a specific downstream task. This is clearly a limitation: such methods cannot be directly applied to "explain" embeddings learned in a self-supervised manner.

In this paper, we develop an XAI framework that does not rely on any downstream network or task, and we then show how we can adopt it to evaluate the quality of an embedding. This requires a generalization of the concept of explanation: what we try to achieve here is to visualize and compare embeddings learned by any neural network.

Our explainability framework is local (we provide a method to infer explanations for a single data input), independent of any downstream task, and flexible (the framework is model-agnostic even though most of our examples and experiments are given for CNNs applied to image analysis). The scores we derive are global and can interpret a whole embedding vector.

1.1   Related Work

To visualize global concepts learned by trained CNNs, one can employ techniques such as filter visualization [27,39,45] or activation maximization techniques. Those aim at extracting visual patterns that maximize an internal neuron or predefined direction in the weight space [28–30]. In this context, [41] visualizes hidden neurons to gain insights on the property of transfer learning.

In the subfield of local explanations, saliency methods are commonly used to generate and visualize attributions for specific inputs. In our work, we compare three common strategies: Vanilla Gradients [4,39], Activations × Gradients (which generalizes Gradient × Input [38] to any hidden layer), and Grad-CAM [37]. Although our techniques can be similarly applied to any saliency method, the three above suffice to show our proof of concept, and avoid the computational overhead that comes with, for example, Integrated Gradients [40]. [9] proposed a variation of the Grad-CAM method for Embedding Networks. Their approach however fundamentally differs from ours, as the authors explicitly utilize a downstream loss function for computing attributions. The authors of [8], instead, extend saliency methods to visualize relevant features in latent space for generative models.

An alternative strategy to increase model interpretability is to restrict the architecture to intrinsically interpretable ones [11] or to impose other constraints during the training process [20,26,46,47]. One frequently used constraint is to enforce the disentanglement of the learned representation. However, this increased interpretability through constraints often comes at the cost of predictive performance [26,46]. We will show that this need not be the case: our XAI-derived scores do help the model achieve higher predictive power.

Several works [3,6,14,32,42] demonstrated that neural networks learn high-level concepts in the hidden layers. In particular, [21] showed that (1) such

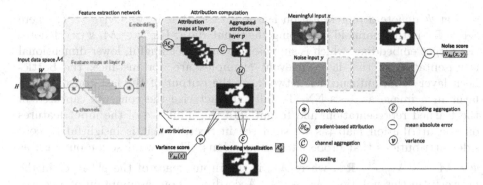

Fig. 1. Schematic description of the embedding explanation framework, including how the noise and variance scores are calculated.

concepts can be represented as directions in the latent space of hidden layers, and (2) deeper layers tend to learn more complex concepts as opposed to shallow layers. The disadvantage of their approach is that such meaningful directions are learned with the aid of additional labelled data. Our proposal generalizes this basic idea to learned embeddings by aggregating the concepts, learned in hidden layers, that contribute to activate the target representation. Our approach is partly motivated by the work [15]. The authors show that, often, single filters fail to capture high-level concepts, and that filter aggregation is instead required.

1.2 Contributions

We can summarize our main contributions as follows[1]:

- We propose a simple and flexible aggregation scheme for explaining and visualizing embeddings of (convolutional) neural networks (Sect. 2). To the best of our knowledge, the present work is the first systematic attempt to do so without any consideration of a downstream task or loss.
- We propose in Sect. 3 metrics to quantify the quality of these embeddings.
- We show that these metrics correlate with desired embedding properties (specifically, informativeness and disentanglement) (Sect. 4.1, 4.2, 4.3) and detect effects like dataset drift (Sect. 4.4).
- We show that training with the proposed metrics as constraints improves the quality of the embeddings (Sect. 4.5).

2 Visualizing Explanations of Embeddings Through Aggregation

In this section, we present a simple and intuitive procedure for visualizing latent embeddings of a neural network.

---

[1] The code accompanying this work can be found at https://github.com/bayer-science-for-a-better-life/XAI4Embeddings.

Let Ψ denote a representation learning task, that is, $\Psi : \mathcal{M} \to \mathbb{R}^N$, where $\mathcal{M} \simeq \mathbb{R}^d$ is the manifold describing the input data. For $\mathbf{x} \in \mathcal{M}$, $\Psi(\mathbf{x})$ denotes the target embedding, which is supposed to be a meaningful, lower-dimensional representation of the data. Relevant examples are, for instance, the bottleneck layer of an autoencoder network, or the output of the last convolutional layer in a image analysis NN. To fully characterize the concepts captured in the learned representation, and to mitigate the influence of the input features on the attribution map (as we shall see in Sect. 4.1), it is insightful to consider attributions that probe latent dimensions. Thus, we describe our task as $\Psi : \mathcal{M} \xrightarrow{\phi_p} \mathcal{M}_p \xrightarrow{\xi_p} \mathbb{R}^N$, where $\mathcal{M}_p$ is the input space of the pth layer in the network (in this notation, $\mathcal{M}_0 \equiv \mathcal{M}$). According to our assumption of a convolution structure, $\mathcal{M}_p \simeq \mathbb{R}^{C_p \times d_p}$, where C_p is the number of channels and d_p is the spatial dimension of the latent representation.

2.1 Attributions for Embeddings

To generate explanations for embeddings without any reference to a downstream task, we regard each target embedding component $\Psi(\mathbf{x})_i$, for $i = 1, \ldots, N$, as a stand-alone output node. Consequently, we interpret its corresponding saliency attributions $\partial \Psi(\mathbf{x})_i / \partial \mathbf{x}$ as feature importance for the activation of the corresponding latent component. This approach can be straightforwardly extended to any intermediate layer, where we regard the attribution values $\partial \xi_p(\mathbf{x})_i / \partial \phi_p(\mathbf{x}) \in \mathcal{M}_p$ as importance weights for the activation of the ith representation component with respect to the pth layer neuron activations $\partial \phi_p(\mathbf{x})$.

In general, $\dim \mathcal{M}_p \neq \dim \mathcal{M}$, as the above procedure will generate, for each i, a map for each of the C_p channels in the feature layer p. To generate a unique map for the attribution, we aggregate the maps $\partial \xi_p(\mathbf{x})_i / \partial \phi_p(\mathbf{x})$ along the channel dimension of layer p by means of a map $\mathcal{C} : \mathcal{M}_p \mapsto \mathbb{R}^{d_p}$, such that
$$\mathcal{C} : \partial \xi_p(\mathbf{x})_{i=1,\ldots,N} / \partial \phi_p(\mathbf{x}) \mapsto (\widehat{A}_\Psi^p)_{i=1,\ldots,N} \in \mathbb{R}^{d_p \times N}.$$
In most representation learning applications $N \sim (10^2, 10^3)$, and it is unfeasible to examine saliency maps for *all* latent dimensions i. A simple solution to generate one single map per input sample is to aggregate the component-wise attribution maps via $\mathcal{E} : (\widehat{A}_\Psi^p)_i \in \mathcal{M} \mapsto \widehat{A}_\Psi^p \in \mathcal{M}_p$.

It is desirable to generate the final attribution in the original input space, in order to formulate hypothesis about explanations on the input features. However, it can happen that $d_0 > d_p$, for instance due to the presence of pooling layers. When this is the case, we apply an upscaling map $\mathcal{U} : \mathbb{R}^{d_p} \to \mathbb{R}^{d_0}$. Given the property of a convolutional layer that the value of each superpixel depends on its receptive field, the simplest choice for $\mathcal{U}$ is to consider the map in $\mathbb{R}^{d_p = H_p \times W_p}$ as a low-resolution map in $\mathbb{R}^{d = H \times W}$. This is the choice we implemented in all our examples and experiments.[2]

---

[2] Another upsampling scheme, for instance, involves performing a transposed convolution of the lower-dimensional matrix with a fixed Gaussian kernel to obtain a full-resolution map [25].

Putting all together, given a learning task Ψ, we define the attribution method A_Ψ^p as a map

$$\mathcal{M} \xrightarrow[\text{forw.}]{\Psi} \mathbb{R}^N \xrightarrow[\text{back}]{\partial \xi_p} \mathcal{M}_p^N \xrightarrow[\text{aggr.}]{\mathcal{C}} \mathbb{R}^{d_p \times N} \xrightarrow[\text{aggr.}]{\mathcal{E}} \mathbb{R}^{d_p} \xrightarrow[\text{upscale}]{\mathcal{U}} \mathcal{M} .$$

We depicted this chain of operations in Fig. 1. In the preceding discussion, to keep notations simple, we explicitly considered vanilla gradients $\partial \xi_p$ as the reference saliency method. This however can be replaced with any available saliency method. Figure 2 shows, for two input samples, examples of embedding attributions for different saliency and aggregation strategies. We notice that for deeper layers the attributions focus on some high-level concepts (e.g., eyes and nose for Fig. 2b).

Following [3,6,21], latent dimensions contain meaningful directions that can be learned through linear classifiers and that correspond to humanly-understandable concepts. The attribution maps $(\widehat{A}_\Psi^p)_{i,c} : \mathcal{M} \rightarrow \mathbb{R}^{d_p}$, where $c = 1, \ldots, C_p$, is to be understood as quantifying the concept(s) learned by the model in the cth filter of the pth layer. Thus, in our approach, we regard the channel aggregation map $\mathcal{C}$ as a "concept" aggregation map. On the other hand, aggregation along the latent embedding dimension is dictated by the need to "summarize" explanations across the whole representation. Given a downstream task $\Theta : \mathbb{R}^N \rightarrow \mathbb{R}$, however, each embedding dimension Ψ_i acts simply as an input feature. With regard to explainability, we interpret the explanations for $\Psi_{i=1,\ldots,N}$ as a basis of explanations for Θ. Namely, explanations A_Θ for the task Θ would act as weights for the more elementary explanations A_{Ψ_i}.

2.2   Aggregation Schemes

Here we review possible aggregation strategies for both the channel and embedding dimensions. To formalize our discussion, we represent the set of attribution maps as a multiset $\mathcal{X}$, that is, a set allowing for repeating elements. Both the channel ($\mathcal{C}$) and embedding ($\mathcal{E}$) maps can be thought of as an aggregation map $\mathcal{A}(\mathcal{X})$ over a multiset $\mathcal{X}$. We also propose a new aggregation strategy, given by $\mathcal{A} = \text{Var}[\mathcal{X}]$, that yields sparser attribution values.

Mean Aggregation. The simplest aggregation method, is the *mean* aggregator, $\mathcal{A}_{\text{mean}}(\mathcal{X}) = \frac{1}{|\mathcal{X}|} \sum_{x \in \mathcal{X}} x$. The mean aggregator captures the distribution of elements in a multiset [44], but not the multiset itself. For example, for $\mathcal{X}_1 = \{-1, 1, 0, 0\}$ and $\mathcal{X}_2 = \{0, 0, 0, 0\}$ we obtain $\mathcal{A}_{\text{mean}}(\mathcal{X}_1) = \mathcal{A}_{\text{mean}}(\mathcal{X}_2) = 0$. Such aggregations "with signs" potentially suffer from the risk of signal cancellation.

Abs Aggregation. Another simple aggregator is given by the *mean absolute* aggregator, $\mathcal{A}_{\text{abs}}(\mathcal{X}) = \frac{1}{|\mathcal{X}|} \sum_{x \in \mathcal{X}} |x|$. The mean absolute aggregator captures the distribution of elements in a multiset without signs. Consequently, the resulting attributions tend to be quite dense. In fact, $\mathcal{A}_{\text{abs}} = 0$ if and only if all elements in $\mathcal{X}$ are zero. This feature could be detrimental in our setting, as sparsity is often a desired property in explainability, and especially challenging to achieve in post-hoc explanations.

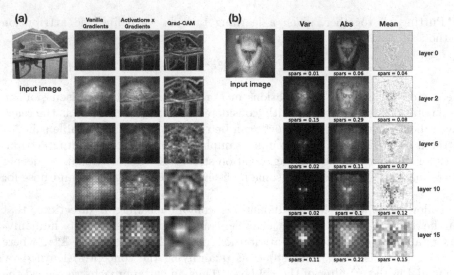

Fig. 2. Example of embeddings for (a) different attribution schemes ($\mathcal{C} = \mathcal{A}_{abs}$, $\mathcal{E} = \mathcal{A}_{var}$) and (b) aggregation strategies (Activations × Gradients). Below each map we report its corresponding sparsity score, given as the average value over the normalized 2D attribution map. We report in the appendix further examples and combinations of attribution and aggregation schemes.

Variance Aggregation. To remedy this lack of sparsity, we introduce a novel aggregation scheme, the *variance* aggregator, $\mathcal{A}_{var} = \text{Var}[\mathcal{X}]$. The variance aggregator is somewhat complementary to the mean aggregator. In fact, for $\mathcal{X}_1 = \{-1, 1, 0, 0\}$, we have $\mathcal{A}_{var}(\mathcal{X}_1) = \frac{2}{3}$ while $\mathcal{A}_{mean}(\mathcal{X}_1) = 0$. On the other hand, for $\mathcal{X}_2 = \{1, 1, 1, 0\}$, $\mathcal{A}_{var}(\mathcal{X}_2) = \frac{1}{4}$ while $\mathcal{A}_{mean}(\mathcal{X}_2) = \frac{3}{4}$. Thus, the variance aggregator assigns higher values to multisets with a wider range of values and penalizes biased multisets where all values concentrate around its mean, regardless of its magnitude. We derive in the Supplementary Information (SI) a simple argument that shows, under a few basic assumptions, that the variance aggregator yields a sparser map than the mean absolute aggregator. We provide evidence that our claim extends to real data by displaying different aggregation methods in Fig. 2b. For each attribution map, we computed a measure of sparsity as the average value over the (normalized to the range $[0, 1]$) 2D attribution map. For the mean aggregator, the sparsity is computed on the absolute value of the map. As claimed, for all layers, the variance produces a sparser map than the mean absolute aggregator.

Comments and Practical Advices. Finally, we provide practical guidance as to the combinations of aggregation schemes for the maps $\mathcal{C}, \mathcal{E}$. We find the combination $\mathcal{C} = \mathcal{A}_{abs}$, $\mathcal{E} = \mathcal{A}_{var}$ (and viceversa) especially insightful to identify the prevailing features dominating the representation, while $\mathcal{E} \equiv \mathcal{C} = \mathcal{A}_{abs}$ is helpful to detect features that are **not** captured by the embedding (see Fig. 2). We find instead $\mathcal{E} \equiv \mathcal{C} = \mathcal{A}_{mean}$ potentially useful when the embedding explanations are combined in a generalized chain rule with a downstream task Θ as mentioned above, especially when it is desirable to distinguish feature contributing positively or negatively. When $\mathcal{C} \equiv \mathcal{E} = \mathcal{A}_{\text{var}}$, we observed that the map is often too sparse.

3 Explainability-Derived Scores

In this section, by employing the embedding explanations described in the previous section, we derive useful metrics to quantify desired properties of a learned latent representation: (1) informativeness, the ability of a latent representation to capture meaningful features of the input sample, and (2) disentanglement, the property quantifying the degree to which latent features are independent of one another. We will show that our proposed scores correlate with the desired properties as well as with the more standard approach of predictive performance on a downstream task.

3.1 Informativeness: The Noise Score

The motivating idea of the noise score is that attributions for an informative representation should, on average, substantially differ from attributions generated from a less meaningful representation. Explicitly, let $x \in \mathbb{R}^d$ be a (meaningful) input image, and let $x_{\text{noise}} \in \mathbb{R}^d$ be such that $x_{\text{noise}} \sim U(0,1)^d$. We define the *noise score* for representation task Ψ and layer p as the Mean Absolute Error (MAE) between (normalized) attributions of a meaningful data input and a noise-generated input

$$N_{A_\Psi^p}(x, x_{\text{noise}}) = \overline{|A_\Psi^p(x) - A_\Psi^p(x_{\text{noise}})|} . \tag{1}$$

We schematically depicted the above definition in Fig. 1. The attribution maps in (1) are normalized to the range $[0, 1]$ to ensure that the score does not merely reflect the magnitude of the respective attribution values. With such a normalization, we have $\sup N_{A^p}(x, y) = 1$, which occurs if $A_\Psi^p(x) - A_\Psi^p(y) = \pm 1$, while $\inf N_{A^p}(x, y) = 0$, which occurs when $A_\Psi^p(x) \equiv A_\Psi^p(y)$.

We will show in the next section that (1) distinguishes different representations for which we know their relative informativeness. However, it is often convenient to have a global reference value N^0, to establish an intrinsic metric for *informativeness*. Since we do not know the underlying distribution of A_Ψ^p, we can sample a benchmark value as follows:

$$N_{A_\Psi^p}^0 = \overline{|A_\Psi^p(y_{\text{noise}}) - A_\Psi^p(x_{\text{noise}})|} , \tag{2}$$

where $y_{\text{noise}} \sim U(0,1)^d$.

The Score Curve. Given a representation task Ψ, we can compute (1) and (2) for each intermediate layer p of the network. The resulting *noise score curve* provides a more complete picture of how effectively the different layers organize information in the target representation.

3.2 Conciseness: The Variance Score

A second beneficial property of a representation is disentanglement [10,13,33]. Disentanglement, in the sense of decomposability [24], implies that the latent features are independent of one another. As a consequence, we also intuitively expect the attributions for each of the latent features not to overlap among each other significantly. Of course, a pair of latent features $\Psi_{1,2}$ can be independent but have very similar attribution maps for a given input, as they might encode independent concepts that happen to overlap in the given sample. Still, we expect the majority of the input space to be represented by some high-level concepts, and a decomposable representation should cover a large portion of it. Since our choice of measuring disentanglement is correlated but differs from the more standard definition, we coin a new term: the *conciseness* of a representation is a measure of the variance of attribution maps across the latent features.

Explicitly, let $x \in \mathbb{R}^d$ be a (meaningful) sample input. We define the *variance score* for the representation task Ψ at layer p as the mean variance of the channel-aggregated (but not embedding-aggregated) attribution maps $(\widehat{A}_\Psi^p)_i(x)$, i.e.,

$$V_{A_\Psi^p}(x) = \overline{\mathrm{Var}\,\widehat{A}_\Psi^p(x)} \ . \tag{3}$$

Figure 1 illustrates how (3) relates to the aggregation strategies of Sect. 2. The above definition enables a direct comparison of embeddings: a representation Ψ is more concise than representation Ψ' if $V_{A_\Psi^p}(x) > V_{A_{\Psi'}^p}(x)$.

In order to determine the intrinsic conciseness of a representation, we recall Popoviciu's inequality [31] for a bounded random variable Z, which reads $\mathrm{Var}\,Z \leq \frac{(\sup Z - \inf Z)^2}{4}$, yielding in our case $V_{A_\Psi^p}(x) \leq 1/4$, assuming that each dimension map $(\widehat{A}_\Psi^p)_i$ is normalized in the range $[0,1]$. The only random variable Z whose variance assumes the maximum value is such that $Z = 0, 1$ each with probability $\frac{1}{2}$. In terms of our map, this would represent that a "superpixel" is either considered on/off in each representation component (with equal distribution). Note that this is independent from the number of drawings, or in our case the embedding size. Hence, (3) is suitable for comparing representations of any size, as we will do in Sect. 4.3.

4 Experiments and Results

In this section we describe our experiments and illustrate the insights we gain from the metrics we defined in the previous section. We apply our techniques to three widely used architectures: Inception V3 [42], ResNet18 [19] and AlexNet [22].[3] For each of these, the target representation will be the output of the last convolutional (or eventually pooling) layer.

We conduct several tests to assess the sensitivity of our scores to informativeness, disentanglement and predictive performance. Specifically, we compare

---

[3] Resnet18 has a BSD 3-clause license, Inception V3 has an MIT license, AlexNet has an Apache V2 license.

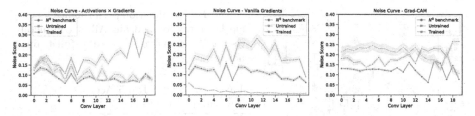

Fig. 3. Average noise score curves (over 50 input samples) for ResNet18 trained on ImageNet [34] for different attribution strategies and $\mathcal{C} = \mathcal{E} = \mathcal{A}_{abs}$.

the values of our scores for a given task and model to the one computed from networks with random weights. In addition of being natural benchmarks for the desired properties listed above, randomly initialized networks do correspond to non-trivial representations [43]. Thus, our scores can be interpreted in this case as probing the model architecture as a prior to the learning task [3,36].

4.1 Detecting Model's Parameter (in)dependence

We begin by comparing the noise score (1) for a fixed network architecture and fixed task Ψ. Score curves for different attribution strategies are presented in Fig. 3. For Activations × Gradients, the noise score fail to distinguish between the trained and the untrained network in early layers. This agrees with the findings of [2], where the authors show that upon visual inspection the defining structure of the input is still recognizable for a network with randomly initialized weights. Our analysis shows that this does not occur for explanations in deeper layers, as the two curves separate further as we go deeper in the network. Thus, while Activations × Gradients is potentially misleading in shallow layers (due to the bias introduced by the input values), it is a meaningful attribution method in deeper layers (we defer explicit examples of such maps to the SI).

For Vanilla Gradients, we notice instead that the two curves (trained and untrained) are well separated even in the early layers. This confirms the analysis of [2], where the authors found a significant discrepancy between the corresponding saliency maps. The difference is however less conspicuous in comparison to the benchmark curve computed from (2). This shows that Vanilla Gradients is more sensitive to weight parameters than input parameters (we recall that the N^0 benchmark curve (2) is computed for a trained network). This is not the case for Activations × Gradients, where the noise curves for the untrained network and the benchmark exhibit a very similar behaviour.

Finally, we observe an overall poor performance of Grad-CAM, except in the very deep layers, where the noise score successfully distinguishes the trained network from both benchmarks [2]. This is consistent with the usual practice of considering the output of the last convolution layer for a Grad-CAM visualization.

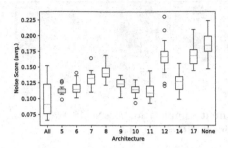

Fig. 4. Average noise scores (25 samples) for ResNet18 networks with layer-wise randomly initiated weights. Each data point is obtained by averaging the noise score for each layer of the noise curve. x-axis values correspond to the re-initialized layer's number.

Table 1. Classification performance for single layer randomization. All = completely re-initialized network, None = full trained network.

Layer	Top 1 Acc	Top 5 Acc
All	0.0	0.7
5	0.0	1.1
6	0.2	0.9
7	0.7	1.8
8	0.3	2.8
9	1.8	4.2
10	0.2	0.3
11	0.2	0.3
12	63.7	85.1
14	4.3	10.1
17	30.0	54.3
None	74.2	91.8

4.2 Detecting Downstream Performance

The noise score (1) aims at quantifying the amount of information captured by the target embedding. It is therefore expected to correlate with a given downstream task performance. We test this expectation by comparing classification performance and noise scores of embeddings obtained through an independent layer randomization. Explicitly, we fix the weights of all the layers to their trained value except for one layer, whose weights we randomize. We report in Table 1 the classification performance for the ResNet18 architecture, and in Fig. 4 we depict the corresponding embeddings' noise scores, defined as the average value of the corresponding noise curve.

Table 1 shows that layer randomizations have different effects on the overall performance of the representation, as some networks (12, 17) are still predictive. In Fig. 4 we observe that embeddings which are still predictive exhibits a higher average noise score. The Spearman rank-order correlation coefficients between average noise score and downstream performance are 0.89 (Top5) and 0.91 (Top1), showing a very strong correlation between the noise score and the downstream performance of the representations.

4.3 Detecting Representations' Conciseness

Increasing the dimension of a representation increments its expressive power. However, large embeddings incur in the risk of noisy and redundant representations, which in turn have detrimental effects on the learning efficacy.

Here we provide evidence that the variance score (3) is suited to detect such pathology. Namely, we compute the variance curve for a given task (image classification on the ImageNet dataset [34]) and attribution scheme for different archi-

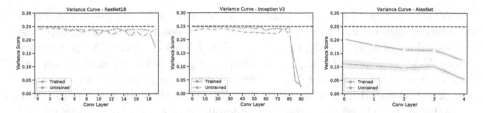

Fig. 5. Variance curves for three popular networks trained on Imagenet. ($\mathcal{C} = \mathcal{A}_{\mathrm{mean}}$, attr.= Activations × Gradients.) The blue dashed line depicts the theoretical maximum value. (Color figure online)

tectures. The corresponding variance curves are reported in Fig. 5. The attributions $\widehat{A}_y^p$ have been rescaled to the values $0, 1$ (after normalization) according to the threshold 0.5. The variance curves of the untrained models indicate the conciseness prior of the pure model architecture, which is affected, for example, by the choice of final non-linearity. In fact, we can assume that randomly initialized networks will tend to maximize representation conciseness, compatible with the architecture prior. In our experiments, we observe that the AlexNet architecture has a strong effect on the variance of the embedding (in average around 75% of the upper bound), while for Inception V3 and ResNet18 both curves approach the theoretically maximum value of $1/4$ (see Sect. 3.2).

Next, we observe that for the trained Inception V3 and ResNet18, whose target representation dimensions are 2048 and 512 respectively, the variance score is in average very close to its upper bound. On the other hand, the trained AlexNet (embedding dimension 9216) shows a strong decline from the randomly initialized version. This shows that the lack of variance in the embedding explanations is not merely due to the architecture inductive bias (as in the case for the random weights network), but also on the representation learning itself. It is expected that such a high embedding size induces redundancy and therefore more entangled embeddings. Accordingly, our experiment provides experimental evidence that the conciseness of a representation correlates with the desired property of disentanglement.

4.4   Detecting Dataset Drift

We can employ the noise score to detect the amount of drift from the training dataset. To test this, we train a simple autoencoder model on the MNIST dataset [23].[4] The encoder network consists of two convolutional layers followed by a linear layer. We refer to the SI for further details concerning hyperparameters, training details and choice of architecture. We generate a drift by considering shifted data samples (normalized in range $[0, 1]$) $\mathbf{x}_\lambda = \mathbf{x}+\lambda\mathbf{y}$, where $\mathbf{x}$ is a sample from the original dataset, and the drift is generated by a normal distribution

---

[4] MNIST dataset is available under the terms of the Creative Commons Attribution-Share Alike 3.0 license.

$\mathbf{y} \sim \mathcal{N}(\mu = 0, \sigma = 1)$ and controlled by the parameter λ. We present in Fig. 6 the relative difference of the noise scores for the second convolutional layer for various values of λ. Explicitly, this is defined as $(N(\mathbf{x}) - N(\mathbf{x}_\lambda))/N(\mathbf{x})$. Here we denote $N(\mathbf{x}) = N_{A_\Psi^p} = (\mathbf{x}, \mathbf{x}_{noise})$ for simplifying notation. Quantitatively, we obtain a Spearman coefficient of $\rho = 0.988$ between the relative noise scores and the corresponding drift parameter λ. Our results confirm that the noise score is negatively correlated with the shift amount. Hence, the noise score can be used as a metric for dataset drift detection or, more generally, to quantify the representation quality degradation for datasets unseen during training time.

4.5   Enhancing Representations with Score Constraints

We further test the usefulness of our scores by incorporating them as constraints during model training. We train an autoencoder model Ω (with encoder Ψ) on the MNIST dataset [23] with a linear layer accessing the bottleneck embedding as a 10-class classifier. The training loss is therefore $\mathcal{L}_{\text{train}}(\mathbf{x}, y) = \mathcal{L}_{\text{rec}}(\mathbf{x}) + \mathcal{L}_{\text{class}}(\mathbf{x}, y) - \lambda_1 N_{A_\Psi}(\mathbf{x}, \mathbf{y}_{\text{noise}}) - \lambda_2 V_{A_\Psi}(\mathbf{x})$, where $\mathcal{L}_{\text{rec}}(\mathbf{x}) = |\mathbf{x} - \Omega(\mathbf{x})|^2$ is the autoencoder reconstruction error and $\mathcal{L}_{\text{class}}$ is the classification loss (Cross Entropy Loss). The two coefficients $\lambda_{1,2}$ control the ratios between the model loss and the score constraints. The encoder network Ψ consists of two convolutional layers followed by a fully connected layer, whose output is our target bottleneck representation. The scores are computed with respect to the second convolutional layer. In order not to affect excessively the training speed, we applied the scores every 20 mini-batches. We did not perform any hyperparameter optimization: we trained the model for a fixed number of epochs (dependent on the bottleneck dimension), and we evaluate our results on a held-out test set. We refer to the SI for further details concerning hyperparameters, architecture and training details. We compare the classification test performance of the model for various values of the coefficients $\lambda_{1,2}$, and we report our findings in Table 2. We note that, overall, the score constraints led to representations that achieved a higher test accuracy on the classification task. We further notice that representation learning benefited from the variance score constraint for higher embedding size: here, redundancy and entanglement affect the learning, and forcing more concise representations reduces these undesirable effects. On the contrary, the noise score constraint has bigger impact on the models with particularly small bottlenecks, for which having a very expressive representation is key. Finally, training including both scores outperforms the original model in all the cases.

5   Conclusions

In this work, we have proposed aggregation schemes to generalize gradient attribution methods to any two intermediate layers of a neural network. In particular, this framework can be used to probe the explanations of embeddings with respect to intermediate feature maps without the need for a downstream task or a direct mapping back to the input space. We derived two useful metrics: the noise score

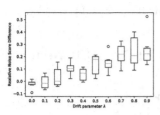

Fig. 6. Correlation between noise score and dataset drift relized by introduction of noise shift.

Table 2. Classification accuracies for score-constrained embeddings on the MNIST dataset. The performances are averaged over 4 runs. NS = noise score, VS = variance score.

Model	λ_1	λ_2	dim = 2	dim = 3	dim = 5	dim = 10
orig.	0	0	88.3 ± 0.7	93.74 ± 0.3	97.2 ± 0.2	97.7 ± 0.2
NS	0.01	0	89.1 ± 0.5	94.3 ± 0.4	97.4 ± 0.1	97.8 ± 0.2
NS	0.1	0	87.8 ± 0.0	94.3 ± 0.2	97.1 ± 0.3	97.8 ± 0.3
NS	1.0	0	$\mathbf{89.3 \pm 0.5}$	$\mathbf{95.1 \pm 0.5}$	97.3 ± 0.1	97.9 ± 0.1
VS	0	0.01	88.6 ± 0.9	94.8 ± 0.8	$\mathbf{97.6 \pm 0.1}$	$\mathbf{98.0 \pm 0.2}$
VS	0	0.1	88.5 ± 1.0	94.5 ± 0.7	97.4 ± 0.2	$\mathbf{98.0 \pm 0.2}$
VS	0	1.0	88.7 ± 0.9	94.7 ± 0.6	97.5 ± 0.2	97.8 ± 0.2
NS+VS	0.1	0.1	88.5 ± 2.1	94.6 ± 0.8	97.4 ± 0.2	97.8 ± 0.2

can detect the informativeness of a representation, and this in turn correlates with downstream task performance; the variance score can be used to probe the disentanglement of an embedding. Both scores can be used as constraints for representation learning, and were shown in a proof-of-concept experiment to boost the performance of the learned representation on the downstream task of interest.

This work is the first thorough study on how XAI techniques can be fruitfully implemented to evaluate and enhance representation learning independently of a downstream task. It would be interesting to apply our framework beyond the convolutional realm, for instance, to graph representation learning or neural machine translation. Our proposed variance aggregator can be seen as a first step towards explainability from the point of view of projection pursuit [16]: it would be of interest to explore, both theoretically and experimentally, more general aggregation strategies based on higher momenta (e.g., lopsidedness). Moreover, our proposed score constraints should be tested in more complex learning problems. One limitation of our current approach is the increase of computational time due to the computation of the scores and the extra back-propagations during training. It would be important to derive "lighter" scores, which estimate (1) and (3) but with a lower memory and computation footprint. We plan to return to these issues in future work.

A   Variance Aggregator is Sparser than Mean Absolute Aggregator

We present a simple argument supporting our claim that the variance aggregator $\mathcal{A}_{\mathrm{var}}$ is sparser than the mean absolute aggregator $\mathcal{A}_{\mathrm{abs}}$. Let $\mathcal{X}$ be a multiset whose elements assume values in the range $[0, 1]$. In our case, this can be achieved by normalizing the multiset. Given the positiveness of $\mathcal{X}$, the mean absolute aggregator simply reduces to the mean of $\mathcal{X}$, i.e., $\mathcal{A}_{\mathrm{abs}} = \mathbb{E}[\mathcal{X}]$. Now we have that

$$\mathbb{E}[\mathcal{X}]^2 = \mathbb{E}[\mathcal{X}^2] - \text{Var}[\mathcal{X}] \le \mathbb{E}[\mathcal{X}] - \text{Var}[\mathcal{X}] \implies \text{Var}[\mathcal{X}] \le \mathbb{E}[\mathcal{X}](1 - \mathbb{E}[\mathcal{X}]),$$
$$(4)$$

where we used the fact that $\mathbb{E}[\mathcal{X}^2] \le \mathbb{E}[\mathcal{X}]$ since $x^2 \le x$ for $x \in [0,1]$. Next, let us assume that $\text{Var}[Z] > \mathbb{E}[Z]$, then

$$\mathbb{E}[\mathcal{X}] < \mathbb{E}[\mathcal{X}](1 - \mathbb{E}[\mathcal{X}]) \implies \mathbb{E}[\mathcal{X}] < 0, \qquad (5)$$

which violates the assumption of positiveness of $\mathcal{X}$. Thus, we have shown that $\mathcal{A}_{\text{var}} = \text{Var}[\mathcal{X}] \le \mathbb{E}[\mathcal{X}] = \mathcal{A}_{\text{abs}}$. In particular, the equality is achieved only for the multiset $\mathcal{X}$ for which all elements equal zero, where $\mathcal{A}_{var} = \mathcal{A}_{\text{abs}} = 0$. This simple argument shows that under some basic assumptions, given the *same* underlying distribution $\mathbb{E}[\text{Var} Z] < \mathbb{E}[\mathbb{E}[Z]]$, and therefore the variance aggregation induces a sparser attribution map.

B   Architecture, Hyperparameter and Training Strategy

B.1   Detecting Dataset Drift

In Sect. 4.4 of the main text we report the results of training an autoencoder model on the MNIST dataset, showing that the noise score captures the effect of dataset drift. The encoder model consists of 3 convolutional layers of size $[8/5/1/2, 4/5/1/2, 2/5/1/2]$.[5] After each convolutional layer we apply batch normalization and max pooling (kernel $= 2$). This produces a 32-dimensional bottleneck representation. The decoder network consists of 3 (transposed) convolutional layers of size $[4/5/1/2, 8/5/1/2, 1/5/1/2]$. A sampling interpolation (scale factor $= 2$) precedes each convolutional layer, and we apply batch normalization after the first two convolutional layers. We used ReLU as activation function, except for the final output of the decoder, where instead we apply a sigmoid function to make sure the final output is in the range $[0,1]$. We use Mean Squared Error (MSE) as our reconstruction loss. We use the Adam optimizer with a fixed learning rate of 10^{-3}, and we train for 5 epochs.

B.2   Training with Scores as Constraints

In Sect. 4.5 of the main text we report our experiments regarding training an autoencoder model on the MNIST dataset with our scores as constraints. The encoder model consists of 2 convolutional layers of size $[8/5/1/2, 4/5/1/2]$ followed by a fully connected layer of size s. We apply batch normalization after each convolutional layer. We conducted several experiments for $s = 2, 3, 5, 10$. We used softplus as the encoder activation function. This is because when the score constraints enter the training loss, we need to compute second derivatives with respect to the weights, which vanish if the activation functions are piecewise linear. The classification branch of the network is a 10-dimensional fully

---

[5]   The notation U/K/S/P completely defines a convolutional layer: U = number of units, K = kernel size, S = stride, P = padding.

connected layer accessing the bottleneck. The decoder network consists of two fully connected layers of size $[32, 28 \times 28]$. We used ReLU as a decoder activation function, and MSE as our reconstruction loss. We use the Adam optimizer with a fixed learning rate of 10^{-3}, and we train for a fixed number of epochs $n_{ep}(s)$ depending on the bottleneck size: $n_{ep}(2) = 20$, $n_{ep}(3) = 15$, $n_{ep}(5) = 10$, and $n_{ep}(10) = 5$.

B.3 Computation Time

We report in Table 3 the training time for the autoencoder models, whose results we presented in Sect. 4.5 of the main text. When our scores are added to the training as constraints, we observe an increasing computational time cost when the dimension of the target bottleneck embedding Ψ increases. This is mainly due to the computation of the scores themselves, as this involves a full backpropagation for each of the latent dimensions of Ψ. We observe that the variance score has a lesser computational footprint than the noise score. One reason is that the former does not require the computation of attributions for the noise-generated input. We expect that this alone introduces a factor of 2 on the computing time, and thus it cannot explain the full difference. We hypothesize that some inefficiency occurs when we compute attributions for the noise input *after* having computed attributions for the meaningful input. In fact, in order to keep track of gradients, we set the option `create_graph=True` in the function `torch.autograd.grad` in PyTorch, and this might lead to an overall heavy computational derivative graph.

Table 3. Execution time $[\frac{seconds}{epoch}]$ for the models reported in Sect. 4.5 of the main text. All the models were trained on a single NVIDIA Tesla V100-16GB GPU.

Model	dim = 2	dim = 3	dim = 5	dim = 10
orig	12	12	12	12
VS	18	18	19	22
NS	134	225	483	1569
NS+VS	135	222	500	1567

C   Further Embedding Visualization Examples

In the main text we restricted, for space reasons, to just a few examples regarding the possible combinations of attribution and aggregation strategies. In Fig. 7 below we provide a more complete set of embedding visualization for the two input pictures of Fig. 2 of the main text. Specifically, for each example, we list, for each of the attribution schemes (Vanilla Gradients, Activations × Gradients, Grad-CAM), all possible combinations (for our channel and embedding aggregation maps $\mathcal{C}$ and $\mathcal{E}$, respectively) of basic aggregation strategies we discussed in the main text ($\mathcal{A}_{mean}$, $\mathcal{A}_{abs}$, $\mathcal{A}_{var}$). Note that when $\mathcal{C} = \mathcal{A}_{var}, \mathcal{A}_{abs}$, then $\mathcal{E} = \mathcal{A}_{mean}$ acts equivalently to $\mathcal{E} = \mathcal{A}_{abs}$.

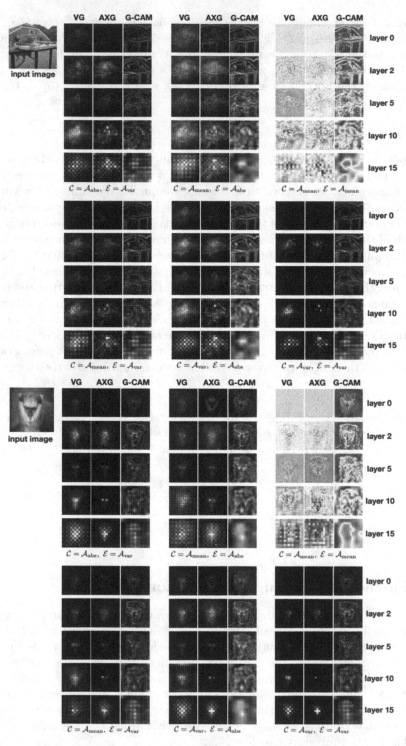

Fig. 7. Embedding visualization for two examples for different attribution schemes and aggregation strategies.

References

1. Liu, Z., Lin, Y., Sun, M.: Representation Learning for Natural Language Processing. Springer, Singapore (2020). https://doi.org/10.1007/978-981-15-5573-2
2. Adebayo, J., Gilmer, J., Muelly, M., Goodfellow, I., Hardt, M., Kim, B.: Sanity checks for saliency maps. In: NeurIPS (2018)
3. Alain, G., Bengio, Y.: Understanding intermediate layers using linear classifier probes. ArXiv abs/1610.01644 (2017)
4. Baehrens, D., Schroeter, T., Harmeling, S., Kawanabe, M., Hansen, K., Müller, K.: How to explain individual classification decisions. ArXiv abs/0912.1128 (2010)
5. Barredo Arrieta, A., et al.: Explainable artificial intelligence (XAI): concepts, taxonomies, opportunities and challenges toward responsible AI. Inf. Fusion 58, 82–115 (2020). https://doi.org/10.1016/j.inffus.2019.12.012, https://www.sciencedirect.com/science/article/pii/S1566253519308103
6. Bau, D., Zhou, B., Khosla, A., Oliva, A., Torralba, A.: Network dissection: quantifying interpretability of deep visual representations. In: 2017 IEEE Conference on Computer Vision and Pattern Recognition (CVPR), pp. 3319–3327 (2017)
7. Bengio, Y., Courville, A.C., Vincent, P.: Representation learning: a review and new perspectives. IEEE Trans. Pattern Anal. Mach. Intell. 35, 1798–1828 (2013)
8. Brocki, L., Chung, N.C.: Concept saliency maps to visualize relevant features in deep generative models. In: 2019 18th IEEE International Conference On Machine Learning And Applications (ICMLA), pp. 1771–1778 (2019). https://doi.org/10.1109/ICMLA.2019.00287
9. Chen, L., Chen, J., Hajimirsadeghi, H., Mori, G.: Adapting grad-CAM for embedding networks. In: Proceedings of the IEEE/CVF Winter Conference on Applications of Computer Vision (WACV) (2020)
10. Do, K., Tran, T.: Theory and evaluation metrics for learning disentangled representations. ArXiv abs/1908.09961 (2020)
11. Doshi-Velez, F., Kim, B.: Towards a rigorous science of interpretable machine learning. arXiv Machine Learning (2017)
12. Došilović, F.K., Brčić, M., Hlupić, N.: Explainable artificial intelligence: a survey. In: 2018 41st International Convention on Information and Communication Technology, Electronics and Microelectronics (MIPRO), pp. 0210–0215. IEEE (2018)
13. Eastwood, C., Williams, C.K.: A framework for the quantitative evaluation of disentangled representations. In: ICLR (2018)
14. Engel, J., Hoffman, M., Roberts, A.: Latent constraints: learning to generate conditionally from unconditional generative models. ArXiv abs/1711.05772 (2018)
15. Fong, R., Vedaldi, A.: Net2Vec: quantifying and explaining how concepts are encoded by filters in deep neural networks. In: Proceedings of the IEEE Conference on Computer Vision and Pattern Recognition (CVPR) (2018)
16. Friedman, J., Tukey, J.: A projection pursuit algorithm for exploratory data analysis. IEEE Trans. Comput. C-23(9), 881–890 (1974). https://doi.org/10.1109/T-C.1974.224051
17. Gunning, D.: Explainable artificial intelligence (XAI) (2017)
18. Hamilton, W.L.: Graph representation learning. Synthesis Lect. Artif. Intell. Mach. Learn. 14(3), 1–159 (2020)
19. He, K., Zhang, X., Ren, S., Sun, J.: Deep residual learning for image recognition. CoRR abs/1512.03385 (2015). http://arxiv.org/abs/1512.03385
20. Henderson, R., Clevert, D.A., Montanari, F.: Improving molecular graph neural network explainability with orthonormalization and induced sparsity. ArXiv abs/2105.04854 (2021)

21. Kim, B., et al.: Interpretability beyond feature attribution: quantitative testing with concept activation vectors (TCAV). In: ICML (2018)
22. Krizhevsky, A.: One weird trick for parallelizing convolutional neural networks. ArXiv abs/1404.5997 (2014)
23. LeCun, Y., Cortes, C.: The MNIST database of handwritten digits (2005)
24. Lipton, Z.C.: The Mythos of Model Interpretability. arXiv e-prints arXiv:1606.03490 (2016)
25. Liznerski, P., Ruff, L., Vandermeulen, R.A., Franks, B.J., Kloft, M., Muller, K.: Explainable deep one-class classification. ArXiv abs/2007.01760 (2020)
26. Liznerski, P., Ruff, L., Vandermeulen, R.A., Franks, B.J., Kloft, M., Müller, K.: Explainable deep one-class classification. CoRR abs/2007.01760 (2020). https://arxiv.org/abs/2007.01760
27. Mahendran, A., Vedaldi, A.: Understanding deep image representations by inverting them. In: 2015 IEEE Conference on Computer Vision and Pattern Recognition (CVPR), pp. 5188–5196 (2015)
28. Mordvintsev, A., Olah, C., Tyka, M.: Inceptionism: going deeper into neural networks (2015)
29. Nguyen, A., Yosinski, J., Clune, J.: Understanding neural networks via feature visualization: a survey. In: Samek, W., Montavon, G., Vedaldi, A., Hansen, L.K., Müller, K.-R. (eds.) Explainable AI: Interpreting, Explaining and Visualizing Deep Learning. LNCS (LNAI), vol. 11700, pp. 55–76. Springer, Cham (2019). https://doi.org/10.1007/978-3-030-28954-6_4
30. Olah, C., Schubert, L., Mordvintsev, A.: Feature visualization. Distill (2017). https://distill.pub/2017/feature-visualization/
31. Popoviciu, T.: Sur les équations algébriques ayant toutes leurs racines réelles (1935)
32. Raghu, M., Gilmer, J., Yosinski, J., Sohl-Dickstein, J.: SVCCA: singular vector canonical correlation analysis for deep learning dynamics and interpretability. In: NIPS (2017)
33. Ridgeway, K., Mozer, M.: Learning deep disentangled embeddings with the F-statistic loss. In: NeurIPS (2018)
34. Russakovsky, O., et al.: ImageNet large scale visual recognition challenge. Int. J. Comput. Vision 115, 211–252 (2015)
35. Samek, W., Müller, K.-R.: Towards explainable artificial intelligence. In: Samek, W., Montavon, G., Vedaldi, A., Hansen, L.K., Müller, K.-R. (eds.) Explainable AI: Interpreting, Explaining and Visualizing Deep Learning. LNCS (LNAI), vol. 11700, pp. 5–22. Springer, Cham (2019). https://doi.org/10.1007/978-3-030-28954-6_1
36. Saxe, A.M., Koh, P.W., Chen, Z., Bhand, M., Suresh, B., Ng, A.: On random weights and unsupervised feature learning. In: ICML (2011)
37. Selvaraju, R.R., Cogswell, M., Das, A., Vedantam, R., Parikh, D., Batra, D.: Grad-CAM: visual explanations from deep networks via gradient-based localization. In: 2017 IEEE International Conference on Computer Vision (ICCV), pp. 618–626 (2017). https://doi.org/10.1109/ICCV.2017.74
38. Shrikumar, A., Greenside, P., Kundaje, A.: Learning important features through propagating activation differences. ArXiv abs/1704.02685 (2017)
39. Simonyan, K., Vedaldi, A., Zisserman, A.: Deep inside convolutional networks: visualising image classification models and saliency maps. CoRR abs/1312.6034 (2014)
40. Sundararajan, M., Taly, A., Yan, Q.: Axiomatic attribution for deep networks. ArXiv abs/1703.01365 (2017)
41. Szab'o, R., Katona, D., Csillag, M., Csisz'arik, A., Varga, D.: Visualizing transfer learning. ArXiv abs/2007.07628 (2020)

42. Szegedy, C., Vanhoucke, V., Ioffe, S., Shlens, J., Wojna, Z.: Rethinking the inception architecture for computer vision. In: 2016 IEEE Conference on Computer Vision and Pattern Recognition (CVPR), pp. 2818–2826 (2016)
43. Ulyanov, D., Vedaldi, A., Lempitsky, V.: Deep image prior. In: 2018 IEEE/CVF Conference on Computer Vision and Pattern Recognition, pp. 9446–9454 (2018)
44. Xu, K., Hu, W., Leskovec, J., Jegelka, S.: How powerful are graph neural networks? ArXiv abs/1810.00826 (2019)
45. Zeiler, M.D., Fergus, R.: Visualizing and understanding convolutional networks. In: Fleet, D., Pajdla, T., Schiele, B., Tuytelaars, T. (eds.) ECCV 2014. LNCS, vol. 8689, pp. 818–833. Springer, Cham (2014). https://doi.org/10.1007/978-3-319-10590-1_53
46. Zhang, Q., Wu, Y., Zhu, S.: Interpretable convolutional neural networks. In: 2018 IEEE/CVF Conference on Computer Vision and Pattern Recognition, pp. 8827–8836 (2018)
47. Zhou, B., Bau, D., Oliva, A., Torralba, A.: Interpreting deep visual representations via network dissection. IEEE Trans. Pattern Anal. Mach. Intell. 41, 2131–2145 (2019)
48. Zhuang, F., et al.: A comprehensive survey on transfer learning. Proc. IEEE 109(1), 43–76 (2021)

Gated Variable Selection Neural Network for Multimodal Sleep Quality Assessment

Yue Chen[1], Takashi Morita[2], Tsukasa Kimura[2], Takafumi Kato[3], Masayuki Numao[2], and Ken-ichi Fukui[2(✉)]

[1] Graduate School of Information Science and Technology, Osaka University, Suita, Japan
[2] SANKEN (The Institute of Scientific and Industrial Research), Osaka University, Osaka, Japan
fukui@ai.sanken.osaka-u.ac.jp
[3] Graduate School of Dentistry, Osaka University, Osaka, Japan

Abstract. Sleep quality can be affected by several factors, such as sleep environment, lifestyles and so on. This research proposed a novel deep learning architecture with multiple-factors for sound-based sleep quality assessment. Utilizing sleep sound for sleep quality evaluation is low-cost and contactless, also, sound data can reflect several physical behaviors such as snore, cough and body movements. This research utilized VAE-LSTM to learn sleep patterns in sleep sound and applied Gated Variable Selection Network (GVSN) to select useful information in factors. We recorded whole night sleep sounds of more than 100 subjects by microphone at home and collected questionnaires for the experiment. The results show that the proposed method can perform accurate sleep quality prediction as well as factor importance analysis.

Keywords: Gated Variable Selection · Sleep Quality Assessment · Sleep Sound · Factor Analysis

1 Introduction

Sleep helps people regain physical and mental strength, relieve stress, improve learning capacity and stay healthy. Traditional tools for clinical and scientific research in sleep medicine is Polysomnography (PSG) [1], which records people's brain waves, the oxygen level in blood, heart rate and breathing, as well as body movements. Based on PSG signals, sleep experts are able to discover disorders such as sleep apnea, epilepsy and manually label sleep stages (i.e., REM or Non-REM sleep and its depth of sleep). PSG machines are expensive and requires the patients to go to a specialized sleep clinic or hospital, which limits its application scene.

With the rapid development of sensor technologies and computer science, in-home health care devices have become popular. Such as sensors under the mattress [8], smart watch or smart wristband, radio sensors [10] and wearable single-EEG electronics [3]. The consumer wearable devices perform well at detecting wakefulness, but have low accuracy on sleep staging [2].

Supported by JSPS KAKENHI Grant Number JP22K19832.

In this research, sleep sound is chosen as sleep monitoring technology. Comparing to other technologies, it is low-cost, contactless and thus does not have an external impact on people's sleep. Besides, sound contains more physical behaviors like snore cough, bruxism, body movements, which are seen as important indices when sleep experts evaluate sleep quality, while other devices only have the ability to capture part of them. Wu et al. [14] compared the sleep event cluster map generated from the sleep sound and the sleep stage sequences based on PSG data. The consistency provided strong support for the effectiveness of using sleep sound for sleep study.

On the other hand, sleep quality can be affected by several factors, such as environmental factors like temperature, humidity, loudness, or physical factors like gender and BMI. For sleep monitoring, considering the influence by environmental and physical factors is necessary. Figuring out which factors are important may give a direction for people to get a better sleep.

This research uses events extracted from sleep sounds as objective signals and sleep satisfaction answered by the subjects as sleep quality index, aims to build a deep learning model for sound-based sleep quality estimation as well as automatically figure out important environmental and physical factors.

In this research, Variational Autoencoder (VAE) [6] is applied to gather compact latent vectors of sound events, later the sequences of latent vectors are fed into a Long-short Term Memory (LSTM) model to learn sleep patterns. Gated Variable Selection Network (GVSN) [9] which uses Gated Residual Network (GRN) as the base model is used for selecting useful information and drop unused information in environmental and physical factors. This research proposes two kinds of models: initialization model and hierarchical selection model, with two differences. The first difference is the factor organized way. In the first model, all factors are fed into a GVSN without group, while the second model groups the factors by type and feeds every type of factors into a unique GVSN model. The second difference is the fusion way of GVSN and LSTM model. In initialization model, factors are fed to initialize LSTM model before the input of sleep events while in hierarchical model, factors and sleep events are on the same level.

The experiment in this research used in-home sound recording data of near 2000 nights from more than 100 subjects to confirm the effectiveness of proposed architectures.

2   Related Works

To the best of our knowledge, researches based on sleep sound recording mostly study sleep apnea [11,12], sound-based sleep quality evaluation researches are still few. Wu et al. [13] applied Hidden Markov Model (HMM) and Support Vector Machine (SVM) to predict subjective sleep quality based on sleep events extracted from laboratory recorded sound data. Kalintha et al. [5] raised a new concept named SleepAge as sleep scoring label which considering the relationship between age and sleep quality and applied several deep learning methods on mel-frequency spectrograms of in-home recorded sleep sound to predict SleepAge.

Hong et al. [4] poposed an end-to-end deep learning model for sound-based sleep staging designed to work with audio from microphone chips.

The mentioned sound-based researches for sleep quality assignment only used sleep sound as input, without considering the environmental and physical factors which may affect sleep quality. This research not only adds the factors to increase evaluation accuracy but also tries to learn the impact giving to sleep quality by each factor.

3   Methodology

3.1   Overview

The whole process of this research is shown in Fig. 1. Sleep sounds are first recorded, then during prepossessing part, sleep sound events are extracted, then VAE is applied for dimensionality reduction; meanwhile, factors such as temperature level, BMI are gathered from sleep questionnaire answered by subjects. The prepossessed sequences of sound events and factors are the inputs of the proposed architectures to learn sleep patterns and predict the sleep quality, which is sleep satisfaction answered by the subjects in this research as well as identify the importance of each factor. Two kinds of architectures are proposed in this research: GVSN-LSTM Initialization model and GVSN Hierarchical Selection model.

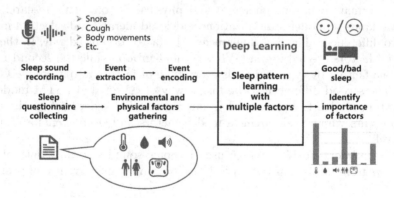

Fig. 1. Whole process of the proposed method

3.2   Sleep Sound Prepossessing

First of all, for each night, sleep sound was recorded in-home during sleep by microphone. Secondly, the sleep events were extracted by Kleinberg's Burst Detection algorithm [7,14]. The example of extracted events (time domain) is shown in Fig. 2(a). At last, Fast Fourier Transform (FFT) was applied. FFT algorithm converts time domain signals to frequency domain signals (spectrum). This research uses discrete points of the spectrum of the extracted events as sound events which are fed into neural networks. In this research, the recording frequency is $fs = 48000$ (Hz), thus the valid range is 0 to $fs/2 = 24000$ (Hz), and we set the frequency interval as 10 Hz, then there are 2400 data points for each event. The example of transferred event spectrums (frequency domain) is shown in Fig. 2(b).

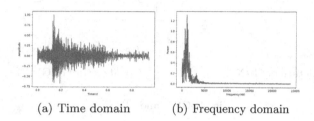

(a) Time domain   (b) Frequency domain

Fig. 2. Extracted sound event

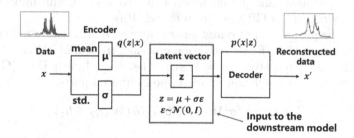

Fig. 3. Event encoding by VAE

3.3   Sleep Sound Event Encoding

High dimensionality may cause huge amount of calculations and thus will take a long time for training. In this research, Variational AutoEncoder (VAE) is used for dimensionality reduction. VAE algorithm has the ability to learn effective embedding from the original data and compress to low-dimensional space. The decoder is used to ensure that the latent space can capture most of the information from the data space, and the decoder uses the latent space output as input to determine whether the data can be completely restored. In this research, encoder and decoder are both used during VAE training part, and only encoder is used for sleep sound encoding. As shown in Fig. 3, the sound event inputs for the further model is encoded to latent representations by a pre-trained VAE model.

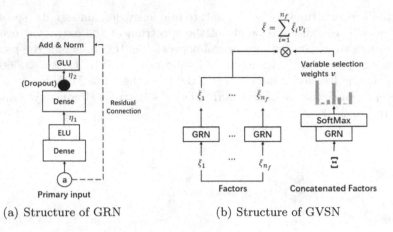

(a) Structure of GRN   (b) Structure of GVSN

Fig. 4. GRN and GVSN

3.4 Gated Residual Network

The Gated Residual Network (GRN) uses skip connection which avoids network degeneration problems and gating which helps to select useful information in factors. The structure of GRN is shown in Fig. 4(a).

In GRN, the primary input a first passes through a fully connected layer with Exponential Linear Unit (ELU) activation function: $\eta_1 = ELU(W_1 a + b_1)$. After another fully connected layer: $\eta_2 = W_2 \eta_1 + b_2$, Gate Linear Unit (GLU) will be applied to provide the flexibility to suppress unused parts:

$$GLU(\eta_2) = (\sigma(W_3 \eta_2 + b_3)) \odot (W_4 \eta_2 + b_4), \qquad (1)$$

where $\sigma(\cdot)$ is Sigmoid activation function and $\odot$ is Element-wise Hadamard product. At last, a standard layer normalization is applied.

3.5 Gated Variable Selection Network

In Gated Variable Selection Network (GVSN) which is shown in Fig. 4(b), GRN is applied to select useful information in each factor ξ_i and get a transformed embedding $\widetilde{\xi}_i$. These GRN networks are independent, that is, the parameters are not shared.

Meanwhile, the factors are concatenated into vector Ξ, and the model feeds Ξ to another GRN and Softmax layer to generate variable selection weights v. The variable selection weights are changed according to the distribution of the factor values, which give the flexibility for different factor inputs.

At last, the transformed embeddings are multiplied with variable selection weights:

$$\widetilde{\xi} = \sum_{i=1}^{n_f} \widetilde{\xi}_i v_i, \qquad (2)$$

where n_f is the number of factors.

GVSN gives different weights for each factor and changes based on the situation of each night, thus useful information will be enhanced and unused information will be ignored adaptively.

3.6   Proposed Model 1: GVSN-LSTM Initialization Model

The structure of GVSN-LSTM Initialization model is shown in Fig. 5. The GVSN-LSTM Initialization model firstly utilizes the GVSN to select useful factors:

$$\widetilde{\xi} = GVSN([\xi_1, \xi_2, ..., \xi_{n_f}]) \tag{3}$$

which is calculated by Eq. 2. Factors used in this research includes environmental factors (temperature level, humidity level, loudness level), physical factors (gender, BMI) and other factors (total recording time, number of extracted sound events).

Then the network applies two different GRN models to obtain the initial hidden state and cell state for LSTM on the selected factor information $\widetilde{\xi}$:

$$h_0 = GRN_h(\widetilde{\xi}) \tag{4}$$

$$c_0 = GRN_c(\widetilde{\xi}) \tag{5}$$

These two different GRN models are independent, that means the parameters are not shared. The meaning of the "Initialization" is to use the output of the two GRN models to initialize the hidden state h_0 and cell state c_0 in LSTM model.

Meanwhile, the LSTM receives sequence of whole night sleep sound events $\widetilde{X} = [\widetilde{x}_1, \widetilde{x}_2, ...\widetilde{x}_n]$ which are encoded by pre-trained VAE as input and applies a single hidden layer with different hidden units in the experiment, then a SoftMax layer is applied on the output of LSTM to generate the probability of good or bad sleep for evaluation:

$$\widetilde{y} = SoftMax(LSTM(\widetilde{X})), \tag{6}$$

where SoftMax activation function represents a Normalized Exponential function, it maps the output of multiple neurons to the $(0,1)$ interval, which can be understood as a probability to perform classification. The loss function is cross entropy.

In GVSN-LSTM Initialization model, the selected information in factors is used to initialize the LSTM model, further the sequence of sound events is fed. Environmental factors and physical factors are regarded as a kind of prior knowledge when learning sleep patterns.

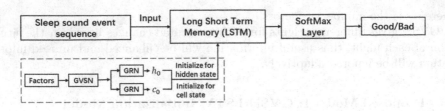

Fig. 5. The proposed model 1: GVSN-LSTM Initialization model

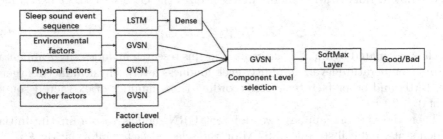

Fig. 6. The proposed model 2: GVSN Hierarchical Selection model

3.7 Proposed Model 2: GVSN Hierarchical Selection Model

The structure of GVSN Hierarchical Selection model is shown in Fig. 6. "Hierarchical" means that there are two selection levels in the model: factor selection level and component selection level.

In factor selection level, different kinds of factors are fed into different GVSN models to learn effective information and give higher weights to useful factors:

$$\widetilde{\boldsymbol{\xi}}_{c_i} = GVSN_{c_i}(\boldsymbol{\xi}_{c_i}), \tag{7}$$

where c_i in [env, phy, other] represents the kinds of factors. Here, $\widetilde{\boldsymbol{\xi}}_{env}$ represents environmental factors, $\widetilde{\boldsymbol{\xi}}_{phy}$ represents physical factors, and $\widetilde{\boldsymbol{\xi}}_{other}$ represents other factors.

Meanwhile, the latent sound feature is learned by same structure LSTM as in Initialization model but with randomly sampled hidden state and cell state applying on sequence of sleep sound events $\widetilde{\boldsymbol{X}} = [\widetilde{\boldsymbol{x}}_1, \widetilde{\boldsymbol{x}}_2, ...\widetilde{\boldsymbol{x}}_n]$ which is encoded by pre-trained VAE. Dense layers are further applied to learned sound event features to transfer the output of LSTM to same dimension as output $\widetilde{\boldsymbol{\xi}}_{c_i}$ of GVSN models:

$$\widetilde{\boldsymbol{\xi}}_{sound} = Dense(LSTM(\widetilde{\boldsymbol{X}})), \tag{8}$$

Here, GVSN for factor selection and LSTM are on same hierarchy.

The transformed sound features $\widetilde{\boldsymbol{\xi}}_{sound}$ and factors $\widetilde{\boldsymbol{\xi}}_{c_i}$ are different components, which are fed into another GVSN module for component level selection. The component level selection is to learn the useful fusion information of sound events and factors. After selection module, a SoftMax dense layer is applied to evaluate the sleep quality:

$$\widetilde{y} = SoftMax(GVSN_{com}(\widetilde{\xi})),\qquad(9)$$

where $\widetilde{\xi} = [\widetilde{\xi}_{sound}, \widetilde{\xi}_{env}, \widetilde{\xi}_{phy}, \widetilde{\xi}_{other}]$. The loss function is also cross entropy.

The hierarchy in the model can learn multimodal data up from the bottom: at the bottom, the model judges the factor's importance in each type of factors and selects useful factors; at the top, the model judges the component importance and enhance important component to learn sleep pattern.

4 Experiment

4.1 Dataset

All subjects were asked to record whole night sleep sound during sleep during 28 days by smartphone microphone. Meanwhile, subjects were asked to fill in the questionnaires, they answered questions about profile before the experiment; everyday before sleep, they answered questions about physical and psychological states; after sleep, they answered questions about the subjective sleep quality and subjective perception of the environment during sleep; after the experiment, they answered questions about lifestyle. The experiment was approved by the ethical committee at SANKEN, Osaka University.

In order to reduce the experimental error, we chose the subjects who did not use the air-conditioner and other home devices. We chose "sleep satisfaction" answered by subjects as target in the experiment and removed the nights which were "neither satisfied nor unsatisfied". "Satisfied" and "very satisfied" answered by the subjects were seen as "good sleep", when "Unsatisfied" and "very unsatisfied" were seen as "bad sleep". We removed the subjects whose recorded sleep nights were less than 10 days and balanced numbers of good/bad sleep classes. There were 161 subjects with 1876 days, the distribution of age and sleep quality is presented in Table 1.

Table 1. Age and sleep quality distribution

Age	#Subjects	Sleep quality	#Nights
20 s	63	Good sleep	372
		Bad sleep	372
30 s/40 s	58	Good sleep	382
		Bad sleep	382
50 s/60 s	40	Good sleep	184
		Bad sleep	184

The environmental factors and physical factors used in the experiments were generated from questionnaires answered by subjects. We divided the temperature into five levels from hot to cold, where number "1" represented very hot, and number "5" represented very cold. Humidity was also divided into five levels from high humidity to low humidity, meanwhile loudness was divided into three levels from noisy to quiet. We also divided gender into two classes by labeling "1" for men and "2" for women. Meanwhile, we calculated Body Mass Index (BMI) by $kg/(m^2)$ where kg was the weight of a person in kilograms and m^2 was his height in metres squared. Besides, we generated some other factors from sound data, we used the total time of whole night recorded sound data (hours) as total recording time, which could reflect total sleep time to some extent. We also used number of extracted sound events. The factors in this research are **Environmental factors**: Temperature level, humidity level, Loudness level; **Physical factors**: Gender, BMI; **Other factors**: Total recording time, Number of extracted sound events.

4.2   Experiment Settings

For latent representation learning, the reconstruction loss function was Kullback-Leibler (KL) divergence, and the latent space was set to 64. The training proceeds by mini-batch learning in which gradients were updated once for a single batch of data, where the batch size is set to 512. The number of iterations was set to 2000. After the VAE model was pre-trained, events were fed for gathering latent representation.

The number of events is too large to train LSTM, therefore, we randomly selected 500 events while maintaining enough number to represent sleep pattern, if the number of events was smaller than 500, we added **0** padding.

For sound pattern learning, we set the hidden units of LSTM by different options for each model, the dropout rate of LSTM was set to 0.5 to prevent overfitting. In GVSN-LSTM Initialization model, the GRN hidden layer size was same to number of LSTM hidden units for initialization; in GVSN Hierarchical model, the GRN hidden layer size was set to 16 for each GRN in factor selection level and component selection level; no dropout was applied in GRN for each model. For each model, the batch size was set to 128, the number of epochs was set to 50 with early stopping strategy.

We experimented each model for different age group. We set up different options for hidden units to observe the influence of model complexity. There were 5 options of LSTM hidden units for 20 s age group: 16, 32, 64, 128, 256 and 4 options for other age groups: 32, 64, 128, 256.

4.3   Sleep Evaluation Accuracy

The experiment results of 20 s age group with 5-fold cross validation are shown in Table 2. The results showed that GVSN-LSTM Initialization model with multi-modal data performed better than LSTM model which just used sound data when the number of LSTM hidden units increased, and GVSN Hierarchical Selection model outperformed other two models. The results showed that the architecture to process multimodal data can efficiently extract valuable information in factors aimed at improving the accuracy of sleep quality assessment. Another point to pay attention is that GVSN Hierarchical model could reach high accuracy with only few LSTM hidden units while others used big amount of hidden units.

Table 2. Comparison of accuracy (average and standard deviation) in 20 s

LSTM hidden	LSTM (Sound only)	Initialization (Multimodal)	Hierarchical (Multimodal)
16	0.518 ± 0.026	0.512 ± 0.058	0.568 ± 0.091
32	0.518 ± 0.063	0.540 ± 0.041	$*0.604 \pm 0.059$
64	0.558 ± 0.052	0.562 ± 0.053	0.600 ± 0.026
128	0.548 ± 0.019	0.566 ± 0.023	0.578 ± 0.047
256	0.546 ± 0.024	0.578 ± 0.047	0.572 ± 0.035

Table 3. Comparison of accuracy (average and standard deviation) in 30 s/40 s

LSTM hidden	LSTM (Sound only)	Initialization (Multimodal)	Hierarchical (Multimodal)
32	0.548 ± 0.025	0.532 ± 0.019	0.568 ± 0.038
64	0.532 ± 0.020	0.554 ± 0.017	$*0.586 \pm 0.033$
128	0.526 ± 0.037	0.556 ± 0.032	0.546 ± 0.040
256	0.560 ± 0.035	0.562 ± 0.046	0.538 ± 0.041

Table 4. Comparison of accuracy (average and standard deviation) in 50 s/60 s

LSTM hidden	LSTM (Sound only)	Initialization (Multimodal)	Hierarchical (Multimodal)
32	0.526 ± 0.030	0.508 ± 0.060	0.538 ± 0.041
64	0.540 ± 0.069	0.544 ± 0.048	0.508 ± 0.045
128	0.549 ± 0.050	0.558 ± 0.063	0.546 ± 0.043
256	0.550 ± 0.023	$*0.558 \pm 0.048$	0.544 ± 0.058

Results of 30 s/40 s age group are shown in Table 3, the results also showed that GVSN-LSTM Initialization model outperformed LSTM with larger LSTM dimension, when GVSN Hierarchical model performed better than GVSN-LSTM initialization modal and could reach good result in low LSTM hidden dimension.

Results of 50 s/60 s group are shown in Table 4. Although Initialization model was slightly better than Hierarchical and LSTM model. Actually, the results were not good on all models for 50 s/60 s age group. It might be caused by the data, the dataset for 50 s/60 s age group is very small.

4.4 Factor Weights Analysis

To visualize which factor may have significant value to sleep quality, we chose the best GVSN Hierarchical results. Figure 7 shows the factor weights on the component level while Fig. 8 shows the factor weights on the factor level.

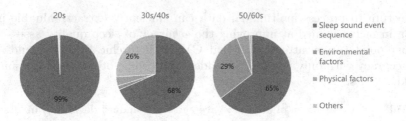

Fig. 7. Factor weight visualization on component level

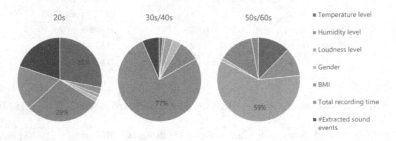

Fig. 8. Product of component weight and factor weight (Ignoring sleep sound event)

For 20 s group, on the component level, sleep sound event sequence dominated 99%, which showed the irreplaceable of information in sleep sounds. Different ages had different factor importance weights. On the component level, regardless of age, events that occur during sleep played a crucial role in determining sleep quality. However, as age grew, other components became more important. For 30 s/40 s age group, the importance of total recording time which reflects total sleep time and number of events grew; for 50 s/60 s age people, environment became the second most important component instead of sleep length and number of events. On factor selection level, Loudness played more principle role in 50 s/60 s age group, which meant 50 s/60 s age people should pay more attention to their sleep environmental loudness; in physical factors, no matter which age group, BMI had more significant effect than gender. For 20 s age group, there were no so much difference between total recording time and number of extracted events while for 30 s/40 s age group, total recording time became vitally important.

5   Conclusion

This research proposed a novel deep learning architecture which utilized Gated Variable Selection Network to select useful information in environmental and physical factors as well as Long Short Term Memory to recognize sleep patterns from sleep sound events, two kinds of fusion models were proposed: Initialization and Hierarchical models.

The experiment results on near 2000 nights from more than 100 subjects showed effectiveness of considering environmental and physical factors. On the other hand, the results GVSN Hierarchical model showed that for each age group, the effect of each factor was distinctive. Targeted recommendations may be a better approach than the general recommendations of existing sleep data monitoring. Also, more data and available factors may improve the accuracy.

References

1. Berry, R.B., et al.: The AASM Manual for the Scoring of Sleep and Associated Events: Rules, Terminology and Technical Specifications. American Academy of Sleep Medicine (2020)
2. Chinoy, E.D., et al.: Performance of seven consumer sleep-tracking devices compared with polysomnography. Sleep **44**(5) (2020). Article number zsaa291
3. Eldele, E., et al.: An attention-based deep learning approach for sleep stage classification with single-channel EEG. IEEE Trans. Neural Syst. Rehabil. Eng. **29**, 809–818 (2021)
4. Hong, J., et al.: End-to-end sleep staging using nocturnal sounds from microphone chips for mobile devices. Nat. Sci. Sleep **14**, 1187–1201 (2022)
5. Kalintha, W., Kato, T., Fukui, K.: SleepAge: sleep quality assessment from nocturnal sounds in home environment. Procedia Comput. Sci. **176**, 898–907 (2020)
6. Kingma, D.P., Welling, M.: Auto-encoding variational bayes. arXiv preprint arXiv:1312.6114 (2013)
7. Kleinberg, J.: Bursty and hierarchical structure in streams. In: Proceedings of the Eighth ACM SIGKDD International Conference on Knowledge Discovery and Data Mining, pp. 91–101 (2002)
8. Kortelainen, J.M., Mendez, M.O., Bianchi, A.M., Matteucci, M., Cerutti, S.: Sleep staging based on signals acquired through bed sensor. IEEE Trans. Inf. Technol. Biomed. **14**(3), 776–785 (2010)
9. Lim, B., Arık, S.Ö., Loeff, N., Pfister, T.: Temporal fusion transformers for interpretable multi-horizon time series forecasting. Int. J. Forecast. **37**(4), 1748–1764 (2021)
10. Lin, F., et al.: SleepSense: a noncontact and cost-effective sleep monitoring system. IEEE Trans. Biomed. Circuits Syst. **11**(1), 189–202 (2017)
11. Luo, J., et al.: A novel deep feature transfer-based OSA detection method using sleep sound signals. Physiol. Meas. **41**(7), 075009 (2020)
12. Nakano, H., Furukawa, T., Tanigawa, T.: Tracheal sound analysis using a deep neural network to detect sleep apnea. J. Clin. Sleep Med. **15**(8), 1125–1133 (2019)
13. Wu, H., Kato, T., Numao, M., Fukui, K.: Statistical sleep pattern modelling for sleep quality assessment based on sound events. Health Inf. Sci. Syst. **5**, 1–11 (2017)
14. Wu, H., Kato, T., Yamada, T., Numao, M., Fukui, K.: Personal sleep pattern visualization using sequence-based kernel self-organizing map on sound data. Artif. Intell. Med. **80**, 1–10 (2017)

Generalized Thermostatistics and the Nonequilibrium Landscape Description of Neural Network Dynamics

Roseli S. Wedemann[1]([✉]) [iD] and Angel R. Plastino[2,3] [iD]

[1] Instituto de Matemática e Estatística, Universidade do Estado do Rio de Janeiro,
Rua São Francisco Xavier 524, Rio de Janeiro, RJ 20550-900, Brazil
roseli@ime.uerj.br

[2] CeBio y Departamento de Ciencias Básicas, Universidad Nacional del Noroeste
de la Provincia de Buenos Aires, UNNOBA, Conicet,
Roque Saenz Peña 456, Junin, Argentina
arplastino@unnoba.edu.ar

[3] Centro Brasileiro de Pesquisas Físicas (CBPF), Rua Xavier Sigaud 150,
Rio de Janeiro, RJ 22290-180, Brazil

Abstract. Generalized thermostatistical formalisms arising from extensions or generalizations of the standard logarithmic entropy are attracting considerable attention nowadays, specially associated with the study of complex systems. Probability distributions optimizing non-standard entropies are common in Nature and are observed in diverse types of complex systems, including those relevant to neuroscience and artificial intelligence (AI). Nonlinear Fokker-Planck dynamics constitutes one of the main mechanisms that can give rise to these distributions. We present a family of nonlinear Fokker-Planck equations associated with general, continuous, neural network, dynamical models for associative memory. Such models are relevant in AI, and in the study of mental life, because memory is an essential ingredient in many phenomena explored by neuroscience and psychology. We investigate how the nonlinear Fokker-Planck approach to network dynamics is related to the nonequilibrium landscape description of this dynamics analyzed in [36]. We prove that, within general nonequilibrium thermostastical settings, the landscape treatment uncovers deep links between the Liapunov function of the network dynamics, the deterministic phase-space flow of the network, and the properties of the diffusion term in the nonlinear Fokker-Planck equations. These connections, in turn, lead to H-theorems involving free-energy-like functionals related to the generalized entropies. This contribution extends and generalizes our previous studies that focused only on the S_q entropies [35]. We illustrate our present developments by applying them to the celebrated Cohen-Grossberg family of neural network models.

Keywords: Continuous neural network dynamics · Nonlinear Fokker-Planck equations · Nonequilibrium landscape theory · Generalized thermostatistical formalisms · Cohen-Grossberg neural networks · Associative memory

© The Author(s), under exclusive license to Springer Nature Switzerland AG 2023
L. Iliadis et al. (Eds.): ICANN 2023, LNCS 14258, pp. 300–311, 2023.
https://doi.org/10.1007/978-3-031-44192-9_24

1   Introduction

Models for associative memory based on artificial neural networks, such as the celebrated Hopfield one [11], offer paradigmatic descriptions of the physical processes and algorithmic structures underlying both normal and pathological mental phenomena. Besides having been used to solve many problems in artificial intelligence (AI), they are also used for studying the mind, because memory is central to most of the processes investigated by psychiatry, psychoanalysis and neuroscience [5,14,23]. Applications to neuroscience rest on the hypothesis that memory is recorded in the architecture of the brain's neural network. Following this theoretical framework, in recent years, we have developed associative memory, neural network models for various mental phenomena, including creativity, neurosis, and the interaction between conscious and unconscious mental processes [4,21,28,30,33,34]. In these models, memory retrieval was implemented using a generalized simulated annealing (GSA) algorithm [26] related to the S_q-thermostatistics [24,25].

Extensions or generalizations of the maximum entropy principle based on non-standard entropic functionals [1,2,12,13,16,19] have proved to be useful for the study of diverse problems in physics and elsewhere, particularly in connection with complex systems [10,25]. Complex systems and processes, including those related to neurosciences and AI, often exhibit probability distributions or densities that do not comply with the standard exponential form usually associated with the Boltzmann-Gibbs thermostatistics. In many cases, thermo-statistical frameworks based on non-standard entropic measures seem to be at work. In this regard, the GSA prescription appears to be relevant, since it simulates, within the context of discrete-state neural networks, a concrete dynamics generating the S_q-maximum entropy distributions [21,28]. For example, some network configurations have been identified, for which the avalanches occurring during the GSA-based memory retrieval process obey S_q-maximum entropy, power-law-like distributions [21]. These distributions, arising from a generalized, non-standard maximum entropy scheme, are compatible with various power-law distributions observed in neuroscience, both in theoretical, numerical studies [17], and in experimental research [3,21,22]. In particular, the generalized maximum entropy distributions are consistent with the distributions of spatial reach and time duration of signal propagation, measured during brain stimulation and captured by fMRI images [3,22]. Other aspects of our numerical simulation models [28,34] also exhibit power-law-like behavior. These results motivate us to investigate further the use of ideas coming from generalized thermostatistical frameworks, based on non-standard entropies, in connection with neural network models and their dynamical behavior. In particular, we shall consider here nonlinear instances of the Fokker-Planck approach, which provide possible mechanisms leading to probability distributions that optimize a general non-logarithmic entropy.

Considering the biological applications that we have mentioned, we shall consider networks of neurons with states described by continuous (phase space) variables that evolve according to an appropriate set of coupled, ordinary differential equations [6,11]. In the absence of noise, these networks can be regarded as deterministic, continuous dynamical systems. The Fokker-Planck approach allows the incorporation of the effects of noise when studying the networks' behavior [15, 29, 31, 32]. An interesting and promising development that has been taking place in recent years concerns the so-called nonequilibrium, landscape theory of network, or network-like, dynamics [8, 27, 36]. Within this approach, the nonequilibrium behavior of the system corresponds to time-dependent solutions of a Fokker-Planck equation, and is analyzed in terms of an abstract potential landscape and an associated phase-space flow, that involve the effects due to both the deterministic part of the dynamics (drift field) and the noisy part (diffusion term). So far, applications of this approach have considered mostly linear Fokker-Planck equations [8, 27, 36] or restricted cases of nonlinear Fokker-Planck equations [35]. The aim of the present contribution is to explore a generalization of the nonequilibrium, landscape theory of neural networks [8, 27, 36], based on a family of nonlinear Fokker-Planck formalisms linked to generalized, non-logarithmic, entropic functionals S_G. We shall show how the generalization of the nonequilibrium landscape formulation entails dynamical structures, independent of the specific form of the Fokker-Planck nonlinearity, that shed light on the connections linking the Liapunov function of the network dynamics with the drift field, and with the (state-dependent) diffusion coefficients of the Fokker-Planck equations associated with the networks. These relations lead, in turn, to the formulation of an H-theorem for the nonlinear Fokker-Planck equation (NLFPE), and to the stationary solution, which has the shape of a density that optimizes a generalized entropy. In order to illustrate these ideas, we shall consider their application to the continuous Cohen-Grossberg neural networks [6].

2   Thermostatistical Formalisms Associated with Generalized Entropies

At the core of generalized thermostatistical formalisms are entropic variational principles, based on the constrained optimization of appropriate entropic functionals [1, 2, 12, 13, 16, 19]. A general trace-form entropic functional, evaluated on a probability density $\mathcal{P}(\boldsymbol{z})$, has the form

$$S_G[\mathcal{P}] = \kappa \int \mathcal{C}(\mathcal{P}(\boldsymbol{z})/P_c)\, d^N \boldsymbol{z}\,, \tag{1}$$

where $\boldsymbol{z} \in \Re^N$ represents a point in an N-dimensional phase space, P_c is a constant with dimensions of inverse phase-space volume, and the constant κ determines the units in which the entropic functional S_G is measured. We assume that the function $\mathcal{C}(x)$, for $x \geq 0$, satisfies $\mathcal{C}(x) \geq 0$, $\mathcal{C}''(x) < 0$, and $\mathcal{C}(0) = 1$.

The generalized thermostatistical formalism derived from the entropic functional (1) is based on the optimization of (1), under the constraints imposed by normalization

$$\int \mathcal{P}(\boldsymbol{z})\, d^N \boldsymbol{z} = 1\,, \tag{2}$$

and by the mean value

$$\int \mathcal{P}(z)\,\varepsilon(z)\,d^N z = \mathcal{E}, \tag{3}$$

of an energy function $\varepsilon(z)$. The ensuing variational problem is

$$\delta\left[S_G - \alpha\left(\int \mathcal{P}(z)\,d^N z\right) - \beta\mathcal{E}\right] = 0, \tag{4}$$

where α and β are the Lagrange multipliers associated with the normalization and the mean energy constraints. The solution to the variational problem is given by the entropy-optimizing probability density

$$\mathcal{P}_{EO}(z) = P_c\,\mathcal{A}\Big(\alpha + \beta\,\varepsilon(z)\Big), \tag{5}$$

where the function $\mathcal{A}(x)$ is the inverse function of $\mathcal{C}'(x)$ (that is, $\mathcal{A}\left(\mathcal{C}'(x)\right) = \mathcal{C}'\left(\mathcal{A}(x)\right) = x$). For the Boltzmann entropy, $S_B = -\kappa\int(\mathcal{P}/P_c)\ln(\mathcal{P}/P_c)d^N z$, one has, $\mathcal{C}(x) = -x\ln x$, $\mathcal{C}'(x) = -1 - \ln x$, $\mathcal{C}''(x) = -1/x$, and $\mathcal{A}(x) = \exp(-1-x)$. For the Tsallis entropy, one has $S_q = \frac{\kappa}{(q-1)}\int\left[(\mathcal{P}/P_c) - (\mathcal{P}/P_c)^q\,d^N z\right]$. Nonextensive, thermostatistical formalisms based on generalized, non-standard entropies are regarded as an important tool in the study of complex systems. A few of the dynamical mechanisms that lead to probability densities optimizing generalized entropies have been identified. One of the most studied is the one based on diffusion, Fokker-Planck, or reaction-diffusion equations with nonlinear diffusion terms [7,9,18].

3   Entropic Forms, Nonlinear Fokker-Planck Dynamics, and Nonequilibrium Landscapes for Networks

A continuous neural network is a multi-dimensional dynamical system. The network's state, at each time t, is represented by a point in an N-dimensional phase-space with coordinates $\{z_1, z_2, \cdots, z_N\}$. Here z_i corresponds to the state of the ith neuron. In the absence of noise (that is, absence of random perturbations), the network's dynamics is deterministic, and obeys the set of coupled, ordinary differential equations,

$$\frac{dz_i}{dt} = K_i(z_1, z_2, \cdots, z_N), \qquad i = 1, \ldots, N. \tag{6}$$

In vector notation, the equations of motion can be cast in a compact fashion, as $\frac{dz}{dt} = K(z)$, with $z, K \in \Re^N$. The vector z, describing the system's state, moves in phase-space according to the flux represented by the vectorial field K. The Hopfield model constitutes an important example of a continuous neural network. Its equations of motion have the form (6), with $K_i(z) = \frac{1}{\tau_i}\left[-z_i + \sum_{j=1}^{N}\omega_{ij}g(z_j)\right]$.

It often happens, when N is very large, that it is not feasible, or conceptually convenient, to follow the evolution of a single, individual realization of the system. Instead, it proves convenient to adopt the strategy of statistical mechanics, and consider a statistical ensemble comprising identical copies of the system, evolving from different initial conditions. The statistical ensemble is mathematically represented by a phase-space probability density $\mathcal{P}(z_1, \cdots, z_N, t)$, that evolves according to the Liouville equation $(\partial\mathcal{P}/\partial t) + \boldsymbol{\nabla} \cdot (\mathcal{P}\boldsymbol{K}) = 0$. This evolution equation is a continuity equation in phase space. Here, $\boldsymbol{\nabla} = (\partial/\partial z_1, \ldots, \partial/\partial z_N)$ denotes the N-dimensional $\boldsymbol{\nabla}$-operator. The evolution of biological neural networks usually has a non-deterministic component, due to the effects of noise. These effects can be taken into account, by adding an extra diffusion-like term to the Liouville continuity equation. One then obtains the linear Fokker-Planck equation (FPE)

$$\frac{\partial\mathcal{P}}{\partial t} = D\nabla^2\mathcal{P} - \boldsymbol{\nabla} \cdot (\mathcal{P}\boldsymbol{K}), \tag{7}$$

where D is a constant, reflecting the global diffusion features of the system's dynamics. The last term on the right hand side of (7) is called the *drift* term and $\boldsymbol{K}$ is referred to as the *drift* field, or alternatively, the *phase-space flow*.

A generalization of the linear FPE (7), incorporating nonlinear diffusion [9, 20], is given by

$$\frac{\partial\mathcal{P}}{\partial t} = DP_c\nabla^2[\mathcal{B}(\mathcal{P}/P_c)] - \boldsymbol{\nabla} \cdot [\mathcal{P}\boldsymbol{K}], \tag{8}$$

where the function $\mathcal{B}(\mathcal{P}/P_c))$ inside the Laplacian operator describes a nonlinear diffusion process. The diffusion process can be related to an entropic form [20], for which the function $\mathcal{C}(x)$ is related to $\mathcal{B}(x)$ through

$$x^{-1}\mathcal{B}'(x) = -\mathcal{C}''(x). \tag{9}$$

Evolution equations of the form (8) constitute important tools for studying diverse phenomena in complex systems. They describe possible dynamical mechanisms leading to probability densities that optimize generalized entropies. A considerable amount of work by the complex systems research community has been devoted to this line of enquiry [7,9,18,20,25]. In this contribution, we propose a nonlinear Fokker-Planck dynamics for neural network dynamical models, such as the Cohen-Grossberg one, as a possible phenomenological mechanism explaining or describing the origin of the power-law-like distributions observed in some studies of brain neural networks. In recent works [15,29,31,35], we already considered some aspects of the nonlinear Fokker-Planck approach to neural network dynamics. Those efforts were centered on Hopfield neural networks, or on linear, neural-like networks devised to explore conceptual issues concerning the problem of synaptic asymmetries. Now we adopt a different perspective, exploring the relation between the nonlinear Fokker-Planck treatment of, and the nonequilibrium landscape approach to continuous, neural network dynamics.

The diffusion term in (8) describes homogeneous and isotropic diffusion, since the diffusion coefficient does not depend itself on the phase-space variables. When applying the Fokker-Planck formalism to the dynamics of networks, where noisy diffusion depends on local properties of synapses that convey the interaction between pairs of neurons, it is necessary to consider a more general scenario involving *inhomogeneous* and *anisotropic* diffusion. Consequently, we will consider the more general NLFPE

$$\frac{\partial P}{\partial t} = DP_c \sum_{ij} \frac{\partial}{\partial z_i} \left[G_{ij} \frac{\partial}{\partial z_j} \mathcal{B}(P/P_c) \right] - \sum_i \frac{\partial}{\partial z_i}(K_i P), \tag{10}$$

where the functions describing local diffusion, $G_{ij} = G_{ij}(z)$, which depend on the phase-space location z, constitute the elements of a positive definite matrix $\{G_{ij}\}$. Our next step is to apply the landscape approach discussed in [8, 27, 36] in the context of linear FPEs, to the nonlinear, evolution Eq. (10). Following [36], we consider first the stationary case of the NLFPE,

$$0 = DP_c \sum_{ij} \frac{\partial}{\partial z_i} \left[G_{ij} \frac{\partial}{\partial z_j} \mathcal{B}(P/P_c) \right] - \sum_i \frac{\partial}{\partial z_i}(K_i P), \tag{11}$$

and introduce an appropriate ansatz for the stationary situation,

$$P(z) = P_c \mathcal{A}(W(z)), \tag{12}$$

defined in terms of the abstract potential landscape $W(z)$. Note that to construct this ansatz we use the function $\mathcal{A}(x)$ that characterizes the form of the entropy-optimizing probability densities. For the standard linear FPEs, the ansatz (12) coincides with the ansatz $P(z) = \exp(-W(z))$, used in [36].

Calculating the derivatives in the two terms of Eq. (11), we obtain

$$\frac{\partial(K_i P)}{\partial z_i} = P \frac{\partial K_i}{\partial z_i} + K_i P_c \mathcal{A}'(W) \frac{\partial W}{\partial z_i}, \tag{13}$$

and, taking into account that $\mathcal{A}(x)$ is the inverse function of $\mathcal{C}'(x)$, and that the functions $\mathcal{B}(x)$ and $\mathcal{C}(x)$ are related through (9),

$$P_c \frac{\partial}{\partial z_i} \left[G_{ij} \frac{\partial}{\partial z_j} \mathcal{B}(P/P_c) \right] = P_c \frac{\partial}{\partial z_i} \left[G_{ij} \mathcal{B}'(\mathcal{A}(W)) \mathcal{A}'(W) \frac{\partial W}{\partial z_j} \right]$$

$$= -P_c \frac{\partial}{\partial z_i} \left[G_{ij} \mathcal{A}(W) \mathcal{C}''(\mathcal{A}(W)) \mathcal{A}'(W) \frac{\partial W}{\partial z_j} \right]$$

$$= -P_c \frac{\partial}{\partial z_i} \left[G_{ij} \mathcal{A}(W) \left(\frac{d}{dW} \mathcal{C}'(\mathcal{A}(W)) \right) \frac{\partial W}{\partial z_j} \right] = -P_c \frac{\partial}{\partial z_i} \left[G_{ij} \mathcal{A}(W) \frac{\partial W}{\partial z_j} \right]$$

$$= - \left[\left(P \frac{\partial G_{ij}}{\partial z_i} + P_c \mathcal{A}'(W) G_{ij} \frac{\partial W}{\partial z_i} \right) \frac{\partial W}{\partial z_j} + P G_{ij} \frac{\partial^2 W}{\partial z_i \partial z_j} \right]. \tag{14}$$

Substituting (13) and (14) in (11), taking into account the ansatz (12) for P, and factoring P_c, we obtain

$$\sum_i \left(\mathcal{A}(W) \frac{\partial K_i}{\partial z_i} + K_i \mathcal{A}'(W) \frac{\partial W}{\partial z_i} \right) =$$

$$-D \sum_{ij} \left[\left(\mathcal{A}(W) \frac{\partial G_{ij}}{\partial z_i} + \mathcal{A}'(W) G_{ij} \frac{\partial W}{\partial z_i} \right) \frac{\partial W}{\partial z_j} + \mathcal{A}(W) G_{ij} \frac{\partial^2 W}{\partial z_i \partial z_j} \right]. \quad (15)$$

Equation (15) can be recast as

$$\mathcal{A}(W) \left\{ \sum_i \left[\frac{\partial K_i}{\partial z_i} + D \sum_j \left(\frac{\partial G_{ij}}{\partial z_i} \frac{\partial W}{\partial z_j} + G_{ij} \frac{\partial^2 W}{\partial z_i \partial z_j} \right) \right] \right\}$$
$$+ \mathcal{A}'(W) \left\{ \sum_i \left[K_i \frac{\partial W}{\partial z_i} + D \sum_j \left(G_{ij} \frac{\partial W}{\partial z_i} \frac{\partial W}{\partial z_j} \right) \right] \right\} = 0. \quad (16)$$

We now analyze the structure of the above equation, in order to determine a set of relations linking the Liapunov function and the drift field (phase-space flow) of the network, with the diffusion-related functions $G_{ij}(z)$. We shall show that, for networks complying with those relations, the concomitant FPE satisfies important properties that hold for thermostatistical formalisms based on general entropic functionals. That is, we shall identify structures that are independent of the particular forms of the entropic functional (characterized by the function $\mathcal{C}(x)$) and of the diffusion nonlinearity (given by the function $\mathcal{B}(x)$). Given that the form of the function $\mathcal{A}(x)$ is ultimately determined by the form of $\mathcal{C}(x)$, a natural way of deriving the above mentioned set of relations is to require that each of the two terms in Eq. (16), which are respectively multiplied by $\mathcal{A}(x)$ and by $\mathcal{A}'(x)$, individually vanish. This procedure leads to the equations

$$\sum_i \left[\frac{\partial K_i}{\partial z_i} + D \sum_j \left(\frac{\partial G_{ij}}{\partial z_i} \frac{\partial W}{\partial z_j} + G_{ij} \frac{\partial^2 W}{\partial z_i \partial z_j} \right) \right] = 0$$
$$\sum_i \left[K_i \frac{\partial W}{\partial z_i} + D \sum_j \left(G_{ij} \frac{\partial W}{\partial z_i} \frac{\partial W}{\partial z_j} \right) \right] = 0. \quad (17)$$

In the computations that follow, it will prove convenient to use the re-scaled potential $\Psi = DW$. The connection between the drift field, the diffusion parameters and the potential Ψ then become

$$\boldsymbol{K} \cdot \nabla \Psi = - \sum_{ij} \left(G_{ij} \frac{\partial \Psi}{\partial z_i} \frac{\partial \Psi}{\partial z_j} \right), \quad (18)$$

and

$$\sum_i \left[\frac{\partial K_i}{\partial z_i} + \sum_j \left(\frac{\partial G_{ij}}{\partial z_i} \frac{\partial \Psi}{\partial z_j} + G_{ij} \frac{\partial^2 \Psi}{\partial z_i \partial z_j} \right) \right] = 0. \quad (19)$$

The above pair of equations imply that

$$K_i = - \left(\sum_j G_{ij} \frac{\partial \Psi}{\partial z_j} \right) + \Pi_i, \quad (20)$$

where $\boldsymbol{\Pi} = (\Pi_1, \dots \Pi_N)$ is a divergenceless vector field that, at each point $\boldsymbol{z}$ in phase space, is orthogonal to the gradient of the potential Ψ. That is,

$$\nabla \cdot \boldsymbol{\Pi} = 0, \quad \text{and} \quad \boldsymbol{\Pi} \cdot \nabla \Psi = 0. \tag{21}$$

When we consider the equations of motion (6) for one single realization of our network and (18), we have

$$\frac{d\Psi(\boldsymbol{z})}{dt} = \nabla \Psi \cdot \frac{d\boldsymbol{z}}{dt} = \nabla \Psi \cdot \boldsymbol{K}$$
$$= -\sum_{i,j} G_{ij} \frac{\partial \Psi}{\partial z_i} \frac{\partial \Psi}{\partial z_j} \leq 0, \tag{22}$$

where the inequality follows from the positive definite character of the matrix $\{G_{ij}\}$. It is plain from Eq. (22) that the potential $\Psi(\boldsymbol{z})$ constitutes a Liapunov function (that is, provides an energy landscape) for the network dynamics. The phase-space flow $\boldsymbol{K}$ of the network always points downhill on the potential landscape $\Psi(\boldsymbol{z})$.

On the basis of the above results, we can obtain an H-theorem for the Fokker-Planck dynamics of a network governed by any evolution equation (10) that complies with (20–21). Introducing the free-energy-like functional,

$$\mathcal{H} = \langle \Psi \rangle - \left(\frac{D}{\kappa}\right) S_G[\mathcal{P}(\boldsymbol{z}, t)], \tag{23}$$

where $\langle \Psi \rangle = \int \Psi \mathcal{P} \, d^N \boldsymbol{z}$, it follows from the FPE (10) and the conditions (20–21), that $\mathcal{H}$ satisfies the H-theorem,

$$\frac{d\mathcal{H}}{dt} = -\int \mathcal{P} \sum_{ij} \left\{ G_{ij} \left[\left(\frac{DP_c}{\mathcal{P}}\right) \frac{\partial}{\partial z_i} \mathcal{B}(\mathcal{P}) + \frac{\partial \Psi}{\partial z_i} \right] \right.$$
$$\left. \times \left[\left(\frac{DP_c}{\mathcal{P}}\right) \frac{\partial}{\partial z_j} \mathcal{B}(\mathcal{P}) + \frac{\partial \Psi}{\partial z_j} \right] \right\} d^N \boldsymbol{z} \leq 0. \tag{24}$$

This H-theorem holds for any form of the nonlinearity $\mathcal{B}((\mathcal{P}))$ appearing in the diffusion term of the FPE, provided that the phase-space flow of the network complies with conditions (20–21). Moreover, under these conditions, the stationary solution of (10) is $\mathcal{P}_{\text{st}}(\boldsymbol{z}) = \mathcal{A}[(1/D)(\phi_0 + \Psi(\boldsymbol{z}))]$. An appropriate choice of the constant ϕ_0 leads to a normalized stationary density $\mathcal{P}_{\text{st}}(\boldsymbol{z})$.

4 Fokker-Planck Approach to Cohen-Grossberg Neural Network Models

The Cohen-Grossberg networks form a family of continuous network models that, besides including the famous Hopfield model as a particular case, also includes other relevant dynamical systems, such as the Lotka-Volterra systems in population dynamics and ecology [6]. The equations of motion of the Cohen-Grossberg neural network models [6] are of the form $dz_i/dt = K_i(z)$, with

$$K_i(z) = a_i(z_i) \left[b_i(z_i) - \sum_{j=1}^{N} c_{ij} d_j(z_j) \right], \quad i = 1, \ldots, N, \tag{25}$$

where the continuous variable z_i describes the state of ith neuron, the c_{ij}'s are constant weights, and the $a_i(z_i)$'s, $b_i(z_i)$'s, and $d_i(z_i)$'s are functions of the variables z_i satisfying $a_i(z_i) d'_i(z_i) \geq 0$. Different choices for the functions $a_i(z_i)$, $b_i(z_i)$, and $d_i(z_i)$ correspond to different instantiations of the Cohen-Grossberg model. When the weights are symmetric ($c_{ij} = c_{ji}$), the Cohen-Grossberg model has a Liapunov function (also called energy function), given by [6]

$$\Omega = -\sum_{i=1}^{N} \int_0^{z_i} b_i(x) d'_i(x) dx + \frac{1}{2} \sum_{j,k=1}^{N} c_{jk} d_j(z_j) d_k(z_k). \tag{26}$$

The components K_i of the Cohen-Grossberg model's phase-space flow can be expressed in terms of the partial derivatives of the Liapunov function Ω, as

$$K_i(z_1, z_2, \ldots, z_N) = -\frac{a_i(z_i)}{d'_i(z_i)} \left(\frac{\partial \Omega}{\partial z_i} \right). \tag{27}$$

The well-known Hopfield model corresponds to a special instance of the Cohen-Grossberg one. Indeed, for $a_i(z_i) = -1/\tau_i$, $b_i(z_i) = z_i$, $c_{ij} = \omega_{ij}$, and $d_i(z_i) = g(z_i)$, the equations of motion (25) coincide with those of the continuous Hopfield neural network (see the paragraph after (6)). Therefore, the Hopfield model is recovered when we have constant a_i's, linear b_i's, and the d_i's all given by the same function $g(z_i)$.

The form of the equations of motion (27) governing the Cohen-Grossberg model imply that the corresponding network dynamics is compatible with a FPE of the form (10), with

$$G_{ij}(z) = \left[a_i(z_i)/d'_i(z_i) \right] \delta_{ij}, \tag{28}$$

where δ_{ij} stands for Kronecker's delta. It then follows that the Fokker-Planck equations for the Cohen-Grossberg model satisfies an H-theorem, $d\mathcal{F}/dt \leq 0$, with $\mathcal{F} = \langle \Omega \rangle - D S_{q^*}[\mathcal{P}]$, and has a stationary solution with the form $\mathcal{P}_{\text{st}}(z) = \mathcal{A}[-(1/D)(\alpha_0 + \Omega)(z)]$, where α_0 is a constant.

5 Concluding Remarks

Within the context of general thermostatistical scenarios, we have investigated the nonlinear Fokker-Planck treatment of the dynamics of networks, and the associated nonequilibrium landscape approach. We extended the nonequilibrium landscape formalism advanced in [36], to frameworks based on generalized entropic measures. We have shown that the landscape approach helps to find connections relating the phase-space flow of the network, its Liapunov function, and the functions describing the inhomogeneity and anisotropy of the diffusion term. These connections, in turn, provide an elegant way for establishing the H-theorem satisfied by the network's Fokker-Planck dynamics.

The developments that we have established in this work were motivated by the power-law-like distributions that are observed in numerical simulations [21, 28] and in experimental data [3, 22], in the field of neuroscience. The study of dynamical mechanisms that, like the Fokker-Planck framework, produce this kind of distributions is of considerable relevance, since the classical Boltzmann thermostatistical approach, which is widely used in the field of neural network models, generates exponential distributions that do not account for the above mentioned numerical and empirical data that reveal power-law behavior. Our current considerations and developments lend support to the idea that generalized entropic measures are useful theoretical tools for modeling and simulating some aspects of the dynamics of complex networks, both natural (such as brain neural networks) as well as the artificial ones that are widely applied to solve a variety of problems in artificial intelligence [26].

Acknowledgments. We acknowledge support from the Brazilian funding agencies: Conselho Nacional de Desenvolvimento Científico e Tecnológico (CNPq), Fundação Carlos Chagas Filho de Amparo à Pesquisa do Estado do Rio de Janeiro (FAPERJ) and Coordenação de Aperfeiçoamento de Pessoal de Nível Superior (CAPES). We are grateful for the kind hospitality of the Centro Brasileiro de Pesquisas Físicas (CBPF), where part of this research was conducted.

References

1. Amigó, J.M., Balogh, S.G., Hernández, S.: A brief review of generalized entropies. Entropy **20**(11), 813.1–21 (2018). https://doi.org/10.3390/e20110813
2. Beck, C.: Generalised information and entropy measures in physics. Contemp. Phys. **50**(4), 495–510 (2009). https://doi.org/10.1080/00107510902823517
3. Beggs, J.M., Plenz, D.: Neuronal avalanches in neocortical circuits. J. Neurosci. **23**, 11167–11177 (2003). https://doi.org/10.1523/JNEUROSCI.23-35-11167.2003
4. de Carvalho, L.A.V., Mendes, D.Q., Wedemann, R.S.: Creativity and delusions: the dopaminergic modulation of cortical maps. In: Sloot, P.M.A., Abramson, D., Bogdanov, A.V., Dongarra, J.J., Zomaya, A.Y., Gorbachev, Y.E. (eds.) ICCS 2003. LNCS, vol. 2657, pp. 511–520. Springer, Heidelberg (2003). https://doi.org/10. 1007/3-540-44860-8_53
5. Cleeremans, A., Timmermans, B., Pasquali, A.: Consciousness and metarepresentation: a computational sketch. Neural Netw. **20**, 1032–1039 (2007). https://doi. org/10.1016/j.neunet.2007.09.011
6. Cohen, M.A., Grossberg, S.: Absolute stability of global pattern formation and parallel memory storage by competitive neural networks. IEEE Trans. Syst. Man Cybern. **13**, 815–826 (1983). https://doi.org/10.1109/TSMC.1983.6313075
7. Czégel, D., Balogh, S., Pollner, P., Palla, G.: Phase space volume scaling of generalized entropies and anomalous diffusion scaling governed by corresponding nonlinear Fokker-Planck equations. Sci. Rep. **8**, 1883 (2018). https://doi.org/10.1038/ s41598-018-20202-w

8. Fang, X., Kruse, K., Lu, T., Wang, J.: Nonequilibrium physics in biology. Rev. Mod. Phys. **91**(4), 045004 (2019). https://doi.org/10.1103/RevModPhys.91.045004

9. Franck, T.D.: Nonlinear Fokker-Planck Equations: Fundamentals and Applications. Springer, Berlin, Heidelberg (2005). https://doi.org/10.1007/b137680

10. Hanel, R., Thurner, S.: A comprehensive classification of complex statistical systems and an axiomatic derivation of their entropy and distribution functions. Europhys. Lett. **93**(2), 20006.1–6 (2011). https://doi.org/10.1209/0295-5075/93/20006

11. Hopfield, J.J.: Neurons with graded responses have collective computational properties like those of two-state neurons. Proc. Natl. Acad. Sci. **81**, 3088–3092 (1984). https://doi.org/10.1073/pnas.81.10.3088

12. Ilić, V.M., Korbel, J., Gupta, S., Scarfone, A.M.: An overview of generalized entropic forms. Europhys. Lett. **133**(5), 50005.1–7 (2021). https://doi.org/10.1209/0295-5075/133/50005

13. Jizba, P., Korbel, J.: Maximum entropy principle in statistical inference: case for non-Shannonian entropies. Phys. Rev. Lett. **122**, 120601.1–6 (2019). https://doi.org/10.1103/PhysRevLett.122.120601

14. Kandel, E.: Psychiatry, Psychoanalysis, and the New Biology of Mind. American Psychiatric Publishing Inc., Washington D.C., London (2005)

15. de Luca, V.T.F., Wedemann, R.S., Plastino, A.R.: Neuronal asymmetries and Fokker-Planck dynamics. In: Kůrková, V., Manolopoulos, Y., Hammer, B., Iliadis, L., Maglogiannis, I. (eds.) ICANN 2018. LNCS, vol. 11141, pp. 703–713. Springer, Cham (2018). https://doi.org/10.1007/978-3-030-01424-7_69

16. Naudts, J.: Generalised Thermostatistics. Springer, London (2011). https://doi.org/10.1007/978-0-85729-355-8

17. Papa, A.R.R., da Silva, L.: Earthquakes in the brain. Theory Biosci. **116**, 321–327 (1997)

18. Plastino, A.R., Plastino, A.: Non-extensive statistical mechanics and generalized Fokker-Planck equation. Phys. A **222**(1), 347–354 (1995). https://doi.org/10.1016/0378-4371(95)00211-1

19. Saadatmand, S.N., Gould, T., Cavalcanti, E.G., Vaccaro, J.A.: Thermodynamics from first principles: Correlations and nonextensivity. Phys. Rev. E **101**, 060101.1–5 (2020). https://doi.org/10.1103/PhysRevE.101.060101

20. Schwämmle, V., Nobre, F.D., Curado, E.M.F.: Consequences of the H theorem from nonlinear Fokker-Planck equations. Phys. Rev. E **76**(4), 041123 (2007). https://doi.org/10.1103/PhysRevE.76.041123

21. Siddiqui, M., Wedemann, R.S., Jensen, H.J.: Avalanches and generalized memory associativity in a network model for conscious and unconscious mental functioning. Phys. A **490**, 127–138 (2018). https://doi.org/10.1016/j.physa.2017.08.011

22. Tagliazucchi, E., Balenzuela, P., Fraiman, D., Chialvo, D.R.: Criticality in large-scale brain fMRI dynamics unveiled by a novel point process analysis. Front. Physiol. | Fractal Physiol. **3**, 15 (2012). https://doi.org/10.3389/fphys.2012.00015

23. Taylor, J.G.: A neural model of the loss of self in schizophrenia. Schizophr. Bull. **37**(6), 1229–1247 (2011). https://doi.org/10.1093/schbul/sbq033

24. Tsallis, C.: Possible generalization of Boltzmann-Gibbs statistics. J. Stat. Phys. **52**, 479–487 (1988). https://doi.org/10.1007/BF01016429

25. Tsallis, C.: Introduction to Nonextensive Statistical Mechanics, Approaching a Complex World. Springer, New York (2009). https://doi.org/10.1007/978-0-387-85359-8

26. Tsallis, C., Stariolo, D.A.: Generalized simulated annealing. Phys. A **233**, 395–406 (1996). https://doi.org/10.1016/S0378-4371(96)00271-3

27. Wang, J., Xu, L., Wang, E.: Potential landscape and flux framework of nonequilibrium networks: robustness, dissipation, and coherence of biochemical oscillations. Proc. Natl. Acad. Sci. **105**(34), 12271–12276 (2008). https://doi.org/10.1073/pnas.0800579105
28. Wedemann, R.S., Donangelo, R., de Carvalho, L.A.V.: Generalized memory associativity in a network model for the neuroses. Chaos **19**(1), 015116-(1–11) (2009). https://doi.org/10.1063/1.3099608
29. Wedemann, R.S., Plastino, A.R.: Asymmetries in synaptic connections and the nonlinear Fokker-Planck formalism. In: Villa, A.E.P., Masulli, P., Pons Rivero, A.J. (eds.) ICANN 2016. LNCS, vol. 9886, pp. 19–27. Springer, Cham (2016). https://doi.org/10.1007/978-3-319-44778-0_3
30. Wedemann, R.S., Plastino, A.R.: Física estadística, redes neuronales y Freud. Núcleos **3**, 4–10 (2016)
31. Wedemann, R.S., Plastino, A.R.: q-maximum entropy distributions and memory neural networks. In: Lintas, A., Rovetta, S., Verschure, P.F.M.J., Villa, A.E.P. (eds.) ICANN 2017. LNCS, vol. 10613, pp. 300–308. Springer, Cham (2017). https://doi.org/10.1007/978-3-319-68600-4_35
32. Wedemann, R.S., Plastino, A.R., Tsallis, C.: Curl forces and the nonlinear Fokker-Planck equation. Phys. Rev. E **94**(6), 062105 (2016). https://doi.org/10.1103/PhysRevE.94.062105
33. Wedemann, R.S., de Carvalho, L.A.V.: Some things psychopathologies can tell us about consciousness. In: Villa, A.E.P., Duch, W., Érdi, P., Masulli, F., Palm, G. (eds.) ICANN 2012. LNCS, vol. 7552, pp. 379–386. Springer, Heidelberg (2012). https://doi.org/10.1007/978-3-642-33269-2_48
34. Wedemann, R.S., de Carvalho, L.A.V., Donangelo, R.: Access to symbolization and associativity mechanisms in a model of conscious and unconscious processes. In: Samsonovich, A.V., Jóhannsdóttir, K.R. (eds.) Biologically Inspired Cognitive Architectures 2011, Frontiers in Artificial Intelligence and Applications, vol. 233, pp. 444–449. IOS Press, Amsterdam, Netherlands (2011). https://doi.org/10.3233/978-1-60750-959-2-444
35. Wedemann, R.S., Plastino, A.R.: Nonlinear, nonequilibrium landscape approach to neural network dynamics. In: Farkaš, I., Masulli, P., Wermter, S. (eds.) ICANN 2020. LNCS, vol. 12397, pp. 180–191. Springer, Cham (2020). https://doi.org/10.1007/978-3-030-61616-8_15
36. Yan, H., Zhao, L., Hu, L., Wang, X., Wang, E., Wang, J.: Nonequilibrium landscape theory of neural networks. Proc. Natl. Acad. Sci. **110**(45), E4185–E4194 (2013). https://doi.org/10.1073/pnas.1310692110

Guiding the Comparison of Neural Network Local Robustness: An Empirical Study

Hao Bu and Meng Sun[✉]

School of Mathematical Sciences, Peking University, Beijing, China
{buhao,sunm}@pku.edu.cn

Abstract. Local robustness refers to whether a deep neural network (DNN) can correctly classify an image under certain perturbations (e.g. Gaussian noise and the L_∞ perturbation). Since the discovery of adversarial examples, the local robustness of DNNs has received much attention, and researchers have proposed many formal verification techniques to measure it. One important application of these verification techniques is to compare the local robustness of different DNNs. However, these techniques contain some parameters that need to be manually set, and it is unclear whether the selection of parameters will affect the comparison results. In this paper, we conduct an empirical study to explore DNNs' local robustness towards perturbations. We find that two widely-used assumptions in existing papers are not always true in practice. Based on our experimental results, we discuss defects of existing local robustness comparison methods and provide some possible solutions.

Keywords: Local robustness · Quantitative verification · Semantic perturbation

1 Introduction

With the widespread usage of deep neural networks (DNNs) in critical applications like face recognition, researchers attach much importance to the local robustness of DNNs. Given an image, local robustness refers to whether the network can correctly classify all possible perturbed images (*qualitative verification*) [8,9,12,15,18]. The most studied perturbation is the L_∞ perturbation, and it is equivalent to proving the absence of adversarial examples in the given L_∞ neighborhood. Later, researchers also consider semantic perturbations such as Gaussian noise, contrast and fog [6,13]. However, qualitative verification for DNN local robustness is computationally hard. Even for the L_∞ perturbation and simple network structures, the verification problem is NP hard [9]. As an alternative, researchers propose *quantitative verification* [1–5,7,10,14,16,17]. Different from qualitative verification which considers *all* possible perturbed images, quantitative verification uses statistical methods to approximate the *probability* that the network can correctly classify the perturbed image. Existing quantitative verification techniques can be divided into two categories, one is based on parameter estimation, and the other is based on hypothesis testing.

© The Author(s), under exclusive license to Springer Nature Switzerland AG 2023
L. Iliadis et al. (Eds.): ICANN 2023, LNCS 14258, pp. 312–323, 2023.
https://doi.org/10.1007/978-3-031-44192-9_25

One important application of these local robustness verification methods is to compare the robustness of different networks. Specifically, given an image and several networks, people try to use qualitative verification or quantitative verification methods to decide which network is more robust around the given image. Compared with adversarial attacks-based methods, these verification-based methods can provide theoretical guarantees thus are more reliable. When using qualitative verification methods, people usually calculate the *maximal robustness radius* (also called *certified lower bound*) of the network on the given image [18]. The maximal robustness radius refers to the maximal perturbation size under which the network can still correctly classify all possible perturbed images. The bigger the maximal robustness radius is, the more robust it is around the given image. When using quantitative verification methods, there are two mainstream approaches to compare the robustness of different networks. The first approach [4,10] is to set a certain perturbation size, then use parameter estimation-based methods to estimate the correctly classified probability. The higher the probability is, the more robust it is. The second approach [1,7,11] is to set a target probability $1 - \varepsilon$, then use hypothesis testing-based methods to calculate the largest perturbation size under which the network can correctly classify the perturbed image with more than $1 - \varepsilon$ probability. The larger perturbation the network can withstand, the more robust it is.

When people use quantitative verification methods to compare the local robustness of different networks, they need to manually set some parameters (the perturbation size or the target probability). However, it is unclear whether the selection of parameters will affect the comparison results. For example, when using parameter estimation-based methods, is it possible that network A is more robust than network B on small perturbation size, while network B is more robust than network A on large perturbation size? Moreover, when people use hypothesis testing-based methods, they usually use binary search to calculate the largest perturbation size that the network can withstand. However, the validity of binary search depends on the monotonicity between the correctly classified probability and the perturbation size. It is unclear whether the correctly classified probability always decreases as the perturbation size increases. Although many existing works [1,4,7,10,11] explicitly or implicitly assume these properties to be true (i.e. parameter selections do not affect the comparison results; correctly classified probability always decreases as the perturbation size increases), no one has studied whether these properties hold true in practice, which makes the validity of these works questionable.

In this paper, we conduct an empirical study on two image classification datasets (CIFAR-10 and ImageNet), four perturbations (contrast, Gaussian noise, fog and L_∞ perturbation) and eight network structures to explore the validity of the aforementioned properties. Specifically, for a combination of network, image and perturbation, we calculate its *probability perturbation curve*, which displays the correctly classified probabilities under different perturbation sizes. The aforementioned properties can be characterized using the probability perturbation curve. Specifically, if the curves of different networks intersect, then the selection of parameters will affect the comparison results. If the curve is not monotonically decreasing, then the correctly classified probability may increase when the perturbation size increases. Our experimental results show that for about 50% images, different parameters can lead to different comparison results. Moreover, for about 8% images, the correctly classified probability does not always decrease when the perturbation size increases. In summary, the main contributions of this paper are as follows.

(1) We conduct a comprehensive empirical study to explore DNNs' local robustness and find counterintuitive phenomena on many images. We analyze possible causes of these unusual phenomena.
(2) We discuss negative impacts of the above findings on existing verification-based local robustness comparison methods. We propose some possible solutions to alleviate these influences.

Note that this paper is not intended to improve or criticize existing qualitative or quantitative verification methods, but to discuss the validity of using these methods to compare the local robustness of different networks.

Notations of this paper: given a network $\mathcal{N}$, an image x that can be correctly classified, a perturbation $\mathcal{T}$ and a parameter θ that controls the perturbation size. The perturbed image $\mathcal{T}_\theta(x)$ is a random vector with a certain probability distribution. Common perturbations include the L_∞ perturbation ($\mathcal{T}_\theta(x)$ is sampled from the uniform distribution in the L_∞ ball centered at x with a radius of θ) and Gaussian noise ($\mathcal{T}_\theta(x)$ is sampled from the normal distribution with x as its mean and $\theta \cdot I$ as its covariance matrix).

2   Related Work

2.1   Qualitative Verification

Qualitative verification aims to answer if the network $\mathcal{N}$ can correctly classify *all* possible perturbed images $\mathcal{T}_\theta(x)$, and most techniques are designed for the L_∞ perturbation. There are two main approaches for L_∞ perturbation's qualitative verification. The first relies on satisfiability modulo theories (SMT) solvers [8, 9]. These techniques usually require the activation functions to be piecewise-linear (e.g. ReLU), and they are both sound and complete. However, as the verification problem is NP hard [9], existing techniques cannot scale to large networks. The second relies on abstract interpretation [15], optimization [12] or layerwise propagation [18]. These techniques can deal with relatively large networks and nonlinear activation functions (e.g. sigmoid), however, they have to sacrifice the completeness. Moreover, they usually do not perform well on complex networks with pooling or batch normalization layers.

In addition to the L_∞ perturbation, researchers also consider semantic perturbations like contrast and rotation [13], which are more difficult to deal with.

2.2   Quantitative Verification

Quantitative verification measures the probability $p \triangleq Pr(\mathcal{N}(x) = \mathcal{N}(\mathcal{T}_\theta(x)))$ that the perturbed image is correctly classified. Qualitative verification can be regarded as a special case of quantitative verification in which people try to answer if the probability p is 1. Usually it is infeasible to calculate the exact value of p, so people use statistical methods to make the verification feasible, with the price of introducing some statistical uncertainty.

Existing quantitative verification techniques can be divided into two categories: hypothesis testing-based [1–3,7,14,16] and parameter estimation-based [4,5,10,17]. The first performs hypothesis testing for the probability p. Given a threshold ε and an uncertainty bound δ, people try to answer if p is higher than $1 - \varepsilon$ with more than $1 - \delta$ confidence. The second directly estimates the probability p. Given a precision target ε and an uncertainty bound δ, people try to obtain an estimated value $\hat{p}$, such that $Pr(|\hat{p} - p| > \varepsilon) < \delta$.

Due to the statistical nature of quantitative verification, it can efficiently deal with complex perturbations, nonlinear activation functions and large networks.

3   Problem Formulation

When using quantitative verification methods to compare the local robustness of different networks, there are two main approaches. For hypothesis testing-based methods, people calculate the *maximal probability robustness radius* to compare the local robustness of different networks.

Method 1. *Given a threshold ε, people hope to find the largest perturbation size θ, such that for all $\theta' \leq \theta$, the correctly classified probability $p = Pr(\mathcal{N}(x) = \mathcal{N}(\mathcal{T}_{\theta'}(x))) \geq 1 - \varepsilon$. The largest θ found is called the maximal probability robustness radius. The larger the maximal probability robustness radius is, the more robust the network is towards the given image.*

For parameter estimation-based methods, people set a certain perturbation size to compare the local robustness of different networks.

Method 2. *Given a perturbation size θ, people estimate the correctly classified probability $p = Pr(\mathcal{N}(x) = \mathcal{N}(\mathcal{T}_{\theta}(x)))$. The larger the probability is, the more robust the network is towards the given image.*

In Method 1, we need to set the threshold ε, and in Method 2, we need to set the perturbation size θ. In previous works [1,4,7,10,11], these two parameters are usually set empirically without concrete reasons. Therefore, it is natural to ask whether the selection of these parameters will affect the comparison results. Moreover, when using Method 1, people usually use binary search to calculate the maximal probability robustness radius, which implicitly assumes that p decreases monotonically as θ increases. Although this assumption seems intuitive, it is unclear whether there are counterexamples in practice. To formally define these two problems, we define the *probability perturbation curve* first.

Definition 1. *Given a network $\mathcal{N}$, an image x that can be correctly classified and a perturbation $\mathcal{T}$, for different perturbation sizes θ, there are different correctly classified probabilities $p = Pr(\mathcal{N}(x) = \mathcal{N}(\mathcal{T}_{\theta}(x)))$. The resulting curve is called the probability perturbation curve.*

Question 1. Given a network $\mathcal{N}$, an image x that can be correctly classified and a perturbation $\mathcal{T}$, is the probability perturbation curve always monotonically decreasing?

Question 2. Given two networks $\mathcal{N}_1$, $\mathcal{N}_2$, an image x that can be correctly classified by both networks and a perturbation $\mathcal{T}$, do these two probability perturbation curves never intersect?

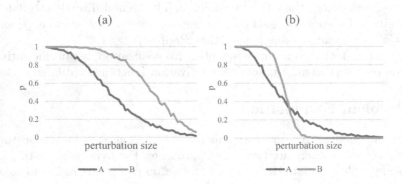

Fig. 1. Examples of probability perturbation curves.

For example, in Fig. 1(a), the two probability perturbation curves do not intersect. In this case, the selection of parameters (threshold ε when using hypothesis testing-based methods and perturbation size θ when using parameter estimation-based methods) does not affect the comparison results (network B is more robust than network A). However, in Fig. 1(b), these two curves intersect, so different parameters may produce different comparison results. For example, if we use Method 2 and select a small θ (left of the intersection point), then network B is more robust. However, if we select a large θ (right of the intersection point), then network A is more robust. Currently, no one has given positive or negative answers to Question 1 or 2.

Note that using qualitative verification methods to compare the local robustness is equivalent to using Method 1 with $\varepsilon = 0$. Therefore, from now on, we only consider quantitative verification methods.

4   Empirical Study

4.1   Design

We use CIFAR-10 and ImageNet (ILSVRC2012) as the datasets of our study. We consider four perturbations: L_∞ perturbation, fog, contrast and Gaussian noise. L_∞ perturbation is widely used in papers about robustness verification and adversarial attacks. The perturbed image is sampled from the uniform distribution in the L_∞ ball centered at x with a radius of θ. Fog is a complex semantic perturbation which adds random fog to the original image x. Contrast is a simple semantic perturbation. Higher contrast values lead to more distinguishable images and lower contrast values lead to flatter images. Gaussian noise perturbation simply adds Gaussian noise to the image. The implementations of fog, contrast and Gaussian noise come from the standard benchmark CIFAR-10-C (ImageNet-10-C) [6]. For each perturbation, we can use a parameter θ to control the perturbation size. Figure 2 shows some examples of these four perturbations.

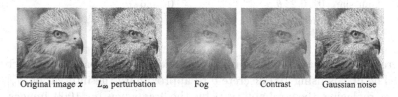

Original image x L_∞ perturbation   Fog   Contrast   Gaussian noise

Fig. 2. Examples of perturbed images.

For CIFAR-10, we train four popular networks. For ImageNet, we use four pre-trained networks from TorchVision. Table 1 presents detailed information.

Table 1. Summary of DNN models.

Dataset	Network	Accuracy	Dataset	Network	Accuracy
CIFAR-10	VGG16	89.27%	ImageNet	ShuffleNet	69.36%
	DenseNet121	90.72%		GoogLeNet	69.78%
	ResNet101	90.45%		RegNet	72.83%
	MobileNetV2	90.25%		MNASNet	73.46%

We randomly select 100 images from the CIFAR-10 testing set and the ImageNet validation set respectively, with the restriction that they can be correctly classified by all networks. For each perturbation, we set a lower bound θ_l and an upper bound θ_u to ensure the perturbed image can still be recognized by humans. As there are infinite possible values for θ, we uniformly select 100 values from $[\theta_l, \theta_u]$ (i.e. $\theta_l + \frac{i}{100} \cdot (\theta_u - \theta_l)$, $i = 1, 2, \cdots, 100$). Table 2 presents the bounds of θ. The "Implementation" column refers to the mapping relationship between θ in this paper and the original implementations in [6]. As it is infeasible to calculate the exact value of p, for each θ, we generate 1000 perturbed images and use the frequency of correctly classified images as the probability p. For example, given an image x, the L_∞ perturbation and $\theta = 0.1$, we uniformly generate 1000 images from the L_∞ ball centered at x with the radius of 0.1. If the network can correctly classify 985 images out of these 1000 perturbed images, we consider the correctly classified probability p to be 0.985 when $\theta = 0.1$. In this way, we can obtain an approximated probability perturbation curve for each combination of image, network and perturbation, with a total of 3200 curves. Each curve is obtained by generating and classifying $100 \times 1000 = 100000$ images.

Table 2. Bounds of perturbation size θ.

	CIFAR-10			ImageNet		
	θ_l	θ_u	Implementation	θ_l	θ_u	Implementation
L_∞	0	0.4	θ	0	1	θ
Fog	0	1	$(0.5 + 2\theta, 2 - 0.5\theta)$	0	1	$(1.5 + 2\theta, 2 - 0.6\theta)$
Contrast	0	0.7	$U[\theta - 0.1, \theta + 0.1]^*$	0	0.8	$U[\theta - 0.1, \theta + 0.1]^*$
Gaussian	0	0.2	θ	0	0.6	θ

*: Uniform distribution in $[\theta - 0.1, \theta + 0.1]$

There are two approximations in our approximated probability perturbation curves. The first is using 100 discrete θ to approximate the interval $[\theta_l, \theta_u]$. The second is replacing the probability p by the frequency on 1000 images. The first approximation may produce false negatives (e.g. the curve is monotonically decreasing on those 100 points but is not monotonically decreasing on $[\theta_l, \theta_u]$). The second approximation can produce both false negatives and false positives. As we hope to give negative answers to Question 1 and 2, we give priority to reducing false positives. Specifically, when we analyze the experimental data, we use relatively conservative thresholds and manually check all suspicious cases to further exclude possible outliers. We also publish all experimental data and code in https://github.com/H-Bu/robust-empirical for further validation. All experiments are conducted on an NVIDIA Titan Xp GPU.

4.2 Question 1: Is the Probability Perturbation Curve Always Monotonically Decreasing?

For all 3200 probability perturbation curves, we use the following criterion to obtain candidate curves: *there exists $\theta_1 < \theta_2$, such that $p_1 + 5\% < p_2$, where p_i is the network's correctly classified probability under perturbation size θ_i ($i = 1, 2$).* Then we manually check all candidate curves that meet the above criterion to exclude outliers. We use a relatively conservative threshold (5%) in our criterion to reduce the false positive rate. The results are shown in Table 3. For example, for CIFAR-10, fog and the VGG network, there are 7% images with non-monotonically decreasing probability perturbation curves.

Table 3. Non-monotonically decreasing curves (%).

CIFAR-10					ImageNet				
	L_∞	Fog	Contrast	Gaussian		L_∞	Fog	Contrast	Gaussian
VGG	6	7	0	3	Shuffle	8	8	1	4
Dense	4	7	3	4	Google	7	5	4	15
Res	16	2	1	16	Reg	11	14	1	9
Mobile	6	10	2	3	MNAS	13	10	1	8

For the L_∞ perturbation, fog and Gaussian noise, there are about 6%–10% images with non-monotonically decreasing curves on average. For the contrast perturbation, the percentage is much lower. We present some representative probability perturbation curves in Fig. 3.

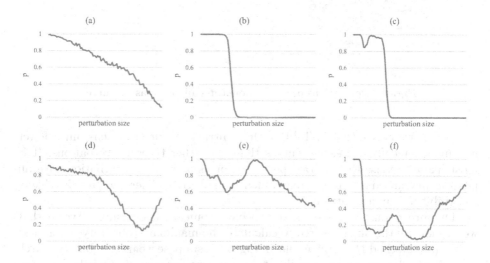

Fig. 3. Some representative probability perturbation curves.

Figure 3(a) and (b) represent the most common cases: the correctly classified probability p decreases as the perturbation size increases. However, for those non-monotonically decreasing cases, the curves can be very complex. When the perturbation size is within some intervals, the correctly classified probability p even increases as the perturbation size increases, which is counterintuitive.

The reason for those non-monotonically decreasing curves might be the non-convex decision boundary around the original image x. As an example, for the L_∞ perturbation, the perturbed image is sampled from the uniform distribution in the L_∞ ball centered at x. Figure 4 illustrates a possible decision boundary and its corresponding probability perturbation curve. For ease of illustration, we assume the image only has two dimensions, so an L_∞ ball is a square centered at x (the black dot). The blue area has the same classification result with x, and the other area (orange or white) has different classification results with x. When the perturbation size θ is smaller than a, the L_∞ square is completely contained in the blue area, therefore, the correctly classified probability p is 1. When $a < \theta < b$, the larger θ is, the lower the proportion of blue area is, so p decreases as θ increases. When $b < \theta < c$, the orange area disappears, so p increases as θ increases. When $\theta > c$, there is no more blue area outside, so p decreases as θ increases and eventually approaches 0.

In practice, the L_∞ ball has hundreds and thousands of dimensions, so the decision boundary can be much more complicated than that in Fig. 4. As an

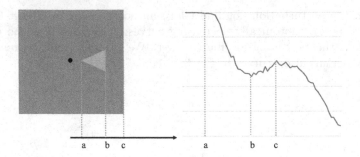

Fig. 4. Explanations of a non-monotonically decreasing curve.

exception, we notice that in Table 3, the contrast perturbation has much fewer non-monotonically decreasing curves than the other three perturbations. It is most likely because the contrast perturbation is a simple perturbation with all possible perturbed images in a one-dimension subspace. Therefore, it is less likely to exhibit a complex pattern.

The direct consequence of those non-monotonically decreasing curves is that we cannot use the binary search to calculate the maximal probability robustness radius (see Method 1). For example, in Fig. 3(e), suppose we use the binary search to calculate the maximal probability robustness radius such that p is higher than 0.8. At first, we check the midpoint of the perturbation size interval, and find p is near 1, so we select the right half of the interval and will finally converge in it. However, the radius we intend to find is in the left half of the interval. Actually, we have noticed similar problems in existing work. For example, in [11], the authors use PROVERO [2] (a hypothesis testing-based quantitative verification method) and binary search to calculate the maximal probability robustness radius for the L_∞ perturbation, and they find that in some cases, the calculated radius is unexpectedly large (see Fig. 6 of their paper).

To alleviate this problem, a possible solution is to combine the grid search and binary search. Specifically, we begin from the lower bound θ_l and iteratively increase the perturbation size with a relatively small step. When we find the first perturbation size θ that makes p smaller than the given threshold $1 - \varepsilon$, we perform binary search around θ until we achieve target precision. In practice, we find this method can produce correct results in most cases.

4.3 Question 2: Do Two Networks' Probability Perturbation Curves Never Intersect?

For each combination of image and perturbation, we consider its corresponding four probability perturbation curves (on four networks). If two networks' probability perturbation curves intersect, we count once. As we consider four networks simultaneously, there can be $C_4^2 = 6$ intersections at most for each combination. We use the following criterion to define an intersection between two networks $\mathcal{N}_1$ and $\mathcal{N}_2$: *there exist θ_1 and θ_2, such that $p_{11} > p_{12} + 5\%$ and $p_{21} + 5\% < p_{22}$, where*

p_{ij} is $\mathcal{N}_j$'s *correctly classified probability under perturbation size* θ_i $(i, j = 1, 2)$. The results are shown in Table 4. For example, for CIFAR-10 and fog, there are 15% images with two intersections, and there are 54% images with at least one intersection.

Table 4. Numbers of intersections (%).

	CIFAR-10							ImageNet						
	$\geqslant 1$	1	2	3	4	5	6	$\geqslant 1$	1	2	3	4	5	6
L_∞	49	29	11	8	1	0	0	52	32	10	6	1	2	1
Fog	54	27	15	8	3	1	0	53	31	17	4	0	1	0
Contrast	6	4	2	0	0	0	0	4	3	1	0	0	0	0
Gaussian	48	33	11	2	2	0	0	56	29	15	8	1	2	1

For the L_∞ perturbation, fog and Gaussian noise, there are about 50% images with at least one intersection. For the contrast perturbation, the percentage is much lower. The reason is similar to the previous question (i.e. contrast is a simple perturbation). We present some representative examples in Fig. 5. The four subgraphs (a-d) have 0, 1, 3 and 6 intersections respectively.

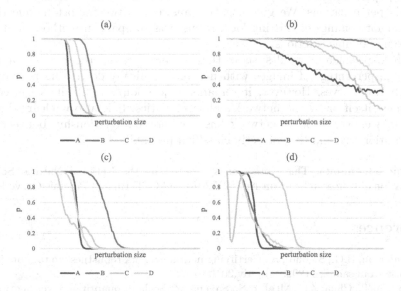

Fig. 5. Examples of curve intersections.

As we have discussed in Sect. 3, if there are intersections between two networks' curves, then different parameters may affect the robustness comparison results when using Method 1 or 2. In fact, if two curves intersect, it is hard to tell which network is more robust. For example, in Fig. 5(b), it is clear that network B is the most robust, and network D is the second. However, it is hard to decide between network A and C. Our results in Table 4 show that intersections are quite common in practice, so in many cases, it is improper to simply use Method 1 or 2 to compare the local robustness of different networks. Moreover, even there is no intersection between curves, sometimes it is still hard to select a proper parameter. For example, in Fig. 5(a), it is intuitive that network B is the most robust, followed by network D, C and A in turn. However, when we use Method 2 to compare their robustness, it is hard to select a perturbation size θ that can distinguish among these four networks. Specifically, if we choose a small θ, the correctly classified probabilities p of all networks are 1, and if we choose a large θ, the probabilities p of all networks are 0.

The main problem of Method 1 and 2 is that they only consider a single parameter, which cannot represent all possible cases. Therefore, we suggest using the probability perturbation curve to compare different networks. For example, we can use the area under the curve as the robustness value. The larger the area is, the more robust the network is towards the given image and perturbation.

5   Conclusion

In this paper, we conduct an empirical study to explore DNN's local robustness towards perturbations. We give negative answers to two important questions, discuss shortcomings of existing local robustness comparison methods and provide some possible solutions.

Our experimental results show that in most cases, there exists a non-negligible percentage of images with non-monotonically decreasing probability perturbation curves. However, it remains a question whether it is caused by the image itself or by the network's characteristics. It is also unclear whether we should expect an ideal network has a monotonic relationship between the perturbation size and the correctly classified probability.

Acknowledgements. This work was sponsored by the National Natural Science Foundation of China under grant No. 62172019 and CCF-Huawei Populus Grove Fund.

References

1. Anderson, B.G., Sojoudi, S.: Certifying neural network robustness to random input noise from samples (2020). arXiv:2010.07532
2. Baluta, T., Chua, Z.L., Meel, K.S., Saxena, P.: Scalable quantitative verification for deep neural networks. In: 43th International Conference on Software Engineering, pp. 312–323 (2021)
3. Bu, H., Sun, M.: Certifying semantic robustness of deep neural networks. In: 27th International Conference on Engineering of Complex Computer Systems, pp. 51–60 (2023)

4. Bu, H., Sun, M.: Measuring robustness of deep neural networks from the lens of statistical model checking. In: 2023 International Joint Conference on Neural Networks (2023)
5. Cardelli, L., Kwiatkowska, M., Laurenti, L., Paoletti, N., Patane, A., Wicker, M.: Statistical guarantees for the robustness of Bayesian neural networks. In: 28th International Joint Conference on Artificial Intelligence, pp. 5693–5700 (2019)
6. Hendrycks, D., Dietterich, T.: Benchmarking neural network robustness to common corruptions and perturbations. In: International Conference on Learning Representations (2019)
7. Huang, C., Hu, Z., Huang, X., Pei, K.: Statistical certification of acceptable robustness for neural networks. In: 30th International Conference on Artificial Neural Networks, pp. 79–90 (2021)
8. Huang, X., Kwiatkowska, M., Wang, S., Wu, M.: Safety verification of deep neural networks. In: 29th International Conference on Computer Aided Verification, pp. 3–29 (2017)
9. Katz, G., Barrett, C., Dill, D.L., Julian, K., Kochenderfer, M.J.: Reluplex: an efficient SMT solver for verifying deep neural networks. In: 29th International Conference on Computer Aided Verification, pp. 97–117 (2017)
10. Levy, N., Katz, G.: RoMA: a method for neural network robustness measurement and assessment. In: 29th International Conference on Neural Information Processing (2022)
11. Li, R., Yang, P., Huang, C.C., Sun, Y., Xue, B., Zhang, L.: Towards practical robustness analysis for DNNs based on PAC-model learning. In: 44th International Conference on Software Engineering, pp. 2189–2201 (2022)
12. Lin, W., et al.: Robustness verification of classification deep neural networks via linear programming. In: IEEE/CVF Conference on Computer Vision and Pattern Recognition, pp. 11418–11427 (2019)
13. Mohapatra, J., Weng, T.W., Chen, P.Y., Liu, S., Daniel, L.: Towards verifying robustness of neural networks against a family of semantic perturbations. In: IEEE/CVF Conference on Computer Vision and Pattern Recognition, pp. 244–252 (2020)
14. Pautov, M., Tursynbek, N., Munkhoeva, M., Muravev, N., Petiushko, A., Oseledets, I.: CC-Cert: a probabilistic approach to certify general robustness of neural networks. In: AAAI Conference on Artificial Intelligence (2022)
15. Singh, G., Gehr, T., Mirman, M., Püschel, M., Vechev, M.: Fast and effective robustness certification. In: Proceedings of the Advances in Neural Information Processing Systems (2018)
16. Tit, K., Furon, T., Rousset, M.: Efficient statistical assessment of neural network corruption robustness. In: Proceedings of the Advances in Neural Information Processing Systems (2021)
17. Webb, S., Rainforth, T., Teh, Y.W., Kumar, M.P.: A statistical approach to assessing neural network robustness. In: International Conference on Learning Representations (2019)
18. Zhang, H., Weng, T.W., Chen, P.Y., Hsieh, C.J., Daniel, L.: Efficient neural network robustness certification with general activation functions. In: Proceedings of the Advances in Neural Information Processing Systems (2018)

Information-Theoretically Secure Neural Network Training with Flexible Deployment

Hengcheng Zhou[✉]

Shanghai Jiao Tong University, Shanghai, China
zhc12345@sjtu.edu.cn

Abstract. Neural networks have been widely used in image processing, speech recognition, and other fields. When multiple parties collaborate to train neural network models by combining their individual data, some data are sensitive and cannot be leaked to anyone other than the data holder. In this paper, we propose new protocols for private neural network training that protect the privacy of sensitive data when they are integrated from different sources. Our protocols can reach information-theoretic security and allow for the flexible configuration of the number of parties based on actual requirements. We conduct experiments in settings with different numbers of participants, where we train neural networks on the MNIST dataset. The experimental results demonstrate that our protocols can successfully implement the task of neural network training while offering the benefit of flexible deployment.

Keywords: Secure multi-party computation · Information-theoretic security · Secret sharing · Neural network training

1 Introduction

Data privacy has received increasing attention in recent years. With the promulgation of policies such as the General Data Protection Regulation(GDPR), protecting data privacy is not just an expectation, but a mandatory requirement. Neural networks, as important machine learning models, typically need to process a large amount of data for better performance. When data come from multiple parties, sensitive data should be kept private while being processed by neural network models. This is of great significance in the social background of the emphasis on data privacy and the rapid development of artificial intelligence.

Privacy-preserving machine learning via secret-sharing-based secure multi-party computation (MPC) [18,19] provides a promising solution by enabling different parties to train the models on their joint data while protecting the privacy of their own inputs. With secret-sharing, the parties first split their original data into several parts and share them with other parties. Then the parties perform the computation on these shares. After they get the shares of the final calculation results, they send these shares to some specific parties for secret reconstruction. Security is guaranteed by the secret sharing scheme used,

L. Iliadis et al. (Eds.): ICANN 2023, LNCS 14258, pp. 324–336, 2023.
https://doi.org/10.1007/978-3-031-44192-9_26

which ensures that an adversary cannot deduce the original secret value from the shares it has access to. In the computational setting, the adversary is limited to run in polynomial time. When we consider the information-theoretic setting, the adversary is computationally unbounded. The information-theoretic setting is undoubtedly better suited to the needs of society since the security doesn't rely on any cryptographic hardness assumption.

The goal of training neural networks while protecting privacy has received a lot of attention. The private neural network training was first implemented by SecureML [12]. SecureML was designed for two parties and was based on the ABY framework [8], which supported the conversion between arithmetic, boolean, and Yao sharing to benefit from different schemes. ABY^3 [11] extended the conversion framework under the setting of three participants and implemented the training of neural networks on this basis. Using additive secret sharing, SecureNN [15] implemented information-theoretically secure neural network training and prediction between three and four participants. BLAZE [13] and FALCON [16] were both designed for three parties, among which BLAZE was capable of resisting a malicious adversary and FALCON was the first secure deep learning framework to handle large-scale networks and data sets. Trident [5] and Tetrad [10] proposed secure neural network protocols specifically for the four-party case. These protocols are designed for specific participant numbers, with the primary aim to increase execution effectiveness. None of the aforementioned methods can achieve information-theoretic security while preserving the ability to flexibly adjust the number of participants. It should be noted that when we talk about altering the number of parties, we mean changing the number of parties who directly participate in the computation rather than supporting any number of participants through certain specific servers. We hope that the data owners will directly participate in the calculation instead of utilizing other servers.

1.1 Our Contributions

We provide private protocols for the training of neural networks with information-theoretic security. Based on Shamir's secret sharing scheme [14], our protocols support the flexible setting of the number of participants n and adversaries t. The main features of our protocols are as follows:

- Our protocols can support computation between general n ($n \geqslant 3$) parties.
- Our protocols are information-theoretically secure when the number of semi-honest adversaries $t < n/2$.
- Our protocols support the flexible setting of n and t according to actual needs. And the cost of communication increases linearly with n as the number of parties increases.

2 Preliminaries

2.1 Notation and Security Model

Let $P_1, \cdots, P_n$ be n $(n \geqslant 3)$ participants. The computation in our protocols is performed in a finite field $\mathbb{F}_p$, where p is a prime number of length ℓ. We represent $\mathbb{F}_p$ as $\{-(p-1)/2, \cdots, (p-1)/2\}$ in order to operate directly on negative numbers. And we denote the set $\{1, 2, \cdots, e\}$ by $[e]$, where e is a positive integer.

We focus on the semi-honest setting, which means that the adversary needs to strictly follow the protocol specification. We assume peer-to-peer secure channels between all pairs of participants. The security of our protocols is analyzed under the universal composability (UC) framework [1]. This framework supports the modular design of MPC protocols, which allows us to design the protocol we want based on existing secure protocols. To design a protocol Π that realizes an ideal functionality $\mathcal{F}$, we can utilize an existing sub-protocol Π_s which securely realizes $\mathcal{F}_s$. We obtain $\Pi_{\mathcal{F}_s}$ by changing any invocation of Π_s in Π to the ideal functionality $\mathcal{F}_s$. If $\Pi_{\mathcal{F}_s}$ securely realizes $\mathcal{F}$, then Π securely realizes $\mathcal{F}$.

2.2 Neural Network Training

In this paper, we focus on the training of Deep Neural Networks (DNNs). For an L-layer neural network, we use a_j^l, b_j^l to denote the activation and bias of the jth neuron in the lth layer, where $1 \leqslant l \leqslant L$. We call the 0th layer the input layer and the Lth layer the output layer. We denote the number of neurons in the lth layer by d^l. Particularly, we use d to denote the number of neurons in the input layer and a^0 to denote the input of the neural network. We denote the weight matrix correspond to the $(l-1)^{\text{th}}$ layer and the lth layer by w^l and we define $z^l = w^l a^{l-1} + b^l$. The training process of a neural network consists of two stages: forward propagation and backward propagation. The forward propagation proceeds according to the formula: $a^l = \sigma\left(z^l\right)$, where σ is the activation function. The backward propagation is used to compute gradients and update parameters. We use $\mathcal{L}$ to denote the loss function. For convenience, we define $\delta^l = \partial\mathcal{L}/\partial z^l$. After we get $\delta^{l+1}(1 \leqslant l < L)$, we can calculate δ^l according to the formula $\delta^l = \left(w^{l+1}\right)^T \delta^{l+1} \odot \sigma'\left(z^l\right)$, where $\odot$ represents the Hadamard product. With δ^l, we can compute $\partial\mathcal{L}/\partial w^l = \delta^l \left(a^{l-1}\right)^T$ and $\partial\mathcal{L}/\partial b^l = \delta^l$ to update w^l and b^l.

We consider two loss functions, the cross-entropy loss and the Multiclass Support Vector Machine (SVM) loss [17]. The difference between using the two loss functions lies in the calculation of δ^L. When we connect the output of the neural network to the softmax function SM and use the cross-entropy loss, we can compute $\delta^L = \text{SM}(z^L) - y$, where y is the label and the softmax function is computed as $\text{SM}(z_i^L) = e^{-z_i^L} / \Sigma_{j=1}^{d^L} e^{-z_j^L}, i \in [d^L]$. When we consider the SVM loss, for $j \in [d^L]$, we can compute δ_j^L as follows:

$$\delta_j^L = \begin{cases} 0, & \text{if } j \neq s \text{ and } z_j^L - z_s^L + \Delta < 0; \\ 1, & \text{if } j \neq s \text{ and } z_j^L - z_s^L + \Delta \geqslant 0; \\ -(\sum_{i \neq s} \mathbf{1}(z_i^L - z_s^L + \Delta \geqslant 0)), & \text{if } j = s, \end{cases} \quad (1)$$

where Δ is a hyperparameter and $s \in [d^L]$ represents the index corresponding to the label. The indicator function $\mathbf{1}$ in Eq. 1 returns 1 if the inside condition is true and 0 otherwise.

2.3 Shamir's Secret Sharing Scheme

Shamir's scheme is a $(t+1)$-out-of-n secret sharing scheme, which means at least $t + 1$ shares are needed to recover the secret. Let $\alpha_1, \cdots, \alpha_n \in \mathbb{F}_p$ be n predetermined distinct nonzero elements. In order to share $u \in \mathbb{F}_p$, the dealer first generates a polynomial $f(x)$ of degree t over $\mathbb{F}_p[x]$ such that $f(0) = u$ and all other coefficients are uniformly random, and then send the share $u_i = f(\alpha_i)$ to party P_i. The vector $(u_1, \cdots, u_n)$ is called a t-sharing of u, which is denoted by $\langle u \rangle_t$ and can be denoted by $\langle u \rangle$ for simplicity. Similarly, the $2t$-sharing of u is denoted by $\langle u \rangle_{2t}$. We can secret-share vectors or matrices by sharing each element in them. Particularly, we call $(\langle r \rangle_t, \langle r \rangle_{2t})$ a double-sharing, where r is uniformly random in $\mathbb{F}_p$. The reconstruction of a secret from its shares can be achieved through the Lagrange interpolation method. In the semi-honest setting, we can have only one participant perform the task of secret reconstruction. When a secret needs to be recovered, each party first sends its share to a specific party, who can then calculate the result and send it to the rest of the participants. We denote the protocol for recovering the secret u from $\langle u \rangle_t$ or $\langle u \rangle_{2t}$ by Π_{Reveal}.

Given two sharings $\langle a \rangle$, $\langle b \rangle$ and two public value $g, h \in \mathbb{F}_p$, we can compute $\langle ga + hb \rangle = g\langle a \rangle + h\langle b \rangle$ by having each party perform the calculation locally on its own shares. And we follow the method in [7] to perform the multiplication of $\langle a \rangle$ and $\langle b \rangle$ with the use of a double-sharing $(\langle r \rangle_t, \langle r \rangle_{2t})$. To compute $\langle c \rangle$ satisfying $c = ab$, we first compute the sharing $\langle ab \rangle_{2t}$ by locally multiply the shares of $\langle a \rangle$ and $\langle b \rangle$. Then we can obtain the result by calculating $\langle c \rangle = \Pi_{Reveal}(\langle ab \rangle_{2t} - \langle r \rangle_{2t}) + \langle r \rangle_t$. This multiplication is information-theoretically secure and we denote it by Π_{Mult}. Since $2t$-sharings are used, the protocol Π_{Mult} requires $t < n/2$.

2.4 Encoding of Real Numbers

Shamir's scheme requires computation to be performed in a finite field, whereas the real-life data processed by neural networks are typically real numbers. To be able to handle real data, we follow the method in [4] to represent real numbers as fixed-point numbers, and then encode these fixed-point numbers into $\mathbb{F}_p$. We use $\mathbb{Z}_{\langle k \rangle} = \{\bar{x} \in \mathbb{Z} \mid -2^{k-1} \leqslant \bar{x} \leqslant 2^{k-1} - 1\}$ to represent signed integers and use $\mathbb{Q}_{\langle k, f \rangle} = \{\tilde{x} \in \mathbb{Q} \mid \tilde{x} = \bar{x} \cdot 2^{-f}, \bar{x} \in \mathbb{Z}_{\langle k \rangle}\}$ to represent the fixed-point numbers corresponding to $\mathbb{Z}_{\langle k \rangle}$, where f and k represent the precision of fixed-point numbers and the length of signed integers, respectively. To convert an element from $\mathbb{Q}_{\langle k,f \rangle}$ to $\mathbb{Z}_{\langle k \rangle}$, we use the function $\text{int}_f : \mathbb{Q}_{\langle k,f \rangle} \mapsto \mathbb{Z}_{\langle k \rangle}$, $\text{int}_f(\tilde{x}) = \tilde{x} \cdot 2^f$. And we use the function $\text{fld} : \mathbb{Z}_{\langle k \rangle} \mapsto \mathbb{F}_p$, $\text{fld}(\bar{x}) = \bar{x}(\text{mod} p)$ to map an element in $\mathbb{Z}_{\langle k \rangle}$ into $\mathbb{F}_p$. The field $\mathbb{F}_p$ needs to satisfy $p > 2^{k+\kappa+1}$, where κ is the security parameter.

3   Building Blocks of Our Protocols

3.1   Basic Operations

Randomness. We use Double-Random and Random from [7] to generate double-sharings and sharings of random values, respectively. These two protocols are both information-theoretically secure against semi-honest adversaries. We use Π_{DouRan} and Π_{Ran} to denote Double-Random and Random, respectively. And we denote the protocol for generating the sharing of a uniformly random bit by Π_{RanBit}. Π_{RanBit} follows the same steps of RAN_2 proposed in [6] except that Π_{Ran}, Π_{Mult} and Π_{Reveal} are used as the underlying protocols. The security analysis of RAN_2 in [6] is also applicable to Π_{RanBit}. When invoking Π_{Ran}, Π_{Mult} and Π_{Reveal} as sub-protocols, the protocol Π_{RanBit} is information-theoretically secure. With Π_{RanBit}, we can generate the sharing of a random number of any length, and we use Π_{RanInt} to denote this protocol. The security of Π_{RanInt} follows from Π_{RanBit}.

Sharing of Zero. We can generate $n - t$ sharings of 0 at one time in the way that Π_{Ran} generates the sharings of random values. And we denote the protocol for generating the random sharings of 0 by Π_{Zero}.

Fixed-Point Arithmetic. For fixed-point addition, both the addition of sharings and the addition by a public value can be performed locally. But when it comes to fixed-point multiplication, we need to truncate the result to maintain the same precision. In [2], FXMul uses the truncation protocol Div2mP to truncate the multiplication result, thus realizing the multiplication of fixed-point encoded sharings. Div2mP will use secret-shared random values generated based on pseudorandom functions. Similar to the protocol Π_{Trun} in [20], we use Π_{RanInt} to generate the sharings of random numbers required in Div2mP to obtain our truncation protocol Π_{Trunc} with information-theoretic security. Algorithm 1 shows the details of Π_{Trunc}, where m is the number of digits to be truncated. Compared with Div2mP, besides the way of generating random numbers, Π_{Trunc} calculates the final result without using the input $\langle a \rangle$ so that $\langle a \rangle$ is only used in the secret reconstruction operation in step 4. The purpose of this is that even when the input of Π_{Trunc} is a $2t$-sharing, Π_{Trunc} can still output a t-sharing. So when we need to calculate the product of two fixed-point encoded sharings $\langle a \rangle$ and $\langle b \rangle$, we can first calculate $\langle ab \rangle_{2t}$ locally, refresh it with a zero $2t$-sharing and then input it into Π_{Trunc}. We use Π_{FxMult} to denote this protocol. The security of Π_{FxMult} follows from Π_{Trunc}.

As for the multiplication by a public value, after encoding the public value into $\mathbb{F}_p$, this kind of multiplication can be performed by locally multiplying the shares by the public value and then using Π_{Trunc} to truncate the result. Note that encoding and truncation are unnecessary when the public value is an integer.

3.2 Fully Connected Layer

The operations involved in a fully connected layer are matrix multiplication and matrix addition. We can compute matrix addition locally. For two secret-shared matrices $\langle A \rangle$ and $\langle B \rangle$, we follow the steps of Π_{FxMult} to calculate their product, except that the multiplication involved is matrix multiplication. We denote the matrix multiplication protocol with truncation by $\Pi_{MatMult}$.

Algorithm 1. Π_{Trunc}

Input: $\langle a \rangle$, k, m;
Output: $\langle b \rangle$;
 1: The parties invoke Π_{RanInt} to get $\langle r' \rangle$, where r' is a random number of length m;
 2: The parties invoke Π_{RanInt} to get $\langle r'' \rangle$, where r'' is a random number of length $k + \kappa - m$;
 3: $\langle r \rangle = 2^m \langle r'' \rangle + \langle r' \rangle$;
 4: $c = \Pi_{Reveal}(2^{k-1} + \langle a \rangle + \langle r \rangle)$;
 5: $c' = c \bmod 2^m$;
 6: $\langle b \rangle = (c - c' - 2^{k-1})2^{-m} - \langle r'' \rangle$;

3.3 ReLU and Derivative of ReLU

In this paper, we use ReLU as the activation function. It is defined as $\mathrm{ReLU}(x) = \max(0, x)$. And its derivative $\mathrm{DReLU}(x)$ is defined to be 1 if $x \geqslant 0$ and 0 otherwise. To implement ReLU and its derivative, first we propose Π_{LZ} based on LTZ in [3]. Given $\langle a \rangle$, LTZ returns $\langle 1 \rangle$ if $a < 0$ and returns $\langle 0 \rangle$ otherwise. In [3], there are several ways to implement LTZ, and the solution we choose is to invoke BitLTC1 as a sub-protocol. LTZ uses pseudorandom functions to generate the required sharings of random numbers and 0, thus reducing the security of the protocol. We can obtain the protocol Π_{LZ} with information-theoretic security by using the protocols proposed in Sect. 3.1 to generate the sharings of random values and the sharings of 0 required in LTZ.

The protocol Π_{DReLU} for computing DReLU can then be implemented based on Π_{LZ}. For input $\langle a \rangle$, Π_{DReLU} first calls Π_{LZ} to get $\langle b \rangle = \Pi_{LZ}(\langle a \rangle)$ and then outputs $\langle c \rangle = 1 - \langle b \rangle$. The security and correctness of Π_{DReLU} directly follow from those of Π_{LZ}. Note that $\mathrm{ReLU}(x) = x \cdot \mathrm{DReLU}(x)$. Hence the protocol Π_{ReLU} for computing ReLU can be constructed by invoking Π_{DReLU} and Π_{Mult}. The security and correctness of Π_{ReLU} follow from those of Π_{DReLU} and Π_{Mult}.

3.4 Loss Function

In this paper, we consider the cross-entropy loss and the SVM loss. Note that for the training of a neural network, we only need to calculate δ^L instead of the loss function.

The Cross-Entropy Loss. We have $\delta^L = SM(z^L) - y$ when using the cross-entropy loss. Same to the processing in [15], we use the function ASM to calculate SM, where $ASM(z_i^L) = ReLU(z_i^L)/\Sigma_{j=1}^{d^L} ReLU(z_j^L), i \in [d^L]$. We have already implemented ReLU, so we only need to implement division to calculate ASM. Algorithm 2 shows our division protocol Π_{Div}. Given $\langle a \rangle$ and $\langle b \rangle$, Π_{Div} returns $\langle s \rangle$ such that $s = \left\lfloor \frac{a \cdot 2^f}{b} \right\rfloor$. In Π_{Div}, the result is computed bit by bit. Note that the result of ASM is between 0 and 1, so the final result can be limited to $f + 1$ bits. In addition, since the value returned by ReLU is nonnegative, we don't have to deal with the case of negative numbers. The security of Π_{Div} follows from the security of Π_{DReLU} and Π_{Mult}.

Algorithm 2. Division Π_{Div}

Input: $\langle a \rangle$, $\langle b \rangle$;
Output: $\langle s \rangle$;
1: $\langle a \rangle = 2^f \cdot \langle a \rangle$;
2: **for** $i = f$ to 0 **do**
3:    $\langle d_i \rangle = 2^i \cdot \langle b \rangle$;
4:    $\langle c_i \rangle = \Pi_{DReLU}(\langle a \rangle - \langle d_i \rangle)$;
5:    $\langle a \rangle = \langle a \rangle - \Pi_{Mult}(\langle c_i \rangle, \langle d_i \rangle)$;
6: **end for**
7: $\langle s \rangle = \sum_{i=0}^{f} 2^i \langle c_i \rangle$;

With Π_{Div}, we can then propose $\Pi_{\delta_A^L}$ to compute δ^L. To avoid the situation where the divisor is 0, for $i \in [d^L]$, we calculate $\langle \delta_i^L \rangle$ according to the formula:

$$\delta_i^L = \frac{\Pi_{ReLU}(z_i^L) + 1 - \bigvee_{j=1}^{d^L} \Pi_{LZ}(-z_j^L)}{\Sigma_{j=1}^{d^L} \Pi_{ReLU}(z_j^L) + d^L(1 - \bigvee_{j=1}^{d^L} \Pi_{LZ}(-z_j^L))} - y_i. \qquad (2)$$

Note that we can also calculate $\Pi_{ReLU}(x)$ as $x \cdot \Pi_{LZ}(-x)$, so in Eq. 2 we don't need extra steps to calculate $\Pi_{LZ}(-z_j^L)$. We utilize PreOrC in [3] to compute $\bigvee_{j=1}^{d^L} \Pi_{LZ}(-z_j^L)$. Given $\{\langle a_1 \rangle, \cdots, \langle a_l \rangle\}$, PreOrC computes $\{\langle p_1 \rangle, \cdots, \langle p_l \rangle\}$ satisfying $\langle p_i \rangle = \bigvee_{j=1}^{i} \langle a_j \rangle, i \in [l]$. We can just generate $\langle p_l \rangle$ in PreOrC to get the protocol for computing unbounded fan-in Or, which we denote as Π_{Or^*}. The security of Π_{Or^*} follows directly from PreOrC, which is information-theoretically secure [3]. And the security of $\Pi_{\delta_A^L}$ follows from Π_{LZ}, Π_{ReLU}, Π_{Div} and Π_{Or^*}.

The SVM Loss. When we use the SVM loss as the loss function, we propose $\Pi_{\delta_B^L}$ to compute δ^L. Algorithm 3 shows the detailed steps of $\Pi_{\delta_B^L}$. According to Sect. 2.2, the key point of this protocol is to judge whether $z_j^L - z_s^L + \Delta \geqslant 0 (j \in [d^L])$, which can be achieved by invoking Π_{DReLU}. The purpose of subtracting $(\Delta + 1)\langle y_j \rangle$ in step 4 is to eliminate the effect of the $j = s$ case on the result. We want to make sure that when $j = s$, the value of m_j is less than 0 and can be filtered out by Π_{DReLU}. The Δ is in the form of fixed-point encoding. Therefore, when calculating $(\Delta + 1)\langle y_j \rangle$, we need to invoke Π_{Trunc} to perform a truncation. We use Δ_0 to denote the number in $\mathbb{Q}_{\langle k,f \rangle}$ corresponding to Δ. When we restrict the value of Δ_0 to be an integer, the truncation used in step 4 can be avoided. In this case, step 4 becomes $\langle m_j \rangle = \langle z_j^L \rangle - \langle a \rangle + \Delta - (\Delta_0 + 1)\langle y_j \rangle$. The protocol $\Pi_{\delta_B^L}$ is information-theoretically secure since it only consists of invocations of secure sub-protocols and local computation.

Algorithm 3. $\Pi_{\delta_B^L}$

Input: $\langle z^L \rangle$, $\langle y \rangle$;
Output: $\langle \delta^L \rangle$;
1: $\langle n \rangle = \langle z^L \rangle \odot \langle y \rangle$;
2: $\langle a \rangle = \sum_{i=1}^{d^L} \langle n_i \rangle$;
3: **for** $j = 1$ to d^L **do**
4:    $\langle m_j \rangle = \langle z_j^L \rangle - \langle a \rangle + \Delta - (\Delta + 1)\langle y_j \rangle$;
5: **end for**
6: Given $\langle m \rangle$, the parties invoke Π_{DReLU} to compute $\langle k \rangle$;
7: $\langle t \rangle = \sum_{i=1}^{d^L} 2^f \langle k_i \rangle$;
8: **for** $i = 1$ to d^L **do**
9:    $\langle \delta_i^L \rangle = \langle -t \rangle \langle y_i \rangle + 2^f \langle k_i \rangle$;
10: **end for**

---

4 Secure Neural Network Training

With all the sub-protocols described above, we can combine them to perform the training of neural networks. We separate the computation process into an offline phase and an online phase. The offline phase is used to perform data-independent operations, such as the generation of the sharings of random numbers. In order to integrate data from different sources, the parties first encode their own data into $\mathbb{F}_p$ and then secret-share them. We denote the entire set of features and labels by $x = (x_1, x_2, \cdots, x_N) \in \mathbb{F}_p^{d \times N}$ and $y = (y_1, \cdots, y_N) \in \mathbb{F}_p^{d^L \times N}$, respectively. The participants also need to initialize $\langle w^l \rangle$ and $\langle b^l \rangle$, where $1 \leqslant l \leqslant L$. When the training phase is over, the participants can reconstruct w^l and b^l from the sharings $\langle w^l \rangle$ and $\langle b^l \rangle$, and decode them locally to get their values in $\mathbb{Q}_{\langle k,f \rangle}$.

Algorithm 4 shows the protocol for an iteration of secure neural network training using the stochastic gradient descent algorithm with L2 regularization, where η represents the learning rate and λ is the hyperparameter relating to the regularization. This protocol uses the cross-entropy loss and is denoted by Π_{DNN_A}. When we consider the SVM loss, we denote the training protocol by Π_{DNN_B}. The calculation steps of Π_{DNN_B} are the same as those of Π_{DNN_A}, except that $\Pi_{\delta_A^L}$ in Π_{DNN_A} is replaced by $\Pi_{\delta_B^L}$. It should be noted that all multiplications in Algorithm 4 require truncation, with the exception of the calculation of the Hadamard product in step 8. The protocol Π_{DNN_A} is information-theoretically secure since it only consists of local computation and invocations of secure sub-protocols. Similarly, the protocol Π_{DNN_B} is also information-theoretically secure.

Algorithm 4. Secure Neural Network Training Π_{DNN_A}

Input: $\langle a^0 \rangle$, $\langle y \rangle$;
1: **for** $l = 1$ to $L - 1$ **do**
2:     $\langle z^l \rangle = \langle w^l \rangle \langle a^{l-1} \rangle + \langle b^l \rangle$;
3:     Given $\langle z^l \rangle$, the parties invoke Π_{ReLU} to compute $\langle a^l \rangle$;
4: **end for**
5: $\langle z^L \rangle = \langle w^L \rangle \langle a^{L-1} \rangle + \langle b^L \rangle$;
6: Given $\langle z^L \rangle$ and $\langle y \rangle$, the parties invoke $\Pi_{\delta_A^L}$ to compute $\langle \delta^L \rangle$;
7: **for** $l = L - 1$ to 1 **do**
8:     $\langle \delta^l \rangle = \langle (w^{l+1})^T \rangle \langle \delta^{l+1} \rangle \odot \Pi_{DReLU}\left(\langle z^l \rangle\right)$;
9: **end for**
10: **for** $l = L$ to 1 **do**
11:     $\langle b^l \rangle = \langle b^l \rangle - \eta \langle \delta^l \rangle$;
12:     $\langle w^l \rangle = (1 - \eta\lambda)\langle w^l \rangle - \eta\langle \delta^l \rangle \langle (a^{l-1})^T \rangle$;
13: **end for**

---

5   Evaluation

5.1   Complexity Analysis

We use communication and round complexity to reflect the interaction between participants. We measure the communication complexity as the number of invocations of Π_{Reveal} and the round complexity as the number of sequential invocations of this protocol. Table 1 shows the complexity of the online phase of the supporting protocols for neural network training, where u and v indicate that the output of $\Pi_{MatMult}$ is a secret-shared matrix with u rows and v columns.

In Π_{Reveal} we let one specific party compute the public value of the secret, therefore each invocation requires $2(n-1)\ell$ bits of messages. This indicates that for all protocols in Table 1, a total of $\mathcal{O}(n)$ bits of messages need to be transmitted. Therefore, our protocols can readily adapt to changes in participant numbers without having to worry about communication overhead rapidly increasing.

Table 1. Communication and round complexity

Protocol	Rounds	Invocations
Π_{Mult}	1	1
Π_{Trunc}	1	1
Π_{FxMult}	1	1
$\Pi_{MatMult}$	1	uv
Π_{DReLU}	3	$k+1$
Π_{ReLU}	4	$k+2$
Π_{Div}	$4f+4$	$(f+1)(k+2)$
$\Pi_{\delta_A^L}$	$4f+10$	$(d^L+f+1)(k+2)+d^L+1$
$\Pi_{\delta_B^L}$	5	$d^L(k+3)$

5.2 Experimental Results

The experiments were carried out on a single server equipped with 2 24-core 2.20 GHz Intel Xeon Gold 5220R CPUs and 128 GB of RAM in the LAN setting. We accelerated the computation of local matrix multiplication using an NVIDIA RTX 3090 GPU. We set the number of adversaries t to 1. And we set the prime of the finite field to be $2^{126} - 137$.

We conducted experiments on two neural networks. The first network we considered came from SecureML [12], which we called Network A. Network A was a 3-layer DNN and used the cross-entropy loss function. It had two hidden layers, each with 128 neurons. The activation function used in Network A was ReLU. We replaced the softmax function and the cross-entropy loss used in Network A with the SVM loss, resulting in a second network, which we called Network B.

The experiments were performed on the MNIST dataset [9], which contained a training set of 60, 000 samples and a testing set of 10, 000 samples. Each sample contains a 28×28-pixel image of a handwritten digit and a label between 0 and 9. We considered the image to be a vector with 784 elements, each with a value between 0 and 255. We used the mini-batch gradient descent algorithm and generated all the required sharings of random numbers and sharings of 0 in the offline phase. All the data were normalized between 0 and 1. And the labels were represented as one-hot vectors. We set the mini-batch size to 128 and the learning rate to 2^{-8} for both networks. For Network A, we set f to 15, which represents the length of the fractional part. After 10 epochs of training, the accuracy of Network A on the testing set reached 88.76%. For Network B, we set f to 13. After 10 epochs of training, the accuracy of Network B on the testing set reached 96.02%.

We also compared the results of secure training with plaintext computation. Table 2 shows the prediction accuracy of Network A and Network B on the testing set for private and plaintext training. The experiments demonstrate that the computing results of private training are very close to those of plaintext training, implying that our protocols can achieve the effect of plaintext computation. The experiments in Table 2 were all carried out in the scenario of 3 participants. It should be noted that increasing the number of parties in our protocols does not lead to additional errors other than increasing the running time. So experiments conducted with 3 parties can represent the calculation results of experiments with any other number of parties. We then conducted experiments with different numbers of participants to analyze the efficiency of our protocols. Table 3 displays the training time for a single epoch of our neural network models when the number of participants is changed while the other settings remain the same. It can be seen from the experimental results that Network B has higher execution efficiency because it avoids the use of division. Furthermore, since the number of field elements that our protocols need to communicate are $\mathcal{O}(n)$, we can see that the training time grows basically linearly as the number of parties increases.

Table 2. Accuracy comparison between private and plaintext training

Epochs	Network A		Network B	
	private	plaintext	private	plaintext
1	77.30%	77.28%	90.93%	90.96%
2	83.38%	83.36%	92.46%	92.40%
3	85.79%	85.80%	93.38%	93.38%
4	87.07%	87.01%	94.43%	94.38%
5	87.70%	87.77%	94.89%	95.00%

Table 3. Training time between different numbers of parties

Number of Parties	Network A	Network B
3	1.87h	1.39h
4	2.05h	1.58h
5	2.23h	1.67h
6	2.35h	1.83h
7	2.51h	1.96h

We underline that the major goal of this paper is to enable secure neural network training with information-theoretic security and the flexible configuration of the number of participants. To get this goal, we unavoidably compromise execution efficiency. The experimental results show that our protocols successfully achieve the training of neural networks while keeping the training time within a tolerable range.

6   Conclusion

In this paper, we propose protocols for secure neural network training which offer high security as well as high flexibility. Our protocols are information-theoretically secure so that security can be guaranteed regardless of the computing power of the adversaries. Our protocols support the flexible configuration of participant numbers and adversary thresholds. And the amount of communication required by our protocols is linear in n, making our protocols very flexible to deploy.

Acknowledgments. This work was supported in part by the National Key Research and Development Program under Grant 2022YFA1004900. We warmly thank Professor Chaoping Xing from Shanghai Jiao Tong University for his guidance on the design of our private protocols.

References

1. Canetti, R.: Universally composable security: a new paradigm for cryptographic protocols. In: Proceeding of Foundations of Computer Science, pp. 136–145 (2001)
2. Catrina, O.: Round-efficient protocols for secure multiparty fixed-point arithmetic. In: 2018 International Conference on Communications (COMM), pp. 431–436 (2018)
3. Catrina, O., Hoogh, S.: Improved primitives for secure multi-party integer computation. In: International Conference on Security and Cryptography for Networks, pp. 182–199 (2010)
4. Catrina, O., Saxena, A.: Secure computation with fixed-point numbers. In: International Conference on Financial Cryptography and Data Security, pp. 35–50 (2010)
5. Chaudhari, H., Rachuri, R., Suresh, A.: Trident: efficient 4pc framework for privacy preserving machine learning. In: Symposium on Network and Distributed System Security (NDSS) (2020)
6. Damgård, I., Fitzi, M., Kiltz, E., Nielsen, J., Toft, T.: Unconditionally secure constant-rounds multi-party computation for equality, comparison, bits and exponentiation. In: Proceedings of the 3th Theory of Cryptography Conference (TCC), pp. 285–304 (2006)
7. Damgård, I., Nielsen., J.B.: Scalable and unconditionally secure multiparty computation. In: Annual International Cryptology Conference, pp. 572–590 (2007)
8. Demmler, D., Schneider, T., Zohner, M.: ABY - a framework for efficient mixed-protocol secure two-party computation. In: Network & Distributed System Security Symposium (2015)
9. Deng, L.: The MNIST database of handwritten digit images for machine learning research. IEEE Signal Process. Mag. **29**(6), 141–142 (2012)
10. Koti, N., Patra, A., Rachuri, R., Suresh, A.: Tetrad: actively secure 4pc for secure training and inference. In: Symposium on Network and Distributed System Security (NDSS) (2022)
11. Mohassel, P., Rindal, P.: ABY^3: a mixed protocol framework for machine learning. In: Proceedings of the 2018 ACM SIGSAC Conference on Computer and Communications Security, pp. 35–52 (2018)
12. Mohassel, P., Zhang, Y.: SecureML: a system for scalable privacy-preserving machine learning. In: IEEE Symposium on Security and Privacy, pp. 19–38 (2017)

13. Patra, A., Suresh, A.: BLAZE: blazing fast privacy-preserving machine learning. In: Symposium on Network and Distributed System Security (NDSS) (2020)
14. Shamir, A.: How to share a secret. Commun. ACM **22**(11), 612–613 (1979)
15. Wagh, S., Gupta, D., Chandran, N.: SecureNN: 3-party secure computation for neural network training. Proc. Priv. Enhanc. Technol. **2019**(3), 26–49 (2019)
16. Wagh, S., Tople, S., Benhamouda, F., Kushilevitz, E., Mittal, P., Rabin, T.: FALCON: honest-majority maliciously secure framework for private deep learning. Proc. Priv. Enhanc. Technol. **2021**(1), 188–208 (2021)
17. Weston, J., Watkins, C.: Support vector machines for multi-class pattern recognition. In: Proceedings of the 7th European Symposium on Artificial Neural Networks (ESANN), pp. 219–224 (1999)
18. Yao, A.: Protocols for secure computations. In: 23rd Annual Symposium on Foundations of Computer Science, pp. 160–164 (1982)
19. Yao, A.: How to generate and exchange secrets. In: 27th Annual Symposium on Foundations of Computer Science, pp. 162–167 (1986)
20. Zhou, H.: Information-theoretically secure multi-party linear regression and logistic regression. In: 2023 IEEE/ACM 23rd International Symposium on Cluster, Cloud and Internet Computing Workshops (CCGridW), pp. 192–199 (2023)

LRP-GUS: A Visual Based Data Reduction Algorithm for Neural Networks

Arnaud Guibert[1]([✉])[iD], Christophe Hurter[1][iD], and Nicolas Couellan[1,2][iD]

[1] École Nationale de l'Aviation Civile, Université de Toulouse,
7 Avenue Edouard Belin, 31400 Toulouse, France
arnaud.guibert@enac.fr
[2] Institut de Mathématiques de Toulouse, UMR 5219, Université de Toulouse,
CNRS, UPS, 118 route de Narbonne, 31062 Cedex 9 Toulouse, France

Abstract. Deriving general rules to estimate a neural network sample complexity is a difficult problem. Therefore, in practice, datasets are often large to ensure sufficient class samples representation. This comes at the cost of high power consumption and long training time. This paper introduces a novel data reduction method for Deep Learning classifiers, called LRP-GUS, focusing on visual features. The idea behind LRP-GUS is to reduce the size of our training dataset by exploiting visual features and their relevance. The proposed technique is tested on the MNIST and Fashion-MNIST datasets. We evaluate the method using compression rates, accuracy and F_1 scores per class. For instance, our method achieves compression rates of 96.10% for MNIST and 75.94% for Fashion-MNIST, at the cost of a drop of 3% test accuracy for both datasets.

Keywords: Data reduction · Machine Learning · Visual features · XAI

1 Introduction

Training Convolutional Neural Networks (CNNs) requires a lot of resources and time, as feature extraction is integrated in the model itself. One solution to solve this issue is to reduce the training dataset size, using data reduction methods to get a lower number of instances, thus training the model faster without affecting the model's performance and robustness. In a way, this can be seen as an experimental estimation of the CNN sample complexity [2]. In this article, we introduce a new data reduction iterative method called Layerwise Relevance Propagation - Guided Undersampling (LRP-GUS), computing reduced dataset class sizes, based on visual features learnt by the model. Our final goal is to generate a training subset from the original training set: once it is computed, new classifiers with a high enough accuracy can be trained on it, faster than if they were trained on the full training set. We use LRP [3] as our decision basis for class undersampling. This method maps the output of a model to its input space, showing the importance of the input pixels in the model's decision as a

© The Author(s), under exclusive license to Springer Nature Switzerland AG 2023
L. Iliadis et al. (Eds.): ICANN 2023, LNCS 14258, pp. 337–349, 2023.
https://doi.org/10.1007/978-3-031-44192-9_27

saliency map. This saliency map is an image with positive and negative pixel values, showing how each input pixel helped the model to make its decision.

We tested our iterative method on two benchmark image datasets with 10 classes: MNIST [21] (the handwritten digits from 0 to 9) and Fashion-MNIST [32] (various pieces of clothing). Both datasets are composed of 60,000 training images and 10,000 testing images. We trained a distinct CNN architecture for each dataset, to reach an acceptable initial generalization accuracy. With a stop condition of a maximum 3% accuracy drop, our method achieved high training dataset reduction, 96.10% for MNIST and 75.94% for Fashion-MNIST.

This paper is organized as follows: Sect. 2 lists methods aiming for data reduction and undersampling datasets. Our method and the reason for using visual features are detailled in Sect. 3. Section 4 describes the experimental framework, and examines the results obtained in this study on the MNIST and Fashion-MNIST datasets. We discuss the results and their limitations in Sect. 5. Section 6 concludes the paper and discusses potential future work.

2 Related Work

Data reduction is a problem that has been widely documented in the recent years [5,10]. It consists of selecting instances from the initial training set, based on different metrics. Its end goal is often to find an acceptable trade-off between the accuracy and the compression rate from the full training set. However, some methods focus on staying above a given accuracy at all costs while others focus on compressing the training data as much as possible. While Deep Learning methods can benefit from a good data compression, it can also be detrimental [9,29] both for the generalization and the convergence speed of the model [1]. Class imbalance methods can also tackle the same issue. They consist in averaging the number of instances per class in a dataset to ensure a balanced class representation, because consequent differences in class representation can hinder the performance of classifiers [15]. Class imbalance can refer to different distributions of datasets, but all of them have an important gap between the minority class and the majority class [10].

Data Reduction: Data reduction techniques try to reduce the initial training dataset while keeping the accuracy as high as possible. Researchers have tried various ways to apply this to existing datasets, such as the pure k-Nearest Neighbors selection approach [7], and a few variants [13,30] focusing on border instances or changing the metric formula. Editing methods focus on cleaning the data, by removing noisy instances and smoothing the inter-class borders [14,31]. While Euclidean distance is a common choice, some authors have used other distances: MeanShift [6] is an example of such method using dissimilarity measures. Finally, clustering methods are also widely used for data reduction. A few examples are Prototype Selection by Clustering [25] that handles instances clusters based on their homogeneity, Symbolic Nearest Mean Classifier [8] and Reduction through Homogeneous Clusters [26]. All these methods only consider the data and their relative proximity in the data space without looking at the evolution of the model during its training phase. In this article, we fill this gap by implicitly constructing a metric based on the data and the model. Our goal is to have a better estimate of the sample complexity [2].

Class Imbalance: Class imbalance methods can be divided in two groups: over-sampling and undersampling methods. We will only focus on undersampling methods since we aim to reduce the dataset size. However, undersampling is not as popular among class imbalance research as oversampling because it tends to degrade the model performance [4]. The most basic method is called random majority undersampling, or RUS. It discards majority classes instances at random until the dataset is more balanced. This method is effective because of the reduced power consumption and training time of the model, but it can perform poorly because of the uncontrolled loss of information from the initial data [12]. One-Sided Selection [19] is an early technique that identifies redundancy of samples close to the class boundaries to remove them. Edited Nearest Neighbor [20] is a technique that detects redundant or insignificant majority samples based on a 3 Nearest Neighbor rule. SMUTE and CSMOUTE [17] are other examples of undersampling techniques, known to work particulary well with complex classifiers like Artificial Neural Networks. Other techniques also use other families of methods like clustering or genetic algorithms to select their instances [11,18,22,33].

XAI Methods: eXplainable AI (XAI) methods map the output of a model to its input space. For image classification, they show the importance of the input pixels in the model's decision as a saliency map. Those maps can take multiple forms, depending on the method. Grad-CAM [28] is one such method, outputting a positive saliency map focusing on the important pixels. The intensity of that saliency map shows which pixels contributed the most for the classification. Local Interpretable Model-Agnostic Explanations (LIME) [27] is another method, quantifying the response of the model to a given instance. It trains an explainable model based on random instances chosen around the reference instance. Other methods, like LRP [3] and SHapley Additive exPlanations [23], take a different approach. They output a saliency map with both positive and negative values. The positive values show the inputs helping the classification, while the negative ones show inputs not helping it. To the best of our knowledge, XAI methods are always used as a visual tool for humans to interpret on, and not as a secondary mean to quantitatively optimize a primary objective.

All data reduction methods aim to compress the initial dataset size while keeping an acceptable generalization accuracy. Our method is more focused on the model's reaction to the dataset and tries to balance the dataset using the relevance of the visual features it has learnt. We used LRP to extract the visual feature relevances learnt by the model and assert them. To the best of our knowledge, this is the first algorithm using visual features and XAI methods to reduce the size of a dataset.

3   The LRP-GUS Method

LRP-GUS aims to create a training subset that balances the difficulty for a model to learn every class separately. We used a hybrid method based on RUS and XAI methods to build such a dataset balanced with respect to visual features. In this section, we will discuss our XAI method choice, then we will explain our algorithm step by step.

Neural Networks are infamously known for being *black box* algorithms, meaning it is difficult to analyze their decision process when predicting a class for an input. This is because they have a complex decision boundary compared to traditional methods like k-NN or Decision Trees. XAI methods have been developed to understand how a model makes its prediction. They are popular in image classification tasks as they return saliency maps that are human-readable. Details about the goal and output of such methods are explained in Sect. 2.

Out of all available methods, we focus on Layerwise Relevance Propagation (LRP) because it provides a direct binary criterion that can be easily exploited at a higher level as we propose. Indeed, in the output class LRP maps, the positive pixels are those contributing to the class decision. Grad-CAM does not provide such information, and LIME requires to train one surrogate model for each classifier and is therefore not suitable for the framework we propose. Several LRP decision rules exist focusing on positive or negative activations and/or weights of the network. Each rule specializes in handling input, upper, middle, or lower layers specifically. Such rules include LRP-0, LRP-ϵ, LRP-γ and the z^β-rule. A composite LRP rule [24] was shown to give better explanations on more complex network architectures. However, since our models for Fashion-MNIST and MNIST are relatively small, as described in Sect. 4.1, we use a pure LRP-ϵ rule (with parameter $\epsilon = 10^{-4}$) for our entire model. An example of LRP outputs on MNIST is shown on Fig. 1.

Notations: Let $D = \{(x_i, y_i) \mid 1 \leq i \leq |D|\} \subset \mathbb{R}^d \times \{1, ..., c\}$ be a dataset for supervised classification with c classes. Let $T \subset D$ and $U \subset D$ be a training set and test set respectively. For any pair of sets A and B so that $A \subset B$, we define the compression rate: $r(A, B) = 1 - \frac{|A|}{|B|}$. Let also, for any $I \subset D$, $I^{(k)} = \{(x, y) \in I \mid y = k\}$ be the k-class set of I for a given class $k \in \{1, ..., c\}$. We also define the negative intensity function n for all samples $x \in \mathbb{R}^d$ as the sum of negative values such that $n(x) = \sum_{i=1}^{d} \min(0, x_i)$.

Finally, we define the normalized LRP function. It applies to: an instance from the input space $x \in \mathbb{R}^d$, a class $y \in \{1, ..., c\}$, and a neural network M. The LRP function can therefore be written as: $l_M : (x, y) \mapsto l_M(x, y) \in \mathbb{R}^d$. To compute an average LRP map across various LRP saliency maps, we propose a normalized version of the LRP function above, using absolute maximum normalization. This normalization ensures the sign of the pixels in the LRP maps remains unchanged. Therefore, we define the normalized LRP function as:

$$\hat{l}_M : (x, y) \mapsto \frac{l_M(x, y)}{\max(|l_M(x, y)|)} \tag{1}$$

LRP Saliency Maps: To illustrate the construction of LRP maps, consider the following example. A model M is trained on the MNIST training dataset, using a network architecture and parameters defined in Sect. 4.1. We picked two images from the MNIST training set (digit 0 and digit 6) to compute the normalized LRP function $\hat{l}_M$. Figure 1 shows the resulting maps for both digits. The model has learnt a good decision frontier between the class 0 and the other classes as only the LRP heatmap computed using the true class ($y = 0$) displays a lot of positive pixels. The second digit, on the other hand, displays positive visual patterns for almost all classes, not only for its true class 6. This highlights our model can learn clear boundaries for some digits (0 in this case) while the boundaries for others (6 here) are less sharp.

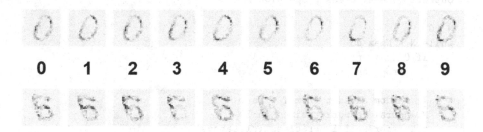

Fig. 1. Normalized LRP maps for 2 MNIST digits. The class y chosen in the LRP formula varies from left (class 0) to right (class 9). In the heatmaps, grey corresponds to scores close to zero, red to positive scores and blue to negative scores. See text for interpretation. (Color figure online)

The Algorithm: LRP-GUS uses both LRP and Random Undersampling to iterate. The goal is not to pick specific important instances for accuracy, but to find which classes have the most difficult patterns to learn, and thus which ones need more instances to build a balanced CNN.

We start from an initial class proportion $p_k \in \mathbb{N}^c$, where for all $j \in \{1,...,c\}$, $(p_k)_j$ defines the number of training samples for class j. We use RUS on the training set T to extract an iteration subset I with proportions defined by p_k. We build a neural network classifier M using this extracted dataset I as a training set. We then use the normalized LRP function $\hat{l}_M$ on the training dataset I, with the inputs true class as parameter, and the negative intensity n to compute a vector $f_k \in \mathbb{R}^c$ of scores per class as follows:

$$\forall j \in \{1,...,c\}, (f_k)_j = n\left(\frac{1}{|I^{(j)}|} \sum_{(x,y) \in I^{(j)}} \hat{l}_M(x,y)\right) \tag{2}$$

We then pick a class c_k to increase or decrease its proportion based on the value and sign of the difference between scores at consecutive iterations: $\Delta f_k = f_k - f_{k-1}$. The class c_k must respect a constraint percentage lim so that the new proportion is not too far away from the class proportions mean. We increase or decrease the proportion of that class by a percentage, and end up with a dataset class proportion p_{k+1} for the next iteration, and the scores f_k of the current iteration. If at any point, all the classes violate the constraint, the algorithm stops. Our algorithm outputs a new dataset proportion with less global instances than the initial dataset T, thus reducing the time and energy required to train new models using it. The pseudocode can be found in Table 1.

Table 1. Algorithm pseudocode

```
input: Training set T, Score vector f, Dataset class proportion p,
       Percentages up, down and lim, Max number of iterations Nmax
output: Dataset class proportion p

N  0
while N < Nmax do
    if 0 is in p:
        stop condition

    I  random dataset from T with p
    M  neural network trained on I
    f_k  scores of I per class (cf. above)
    c_k  class whose proportion will be changed

    if (f_k - f)(c_k) > 0 do
        p(c_k)  (1 - down) * p(c_k)
    else do
        p(c_k)  (1 + up) * p(c_k)
    f  f_k
    N  N + 1

return p
```

4   Results

4.1   Experimental Setup

Experiments were carried out on the MNIST and Fashion-MNIST datasets. MNIST is known for its separability with most handwritten digits sharing common features from their own class, and differences with other classes. Fashion-MNIST is a bit more complex, as some classes visually overlap, making it difficult for a model or even a human to classify them. Each dataset was trained on a separate architecture. Since our goal is to compress the dataset, the chosen architectures and hyperparameters were selected to guarantee both CNNs were "good enough" classifiers (with a high accuracy on the full training set). While there is room for hyperparameters improvement, this is not the goal of this paper.

Our MNIST network architecture is based on an existing model, LeNet-5 [21]. It is a small and compact CNN. We tuned and changed a few parameters in layers, as described in Table 2. All convolution layers are followed by a ReLU activation function, and the fully connected is followed by a Softmax. Our model uses an Adam optimization [16] algorithm with default α, β_1, β_2 and ϵ parameters. A batch size of 64 was chosen. The model training was stopped after 15 epochs. The Fashion-MNIST architecture introduces more layers, dropout and batch normalization, described in Table 3. The activation functions are the same as in the MNIST model. It uses an Adam optimization algorithm with default parameters, a batch size of 128 and the model training was stopped after 15 epochs.

Table 2. MNIST model

Layer	Size	Kernel	Strides
Input	28*28*1	–	–
Conv2D	26*26*32	3	1
Max Pool	13*13*32	2	2
Conv2D	11*11*64	3	1
Max Pool	5*5*64	2	2
Dropout (.5)	5*5*64	–	–
FC	10	–	–

Table 3. Fashion-MNIST model

Layer	Size	Kernel	Strides
Input	28*28*1	–	–
Conv2D	28*28*16	1	1
Conv2D	28*28*32	3	1
Max Pool	14*14*32	2	2
BatchNorm	14*14*32	–	–
Dropout (.2)	14*14*32	–	–
Conv2D	12*12*64	3	1
Max Pool	6*6*64	2	2
BatchNorm	6*6*64	–	–
Dropout (.2)	6*6*64	–	–
FC	256	–	–
Dropout (.2)	256	–	–
FC	10	–	–

4.2 MNIST

The following initial set of parameters was chosen: score vector $f = 0$ for all classes, dataset class proportion $p = 2000$ for all classes, percentages $up = 5\%$, $down = 20\%$ and $lim = 40\%$ and a maximum number of iterations $Nmax = 1000$. The generalization accuracy with respect to the compression rate is displayed in Fig. 2a and the evolution of the dataset proportions p and the F_1 scores per iteration are shown in Fig. 2b.

The stop condition for our algorithm is a maximum accuracy drop of 3% compared to the full training set T accuracy. This target is shown as the horizontal black line on Fig. 2a. We deduce the *cutoff* iteration i_c from the intersection with the curve. The vertical line $x = i_c$ on Fig. 2b gives the *cutoff* dataset T_c and the algorithm final proportion p.

Table 4 shows the repartition of classes in both datasets T and T_c. We can see the introduced imbalance in our subset, while the original training set is almost balanced. Thus, we trained 20 models on the original training dataset T, our cutoff dataset T_c and on a new dataset T_c (bal), with the same size as T_c, but a forced proportional split of instances between classes. Performance results for those datasets, along with the compression rate are also displayed in Table 4.

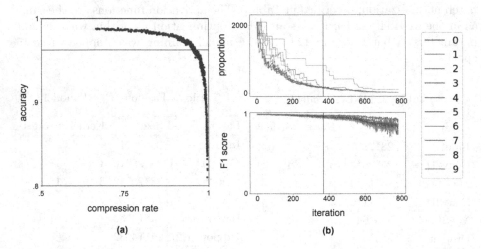

Fig. 2. (a) Evolution of accuracy by compression rate and (b) F_1 scores and class proportions per iteration for our experiments on the MNIST dataset. See text for interpretation.

4.3   Fashion-MNIST

The following initial set of parameters was chosen: score vector $f = 0$ for all classes, dataset class proportion $p = 4000$ for all classes, percentages $up = 5\%$, $down = 20\%$ and $lim = 40\%$ and a maximum number of iterations $Nmax = 500$. The generalization accuracy by the compression rate is displayed in Fig. 3a and the evolution of the dataset proportions p and the F_1 scores per iteration are shown in Fig. 3b.

The interpretation of the black lines is the same as for MNIST (see Sect. 4.2). Table 5 shows the repartition of classes in both datasets T and T_c. We also trained 20 models on the original training dataset T, our cutoff dataset T_c and on a new dataset T_c (bal). Performance results on those datasets, along with the compression rate are also displayed in Table 5.

Table 4. Experiment results on MNIST. (a) Proportions of classes in T and T_c. (b) Compression rate, mean and standard deviation for accuracy and F_1 scores. Computed with 20 models for each dataset T, T_c and T_c (bal).

(a)

class	T		T_c	
-	N	%	N	%
0	6923	9.9	185	7.9
1	6742	11.2	819	35.0
2	5958	9.9	173	7.4
3	6131	10.2	173	7.4
4	5842	9.7	162	6.9
5	5421	9.0	152	6.5
6	5918	9.9	162	6.9
7	6265	10.4	154	6.6
8	5851	9.8	180	7.7
9	5949	9.9	180	7.7

(b)

-	T		T_c		T_c (bal)	
-	μ	σ	μ	σ	μ	σ
r	-		96.10		96.10	
accu.	99.24	5e-4	96.35	2e-3	96.63	2e-3
F_1 (0)	99.55	0.10	97.67	0.36	97.75	0.36
F_1 (1)	99.57	0.06	98.50	0.38	98.42	0.23
F_1 (2)	99.17	0.14	95.11	0.49	95.57	0.33
F_1 (3)	99.36	0.10	95.49	0.46	96.35	0.64
F_1 (4)	99.41	0.14	97.52	0.38	97.65	0.38
F_1 (5)	99.02	0.11	95.93	0.62	96.80	0.52
F_1 (6)	99.23	0.13	97.52	0.28	97.65	0.31
F_1 (7)	98.99	0.17	95.32	0.24	95.33	0.63
F_1 (8)	99.09	0.12	94.86	0.41	95.03	0.48
F_1 (9)	98.95	0.19	95.36	0.42	95.62	0.37

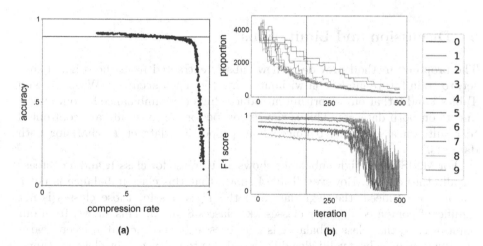

(a)   (b)

Fig. 3. (a) Evolution of accuracy by compression rate and (b) F_1 scores and class proportions per iteration for our experiments on the Fashion-MNIST dataset. See text for interpretation.

Table 5. Experiment results on Fashion-MNIST. (a) Proportions of classes in T and T_c. (b) Compression rate, mean and standard deviation for accuracy and F_1 scores. Computed with 20 models for each dataset T, T_c and T_c (bal).

	(a)			
class	T		T_c	
-	N	%	N	%
0	6000	10.0	1068	7.4
1	6000	10.0	1012	7.0
2	6000	10.0	1097	7.6
3	6000	10.0	967	6.7
4	6000	10.0	1130	7.8
5	6000	10.0	3205	22.2
6	6000	10.0	1130	7.8
7	6000	10.0	2685	18.6
8	6000	10.0	1130	7.8
9	6000	10.0	1012	7.0

	(b)					
-	T		T_c		T_c (bal)	
-	μ	σ	μ	σ	μ	σ
r	-		75.94		75.94	
accu.	92.46	3e-3	88.98	1e-2	89.53	1e-2
F_1 (0)	87.61	0.42	83.22	2.43	83.89	2.66
F_1 (1)	99.02	0.19	98.12	0.18	98.33	0.20
F_1 (2)	87.99	1.25	82.19	2.40	82.72	2.96
F_1 (3)	93.02	0.37	89.36	0.56	90.00	0.62
F_1 (4)	87.94	0.93	81.46	1.75	82.55	2.62
F_1 (5)	98.55	0.24	98.04	0.27	97.50	0.43
F_1 (6)	77.88	0.59	69.55	1.97	71.06	1.83
F_1 (7)	96.82	0.47	95.53	0.86	95.46	0.49
F_1 (8)	98.66	0.15	97.18	0.39	97.50	0.37
F_1 (9)	97.10	0.41	96.03	1.02	96.26	0.29

5   Discussion and Limitations

The proposed method provides a new subset, extracted from the original subset, to train future models on without losing too much accuracy. We can see on Tables 4 and 5 that our algorithm introduces high class imbalance for our experiments on both datasets. This is the reason performance results are confronted to results on a separated balanced final proportion dataset T_c (bal) for both datasets.

For MNIST, the high imbalance shows an increase for class 1, and a decrease for all other classes. However, Table 4 shows that this class imbalance is not a major issue. Indeed, the degradation of the F_1 scores for those classes is not significant compared to other classes like classes 8 and 9. This shows, from our point of view, that class imbalance is not necessarily detrimental in Deep Learning, but may even be a valid idea during training to balance inter-class relevance. For example, the digit 6 proportion was lowered in the dataset from 10% to 7% but its F_1 score barely decreased (−2%). In contrast, other classes like digit 1 need more representation to maintain a good F_1 score. However, the balanced dataset T_c (bal) has better F_1 scores for all classes.

For Fashion-MNIST, the high imbalance shows an increase for classes 5 and 7, and a decrease for all other classes. However, we noticed multiple runs on that dataset returned different proportions. Table 5 shows that the results are more contrasted this time. Classes 5 and 7 were increased in proportion and had their F_1 scores decreased by only 0.5% and 1% respectively, which is successful to us. However, many classes that were reduced in proportion suffered a significant F_1 score drop (−6% for *pullover*, −6.5% for *coat* or −8% for *shirt*). The drop in proportion of those classes, visually overlapping with each other, was detrimental for their F_1 scores and overall accuracy. Like our MNIST results, the balanced dataset T_c (bal) generalizes a bit better for all classes.

It should also be mentioned from Tables 4 and 5 that there is an increase of the standard deviation σ when reducing the dataset sizes. This should not be a surprise as reducing the number of instances in a class reduces its intraclass variance, thus reducing its generalization to unknown instances.

Both experiments on MNIST and Fashion-MNIST show that our algorithm is aggressive in compression rate, as it tends to force an important degradation of global accuracy and F_1 scores per class. One explanation may be the choice of the *up* and *down* parameters, as picking $+5\%$ and -20% forces a quick degradation of the dataset. Moreover, our stop condition based on accuracy is also limited to datasets and models achieving high initial accuracy. Other possible methods for choosing our *cutoff* iteration are still under investigation.

6 Conclusion

Our method, LRP-GUS, extracts a training subset that reflects more homogeneous visual features learnt across all classes of any given dataset. We used an XAI method, LRP, to assess the visual features and select the class proportions that should be modified. To the best of our knowledge, this is the first data reduction method exploiting such visual features. LRP-GUS achieved high compression rates, 96.10% for MNIST and 75.94% for Fashion-MNIST, at the cost of a drop of 3% test accuracy for both datasets. This shows that deep learning models can be trained on extracted imbalanced subsets while controlling a good trade-off with the predictive performance. This is encouraging as some datasets come with a natural high imbalance (fraud detection, meteo prediction, ...).

As our algorithm is highly dependent of the choice of the *cutoff* iteration, its choice is crucial. In the proposed work, it was selected as corresponding to a drop of 3% accuracy. More clever choices based on automatic detection of regime shift in the accuracy-compression rate graph may be more appropriated. The current non-refined choice of *cutoff* introduces extra class imbalance that may explain the contrasted results when comparing the final reduced dataset and a random balanced dataset with the same compression rate. We believe visual features can give a good explanation about a model's performance, thus allowing to choose instances and train a better model. The results displayed in this paper show the viability of our method in the form of preliminary results. Further investigation will focus on making a proper comparison with data reduction methods. In addition, future work could also investigate other XAI methods beyond LRP like LIME, or by extension SHAP.

Aknowledgements. This work was financed by the European Unions Horizon 2020 within the framework SESAR 2020 research and innovation program under grant agreement N. 894238, project Transparent Artificial Intelligence and Automation to Air Traffic Management Systems, ARTIMATION.

References

1. Anand, R., Mehrotra, K.G., Mohan, C.K., Ranka, S.: An improved algorithm for neural network classification of imbalanced training sets. IEEE Trans. Neural Netw. **4**(6), 962–969 (1993)
2. Anthony, M., Bartlett, P.L., Bartlett, P.L., et al.: Neural Network Learning: Theoretical Foundations, vol. 9. Cambridge University Press, Cambridge (1999)
3. Bach, S., Binder, A., Montavon, G., Klauschen, F., Müller, K.R., Samek, W.: On pixel-wise explanations for non-linear classifier decisions by layer-wise relevance propagation. PLoS ONE **10**(7), e0130140 (2015)
4. Batista, G.E., Prati, R.C., Monard, M.C.: A study of the behavior of several methods for balancing machine learning training data. ACM SIGKDD Explor. Newsl. **6**(1), 20–29 (2004)
5. Buda, M., Maki, A., Mazurowski, M.A.: A systematic study of the class imbalance problem in convolutional neural networks. Neural Netw. **106**, 249–259 (2018)
6. Cheng, Y.: Mean shift, mode seeking, and clustering. IEEE Trans. Pattern Anal. Mach. Intell. **17**(8), 790–799 (1995)
7. Cover, T., Hart, P.: Nearest neighbor pattern classification. IEEE Trans. Inf. Theory **13**(1), 21–27 (1967)
8. Datta, P., Kibler, D.: Learning symbolic prototypes. In: ICML, pp. 75–82 (1997)
9. Estabrooks, A., Jo, T., Japkowicz, N.: A multiple resampling method for learning from imbalanced data sets. Comput. Intell. **20**(1), 18–36 (2004)
10. Garcia, S., Derrac, J., Cano, J., Herrera, F.: Prototype selection for nearest neighbor classification: Taxonomy and empirical study. IEEE Trans. Pattern Anal. Mach. Intell. **34**(3), 417–435 (2012)
11. Ha, J., Lee, J.S.: A new under-sampling method using genetic algorithm for imbalanced data classification. In: Proceedings of the 10th International Conference on Ubiquitous Information Management and Communication, pp. 1–6 (2016)
12. Hasanin, T., Khoshgoftaar, T.: The effects of random undersampling with simulated class imbalance for big data. In: 2018 IEEE International Conference on Information Reuse and Integration (IRI), pp. 70–79. IEEE (2018)
13. Hastie, T., Tibshirani, R.: Discriminant adaptive nearest neighbor classification and regression. Adv. Neural Inf. Process. Syst. **8**, 409–415 (1995)
14. Jain, A.K., Duin, R.P.W., Mao, J.: Statistical pattern recognition: a review. IEEE Trans. Pattern Anal. Mach. Intell. **22**(1), 4–37 (2000)
15. Japkowicz, N., Stephen, S.: The class imbalance problem: a systematic study. Intell. Data Anal. **6**(5), 429–449 (2002)
16. Kingma, D.P., Ba, J.: Adam: a method for stochastic optimization. arXiv preprint arXiv:1412.6980 (2014)
17. Koziarski, M.: CSMOUTE: combined synthetic oversampling and undersampling technique for imbalanced data classification. In: 2021 International Joint Conference on Neural Networks (IJCNN), pp. 1–8. IEEE (2021)
18. Krawczyk, B., Galar, M., Jeleń, Ł, Herrera, F.: Evolutionary undersampling boosting for imbalanced classification of breast cancer malignancy. Appl. Soft Comput. **38**, 714–726 (2016)
19. Kubat, M., Matwin, S., et al.: Addressing the curse of imbalanced training sets: one-sided selection. In: ICML, vol. 97, p. 179. Citeseer (1997)
20. Laurikkala, J.: Improving identification of difficult small classes by balancing class distribution. In: Quaglini, S., Barahona, P., Andreassen, S. (eds.) AIME 2001. LNCS (LNAI), vol. 2101, pp. 63–66. Springer, Heidelberg (2001). https://doi.org/10.1007/3-540-48229-6_9

21. LeCun, Y., Bottou, L., Bengio, Y., Haffner, P.: Gradient-based learning applied to document recognition. Proc. IEEE **86**(11), 2278–2324 (1998)
22. Lin, W.C., Tsai, C.F., Hu, Y.H., Jhang, J.S.: Clustering-based undersampling in class-imbalanced data. Inf. Sci. **409**, 17–26 (2017)
23. Lundberg, S., Lee, S.I.: A unified approach to interpreting model predictions (2017)
24. Montavon, G., Binder, A., Lapuschkin, S., Samek, W., Müller, K.-R.: Layer-wise relevance propagation: an overview. In: Samek, W., Montavon, G., Vedaldi, A., Hansen, L.K., Müller, K.-R. (eds.) Explainable AI: Interpreting, Explaining and Visualizing Deep Learning. LNCS (LNAI), vol. 11700, pp. 193–209. Springer, Cham (2019). https://doi.org/10.1007/978-3-030-28954-6_10
25. Olvera-López, J.A., Carrasco-Ochoa, J.A., Martínez-Trinidad, J.: A new fast prototype selection method based on clustering. Pattern Anal. Appl. **13**(2), 131–141 (2010)
26. Ougiaroglou, S., Evangelidis, G.: Efficient dataset size reduction by finding homogeneous clusters. In: Proceedings of the Fifth Balkan Conference in Informatics, pp. 168–173 (2012)
27. Ribeiro, M.T., Singh, S., Guestrin, C.: Why should i trust you? Explaining the predictions of any classifier. In: Proceedings of the 22nd ACM SIGKDD International Conference on Knowledge Discovery and Data Mining, pp. 1135–1144 (2016)
28. Selvaraju, R.R., Cogswell, M., Das, A., Vedantam, R., Parikh, D., Batra, D.: Grad-CAM: visual explanations from deep networks via gradient-based localization. In: Proceedings of the IEEE International Conference on Computer (Cision), pp. 618–626 (2017)
29. Weiss, G.M., Provost, F.: The effect of class distribution on classifier learning: an empirical study. Technical report, Rutgers University (2001)
30. Wilson, D.R., Martinez, T.R.: Improved heterogeneous distance functions. J. Artif. Intell. Res. **6**, 1–34 (1997)
31. Wilson, D.R., Martinez, T.R.: Reduction techniques for instance-based learning algorithms. Mach. Learn. **38**(3), 257–286 (2000)
32. Xiao, H., Rasul, K., Vollgraf, R.: Fashion-MNIST: a novel image dataset for benchmarking machine learning algorithms. arXiv preprint arXiv:1708.07747 (2017)
33. Yen, S.J., Lee, Y.S.: Cluster-based under-sampling approaches for imbalanced data distributions. Expert Syst. Appl. **36**(3), 5718–5727 (2009)

Mining and Injecting Legal Prior Knowledge to Improve the Generalization Ability of Neural Networks in Chinese Judgments

Yaying Chen[1], Ji Ma[2], Nanfei Gu[3], Xintong Wang[4], and Minghua He[1(✉)]

[1] College of Computer Science and Technology, Jilin University, Changchun, China
hemh2120@gmail.com
[2] College of Communication Engineering, Jilin University, Changchun, China
[3] School of Law, Jilin University, Changchun, China
[4] Law School, Fudan University, Shanghai, China

Abstract. Data mining often faces the problem of too many missing values in real datasets and of the inability to quantify the value of mined knowledge, which constrains the generalization ability of neural networks. In publicly available legal datasets, established data filling methods ignores the invisible constraints among non-random missing data. To address this issue, optimal Bayesian network and posterior probability are adopted to predict missing values, which can estimate the true distribution of missing variables through mining the implicit constraints in existing available variable data. At the same time, the average treatment effect on the treated (ATT) is adopted to mine the adjudication paths in legal datasets which are injected into Bi-LSTM as prior knowledge. We have demonstrated through extensive experiments that the injection of prior knowledge is effective in improving the generalization ability of neural networks. In addition, through the Legal Judgment Prediction (LJP) task, the value of the mined prior knowledge can be evaluated, the most critical adjudication path can be identified which contributes to the promotion of judicial uniformity.

Keywords: Data Mining · Missing Value Processing · Legal Prior Knowledge

1 Introduction

Neural networks has been widely used in the field of data mining and have obtained excellent achievements, but datasets with high missing values still have a negative impact on its performance. Faced with many real and challenging judgments, mining the judging path and injecting it into the neural network can help the model better understand the relationship between legal elements and

Y. Chen and J. Ma—Contribute equally to this work.

© The Author(s), under exclusive license to Springer Nature Switzerland AG 2023
L. Iliadis et al. (Eds.): ICANN 2023, LNCS 14258, pp. 350–362, 2023.
https://doi.org/10.1007/978-3-031-44192-9_28

predict judgment results. Besides, it can effectively enhance the predictive performance and interpretability of the model in challenging datasets and improve the generalization ability of neural networks.

In the past few years, the progress of data mining technology has made significant contributions to improving the efficiency and accuracy of judicial adjudications. Established studies have created legal consultation systems to help people in the process of defending their rights by mining many judicial documents [3]. Some researchers have also considered the mining of legal arguments to try to solve the controversial issues and make efforts to achieve judicial uniformity [2]. Based on the deep learning algorithms, these legal artificial intelligence lays greater emphasize on data quality. However, existing work to some extent overlooks the improvement of data mining quality, especially due to the diversity of judging paths and complexity of Chinese semantics, problems related to missing labels often occur when the model conducts data mining towards real judgments. The absence of legal datasets is a non-random absence, which not only disrupts the inherent correlation inside data itself, but also leads to serious biases in prior knowledge mining and judgment result prediction. At the same time, there are significant limitations for legal artificial intelligence which requires high interpretability due to the lack of prior knowledge of judging path in predicting judicial adjudications results.

Improving the data mining capabilities of neural networks in complex legal datasets has important research value, but it faces significant challenges in practice. 1) Select an appropriate processing method to meet the filling requirements of non random missing data in the datasets. Traditional missing value filling methods often disrupt the correlation of data itself, leading to bias in prior knowledge mining and the prediction of judgment results. 2) Mine prior knowledge in judgments to enhance the predictive ability and interpretability of the model. The existing algorithms of adjudications often represent cases as unstructured text when predicting judgment results, and they lack the ability to interpret as well as infer models. 3) Effectively inject judging path as prior knowledge into neural networks. The existing data mining models cannot accurately evaluate the effectiveness of results and point out the correct path of judgments. Because of their indirect impact, the existing data mining models may restrict the prospects of application.

In this paper, based on high-quality filling of missing data, we effectively improve the data mining ability of neural networks in complex legal datasets through mining and injecting prior knowledge. First, based on the characteristics of the datasets and combined with the suggestions of legal experts, a general framework that meets the logic of adjudication is to be constructed, and high-quality data will be filled through the optimal Bayesian network, which effectively preserves the potential relationship between the original data. Secondly, prior knowledge in the datasets is to be mined and employed as a quantitative indicator to evaluate the potential relationship of data contained in the optimal Bayesian network, to better clarify the main path of judgments. Finally, By injecting the mined causal effects as prior knowledge into the neural network and comparing the accuracy improvement of different prior knowledge in the legal judgment prediction task, we are able to quantify the prior knowledge. Thus, it can better determine the correct judging path and promote the unity of justice.

Our main contributions are as follows: 1) A method based on optimal Bayesian network and posterior probability to deal with missing data was proposed, which effectively solves the problem of non-random missing in legal datasets. 2) The model can mine judging path in judgments much accurately, as well as improve the predictive and interpretability of the model much effectively. 3) We incorporate the judging path as prior knowledge into the downstream training to improve the accuracy of legal judgment model prediction and to enhance the quality of prior knowledge. Through these three aspects of efforts, the data mining ability of neural networks in complex datasets can be effectively improved, and the generalization ability of the model can be enhanced.

2   Related Work

2.1   Mining and Injecting Prior Knowledge

With the rapid development of machine learning and deep learning technologies in recent years, scholars have also attempted to embed prior knowledge into neural network to improve their accuracy and interpretability. However, due to the existence of potential confounding variables and counterfactual frameworks, this technology still requires further research and development to better apply it in various real-life scenarios. The LiNGAM [9] proposed by Shimizu et al. accomplishes the task of discovering the complete causal outcomes of continuous-valued data through the statistical method of independent component analysis, which can help researchers to better analyze the causal relationships in the observed data. The CGNN [4] proposed by Goudet et al. discover functional causal models from observable data by discovering bivariate and multivariate causal structures by observing the conditional independence and asymmetry of the distribution of the data, and it can handle multiple types of data efficiently. HetSANN [6] proposed by Hong et al. used an attention mechanism based on relation types to achieve aggregation of multi-relational information, and improves the accuracy of legal judgment models by injecting causal relationships.

2.2   Legal Judgment Prediction

Legal Judgment Prediction (LJP) is currently a hot topic in the field of natural language processing and artificial intelligence, which has attracted widespread attention and research from scholars both domestically and abroad. ECHR [1] had released a new dataset of predicted UK legal judgments, derived from cases heard by the real European Court of Human Rights. PS-LJP [8] was a process-supervised LJP model that introduces process supervision to ensure the accuracy of the obtained dependency information when modeling dependencies between sequence sub-datasets, and a genetic algorithm to optimize the parameters. LADAN [12] considered the problem of miscarriage of justice in similar legal cases, attempting to use graph neural networks to automatically learn the nuances between confusing legal texts, and improving the attention mechanism so that the model fully exploits the learned differences to thoughtfully extract valid discriminative features from factual descriptions.

3   Datasets and Methodology

In this section, we first introduce the legal dataset used, which exhibits stronger inter-data correlations but also contains more missing values. Then, we employ a Bayesian network to impute missing values and use the HillClimbing algorithm and the K2 score to make the model more interpretable. Finally, we use average treatment effects on treated (ATT) to extract prior knowledge and inject it into Bi-LSTM for better performance improvement.

3.1   Datasets

The dataset used in this study is Chinese judgments about the determination of labor relations for overage labors from China Judgements Online. The dataset D is divided into two parts, the training set D_1 and the testing set D_2. The training set D_1 is designed to mine potential referee paths, populate the dataset and identify critical referee paths, while the purpose of the testing set D_2 is to test our method's performance on the LJP task. To make the study more focused, the retrial instance judgments are merged directly into the second instance judgments. The training set D_1 consists of 1306 judgments, of which 663 are first instance judgments and 643 are second instance judgments; the testing set D_2 consists of 561 judgments, of which 284 are first instance judgments and 277 are second instance judgments. The distribution about the number of dataset can be seen in Fig. 1a. At the same time, there is so much missing in the judgments, which is in accordance with the judicial practice, because the judges' standards are not uniform when they use the law. In order to follow up with more systematic and finer data filling, we need to clarify the distribution of missing values. After statistics, the missing values of the dataset are shown in Fig. 1b. Most of the judgments have around 4 missing values, which poses a greater challenge for the filling of missing values.

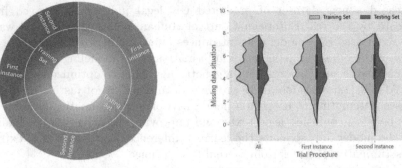

| (a) Dataset Division | (b) Missing Distribution of the Dataset |

Fig. 1. Details of the Dataset and Missing Value

To quantitatively analyze the complex judgments, feature extraction is required. The specific contents of the labels can be found in Table 1.

Table 1. Tag System for Dataset, the original data with contextual meaning is presented in Chinese, which is translated into English for clarity.

A Case Basic Fact 案件基本事实部分
A.1 When do labors to reach the mandatory age for retirement 劳动者何时达到法定退休年龄✓
A.2 Whether have a written contract 有无书面合同✓
A.3 Whether enjoy the benefits of the old-age insurance 有无享受养老保险待遇✓
A.4 Whether recognized of the basic old-age insurance 是否认定为基本养老保险待遇✓
A.5 Labor gender 劳动者性别✓
A.6 Kind of old-age insurance 养老保险待遇类型✓
B Judicial Opinion 裁判依据
B.1 Article 44 of the Labor Contract Law 《劳动合同法》第四十四条✓
B.2 Article 7 of the Labor Contract Law 《劳动合同法》第七条✓
B.3 Article 21 of the Implementing Regulations of the Labor Contract Law 《劳动合同法实施条例》第二十一条✓
B.4 Article 7 of the Interpretation on Several Issues concerning the Application of Law in the Trial of Labor Dispute Cases (III) 《关于审理劳动争议案件适用法律若干问题的解释（三）》第七条✓
C Judgement Results 裁判结果
C Judgement results 裁判结果✓

3.2 Missing Value Processing

Task Defnition. Let $D \in R^{n \times m}$ be a two-dimensional matrix consisting of n data points and m feature points. $M \in \{0,1\}^{n \times m}$ is a mask matrix indicating whether there are missing feature values. Where D_{ij} and M_{ij} denote the values of the ith row and jth column in D or M, respectively, and when D_{ij} takes the value of 0 indicates the presence of missing. Our goal is to predict the missing feature values D_{ij} fetch when M_{ij} takes the value of 0.

Construction of the Optimal Bayesian Network. Optimal Bayesian Networks are capable of adaptively learning the joint probability distribution between data, for which we can make predictions on the basis of data association. Considering that the data in this dataset are non-randomly missing, we model the problem as a probabilistic graphical model and represent the conditional probability relationships between variables with directed edges with weights.

To ensure interpretability in the construction of the Bayesian network, we have adopted the following approach. On the one hand, as the feature points of any data sample can be classified into three categories - factual status, evidence, and judgment results - we constructed a general framework for the logic of legal judgment documents, as shown in Fig. 2a. The prior framework of the network is divided into three layers: the factual status layer, the evidence layer, and the judgment result layer. On the other hand, by combining this general framework with the hill-climbing algorithm and K2 scoring, we further performed structure learning of the optimal Bayesian network on the test set. Finally, we obtained the optimum Bayesian network G, as shown in Fig. 2b.

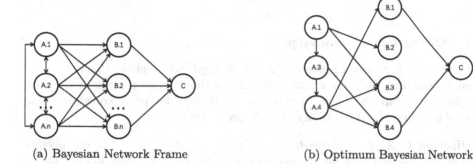

(a) Bayesian Network Frame   (b) Optimum Bayesian Network

Fig. 2. The Framework of Optimum Bayesian Network

Predicting Missing Values. Once we have obtained the optimal Bayesian network G, it is necessary to further determine the characteristics of the nodes' values. Therefore, by using the maximum likelihood estimation algorithm, we fit the distributional features of the data in the dataset to the optimal Bayesian network G. This allows us to obtain a new directed acyclic graph parameterized by the edges in G, denoted as G'. Finally, we integrate the predicted values for both non-missing and missing values of X_i into the dataset D_c.

Based on the results obtained from Fig. 3, it is possible to establish a set of rules for imputing missing values in order to better satisfy the requirements of data relationships. For example, if the weights of directed edges between A4, B1, and C are all close to 1 and greater than 0, we can assume that there is a strong causal relationship between these three variables. In combination with the opinions of legal experts, we can start with the variable C, which possesses relatively few missing values, as well as properties related to labor relations. If

B1 is not missing, we can impute "yes" to A4. By mining relationships between data and leveraging the knowledge of legal experts, we can fill in the missing values more accurately and with more interpretability.

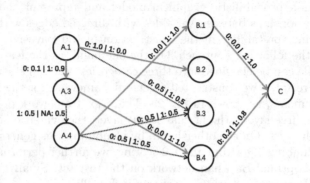

Fig. 3. Weights on the Edges Represent the Strength of Causal Relationships

3.3 Mining Prior Knowledge

To obtain the key causal pathways present in legal judgments of this nature, we need to evaluate the prior knowledge. We use the average treatment effect on the treated group (ATT) as the evaluation criterion for prior knowledge, and nature based on the ATT values of each directed edge.

Definition 1. *ATT (average treatment effect on the treated) is the average causal effect of intervention on individuals in the treated group, defined by the following formula:*

$$\tau_{ATT} = E(\tau|D = 1) = E[Y(1)|D = 1] - E[Y(0)|D = 1] \tag{1}$$

where τ is the individual level causal effect of intervention, Y is the outcome variable, and D is the indicator variable for intervention.

The estimation of ATT usually involves observing the sample of the treatment group to understand how the results of the control group change after the intervention. It is an important causal inference indicator since it can help researchers evaluate the actual impact of a specific intervention measure on the treatment group. Under the conditional independence assumption (CIA), the propensity-score matching (PSM) estimator of ATT can generally be expressed as:

$$\tau_{ATT}^{PSM} = E_{P(X)|D=1}\{E[Y(1)|D = 1, P(X)] - E[Y(0)|D = 0, P(X)]\} \tag{2}$$

In this equation, the PSM estimator of ATT is equal to the expected difference between the outcome of individuals with treatment and those of individuals without treatment, both conditioned on the covariate vector P(X), and weighted by the probability of receiving treatment for individuals in the treatment group.

3.4 Injecting Prior Knowledge

To achieve the injection of prior knowledge, we use RNN to generate labels for the referee paths, each label depends on its antecedent label, which reflects the correlation between the labels. Subsequently, we use the decoded results as representations of causal knowledge and merge them with the original feature vectors to inject causal knowledge.

In the first step, we map the input sequence X and prior knowledge K to a common space, obtaining two matrices $P \in \mathbb{R}^{d \times T}$ and $Q \in \mathbb{R}^{d \times M}$. Here, d represents the dimension of the common space, T indicates the length of the input sequence, and M denotes the number of prior knowledge:

$$P = W_x X,$$
$$Q = W_k K,$$

(3)

where d_x and d_k represent the feature dimensions of the input sequence and prior knowledge, respectively.

In the second step, we compute the attention weight vector $\alpha_t \in \mathbb{R}^M$ for prior knowledge with dot product attention mechanism. Specifically, we use P_t to denote the input sequence with time step t, and then we use the softmax function to compute α_t to obtain the attentional representation of prior knowledge by normalizing the results obtained.

In the third step, we compute the input sequence representation with incorporated prior knowledge $\tilde{X} \in \mathbb{R}^{2d \times T}$. Specifically, we combine the input sequence X with the attention weight vectors for all prior knowledge to obtain:

$$\tilde{X} = [X; Q\alpha_1, Q\alpha_2, \dots, Q\alpha_T]$$

(4)

Here, $[X; Q\alpha_1, Q\alpha_2, \dots, Q\alpha_T]$ denotes the matrix obtained by concatenating X with all of $Q\alpha_t$.

In the fourth step, we involve using an RNN for decoding and generating the corresponding labels L for the referee paths. Specifically, at each time step t, we compute the current hidden state $h_t \in \mathbb{R}^h$ and the predicted label $l_t \in \mathbb{R}^C$ using the current input vector $\tilde{x}_t \in \mathbb{R}^{2d}$, the previous RNN hidden state $h_{t-1} \in \mathbb{R}^h$, and the preceding label $l_{t-1} \in \mathbb{R}^C$:

$$h_t = \mathrm{LSTM}(\tilde{x}_t, h_{t-1}, l_{t-1}),$$
$$l_t = \mathrm{softmax}(W_l h_t + b_l).$$

(5)

Here, Bi-LSTM is a standard Bi-LSTM model, $W_l \in \mathbb{R}^{C \times h}$ and $b_l \in \mathbb{R}^C$ are weight and bias vectors used for label generation, and softmax is the Softmax function used to transform scores into probability distributions.

In the fifth step, we combine the prior knowledge features with the original features to compute a new feature vector $\tilde{F} \in \mathbb{R}^{(d_x + d_k) \times N}$. We can then use $\tilde{F}$ for the classification task and retrain the classifier to improve the prediction performance. Specifically, we define the feature vector set $F \in \mathbb{R}^{d_x \times N}$ and the set of referee path labels $L \in \mathbb{R}^{C \times N}$, concatenate them, and obtain:

$$\tilde{F} = [F; L] \tag{6}$$

4   Experiments and Results

In this section, we first conduct comparative experiments to determine the best model for our dataset for the LJP task. Then, we explore the effect of different qualities of prior knowledge on the model as a way to find the critical judging path. The experimental results demonstrate the effectiveness of our approach.

4.1   Comparison Model

To quantify the quality of a prior knowledge, we first performed the LJP task, and we chose the mainstream model as the comparison model along with four commonly used models - BiLSTM [5], CNN-BiLSTM [7], BERT [10], and Lawformer [11], to compare their effectiveness in our experiments.

Our analysis of different NLP models in the LJP task revealed that BiLSTM and CNN-BiLSTM, with their BiLSTM structures, effectively captured information from text sequences in forward and backward directions. While BERT and Lawformer, based on transformer architecture, were shown to extract knowledge through unsupervised learning on large-scale data and fine-tune on specific tasks. BERT demonstrated its versatility, making it suitable for various NLP tasks, while Lawformer was designed specifically for legal NLP tasks, and CNN-BiLSTM for text classification.

We used the aforementioned models to predict the results of current legal judgments tasks using the same dataset. To avoid errors caused by imbalanced sample class proportions, we used weighted average calculation method to obtain the $Precision_{weighted}$, $Recall_{weighted}$, and $F1 - Score_{weighted}$ as quantitative indicators of the prediction performance. The final prediction results of all models are shown in Fig. 4. As can be seen from the results, the BiLSTM model performs significantly better than other models on this dataset, making it more suitable for the current legal judgment task.

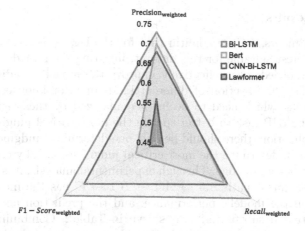

Fig. 4. Comparison of Performance Metrics for Different Prediction Models

4.2 Finding the Critical Judging Path

According to the ATT values of the final directed edge, we determined the key judgment path for this type of case, which is shown in Fig. 5. According to the calculation results, we can determine that the key judgment path for the issue of over-age workers in our dataset can be roughly divided into the following three paths: $A.4 \rightarrow B.1 \rightarrow C$; $A.3 \rightarrow A.4 \rightarrow B.1 \rightarrow C$; $A.3 \rightarrow B.4 \rightarrow C$.

To further determine the most critical judgment criteria, we injected these judgment paths as prior knowledge into BiLSTM, and used the degree of change in BiLSTM's $Precision_{weighted}$, $Recall_{weighted}$, and $F1 - Score_{weighted}$ as indicators to quantify the impact of injecting prior knowledge on the model's performance. When a certain judgment path injection results in the maximum improvement, the corresponding path is considered as the most critical.

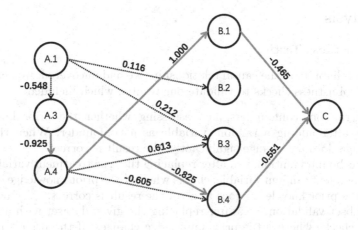

Fig. 5. Bayesian Graphical Estimation of Key Pathways

4.3 Main Results

Through experiments, we can confirm that for the legal prediction model BiL-STM which is most suitable for this dataset, injecting the mined key judgment path as prior knowledge can effectively improve the model's prediction performance. However, the injection of different kinds of prior knowledge produces differential effects, which need to be further analyzed by the prediction effect evaluation of the LJP task to better specify the most critical judging path.

In legal application, there should be only one determined judgment criterion, but our model can determine the most critical judgment path by comparing the importance of prior knowledge. Through experimental analysis, it is evident that injecting the judgment path $A.3 \rightarrow A.4 \rightarrow B.1 \rightarrow C$ has the most significant improvement on the model's performance, and the prediction accuracy of the model has increased substantially, as shown in Table 2. Combining the above analysis, we are confident to conclude that the judgment path $A.3 \rightarrow A.4 \rightarrow B.1 \rightarrow C$ is the most critical judgment path, and in determining the labor relationship of over-age workers, the judgment path $A.3 \rightarrow A.4 \rightarrow B.1 \rightarrow C$ should be adopted to better unify justice. The above experimental results can also prove that by injecting high-quality prior knowledge can effectively improve the generalization ability of neural networks in legal datasets and enhance the quality of data mining.

Table 2. Performance Comparison of Entity Relation Extraction with Different Knowledge Graph Embeddings

	$Precision_{weighted}$	$Recall_{weighted}$	$F1 - Score_{weighted}$
Bi-LSTM + Normal	0.73	0.73	0.72
Bi-LSTM + $A.4 \rightarrow B.1 \rightarrow C$	0.72	0.72	0.72
Bi-LSTM + $A.3 \rightarrow A.4 \rightarrow B.1 \rightarrow C$	**0.77**	**0.76**	**0.77**
Bi-LSTM + $A.3 \rightarrow B.4 \rightarrow C$	0.74	0.73	0.73

5 Analysis

5.1 Robustness Testing

To test the reliability of the causal relationships we had uncovered, we performed a series of robustness checks to validate our results, which included:

1. Adding random confounders, i.e., assessing whether the prior knowledge changes after adding a random variable as a confounder. When the prior knowledge does not change significantly, the result is correct.
2. The placebo intervention, i.e., after replacing the true treatment variable with an independent random variable, checks whether the prior knowledge changes. When the prior knowledge goes to zero, the result is correct.
3. Data subset validation, i.e., after replacing the given dataset with a random subset, checks whether the prior knowledge changes. If the prior knowledge does not change, the result is correct.

The final results of our validation are shown in Fig. 6. It can be observed that the mined causal relationships have sufficient reliability in our dataset. And it is reasonable to believe that our proposed model can also show superior results with strong generalization ability on other legal datasets.

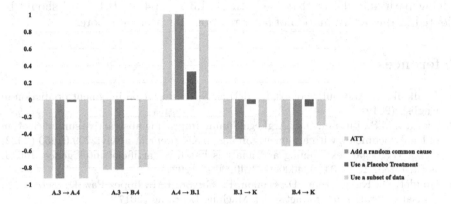

Fig. 6. Robustness Detection Metrics

5.2   Juridical Validation of the Results

From the main results of the comparative experiment, it can be concluded that the strongest correlation exists between A.4 "Whether recognized of the basic old-age insurance" and C "Judgement results". In addition, in cause-effect relationship discovery, A.5 "Labor gender", A.2 "Whether have a written contract" and C "Judgement results" aren't causally related basically, which further verifies the accuracy of analysis results. In summary, the judge should adopt A.4, "Whether recognized of the basic old-age insurance" as the only adjudication path in the identification of overage laborers' labor relations, which not only reflects the judges' collective experience extracted from many judgments, but also meets the requirement of legal hierarchy.

6   Conclusion

In this paper, a more interpretable method of filling missing values based on real legal datasets is proposed, and that injecting prior knowledge can effectively improve the generalization ability of neural network while it is able to effectively evaluate the importance of mined knowledge is demonstrated. Specifically, to improve the transparency and interpret-ability of the application of Bayesian network, a combination of hill-climbing algorithm and K2 scoring algorithm for missing value filling is employed, which can better satisfy the filling of non-random missing datasets. Secondly, the average intervention effect (ATT) is used as an assessment criterion for prior knowledge to better identify the critical adjudication paths in legal datasets. It is experimentally found that injecting the critical adjudication path as prior knowledge into the neural network can effectively improve the prediction performance of the model. Finally, the model can compare the importance of prior knowledge to identify the most important judging path and clarify that the path of $A.3 \rightarrow A.4 \rightarrow B.1 \rightarrow C$ should be adopted in the determination of labor relations for overage laborers.

References

1. Chalkidis, I., Androutsopoulos, I., Aletras, N.: Neural legal judgment prediction in English (2019)
2. Elaraby, M.S., Litman, D.J.: ArgLegalSumm: improving abstractive summarization of legal documents with argument mining. arXiv preprint arXiv:2209.01650 (2022)
3. Geng, B.: Legal text mining and analysis based on artificial intelligence. Int. J. Artif. Intell. Tools **31**, 2240006:1–2240006:16 (2021)
4. Goudet, O., Kalainathan, D., Caillou, P., Guyon, I.M., Lopez-Paz, D., Sebag, M.: Causal generative neural networks. Machine Learning (2017)
5. Graves, A., Schmidhuber, J.: Framewise phoneme classification with bidirectional LSTM and other neural network architectures. Neural Netw. Official J. Int. Neural Netw. Soc. **18**(5–6), 602–10 (2005)
6. Hong, H., Guo, H., Lin, Y., Yang, X., Li, Z., Ye, J.: An attention-based graph neural network for heterogeneous structural learning. In: AAAI Conference on Artificial Intelligence (2019)
7. Saha, R., Jyhne, S.: Interpretable text classification in legal contract documents using tsetlin machines. In: 2022 International Symposium on the Tsetlin Machine (ISTM), pp. 7–12 (2022)
8. Shang, X.: A computational intelligence model for legal prediction and decision support. Comput. Intell. Neurosci. **2022** (2022)
9. Shimizu, S., Hoyer, P.O., Hyvärinen, A., Kerminen, A.J.: A linear non-gaussian acyclic model for causal discovery. J. Mach. Learn. Res. **7**, 2003–2030 (2006)
10. Wahab, A., Sifa, R.: Dibert: Dependency injected bidirectional encoder representations from transformers. In: 2021 IEEE Symposium Series on Computational Intelligence (SSCI), pp. 1–8 (2021)
11. Xiao, C., Hu, X., Liu, Z., Tu, C., Sun, M.: Lawformer: a pre-trained language model for Chinese legal long documents. arXiv preprint arXiv:2105.03887 (2021)
12. Xu, N., Wang, P., Chen, L., Pan, L., Wang, X., Zhao, J.: Distinguish confusing law articles for legal judgment prediction. In: Annual Meeting of the Association for Computational Linguistics (2020)

Mixed-Mode Response of Nigral Dopaminergic Neurons: An *in Silico* Study on SpiNNaker

Pavan Kumar Enuganti and Basabdatta Sen Bhattacharya[✉] [iD]

BITS Pilani, K K Birla Goa Campus, Goa, India
{p20180053,basabdattab}@goa.bits-pilani.ac.in
https://binnlabs-goa.in

Abstract. We present a work-in-progress on the mixed-mode (burst, non-burst) spiking response of the Substantia-Nigra-pars-compacta (SNc) using a conductance-based Izhikevich's spiking neuron (IZK) model on SpiNNaker. The SNc is a primary source of Dopamine (DA) that is essential for reward-based learning and prediction in the brain and forms a part of the Basal Ganglia (BG). The bursting phases of the mixed-mode facilitate reward-related DA release whereas the non-burst phases maintain the base-levels of DA in the extracellular space. Previously, we have implemented a BG model where the modulatory effects of DA on the network synapses were simulated using static conductances. Recently, we have implemented the time-varying effects of reward-based DA release in a balanced-random-network. However, both these works did not include the SNc population. Here, we present an SNc population simulated on SpiNNaker and parameterised to display mixed-mode response; our goal is to integrate it into the existing BG model. We observe that the IZK model parameter d is crucial for model response transition between the burst and non-burst modes. Furthermore, inhibition play a pivotal role in transition from burst to mixed-mode response as reported in physiological studies. In addition, we have identified the constant current inputs in the model that facilitate mixed-mode response. With appropriate parameterisation of the efferents from the existing BG model to the SNc population, the burst to non-burst ratio in the mixed-mode response conforms to physiological observations. Continuing research is looking into using the SNc population to model reward-based learning and decision-making by the brain.

Keywords: Dopamine · Mixed-mode · Burst mode · Non-burst mode · Substantia Nigra pars Compacta · SNc · SpiNNaker · Basal Ganglia

This research was supported by the Science and Engineering Research Board of India (SERB) Grant no. CRG/2019/003534. Access to SpiNNaker server was via the Human Brain Project; support for all SpiNNaker-based work was provided by the SpiNNaker team, the University of Manchester.

L. Iliadis et al. (Eds.): ICANN 2023, LNCS 14258, pp. 363–374, 2023.
https://doi.org/10.1007/978-3-031-44192-9_29

1   Introduction

The Substantia Nigra pars compacta (SNc), a neuron population that forms part of the Basal Ganglia (BG) complex in the midbrain of rodents and mammals, is known to be one of the main sources of the neuro-chemical Dopamine (DA) in the brain. The crucial role of DA on behavioral state changes in the brain has been studied extensively by not only neuro-physiologists [21] and psychologists [1], but also physical scientists [3]; the latter group in particular use computational tools to understand the mechanisms that underpin both short- and long-term brain state changes due to DA. There are a plethora of computational models that are proposed over the past decades, for example Humphries et al. [10] use mathematical modulation (time invariant) of excitatory and inhibitory synapses by DA in a computational model of the BG; Izhikevich [13] have implemented DA-ergic neuromodulation using synaptic trace-based differential (time-varying) equations. The role of the SNc population in both [10] and [13] are implicit. On the other hand, there are models that implement the SNc population explicitly, for example Cullen and Wong-Lin [3] have implemented nigral (i.e. of the SNc) DA-ergic neuron models to simulate pre-synaptic dynamics of DA, which in turn was based on the models by Best et al. [2]; Merrison-Hort et al. have implemented the SNc population in a BG model to understand disorders in Parkinsonian tremor [14].

Previously, we have implemented a BG model of action-selection on SpiN-Naker [6] based on a series of works by Gurney et al. [9,10] where the neuromodulatory effects of DA-ergic neurons are implemented by direct (static, as in [10]) intervention on the model synaptic conductances, i.e. the spiking behaviour of SNc was not modelled explicitly. However, a survey of existing neurophysiological literature suggest that the nigral DA-ergic neurons fire a burst of spikes (burst mode) corresponding to receiving or expecting rewards that is crucial to learning and decision-making by the brain [11,21,25]. On the other hand, non-burst firing modes are thought to be important in maintaining the base levels of extracellular DA in the absence of any new 'events'. Thus, the DA-ergic neurons are reported to fire in a 'mixed-mode' consisting of both firing phases viz. burst and non-burst occurring spontaneously [11] [8]. Furthermore, if an extrinsic depolarising current is applied to a nigral DA-ergic neuron when it is in a non-burst phase of the mixed-mode response, there is a phase transition into burst mode [7]. Thus, such extrinsic application of depolarising current may be thought to mimic the occurrence of an event e.g. arrival of a reward or punishment. Recently, we have simulated instrumental conditioning on SpiNNaker with a balanced-random-network where the reward delivery was with a short (4 ms) current pulse that mimicked a 'phasic' release of DA in the extracellular space corresponding to burst mode firing. This was originally done in [13] and subsequently implemented on sPyNNaker [20] (the software toolchain of SpiN-Naker) as demonstrated by Mantas et al. [15]. In this work, our objective is to parameterise a SNc spiking neuron such that it displays a spontaneous mixed-mode behaviour in the presence of stochastic noise as well as constant current inputs when simulated using the conductance-based Izhikevich neuron model [13]

implemented on SpiNNaker; this will then be used to define a SNc neuron population that can be integrated into our existing BG model [23]. Towards this, we
find that Cullen and Wong-Lin have also used the IZK neuron model in their
work, albeit the current-based version [3,12]. Thus, unlike in their work, any
one set of parameters in our conductance-based IZK model could not mimic a
mixed-mode behaviour and needed further analysis.

At first, we parameterised one DA-ergic neuron model to simulate bursting behaviour in response to a constant current (I_{dc}) input. We observed that
the parameter d of the IZK model was crucial in eliciting burst or non-burst
mode response; the bifurcation point was observed to be for $d > 2$. Furthermore,
by setting d for a bursting mode response, and applying a set of excitatory
and inhibitory stochastic inputs, we could mimic a mixed-mode response where
there was a combination of non-burst and burst mode firing as reported in literature [11]. Based on these observations, we then implemented a SNc population
consisting of eight neurons [17] and provided six projections (two excitatory,
four inhibitory) from the existing BG model on SpiNNaker and informed by
existing literature [25]. Our results show that indeed, with increased inhibitory
afferents, the independently bursting mode of the SNc population (with $d \leq 2$)
transformed into a mixed-mode response. Furthermore, varying I_{dc} affected the
proportion of burst and non-burst spikes in the SNc neuron response where the
bursting behaviour increased with increasing I_{dc}, similar to that reported in
physiological research. The burst to non-burst spike count ratio is in the range
$(2-3) : 1$ for $d = 2$ and $(5-6) : 1$ for $d = 1$ for the tested range of $I_{dc} \in [0, 4]$. We
note that the range for $d = 2$ conform to physiological report of $\approx 75\%$ spikes
participating in the burst mode for both anaesthetised and awake rodents. We
have not presented the recurrent or efferent connections of the SNc here and is
a work-in-progress.

In Sect. 2, we present a brief overview of existing literature and methods of
simulation. In Sect. 3, we present the results. In Sect. 4, we conclude the paper.

2   Methods

2.1   Literature Survey

In a study of extracellular recordings from the SNc of anaesthetised rats, Grace
and Bunney [8] reported two response modes in the neurons: spontaneous firing by what they termed 'active' cells, as opposed to 'inactive' cells that fired
only when evoked explicitly with extrinsic currents and with regular inter-spike
intervals (isi). Of the former variety that comprised around 70% of the recorded
sample, two further firing modes were observed viz. slow irregularly spaced single spike mode, referred to herewith as 'non-burst' firing mode, with an average
firing rate between $4-5$ Hz and mostly within the range $1-9$ Hz; the burst firing
mode had $\approx 2-6$ spikes per burst for most cases, with increasing isi within the
burst (referred to hereafter as intra-burst interval); the average intra-burst interval was in the range 60–86 ms [7]. The isi of the non-burst mode firing neurons
showed a unimodal normal distribution around $200-250$ ms mean; the isi of the

burst firing neurons showed a bimodal distribution where all isi<= 100 ms indicated bursts, the remaining indicated either inter-burst intervals or non-burst
spikes. Thus, the burst firing neurons had a mixed-mode response where there
were intermittent non-bursting spikes. However, in a study on freely moving rats
that was reported by Hyland et al. [11], all recorded SNc neurons responded in
mixed-mode, i.e. they fired at least some spikes in burst even if for cases where
most spikes were in the non-burst mode. Thus, they classed the responsive DA-
ergic neurons to be low- and high-bursting. Furthermore, observations that were
made on anesthetized rats in [7,8] were largely confirmed in freely moving rats,
albeit at an overall increased level of activity. Thus, the instantaneous intra-burst
frequency is higher for awake behaving animals both for spontaneous firing as
well as when triggered by salient stimuli; within the sample, spontaneous burst
firing mode had a lower instantaneous intra-burst frequency than bursts elicited
by extrinsic factors. The average intra-burst interval was observed as $\leq$ 80 ms
and up to 74% of the total number of spikes belonged to the burst mode. We
too have observed similar behaviour in our model (See Sect. 3.2).

The non-bursting spikes are thought to be due to mainly a slow depolarising
current for a characteristic high threshold voltage of DA-ergic neurons, as well
as due to an after hyperpolarisation following a spike so as to delay the onset of
the next spike [8]. The neurons are seen to transit to a burst firing mode with
the extrinsic application of excitatory agent that caused increased levels of membrane depolarisation; the authors hypothesize a potassium channel blocking mechanism that facilitates such transition. A review by Tepper [25] indicates that other
researches have also observed burst firing in SNc cells in response to an excitatory
(glutamatergic) trigger, one of the main sources of which to the SNc is the Subthalamic Nucleus (STN) and the frontal cortex. We have observed an increase in
the burst firing mode with increasing external current levels (see Figs. 4 and 5).

Overall, it seems that for the SNc neurons, the firing patterns are what is
more important than the firing rate [25]. In particular, burst firing phases of the
SNc neurons effects phasic DA release in the extracellular space, that in turn
contributes to reward-based reinforcement learning by modulating excitatory
and inhibitory synapses of the efferent neural ensembles. In this regard, Hyland
et al. [11] did instrumental (also known as 'operant') conditioning during their
above-mentioned study on awake behaving rats. They observed that the SNc
neurons responded with burst spikes when reward was delivered; burst firing was
also observed when reward predicting stimulus was delivered. Their experimental
observations agreed with previous research by Schultz [21] on awake monkeys
where SNc neuron fired in burst when animals were trained to expect their
reward in response to a reward predicting cue. Upon being trained though, such
burst firing of nigral DA-ergic neurons was in response to an error in the expected
value of the predicted reward.

While the reward prediction error theory is widely accepted currently, Redgrave and Gurney [18,19] propose an alternative hypothesis on burst firing and
consequent phasic release of DA. Their observation is based on the time to visual
signal processing in the cortex and subsequent action taken by the motor system
for response to positive or negative stimuli, which is mediated by the dopamin-

ergic pathway of decision making and action-selection. The phasic release of DA in response to a burst is characterised by a short latency in addition to the short duration. Within that time, a more plausible hypothesis would be that the phasic DA release indicates a sensory prediction error [18], providing a positive or negative reinforcement (reward or punishment respectively) to bias the previously selected action caused by a sensory stimulus. The emphasis is on the short latency of the phasic DA signals. Interestingly Dreyer et al. [4] discuss how non-burst firing, associated with basal DA concentration in the extracellular space, affect the transient phasic DA release. (Here too the authors emphasise the relevance of burst firing for reward and learning in the brain). Cullen & Wong-Lin [3] have referred to the transient bursting phase of DA-ergic neurons to be facilitating behavioural changes and learning (after [22,24]). To observe the response latency in our model, we have presented a study on the first burst corresponding to the transient response phase (see Sect. 3.1).

We note that our implementations of the conductance-based IZK model on SpiNNaker thus far has been in the non-burst mode [5,23]; this work will be the first instance where we are implementing a burst-mode behaviour. Below, we mention the methods used in our experimental set-up to study the burst mode, followed by the mixed-mode behaviour in a model SNc neuron in context to our literature survey presented here.

2.2 Experimental Set-Up *in Silico*

Izhikevich's Model of a Spiking Neuron: The conductance-based IZK model is defined in Eqs. (1–3):

$$\frac{dv(t)}{dt} = 0.04v^2(t) + 5v(t) + 140 - u(t) + I_{dc} + I_{syn}(t) \qquad (1)$$

$$\frac{du(t)}{dt} = a(bv(t) - u(t)); \text{If } v(t) > 30, \text{then } v(t) \leftarrow c; u(t) \leftarrow u(t) + d \qquad (2)$$

$$I_{syn}(t) = \bar{g} \cdot e^{-t/\tau_{syn}} \cdot (E_{syn} - v(t)) \qquad (3)$$

where, $a = 0.0025$ (ms^{-1}), $b = 0.2$ (mV^{-1}), $c = -55$ mV, $d = 2$ after [3] for burst mode response; $v(t)$ and $u(t)$ are the membrane potential and recovery variables with initial values of -70 mV and -14 respectively; $\bar{g}, E_{syn} = \{-70, 0\}$ mV, $\tau_{syn} = \{6, 4\}$ are the maximum post-synaptic conductance, reversal potential and decay time constant respectively for {excitatory, inhibitory} synapses, I_{dc}, I_{syn} are the constant and synaptic current inputs, and are variable in this work (see below).

Studying the Burst Mode Characteristics: After [11], we considered a spike 'f' at time t^f as a part of a burst if the inter-spike interval with the previous spike in the train $((t^f - t^{f-1}) \leq 80$ ms; else, either f is a part of the next burst $((t^{f+1} - t^f) \leq 80$ ms), or f is a non-burst spike $((t^{f+1} - t^f)$ & $(t^f - t^{f-1}) > 80$ ms). We observed that the parameter $d \leq 2$ elicited burst behaviour in the model, all other parameter values being the same as defined above; $\forall d > 2$, the model displayed non-burst behaviour after an initial burst. Our objective is to conform to physiological observations specified in Sect. 2.1. Thus, we made a thorough analysis of the burst mode behaviour for $d = 1, 2$, the only two (integer) values for which the model displayed burst mode. Furthermore, varying I_{dc} affected the number of spikes within a burst, the intra-burst intervals, as well as the number of bursts and inter-burst intervals. The simulations for this study were for 1 s at resolution of 0.1 ms. The observations on bursting behaviour with varying I_{dc} is presented in Sect. 3.1.

Simulation Method for Mixed-mode Output: To simulate real world inputs to the SNc neuron model, we now provide it with noisy inputs (I_{syn} in Eqn (1)) from two excitatory (3, 12 Hz) and four inhibitory (0.5, 0.5, 22 and 29 Hz) Poisson sources. This experimental set-up is based on the BG receiving excitatory inputs from two external sources and inhibitory inputs from other populations within the BG (see Fig. 1 and the below subsection for details). We note that the inhibitory inputs play a crucial role in transition of the burst mode of the neuron (d=1, 2) to a mixed-mode. The synaptic efficacies were defined by the post-synaptic maximum membrane conductance ($\bar{g}$ in Eq. (3)), and were set thus: (0.01, 0.05) μS respectively for the excitatory, (1.5, 1.5, 4, 4) μS respectively for the inhibitory. The response of the neuron corresponding to each value of $I_{dc} \in [0, 4; 0.5]$ was averaged over 10 trials, where each trial run was for 10 s at a resolution of 0.1 ms; the Poisson inputs ($\sum I_{syn}$) were provided from 500 ms to 9.5 s that helped to compare the spike train response for I_{dc} (burst mode) during the initial and last 500 ms intervals with $I_{dc} + \sum I_{syn}$ (mixed-mode) for the remaining time.

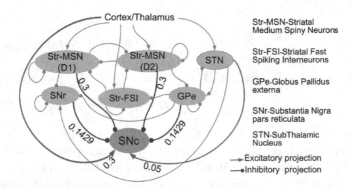

Fig. 1. The SNc population receiving afferents, informed by existing physiological literature [17] [16] from selected populations of the existing BG network on SpiNNaker [23]. The weights of the excitatory and inhibitory synapses are defined by the post-synaptic membrane conductance parameter $\bar{g}$ in Eqn. (3), and are set here such that the SNc population response is in mixed-mode with burst and non-burst phases conforming to physiological literature. The values (units:μS) are shown against each afferent.

Simulation Method for SNc Population and its Afferents in the BG Network: We have implemented a SNc population consisting of eight [17] IZK neuron models as parameterised above and receiving afferents from selected populations (Medium Spiny Neuron (MSN) of D1 and D2 types, Global Pallidus externa (GPe), Subthalamic Nucleus (STN) and Substantia Nigra pars reticulata (SNr)) of the existing BG network [17] as shown in Fig. 1; there is also an afferent from the cortical region [16]. The conductance values and synaptic types (excitatory, inhibitory) are mentioned in the Fig. 1. All connections are one-to-one. The output firing rates of the MSN (D1, D2), GPe, STN and SNr in the existing BG network are (0.6, 0.3), 29, 12 and 22 Hz respectively and is of irregular type [23]; the cortical input is a 3 Hz Poisson source. (This is the basis of the above-mentioned firing rates that were set for the Poisson inputs to the single SNc neuron model). The response of the population was averaged across all the eight neurons corresponding to each value of $I_{dc} \in [0, 4; 0.5]$. Simulation run time was for 10 s at a resolution of 0.1 ms.

3 Results

3.1 Bursting with Constant Input

Figures 2 (a) and (b) shows the characteristic of the first burst response for d = 1, 2 when I_{dc} is increased progressively in the range $3 - 19$ nA. The spike count within the burst (Fig. 2(a)) increases linearly with a steeper slope (3.4:1) for d = 1 than d = 2. The intra-burst intervals are in the range $1.2 - (9 - 11)$ over both values of d, although all but the last isi is ≈ 4 ms or less; this trend is similar for both d = 1 and 2, and is shown in Fig. 2 (c) (see along the diagonals). Thus, the instantaneous intra-burst frequency decreases as the burst proceeds for all I_{dc}. The time of the first spike of the burst, i.e. the neuron response time, decrease exponentially (Fig. 2(b)) with increasing I_{dc}. This observations is in accord with the short latency of DA signals proposed to be fundamental for the sensory prediction error hypothesis [19].

A second burst in the neuron response was observed for $I_{dc} \geq 4$, and the 1st inter-burst interval (i.e. between the 1st and 2nd bursts) decreased exponentially with increasing current (not shown here for conciseness). However, the inter-burst intervals from the 2nd and onwards are fairly constant for each value of I_{dc} with low variability around a mean. Figure 3 shows the mean of the (2nd and onwards) inter-burst intervals (left y-axis) and the total number of bursts (right y-axis) for increasing I_{dc}; the former decreases exponentially and indicates burst frequencies of $\approx 2 - 10$ Hz. Our results agree with experimental report of increasing burst frequency with depolarising extrinsic currents [25]. For d = 2, the burst count plot approaches a 'steady state' around $\approx < 10$; for d = 1 though, the burst count continued to increase linearly at the last tested value $I_{dc} = 19$.

3.2   Mixed-mode Response of a Single Neuron

Figure 4 show the mixed-mode model response for current inputs $I_{dc} + \sum I_{syn}$ (see Sect. 2.2 for methods). Firstly, we note that the larger number of inhibitory than excitatory I_{syn} effects a transition from the burst mode to mixed-mode, agreeing with reports in physiological literature [25]. The ratio of the spike counts participating in burst and non-burst ($\nu_b : \nu_{nb}$) in Fig. 4 (b) is in the range

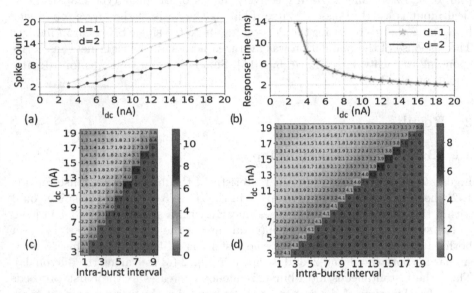

Fig. 2. The first burst response of the SNc neuron implemented with Izhikevich's spiking neuron model and comparing for model parameter d = 1 and 2 with increasing I_{dc}: (a) spike count within the burst; (b) time of the first spike of the first burst. (c) The intra-burst interval of the first burst shown as heat-map. The overall increase in spike count within the burst for d = 1 (right) compared to d = 2 (left) is distinct with the wider matrix. The values along the (approx) diagonals show the intervals between the last two spikes of the burst.

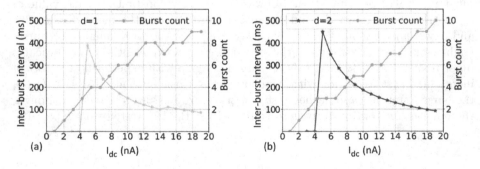

Fig. 3. The inter-burst intervals (left y-axis) as well as the burst count (right y-axis) with increasing values of I_{dc} for (a) d=1 and (b) d=2.

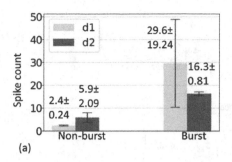 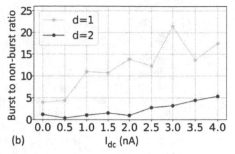

Fig. 4. (a) Mean (μ) $\pm$ variance (σ) (for a sample value of $I_{dc} = 2.5$ nA), and the (b) ratio ($\nu_b : \nu_{nb} \forall I_{dc} \in [0, 4]$ nA) of the spike counts within non-burst and burst phases of the mixed-mode response (see Sect. 3.2) averaged over ten trials for d = 1,2.

$\approx (2 - 5) : 1$ with $I_{dc} \in [2.5, 4]$ nA for $d = 2$; the ratio is a factor of $\approx 3 - 4$ higher for $d = 1$. Note that I_{syn} is not varied here; only the I_{dc} is varied to set the network bias for a desired response. We observe that for $I_{dc} \in [2.5 - 3]$ nA, $\nu_b : \nu_{nb} \simeq 3 : 1$ i.e. $\simeq 75\%$ of the response is in the burst mode, which is in agreement with physiological studies [11]. A sample response for $I_{dc} = 2.5$ is shown in Fig. 4 (a). The increased burst for $d = 1$ and the high variance implies a comparatively stable mixed-mode response of the network for $d = 2$.

3.3 Mixed-Mode Population Response

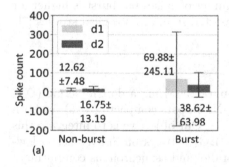 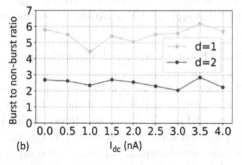

Fig. 5. (a) $\mu \pm \sigma$ for a sample value of $I_{dc} = 2.5$ nA, and (b) $\nu_b : \nu_{nb} \forall I_{dc} \in [0, 4]$ nA for the average SNc population mixed-mode response. The $\sum I_{syn}$ is fixed and is set by $\bar{g}$ of the afferents shown in Fig. 1.

Figure 5 (b) shows the $\nu_b : \nu_{nb}$ for the SNc population mixed-mode response when parameterised with $\bar{g}$ shown in Fig. 1 for afferents from the BG network. As before, all I_{syn} is constant; only the I_{dc} is varied to set the network bias for a desired response. We observe that $\nu_b : \nu_{nb} \in (2 - 3) : 1 \forall I_{dc} \in [0, 4; 0.5]$ nA when $d = 2$, and is close to the range ($\approx 75\%$) reported in literature [11]. The ratio

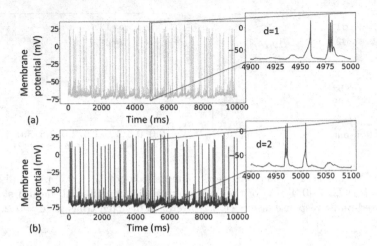

Fig. 6. The membrane potential of a sample neuron in the SNc population (Fig. 1) responding in mixed-mode (see inset) for (a) d = 1 and (b) d = 2.

is higher for $d = 1$, although it is much more stable than for an independent neuron in Fig. 4 (b). A sample response for $I_{dc} = 2.5$ is shown in Fig. 5 (a) when the $\nu_b : \nu_{nb} = 2.3 : 1$. Once again, we note that even if the ratio is stable for $d = 1$ in Fig. 5 (b), the variance is very high across the population response, once again indicating an unstable mixed-mode response compared to that for $d = 2$. Membrane potential for a sample neuron from the SNc population is shown in Fig. 6 for $d = 1, 2$, $I_{dc} = 2.5$ nA. The inset shows the mixed-mode for both values of d, although the observed range of the number of spikes per burst is higher for $d = 1$; however, this is within the range reported from physiological studies [7].

4   Discussion and Conclusion

We have presented a work-in-progress on parameterising a dopaminergic (DA-ergic) neuron population of the Substantia Nigra pars compacta (SNc) for both burst and non-burst (mixed-)mode behaviour. Our objective is to integrate this population into an existing Basal Ganglia (BG) network on SpiNNaker, a low-power neuromorphic hardware allowing parallel and asynchronous computing.

Several wet-lab experiments on SNc recordings from anaesthetised as well as awake behaving mammals and rodents show that the burst firing phase of these neurons are associated with phasic release of DA in the extracellular space, which in turn affects the reward system of the brain; at the same time, the non-burst firing phases regulate a basal concentration of DA in the absence of any event. Thus, these nigral DA-ergic neurons show a mixed-mode firing pattern where the proportion of spikes in the burst and non-burst phases is dependent on time-varying extrinsic and intrinsic factors. Recently, we have simulated phasic release of dopamine for instrumental conditioning in a simple coupled oscillator implemented on SpiNNaker. However, the phasic release was simulated by short current pulses explicitly timed to mimic the burst durations of SNc neurons. In this work, we have demonstrated a set of parameters for our SNc population model that can induce mixed-mode response with a burst to non-burst ratio of 3:1; furthermore, the response varies with variable values of constant and stochastic current inputs; also, the number of spikes in one burst in steady state is between 2 to 3. All of these observations conform to experimental literature. In addition, we have demonstrated the dynamics of the time to the first burst response as well as the instantaneous intra-burst frequency with varying values of the constant current input, an aspect that provides insights to Redgrave & Gurney's sensory prediction error hypothesis of DA. After identifying a set of parameter ranges that conform to the above-mentioned observations, we defined a population of SNc neurons and provided projections from selected neural populations, informed by physiological literature, of the existing BG network on SpiNNaker. Upon appropriate parameterisation of the afferent projections, our results show a mixed-mode response in the SNc population neurons.

We would like to note that the recurrent synaptic projections in the SNc as well as its efferents on to the BG network populations are not included in this study. This will be taken up in the next phase of our work and will be based upon our findings presented here. The simulation and analysis presented here will also serve as an important and useful resource for researchers who aim to simulate biologically plausible spike response of nigral dopaminergic neurons using conductance-based Izhikevich's spiking neuron models.

References

1. Berridge, K.C.: The debate over dopamine's role in reward: the case for incentive salience. Psychopharmacology **191**, 391–431 (2007)
2. Best, J.A., Frederik Nijhout, H., Reed, M.C.: Mathematical models of neuromodulation and implications for neurology and psychiatry. In: Érdi, P., Sen Bhattacharya, B., Cochran, A.L. (eds.) Computational Neurology and Psychiatry. SSB, vol. 6, pp. 191–225. Springer, Cham (2017). https://doi.org/10.1007/978-3-319-49959-8_8
3. Cullen, M., Wong-Lin, K.: Integrated dopaminergic neuronal model with reduced intracellular processes and inhibitory autoreceptors. IET Syst. Biol. **9**(6), 245–258 (2015)
4. Dreyer, J.K., Herrik, K.F., Berg, R.W., Hounsgaard, J.D.: Influence of phasic and tonic dopamine release on receptor activation. J. Neurosci. **30**(42), 14273–14283 (2010)
5. Enuganti, P.K. et al.: Instrumental conditioning with neuromodulated plasticity on SpiNNaker. In: Tanveer, M., Agarwal, S., Ozawa, S., Ekbal, A., Jatowt, A. (eds.) Neural Information Processing. ICONIP 2022. LNCS, vol. 13624, pp. 148–159. Springer, Cham (2023). https://doi.org/10.1007/978-3-031-30108-7_13
6. Furber, S.B., Galluppi, F., Temple, S., Plana, L.A.: The spinnaker project. Proc. IEEE **102**(5), 652–665 (2014)
7. Grace, A.A., Bunney, B.S.: The control of firing pattern in nigral dopamine neurons: burst firing. J. Neurosci. **4**(11), 2877–2890 (1984)
8. Grace, A.A., Bunney, B.S.: The control of firing pattern in nigral dopamine neurons: single spike firing. J. Neurosci. **4**(11), 2866–2876 (1984)

9. Gurney, K., Prescott, T.J., Redgrave, P.: A computational model of action selection in the basal ganglia. i. a new functional anatomy. Biol. Cybern. **84**(6), 401–410 (2001)

10. Humphries, M.D., Stewart, R.D., Gurney, K.: A physiollogically plausible model of action selection and oscillatory activity in the basal ganglia. J. Neurosci. **26**(50), 12921–12942 (2006)

11. Hyland, B.I., Reynolds, J., Hay, J., Perk, C., Miller, R.: Firing modes of midbrain dopamine cells in the freely moving rat. Neuroscience **114**(2), 475–492 (2002)

12. Izhikevich, E.M.: Simple model of spiking neurons. IEEE Trans. Neural Netw. **14**(6), 1569–1572 (2003)

13. Izhikevich, E.M.: Solving the distal reward problem through linkage of STDP and dopamine signaling. Cereb. Cortex **17**(10), 2443–2452 (2007)

14. Merrison-Hort, R., Yousif, N., Ferrario, A., Borisyuk, R.: Oscillatory neural models of the basal ganglia for action selection in healthy and parkinsonian cases. In: Érdi, P., Sen Bhattacharya, B., Cochran, A.L. (eds.) Computational Neurology and Psychiatry. SSB, vol. 6, pp. 149–189. Springer, Cham (2017). https://doi.org/10.1007/978-3-319-49959-8_7

15. Mikaitis, M., Garcia, G.P., Knight, J., Furber, S.: Neuromodulated synaptic plasticity on the spinnaker neuromorphic system. Front. Neurosci. **30**(30), 10127–10134 (2018)

16. Naito, A., Kita, H.: The cortico-pallidal projection in the rat: an anterograde tracing study with biotinylated dextran amine. Brain Res. **653**(1–2), 251–257 (1994)

17. Oorschot, D.E.: Total number of neurons in the neostriatal, pallidal, subthalamic, and substantia nigral nuclei of the rat basal ganglia: a sterological study using the cavalieri and optical disector methods. J. Comp. Neurol. **366**, 580–599 (1996)

18. Redgrave, P., Coizet, V., Reynolds, J.: Phasic dopamine signaling and basal ganglia function. In: Handbook of Behavioral Neuroscience, vol. 20, pp. 549–559. Elsevier (2010)

19. Redgrave, P., Gurney, K.: The short-latency dopamine signal: a role in discovering novel actions? Nat. Rev. Neurosci. **7**(12), 967–975 (2006)

20. Rhodes, O., et al.: sPyNNaker: A software package for running PyNN simulations on spinnaker. Front. Neuroscience **12**, 816 (2018)

21. Schultz, W.: Predictive reward signal of dopamine neurons. J. Neurophysiol. **80**(1), 1–27 (1998). https://doi.org/10.1152/jn.1998.80.1.1. PMID: 9658025

22. Schultz, W.: Neuronal reward and decision signals: from theories to data. Physiol. Rev. **95**(3), 853–951 (2015)

23. Sen-Bhattacharya, B., et al.: Building a spiking neural network model of the basal ganglia on spinnaker. IEEE Trans. Cogn. Dev. Syst. **10**(3), 823–836 (2018)

24. Steinberg, E.E., Keiflin, R., Boivin, J.R., Witten, I.B., Deisseroth, K., Janak, P.H.: A causal link between prediction errors, dopamine neurons and learning. Nat. Neurosci. **16**(7), 966–973 (2013)

25. Tepper, J.M.: Neurophysiology of substantia Nigra dopamine neurons: modulation by GABA. Handbook Behav. Neurosci. **20**, 275–296 (2010)

Pan-Sharpening with Global Multi-scale Context Network

Lu Lin[1], Chen Yin[2(✉)], and Zhenkun Gao[2]

[1] Fujian Police College, Fuzhou, China
[2] Xiamen University, Xiamen, China
chenyin@stu.xmu.edu.cn

Abstract. Pan-sharpening is a widely used technique that fuses low-resolution multispectral images and high-resolution panchromatic images to produce high-resolution multispectral images. However, existing convolution neural network models have a limited perception field, while existing transformer models ignore multi-scale information and have high computational complexity. Considering these issues, in this work, we propose a Global Multi-Scale Context Network (GMSCN) for pan-sharpening tasks that combines the advantages of global modeling and multiscale modeling. Our network consists of two core modules: the Multi-Scale Non-Local Block (MSNB) and the Mixed Scale Fusion Block (MSFB). The MSNB module incorporates multiscale feature extraction capabilities with a lightweight non-local block to reduce computational complexity, while the MSFB module promotes interaction and integration of multiscale features. Experiments on various datasets have demonstrated that our proposed method achieves state-of-the-art performance.

Keywords: Pan-sharpening · Non-local · Remote-sensing

1 Introduction

In industries such as agriculture and manufacturing, there is an increasing demand for high-resolution multispectral remote sensing images. Unfortunately, existing satellite sensors often face technical and cost constraints that prevent them from directly obtaining these images. As a result, a common approach is for satellites to collect low-resolution multispectral (MS) and high-resolution panchromatic (PAN) images using separate sensors. The panchromatic images typically have a resolution that is a multiple of the multispectral images. To address this issue, pan-sharpening technology has emerged as a powerful tool for fusing these two types of images and generating high-resolution multispectral images. This technology has garnered significant attention since its inception.

In the field of pan-sharpening, mainstream technologies can be divided into traditional methods and deep learning-based methods. Before the advent of deep learning, traditional methods such as component substitution [7,9], multiresolution analysis [4,14], and model-based methods were the dominant approaches for producing high-quality spatial details, but they often struggled to maintain spectral information. However, with the explosive progress of deep learning

L. Iliadis et al. (Eds.): ICANN 2023, LNCS 14258, pp. 375–385, 2023.
https://doi.org/10.1007/978-3-031-44192-9_30

technology in recent years, deep learning-based methods have taken over the pan-sharpening field. PNN [13] was the first to introduce this technology into the field and achieved impressive results by designing a simple three-layer convolution neural network. Since then, a plethora of convolution neural network models have been proposed, but they suffer from a congenital deficiency of limited perception fields, which constrains model performance improvement.

Recently, inspired by NLP tasks [16], transformer models have been introduced into computer vision and have demonstrated excellent performance in a variety of tasks [5,12], including pan-sharpening tasks. The Transformer model's global receptive field has attracted much attention because it solves the limitations of the CNN model. Generally speaking, a larger model perception field will improve the model's performance. INNformer [21] introduced transformer technology into pan-shaprening and proved the model's strong performance. However, the application of transformer models in pan-sharpening is still insufficient. First, it considers global information but ignores multi-scale information, which is crucial for remote sensing images that exhibit large scale differences. Furthermore, transformer models' computational complexity makes them challenging to deploy on devices.

Based on our analysis, we have developed the Global Multi-Scale Context Network (GMSCN) to improve the performance of pan-sharpening tasks by combining the advantages of global information and multi-scale modeling. Our network comprises two core modules: the Multi-Scale Non-local Block (MSNB) and the Mixed Scale Fusion Block (MSFB). We have designed a lightweight MSNB to reduce the computational burden while enabling multi-scale global information modeling. Our MSFB uses dilation convolution to extract multi-scale features and perform cross-scale feature fusion.

Our model prioritizes multi-scale modeling capabilities based on global feature extraction, which addresses the problem that other global feature extraction methods overlook multi-scale information. We conducted experiments on various datasets, and the results demonstrate the effectiveness of our approach.

Our research has made the following contributions:

- We propose a novel Global Multiscale Context Network (GMSCN) for pansharpening that overcomes the limitations of previous methods. This network architecture effectively extracts global information while also performing multiscale modeling to enhance the quality of the results.
- To address the computational complexity of the nonlocal module, we introduce a lightweight Multiscale Non-local Block (MSNB) and a Mixed Scale Fusion Block (MSFB) for feature fusion. Our approach achieves global modeling and multiscale feature extraction while minimizing computational complexity.
- Our proposed method achieves state-of-the-art performance on various benchmark datasets. We demonstrate through extensive experiments that our approach outperforms existing pan-sharpening methods both quantitatively and qualitatively.

2   Related Work

2.1   Pan-Sharpening

Pan-sharpening is a technique that fuses low-resolution multispectral images and high-resolution panchromatic images to produce high-resolution multispectral images. Traditional pan-sharpening methods can be divided into component substitution [7,9,10], multi-resolution analysis [4,14], and model-based approaches [6]. Component substitution methods replace the spatial components of the multispectral images with the spatial components of the panchromatic images, resulting in high-quality details but ignoring spectral information. Multi-resolution analysis methods decompose images into multiple components, perform pan-sharpening at multiple scales, and improve the ability to maintain spectral information. Model-based methods treat pan-sharpening as an optimization problem and generate images using various optimization methods, but require many manually designed features that limit model performance.

Recently, deep learning-based methods have dominated the pan-sharpening field. PNN [13] was the first to introduce deep learning into this field, and subsequent works, such as PANNET [19], have expanded on this by introducing residual connections. MSDCNN [20] incorporates multi-scale modeling to capture multi-scale features, while SRPPNN [1] improves model performance by designing particularly deep networks. GPPNN [18] combines model-based methods and designs interpretable models through deep unfolding technology. However, the limited receptive field of CNNs restricts model performance, and the computational burden is high.

More recently, transformer-based methods have emerged in pan-sharpening. Innformer [21] combines CNNs and transformers, effectively utilizing a combination of local and global features. However, multiscale details are ignored, and the computational burden is high. In contrast, our proposed method combines global receptive fields and multiscale modeling capabilities with a smaller computational load, achieving state-of-the-art performance on various datasets.

2.2   Long Range Modeling

Convolutional neural networks (CNNs) are widely used in image processing, but they have limitations in capturing global information efficiently. The size of the receptive field is crucial to the performance of the model, but traditional methods such as pooling can result in information loss. To address this issue, dilation convolution has been proposed in DeepLab [3] to enhance the receptive field without losing details. However, it still lacks the ability to capture global information effectively.

To overcome these limitations, non-local [17] methods have been introduced, inspired by self-attention mechanisms in natural language processing, to capture global features. But the computational complexity of non-local methods is significant, which limits their practical use. Recently, global modeling capabilities have been expanded with the introduction of transformer-based models such as

Vision Transformer (ViT) [5] and Swing Transformer [12]. However, these methods often sacrifice local details and require substantial computational resources.

3   Method

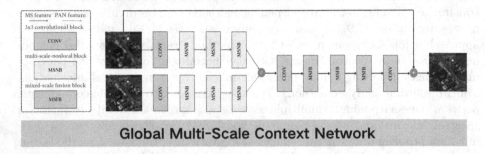

Fig. 1. The overall architecture of our proposed model, which is composed of two core modules: Multi-scale Non-local Block (MSNB) and Mixed-scale Fusion Block (MSFB).

In order to enhance global feature extraction and multiscale modeling capabilities, we proposed a novel Global Multiscale Context Network, as illustrated in the Fig. 1. Our GMCNet comprises two branches and two core modules, namely Multiscale Non-local Block (MSNB) and Multiscale Feature Fusion Block (MSFB). Firstly, the MS image is upsampled to the same size as the PAN image and both are projected into the feature space via convolution. Subsequently, the PAN and MS branches extract the corresponding multiscale features of the images. The extracted features are pre-fused through convolution and then fed into the cascaded MSFB for multiscale feature fusion and interaction. Finally, a 1×1 convolution is applied to adjust the channel dimension of the feature map, which is then residual connected with the input upsampled MS to obtain the final output. With MSNB, we extract multiscale global features, while MSFB fuses multiscale features efficiently. Our GMCNet achieves the ability to capture multiscale features and global context with reduced computational complexity, thereby enabling better attention to image details.

3.1   Multi-scale Non-local Block

As depicted in the Fig. 2, we compare the original Non-local module structure to our MSFB. Given an input feature map X, the calculation process of the Non-local module can be expressed as:

$$Q = W_Q \times \theta(X) \qquad (1)$$
$$K = W_k \times \phi(X) \qquad (2)$$
$$V = W_V \times \gamma(X) \cdot Softmax(Q \times K) \qquad (3)$$
$$Z = W_Z \times \iota(V) + X \qquad (4)$$

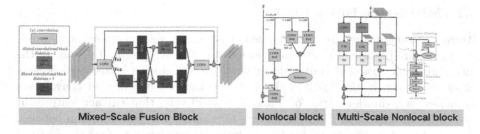

Fig. 2. The left half shows our MSFB module, promoting multi-scale feature interaction and fusion. MSNB, on the other hand, reduces computational complexity and focuses on detailed features while capturing global features.

Here, Z is the module's output, and W_Q, W_K, W_V, and W_Z are linear transformation matrices. Operations θ, ϕ, γ, and ι are used to reshape. Due to its global scope of operations, the Non-local module requires a significant amount of computation and lacks the ability to sense multiple scales. Previous research [2] has revealed that the self-attention weights generated at each location of X are essentially identical. Thus, the W_q matrix is unnecessary, and removing W_z has little effect on the performance of non-local modules. Inspired by these, we designed MSFB to achieve lightweight self-attention and combine multi-scale feature extraction benefits. Specifically, given the input X, we use convolution and pooling to downsample X by two and four times to generate X_2 and X_4. The original size is designated as X_1. We start with context modeling and transform on input feature X_i, expressed as:

$$K_i = \theta(X_i) \times Softmax(\gamma(W_k X_i)) \tag{5}$$
$$V_i = W_{v2} \times LN(W_{v1} K) \tag{6}$$
$$attention_i = sigmoid(V_i) \tag{7}$$

where LN stands for layer norm, and W_v and W_k represents linear transform matrix, θ and γ are reshape operations. The overall process of the module can be expressed as:

$$X_1, X_2, X_4 = X, down2(X), down4(X) \tag{8}$$
$$attention_i = Transform(ContextModeling(X_i)) \tag{9}$$
$$Z = \sum_i (attention_i \times X) \tag{10}$$

where $down2$ and $down4$ are convolution blocks comprised of $Conv_{3 \times 3}$ and pooling operations. By applying multi-scale non-local operations to input features, we generate attention weights of different scales and add the multi-scale global features together. This enables multi-scale global feature modeling, reduces computational effort, and achieves efficient global modeling.

3.2   Mixed-scale Fusion Block

Remote sensing images are characterized by a wide range of geomorphic features, which require the use of multiscale features for effective fusion. To promote the interaction and fusion of multiscale features, we introduce a Mixed Scale Fusion block, as shown in the Fig. 2. This module comprises two dilated convolution branches with dilation ratios of 2 and 3, respectively, that extract features at two different scales and facilitate feature interaction via concatenation between the two branches. Finally, a 1×1 convolution is employed to fuse the features of the two scales.

Given an input feature F_i, we first expand the number of channels to twice the original size using a 1×1 convolution and then split the channel dimensions to obtain F_{C1} and F_{C2}, which are then fed into the two branches:

$$F_{C1}, F_{C2} = Split(Conv1 \times 1(F_i)) \tag{11}$$

In the two branches, we employ dilated convolutions with dilation ratios of 2 and 3, respectively, to process features, and perform cross-scale feature interaction through concatenation. Finally, a 1×1 convolution is used for feature fusion, and a residual connection is established with the input:

$$F_{C1} = Relu(conv_{d=2}(F_{C1})) \tag{12}$$
$$F_{C2} = Relu(conv_{d=3}(F_{C2})) \tag{13}$$
$$P_1 = Relu(conv_{d=2}(C(F_{C1}, F_{C2}))) \tag{14}$$
$$P_2 = Relu(conv_{d=3}(C(F_{C1}, F_{C2}))) \tag{15}$$
$$F_{i+1} = F_i + conv_{1\times1}(C(P_1, P_2) \tag{16}$$

3.3   Loss Function

To prevent overly smooth textures in the output image, we adopt the L1 loss as our objective function. Specifically, given the predicted output image Y and the ground truth image G, the loss function is defined as follows:

$$L = ||Y - G||_1 \tag{17}$$

4   Experiment

4.1   Experiment Details

In this study, we aimed to assess the performance of our model under varying scenarios and seasons. To this end, we evaluated the experimental results using three diverse datasets, including WorldView2, WorldView3, and Gaofen2, which were captured by distinct satellites. This approach enabled us to effectively assess the ability of our model. Given the unavailability of the ground truth, we employed the wald protocol [15] to generate training data. In this

Table 1. Table presents quantitative comparison of the performance of our proposed method against other SOTA approaches. Results demonstrate the best performance are highlighted in red. The upward arrow (↑) indicates that a higher value corresponds to better performance, while the downward arrow (↓) indicates that a lower value corresponds to better performance.

Method	WorldView-II				GaoFen2				Worldview-III			
	PSNR↑	SSIM↑	SAM↓	ERGAS↓	PSNR↑	SSIM↑	SAM↓	ERGAS↓	PSNR↑	SSIM↑	SAM↓	ERGAS↓
SFIM	34.1297	0.8975	0.0439	2.3449	36.9060	0.8882	0.0318	1.7398	21.8212	0.5457	0.1208	8.9730
Brovey	35.8646	0.9216	0.0403	1.8238	37.7974	0.9026	0.0218	1.3720	22.5060	0.5466	0.1159	8.2331
GS	35.6376	0.9176	0.0423	1.8774	37.2260	0.9034	0.0309	1.6736	22.5608	0.5470	0.1217	8.2433
IHS	35.2962	0.9027	0.0461	2.0278	38.1754	0.9100	0.0243	1.5336	22.5579	0.5354	0.1266	8.3616
GFPCA	34.5581	0.9038	0.0488	2.1411	37.9443	0.9204	0.0314	1.5604	22.3344	0.4826	0.1294	8.3964
PANNET	40.8176	0.9626	0.0257	1.0557	43.0659	0.9685	0.0178	0.8577	29.6840	0.9072	0.0851	3.4263
MSDCNN	41.3355	0.9664	0.0242	0.9940	45.6847	0.9827	0.0135	0.6389	30.3038	0.9184	0.0782	3.1884
SRPPNN	41.4538	0.9679	0.0233	0.9899	47.1998	0.9877	0.0106	0.5586	30.4346	0.9202	0.0770	3.1553
GPPNN	41.1622	0.9684	0.0244	1.0315	44.2145	0.9815	0.0137	0.7361	30.1785	0.9175	0.0776	3.2593
Innformer	41.6903	0.9704	0.0227	0.9514	47.3528	0.9893	0.0102	0.5479	30.5365	0.9225	0.0747	3.0997
Ours	41.7193	0.9705	0.0226	0.9505	47.6443	0.9893	0.0099	0.5294	30.7077	0.9247	0.0735	3.0592

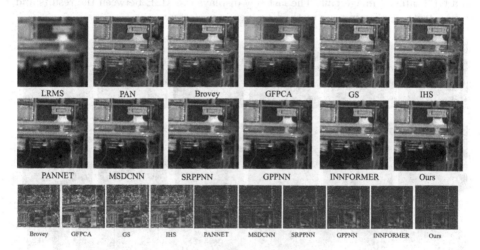

Fig. 3. This figure shows a comparison of our proposed method with nine alternatives on a WV2 satellite image pair. The last row displays the MSE between the results and ground truth, confirming our method's superior performance.

regard, the data was cropped as a patch for training purposes, with a pan patch size of 128×128 and an MS patch size of 32×32.

We compared a selection of commonly used methods, such as SFIM [11], Brovey [7], GS [9], IHS [8], GFPCA [10], along with modern deep learning approaches such as PANNET [19], MSDCNN [20], SRPPNN [1], and GPPNN [18], which have gained prominence in recent years. Additionally, we also evaluated transformer-based techniques, specifically INN-former [21], which exhibit a strong ability for global modeling.

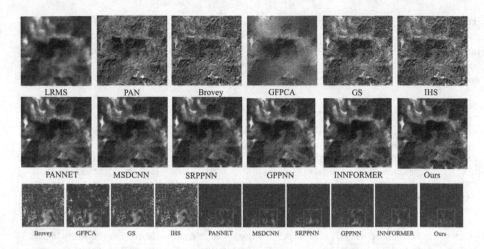

Fig. 4. This figure shows a comparison of our proposed method with nine alternatives on a GF2 satellite image pair. The last row displays the MSE between the results and ground truth, confirming our method's superior performance.

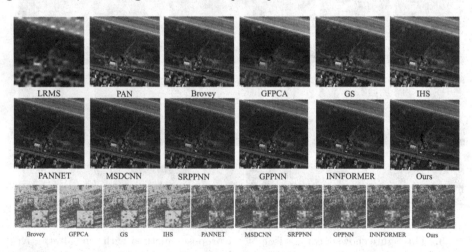

Fig. 5. This figure shows a comparison of our proposed method with nine alternatives on a WV3 satellite image pair. The last row displays the MSE between the results and ground truth, confirming our method's superior performance.

Several common evaluation metrics were adopted to assess the quality of the generated images. These metrics encompassed PSNR, SSIM, SAM, and ERGAS, which are widely recognized and utilized to measure the fidelity and accuracy of reconstructed images.

Our model was developed and implemented using PyTorch deep learning framework. The model was trained for 1000 epochs on an RTX 2080 GPU using

Stochastic Gradient Descent optimizer. We used a learning rate of 2e-4 and a batch size of 16 for training.

4.2 Comparison with SOTA Methods

Quantitative and qualitative comparisons of the experimental results indicate that our proposed method outperforms other state-of-the-art methods. The results of the quantitative comparison of the three datasets are presented in Table 1. The table shows that our method achieves superior performance compared to the comparison methods on all evaluation indicators, including surpassing the most advanced INN-former model. These results demonstrate the effectiveness of our approach of introducing multiscale features to improve the model performance. Specifically, on the GF2 dataset, our model achieves a PSNR improvement of 0.2914 dB compared to the most advanced INN-former, which highlights the significant benefits of incorporating multiscale information to improve the model's global modeling capabilities. Similar trends are observed in other datasets and evaluation indicators.

In our quantitative analysis, we conducted a visual comparison on representative samples from the WV2, GF2 and WV3 datasets. The results, shown in the Figs. 3, 4 and 5, demonstrate the superiority of our model over several other representative methods. The last row of the figure displays the resulting images and their corresponding MSE values with ground truth image, with brighter regions indicating larger differences from the ground truth. As indicated in the figure, our method produces images with the smallest brightness discrepancy, the most similar texture to the ground truth, and the closest spectrum. These findings showcase the effectiveness of our approach in multiscale modeling and global information capture. In particular, our method excels in capturing image details and enhancing the sensing of small targets.

Table 2. This table summarizes ablation experiments on three datasets, analyzing the impact of removing components from our proposed method. Results highlight the importance of each component and offer insights for refinement.

Config	MSNB	MSFB	WorldView-II				GaoFen2				WorldView-III			
			PSNR↑	SSIM↑	SAM↓	ERGAS↓	PSNR↑	SSIM↑	SAM↓	ERGAS↓	PSNR↑	SSIM↑	SAM↓	ERGAS↓
(I)	✗	✓	41.6551	0.9705	0.0226	0.9578	47.3723	0.9884	0.0103	0.5476	30.6247	0.9235	0.0735	3.0746
(II)	✓	✗	41.5310	0.9694	0.0230	0.9710	47.5306	0.9890	0.0102	0.5374	30.5344	0.9228	0.0744	3.0997
Ours	✓	✓	41.7193	0.9705	0.0226	0.9505	47.6443	0.9893	0.0099	0.5294	30.7077	0.9247	0.0735	3.0592

4.3 Ablation Experiment

To further demonstrate the effectiveness of our proposed module, we conducted ablation experiments on three datasets using the same evaluation indicators. Our model consists of two core modules, the Multi-Scale Non-Local Block and Mixed

Scale Fusion Block. We designed two sets of ablation experiments, replacing MSNB and MSFB with ResBlocks with similar parameter quantities to evaluate the effectiveness of the proposed model. As shown in the Table 2, when our core modules were removed, the network's performance decreased to varying degrees, proving the important role of multiscale feature extraction and global information modeling in improving the pan-sharpening task.

5   Conclusion

This article proposes a novel approach to address the issue that other global feature modeling methods neglect multiscale detail features. We present a global multiscale context network, which comprises a Multi-scale Non-local Block and a Mixed Scale Fusion Block, to effectively capture both global and multiscale features of images. Through extensive experiments on multiple datasets and evaluation indicators, we demonstrate the superiority of our proposed method over state-of-the-art methods. Ablation experiments are also conducted to further validate the effectiveness of our approach, highlighting the promising potential of integrating multiscale features and global feature modeling capabilities.

References

1. Cai, J., Huang, B.: Super-resolution-guided progressive pansharpening based on a deep convolutional neural network. IEEE Trans. Geosci. Remote Sens. **59**(6), 5206–5220 (2021). https://doi.org/10.1109/TGRS.2020.3015878
2. Cao, Y., Xu, J., Lin, S., Wei, F., Hu, H.: GCNet: non-local networks meet squeeze-excitation networks and beyond. In: Proceedings of the IEEE/CVF International Conference on Computer Vision Workshops (2019)
3. Chen, L.C., Papandreou, G., Kokkinos, I., Murphy, K., Yuille, A.L.: Semantic image segmentation with deep convolutional nets and fully connected CRFs. arXiv preprint arXiv:1412.7062 (2014)
4. DadrasJavan, F., Samadzadegan, F., Fathollahi, F.: Spectral and spatial quality assessment of IHS and wavelet based pan-sharpening techniques for high resolution satellite imagery. Adv. Image Video Process. **6**(2), 1 (2018)
5. Dosovitskiy, A., et al.: An image is worth 16×16 words: Transformers for image recognition at scale. arXiv preprint arXiv:2010.11929 (2020)
6. Fasbender, D., Radoux, J., Bogaert, P.: Bayesian data fusion for adaptable image pansharpening. IEEE Trans. Geosci. Remote Sens. **46**(6), 1847–1857 (2008)
7. Gillespie, A.R., Kahle, A.B., Walker, R.E.: Color enhancement of highly correlated images. ii. channel ratio and "chromaticity" transformation techniques - sciencedirect. Remote Sens. Environ. **22**(3), 343–365 (1987)
8. Haydn, R., Dalke, G.W., Henkel, J., Bare, J.E.: Application of the IHS color transform to the processing of multisensor data and image enhancement. Natl. Acad. Sci. United States of America **79**(13), 571–577 (1982)
9. Laben, C.A., Brower, B.V.: Process for enhancing the spatial resolution of multispectral imagery using pan-sharpening (2000). uS Patent 6,011,875

10. Liao, W., Xin, H., Coillie, F.V., Thoonen, G., Philips, W.: Two-stage fusion of thermal hyperspectral and visible RGB image by PCA and guided filter. In: Workshop on Hyperspectral Image and Signal Processing: Evolution in Remote Sensing (2017)
11. Liu., J.G.: Smoothing filter-based intensity modulation: a spectral preserve image fusion technique for improving spatial details. Int. J. Remote Sens. **21**(18), 3461–3472 (2000)
12. Liu, Z., et al.: Swin transformer: Hierarchical vision transformer using shifted windows. In: Proceedings of the IEEE/CVF International Conference on Computer Vision, pp. 10012–10022 (2021)
13. Masi, G., Cozzolino, D., Verdoliva, L., Scarpa, G.: Pansharpening by convolutional neural networks. Remote Sens. **8**(7), 594 (2016)
14. Schowengerdt, R.A.: Reconstruction of multispatial, multispectral image data using spatial frequency content. Photogram. Eng. Remote Sens. **46**(10), 1325–1334 (1980)
15. Thomas, C., Ranchin, T., Wald, L., Chanussot, J.: Synthesis of multispectral images to high spatial resolution: a critical review of fusion methods based on remote sensing physics. IEEE Trans. Geosci. Remote Sens. **46**(5), 1301–1312 (2008)
16. Vaswani, A., et al.: Attention is all you need. In: Advances in Neural Information Processing Systems, vol. 30 (2017)
17. Wang, X., Girshick, R., Gupta, A., He, K.: Non-local neural networks. In: Proceedings of the IEEE Conference on Computer Vision and Pattern Recognition, pp. 7794–7803 (2018)
18. Xu, S., Zhang, J., Zhao, Z., Sun, K., Liu, J., Zhang, C.: Deep gradient projection networks for pan-sharpening. In: IEEE Conference on Computer Vision and Pattern Recognition, pp. 1366–1375, June 2021
19. Yang, J., Fu, X., Hu, Y., Huang, Y., Ding, X., Paisley, J.: Pannet: a deep network architecture for pan-sharpening. In: IEEE International Conference on Computer Vision, pp. 5449–5457 (2017)
20. Yuan, Q., Wei, Y., Meng, X., Shen, H., Zhang, L.: A multiscale and multidepth convolutional neural network for remote sensing imagery pan-sharpening. IEEE J. Sel. Top. Appl. Earth Obser. Remote Sens. **11**(3), 978–989 (2018)
21. Zhou, M., Huang, J., Fang, Y., Fu, X., Liu, A.: Pan-sharpening with customized transformer and invertible neural network. In: Proceedings of the AAAI Conference on Artificial Intelligence, vol. 36, pp. 3553–3561 (2022)

Population Coding Can Greatly Improve Performance of Neural Networks: A Comparison

Marius Jahrens[ID], Hans-Oliver Hansen[✉][ID], Rebecca Köhler,
and Thomas Martinetz[ID]

Institute for Neuro- and Bioinformatics, University of Lübeck, Lübeck, Germany
{m.jahrens,h.hansen,thomas.martinetz}@uni-luebeck.de,
rebecca.koehler@student.uni-luebeck.de

Abstract. Artificial neural networks oftentimes operate on continuous inputs. While biological neural networks usually represent information through the activity of a population of neurons, the inputs of an artificial neural network are typically provided as a list of scalars. As the information content of each of the input scalars depends heavily on the problem domain, representing them as individual scalar inputs, irrespective of the amount of information they contain, may prove to be suboptimal for the network. We therefore compare and examine four different Population Coding schemes and demonstrate on two toy datasets and one real world benchmark that applying Population Coding to information rich, low dimensional inputs can vastly improve a network's performance.

Keywords: Machine Learning · Population Coding · Information Representation

1 Introduction

Recently, multiple publications have shown that it is beneficial for neural networks to encode continuous inputs as vector encodings [5,6], also known as Population Coding. For that, the scalar components of the network input are represented as vectors such that the value of a scalar will not be defined by the extent of a single stimulus, but by the pattern in the vector.

In nature, this principle can be observed in the activation patterns that represent joint position or eye position as well as an organism's location in space, i.e. grid cells as described by [1,3,4]. For different purposes different encoding schemes are used. These can be distinguished by the neurons employing unimodal or multimodal activation characteristics. In this paper, we explore examples for both types of encoding schemes.

For a closed set of discrete values, this has been done for a while in the form of learned embeddings, e.g. in language models with a fixed dictionary [2]. For

---

M. Jahrens and H.-O. Hansen—Equal contributions.

L. Iliadis et al. (Eds.): ICANN 2023, LNCS 14258, pp. 386–398, 2023.
https://doi.org/10.1007/978-3-031-44192-9_31

an open set of discrete values, a similar concept can be found in position encodings [8]. However, position encodings are usually only applied to the positional information of elements in a sequence or tensor, rather than to encode the scalar values of an input sample.

The benefit of applying Population Coding to neural network inputs has been demonstrated not only for information rich, independent scalars like cartesian coordinates [6], but also highly correlated scalars like pixel values in images [5]. A more thorough analysis of existing approaches would therefore help determine the usefulness and potential pitfalls of Population Coding in common types of neural networks as well as novel network architectures.

We compare four Population Coding schemes and examine their utility first in a regression setting and on a simple classification task. We show that Population Coding can drastically improve a model's performance in a way that cannot be explained by the increased network depth or number of parameters. Finally, we apply the best of the four Population Coding schemes to a real world benchmark dataset, where Population Coding is substantial for beating the so-far best performing approaches.

2   Related Work

Population Coding was successfully used in several publications to increase a network's performance. The authors of [6] used Positional Encoding on a camera pose vector, a five dimensional input vector (x, y, z, θ, ϕ) with spacial coordinates x, y and z as well as orientation θ and ϕ to learn the corresponding RGB-values on the line of sight. Encoding the low-dimensional inputs was essential to achieve good results on their regression problem.

In [5] another Population Coding scheme called Magnitude Encoding was employed to get a new representation of the individual intensity values of grey scale images. The model processes multiple images per sample and uses late fusion, so the improved performance may be attributed to improved information retention. The input encoding turned out to be crucial to solve certain tasks pertaining to color.

The authors of [7] introduced Fourier Feature Mapping and demonstrated the high impact of their encoding scheme on the capacity of multilayer perceptrons (MLPs) to learn high frequency dependencies between input and output.

3   Population Coding

Population Coding schemes are deterministic transformations $f : \mathbb{R}^n \rightarrow \mathbb{R}^{d \cdot n}$ from some domain $\mathbb{R}^n$ into a (real) vector of dimension $d \cdot n$. Across all encodings the input values are assumed to be in the range -1 to 1. For encoding schemes that encode each component separately (defined by a mapping $\mathbb{R} \rightarrow \mathbb{R}^d$), the resulting encoded vector is a concatenation of the n encoded components.

Four types of Population Coding are being evaluated: Positional Encoding (PE), Fourier Feature Mapping (FFM), Tent Encoding (TE), and Magnitude Encoding (ME).

3.1 Positional Encoding

For a multimodal example, we explore Positional Encoding (PE) as described in [6], which uses a combination of sine and cosine functions with exponential frequencies to encode the given input values:

$$f(x) = [\sin(2^0 \pi x), \ldots, \sin(2^j \pi x), \ldots, \sin(2^{L-1} \pi x),$$
$$\cos(2^0 \pi x), \ldots, \cos(2^j \pi x), \ldots, \cos(2^{L-1} \pi x)]$$

for each input scalar x. In this case $d = 2 \cdot L$.

3.2 Fourier Feature Mapping

Fourier Feature Mapping (FFM) was introduced in [7]. In contrast to PE, the components are not encoded individually but instead for their Gaussian mapping, the input vector $\mathbf{p} \in \mathbb{R}^n$ is transformed via random linear operation:

$$f(\mathbf{p}) = [\sin(2\pi \mathbf{b}_1^T \mathbf{p}), \ldots, \sin(2\pi \mathbf{b}_j^T \mathbf{p}), \ldots, \sin(2\pi \mathbf{b}_L^T \mathbf{p}),$$
$$\cos(2\pi \mathbf{b}_1^T \mathbf{p}), \ldots, \cos(2\pi \mathbf{b}_j^T \mathbf{p}), \ldots, \cos(2\pi \mathbf{b}_L^T \mathbf{p})].$$

The random vectors $\mathbf{b}_i$ are drawn independently from a normal distribution. In this case $d = \frac{2 \cdot L}{n}$.

3.3 Tent Encoding

For a unimodal example, we explore Tent Encoding (TE) by the authors of [5], which is based on the tent mapping.

$$t(x) = \begin{cases} x + 1 & x \in [-1, 0] \\ -x + 1 & x \in (0, 1] \\ 0 & \text{else.} \end{cases}$$

In addition to translations $t(\cdot - a)$, TE uses different slopes m that can be adjusted:

$$f(x) = [t(m \cdot (x - \mu_0)), \ldots, t(m \cdot (x - \mu_{L-1}))]$$

with $\mu_i = \frac{2 \cdot i}{L-1} - 1 \quad \forall i = 0, \ldots, L-1$. In this case $d = L$.

3.4 Magnitude Encoding

Magnitude Encoding (ME) as described in [5] uses Gaussian bell curves $g(x) = \exp(-x^2/(2\sigma^2))$. Each input component is encoded via

$$f(x) = [g(x - \mu_0), g(x - \mu_1), \ldots, g(x - \mu_{L-1})]$$

with $\mu_i = \frac{2 \cdot i}{L-1} - 1 \quad \forall i = 0, \ldots, L-1$. In this case $d = L$.

3.5   Plots

Figure 1 shows visualizations of the four coding schemes. Figure 1a shows Positional Encoding for $L = 2$. Figure 1b shows four sine and cosine waves with random parameters for **b**. Tent encoding in Fig. 1c uses parameters $m = 1$ and $L = 5$. The Gaussian curves in Fig. 1d are created with parameters $\sigma = 0.2$ and $L = 5$.

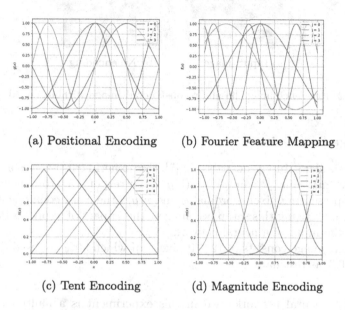

(a) Positional Encoding   (b) Fourier Feature Mapping

(c) Tent Encoding   (d) Magnitude Encoding

Fig. 1. Visualization of the four coding schemes.

4   Experiments

The first experiment demonstrates the behavior of a simple neural network on a 2D regression task and the impact that Population Coding has on its performance. We then form a hypothesis as to which properties of the data are responsible for the large divide between the model's performance with and without Population Coding.

The second experiment is designed based on this hypothesis in order to provide further evidence to support or refute it. Additionally, the second experiment is modeled after more common classification tasks to make it easier to draw conclusions how training and test performance would translate to real world classification problems in terms of overfitting behavior and generalization capability.

Finally, we apply the best performing Population Coding scheme to a real world benchmark.

(a) Input image   (b) No encoding

Fig. 2. Reference image [9] and reconstructed image without encoding.

4.1   Image Regression

Task: In a similar setup as described in [7], this experiment involves a regression to learn the mapping $f : (x, y) \mapsto (r, g, b)$ corresponding to a single image, with x, y representing pixel coordinates and r, g, b the color components of each respective pixel. Using this setup, we analyse the impact of applying Population Coding on the input of a neural network.

The input image consists of 12,000 pixels, of which 90% are used as training data and 10% as test data.

Model: The neural network used in this experiment is a multilayer perceptron (MLP) with four hidden layers, each of size 256, and Rectified Linear Unit (ReLU) activations. The output consists of three channels with sigmoid activations for red, green, and blue (RGB-) values. The mean squared error (MSE) is used as loss function. The MLP is trained over 12,000 epochs with the Adam optimizer with learning rates between 10^{-2} and 10^{-3}, tuned for optimal results for each setting.

The input coordinates are scaled to $[-1, 1]$. Three different population sizes $d \in \{16, 64, 256\}$ are examined. The network's output images are evaluated visually as well as quantitatively by the MSE.

Results: When only passing the two-dimensional coordinates as input without applying Population Coding, the model is unable to learn high-frequency dependencies, as seen in Fig. 2. Once any form of Population Coding is applied, the resolution of the output image increases significantly. A comparison of all evaluated encoding methods is shown in Fig. 3. Using any encoding with population size $d = 16$ already yields a significant improvement in the reconstructed image. Increasing the population size enhances the output's image quality further. Population sizes beyond $d = 256$ show diminishing returns.

When using TE, the best results are achieved when setting m to a quarter of the encoding dimension. Here, the output image produced with $d = 256$ and $m = 64$ can hardly be distinguished from the input image. Comparable results are achieved with ME and $d = 256$.

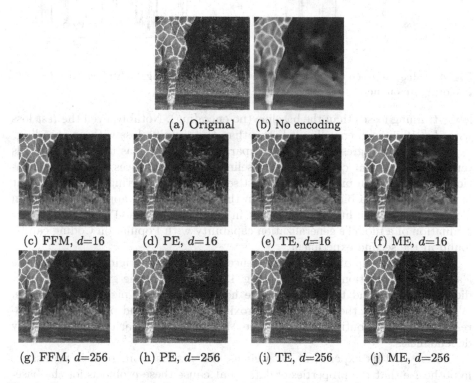

(a) Original   (b) No encoding

(c) FFM, d=16   (d) PE, d=16   (e) TE, d=16   (f) ME, d=16

(g) FFM, d=256   (h) PE, d=256   (i) TE, d=256   (j) ME, d=256

Fig. 3. Output images of each encoding with population sizes $d = 16$ and $d = 256$, standard deviation σ for (f) 0.1 and (j) 0.007, and slope m for (e) 4 and (i) 64.

In Table 1, the training and test loss are shown. The quantitative results correlate with the visual impression. Note that the training loss has a larger impact on the image quality than the test loss, because most of the pixels are in the training set. The use of any encoding, even with only 16 dimensions, leads to

Table 1. Training and test loss achieved within 12,000 epochs of learning for different encodings with dimension d on the regression task.

encoding	none	FFM		PE		TE		ME	
d	1	16	256	16	256	16	256	16	256
train loss	0.016	0.0086	0.0057	0.0063	0.0004	0.0092	0.0005	0.0111	0.0007
test loss	0.018	0.0160	0.0153	0.0156	0.0298	0.0156	0.0177	0.0158	0.0170

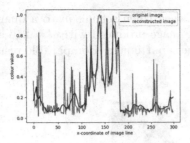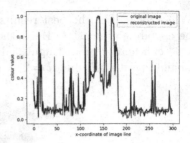

Fig. 4. Values of green channel in row 150; left: no encoding; right: TE with $d = 256$. (Color figure online)

lower training losses than the baseline (no encoding). Notably, even the *test* loss with $d = 16$ in each encoding is better than the training loss with no encoding.

This kind of regression task is comparatively smooth, as neighboring pixels tend to have similar colors. So the baseline already produces good approximations for the unseen pixels from the test set by simply blurring the image. That is why there isn't a big improvement in the test loss when applying Population Coding, despite the huge improvement in the training loss. Therefore, a better evaluation of a model's generalization capability with Population Coding can be found in the second experiment.

A better closeup of the color differences between the original image and the learned reconstructions is shown in Fig. 4, which shows the green channel predictions and ground truth for a single horizontal line of pixels in the image. Without encoding, the values are approximated poorly and peaks are not represented well. In contrast, with TE the MLP is able to learn higher frequency dependencies.

Based on this experiment, as well as the results from related works, we hypothesize that the properties of data, that cause these problems for the baseline model, are twofold: low information redundancy between the input dimensions, and high information content per dimension (i.e. high mutual information of individual input features with regards to the data points' labels).

Failure Cases: PE exhibits poor test performance for large d, which we're attributing to the fact that for large d this encoding produces very rapidly changing encodings for similar input values, leading to an erratic rather than a smooth mapping between input space and encoding space. Visually, this can be observed as white pixels on the giraffe in Fig. 3h, which are pixel coordinates that are not part of the training set. Quantitatively, this is reflected in the poor test loss for $d = 256$ in Table 1.

When using TE, it must be ensured that the tent functions have sufficient width. The width must be at least $8/d$ such that there is an overlap. Otherwise, mirroring artifacts occur as seen in Fig. 5, as the neural network is unable to distinguish between different input scalars that have the same representations. The same phenomenon happens with ME when setting σ too small.

4.2   Classification

Although a regression task on a single image is well suited to demonstrate visually how an MLP can learn to represent highly dynamic input data with and without encoding, it is not indicative of the network's performance on tasks like classification, or regression tasks with a less smooth mapping.

Fig. 5. TE artifacts for $d = 16, m = 5$.

This second experiment is designed to test the hypothesis formulated in the previous section that Population Coding works particularly well for low-dimensional inputs with high information content encoded in the individual scalar values.

Task: For the classification task a range of real numbers is labeled as either *odd* or *even*, based on their integer part.

$$c(x) \mapsto \begin{cases} 'even' & \lfloor x \rfloor \bmod 2 = 0, \\ 'odd' & \text{else.} \end{cases}$$

The dataset consists of 9,000 training samples and 1,000 test samples uniformly sampled from the range $[0, 100)$ and rescaled to $[-1, 1]$. Figure 6 shows a cutout representing the classes on a number axis for the interval $[0, 6.5]$.

Model: The model is a simple MLP with two hidden layers with 64 neurons each, connected via ReLU-activations. Training took place over 10,000 epochs using the Adam optimizer with a fixed learning rate of 10^{-4} and a batch size of 9,000.

For input dimension $d \in \{16, 64, 256\}$, ME is used with $\sigma = 2/d$, and TE is used with $m = d/2$. For ME, this leads to neighboring bell curves interjecting at each other's inflection points and in TE neighboring tents having an overlap

$$0 \quad 1 \quad 2 \quad 3 \quad 4 \quad 5 \quad 6$$
$$x$$

Fig. 6. The two classes in the classification task: Blue is label "even", red is label "odd". (Color figure online)

of half their width. FFM's frequencies were sampled from a normal distribution with $\mu = 0$ and $\sigma = 100$ in order to obtain adequately high frequencies. PE is initialized as explained above, i.e. the lowest frequency is 1, the highest is $2^{d/2-1}$.

Results: The results for this experiment, shown in Table 2, match the expectations from the hypothesis. Inputs without any encoding scheme (other than scaling to the interval $[-1, 1]$) lead to low accuracy, because the MLP is not capable of understanding small differences in input values. Population Coding provides higher test accuracies. They enable the model to differentiate between neighboring input values. Rescaling the input values to a larger domain does not improve the baseline model.

Table 2 shows the average training and test accuracies and their standard deviation (over ten runs), each for input dimensions 16, 64, and 256 for each of the other Population Coding schemes. While each encoding scheme converged after 2,000 epochs, training the model without an input encoding required at least 10,000 epochs to reach convergence.

Table 2. Classification Task Accuracies for different Encoding Schemes, outliers in **bold**.

encoding	d	Training	Test
none	1	0.6182 ± 0.0144	0.5934 ± 0.0228
FFM	16	1.0 ± 0.0	0.9979 ± 0.0
	64	1.0 ± 0.0	0.9976 ± 0.0005
	256	1.0 ± 0.0	0.998 ± 0.0
PE	16	0.9997 ± 0.0001	0.997 ± 0.0001
	64	1.0 ± 0.0	0.945 ± 0.0117
	256	1.0 ± 0.0	$\mathbf{0.5021 \pm 0.0109}$
TE	16	0.9688 ± 0.0023	0.9538 ± 0.0023
	64	0.9998 ± 0.0	0.9998 ± 0.0117
	256	1.0 ± 0.0	0.9977 ± 0.0007
ME	16	0.9844 ± 0.008	0.9826 ± 0.008
	64	0.9999 ± 0.0001	0.998 ± 0.0
	256	1.0 ± 0.0	0.9968 ± 0.0010

The Population Coding schemes performed exceedingly well during training reaching accuracies of almost 100%. Notably, even in low dimensions the experiment on FFM leads to robust results, in spite of the randomness of its frequency selections.

The results clearly show that multilayer perceptrons benefit from encoded input data to differentiate between samples with similar but not identical values. These are the cases where fine nuances can carry a lot of information pertaining to the solution of a given task. Similar effects have been observed in [5] using convolutional neural networks, which indicates that the observed benefits are not limited to MLP based architectures either.

Failure Cases: As expected based on the previous experiment, PE's test accuracy when using high input dimensions drops due to overfitting high frequencies to training data.

4.3 Real World Benchmark Dataset

As a real world benchmark, we choose a task that should benefit greatly from Population Coding if our previous hypothesis is valid. Time series are a good candidate because they generally have a low dimensionality at each time step and features with high information content, i.e. even small variations in the values can be relevant.

In addition, three criteria were applied to choose an appropriate benchmark. Firstly, a variety of published solutions should exist for comparison. Secondly, the publications should include recent methods. And thirdly, the results should leave room for improvement.

Task: Based on these criteria, the ETTh2 dataset [11] was chosen. It consists of a real world long-term series forecasting (LTSF) task, and the authors have included a Transformer based architecture as a baseline. The task is to predict the oil temperature X_t of an electric transformer at every hour t. The data stream for training and testing comprises two years. More specifically, a time series $(X_t)_{t=1}^{L}$ with a look-back window of size $L = 336$ is given, which will be used to predict the oil temperature with time steps $(X_t)_{t=L+1}^{L+T}$ with $T = 720$.

The state-of-the-art model was published in [10], where the authors compared the effectiveness of different Transformer based and non-Transformer based architectures to solve a variety of LTSF tasks. Their experiments show that Transformers, which currently provide the most successful solution to extract semantic correlations between elements of long word sequences, were easily outperformed by simple linear layers.

The benchmark measures the mean squared error (MSE) as well as the mean absolute error (MAE) on the test set.

Model: The authors of [10] achieve state-of-the-art performance on the ETTh2 benchmark with *LTSF-Linear* models. *LTSF-Linear* is a class of models containing only a linear layer that takes the last L time steps as input and produces a forecast for the next T values, hence, the models map from $\mathbb{R}^L$ to $\mathbb{R}^T$. The best performing model, called *NLinear*, first subtracts the input's last value as a simple normalization step and adds it back after propagating through the linear layer.

We use the NLinear model as a baseline and enhance it by applying Magnitude Encoding to the input values. Because this Population Coding scheme produces a sparser representation of the data, a linear layer may not be able to provide good predictions in a single transformation. Therefore, we also evaluate a model with an MLP with three layers replacing the single linear layer, each connected via *tanh* activation. After the last linear layer no activation function is applied. For comparison, the baseline model without Population Coding is tested with and without an MLP as well.

For encoding, we use parameters $d = 64$ and $\sigma = 2/d$. The MLP uses T neurons in every layer.

Results: Table 3 shows the MSE and MAE after testing each model with look-back window size $L = 336$ and prediction dimension $T = 720$. Training took place on ETTh2 with Adam for 20 epochs with early stopping if the validation loss does not improve within six epochs. The learning rate starts at 0.05 and decays with factor 2 each epoch. In order to prevent overfitting when using Magnitude Encoding, a weight decay of 0.001 was applied. The linear models without Population Coding did not benefit from weight decay.

Indeed, our approach using an MLP and Magnitude Encoding outperforms the other models in terms of MSE and MAE, establishing a new state-of-the-art for this benchmark dataset.

Table 3. Mean and standard deviation of the MSE- and MAE-Losses of NLinear and MLP models over five runs with and without Population Coding. "ME" stands for Magnitude Encoding, "WD" stands for Weight Decay. Best results are highlighted in **bold**.

Model	MSE	MAE
Linear (Baseline)	0.225 ± 0.001	0.381 ± 0.001
Linear+ME+WD	0.214 ± 0.003	0.372 ± 0.003
MLP	0.25 ± 0.002	0.403 ± 0.001
MLP+WD	0.21 ± 0.001	0.369 ± 0.001
MLP+ME+WD (ours)	$\mathbf{0.189} \pm 0.006$	$\mathbf{0.349} \pm 0.005$

5 Conclusion

Based on preliminary experiments, we formed the hypothesis that Population Coding can vastly increase the capability to learn high frequency dependencies between input and output of a neural network. Follow-up experiments provided empirical evidence in support of the hypothesis. To test increasingly difficult settings, we started with toy tasks, followed by a synthetic classification problem, leading into real world data for time series forecasting. Across encoding schemes, a correlation between population size and resolution of the learned function can be observed, with diminishing returns for large populations.

We want to highlight the core observation that Population Coding is a versatile tool beyond its typical role as position encoding. The technique proves to be invaluable, demonstrating its efficacy and relevance in a multitude of scenarios.

In order to avoid overfitting, small differences in input values must not lead to drastic changes in the encoded representation. This is shown to be a problem for a class of commonly used position encoding methods, with other encoding schemes being less susceptible to this issue.

Overall, Magnitude Encoding, Tent Encoding as well as Fourier Feature Mapping show the best results among the compared Population Coding schemes.

An interesting prospect is the use of Population Coding to explicitly encode features inside a neural network. While in theory, a neural network can learn these Population Coded features, this work is evidence that in practice it does not do so, at least not for the input layer.

Potential applications include late fusion models as well as sequence models with low dimensional sequence samples like audio waveforms and other time series data. In these scenarios, using Population Coding on the input might drastically improve model performances.

References

1. Averbeck, B., Latham, P., Pouget, A.: Neural correlations, population coding and computation. Nature Rev. Neurosci. **7**, 358–66 (2006). https://doi.org/10.1038/nrn1888
2. Devlin, J., Chang, M., Lee, K., Toutanova, K.: BERT: pre-training of deep bidirectional transformers for language understanding. In: Proceedings of the 2019 Conference of the North American Chapter of the Association for Computational Linguistics: Human Language Technologies, pp. 4171–4186. Association for Computational Linguistics (2019). https://doi.org/10.18653/v1/n19-1423
3. Georgopoulos, A., Schwartz, A., Ketiner, R.: Neuronal population coding of movement direction. Science **233**, 1416–1419 (1986)
4. Hafting, T., Fyhn, M., Molden, S.: Microstructure of a spatial map in the entorhinal cortex. Nature **436**, 801–806 (2005)
5. Jahrens, M., Martinetz, T.: Solving Raven's progressive matrices with multi-layer relation networks. In: 2020 International Joint Conference on Neural Networks (IJCNN), pp. 1–6. IEEE (2020)

6. Mildenhall, B., Srinivasan, P.P., Tancik, M., Barron, J.T., Ramamoorthi, R., Ng, R.: NeRF: representing scenes as neural radiance fields for view synthesis. In: Vedaldi, A., Bischof, H., Brox, T., Frahm, J.-M. (eds.) ECCV 2020. LNCS, vol. 12346, pp. 405–421. Springer, Cham (2020). https://doi.org/10.1007/978-3-030-58452-8_24

7. Tancik, M., et al.: Fourier features let networks learn high frequency functions in low dimensional domains (2020)

8. Vaswani, A., et al.: Attention is all you need. In: Advances in Neural Information Processing Systems, vol. 30. Curran Associates, Inc. (2017). https://proceedings.neurips.cc/paper/2017/file/3f5ee243547dee91fbd053c1c4a845aa-Paper.pdf

9. Zell, H.: Giraffa camelopardalis reticulata 01 (2009). https://upload.wikimedia.org/wikipedia/commons/4/4d/Giraffa_camelopardalis_reticulata_01.JPG, license: CC BY-SA 3.0

10. Zeng, A., Chen, M., Zhang, L., Xu, Q.: Are transformers effective for time series forecasting? (2022). https://doi.org/10.48550/ARXIV.2205.13504. https://arxiv.org/abs/2205.13504

11. Zhou, H., et al.: Informer: beyond efficient transformer for long sequence time-series forecasting. In: The Thirty-Fifth AAAI Conference on Artificial Intelligence, AAAI 2021, Virtual Conference, vol. 35, pp. 11106–11115. AAAI Press (2021)

QuasiNet: A Neural Network
with Trainable Product Layers

Kristína Malinovská[(⊠)][iD], Slavomir Holenda, and Ľudovít Malinovský[iD]

Faculty of Mathematics, Physics and Informatics, Comenius University in Bratislava,
Bratislava, Slovakia
kristina.malinovska@fmph.uniba.sk
http://cogsci.fmph.uniba.sk/cnc/

Abstract. Classical neural networks achieve only limited convergence
in hard problems such as XOR or parity when the number of hidden
neurons is small. With the motivation to improve the success rate of
neural networks in these problems, we propose a new neural network
model inspired by existing neural network models with so called product
neurons and a learning rule derived from classical error backpropagation, which elegantly solves the problem of mutually exclusive situations.
Unlike existing product neurons, which have weights that are preset and
not adaptable, our product layers of neurons also do learn. We tested the
model and compared its success rate to a classical multilayer perceptron
in the aforementioned problems as well as in other hard problems such
as the two spirals. Our results indicate that our model is clearly more
successful than the classical MLP and has the potential to be used in
many tasks and applications.

Keywords: product neuron · multiplication · error backpropagation ·
XOR · parity · 2 spirals

1 Introduction

Multiplication of neuronal activations has been theoretically studied, but it is
used relatively rarely in practice. In the simplest case, a neuron similar to a
classical perceptron computes a weighted sum of the terms of a higher-order
polynomial, and only the summation weights are trained via error backpropagation. Since the number of possible terms grows exponentially with increasing
polynomial degree, the composition of the polynomial can be constrained in various ways. In the more complex case of the so-called product neurons, the network
would learn the exponents of the individual components of each term. However,
this leads to computations in the domain of complex numbers in the general
case if a negative number is raised to a fraction. As a result, multiplication is
only used in particular cases as an optimization technique at pre-selected exact
locations in the model. Most of the time, the network itself does not learn to use
multiplication. Despite these obstacles, both theoretical and practical results

© The Author(s), under exclusive license to Springer Nature Switzerland AG 2023
L. Iliadis et al. (Eds.): ICANN 2023, LNCS 14258, pp. 399–410, 2023.
https://doi.org/10.1007/978-3-031-44192-9_32

argue in favor of using multiplication as a tool to increase the computational power of neural networks.

In this paper, we propose a novel neural network model QuasiNet that has layers of product neurons as well as layers of classical summation neurons. The novelty of our approach is that we define a new way of applying weights at the product layer, which we call quasi-exponentiation. Unlike other models, our method allows trainable product neuron weights using a gradient descent method without the need for computations in the domain of complex numbers. Thus, the network is able to partially learn the polynomial composition, which increases the generality of the model. The multiplication layer is designed in such a way that it can be plugged into the architecture as arbitrarily and easily as a classical Sigmoidal summation layer. The results of our experiments show the incomparably higher efficiency of our model in XOR and parity problems compared to a classical two-layer perceptron with the same architecture and parameters, as well as in other hard problems such as the separation of two-spirals.

2   Related Work

Multiplication has been used in neural models since the late 1950s, and in the 1960s it was popular to use higher-order Sigmoidal neurons for pattern recognition [13]. These were classical Sigmoidal neurons, but the input vector was augmented with terms generated by multiplying and exponentiating the inputs, and these terms were given their own weights. This approach is a natural extension of the classical perceptron, but in the general case leads to an exponential increase in dimensionality, with the upper bound on the degree of the polynomial being mainly a designer's choice. In such networks, back propagation of error can be easily applied, and neurons of this type are also known as *sigma-pi* neurons [16], since they perform a weighted sum of the products of the inputs.

The solution to the dimensionality problem was a family of models in which the number of polynomial terms was restricted to some pre-selected ones. For example, Giles et al. [9] and Spirkovska and Reid [21] show that classical perceptron networks can be significantly outperformed in both learning speed and generalization capability in this way. However, this approach requires some knowledge of the problem to be embedded in the model by its designer. Constructive models have been a response to this. Their essence was to learn in different ways which polynomial terms were needed, starting with a minimal model and gradually adding higher order terms and evaluating their effectiveness [10,15].

A generalization of the above principle is the product neuron model [6], which assumes trainable real weights acting as exponents of the inputs. The authors have solved the problem with the input to the domain of complex numbers by using only the real part of the number. For logical inputs, such a neuron becomes a de facto summation neuron which has cosine as an activation function, leading to further theoretical problems [2].

An alternative approach was suggested by Ghosh and colleagues [8]. Their model first linearly combines the inputs and then directly multiplies this linear combination without using an activation function. The nonlinear activation function is applied only at the output. The only primes of the model are the linear weights, and the weights on the multiplication layer are fixed to one. The result can be analyzed as a polynomial. Hence the product of the sums stands out in the formula, it is said to be a pi-sigma network. Since the weights on the multiplication layer are fixed and only linear weights are learned, the learning algorithm is based on the gradient method.

The authors tested the success of the network on many common tasks such as feature approximation, data classification, feature recognition with translation and rotation invariance, and also verified the network's ability to learn logical functions of parity, symmetry and negation. The achieved success rate is an order of magnitude better in the case of parity compared to the classical multilayer perceptron and comparable to other models with higher order neurons.

From our point of view, the drawback is that [8] fixes the multiplicative weights and does not even try to find a way to learn them. Moreover, the absence of an activation function after the linear transformation reduces the pi-sigma network to a polynomial model with forward-selected terms. [20] propose a solution with a constructive model, similar to the constructive pi-sigma models above.

Analogs of multiplication occur in biological neural networks in various forms. One possibility are the so called dendritic clusters [12] found in the dendritic trees, which can also divide, or could represent an operation similar to the sigma-pi neurons [11]. The ability of neurons to multiply inputs has been found in the auditory [22] and visual [1] cortices. Some authors argue that the physical proximity of synapses leads to multiplicative behavior, whereas distant synapses function in a summation mode [3].

Schmitt [19] analyzes different types of neural networks with multiplicative and sigmoidal neurons and derives general mathematical constraints for each type of network in terms of the Vapnik-Chervonenkis dimension. It concludes that multiplication in neural networks is a suitable choice for increasing the degree of nonlinear interaction and computational power, even for high-order neurons. The paper also provides a qualitative overview of neural models with multiplication, which is still quite relevant despite the current boom of deep networks with a large number of parameters and the use of brute force graphics cards.

In the context of deep neural networks, sum-product multiplication has been studied in sum-product networks [4,14]. Some new models use multiplication of vectors and activation matrices by elements at selected locations of the model [5,7,18,23]. Articles of varying quality can be found on the blogosphere that describe specific applications of multiplication in deep neural networks and show its benefits in concrete examples. Thus, this is still an active and promising research direction.

3 QuasiNet

We propose a novel neural network model we call QuasiNet. Our model resembles the pi-sigma network [8], except that we apply the hyperbolic tangent as an activation function on the hidden layer, thus obtaining hidden activations from the interval $(-1, 1)$. We then multiply these on the output layer. The weights in our model are not fixed, nor do they act as exponents, but are involved in the computation so that at one extreme a given hidden layer activation does not matter (it is reduced to one as if the neuron activations were raised to 0) and at the other extreme it performs at its original function (unchanged as if they were raised to 1). This recalculation, which replaces the exponentiation from the previous models, is in fact polynomial. This property guarantees that complex numbers do not appear anywhere in the computation, and also allows the model to learn which hidden neurons "make sense" to use to achieve the desired output. We show a schematic representation of the model in Fig. 1. For the ease of explaining the workings of the model we will describe a simple case with one summation and one product layer. However, QuasiNet can be extended to any number of connected layers and of various types (both product and summation) and still can be trained with the same standard error backpropagation learning rule [17].

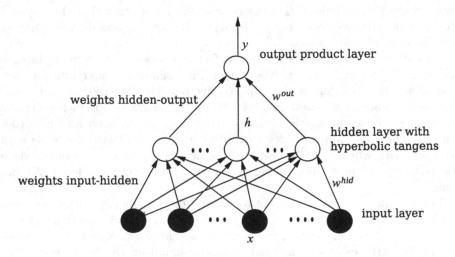

Fig. 1. The schematic depiction of our model adapted from [8].

In our current research, we chose the hyperbolic tangent because by representing the logical values truth and false by -1 and $+1$ we can directly simulate the logical XOR function using multiplication, since sign multiplication behaves exactly like XOR. For other tasks, it may be appropriate to choose a different activation function.

3.1   Forward Pass

Given an input x, including the trainable bias, and weights w^{hid} and w^{out} we compute the activation of neurons on the connected hidden layer h as:

$$h_i = \tanh(\sum_j w_{ij}^{\text{hid}} \cdot x_j), \tag{1}$$

and from that the activation of the connected product layer y, which in this case, is the output layer of the model, can be expressed as

$$y_i = \prod_j \left(1 - \sigma(w_{ij}^{\text{out}})(1 - h_j)\right), \tag{2}$$

or

$$y_i = \prod_j f(h_j, \sigma(w_{ij}^{\text{out}})), \tag{3}$$

where f is defined as:

$$f(h_j, d) = 1 - d(1 - h_j) \tag{4}$$

and σ is the logistic function.

Thus, our model uses the analogy of the product neuron [6] at the output layer, but replaces the input-weight exponentiation by a polynomial function f with one nonlinear parameter:

$$f(h, \sigma(w)) = 1 - \sigma(w)(1 - h) \tag{5}$$

This approach preserves some properties of the exponentiation, namely $h^1 = f(h, 1) = h$ and $h^0 = f(h, 0) = 1$ but does not preserve the property $0^d = 0$. Instead, in the case of zero input, we get $f(0, d) = 1 - d$.

Moreover, our method of applying weights using the function f is continuous and continuously differentiable for all zero input values, while 0^0 is undefined and hence a point of discontinuity and without derivative. By applying the logistic function to the weight, we achieve that the weight can take arbitrary real values, but which correspond to the exponents of 0 and 1 at the extrema. This allows the output weights to learn safely using gradient methods which would otherwise put them outside of the desired values.

3.2   Error Backpropagation

For the output layer, we can use the gradient descent method for the mean squared error to derive the following rule for adapting the hidden-output weights:

$$\frac{\partial E}{\partial w_{ij}^{\text{out}}} = (d_i - y_i) \left(\prod_{k \neq j} 1 - \sigma(w_{ik}^{\text{out}})(1 - h_k) \right) \tag{6}$$

$$(h_j - 1)\sigma(w_{ij}^{\text{out}})(1 - \sigma(w_{ij}^{\text{out}}))$$

and back-propagating the error to the hidden layer:

$$\frac{\partial E}{\partial h_i} = \sum_k (d_k - y_k) \left(\prod_{l \neq i} 1 - \sigma(w_{kl}^{\text{out}})(1 - h_l) \right) \sigma(w_{ki}^{\text{out}}) \tag{7}$$

To speed up the computation, we can replace the partial multiplication in the learning rule by division, in case division by zero does not occur in the computation:

$$\prod_{k \neq j} 1 - \sigma(w_{ik}^{\text{out}})(1 - h_l) = \frac{y_i}{1 - \sigma(w_{ij}^{\text{out}})(1 - h_j)} \tag{8}$$

Then we used the back-propagated error to adapt the input-hidden weights as:

$$\Delta w_{ij}^{\text{hid}} \sim \frac{\partial E}{\partial w_{ij}^{\text{hid}}} = \frac{\partial E}{\partial h_i}(1 - h_i^2)x_j \tag{9}$$

Our QuasiNet model does not need to be further constrained or stabilized; it can be approached in all respects as a multi-layered perceptron. The multiplication layer can also be incorporated into the network in other ways, such as alternating the summation and multiplication layers, multiplying first and then adding, and so on. It is also possible to modify or rescale the f function according to the properties we want to achieve and the model will look very similar.

4   Experimental Results

4.1   XOR and Parity

For the baseline comparison, we used a basic multilayer perceptron (MLP) without any regularization. We implemented our model in Python programming language[1] by modifying the original MLP to make the comparison as faithful as possible. Here we present mainly the results from experiments with the XOR and n-parity problem and preliminary results from other problems. In general, XOR is indeed a parity problem, but we keep the naming for convenience.

The parity problem, i.e., determining whether a binary number has an even or odd number of units, is a classical, rather hard problem for neural networks and is used to test and validate new models. In our experiments, we evaluate the convergence, i.e., how many networks out of 100 reach a stable solution. We consider that the network converged to the solution if it gives the correct output for ten consecutive epochs. We gave networks at most 10 thousand training epochs, in the case of larger n-parity. For both types of networks, we use a uniform learning rate $\alpha = 0.9$ and a Gaussian initialization of the weights with distribution $\mathcal{N}(0; 1.0)$. These hyperparameters were chosen based on previous experimentation.

---

[1] https://github.com/kik-re/prodnet.

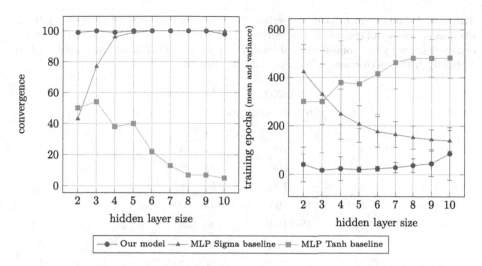

Fig. 2. Results from XOR experiments with varying hidden layer size (max. 500 epochs) in terms of convergence (left) and average training epochs to convergence (right), including non-converging runs in the mean.

In Fig. 2, we show the effect of hidden layer size on the convergence of networks in the XOR task. To emphasize the point that QuasiNet is not successful solely because of encoding the labels of the problem as $-1, 1$ instead of $0, 1$ we include the results for the baseline with two consecutive hyperbolic tangent layers. For the so-called minimal XOR with 2 hidden neurons, we observe a clear superiority of our model. So far, there is no three-layer network model known to us without residual weights that learns this problem to 100% in the minimal architecture with 2 hidden neurons, i.e., that all trained networks find a solution.

In Table 1 we show the results of initial experiments for parity $2 - 7$, where parity 2 represents XOR. For MLP, we no longer found an optimal hidden layer size for parity greater than 5. Given the constraint on the number of training epochs we set above, MLP could not learn the task.

In Fig. 3 we display the results of hidden layer size experiments for parity 7 for both our model and the MLP baseline. Note, that we allowed the MLP baseline to train for 10 thousand epochs, which is significantly more then in the case of our QuasiNet, which in the best case converges in less then 100 epochs. Similarly, the tested hidden layer sizes for the MLP baseline and its success differ dramatically from our model.

In Fig. 4 we display a more detailed experiment with QuasiNet: convergence in parity 8 as a function of the hidden layer size. We also show the mean training epochs. Note, that for deeper evaluation we allowed the model to train for 5000

Table 1. Results from n-parity experiments: minimum size of the hidden layer **h** for maximum number of converging networks. For MLP baseline we report results we have achieved given by the computational limits, very large hidden layer size would lead to a slightly better performance, but not full convergence.

n-parity	QuasiNet		MLP baseline	
	h	convergence	h	convergence
2	2	100	4	100
3	4	100	9	100
4	6	100	12	91
5	7	100	50	44
6	12	100	45	69
7	15	100	45	33

instead of 500 epochs. This experiment illustrates that larger hidden layer size does not lead to better performance. The optimal hidden layer size for out model seems to be rather close to the number of input features.

Last, but not least, we present overall results for parity problem with in terms of best hidden layer size found so far for $2 \leq n \leq 13$ in Fig. 5. In our experiments we observe that most of the nets converge in relative small number of epochs even for large n-parities.

4.2 Multiple Layers and 2 Spirals

The famous 2 spiral problem is commonly used for testing new neural network models. Similarly to parity it poses a problem with mutually exclusive situations, i.e. the point belongs to one spiral or to another. We display the 2 spirals dataset with 2 thousand points we have used and its distribution into training and testing data in Fig. 6. Note, that the spiral coordinates are transformed to the interval $(-1, 1)$ similarly to inputs in parity problem. In our preliminary experiments we have observed that this problem requires more hidden layers for a satisfying performance level.

In Fig. 7 we display training progress of QuasiNet with four hidden layers of neurons, where the hyperbolic tangent and product layers are combined one after another. Namely, the architecture used was: 2 input neurons, 10 tanh neurons, 80 product neurons, 5 tanh neurons and finally 1 output product neuron. Other hyperparameters used were learning rate $\alpha = 0.01$ and a Gaussian initialization of the weights with distribution $\mathcal{N}(0; 0.5)$. The networks were trained for 10 thousand epochs. The mean accuracy for the testing data set was 98.275% and 4 out of 10 networks achieved full convergence, which we deem very successful.

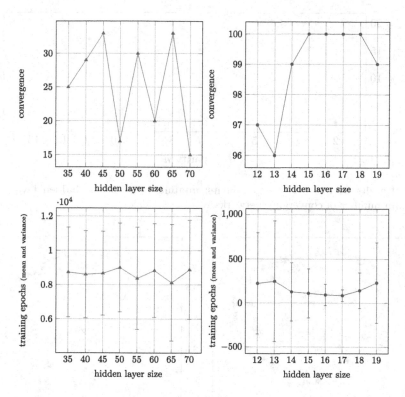

Fig. 3. Results from parity 7 experiments: convergence (top), training epochs (bottom) for MLP baseline (left) and QuasiNet (blue). (Color figure online)

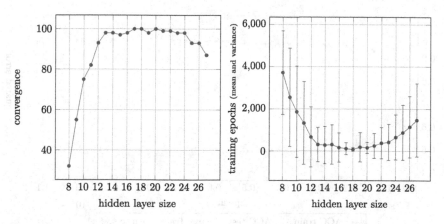

Fig. 4. Results from parity 8 experiments with varying hidden layer size (100 nets, max. 5000 epochs) in terms of convergence (left) and average training epochs to convergence (right), including non-converging runs in the mean.

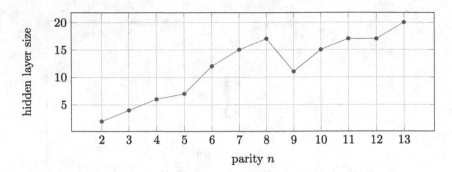

Fig. 5. Results from n-parity experiments: minimum size of the hidden layer **h** for maximum number of converging networks.

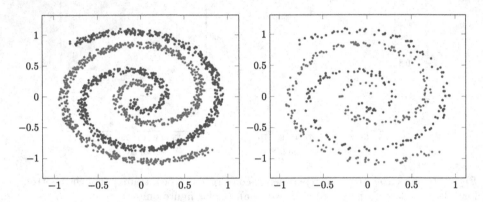

Fig. 6. The 2 spirals dataset (2000 pts) split into 80% training and 20% testing data.

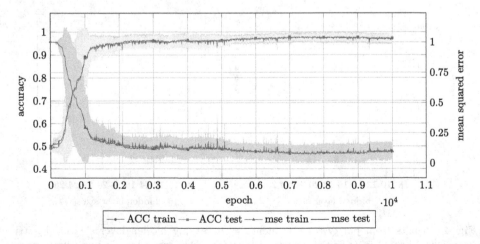

Fig. 7. Results from training of the 2 spirals problem: mean and standard deviation over 10 nets trained for 10000 epochs, only every 10th epoch is shown.

5 Conclusion and Future Work

Our innovative neural network model QuasiNet compensates for particular short-comings of existing neural networks with product neurons and proposes a new way to train the weights of any multiplicative components in neural networks, which avoids the problem with computations in the domain of complex numbers. Our model is mathematically simple, easy to implement, and can be combined with existing models, with the promise of increasing their efficiency in tasks with mutually exclusive situations, which are in general quite difficult for classical neural networks to solve. QuasiNet outperforms the classical MLP baseline in the XOR and n-parity tasks and excels also in the 2 spiral problem task, which is considered one of the hardest problems for neural networks in general. A major advantage of QuasiNet is that it needs a quite small amount of parameters and training epochs to learn hard tasks. From the preliminary queries in the literature and results from related models we assume QuasiNet is at least comparable with the existing baselines. Yet a thorough experimentation and comparison outside of the scope of this debut research paper is to be done to strengthen our claims.

There is a vital need to continue the experimentation with this intriguing new model in terms of testing of various classical neural networks problems and comparing it to existing work. We believe that in the future our model could be also beneficial in the domain of deep learning where it could be used instead of classical fully connected layers in combination with convolutional layers for feature extraction. The fact that the model requires only a fraction of weights compared to the classical fully-connected MLP with Sigmoid or similar activation function could be utilized for analyzing the properties encoded in the feature space of deep networks thus contributing to better explainability of the model. The properties of QuasiNet, its explainability and possibility to encode mutually exclusive properties would also benefit the neural modeling in the domain of cognitive robotics and human-robot interaction where the development of the understanding and interpretation of the sensory input is vital for the robotic system.

Acknowledgements. The research leading to these results has received funding from the project titled TERAIS in the framework of the program Horizon-Widera-2021 of the European Union under the Grant agreement no. 101079338.

References

1. Andersen, R.A., Essick, G.K., Siegel, R.M.: Encoding of spatial location by posterior parietal neurons. Science **230**(4724), 456–458 (1985)
2. Anthony, M., Bartlett, P.L.: Neural Network Learning: Theoretical Foundations, vol. 9. Cambridge University Press, Cambridge (1999)
3. Bugmann, G.: Summation and multiplication: two distinct operation domains of leaky integrate-and-fire neurons. Netw. Comput. Neural Syst. **2**(4), 489–509 (1991)
4. Delalleau, O., Bengio, Y.: Shallow vs. deep sum-product networks. In: Advances in Neural Information Processing Systems, vol. 24 (2011)

5. Diba, A., Sharma, V., Van Gool, L.: Deep temporal linear encoding networks. In: Proceedings of the IEEE Conference on Computer Vision and Pattern Recognition, pp. 2329–2338 (2017)
6. Durbin, R., Rumelhart, D.E.: Product units: a computationally powerful and biologically plausible extension to backpropagation networks. Neural Comput. **1**(1), 133–142 (1989)
7. Erhan, D., Bengio, Y., Courville, A., Vincent, P.: Visualizing higher-layer features of a deep network. University of Montreal **1341**(3), 1 (2009)
8. Ghosh, J., Shin, Y.: Efficient higher-order neural networks for classification and function approximation. Int. J. Neural Syst. **3**(04), 323–350 (1992)
9. Giles, C.L., Maxwell, T.: Learning, invariance, and generalization in high-order neural networks. Appl. Opt. **26**(23), 4972–4978 (1987)
10. Heywood, M., Noakes, P.: A framework for improved training of sigma-pi networks. IEEE Trans. Neural Netw. **6**(4), 893–903 (1995)
11. Mel, B., Koch, C.: Sigma-pi learning: on radial basis functions and cortical associative learning. In: Advances in Neural Information Processing Systems, vol. 2 (1989)
12. Mel, B.W.: Information processing in dendritic trees. Neural Comput. **6**(6), 1031–1085 (1994)
13. Nilsson, N.J.: Learning Machines. McGrawHill, New York (1965)
14. Poon, H., Domingos, P.: Sum-product networks: a new deep architecture. In: 2011 IEEE International Conference on Computer Vision Workshops (ICCV Workshops), pp. 689–690. IEEE (2011)
15. Redding, N.J., Kowalczyk, A., Downs, T.: Constructive higher-order network that is polynomial time. Neural Netw. **6**(7), 997–1010 (1993)
16. Rumelhart, D.E., Hinton, G.E., McClelland, J.L., et al.: A general framework for parallel distributed processing. Parallel Distrib. Process. Explor. Microstruct. Cogn. **1**(45–76), 26 (1986)
17. Rumelhart, D.E., Hinton, G.E., Williams, R.J.: Learning representations by back-propagating errors. Nature **323**(6088), 533–536 (1986)
18. Schenck, C., Fox, D.: SPNets: differentiable fluid dynamics for deep neural networks. In: Conference on Robot Learning, pp. 317–335. PMLR (2018)
19. Schmitt, M.: On the complexity of computing and learning with multiplicative neural networks. Neural Comput. **14**(2), 241–301 (2002)
20. Shin, Y., Ghosh, J.: Ridge polynomial networks. IEEE Trans. Neural Netw. **6**(3), 610–622 (1995)
21. Spirkovska, L., Reid, M.B.: Higher-order neural networks applied to 2D and 3D object recognition. Mach. Learn. **15**(2), 169–199 (1994)
22. Suga, N., Olsen, J., Butman, J.: Specialized subsystems for processing biologically important complex sounds: cross-correlation analysis for ranging in the bat's brain. In: Cold Spring Harbor Symposia on Quantitative Biology, vol. 55, pp. 585–597. Cold Spring Harbor Laboratory Press (1990)
23. Zhu, J., Zeng, H., Du, Y., Lei, Z., Zheng, L., Cai, C.: Joint feature and similarity deep learning for vehicle re-identification. IEEE Access **6**, 43724–43731 (2018)

Razor SNN: Efficient Spiking Neural Network with Temporal Embeddings

Yuan Zhang[1], Jian Cao[1(✉)], Jue Chen[1], Wenyu Sun[2], and Yuan Wang[3]

[1] School of Software and Microelectronics, Peking University, Beijing, China
zhangyuan@stu.pku.edu.cn
[2] Alibaba Group, Hangzhou, China
[3] School of Integrated Circuits, Peking University, Beijing, China

Abstract. The event streams generated by dynamic vision sensors (DVS) are sparse and non-uniform in the spatial domain, while still dense and redundant in the temporal domain. Although spiking neural network (SNN), the event-driven neuromorphic model, has the potential to extract spatio-temporal features from the event streams, it is not effective and efficient. Based on the above, we propose an events sparsification spiking framework dubbed as Razor SNN, pruning pointless event frames progressively. Concretely, we extend the dynamic mechanism based on the global temporal embeddings, reconstruct the features, and emphasize the events effect adaptively at the training stage. During the inference stage, eliminate fruitless frames hierarchically according to a binary mask generated by the trained temporal embeddings. Comprehensive experiments demonstrate that our Razor SNN achieves competitive performance consistently on four events-based benchmarks: DVS 128 Gesture, N-Caltech 101, CIFAR10-DVS and SHD.

Keywords: Efficient SNNs · DVS · Temporal embeddings · Pruning

1 Introduction

Event-based neuromorphic computation utilizes sparse and asynchronous events captured by DVS to represent signals more efficiently. Unlike RGB cameras, DVS encodes the time, location, and polarity of the brightness changes for each pixel at high event rates [10]. Although the events are sparse in the spatial domain, the streams they composed are dense in the temporal domain. This characteristic makes event streams hardly process directly through deep neural networks (DNNs), which are based on dense computation. Fortunately, spiking neural networks (SNNs) have an event-triggered computation characteristic that matches well with processing events. However, it is desirable to accelerate the SNN models to be more suitable and efficient for real-time events tasks and further improve accuracy.

The dynamic mechanism owns attention recipes, which selectively focus on the most informative components of the input, and can be interpreted as the

This work was supported by the National Key Research and Development Program of China (Grant No. 2018YFE0203801).

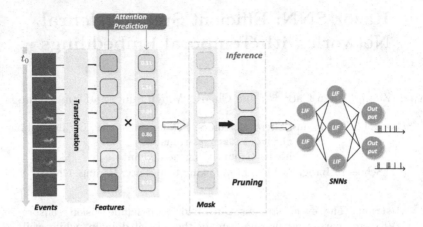

Fig. 1. Event pruning for a spike layer in Razor SNN.

sensitivity of output to the variant input. As for SNNs, inspired by [17] and [24], we propose the **temporal embeddings** combined with the dynamic mechanism for SNNs, to explore the unstructured and data-dependent strategy. Heaps of prior works [2, 10, 24] are dedicated to the spatial-wise attention. Different from above works, the temporal embeddings emphasize on dense ticks of event streams.

As shown in Fig. 1, we present an event pruning mechanism for the temporal domain by embeddings, to adaptively filter out immaterial events and get the SNNs slim. It would reconstruct features and predict attention vectors, to compute the probabilities of dropping the events, while retaining the event-triggered characteristic. We get the pruning architecture as Razor SNN. Our method reveals the possibility of exploiting the dynamic mechanism with temporal embeddings for the acceleration of SNNs and RNNs-like models. The contributions are listed as follows:

* Rethink the DVS events characteristics in both spatial and temporal aspects, and propose the novel pruning method named Razor SNN. It can do inference tasks with less data but higher performance. To the best of our knowledge, this is the first work to design a dynamic mechanism with temporal embeddings for SNNs.
* Our Razor SNN can achieve competitive performances on events recognition tasks, even compared with full-events inputs. Besides, it gets improvement of accuracy for gesture recognition with inference only 65 ms.

2   Related Works

2.1   Object Recognition Using DVS

For events recognition matched with a dynamic vision camera, processing the events as groups is the most common method, to yield sufficient signal-to-noise ratios (SNR) [1]. In this paper, we adopt the frame-based representation that accumulates events occured in a time window and maps into a frame [24]. It is convenient to generate frame-based representation and naturally compatible with the traditional computer vision framework. Besides, SNN algorithms based on frames benefit from faster convergence for training [14]. Timestep and window size is crucial to determine the quality of frame-based representation, the larger window size is, the higher SNR we could have. The prior works have been dedicated to taking various techniques to improve the classification performance based on the large window size. [21, 29] attempt to improve performance by taking training methods, while [4, 23] by changing the connection path of the SNNs, and [6, 8] through hybrid fusion.

2.2 Spiking Neural Networks

Based on the biologically plausible, the spiking neuron computes by transforming dynamic input into a series of spikes. Spike-based SNNs is to assume that the neurons which have not received any input spikes will skip computations, called event-triggered characteristic [15]. There are heaps of research works on launching spiking neural networks for recognition tasks [18]. Diehl et al. proposed a mechanism utilizing Spike Time Dependent Plasticity (STDP) [3], lateral inhibition and homeostasis to recognize. Lee et al. and Delbruck et al. have proposed a supervised learning mechanism mimicking back-propagation of conventional ANNs that can efficiently learn [12]. The first one uses feed-forward layers of spiking neurons and a variant of back-propagation by defining an error function between desired and spiking activity. Wu et al. proposed Spatio-Temporal Backpropagation (STBP), a learning rule for back-propagating error in temporal and spatio domain [20]. This addresses the problem of approximating the derivative of the spike function that inherently brings in the question of biological plausibility. In this work, we adopt LIAF models as the elements of spike-based SNNs and STBP to evaluate the network architecture.

2.3 Model Acceleration of SNNs

There are various solutions that aim to compress or accelerate spiking neural networks. Structural network pruning methods explicitly prune out filters [9]. Knowledge distillation methods [11, 27, 28] can guide the training of a student model with learnt knowledge, such as predictions and features, from a higher-capacity teacher (ANNs or SNNs). Some works design synchronous hardware inference mechanisms with parallelization strategies [13]. In our work, however, we aim to accelerate a SNN model based on feature map reconstruction with constraining width and depth of the model.

3 Razor SNN

3.1 Iterative LIAF Model

We first introduce the Leaky Integrate-and-Fire (LIF) model, a balance between complex dynamic characteristics and simpler mathematical form, and translate

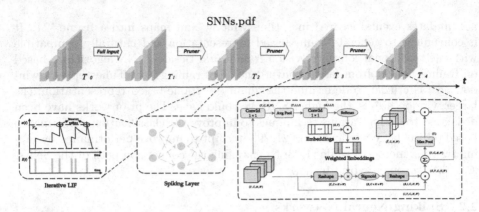

Fig. 2. The complete forward flow of Razor SNN with Event Pruning Mechanism. The feature maps colored green are processed at timestamp T_i. The dashed box in the bottom right corner represents the Event Pruning Mechanism we proposed. Zoom up to view better.

it to an iterative expression with the Euler method [21]. Mathematically it is updated as:

$$u(t + 1) = \tau u(t) + I(t), \tag{1}$$

where $u(t)$ denotes the neuronal membrane potential at time t, τ is a time constant for the leaky behavior and $I(t)$ is the pre-synaptic input. The LIF model is as follows:

$$a_i^{t+1,\, l} = \sum_{j=1}^{l-1} W_{i,j}^n O_j^{t+1,l-1}. \tag{2}$$

Equation 2 comes from the spatial domain. Where a_i is the axon inputs of the ith neuron, $W_{i,j}^n$ is the synaptic weight from the jth neuron in previous layer to the ith neuron and O_j is the output of the jth neuron, whose value can only be 1 or 0. Besides, where the t means the timestamp, l represents the lth layer:

$$u_i^{t+1,\, l} = u_i^{t,l} h\left(O_i^{t,l}\right) + a_i^{t+1,l}. \tag{3}$$

Equation 3 comes from the temporal domain (TD). u_i is the membrane potential of the ith neuron. $h(x)$ means the rate of TD memory loss as follows:

$$h(x) = \tau e^{-\frac{x}{\tau}}. \tag{4}$$

Equation 5 is the output of the ith neuron, responsible for checking whether the membrane potential exceeds the threshold V_{th} and firing a spike or not:

$$O_i^{t+1,\, l} = \begin{cases} 1 & u_i^{t+1,l} \geq V_{th}, \\ 0 & u_i^{t+1,l} < V_{th}. \end{cases} \tag{5}$$

However, introducing the LIF model into the last layer will lose information on the membrane potential and disturb the performance. Instead, we adpot the leaky integrate-and-analog-fire (LIAF) model. LIAF changes the Heaviside step function to ReLU function, then both spatial and temporal domains are analog values.

3.2 Event Pruning Mechanism

The precise observation of significant events is the keystone to Dynamic Event Pruner. Unlike vanilla attention mechanisms, Razor SNN takes the information from neighboring frames into consideration with Global Temporal Embeddings. Besides, Prune the refined events to purify inputs. For simplicity, we follow method [24] that the spatial input of lth layer at tth timestamp $O^{t,\,l-1}$ equals to $X^{t,\,l-1} \in \mathbb{R}^{C \times H \times W}$, where X is the feature maps tensor and C is channel size.

Global Temporal Embeddings. We introduce a set of learnable global temporal embeddings $B \in \mathbb{R}^{E \times T}$ to extract E sequence principles on temporal features. Notably, not all embeddings play the same role. For example, we would assign more attention on the moment when events are dense, while less on that when events are sparse. In this paper, we propose an embedding weighting module to determine the embedding importance independently. Concretely, we conduct a convolution-based module with softmax function (see Fig. 2) to predict, and weight the importance vector w onto the temporal embeddings to generate weighted embeddings $\hat{B}$:

$$\hat{B}^t = \sum_{i=1}^{T} w_i \odot B^t. \tag{6}$$

Reconstruct Events Feature. We accumulate the feature maps within T and flatten X into shape of $(T, C \times H \times W)$ in the paper. Then the Events of Interests (EoI) masks M can be obtained by calculating the similarities between weighted embeddings and the temporal frames in the feature maps:

$$M = \sigma(\hat{B}X), \tag{7}$$

where σ denotes sigmoid activation function. Eventually, multiplying with the masks, we reconstruct Events Feature and get the refined feature $\hat{X}$, which is a better substitute for the vanilla features:

$$\hat{X} = \sum_{i=1}^{E} M \odot X. \tag{8}$$

Pruning Strategy. Due to the refined feature has contained discriminative temporal information provided by the Global Temporal Embeddings, it is what the pruning mechanism based on. We only need to send the refined feature to the adaptive max pooling 3d for extracting importance scores of temporal features $S \in \mathbb{R}^T$, which is as follows:

$$S = max_{i=1}^{H} max_{j=1}^{W} max_{k=1}^{C} \hat{\boldsymbol{X}}, \tag{9}$$

While during inference, we will generate a binary mask $\boldsymbol{M}$ according to the scores, where eliminate pointless frames which are lower than filtering threshold S_{th} we set, and set the attention score of the other frames to 1.

$$\boldsymbol{M} = \boldsymbol{H}(\boldsymbol{S} - \boldsymbol{S}_{th}). \tag{10}$$

$\boldsymbol{H}(\cdot)$ is a Heaviside step function that is same as in Eq. 5. Eventually, we combine the mask $\boldsymbol{M}$ with the input tensor, and the formed input at tth timestamp is:

$$\widetilde{\boldsymbol{X}}^{t,l-1} = \boldsymbol{M}^{t,l-1} \odot \hat{\boldsymbol{X}}^{t,l-1}. \tag{11}$$

3.3   Architecture Design of RazorSNNs

We implement the RazorSNNs with embedding the Event Pruning Mechanism into each spiking layer except the encoder layer (the first layer). The reason is that, we assume SNN cannot extract more spatio-temporal information in this condition and pruning the whole network leads to unstable results. We follow the recent state-of-the-art methods [19,24] to use a x-stage pyramid structure, and the Razor Pruning Architecture is shown in Fig. 2.

4   Experimental Results

In this section, to show our method superiority and effectiveness, we conduct experiments on three popular event-based benchmarks: DVS Gesture, N-Caltech and CIFAR10-DVS.

4.1   Implementation Details

In this paper, we follow the similar notation as Yao et al. [24] to define our network architectures separately for DVS128 Gesture, SHD and CIFAR10-DVS, while N-Caltech's is the same as DVS128 Gesture's. Besides, We take rate coding as loss function, and utilize the Adam optimizer for accelerating the training process. The corresponding hyperparameters details are shown in Table 1 (Table 2).

Table 1. Comprehensive parameters for experiments.

Parameter	Description	Value
dt	Window size	1 ms
V_{th}	Fire threshold	0.3
$e^{-\frac{dt}{\tau}}$	Leakage factor	0.3
S_{th}	Razor ratio	0.4

Table 2. Accuracy of models for the SHD Dataset (%).

Methods	Architecture	SHD
Cramer [5]	LIF RSNN	71.40
Yin [26]	RELU SRNN	88.93
Zenke [25]	SG-based SNN	84.00
Yao [24]	TA-SNN	91.08
Ours	Razor SNN	**92.83**

4.2 Performance Comparison

We compare Razor SNN with various of prior works for event-based data, like CNN method, spike-based SNN, and analog-based SNN, on above mentioned benchmarks. The experiment results are shown in Table 3. From the results, our Razor SNN outperforms the strong baseline with a margin on SHD, CIFAR series and N-Caltech 101, and achieves competitive performance on DVS128 Gesture.

SHD. The SHD dataset [5] is a large spike-based audio classification task that contains 10420 audio samples of spoken digits ranging from zero to nine in English and German languages. Unlike the fourdimensional event stream generated by the DVS camera, the audio spike stream has only two dimensions, i.e., time and position. Our method surpasses the previous state-of-the-art by 1.75%, and verify the effectiveness of the Temporal embedding module.

DVS128 Gesture. Almost all the spike-based SNNs methods evaluate their model on it. Razor SNN surpasses TA-SNN by 0.22% and outperforms all CNN-based methods. Due to unique temporal feature extraction and reconstruction, Razor SNN has superior ability to distinguish the clockwise and counterclockwise of gestures, which are easily confused.

N-Caltech 101. N-Caltech is a spiking version of frame-based Caltech101 dataset, which is a large-scale Events dataset. Few methods tested on N-Caltech because of the complicate background and computational complexity. Notably, Razor SNN still gets a nearly 2.1% increase over the TA-SNN, and outperforms all the SOTA methods. Besides, the temporal embeddings function as the attention module when SNNs meet static image, which is beneficial to classification.

CIFAR10-DVS. Compared to the best result TA-SNN so far, our method gets 1.01% improvement, attributed to its global temporal module catching critical events information and filter temporal noise, which damages SNNs accuracy. Our Razor SNN shows better generalization on large-scale data set, where exists more noisy and pointless events.

Moreover, the number of parameters in Razor SNN only has weak increase compared with the vanilla SNN. So the events pruning mechanism can afford SNNs to achieve higher performance with less cost for practical applications.

Table 3. Comparison of different methods on DVS-Gesture, N-Caltech 101 and CIFAR10-DVS (%).

Methods	Architecture	Gesture	N-Caltech	CIFAR10
Wu [21]	NeuNorm	-	-	60.50
Ramesh [16]	DART	-	66.8	65.78
Kugele [8]	DenseNet	95.56	-	66.75
Wu [22]	LIAF-Net	97.56	-	70.40
Zheng [29]	ResNet19	96.87	-	67.80
Kim [7]	SALT	67.10	55.0	-
Wu [19]	ASF-BP	93.40	60.23	62.50
Yao [24]	TA-SNN	98.61	68.42	72.00
Ours	Razor SNN	**98.83**	**70.50**	**73.01**

4.3 Ablation Studies

The Number of Temporal Embeddings. We perform experiments on DVS Gesture to explore the effects of different numbers of temporal embeddings in Razor SNN. As shown in Table 4, with only 2 embeddings, Event Pruning improves SNN by 0.84% Acc, while more tokens could achieve further improvements. In this paper, we choose a number of **4** for a better performance.

Table 4. Ablation on the number of temporal embeddings.

0 (vanilla)	2	4	6	8
97.99	98.56	**98.83**	98.79	98.34

The Position of Where to Prune. It is vital to figure out that we should insert temporal embeddings into which layers to prune, and we design four sets of experiments to explore. E1, pure SNNs baseline; E2, introduce temporal embeddings into the encoder layer; E3, introduce temporal embeddings into the backbone layers. E4, introduce temporal embeddings into all the layers. As shown in

Fig. 3, we observe that E2 and E3 independently afford improvement in most cases, where E3 achieves the best accuracy when T=120. But E4, who owns E2 and E3 simultaneously, leads to unstable results, and we assume SNNs cannot extract more spatio-temporal information in this condition.

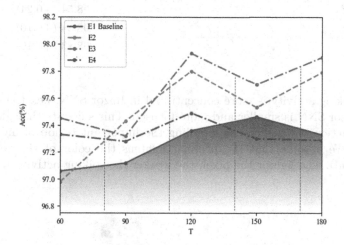

Fig. 3. E1, pure SNNs baseline; E2, introduce embeddings into the encoder layer; E3, introduce embeddings into the backbone layers. E4, introduce embeddings into all the layers.

Effects of Components in Event Pruning Mechanism. We set experiments to show the contribution of each proposed component in Mechanism in Table 5. **+ Embeddings.** Global temporal embeddings benefit most (0.31%) for Razor SNNs due to its consideration of neighboring frames and extraction of temporal features. **+ Embeddings weighting module.** Embedding weighting module decides the embedding importance independently and provide discriminative information and gains by 0.24%. **+ Reconstruct Events Feature.** The refined feature has contained discriminative temporal information, and experiment statics (0.10%) proves that it a better substitute for the original features indeed. **+ Pruning.** Pruning eliminates worthless events contained much noise which disturb the SNNs model.

4.4 Visualization Analysis

To validate the effectiveness of Razor SNN, we visualize the case that when the vanilla SNN fails in recognition, the Razor SNN succeeds. As shown in Fig. 4, each feature indicates the average response of a spiking layer. We make the following two observations about the effect of temporal embeddings and reconstruction of Razor SNN.

Table 5. Ablation experiments on effects of components in Event Pruning Mechanism.

Embeddings	Weighting	Reconstruct	Pruning	Acc (%)
-	-	-	-	97.99 (baseline)
✓	-	-	-	98.30 (**+0.31**)
✓	✓	-	-	98.54 (+0.24)
✓	✓	✓	-	98.64 (+0.10)
✓	✓	✓	✓	98.83 (+0.19)

The spiking activity is more concentrated in Razor SNN, i.e., the deep blue area of Razor SNN is smaller and more focused. This suggests that global temporal extraction is beneficial to handling the important region of intermediate channels. We observe that the pruning lightens the color of the yellow area (background). The lighter the pixel, the weaker the spiking activity rate.

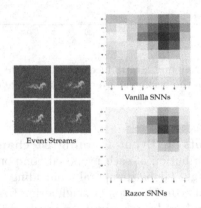

Fig. 4. Visualization of the heat maps generated by vanilla SNNs and Razor SNNs separately. The temporal embeddings and reconstructed features urge SNNs to centre on the gesture instead of distraction somewhere like vanilla models. Best viewed in color.

5   Conclusion

In this paper, we innovatively introduce dynamic attention mechanism based on temporal embeddings into SNNs, and propose the Razor SNNs. Compared with vanilla Spiking Neural Networks, Razor SNNs process signals more efficiently, especially for event streams, pruning pointless event frames progressively. Our method enjoys finer temporal-level feature and prunes worthless events frames. Extensive experiments show that, our Razor SNNs apply to various benchmarks and can achieve state-of-the-art performance consistently.

References

1. Amir, A., et al.: A low power, fully event-based gesture recognition system. In: Proceedings of the IEEE Conference on Computer Vision and Pattern Recognition, pp. 7243–7252 (2017)
2. Cannici, M., Ciccone, M., et al.: Attention mechanisms for object recognition with event-based cameras. In: WACV (2019)
3. Caporale, N., Dan, Y.: Spike timing-dependent plasticity: a hebbian learning rule. Annu. Rev. Neurosci. **31**, 25–46 (2008)
4. Cheng, X., Hao, Y., Xu, J., Xu, B.: LISNN: improving spiking neural networks with lateral interactions for robust object recognition. In: IJCAI, pp. 1519–1525 (2020)
5. Cramer, B., Stradmann, Y., Schemmel, J., Zenke, F.: The heidelberg spiking data sets for the systematic evaluation of spiking neural networks. IEEE Trans. Neural Netw. Learn. Syst. **33**(7), 2744–2757 (2020)
6. Deng, L., et al.: Rethinking the performance comparison between SNNs and ANNs. Neural Netw. **121**, 294–307 (2020)
7. Kim, Y., Panda, P.: Optimizing deeper spiking neural networks for dynamic vision sensing. Neural Netw. **144**, 686–698 (2021)
8. Kugele, A., Pfeil, T., et al.: Efficient processing of spatio-temporal data streams with spiking neural networks. Front. Neurosci. **14**, 439 (2020)
9. Kundu, S., Datta, G., Pedram, M., Beerel, P.A.: Towards low-latency energy-efficient deep snns via attention-guided compression. arXiv preprint arXiv:2107.12445 (2021)
10. Kundu, S., et al.: Spike-thrift: towards energy-efficient deep spiking neural networks by limiting spiking activity via attention-guided compression. In: CVPR (2021)
11. Kushawaha, R.K., Kumar, S., Banerjee, B., Velmurugan, R.: Distilling spikes: knowledge distillation in spiking neural networks. In: 2020 25th International Conference on Pattern Recognition (ICPR), pp. 4536–4543. IEEE (2021)
12. Lee, J.H., Delbruck, T., Pfeiffer, M.: Training deep spiking neural networks using backpropagation. Front. Neurosci. **10**, 508 (2016)
13. Panchapakesan, S., Fang, Z., Li, J.: SyncNN: evaluating and accelerating spiking neural networks on FPGAs. In: 2021 31st International Conference on Field-Programmable Logic and Applications (FPL), pp. 286–293. IEEE (2021)
14. Pérez-Carrasco, J.A., et al.: Mapping from frame-driven to frame-free event-driven vision systems by low-rate rate coding and coincidence processing-application to feedforward convnets. IEEE Trans. Pattern Anal. Mach. Intell. **35**(11), 2706–2719 (2013)
15. Pfeiffer, M., Pfeil, T.: Deep learning with spiking neurons: opportunities and challenges. Front. Neurosci. **12**, 774 (2018)
16. Ramesh, B., Yang, H., et al.: DART: distribution aware retinal transform for event-based cameras. TPAMI **42**(11), 2767–2780 (2019)
17. Rao, Y., et al.: DynamicViT: efficient vision transformers with dynamic token sparsification. In: Advances in Neural Information Processing Systems (2021)
18. Rückauer, B., Känzig, N., Liu, S.C., Delbruck, T., Sandamirskaya, Y.: Closing the accuracy gap in an event-based visual recognition task. arXiv preprint arXiv:1906.08859 (2019)
19. Wu, H., et al.: Training spiking neural networks with accumulated spiking flow. In: Proceedings of the AAAI Conference on Artificial Intelligence, vol. 35, pp. 10320–10328 (2021)

20. Wu, Y., Deng, L., et al.: Spatio-temporal backpropagation for training high-performance spiking neural networks. Front. Neurosci. **12**, 331 (2018)
21. Wu, Y., Deng, L., et al.: Direct training for spiking neural networks: faster, larger, better. In: AAAI (2019)
22. Wu, Z., Zhang, H., et al.: LIAF-Net: leaky integrate and analog fire network for lightweight and efficient spatiotemporal information processing. IEEE Trans. Neural Netw. Learn. Syst. **33**(11), 6249–6262 (2021)
23. Xu, Q., Qi, Y., Yu, H., Shen, J., Tang, H., Pan, G., et al.: CSNN: an augmented spiking based framework with perceptron-inception. In: IJCAI, pp. 1646–1652 (2018)
24. Yao, M., et al.: Temporal-wise attention spiking neural networks for event streams classification. In: ICCV (2021)
25. Yin, B., Corradi, F., Bohté, S.M.: Effective and efficient computation with multiple-timescale spiking recurrent neural networks. In: International Conference on Neuromorphic Systems 2020, pp. 1–8 (2020)
26. Zenke, F., Vogels, T.P.: The remarkable robustness of surrogate gradient learning for instilling complex function in spiking neural networks. Neural Comput. **33**(4), 899–925 (2021)
27. Zhang, L., Cao, J., Zhang, Y., Zhou, B., Feng, S.: Distilling neuron spike with high temperature in reinforcement learning agents. arXiv preprint arXiv:2108.10078 (2021)
28. Zhang, Y., Chen, W., Lu, Y., Huang, T., Sun, X., Cao, J.: Avatar knowledge distillation: self-ensemble teacher paradigm with uncertainty. arXiv preprint arXiv:2305.02722 (2023)
29. Zheng, H., Wu, Y., et al.: Going deeper with directly-trained larger spiking neural networks. arXiv preprint arXiv:2011.05280 (2020)

Real-Time Adaptive Physical Sensor Processing with SNN Hardware

Jordi Madrenas[1]([envelope]) [iD], Bernardo Vallejo-Mancero[1] [iD],
Josep Àngel Oltra-Oltra[1] [iD], Mireya Zapata[2] [iD], Jordi Cosp-Vilella[1] [iD],
Robert Calatayud[1] [iD], Satoshi Moriya[3] [iD], and Shigeo Sato[3] [iD]

[1] Department of Electronic Engineering, Universitat Politècnica de Catalunya,
Barcelona, Catalunya, Spain
jordi.madrenas@upc.edu
[2] Centro de Investigación en Mecatrónica y Sistemas Interactivos - MIST,
Universidad Indoamérica, Quito, Ecuador
[3] Research Institute of Electrical Communication, Tohoku University, Sendai, Japan

Abstract. Spiking Neural Networks (SNNs) offer bioinspired computation based on local adaptation and plasticity as well as close biological compatibility. In this work, after reviewing the Hardware Emulator of Evolving Neural Systems (HEENS) architecture and its Computer-Aided Engineering (CAE) design flow, a spiking implementation of an adaptive physical sensor input scheme based on time-rate Band-Pass Filter (BPF) is proposed for real-time execution of large dynamic range sensory edge processing nodes. Simulation and experimental results of the SNN operating in real-time with an adaptive-range accelerometer input example are shown. This work opens the path to compute with SNNs multiple physical sensor information for perception applications.

Keywords: Spiking Neural Networks (SNNs) · HEENS · Real-time sensor processing · Spike-rate filters · adaptive-range sensors

1 Introduction

1.1 Spiking Neural Networks (SNNs)

SNNs are becoming more and more relevant to Machine Learning (ML) applications. They offer bioinspired computation based on local adaptation and plasticity as well as closer biological compatibility than Artificial Neural Network (ANN) counterparts, which makes them well-suited not only for engineering but also for biomedical applications. Because of their closeness to natural neurons and computation capability, SNNs are considered the third generation of neural networks [1].

Grant PID2021-123535OB-I00 funded by MCIN/AEI/10.13039/501100011033 and by ERDF A way of making Europe.

L. Iliadis et al. (Eds.): ICANN 2023, LNCS 14258, pp. 423–434, 2023.
https://doi.org/10.1007/978-3-031-44192-9_34

As it happens with general ANNs, SNNs demand for most applications a large number of units and synapses, thus requiring intensive computation. Also, general computing platforms and software implementations are not well-suited to cope with real-time response. First, the general-purpose processing units and the Instruction Set Architecture (ISA) are normally oversized for the required data precision and neural operations. Because of this, power consumption is not efficiently utilized. Second, the parallelism degree is generally too low for the required computation. Finally, the system size also limits the application of SNNs to embedded systems, Internet of Things (IoT) applications or edge computing [2].

Furthermore, as biological neural processing is not yet well understood, being ML still far from biological intelligence, there are plenty of opportunities in the development of SNN algorithms and neural topologies. For this purpose, it is necessary to count with efficient hardware that helps software engineers and neuroscientists in the fast verification of experimental prototypes.

1.2   SNN Emulating Hardware

Because of the previously stated facts, the development of hardware platforms that emulate SNNs has become an active research topic. In contrast with *simulation*, we understand by *emulation* when the system responds in real time.

Hardware Implementations of SNNs. SNNs can be deployed with pure analog, mixed-signal or digital technology. Analog implementations are the most compact but less flexible, e.g. [3]. Their niche of application is ultra-low power with a fixed topology and medium complexity. Digital implementations are more scalable and easier to configure at the cost of increased resource and power consumption. Mixed-signal implementations [4] intend to get the best of each domain, but it can be argued that they also can inherit limiting aspects from both. Since the aim of this work is to develop a flexible architecture to allow prototyping of any neural and synaptic model, with good scalability and reconfigurability and easily adapted to sensor interfaces, we have focused on pure digital implementations.

Digital Hardware Examples. To cite a few relevant examples of previously reported digital SNN implementations, we can consider the following ones:

- The SpiNNaker system has been developed under the EU-funded Human Brain Project [5]. The system uses asynchronous spike distribution. It is based on ARM processors, which makes it easily programmable, sacrificing efficiency of dedicated hardware to gain software flexibility.
- TrueNorth [6] is the IBM's proposal of custom neuromorphic Integrated Circuit (IC). It is also event-driven and uses cores with 256 axons, 256 neurons and programmable 256×256 synaptic crossbar, achieving a million neurons per chip. Neurons are however limited to specific models, especially Leaky Integrate and Fire (LIF).

– Loihi 2 [7] was developed by Intel. The chip is manufactured in a 14 nm process and introduces a microcode programmable neural engine, integrating 128 neuromorphic cores and 3×86 cores. This gives the chip more flexibility to define different SNN models.

Each proposed hardware solution shows specific advantages and limitations. Custom chips offer the maximum performance per resource and power, while SpiNNaker offers maximum flexibility. In between, there is room to propose efficient architectures that use programmable logic, reducing the power consumption of conventional processors and offering a high degree of flexibility for prototyping SNNs. This is the case of HEENS, introduced in Sect. 2. In Sect. 3, the HEENS CAE Flow is described, including a spike-rate BPF application example and the proposal of architecture modification to enable adaptive external sensor inputs. In Sect. 4, experimental results of the real-time operation with external accelerometer sensor input are presented. Finally, in Sect. 5 Conclusions and Ongoing Work are pointed out.

2 HEENS Multiprocessor Architecture Review

For the sake of completeness, the main characteristics and properties of the HEENS architecture are summarized here. HEENS is a second-generation architecture based on a previous SNN [8] that supports multiple SNN models, such as LIF [9], Izhikevich model [10], and any one that can be computed locally in an algorithm, with 16-bit precision. Of course, too complex algorithms may not be computed in real-time. Besides this, HEENS introduces Random Access Memory (RAM) decoding for spike routing, which allows for the connection reconfiguration, thus supporting the development of evolutive SNNs.

Figure 1 shows the HEENS multiprocessor node (left) and the Processing Element (PE) (right) block diagrams. A sequencer control unit (left) dispatches the instructions of neural and synaptic algorithms that are executed in parallel by the PEs array. The generated spikes are efficiently transmitted by a serial synchronous Address Event Representation (AER) bus with point-to-point connection [11]. This allows to create a ring of HEENS processors, being this out of scope of this work, that concentrates in a single node. In Fig. 1 (right), the PE diagram is shown. It consists of two banks of 8 16-bit registers, a custom ALU with a multiplier and saturated arithmetic, a 64-bit LFSR for pseudo-random noise generation and two memory blocks. The top one contains the synaptic and neural parameters associated with the neurons mapped to each PE. The bottom one is used as an associative memory that decodes the incoming spike address, detecting the programmed synapses. This way, reconfigurable connectivity is supported without the need of complex interconnect schemes. The architecture has been proposed to:

– Minimize resource usage and power consumption.
– Support of any neural or synaptic algorithm (multi-model) such as LIF, Izikhevich, and others.

- Support synaptic plasticity such as Spike Timing-Dependent Plasticity (STDP).
- Permit complex and reconfigurable connectivity.
- Offer good scalability (by means of point-to-point ring connection).
- Execute in biological time scale (real time ∼1 ms).
- Evaluate continuously neurons within a time frame (noise).
- Support evolution: Simple reconfiguration of connections and neurons.

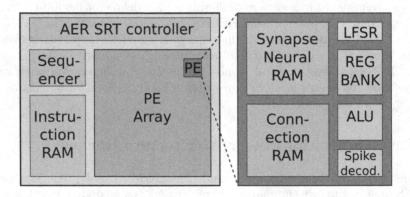

Fig. 1. HEENS node (left) and PE architecture.

The compact and flexible properties of the HEENS architecture, makes it well-suited for applications that can interact with external sensors, discrete or integrated (MEMS [12]).

3 SNN Application Flow

3.1 HEENS CAE Software Tool

The software support to SNN hardware architectures has become fundamental to easily enable the network definition and programming [13].

Figure 2 shows the developed software tools that enable a user-friendly environment [14]. The user simply writes a text netlist of connected neurons, specifying the connection weight and other parameters, and selects the neural model, for instance, LIF or Izhikevich. The model and network compilation are automatically done and uploaded to the FPGA by means of an Ethernet connection, The user then controls the network execution and displays in real-time the raster plot and selected membrane potentials in an HDMI display [15,16].

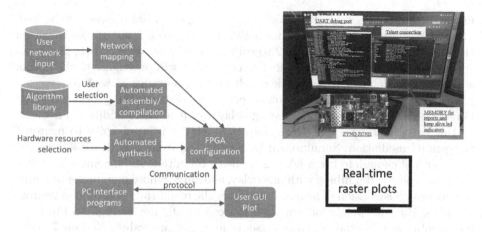

Fig. 2. HEENS CAE flow chart.

3.2   Spike-Rate Band Pass Filter Example

In order to demonstrate the connection of sensors to the HEENS system, a spike-rate BPF example is presented. Although different models could be applied, for this example, a LIF neural model is used, with conventional weighted synapses. The SNN parameters have been defined as:

- Voltage unit, one Least Significant Bit (LSB): $V_{LSB} = 10\ m$ V
- Threshold voltage $V_{th} = -55$ mV $= -5500 \times V_{LSB}$
- Resting potential $V_{rest} = -70$ mV $= -7000 \times V_{LSB}$
- Threshold to Resting voltage Δ V $= 15$ mV $= 1500 \times V_{LSB}$
- Membrane decay time constant: 20 ms
- Emulation cycle time: 1 ms

In general, real time is considered if the emulation time step is in 1 ms slots. The HEENS system can support faster speeds, but this is the one selected for real-time.

Figure 3 shows the time-rate spiking BPF. It is composed of a spike stream generator (neurons 0–2), and a cascade of a Low Pass Filter (LPF) (neurons 3, 4) and a High Pass Filter (HPF) (neurons 5–8). Neurons 0–2 implement a programmable oscillator. Bearing into account that the threshold voltage has been set to 1500, an initial input spike fires neuron 1. The self-feedback produces a continuous oscillation that feeds the neuron 2 input. By means of the d_{OSC} synapse value, the output spike rate can be controlled. This is useful to simulate the filter for different input rates.

The LPF operates as a delay line, with a feedforward inhibition signal. Same as the oscillator, when neuron 2 produces a first spike, neuron 3 oscillates, generating a spike stream, due to its self-feedback. The adjustable delay d_{LPF} determines the number of spikes needed to rise the membrane potential of neuron 4 up to its threshold voltage. If a new input spike appears before neuron 2 can fire, its membrane potential is reset to the resting potential because of the feed-forward inhibition. This means that if the time between input spikes is shorter than the time needed for neuron 2 to spike, it will never do it. Thus, fast input spike rates will be eliminated, while low-rate spikes will propagate to the output with constant delay. Therefore, the cutoff rate is programmed with d_{LPF}.

The HPF operates with a similar principle, distinguishing between times longer or shorter than a discriminating delay, but it requires additional neurons. In this case, neurons 6 and 7 calculate this delay. An input spike to neuron 6 triggers its oscillation. Simultaneously, neuron 8 is excited with a 1400 weight, close but not enough to fire it (Δ V is needed). Simultaneously, neuron 5 receives the same spike and inhibits, with one delay, neuron 8, whose membrane potential is thus reset. Oscillation of neuron 6 increases the membrane potential of neurons 7 and 8. But the weight of neuron 8 is weak (150), not enough to fire it, so its membrane potential remains at some intermediate value. Neuron 7 has a higher weight $d_{HPF} > 150$. Thus, depending on this value, it will fire after some shorter or longer time. If a new input spike appears before neuron 7 fires, it will fire neuron 8, because its membrane potential has been increased by the oscillation of neuron 6, and neuron 7 is reset by the 4–7 inhibition synapse. On the contrary, when neuron 7 fires, it inhibits neurons 6 and 8 resetting the network and preventing that the new incoming spike is transmitted to the output. In summary, if the input spike rate is fast enough compared to the neuron 7 spiking rate, it will be propagated to the output. If slower, it is filtered out.

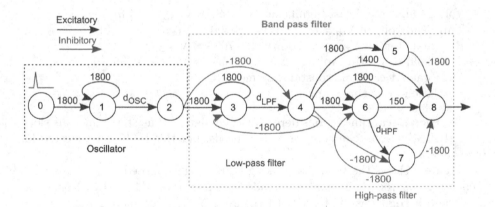

Fig. 3. Spike-rate Band-Pass Filter.

The LPF, the BPF and the HPF response functions are shown in Fig. 4(a). As it can be seen, the rates remain unchanged for the pass bands, but they are filtered out for the out-of-band of each filter.

To obtain the low-pass and high-pass response, besides the BPF of Fig. 3, an additional instance of HPF is used. The LPF is not replicated because the output of neuron 4 in Fig. 3 already provides this response.

Since biological senses tend to reduce the sensitivity to strong input stimuli with time and to potentiate it for weak inputs, an adaptive feedback to the input sensors has been implemented in a simple but effective way, that consists in analyzing the three filter outputs. Assuming that the sensor response intensity is rate-encoded, the feedback circuit will increase (UP neuron) or decrease (DOWN neuron) the sensor sensitivity when the LPF or the HPF are active, respectively, as shown in Fig. 4(b). Both LPF and HPF potentiate their respective neuron and inhibit the counterpart. In the middle rate band, when the BPF is active, inhibition to both output neurons occurs, as the rate is in the nominal range. The weights have been selected for this work demonstration, but they can be adjusted to the needs of particular sensors or time adaptations.

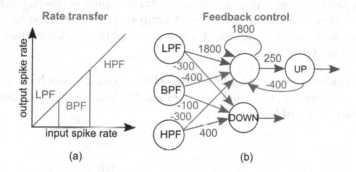

Fig. 4. a) Transfer rate for LPF, HPF and BPF; b) Feedback control.

3.3   Introducing Sensor Inputs

So far, the HEENS implementations have been used to demonstrate the architecture flexibility to emulate multi-model, real-time, self-contained SNNs. The stimuli have been either generated by means of internal noise using the embedded Linear-Feedback Shift Registers (LFSRs), or applying an initial condition to some neurons and sustaining the excitation by means of close-loop neuron oscillators. However, the intended use of the HEENS architecture is to interact in real-time with artificial and natural neural systems, with power consumption as low as possible.

In Fig. 5(a), the proposed scheme for multiple physical sensor processing is shown. The sensor information is converted to AER and input to the SNN processor, which performs the sensor fusion and adaptive processing. The reverse path allows for actuator driving as well as for feedback on sensor devices.

Despite this is a general approach, it requires an additional node to encode, transmit and decode the spikes in AER format. Therefore, for low-power, local processing, it is preferable to directly inject the sensor information encoded in spikes to the HEENS system. This allows to envisage a single-chip solution, including the sensor conditioning and the bioinspired processing, and even the sensors [12], on the same integrated circuit.

For this reason, instead of generating spikes for an external node, in this work, an improved HEENS implementation that supports external sensors is reported. To support the HEENS capability to process external signals from physical sensors, the hardware VHDL code has been modified to directly introduce external spikes. Figure 5(b) shows the new approach concept. The external spikes coming from the sensor conditioning are directly introduced into the PE array. There are in fact two options:

– Synapse introduction: In this approach, a bit of the presynaptic register is loaded with the external incoming spike.
– Neuron combination/replacement: the external spike is directly injected to the postsynaptic spike of the selected neuron. It can be done by means of replacement or by combination, for instance applying a logic function, normally a logic OR.

Both techniques can be introduced in a relatively simple way by slightly modifying the hardware. In this work, as a demonstration, the neuron combination approach has been implemented.

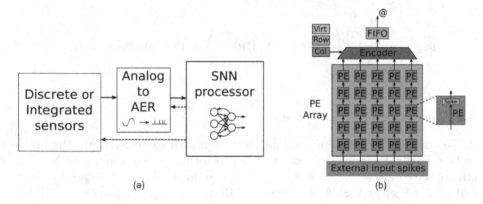

(a)   (b)

Fig. 5. (a) Connection of multiple sensors to HEENS or AER-based SNN hardware; (b) Direct input spike scheme.

4   Experimental Results

The original HEENS implementation of a ZedBoard development plaform [17] has been modified to support external inputs and external outputs. The interaction is through PMOD ports. The present design supports 8 inputs and 24 outputs, but it can be easily expanded or modified.

Figure 6 shows the implemented demonstration example in this work. The HEENS core consists of the PE array, the control processor and the AER SRT controller. For the sake of simplification, the control processor block includes the sequencer, the instruction memory and the dual-core ARM Cortex A9 processor that is included in the ZedBoard FPGA (Zynq Processing System part). As previously indicated, since a single-node is used, the spikes transmitted by the AER block are fed back to the same system. By means of an ethernet connection, the HEENS system can be configured and controlled using the CAE toolbox introduced in the previous Section. The HDMI display allows to present the spike raster plot in real time.

The PE array has been modified to allow external input and output of spikes. The PMOD accelerometer is multiplexed with the switch array (SW in Fig. 6) and the 8-bit value is converted to a spike train by taking the overflow bit of accumulating every millisecond the sensor value on an 8-bit counter (Val 2 spike block). Finally, the Feedback signal that exits the PE array consists of the postsynaptic spikes of the UP and DOWN neurons of Fig. 4(b).

Every time a postsynaptic spike is produced on the UP/DOWN neuron, the input sensor signal is shifted right/left one bit, effectively multiplying/dividing by two, respectively, the sensor value. Thus the amplification or attenuation changes exponentially with the UP/DOWN spikes, which allows to use all the sensor dynamic range by selecting the operating range at every moment. The shifting information is also known, and thus it can also be used to inform the SNN about the current range of operation.

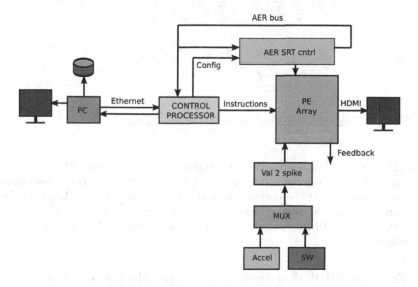

Fig. 6. HEENS direct input/output example.

In this work, an input associated with neuron 0 has been connected to a PMOD ACL accelerometer sensor [18]. The 13-bit acceleration measure is multiplexed to 8 bits. This input is also multiplexed with the ZedBoard switch array, so that it is possible to verify the behavior with manually-selected inputs, or by tilting the accelerometer inclination, measuring an acceleration that goes from 0 to the gravity g, depending on the accelerometer angle.

A 5×5 PE processor including the modification has been synthesized and mapped on a Xilinx ZedBoard evaluation board. Then, the BPF network has been transmitted to the FPGA by means of the HEENS Toolchain Suite (HTS) tool [14]. Figure 7 shows the screen display of the raster plot. The filter selects only a band of the time spikes. The screenshots have been obtained using the HDMI screen display hardware block reported in [16].

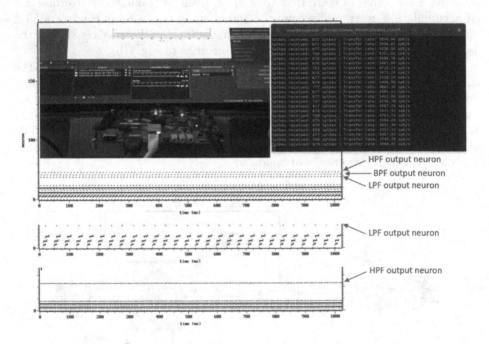

Fig. 7. HEENS real-time operation. At the top left, system picture with the accelerometer connected. At the top right, the monitoring window indicating the spikes transmitted every millisecond. At the bottom, three captures of spike raster plots for different inclinations of the accelerometer, showing in descending order the operation at middle rates (HPF, BPF and LPF spikes), at low rates (LPF-only spikes) and at high rates (HPF-only spikes).

In Fig. 8, the VHDL time simulation shows the adaptive operation performed by the network introduced in Figs. 3 and 4b. The simulation has been performed by means of the Siemens Questa simulator. The detailed explanation is out of scope of this work, but the top signals correspond to the external inputs (a constant 0x3E value is applied) and the central signals labelled spike_disp(*)(*)(*)

show the spikes generated by the LPF, BPF, HPF, UP and DOWN neurons, in descending order. Below them, the membrane potentials of the UP and DOWN neurons are shown.

In this example, a high frequency is applied, thus, only the HPF transmits the input stream to its output, while the LPF and BPF stop it. As it can be observed, approximately every 7 spikes of the HPF produce a spike of the DOWN feedback neuron. The amount of spikes necessary to produce the feedback neuron spike can be adjusted with the presynaptic weights of the DOWN/UP neurons.

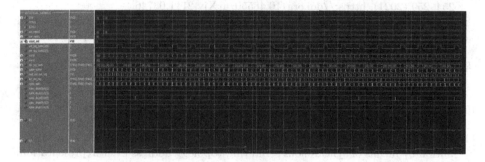

Fig. 8. VHDL simulation showing the adaptive operation of the feedback loop.

5   Conclusion and Future Work

The HEENS architecture and design flow have been introduced. HEENS is well suited for sensors interfacing in SNN applications. A spiking implementation of a time rate BPF has been described and an adaptive physical sensor input scheme has been proposed for real-time execution of sensory edge processing nodes. In the future, a range of sensors will be applied to perform sensor fusion and inference for environment perception applications.

References

1. Maass, W.: Networks of spiking neurons: the third generation of neural network models. Neural Netw. **10**(9), 1659–1671 (1997). https://doi.org/10.1016/S0893-6080(97)00011-7
2. Naveen, S., Kounte, M.R.: Key Technologies and challenges in IoT edge computing. In: Third International conference on I-SMAC (IoT in Social, Mobile, Analytics and Cloud) (I-SMAC), pp. 61–65 (2019). https://doi.org/10.1109/I-SMAC47947.2019.9032541
3. Moriya, S., et al.: Analog-circuit implementation of multiplicative spike-timing-dependent plasticity with linear decay. Nonlinear Theory Appl. IEICE **12**(4), 685–694 (2021). https://doi.org/10.1587/nolta.12.685

4. Pehle, C., et al.: The BrainScaleS-2 accelerated neuromorphic system with hybrid plasticity. Front. Neurosci. **16**, 795876 (2022). https://doi.org/10.3389/fnins.2022. 795876

5. Mayr, C., Hoeppner, S. Furber, S.: SpiNNaker 2: a 10 million core processor system for brain simulation and machine learning (2019). https://doi.org/10.48550/arXiv. 1911.02385

6. Debole, M.V., et al.: TrueNorth: accelerating from zero to 64 million neurons in 10 years. Computer **52**(5), 20–29 (2019). https://doi.org/10.1109/MC.2019.2903009

7. Orchard, G., et al.: Efficient neuromorphic signal processing with Loihi 2. In: IEEE Workshop on Signal Processing Systems, SiPS: Design and Implementation (1), pp. 254–259 (2021). https://doi.org/10.48550/arXiv.2111.03746

8. Sripad, A., et al.: SNAVA-a real-time multi-FPGA multi-model spiking neural network simulation architecture. Neural Netw. **97**, 28–45 (2018). https://doi.org/ 10.1016/j.neunet.2017.09.011

9. Abbott, L.F.: Lapicque's introduction of the integrate-and-fire model neuron. Brain Res. Bull. **50**(5–6), 303–304 (1907). https://doi.org/10.1016/s0361-9230(99)00161-6

10. Izhikevich, E.: Simple model of spiking neurons. IEEE Trans. Neural Netw. **14**(2003), 1569–1572 (2003). https://doi.org/10.1109/TNN.2003.820440

11. Dorta, T., Zapata, M., Madrenas, J., Sánchez, G.: AER-SRT: scalable spike distribution by means of synchronous serial ring topology address event representation. Neurocomputing **171**, 1684–1690 (2016). https://doi.org/10.1016/j.neucom.2015. 07.080

12. Madrenas, J., et al.: Towards efficient and adaptive cyber physical spiking neural integrated systems. In: 2020 27th IEEE International Conference on Electronics, Circuits and Systems (ICECS), pp. 1–4 (2020). https://doi.org/10.1109/ ICECS49266.2020.9294982

13. Galanis, I., Anagnostopoulos, I., Nguyen, C., Bares, G.: Efficient deployment of spiking neural networks on SpiNNaker neuromorphic platform. IEEE Trans. Circuits Syst. II: Express Briefs **68**(6), 1937–1941 (2021). https://doi.org/10.1109/ TCSII.2020.3047425

14. Oltra-Oltra, J.A., et al.: Hardware-software co-design for efficient and scalable real-time emulation of SNNs on the edge. In: 2021 IEEE International Symposium on Circuits and Systems (ISCAS), pp. 1–5 (2021). https://doi.org/10.1109/ ISCAS51556.2021.9401615

15. Zapata, M., Vargas, V., Cagua, A., Alvarez, D., Vallejo, B., Madrenas, J.: Real-time monitoring tool for SNN hardware architecture. In: Artificial Life and Evolutionary Computation. WIVACE 2022. Communications in Computer and Information Science, vol. 1780 (2023). https://doi.org/10.1007/978-3-031-31183-3_24

16. Vallejo-Mancero, B., Nader C., Madrenas, J., Zapata, M.: Real-time display of spiking neural activity of SIMD hardware using an HDMI interface. In: 31st International Conference on Artificial Neural Networks (2022). https://doi.org/10.1007/ 978-3-031-15934-3_60

17. https://www.xilinx.com/products/boards-and-kits/1-8dyf-11.html . Accessed 10 Apr 2023

18. https://digilent.com/reference/pmod/pmodacl/start . Accessed 10 Apr 2023

Regularization for Hybrid N-Bit Weight Quantization of Neural Networks on Ultra-Low Power Microcontrollers

Minh Tri Lê[1,2](✉) ⓘ, Etienne de Foras[1], and Julyan Arbel[2] ⓘ

[1] TDK InvenSense, 38000 Grenoble, France
`minh-tri.le@inria.fr`
[2] Univ. Grenoble Alpes, Inria, CNRS, Grenoble INP, LJK, 38000 Grenoble, France

Abstract. We propose a novel regularization method for hybrid quantization of neural networks, enabling efficient deployment on ultra-low power microcontrollers in embedded systems. Our approach introduces alternative regularization functions and a uniform hybrid quantization scheme targeting $\{2, 4, 8\}$-bits. The method offers flexibility to the weight matrix level, negligible costs, and seamless integration into existing 8-bit post-training quantization pipelines. Additionally, we propose novel schedule functions for regularization, addressing the critical yet often overlooked timing aspect and providing new insights into pacing quantization. Our method achieves a substantial reduction in model byte size, nearly halving it with less than 1% accuracy loss, effectively minimizing power and memory footprints on microcontrollers. Our contributions advance resource-efficient models in resource-constrained devices and the emerging field of tinyML, overcoming limitations of existing approaches and providing new perspectives on the quantization process. The practical implications of our work span diverse real-world applications, including IoT, wearables, and autonomous systems.

Keywords: Deep Learning · TinyML · Regularization · Quantization · Microcontrollers · Sensors

1 Introduction

Neural Networks and Resource-Constrained Devices. As neural networks (NNs) continue to deliver impressive results across a wide range of domains, they are primarily powered by highly overparameterized models, which come with a substantial power consumption cost. This energy barrier inadvertently restricts their deployment in resource-constrained applications, such as ultra-low power microcontroller units (MCUs), like Arm Cortex-M0+ and M4 [18]. MCUs are integral components of embedded systems commonly found in wearables and IoT devices. These systems demand efficient neural network models that can operate within their limited memory (as low as 32 KB), computational capacity (up to 48 MHz), and strict power constraints that must endure for months or even years. The need for innovative solutions for compressing and deploying neural networks on resource-constrained embedded devices emerged into the field of tinyML [12].

© The Author(s), under exclusive license to Springer Nature Switzerland AG 2023
L. Iliadis et al. (Eds.): ICANN 2023, LNCS 14258, pp. 435–446, 2023.
https://doi.org/10.1007/978-3-031-44192-9_35

Quantization. TinyML necessitates the development of novel quantization methods that retain the flexibility of existing approaches while achieving better trade-offs between model size, accuracy, and efficiency for resource-constrained applications. Quantization is a widely used technique for compressing deep neural network models by converting their floating-point parameters into lower-bit precision integers, as illustrated in the following diagram. It has become an essential method for meeting the requirements of MCUs that perform inference based on fixed-point arithmetic [9]. Uniform symmetric post-training quantization (PTQ) at 8-bits is a prevalent approach due to its model-agnosticism, simplicity, and broad embedded hardware support with acceptable performance loss [9,22]. However, it suffers from sensitivity to outliers and performs poorly at low bit precision, such as binary or ternary networks [22].

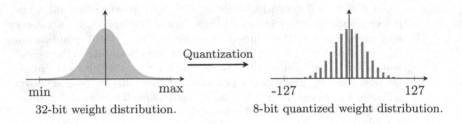

32-bit weight distribution.   8-bit quantized weight distribution.

Contributions. In this paper, we propose a novel regularized quantization method that enables hybrid quantization at the weight matrix level across various combinations of bit precision: {2, 4, 8}-bits. Our approach generalizes regularization functions to {2, 4, 8}-bits, building on the work of [7] at 1-bit. By building upon PTQ, our method maintains its flexibility and compatibility with existing end-to-end pipelines already using 8-bit quantization, specifically targeting resource-constrained devices. Additionally, our approach offers a uniform hybrid quantization scheme across {2, 4, 8}-bits, extendable to any bit precision, thereby reducing the model inference power footprint on MCU platforms. Furthermore, we introduce a scheduled regularization technique for progressive quantization, offering crucial insights on the often overlooked but critical timing aspect of regularization [10] in the case of quantization. Our primary contributions are summarized as follows:

1. We propose generalized regularization functions for {2, 4, 8}-bit quantization, extendable to any bit-precision;
2. We introduce a hybrid quantization scheme at the weight matrix level, designed to reduce the model power footprint for ultra-low power MCUs;
3. We present a novel scheduled regularization approach for progressive weight quantization to {2, 4, 8}-bits;
4. We conduct comprehensive experiments demonstrating the effectiveness of our method across various settings, including activation, regularization, schedule, and layer combination. These experiments provide new insights on how to use and pace regularization with schedule functions for quantization.

Related Work. Prior works have focused on quantization-aware training approaches (QAT) using the straight-through estimator for binary or ternary networks [6,21], or other approximations [13,20] to simulate the quantization effect during training. Other approaches introduce an additional term to the objective function [7,16] of the neural network to encourage weights to converge to a set of points during training, minimizing the loss of accuracy during PTQ. Alternative approaches have used knowledge distillation [2] or Bayesian methods [4] to learn lower-bit precision networks. Moreover, previous studies have shown that lower bit-precision models can achieve better performance by utilizing PReLU activation functions in CNN models [5,11].

Regularization techniques are widely used to improve the generalization performance of neural networks. Various implicit methods include dropout, early stopping, or data augmentation [14], while explicit regularization involves the L_2 penalty. Additionally, the L_1 regularization can be used to encourage weight pruning. Regularization can also be employed for quantization, as demonstrated in [7], where regularization functions are used to quantize models down to 1-bit.

The early training stages are the most critical for convergence, so introducing an explicit high-penalty regularization term for quantization at the beginning can negatively impact and disrupt gradient optimization [1,8]. Moreover, [10] discovered that when using regularization, the initial phase is the most crucial and sensitive period for performance. They also show that starting with late regularization does not improve generalization and can even worsen the outcome in some cases. They conclude that the role of regularization is to steer the initial transient towards regions of the loss with multiple equivalent solutions, rather than bias the final solution towards critical points. Our study fills a gap in the literature by exploring the effect of transient dynamics on regularization for quantization, an aspect that has not been previously investigated.

In the following sections, we present our proposed method encompassing generalized regularization functions, a hybrid quantization scheme, and a scheduled regularization approach (Sect. 2), experimental setup (Sect. 3), and results demonstrating the efficacy of our approach (Sect. 4).

2 Proposed Method

In this section, we introduce our regularization approach for hybrid $\{2, 4, 8\}$-bit quantization of neural networks at the weight matrix level, which is illustrated in the following diagram using a gated recurrent unit (GRU) model, a convolutional neural network (CNN), with a fully-connected (FC) layer as an example.

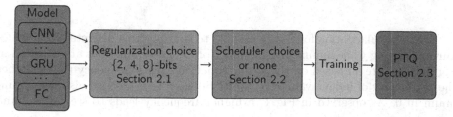

The explicit regularization adds a term to the loss function L in the objective function J as follows [7]:

$$J(W, x, y) = L(f(x, W), y) + \lambda \sum_{i=1}^{M} \text{Reg}(W_i), \tag{1}$$

where, f is the neural network with weights W, λ controls how much the weights are penalized by the regularizer function Reg, and M is the number of weight matrices to quantize. Notice that in the notation $\text{Reg}(W_i)$, the function Reg is applied element-wise to the weight entries of W_i.

2.1 N-bit Generalization

We introduce the following new regularization functions for quantization Reg_N for $N \in \{2, 4, 8\}$:

$$\text{Reg}_N(w) = \begin{cases} 1 - \cos\left(2\pi(2^{N-1} - 1)w\right) & \text{if } |w| \le 1 + \frac{1}{4(2^{N-1}-1)} \\ 1 + 2\pi\left((|w| - 1)(2^{N-1} - 1) - \frac{1}{4}\right) & \text{if } |w| > 1 + \frac{1}{4(2^{N-1}-1)} \end{cases} \tag{2}$$

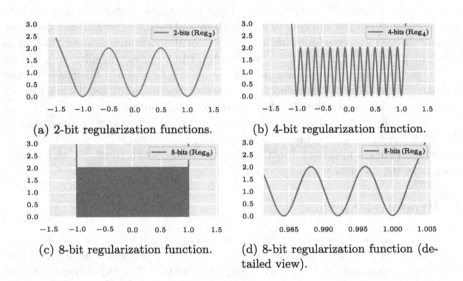

(a) 2-bit regularization functions.

(b) 4-bit regularization function.

(c) 8-bit regularization function.

(d) 8-bit regularization function (detailed view).

Fig. 1. N-bit regularization functions of Eq. (2), for $N \in \{2, 4, 8\}$.

Such a regularization forces the weights to converge to a discrete set of values during training while minimizing the function J. These functions are depicted in Fig. 1. They are all based on the cosine function with a frequency that matches the cardinality of unique values in N-bits between $[-1; +1]$ and also has a minimum in 0. As observed in Fig. 1, a higher frequency leads to steeper minima angles. All Reg_N are continuously differentiable ($\mathcal{C}^1$) on $\mathbb{R}$. For any $N \in \{2, 4, 8\}$, function Reg_N has $2^N - 1$ global minima defined by:

$$\left\{ \frac{k}{2^{N-1} - 1}, k \in \mathbb{Z}, |k| \leq 2^{N-1} - 1 \right\}. \tag{3}$$

The proposed regularization is fully differentiable as well as model-agnostic and enables full or hybrid quantization at the weight matrix level, by selecting the number of bits N. Thus, it can easily be integrated into any training procedure and will be transparent to any embedded deployment process. Moreover, the regularization optimization is executed in conjunction with the training process, resulting in minimal computational overhead.

2.2 Scheduled Regularized Quantization

The high density of global minima, especially in the 8-bit regularization in Fig. 1c, may cause high gradient spikes throughout training and prevent convergence. To overcome this issue, we employ a scheduled regularization scheme [10] that progressively increases the quantization penalty over time, as depicted in Fig. 2. Thus, this allows more time for the weights to properly converge before being trapped by incremental regularization in the global minima, as shown in Fig. 3.

A fast schedule function has similar effects to a steep minima angle: weights should converge faster towards their quantized values, but it may hinder the learning process if the penalty is excessive. Conversely, starting with a slower pace allows more time for the model to learn; however, if the last period is too accelerated, it might cause abrupt gradient surges, negatively impacting the performance.

The schedule function S is scaled to the quantized regularization over time during training as

$$\text{Reg}(W, t) = \text{Reg}(W)S(t). \tag{4}$$

This also has the effect of increasing the angle steepness over time, which traps weights to a minimum. Schedule functions $S(\cdot)$ need to satisfy the following properties:

$$S(t = 1) \approx 0 \text{ and } \geq 0, \quad S(t = t_{\text{final}}) \leq 1, \quad S'(t) \geq 0.$$

We then define eight schedule functions in Table 1 depicted in Fig. 2.

Figure 3 demonstrates the quantization convergence of weights over epochs using a linear schedule. We notice that the weight distribution becomes more and more discrete and converges towards Reg_4 minima, so we can minimize the loss of PTQ accuracy after rounding the weights.

2.3 Post-training Quantization

We choose the simple symmetric linear min-max as the PTQ algorithm for its ease of implementation and seamless deployment to low power embedded devices, as well as reasonable performance results in most scenarios [9,22].

Table 1. Schedule functions for regularization. Here, d is set to 0.01 and 0.001 for schedule inverse linear and inverse polynomial respectively, and rate is set to 0.8 by default. For step-based functions, step is set to 10 by default. For step-based inverse, a higher rate leads to a faster schedule, contrary to step-based bounded.

Scheduler name	Function
Linear	$S(t, t_{\text{final}}) = \frac{t-1}{t_{\text{final}}-1}$
2-polynomial	$S(t, t_{\text{final}}) = \frac{t^2-1}{t_{\text{final}}^2-1}$
N-polynomial	$S(t, t_{\text{final}}, N) = \left(\frac{t}{t_{\text{final}}}\right)^N$
Inverse linear	$S(t, d) = \frac{1}{1+\frac{1}{dt}}$
Inverse polynomial	$S(t, d) = \frac{1}{1+\frac{1}{dt^2}}$
Step-based linear	$S(t, t_{\text{final}}, \text{step}) = \frac{\left\lfloor \frac{t}{\text{step}} \right\rfloor}{\left\lfloor \frac{t_{\text{final}}}{\text{step}} \right\rfloor}$
Step-based inverse	$\text{scale}(t_{\text{final}}, \text{step}, \text{rate}) = \frac{1}{\text{rate}^{\left\lfloor \frac{t_{\text{final}}}{\text{step}} \right\rfloor}}$
	$S(t, \text{step}, \text{rate}) = \frac{1}{\text{scale} \times \text{rate}^{\left\lfloor \frac{t}{\text{step}} \right\rfloor}}$
Step-based bounded	$S(t, \text{step}, \text{rate}) = 1 - \text{rate}^{\left\lfloor \frac{t}{\text{step}} \right\rfloor}$

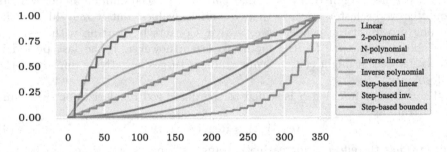

Fig. 2. Schedule functions for quantized regularization for $t_{\text{final}} = 350$.

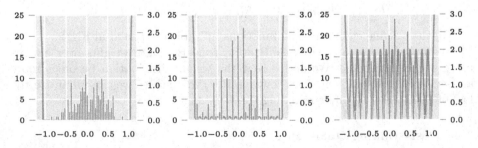

Fig. 3. Scheduled regularization of GRU weights at epoch 1, 25, and 500 (left to right) to 4-bits with Reg_4 regularization and linear schedule in the background.

The model weights are quantized in two straightforward steps. First, we round the regularized weights to their nearest global minima with respect to their regularization function ({2, 4, 8}-bits), and quantize them to int-N integers. Finally, we quantize the remaining weights to 8-bit integers, and bias and activations are quantized to 32-bit integers.

3 Experiments

This section details the experimental design and choices to extensively evaluate our proposed method for regularized quantization on two classification tasks.

3.1 Datasets

Bring-to-See. We experimented with a bring-to-see (BTS) dataset, which refers to the binary detection of the motion of a user's wrist toward their face as a means of waking up a watch or a mobile device. We have raw data from a 3-axis accelerometer at $20\,\mathrm{Hz}$ as input, and each gesture sample is $2\,\mathrm{s}$. Thus, each input is shaped as 40 sequence length, 3 features.

Google Speech Commands v2-12. We also tested the Google speech commands v2-12 (GSCv2-12) dataset [19] consisting of 12 keyword spotting words. The audio samples are pre-processed with MFCC and have a shape of 94 sequence length, 13 features.

3.2 Model

We use a convolutional RNN and specifically convolutional GRU because of their size-performance tradeoff [3] and standard usage for sequence classification. They are also compatible with causal architectures, which is critical for real-time inference [15]. We also use batch normalization, dropout, and spatial dropout [17] layers. Additionally, we evaluate the PReLU activation over ReLU [5,11]. We refer to the baseline model as the configuration in Table 2. For the BTS dataset and GSCv2-12 dataset, each model is trained for 500 and 350 epochs, respectively, using the Nadam optimizer with default parameter on TensorFlow.

3.3 Experimental Design

We aim to address the following questions through our experiments:

Q1. Where to apply {2, 4, 8}-bit quantization, and when?
Q2. Is PReLU superior to ReLU for N-bit quantization?
Q3. Is scheduling beneficial to regularization? When is scheduling versus non-scheduling most effective? Is a faster schedule better than a slower one?

We experiment with our proposed method and provide answers to the previous questions by making two key components vary: the regularization design and the model configuration. The following sections elaborate on the details of the extensive experimental scenarios.

Table 2. Baseline model configuration size and parameters where (c, k) refers to the number of channels and the kernel size of the CNN1D. Weights are stored in 8-bits and activations in 32-bits integers.

Layer	Configuration		Parameters		Size (B)	
	BTS	GSCv2-12	BTS	GSCv2-12	BTS	GSCv2-12
CNN1D (c, k)	(6, 5)	(128, 10)	96	16,768	114	17,512
Batchnorm	✓		24	512	96	2,048
Activation	ReLU/PReLU		c if PReLU else 0		$c \times 4$ if PReLU else 0	
SpatialDropout	✓		✗		✗	
GRU	5	196	195	191,688	285	195,216
Dropout	✓		✗		✗	
Batchnorm	✗	✓	✗	784	✗	3,136
FC	2	12	12	2,364	18	2,400
Total			327(+6)	212,116(+128)	513(+24)	219,952(+512)

Regularization Configuration. We test our {2, 4, 8}-bit regularizations in hybrid settings. We also assess the effectiveness of the schedule functions on generalization and quantization convergence by comparing scenarios with and without a schedule for each regularization choice.

Model Configuration. We evaluate the effects of quantization on various layer combinations: convolution, GRU, both, or both, and the output layer, which we refer to as "all layers". The remaining layers are quantized to 8-bits, as described in Sect. 2.3, enabling hybrid quantization. The hybrid configuration is annotated as $\{N, 8\}$-bits. To minimize the number of combinations, we decided to regularize the two weight matrices of the GRU layer at the same bit precision, even if regularization allows for weight-wise quantization granularity. We also limit the hybrid configuration to two different bit precisions at a time for each model, even though our method allows models to be quantized to any hybrid mix of bit precision, e.g., {2,4,8}-bit model.

In addition, we test the performance of ReLU versus PReLU as convolutional activation, as stated in Sect. 3.2.

3.4   Deployment and Evaluation

The neural networks are deployed and evaluated by accuracy on low power embedded sensors for real-time inference using Arm Cortex-M0+ and M4 MCU [18] for the BTS and GSCv2-12 datasets, respectively. The accuracy of the model was evaluated by selecting the best model on the validation set from five independent training repetitions for all experiments.

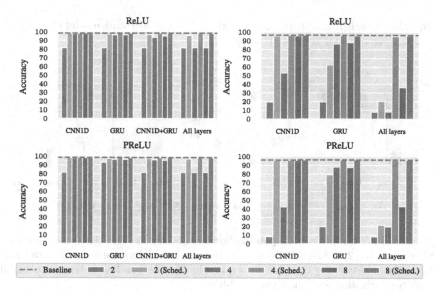

Fig. 4. Hybrid {2, 4, 8}-bit quantization test accuracy results on the BTS (left) and GSCv2-12 dataset (right), without schedule (blue) or with schedule (green). The baseline is trained normally without regularization and quantized to 8-bits. (Color figure online)

4   Results

4.1   Regularization Configuration

Figure 4 shows the effectiveness of our N-bit regularization method for model quantization, especially on {4,8}-bits, or with CNN1D in general, addressing Q1. However, in most cases, 2-bit performance falls behind that of 4-bits and 8-bits, except for CNN1D with scheduling, offering some insights for Q1 and Q3.

To Schedule or Not to Schedule? As discussed in Sect. 4.1, incorporating scheduling with regularization improves the quantization outcomes compared to not using scheduling in most cases, particularly in the most demanding scenario where all layers are quantized, and with higher bit precision like {4,8}-bits, across both datasets. This indicates that progressive quantization does foster a more favorable environment for optimization, addressing Q3.

Finding the Right Pace. In Fig. 4, when considering the median and mean accuracy, slower-paced schedules demonstrate better performance for {2, 4, 8}-bit quantization. This implies that higher bit precision requires lower regularization penalties over time for effective PTQ. Notably, the case without a schedule is the fastest, as it entirely omits progressive regularization. These insights respond to Q3 and emphasize the importance of selecting the suitable scheduler for different quantization settings, and highlight the need for further investigation into customizing scheduling approaches based on the dataset and model characteristics to achieve optimal results (Fig. 5).

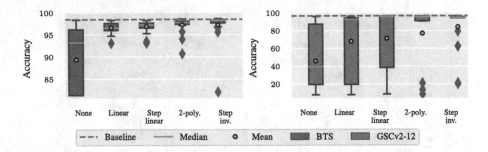

Fig. 5. Scheduler comparison of quantization results on the BTS (left) and GSCv2-12 (right) dataset in $\{2, 4, 8\}$-bits, across all scenarios. Schedulers are ordered from fastest to slowest at mid-training time (as shown in Fig. 2). The baseline is trained normally without regularization and quantized to 8-bits.

4.2   Model Configuration

In relation to Q1, quantizing the CNN1D layer is robust in all cases, with 4-bit scheduled regularization and PReLU surpassing the baseline on BTS. However, the GRU layer is more sensitive to quantization as it is larger, especially on GSCv2-12. Scheduled quantization on the GRU layer at $\{2, 4, 8\}$-bits provides acceptable results on BTS. However, only $\{4, 8\}$-bits is suitable for GSCv2-12, and a 2-bit quantization without a scheduler is overly detrimental in all cases. Quantizing both CNN1D and GRU layers at $\{4, 8\}$-bits and a schedule provides acceptable performance. Applying quantization to all layers with $\{4, 8\}$-bits with a schedule yields less than a 1% loss for both datasets.

In response to Q2, we observe that in the $\{2, 4, 8\}$-bit range, PReLU generally performs better than ReLU (Fig. 4), while ReLU still achieves close results under the best regularization scenarios.

4.3   Key Results

Our findings reveal that employing 4-bit quantization in conjunction with an appropriate scheduler results in the most advantageous size-performance trade-off in all cases (Q1, Q3), with PReLU activation emerging as a superior option when considering $\{2, 4, 8\}$-bits (Q2). However, our method presents certain limitations. For instance, 2-bit quantization may underperform, particularly without schedulers, in large layers, and on the GSCv2-12 dataset, as illustrated in Fig. 4. Moreover, despite expectation, 8-bit regularized quantization does not surpass the 8-bit baseline. Additionally, our method requires the consideration of extra hyperparameters. Despite these drawbacks, our method achieves substantial byte size reductions in baseline models (Table 2) when all layers are quantized to 4-bits: approximately 25.8% reduction with ReLU on BTS, with a 0.3% performance loss, and 47.5% reduction on GSCv2-12, with less than a 0.8% accuracy loss. Furthermore, 2-bit quantization of CNN and GRU on BTS yields a reduction in 37.3% byte size at the cost of a 1.5% performance loss.

In summary, our study emphasizes the importance of carefully selecting model hyperparameters, such as activation, regularization, and scheduler choice, in quantization performance and offers evidence supporting the effectiveness of functional hybrid quantization techniques, both with and without schedulers, in reducing the model size without compromising performance.

5   Conclusion

In this paper, we introduced a novel regularized quantization method for deep neural networks, enabling uniform hybrid quantization at the weight matrix level across various bit precisions ($\{2, 4, 8\}$-bits) in a model-agnostic manner. We also presented a scheduled regularization scheme for quantization, addressing the often-overlooked aspect of time in regularization. Our approach demonstrated the ability to reduce the model byte size by nearly half while maintaining minimal accuracy loss. We showed that our method retains the flexibility benefits of PTQ and seamlessly integrates into any existing training pipelines with minimal computational overhead for resource-constrained devices, providing a uniform hybrid quantization scheme that reduces the model inference power footprint of neural networks. Overall, this work contributes to the expanding field of tinyML, enabling the efficient deployment of deep learning models on ultra-low power MCUs for tinyML applications.

Future work can encompass further exploration of different regularization functions and hybrid combinations to $\{2,4,8\}$-bits, and extending the method to other deep learning architectures beyond CNNs and GRUs. Investigating scheduled regularization to reduce the activation size from 32-bit integers represents another essential direction for achieving substantial improvements in the power efficiency and performance of tinyML systems.

References

1. Achille, A., Rovere, M., Soatto, S.: Critical learning periods in deep networks. In: 7th International Conference on Learning Representations (2019)
2. Alemdar, H., Leroy, V., Prost-Boucle, A., Pétrot, F.: Ternary neural networks for resource-efficient AI applications. In: International Joint Conference on Neural Networks, IJCNN, pp. 2547–2554 (2017)
3. Arik, S.Ö., et al.: Convolutional recurrent neural networks for small-footprint keyword spotting. In: 18th Annual Conference of the International Speech Communication Association, Interspeech (2017)
4. van Baalen, M., et al.: Bayesian bits: unifying quantization and pruning. In: Advances in Neural Information Processing Systems, vol. 33, pp. 5741–5752 (2020)

5. Bulat, A., Tzimiropoulos, G., Kossaifi, J., Pantic, M.: Improved training of binary networks for human pose estimation and image recognition. CoRR abs/1904.05868 (2019)
6. Courbariaux, M., Bengio, Y., David, J.P.: BinaryConnect: training deep neural networks with binary weights during propagations. In: Advances in Neural Information Processing Systems, vol. 28 (2015)
7. Darabi, S., Belbahri, M., Courbariaux, M., Nia, V.: Regularized Binary Network Training. arXiv abs/1812.11800 (2018)
8. Frankle, J., Schwab, D.J., Morcos, A.S.: The early phase of neural network training. In: 8th International Conference on Learning Representations (2020)
9. Gholami, A., Kim, S., Dong, Z., Yao, Z., Mahoney, M.W., Keutzer, K.: A survey of quantization methods for efficient neural network inference. arXiv abs/2103.13630 (2021)
10. Golatkar, A.S., Achille, A., Soatto, S.: Time matters in regularizing deep networks: weight decay and data augmentation affect early learning dynamics, matter little near convergence. In: Advances in Neural Information Processing Systems, vol. 32 (2019)
11. Kim, H., Park, J., Lee, C., Kim, J.: Improving accuracy of binary neural networks using unbalanced activation distribution. In: IEEE Conference on Computer Vision and Pattern Recognition, CVPR, pp. 7862–7871 (2021)
12. Lê, M.T., Arbel, J.: TinyMLOps for real-time ultra-low power MCUs applied to frame-based event classification. In: EuroMLSys 2023: Proceedings of the 3rd European Workshop on Machine Learning and Systems. ACM, New York (2023)
13. Louizos, C., Reisser, M., Blankevoort, T., Gavves, E., Welling, M.: Relaxed quantization for discretized neural networks. In: 7th International Conference on Learning Representations (2019)
14. Shorten, C., Khoshgoftaar, T.M.: A survey on image data augmentation for deep learning. J. Data 6(1), 1–48 (2019). https://doi.org/10.1186/s40537-019-0197-0
15. Takeuchi, D., Yatabe, K., Koizumi, Y., Oikawa, Y., Harada, N.: Real-time speech enhancement using equilibriated RNN. In: 2020 IEEE International Conference on Acoustics, Speech and Signal Processing, ICASSP, pp. 851–855 (2020)
16. Tang, W., Hua, G., Wang, L.: How to train a compact binary neural network with high accuracy? In: Proceedings of the AAAI Conference on Artificial Intelligence, vol. 31, pp. 2625–2631 (2017)
17. Tompson, J., Goroshin, R., Jain, A., LeCun, Y., Bregler, C.: Efficient object localization using convolutional networks. In: IEEE Conference on Computer Vision and Pattern Recognition, CVPR, pp. 648–656 (2015)
18. Unlu, H.: Efficient neural network deployment for microcontroller. CoRR abs/2007.01348 (2020)
19. Warden, P.: Speech Commands: A Dataset for Limited-Vocabulary Speech Recognition. arXiv abs/1804.03209 (2018)
20. Yin, P., Zhang, S., Lyu, J., Osher, S.J., Qi, Y., Xin, J.: BinaryRelax: a relaxation approach for training deep neural networks with quantized weights. SIAM J. Imaging Sci. 11(4), 2205–2223 (2018)
21. Zhu, C., Han, S., Mao, H., Dally, W.J.: Trained ternary quantization. In: 5th International Conference on Learning Representations (2017)
22. Zmora, N., Jacob, G., Zlotnik, L., Elharar, B., Novik, G.: Neural Network Distiller: A Python package for DNN compression research. arXiv abs/1910.12232 (2019)

SGNN: A New Method for Learning Representations on Signed Networks

Ji Jin[1,2], Jialin Bi[2], and Cunquan Qu[1,2(✉)]

[1] Data Science Institute, Shandong University,
Jinan 250100, People's Republic of China
cqqu@sdu.edu.cn
[2] School of Mathematics, Shandong University,
Jinan 250100, People's Republic of China

Abstract. Graph Convolutional Neural Networks (GCNNs) have emerged as a powerful tool for processing graph-structured data and achieving outstanding performance in various scenarios, including node classification, link prediction, and graph visualization. However, in signed networks, which contain links with logically opposite relations, two types of associations can more accurately capture relationships in the real world. In this paper, we propose a novel optimization objective for learning representations in signed networks by capitalizing on the structural balance theory. Additionally, we introduce a new message propagation framework and develop a scalable signed graph neural network model, SGNN, which significantly outperforms existing signed graph embedding models when applied to the link classification task on four empirical networks. Moreover, our message propagation framework enables the construction of deeper GCNNs. Overall, our study presents a new approach for learning meaningful representations on signed networks, utilizing a novel message propagation framework and optimization objective that captures the complex relationships between nodes in a signed graph.

Keywords: Graph neural networks · Signed networks · Embedding learning

1 Introduction

Graph-structured data is widely prevalent in various fields such as social science, physical systems, biological systems, and knowledge graphs [14,16]. As a result, there is much interest in machine learning models for graph-structured data to solve tasks such as link prediction [22], recommendation [23], clustering [11], and node classification [17]. Graph embedding, also be known as network representation learning, is one of the most effective tools for graph data learning, where the basic idea is to project networks into a low-dimensional latent space [2,19,25]. Deep learning-based graph embedding methods can be divided into traditional approaches such as DeepWalk [15] and node2vec [5], and graph neural network (GNN)-based methods [6]. In this study, we mainly focus on the latter class of methods.

L. Iliadis et al. (Eds.): ICANN 2023, LNCS 14258, pp. 447–458, 2023.
https://doi.org/10.1007/978-3-031-44192-9_36

GNN models are a type of deep learning model that utilizes graph data as training data, such as graph convolutional network [9] and graph attention network, which have demonstrated powerful and convincing performance in learning graph-structured data. The primary assumption in GNN models is that the link in networks implies similar representations of nodes in the latent space [13]. Many GNN models are designed under homophily, which means that the connected nodes have the same labels or similar properties [26,28]. Therefore, classic GNN models update the node's representation by gathering nodes' and neighbours' information in different weights. It is a straightforward but efficient operation to use networks' structure directly.

However, most GNN models struggle with heterogeneous edges or nodes. As a special type of heterogeneous network, signed networks, which feature positive and negative links between nodes, are a type of heterogeneous network that presents a unique challenge for GNN models. The primary variations of GNN models used on signed networks are dividing the networks into positive and negative parts, training each network independently, and outputting two embeddings, respectively, such as SGCN [4]. But this approach can sacrifice the inherent structure and properties of the network. We summarize the challenges of embedding for signed networks into the following two points. Firstly, what is the objective function of embedding on signed networks? Secondly, classic GNN models can't be applied on signed networks. How to change their aggregation operations to make them able to aggregate the structure information on signed networks?

In this study, we propose a novel GNN model, SGNN, which completes the aggregation operation in a normal GNN model. It can be directly utilized on signed networks and gathers the information with the sign of the edge. SGNN doesn't need preprocessing on signed networks, unlike other models for signed networks. As a result, SGNN shows noteworthy performance in the representation learning of signed networks compared with other models. Meanwhile, taking advantage of the special aggregation operation, SGNN also demonstrates the ability to restrain the over-smoothing problem of GNN.

The major contributions of this study are as follows:

- We present a novel approach to training signed networks based on the balance theory of signed networks. Our objective function is specifically designed for this purpose.
- To implement our approach, we introduce a new layer that features our proposed aggregation operation. This enables us to explore the scalable SGNN model, which can accurately learn the signed network data without any pre-processing steps required by previous models.
- We conducted experiments using several real social networks and found that our model outperforms existing signed network embedding methods.

2   Related Works

The Graph Convolution Network (GCN) is a well-known GNN model that has exhibited impressive performance in solving graph-related problems. It modifies convolution neural networks to suit graph structures and aggregates neighbors' information to update the gathered information with a learnable parameter. Multiple layers are stacked to aggregate multiple-hop neighbors' messages [1,9]. Other variations of the aggregation operation have been developed to improve performance, such as the GAT model [21] and the SAGE model [6].

Network representation learning or graph embedding is a common way to solve network-based tasks. Traditional methods such as kernel analysis have limitations when facing large-scale networks due to computing power and computational complexity limitations. Deep learning-based network representation learning has brought new opportunities for solving these problems, such as the SNE model [20], DeepWalk [15], and node2vec [5]. However, most classical embedding models are designed for unsigned networks and fail to learn signed networks. These models will learn similar embeddings of connected nodes, which is inappropriate in signed networks, where vectors of negatively connected nodes should be relatively far apart in the embedding space. To address this issue, newly designed models are needed for signed networks to use negative links [5].

The primary way to learn signed networks is by dividing the network into two parts and learning the positive and negative embeddings separately [4,8,24,27]. However, these embedding models cannot use positive and negative connections simultaneously. Therefore, there needs to be more research on signed network embedding.

3 Representation Learning on Signed Networks

3.1 Embedding of Signed Networks

Let us introduce some basic notation before proceeding. Consider a signed network $G(V, E)$, where V is a finite set of nodes and E is the set of edges. Each edge $e_{in} \in E$ can be represented as a triple (i, j, s_{ij}), where i and j are the start and end nodes of the edge, respectively, and s_{ij} represents the sign of the edge. For simplicity, we denote the cardinality of V and E as n and m, respectively. Therefore, a signed network can be represented as an adjacency matrix $A = (s_{ij})_{n \times n}$:

$$A_{ij} = \begin{cases} 1, & \text{if } i \text{ and } j \text{ are positively connected,} \\ -1, & \text{if } i \text{ and } j \text{ are negatively connected,} \\ 0, & \text{if } i \text{ and } j \text{ are not connected.} \end{cases}$$

The adjacency matrix facilitates the classification of node pairs in signed networks into three categories: positive, negative, and absent. This is in contrast to unsigned networks, where node pairs are either connected or not. The theory of structural balance, proposed by Heider [7], is a fundamental theory in the study of signed networks. In undirected signed networks, there are four types of triangles, as depicted in Fig. 1. Triangles (a) and (b) are balanced, whereas triangles (c) and (d) are unbalanced. It is noteworthy that in balanced signed networks, nodes can be partitioned into two communities. For example, in a link e_{ij}, if node i and node j belong to the same community, they perceive each other

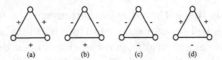

Fig. 1. Undirected signed triads. Based on the number of positive edges, (a) and (b) is balanced. (c) and (d) are unbalanced.

as friends, and the link e_{ij} is positive. Conversely, if node i and node j belong to different communities, the link is negative.

Although most triangles in real-world signed networks are balanced, unbalanced configurations do exist [3]. In this context, we propose a novel approach for understanding relationships in signed networks. Specifically, we assume that each node's position p_i in the latent space represents the node's opinion, such as their political position in social network. Unlike the structural balance theory, which forces nodes into only two clusters due to the existence of unbalanced structures, we do not impose such constraints. Given a threshold w, the distance between two nodes in the latent space represents the sign of a link. If the sign of a node pair is positive, then the two nodes have similar opinions, and $|p_i - p_j| < w$. Otherwise, if the sign of the link e_{ij} is negative, $|p_i - p_j| > w$. Notably, we differ from most existing studies on signed networks in our treatment of absent connections. While these are typically treated as "mild negative links", we assume that absent connections have little influence on the nodes' distance in the latent space. For example, in signed social networks, a missing link typically means that two users have not yet met, rather than that they hate each other.

To learn the node positions in signed networks, we propose an objective function inspired by the link prediction problem. Specifically, we aim to design a likelihood function that evaluates the embedding performance. The likelihood function should satisfy the following condition: if the link e_{ij} is positive, the two points corresponding to nodes i and j should be located close together in the latent space, with a small distance between them. Mathematically, the likelihood function can be expressed as follows:

$$P(i, j) = \sigma(p_i^{\top} p_j) = \frac{1}{1 + \exp(-p_i^{\top} p_j)}, \tag{1}$$

where σ is the sigmoid activation function. To simplify the calculation, p_i and p_j are learned representation vectors of node i and j in the $[-1, 1]^n$ space. The likelihood function describes the similarity between node i and node j.

To compute the objective function for training on signed networks, we sum over all links with their corresponding signs. Specifically, the objective function is defined as follows:

$$P(G) = -\sum_{s_{ij}=1} log(P(i, j)) - \sum_{s_{ij}=-1} log(1 - P(i, j)). \tag{2}$$

The first term in the equation sums over all positive links, while the second term sums over all negative (or absent) links. Minimizing this objective function encourages the learned representations to place similar nodes close together and dissimilar nodes far apart, thereby capturing the underlying structure of the signed network.

This objective function is based on three principles for embedding signed networks:

1. For positively connected nodes, the distance between their embeddings should be minimized.
2. For negatively connected nodes, the distance between their embeddings should be maximized.
3. For disconnected nodes, their embeddings should be independent and not influenced by each other, as they have not yet interacted.

3.2   Aggregation for Signed Networks

Since GNN models have shown excellent performance in graph representation learning, we extend them to signed networks. A standard GNN model layer involves two main operations, namely update and aggregation. The former pre-processes information of each node, while the latter collects information of each node and its neighbors to achieve the convolution effect. A GNN layer can be expressed as follows:

$$
\begin{aligned}
h_i^{(l)'} &= update\left(h_i^{(l-1)}\right), \\
h_i^{(l)} &= \sigma\left(aggregate\left(h_i^{(l)'}, h_{\mathcal{N}_i}^{(l)'}\right)\right),
\end{aligned}
\tag{3}
$$

here, $h_i^{(l)}$ represents the hidden representation of node i in layer l, $\mathcal{N}_i$ is the neighbor set of node i, and σ is the activation function.

To apply GNN to signed networks, we need to define the operation for all three types of connections: positive, negative, and absent. Unlike classic GNN models that naturally output similar representations for a node and its neighbors, we need to break this rule in our specially designed aggregate operation.

To achieve this, we follow the idea of GCN and modify it to suit our purpose. GCN aggregates the representation of each node with its neighbors, pushing each node towards each other. It works well for normal networks since connected nodes should have similar representations. However, the situation is more complex in signed networks. We keep what GCN does for positive links and push each node towards its positive neighbors. However, we also need to move each node away from its negative neighbors. With this design, the model can automatically distinguish different types of connections without complex operations. The schematic is shown in the first part of Fig. 2.

After the modified operation, we can use the signed network structure information during aggregation and design a new GNN model for signed networks. In the next part, we will introduce SGNN in detail.

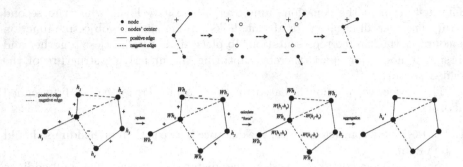

Fig. 2. Here shows the aggregation operation in SGNN layer. It first calculates each center of positive and negative neighbors. Then it pushes each node towards the positive center, away from the negative center.

3.3   SGNN, Signed Graph Neural Network

Classical GNN models use an average operation for node aggregation, which is not sufficient for our purposes. To address this issue, we turn to GCN models with a residual structure, which exhibit better performance and flexibility. The information aggregation step in GCN can be expressed mathematically as follows:

$$h_i^{(l)} = h_i^{(l)'} + \sum_{j \in \mathcal{N}_i} \left(\frac{1}{d_i d_j} * h_j^{(l)'} \right). \tag{4}$$

However, this formulation conceals the interaction between a node and its neighbors. We make a minor but significant modification to Eq. 4:

$$
\begin{aligned}
h_i^{(l)} &= h_i^{(l)'} + \sum_{j \in \mathcal{N}_i} \left(\frac{1}{d_i d_j} * (h_i^{(l)'} + h_j^{(l)'} - h_i^{(l)'}) \right) \\
&= h_i^{(l)'} + \sum_{j \in \mathcal{N}_i} \left(\frac{1}{d_i d_j} * h_i^{(l)'} \right) + \sum_{j \in \mathcal{N}_i} \left(\frac{1}{d_i d_j} * (h_j^{(l)'} - h_i^{(l)'}) \right).
\end{aligned}
\tag{5}
$$

Equation 5 reveals that the first term, $h_i^{(l)'} + \sum_{j \in \mathcal{N}_i} \left(\frac{1}{d_i d_j} * h_i^{(l)'} \right)$, represents the essential information retained by the center node during aggregation. The second term, $\sum_{j \in \mathcal{N}_i} \left(\frac{1}{d_i d_j} * (h_j^{(l)'} - h_i^{(l)'}) \right)$, captures the influence of the neighbors on the center. We can interpret this influence as a "force" that the neighbors exert on the center. Thus, GCN performs information aggregation by calculating the difference between the center and the neighbors as the "force", summing all the "forces", and pushing the center with a weight determined by each neighbor's degree. By assigning a sign to each "force", we can naturally aggregate the signed information without additional manual operations.

In this paper, we propose a novel aggregation operation based on Eq. 5. By introducing a sign for each "force", we enable the aggregation operation to aggregate signed information without additional manual operations. Specifically, we leave the operation unchanged for positive edges, but for negative edges, we change the sign of the "force" to achieve the "pushing away" effect, as shown below:

$$aggregate(h_i^{(l)'}) = h_i^{(l)'} + \sum_{j \in \mathcal{N}_i} \left(\frac{s_{ij}}{2d_id_j} * (h_j^{(l)'} - h_i^{(l)'}) \right). \qquad (6)$$

To make it easy to calculate each "force" and push in or out with each neighbor's sign, we perform an operation that doesn't add much complexity. To demonstrate its effectiveness, we use a simple linear model for the update part of our SGNN model, similar to GCN. The complete model of SGNN is shown below:

$$h_i^{(l)} = \sigma \left(w_l' h_i^{(l-1)} + \sum_{j \in \mathcal{N}_i} (\frac{s_{ij}}{2d_id_j} * (w_l h_j^{(l-1)} - w_l h_i^{(l-1)})) \right), \qquad (7)$$

here, w_l and w_l' are learnable parameters of layer l. When $l = 0$, $h_i^{(0)}$ is the input feature x_i of node i, and the output h_i of the last layer is the embedding position p_i of node i. Through the update and aggregate method, a node's representation can approach that of its positive neighbors and move away from its negative neighbors during the propagation process. The second part of Fig. 2 shows the specific operation of our model for one node during training.

To standardize the output, we embed the results into a $[-1, 1]^k$ Euclidean space, where k represents the embedding dimension. We use the hyperbolic tangent function, also known as tanh, as the activation function. GNN models usually stack only two or three layers because a deeper stack can cause over-smoothing. Similarly, we stack three layers in SGNN. However, because negative links exist, each node pushes away its negative neighbors, which restricts over-smoothing during the propagation process. Therefore, we test the model's performance with a deeper stack by building a model, SGNN-6, which has six layers.

4 Experiments

In this section, we present experiments to evaluate the effectiveness of the proposed model. A good network embedding should capture the internal relationships between nodes in the network. However, determining whether an embedding result is good or bad can be challenging. Therefore, we use a sign classification task to assess the performance of the learned node embeddings.

First, we obtain node embeddings for each model and then evaluate whether the learned node embeddings can improve the performance of link or sign prediction for signed networks. To achieve this, we train a logistic regression model with one layer to prevent an overly-performing classification model from hiding differences between different embeddings. We use the node embeddings as features to classify the sign of a link. Specifically, the model concatenates each pair of node embeddings as input and outputs the link sign. We use the concatenation method for combining embeddings in all experiments since it generally performs better. The classification accuracy indicates the embedding model's performance.

Empirical signed networks often have a significant imbalance between the number of positive and negative edges. Therefore, we use F1 scores to evaluate the classification performance.

4.1 Datasets

The experiments are conducted on four empirical signed networks: Bitcoin-Alpha, Bitcoin-otc [10], Slashdot [18] and Epinions [12]. Table 1 summarizes some of the main statistics for each dataset.

Table 1. Dataset statistics

Dataset	Edges	Nodes	+ Edges	− Edges
Bitcoin-alpha	24,186	3,783	93%	7%
Bitcoin-otc	35,592	5,881	89%	11%
Slashdot	545,671	81,867	77%	23%
Epinions	841,372	131,828	85%	15%

4.2 Performance Comparison

To demonstrate the efficacy of the proposed aggregation operation in signed networks, we conducted a comparison between SGCN and a "signed GCN" model. The signed GCN model utilizes the GCN aggregation operation, but incorporates the sign into the aggregated average. The aggregation operation is presented below:

$$h_i^{(l)} = h_i^{(l)'} + \sum_{j \in \mathcal{N}_i} \left(\frac{s_{ij}}{d_i d_j} * h_j^{(l)'} \right). \tag{8}$$

This aggregation preserves the core concept of GCN models, but it factors in the sign of each connection. Put differently, the "signed GCN" incorporates the signed information during the aggregation process, but in a rudimentary manner. The discrepancy between the two aggregation methods is readily apparent.

In graphs (a) and (b) of Fig. 3, we present the embedding results obtained by our proposed model and the "signed GCN" model. The predicted sign of the target node pairs is based on the inner product of two nodes. The results indicate that the distances between node pairs measured by their embedding vectors' inner product in the SGCN model can effectively distinguish positive and negative connections. However, the "signed GCN" model exhibits a noticeable overlap between the predicted values of positive and negative edges. Additionally, as previously mentioned, the aggregation operation in the classic GCN model tightens each node's embedding, resulting in poor performance that worsens as the model deepens. The SGCN model to some extent circumvents these issues and maintains clear embeddings even after multiple aggregations. To verify this, we conducted additional experiments in which we stacked SGNN and "signed GCN" models to 6 or 9 layers to assess their performance. The results are displayed in graph (b) and (c) of Fig. 3.

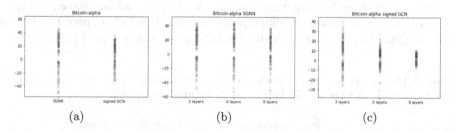

(a)   (b)   (c)

Fig. 3. The results of experiments on BitCoin-alpha. The graph (a) are results for edges sign prediction. The graph (b) and (c) are results of edges sign for different model with different layers. Where the blue dots represent the positive links and red dots represent the negative links for all graphs. (Color figure online)

We can see from our experiments that our model is able to clearly separate the embeddings, which indicates that it is utilizing negative links during propagation. This is in contrast to the "signed GCN", which also uses the sign of links as weights during propagation but is unable to prevent over-smoothing.

To further compare our model with the "signed GCN", we conducted link classification tasks and randomly split each dataset into training and testing sets with a ratio of 80:20. We used the Adam optimizer algorithm with a learning rate of 0.01 to train each model for 100 epochs and performed 20 independent experiments to obtain the average performance of each model. The embedding dimensions is seted to 64 after grid searches in our experiments, which is consistent with the approaches used in SGCN [4] and SIDE [8]. We evaluated the performance of our models on signed link prediction tasks. The F1 scores are reported in Table 2.

Specifically, we compared our model with seven baseline models: four designed specifically for signed networks (SSE, SiNE, SIDE, and SGCN) and three classic GNN models (GCN, GAT, and SAGE) with same experiments setting. The SSE, SiNE, SIDE, and SGCN models are specifically designed for signed networks, and as such, no modifications are needed for the experiments.

Table 2. Link prediction F1 for all datasets.

F1	Bitcoin-alpha	Bitcoin-otc	Slashdot	Epinions
SGNN	0.974	0.966	0.913	0.954
Signed GCN	0.967	0.962	0.903	0.952

The parameters used in this study are based on the original papers that proposed these models. Regarding the GNN models, namely GCN, GAT, and SAGE, we only utilize the unsigned structure of the signed network in the experiment. However, the signed structure is taken into consideration when calculating the loss to ensure the models' effectiveness. Each GNN model consists of three layers, with the activation function being the hyperbolic tangent function. Additionally, the objective function or loss-function used in this study is the one shown in Eq. 2. Moreover, we the our model with 6 layers which called SGNN-6, performs better on some data. To summarize, the final results of F1 can be found in Table 3.

Table 3. Link prediction F1 for all datasets. The maximum F1 score is highlighted in underlined bold, and the second largest one is highlighted in bold.

F1	Bitcoin-alpha	Bitcoin-otc	Slashdot	Epinions
SGNN	**0.974**	**0.966**	**0.913**	**0.954**
SGNN-6	**0.973**	**0.969**	**0.923**	**0.958**
GCN	0.949	0.941	0.867	0.912
SAGE	0.97	0.959	0.879	0.931
GAT	0.948	0.92	0.864	0.913
SSE	0.898	0.923	0.82	0.901
SiNE	0.888	0.878	0.854	0.914
SIDE	0.738	0.75	0.646	0.711
SGCN	0.917	0.925	0.864	0.933

Based on the comparison, the following conclusions can be drawn: Firstly, the proposed SGNN model exhibits the best performance over the baseline models on all datasets, which demonstrates the effectiveness of our model in extracting information from signed networks compared to other models. Secondly, the SGNN-6 model outperforms SGNN, indicating that our model can somewhat alleviate the over-smoothing problem. In summary, the SGNN model and its SGNN-6 variant have shown promising results in extracting useful information from signed networks.

5   Conclusion

This study presents a significant contribution to the field of graph analysis, particularly in the analysis of heterogeneous, signed networks. The proposed framework offers a robust and scalable solution for handling complex signed graphs, providing new insights into their internal relationships and enabling accurate predictions of various tasks. The results of this study can benefit many fields, such as social network analysis, recommendation systems, and cybersecurity, where signed networks are prevalent.

Acknowledgements. The authors was supported in part by National Natural Science Foundation of China under Grant 12001324, in part by Shandong University multidisciplinary research and innovation team of young scholars under Grand 2020QNQT017.

References

1. Bruna, J., Zaremba, W., Szlam, A., LeCun, Y.: Spectral networks and locally connected networks on graphs. arXiv preprint arXiv:1312.6203 (2013)
2. Cao, S., Lu, W., Xu, Q.: Deep neural networks for learning graph representations. In: Proceedings of the AAAI Conference on Artificial Intelligence, vol. 30 (2016)
3. Cygan, M., Pilipczuk, M., Pilipczuk, M., Wojtaszczyk, J.O.: Sitting closer to friends than enemies, revisited. In: Rovan, B., Sassone, V., Widmayer, P. (eds.) MFCS 2012. LNCS, vol. 7464, pp. 296–307. Springer, Heidelberg (2012). https://doi.org/10.1007/978-3-642-32589-2_28
4. Derr, T., Ma, Y., Tang, J.: Signed graph convolutional networks. In: 2018 IEEE International Conference on Data Mining (ICDM), pp. 929–934. IEEE (2018)
5. Grover, A., Leskovec, J.: Node2vec: scalable feature learning for networks. In: Proceedings of the 22nd ACM SIGKDD International Conference on Knowledge Discovery and Data Mining, pp. 855–864 (2016)
6. Hamilton, W., Ying, Z., Leskovec, J.: Inductive representation learning on large graphs. In: Advances in Neural Information Processing Systems, pp. 1024–1034 (2017)
7. Heider, F.: Attitudes and cognitive organization. J. Psychol. **21**(1), 107–112 (1946)
8. Kim, J., Park, H., Lee, J.-E., Kang, U.: Side: representation learning in signed directed networks. In: Proceedings of the 2018 World Wide Web Conference, pp. 509–518 (2018)
9. Kipf, T.N., Welling, M.: Semi-supervised classification with graph convolutional networks. arXiv preprint arXiv:1609.02907 (2016)
10. Kumar, S., Hooi, B., Makhija, D., Kumar, M., Faloutsos, C., Subrahmanian, V.S.: Rev2: fraudulent user prediction in rating platforms. In: Proceedings of the Eleventh ACM International Conference on Web Search and Data Mining, pp. 333–341 (2018)
11. Kunegis, J., Schmidt, S., Lommatzsch, A., Lerner, J., De Luca, E.W., Albayrak, S.: Spectral analysis of signed graphs for clustering, prediction and visualization. In: Proceedings of the 2010 SIAM International Conference on Data Mining, pp. 559–570. SIAM (2010)
12. Leskovec, J., Lang, K.J., Dasgupta, A., Mahoney, M.W.: Community structure in large networks: natural cluster sizes and the absence of large well-defined clusters. Internet Math. **6**(1), 29–123 (2009)

13. McPherson, M., Smith-Lovin, L., Cook, J.M.: Birds of a feather: homophily in social networks. Ann. Rev. Sociol. **27**(1), 415–444 (2001)
14. Newman, M.: Networks. Oxford University Press, Oxford (2018)
15. Perozzi, B., Al-Rfou, R., Skiena, S.: DeepWalk: Online learning of social representations. In: Proceedings of the 20th ACM SIGKDD International Conference on Knowledge Discovery and Data Mining, pp. 701–710 (2014)
16. Phelps, C., Heidl, R., Wadhwa, A.: Knowledge, networks, and knowledge networks: a review and research agenda. J. Manag. **38**(4), 1115–1166 (2012)
17. Sen, P., Namata, G., Bilgic, M., Getoor, L., Galligher, B., Eliassi-Rad, T.: Collective classification in network data. AI Mag. **29**(3), 93 (2008)
18. Fensel, D., Sycara, K., Mylopoulos, J. (eds.): ISWC 2003. LNCS, vol. 2870. Springer, Heidelberg (2003). https://doi.org/10.1007/b14287
19. Tang, J., Qu, M., Wang, M., Zhang, M., Yan, J., Mei, Q.: Line: large-scale information network embedding. In: Proceedings of the 24th International Conference on World Wide Web, pp. 1067–1077 (2015)
20. Van der Maaten, L., Hinton, G.: Visualizing data using t-SNE. J. Mach. Learn. Res. **9**(11) (2008)
21. Veličković, P., Cucurull, G., Casanova, A., Romero, A., Lio, P., Bengio, Y.: Graph attention networks. arXiv preprint arXiv:1710.10903 (2017)
22. Wang, D., Cui, P., Zhu, W.: Structural deep network embedding. In: Proceedings of the 22nd ACM SIGKDD International Conference on Knowledge Discovery and Data Mining, pp. 1225–1234 (2016)
23. Wang, H., et al.: Knowledge-aware graph neural networks with label smoothness regularization for recommender systems. In: Proceedings of the 25th ACM SIGKDD International Conference on Knowledge Discovery & Data Mining, pp. 968–977 (2019)
24. Wang, S., Tang, J., Aggarwal, C., Chang, Y., Liu, H.: Signed network embedding in social media. In: Proceedings of the 2017 SIAM International Conference on Data Mining, pp. 327–335. SIAM (2017)
25. Wang, S., Tang, J., Aggarwal, C., Liu, H.: Linked document embedding for classification. In: Proceedings of the 25th ACM International on Conference on Information and Knowledge Management, pp. 115–124 (2016)
26. Xu, K., Hu, W., Leskovec, J., Jegelka, S.: How powerful are graph neural networks? arXiv preprint arXiv:1810.00826 (2018)
27. Yuan, S., Wu, X., Xiang, Y.: SNE: signed network embedding. In: Kim, J., Shim, K., Cao, L., Lee, J.-G., Lin, X., Moon, Y.-S. (eds.) PAKDD 2017. LNCS (LNAI), vol. 10235, pp. 183–195. Springer, Cham (2017). https://doi.org/10.1007/978-3-319-57529-2_15
28. Zhu, J., et al.: Graph neural networks with heterophily. In: Proceedings of the AAAI Conference on Artificial Intelligence, vol. 35, pp. 11168–11176 (2021)

SkaNet: Split Kernel Attention Network

Lipeng Chen[1,2], Daixi Jia[1,2], Hang Gao[1,2], Fengge Wu[1,2(✉)], and Junsuo Zhao[1,2]

[1] Institute of Software, Chinese Academy of Sciences, Beijing, China
fengge@iscas.ac.cn
[2] University of Chinese Academy of Sciences, Beijing, China

Abstract. Recently, convolutional neural networks (CNNs) and vision transformers (ViTs) have shown impressive results in the area of light-weight models for edge devices. However, the dominant CNNs and ViTs architectures rely heavily on a structured grid or sequence representation of images, which can result in inflexible handling of complex or irregular objects within them. In this paper, we propose SkaNet, an innovative, high-performance hybrid architecture that synergistically integrates the benefits of both CNNs and ViTs, and further enhances these advantages by graph representation learning. Specifically in SkaNet, we introduce a novel linear attention named split kernel attention (SKA) that exploits graph convolution to capture global semantic information and facilitate flexible recognition of irregular objects, splits input tensors into multiple channel groups adaptively, and fuses aforementioned modules into linear attention to efficiently aggregate contextual information. Extensive experiments demonstrate that SkaNet outperforms popular light-weight CNN and ViT-based models on common vision tasks and datasets. For classification on ImageNet-1k, SkaNet-S, with 5.5M parameters, achieves an impressive top-1 accuracy of 79.5%, surpassing MobileViT-S with an absolute gain of 1.1%. Furthermore, SkaNet-S exhibits superior performance in semantic segmentation on PASCAL VOC 2012 and object detection on COCO 2017. Our source code is available on GitHub at: https://github.com/charryglomc/skanet.

Keywords: Convolutional Neural Network · Attention · Graph Representation Learning · Light-weight

1 Introduction

CNNs [11,22,25,27] and the recently introduced ViTs [6,24,35] have significantly advanced great performance in various computer vision tasks, including image classification, semantic segmentation and object detection. From our perspective, both CNNs and ViTs are indispensable and have the following pros and cons: CNNs have better hardware support and are generally easier to train, which is why the majority of existing works employ CNN-based designs to develop efficient models. However, one limitation of CNNs is that they have a local receptive

L. Iliadis et al. (Eds.): ICANN 2023, LNCS 14258, pp. 459–473, 2023.
https://doi.org/10.1007/978-3-031-44192-9_37

field and are unable to effectively model global context [33]. Compared to CNNs, the introduction of ViTs based on self-attention mechanism [6] allows for explicit modeling of global interactions as it facilitates long-range interactions. However, they are typically compute intensive, and may be difficult to handle high resolution images. Besides, self-attention in ViTs only considers spatial dimension adaptation and often ignores channel dimension adaptation, which is a critical aspect for visual tasks. Here, we argue that can we design an efficient mobile architecture by combining the complementary advantages of CNNs and ViTs effectively?

Additionally, image data is typically represented as a regular grid connected by adjacent pixels in Euclidean space. For an input image, CNNs [20] use convolution filters to slide on the image for operation. Recent ViTs [24] split an image into multiple patches of equal size, and expand each patch into a 1D sequence as input. However, objects in most images are not square and irregular, therefore it is not feasible to directly transform images into ordinary grids or sequence structures using CNNS and ViTs. Besides, CNNs and ViTs leverage the locality and sparsity of features in image processing, but lack the capability to understand global semantic information. To overcome this limitation, our model aims to acquire the ability to capture global semantic information and enable flexible recognition of irregular objects.

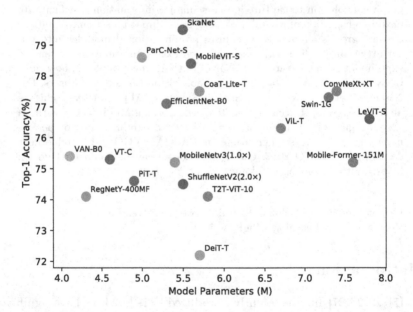

Fig. 1. Results of different models on ImageNet-1K validation set.

In this paper, our goal is to design a novel efficient hybrid architecture in the area of light-weight models for edge devices. For the current state-of-the-art lightweight models, pure CNN-based architectures lack the capability to effectively model global contextual information. The incorporation of ViT-based models has facilitated the modeling of global contextual information and enabled spatial dimension adaptation. Nonetheless, ViT-based models are computationally expensive and do not account for channel dimension adaptation. Directly transforming images into regular grids or sequence structures using CNNs and ViTs is not a flexible or efficient method for identifying irregular objects and comprehending global semantic information within images. To address the aforementioned issues, we present a new linear attention method called SKA. SKA initially partitions the input feature map into patches and considers each patch as an individual node. Subsequently, it constructs a graph for every image based on the representation of the nodes. Through the use of graph convolution, SKA is able to take into account the features of both each node and its neighboring nodes, resulting in a more flexible and efficient approach to visual perception that captures global semantic correlation between nodes. In terms of channel-wise processing, SKA divides input tensors into multiple channel groups to address redundancy issues commonly encountered with high channel counts to enable channel dimension adaptation. Moreover, SKA integrates the aforementioned modules with linear attention to aggregate contextual information effectively. Building upon the SKA method, we propose a new light-weight and high-performance vision network called SkaNet. Extensive experiments demonstrate that with almost equivalent parameter count, our SkaNet-S achieves 79.5% top-1 accuracy on the ImageNet1K classification task, outperforming the previously popular MobileViT-S with an absolute gain of 1.1%. As shown in Fig. 1, Compared with a variety of light-weight models, SkaNet-S achieves accuracy advantages with smaller parameters. For experiments of semantic segmentation and object detection, our proposed SkaNet-S also achieves higher mIOU and mAP, while having fewer parameters.

Our main contributions are summarized as follows:

- We design a novel linear attention named SKA that utilizes graph convolution to capture global semantic information and enable flexible recognition of irregular objects, splits input tensors into multiple channel groups to adapt to channel dimension information. We jointly uses aforementioned modules into linear attention to aggregate contextual information, which brings higher accuracy.
- Based on SKA, we propose SkaNet, a new efficient hybrid architecture, which inherits the advantages of CNNs and ViTs, while abandoning their disadvantages. Besides, our proposed SkaNet also considers the advantages of graph convolution, which enables more flexible and efficient visual perception.
- We conduct extensive experiments in common vision tasks and datasets. Compared with popular light-weight models, our proposed SkaNet achieves good trade-off between model size and accuracy. We hope the action of intruding graph representation learning to light-weight vision network will promote the way toward further research and development of more powerful neural network architectures for computer vision tasks.

2   Related Work

2.1   CNNs, Attention and MLP for Vision

Traditionally, CNNs have been the mainstream network architecture for light-weight vision tasks [14,19,20]. However, with the advent of MobileNet [15] and Xception [4], depth-wise separable convolution has become the most widely used architecture in recent years [1,4]. In 2015, the paper "Multi-scale Context Aggregation by Dilated Convolutions" [38] introduced dilated convolution primarily for semantic segmentation tasks. The paper proposed using dilated convolution to increase the receptive field of convolutional operations, enabling better capture of contextual information within images. Despite this, the lack of global interactions has restricted the performance of the approach.

As attention mechanisms become increasingly popular and are applied in various fields, researchers are continuously proposing new attention mechanisms and improvement strategies. Some examples include multi-head self-attention [6, 24,35] and hierarchical attention [24]. Self-attention allows for explicit modeling of global interactions. However, it still faces some challenges. For instance, the computational complexity of self-attention is relatively high when processing high-resolution images [24]. Additionally, the self-attention mechanism treats 2D images as 1D sequences, which weakens the crucial 2D structure of images.

Multilayer Perceptrons (MLP) has become an essential component in computer vision and is widely used in various vision tasks, such as object detection and segmentation [2]. Following the MLP in VAN [11], we apply it in our SKA. The MLP is made up of a point-wise convolution, a depth-wise convolution, and another point-wise convolution, which facilitates the flow of information in both spatial and channel dimension.

2.2   Graph Convolutional Network

GCNs were first introduced by Thomas N. Kipf et al. in 2017 [17] as an approach that enables neural networks to operate directly on graph data, making it applicable to tasks such as image classification and social network analysis. Since their introduction, researchers have continuously developed and improved GCNs. Notable advancements include non-Euclidean space convolution, where traditional convolutional neural networks require graphs to be transformed into Euclidean space, which can destroy the topology of the graph. Researchers have proposed graph convolutional networks based on spectral graph theory [17] to allow the network to perform convolution operations while maintaining the graph's topology. Additionally, due to the non-trivial topological structure and sparsity of graph data, researchers have proposed many deep graph convolutional network models, such as Graph Attention Networks (GAT) [34] and GraphSAGE [12]. In contrast, traditional methods that transform images into grid or sequence structures using CNNs or ViTs are redundant and inflexible. Our proposed SKA module employs graph convolution to reconstruct the relationships between nodes, flexibly capturing global semantic features in images.

3   Method

3.1   Overall Framework of SkaNet

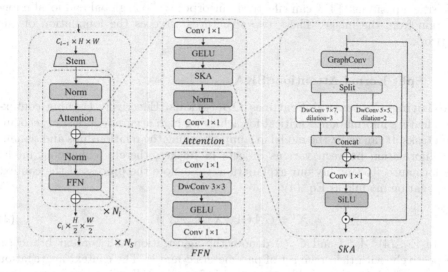

Fig. 2. Left Column: SkaNet is composed of N_s stages, each of which is comprised of one stem and N_i blocks. Typically, N_s is set to 4. specifically in every stage of SkaNet-S, we set N_i to 3, 3, 12, and 2. Middle Column: Structure of Attention and FFN. Right Column: Structure of our proposed module SKA.

Recent research has revealed that CNNs tend to favor pyramid architectures, unlike ViT-based structures [14]. In computer vision tasks, a pyramid structure typically consists of a sequence of downsampled images, which each image is a reduced version of the previous image. These downsampled images can be applied to process images of varying scales and resolutions. To this end, we build pyramidal network structures based on the design principles of ConvNeXt [25], extracting hierarchical features at four distinct scales in four stages. For each stage of the model, as illustrated in the left column of Fig. 2, the input image or the output from the previous stage is initially sampled to decrease the inherent redundancy and computational burden of the image. This process can be represented as:

$$X' = Stem\,(X)\,. \tag{1}$$

where input: $X \in \mathbb{R}^{C \times H \times W}$, output: $X' \in \mathbb{R}^{C' \times \frac{H}{2} \times \frac{W}{2}}$. Subsequently, the features flows into the Attention and feed-forward network (FFN), preceded by a normalization layer. Additionally, a shortcut connection of addition is introduced to better aggregate features.

$$X' = X + \text{Attention}(\text{Norm}(X)), \tag{2}$$
$$X'' = X' + \text{FFN}(\text{Norm}(X')). \tag{3}$$

The middle column of Fig. 2 illustrates the Attention and FFN components. Attention incorporates our proposed SKA module, which can adaptively capture contextual information and global semantic information while paying attention to critical positions. FFN can effectively incorporate both global and local information from the image. These two structures serve as the foundation of our network.

3.2 Split Kernel Attention: SKA

Revisiting Contextual Features Operations. Effectively learning contextual feature information is critical for achieving high accuracy in visual recognition tasks. It can assist the model in comprehending the relationships and semantic information between various objects in images, thereby enhancing model performance. To simplify our explanation, we denote the process of the context aggregation module as Eq. (4):

$$X' = CA\left(A_\phi(X), C_\psi(X)\right). \tag{4}$$

In Eq. (4), $A_\phi(\cdot)$ and $C_\psi(\cdot)$ denote the aggregation and context branches, respectively, with their own set of parameters ϕ and ψ. The context aggregation module calculates the significance of each feature in X using the aggregation branch $A_\phi(X)$, which is then combined with features from the context branch $C_\psi(X)$ through $CA(\cdot, \cdot)$. The final output X' is obtained by this process.

Table 1. Examples of commonly used context aggregation methods, all of which are derived based on Eq. (4), where $\otimes$ represents matrix product, $\odot$ represents element-wise product, and W represents linear projection.

Row	Method	$CA(\cdot, \cdot)$	$A_\phi(\cdot)$	$C_\psi(\cdot)$
1	Self-attention	$\otimes$	Softmax $\left(\frac{XW_Q(XW_K)^T}{\sqrt{d}}\right)$	XW_V
2	SE	$\odot$	Sigmoid $\left((AVG(X)W_\phi)W_\psi\right)$	X
3	LKA	$\odot$	$((XW_{dw})W_{dw-d})W_p$	X

Table 1 presents three different attention mechanisms in rows 1 to 3, along with their strengths and weaknesses. The self-attention mechanism proposed in transformers (row 1) has been extensively studied, but it suffers from high computational complexity when processing long sequences or high input resolutions. In row 2, Hu et al. proposed the squeeze-and-excitation (SE) module, which reduces feature dimensionality by aggregating contextual information for each position. However, condensing each feature map into a scalar value may lead to some loss of information. Row 3 introduces LKA, an adaptive attention method that adjusts the output based on the input feature rather than using a normalized attention map. Nonetheless, LKA still has some limitations in terms of channel adaptivity and extracting global semantic information flexibly. Therefore, we propose a novel attention module in the right column of Fig. 2 named SKA that overcomes these limitations. The SKA module can be denoted as:

$$Attention = \text{SiLU}\left(\text{Conv}_{1 \times 1}\left(\text{CSM}(\text{GraphConv}(X))\right)\right), \quad (5)$$

$$Y = Attention \odot X. \quad (6)$$

We begin with the feature map $X \in \mathbb{R}^{C \times H \times W}$. Next, X undergoes a graph convolution structure that facilitates the exchange and aggregation of node information. This aids in identifying irregular objects and comprehending global semantic information of images. Following this, channel splitting module (CSM) divides the input tensors into several channel groups to adapt to channel dimension information, and a point-wise convolution is used to better capture the relationship between channel dimension. Prior to aggregating the context and aggregation branches, we apply SiLU activation [7] in the context branch, which exhibits a stable training property. $Attention \in \mathbb{R}^{C \times H \times W}$ denotes the attention map. Utilizing the aforementioned $Attention$, the initial X is weighted to prioritize crucial positions in computer vision. Ultimately, we obtain the result $Y \in \mathbb{R}^{C \times H \times W}$, which represents the output of our SKA module.

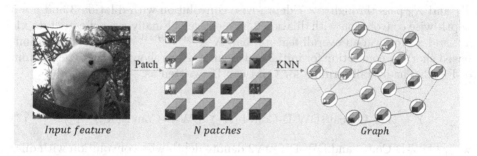

Fig. 3. The process of transforming an input feature into a graph structure.

GraphConv. As it is widely acknowledged, transforming images directly into regular grids or sequential structures using CNNs and ViTs is inflexible when it comes to identifying irregular objects and comprehending global semantic information contained within complex images. Taking inspiration from recent developments in this field [13,21], we begin by partitioning the feature map $X \in \mathbb{R}^{C \times H \times W}$ into N patches, and each node in the graph contains the features of the corresponding patch $X_i \in \mathbb{R}^F$. Here, F represents the dimensionality of the feature vector. For each node v_i, we apply the k-nearest neighbors (KNN) [10] algorithm to locate its K nearest neighbors $v_j(j = 1, 2..., K)$, connecting them via edges e_{ij} within the graph structure, as illustrated in Fig. 3. Finally, a graph $\mathcal{G} = (\mathcal{V}, \mathcal{E})$ is obtained, capturing the relationships between the various nodes.

Here, $\mathcal{V}$ and $\mathcal{E}$ represent the sets of all nodes and edges within the resulting graph structure, respectively. We use the GraphConv operation on the resultant features graph $\mathcal{G} = (\mathcal{V}, \mathcal{E})$ to compute the furthest nodes among neighbors by means of a max operation, and aggregate the features of these two nodes. Next, edge features are updated for the furthest nodes as well as the original node, accomplished via an MLP with a specified number of layer neurons. This leads to the updated graph $\mathcal{G}'$. As such, we can leverage the GraphConv module to effectively learn vision representation within given images.

Channel Splitting Module. The large receptive field in the ViTs makes it easier to capture long-term interactions, which is also considered as one of the key advantages of ViTs. Inspired by some recent efforts [11,22], we started to design a CSM as follows: Our initial design involves utilizing a pair of convolution kernels with a significant difference in size: a 21×21 convolution and a 10×10 convolution. As an extension of the approach used in VAN [11], we then decompose the 21×21 convolution into a combination of a 7×7 depth-wise convolution with dilation 3, a 5×5 depth-wise convolution, and a 1×1 convolution. Similarly, a 10×10 convolution can be decomposed into a 5×5 depth-wise convolution with dilation 2, a 3×3 depth-wise convolution and a 1×1 convolution. To completely integrate different receptive fields, we partition the features $X \in \mathbb{R}^{C \times H \times W}$ along channel dimension into three subsets: $X_1 \in \mathbb{R}^{C_1 \times H \times W}$, $X_2 \in \mathbb{R}^{C_2 \times H \times W}$ and $X_3 \in \mathbb{R}^{C_3 \times H \times W}$. In addition to X_2 for identity mapping, X_1 and X_3 pass through 7×7 depth-wise convolution with dilation 3 and 5×5 depth-wise convolution with dilation 2, respectively. Finally, we concatentate x1, x2, and x3 to form an overall feature map $X' \in \mathbb{R}^{C \times H \times W}$ and use an addition-based shortcut connection for initial feature map X, as shown in the right column of Fig. 2. The overall formula for CSM can be written as:

$$Y = X + \text{Concat}\left(\text{DW-D-Conv1}\left(X_1\right), \text{DW-D-Conv2}\left(X_3\right), X_2\right). \qquad (7)$$

where DW-D-Conv1 and DW-D-Conv2 denote depth-wise convolution with dilation as described above, X_1, X_2, and X_3 represent the feature results obtained after dividing the features in X. Through CSM we design, features with adaptive channels perceptions can be extracted and more attentions can be pushed to local and global interactions.

4   Experiments

To evaluate the general-purpose nature of SkaNet, we conduct extensive experiments to verify the effectiveness of our method: (1) ImageNet-1K [5] dataset for image classification, (2) PASCAL VOC 2012 [8] dataset for semantic segmentation, (3) COCO 2017 [23] dataset for object detection. All experiments are implemented with PyTorch on Centos workstations with NVIDIA RTX5000 GPUs.

4.1   ImageNet Classification

In Table 2, we see that our model achieve very competitive performance with state-of-the-art ViTs and hybrid models, and CNNs.

Comparison with ViTs. At approximately the same amount of parameters, the accuracy of our SkaNet-S on the ImageNet-1K dataset is far superior to recent ViT variants. For example, SkaNet-S obtains 78.9% top-accuracy with the input size of 224×224, surpassing T2T-ViT-10 [39] and DeiT-T [32] by 4.8% and 6.7% absolute margins respectively.

Table 2. ImageNet-1K classification performance of light-weight (around 5M parameters) models.

Frameworks	Model	Date	Resolution	Params(M)	FLOPs(G)	Top-1(%)
ViTs	PVTv2-B0 [36]	Springer'2022	224^2	3.4	0.6	70.5
	T2T-ViT-7 [39]	ICCV'2021	224^2	4.3	1.1	71.7
	T2T-ViT-10 [39]	ICCV'2021	224^2	5.8	1.2	74.1
	DeiT-T [32]	ICML'2021	224^2	5.7	1.08	72.2
Hybrid	Mobile-Former-151M [3]	CVPR'2022	224^2	7.6	1.51	75.2
	ViT-C [6]	NIPS'2021	224^2	4.6	1.10	75.3
	ViL-T [16]	NIPS'2021	224^2	6.7	1.3	76.3
	LeViT-S [9]	ICCV'2021	224^2	7.8	0.31	76.6
	Swin-1G [24]	ICCV'2021	224^2	7.3	1.00	77.3
	CoaT-Lite-T [37]	ICCV'2021	224^2	5.7	160	77.5
	MobileViT-S [27]	ICLR'2022	256^2	5.6	4.02	78.4
CNNs	MobileNetV3 (1.0×) [18]	ICCV'2019	224^2	5.4	0.23	75.2
	ShuffleNetV2 (2.0×) [26]	ECCV'2018	224^2	5.5	0.60	75.4
	EfficientNet-B0 [31]	ICML'2019	224^2	5.3	0.39	77.1
	RegNetY-400MF [28]	CVPR'2020	224^2	4.3	0.40	74.1
	VAN-B0 [11]	arXiv'2022	224^2	4.1	0.88	75.4
	ConvNext-XT [25]	CVPR'2022	224^2	7.4	0.60	77.5
	ParC-Net-S [40]	ECCV'2022	256^2	5.0	3.48	78.6
	SkaNet-S	Ours	224^2	5.5	1.95	**78.9**
	SkaNet-S	Ours	256^2	5.5	2.36	**79.5**

Comparison with Hybrid Models. We also compare the hybrid models proposed in recent years(Mobile-Former(Chen et al. 2022), ViT(Xiao et al.2021), ViL(Kim et al. 2021), LeViT(Graham et al. 2021), Swin(Liu et al. 2021), CoaT(Li et al. 2021) and MobileViT(Mehta et al. 2022)). As shown in Table 2, compared with Swin-1G [24], which is also based on the pyramid structure, our model performance exceeds 1.7% absolute advantage with less parameters. We conduct a fair comparison with MobileViT-S [27] with the same input resolution 256×256, almost the same amount of parameters. SkaNet-S improves by 1.1% top-accuracy compared to MobileViT-S. The results show that our model exceeds their performance.

Comparison with ConvNets. SkaNet-S is significantly better than the previously proposed light-weight CNNs. For example, SkaNet-S achieves an accuracy rate of 78.9% at about 5.5M with 224×224 resolution, which outperforms 3.7% of MobileNetV3 (1.0×) [18], 3.5% of ShuffleNetV2 (2.0×) [26], EfficientNet-B0 [31] 1.8% and 4.8% for RegNetY-400M [28]. For the currently popular model VAN-B0 [11] and ConvNext-XT [25] based on the pyramid architecture, SkaNet-S surpasses them by a healthy margin on various model sizes and settings. Notably, It also surpasses the recently proposed Parc-Net-S [40] by 0.9% at an input resolution of 256 × 256.

4.2   Dense Prediction Tasks

SkaNet for Semantic Segmentation. We evaluate our SkaNet for semantic segmentation task on PASCAL VOC dataset using the commonly used DeepLabv3 framework at an input resolution of 512 × 512. As shown in the Table 3(a), with similar model size, our SkaNet-S outperform MobileViT-S from the perspective of mean intersection over union(mIOU). Our model obtains 80.1 mIOU on the validation dataset, providing a 1.0 points gain over MobileViT-S. These results clearly demonstrate the effectiveness and scalability of our SkaNet on semantic segmentation.

SkaNet for Object Detection. We use SkaNet as a backbone in SSDLite at an input resolution of 320 × 320. SSDLite is that standard convolutions are replaced with separable convolutions in the detection head and then we call this framework as SSDLite. As shown in the Table 3(b), SkaNet-S gives competitive performance compared to MobileVit-S backbone detection accuracy. SkaNet-S achieves the highest 28.9 box AP, with less number of Parameters.

Table 3. (a) Semantic Segmentation with DeepLabv3 on PASCAL VOC 2012. (b) Object Detection with SSDLite on COCO 2017.

Feature backbone	Params(M)	mIoU	Feature backbone	Params(M)	mAP
MobileNetV1 [15]	11.1	75.3	MobileNetV1 [15]	5.1	22.2
MobileNetV2 [29]	4.5	75.7	MobileNetV2 [29]	4.3	22.1
ParC-Net-S [40]	5.8	79.7	ParC-Net-S [40]	5.2	28.8
MobileViT-S [27]	6.4	79.1	MobileViT-S [27]	5.7	27.7
SkaNet-S	6.3	**80.1**	**SkaNet-S**	5.6	**28.9**
(a)			(b)		

4.3   Ablation and Analysis

The Effects of Modules in SKA. We conduct ablation studies to demonstrate that each component of the SKA is integral. Table 4 illustrates that all parts in SKA are essential to achieving improved performance.

Table 4. Ablation on different components of SKA. The results show the benefits of each part in our design. Specifically, "w/o GraphConv" indicates that GraphConv was replaced with $DW_{5\times5}$; "CSM" refers to the channel splitting module in SKA, while "w/o CSM" represents replacing CSM with a 7×7 depth-wise convolution with dilation 3. "w/o Attention" indicates the absence of shortcut connections, while "w/o Attention(Add)" uses a shortcut connection with addition.

Row	Component	Params(M)	FLOPs(G)	Top-1(%)
1	w/o GraphConv	5.4	2.29	78.3
2	w/o CSM	5.6	2.36	78.6
3	w/o CSM (no-Add)	5.5	2.36	79.2
4	w/o $Conv_{1\times1}$	5.2	2.36	78.8
5	w/o SiLU	5.5	2.36	79.0
6	w/o GELU	5.5	2.36	79.3
7	w/o Sigmoid	5.5	2.36	79.1
8	w/o Attention	5.5	2.36	78.4
9	w/o Attention (Add)	5.5	2.36	78.7
10	**SkaNet-S(ours)**	5.5	2.36	**79.5**

- **GraghConv.** By analyzing the possible complex interactions between pixels at different locations in an image, GraghConv gets the ability to capture global semantic information. As shown in row 1 of the results, utilizing Graph-Conv leads to a 1.2% increase in accuracy compared to using $DW_{5\times5}$.
- **CSM.** We utilize the CSM to capture adaptive channel features and long-term dependencies. As shown in rows 2–3 of the results, replacing CSM with a 7×7 depth-wise convolution with dilation 3 results in a drop in accuracy of 0.9%, while removing the shortcut connection with addition leads to a decrease of approximately 0.3%. These findings highlight the crucial role of CSM design in image tasks.
- **Conv1 × 1.** Conv1 × 1 facilitates channel self-adaptability and promotes the exchange of information in the channel direction. In row 4, after adding Conv1 × 1, it can bring 0.7% accuracy improvement to SkaNet-S.
- **Activation Functions.** SiLU is an activation function with smoothness, non-monotonicity, and normalization effect. It has been proved that it performs better than traditional activation functions such as ReLU in some tasks. As Shown in rows 5–7, SiLU yield better performances than using Sigmoid or Tanh activation functions.
- **Attention Mechanism.** The introduction of the attention mechanism can be seen as enabling the network to efficiently aggregate contextual information. We introduce the attention mechanism in our SKA. As shown in row 8–9, Skanet-S improved by 1.1% compared to no attention, and increased by 0.8% compared to addition.

Visualization of CAM. Class activation mapping (CAM) is a commonly used tool for visualizing the differentiation of regions through mapping. In this study, we utilize the Grad-CAM [30] activation feature class mapping on ImageNet-1K in Fig. 4. The transformer architecture based on self-attention mechanism (DeiT-S and MobileViT-S) exhibits more detailed activation maps than CNNs, but they also activated some irrelevant parts. Compared to VAN-T, our SkaNet-S has a greater focus on semantic objects, displaying more refined activation maps.

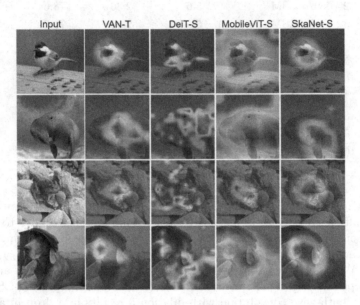

Fig. 4. Visualization of Grad-CAM activation maps of the models trained on ImageNet-1K.

5   Conclusion

In this paper, we propose a novel linear attention named SKA that capture global semantic information, contextual features information, and adapts to channel dimension information. Based on SKA, we present SkaNet, a new light-weight vision network, which leverages the respective advantages of CNNs and ViTs while mitigating their drawbacks. Additionally, SkaNet integrates the benefits of graph convolution, enabling more flexible and efficient visual perception. With preferable complexity-performance trade-offs, our proposed SkaNet can be well applied to downstream tasks.

Acknowledgements. This research was supported by CAS Project for Young Scientists in Basic Research, Grant No. YSBR-040.

References

1. Chen, L.-C., Zhu, Y., Papandreou, G., Schroff, F., Adam, H.: Encoder-decoder with atrous separable convolution for semantic image segmentation. In: Ferrari, V., Hebert, M., Sminchisescu, C., Weiss, Y. (eds.) ECCV 2018. LNCS, vol. 11211, pp. 833–851. Springer, Cham (2018). https://doi.org/10.1007/978-3-030-01234-2_49
2. Chen, S., Xie, E., Ge, C., Chen, R., Liang, D., Luo, P.: CycleMLP: a MLP-like architecture for dense prediction. arXiv preprint arXiv:2107.10224 (2021)
3. Chen, Y., et al.: Mobile-former: bridging mobilenet and transformer. In: Proceedings of the IEEE/CVF Conference on Computer Vision and Pattern Recognition, pp. 5270–5279 (2022)
4. Chollet, F.: Xception: deep learning with depthwise separable convolutions. In: Proceedings of the IEEE Conference on Computer Vision and Pattern Recognition, pp. 1251–1258 (2017)
5. Deng, J., Dong, W., Socher, R., Li, L.J., Li, K., Fei-Fei, L.: ImageNet: a large-scale hierarchical image database. In: 2009 IEEE Conference on Computer Vision and Pattern Recognition, pp. 248–255. IEEE (2009)
6. Dosovitskiy, A., et al.: An image is worth 16×16 words: transformers for image recognition at scale. arXiv preprint arXiv:2010.11929 (2020)
7. Elfwing, S., Uchibe, E., Doya, K.: Sigmoid-weighted linear units for neural network function approximation in reinforcement learning. Neural Netw. **107**, 3–11 (2018)
8. Everingham, M., Van Gool, L., Williams, C.K., Winn, J., Zisserman, A.: The pascal visual object classes (VOC) challenge. Int. J. Comput. Vis. **88**, 303–338 (2010)
9. Graham, B., et al.: LeViT: a vision transformer in convnet's clothing for faster inference. In: Proceedings of the IEEE/CVF International Conference on Computer Vision, pp. 12259–12269 (2021)
10. Guo, G., Wang, H., Bell, D., Bi, Y., Greer, K.: KNN model-based approach in classification. In: Meersman, R., Tari, Z., Schmidt, D.C. (eds.) OTM 2003. LNCS, vol. 2888, pp. 986–996. Springer, Heidelberg (2003). https://doi.org/10.1007/978-3-540-39964-3_62
11. Guo, M.H., Lu, C.Z., Liu, Z.N., Cheng, M.M., Hu, S.M.: Visual attention network. arXiv preprint arXiv:2202.09741 (2022)
12. Hamilton, W., Ying, Z., Leskovec, J.: Inductive representation learning on large graphs. In: Advances in Neural Information Processing Systems, vol. 30 (2017)
13. Han, K., Wang, Y., Guo, J., Tang, Y., Wu, E.: Vision GNN: an image is worth graph of nodes. arXiv preprint arXiv:2206.00272 (2022)
14. He, K., Zhang, X., Ren, S., Sun, J.: Deep residual learning for image recognition. In: Proceedings of the IEEE Conference on Computer Vision and Pattern Recognition, pp. 770–778 (2016)
15. Howard, A.G., et al.: MobileNets: efficient convolutional neural networks for mobile vision applications. arXiv preprint arXiv:1704.04861 (2017)
16. Kim, W., Son, B., Kim, I.: ViLT: vision-and-language transformer without convolution or region supervision. In: International Conference on Machine Learning, pp. 5583–5594. PMLR (2021)
17. Kipf, T.N., Welling, M.: Semi-supervised classification with graph convolutional networks. arXiv preprint arXiv:1609.02907 (2016)
18. Koonce, B.: MobileNetV3. In: Convolutional Neural Networks with Swift for Tensorflow, pp. 125–144. Apress, Berkeley (2021). https://doi.org/10.1007/978-1-4842-6168-2_11

19. Krizhevsky, A., Sutskever, I., Hinton, G.E.: ImageNet classification with deep convolutional neural networks. Commun. ACM **60**(6), 84–90 (2017)
20. LeCun, Y., Bottou, L., Bengio, Y., Haffner, P.: Gradient-based learning applied to document recognition. Proc. IEEE **86**(11), 2278–2324 (1998)
21. Li, G., Muller, M., Thabet, A., Ghanem, B.: DeepGCNs: can GCNs go as deep as CNNs? In: Proceedings of the IEEE/CVF International Conference on Computer Vision, pp. 9267–9276 (2019)
22. Li, S., et al.: Efficient multi-order gated aggregation network. arXiv preprint arXiv:2211.03295 (2022)
23. Lin, T.-Y., et al.: Microsoft COCO: common objects in context. In: Fleet, D., Pajdla, T., Schiele, B., Tuytelaars, T. (eds.) ECCV 2014. LNCS, vol. 8693, pp. 740–755. Springer, Cham (2014). https://doi.org/10.1007/978-3-319-10602-1_48
24. Liu, Z., et al.: Swin transformer: hierarchical vision transformer using shifted windows. In: Proceedings of the IEEE/CVF International Conference on Computer Vision, pp. 10012–10022 (2021)
25. Liu, Z., Mao, H., Wu, C.Y., Feichtenhofer, C., Darrell, T., Xie, S.: A convnet for the 2020s. In: Proceedings of the IEEE/CVF Conference on Computer Vision and Pattern Recognition, pp. 11976–11986 (2022)
26. Ma, N., Zhang, X., Zheng, H.T., Sun, J.: ShuffleNet V2: practical guidelines for efficient CNN architecture design. In: Proceedings of the European Conference on Computer Vision (ECCV), pp. 116–131 (2018)
27. Mehta, S., Rastegari, M.: MobileViT: light-weight, general-purpose, and mobile-friendly vision transformer. arXiv preprint arXiv:2110.02178 (2021)
28. Radosavovic, I., Kosaraju, R.P., Girshick, R., He, K., Dollár, P.: Designing network design spaces. In: Proceedings of the IEEE/CVF Conference on Computer Vision and Pattern Recognition, pp. 10428–10436 (2020)
29. Sandler, M., Howard, A., Zhu, M., Zhmoginov, A., Chen, L.C.: MobileNetV2: inverted residuals and linear bottlenecks. In: Proceedings of the IEEE Conference on Computer Vision and Pattern Recognition, pp. 4510–4520 (2018)
30. Selvaraju, R.R., Cogswell, M., Das, A., Vedantam, R., Parikh, D., Batra, D.: Grad-CAM: visual explanations from deep networks via gradient-based localization. In: Proceedings of the IEEE International Conference on Computer Vision, pp. 618–626 (2017)
31. Tan, M., Le, Q.: EfficientNet: rethinking model scaling for convolutional neural networks. In: International Conference on Machine Learning, pp. 6105–6114. PMLR (2019)
32. Touvron, H., Cord, M., Douze, M., Massa, F., Sablayrolles, A., Jégou, H.: Training data-efficient image transformers & distillation through attention. In: International Conference on Machine Learning, pp. 10347–10357. PMLR (2021)
33. Tuli, S., Dasgupta, I., Grant, E., Griffiths, T.L.: Are convolutional neural networks or transformers more like human vision? arXiv preprint arXiv:2105.07197 (2021)
34. Veličković, P., Cucurull, G., Casanova, A., Romero, A., Lio, P., Bengio, Y.: Graph attention networks. arXiv preprint arXiv:1710.10903 (2017)
35. Wang, W., et al.: Pyramid vision transformer: a versatile backbone for dense prediction without convolutions. In: Proceedings of the IEEE/CVF International Conference on Computer Vision, pp. 568–578 (2021)
36. Wang, W., et al.: PVT v2: improved baselines with pyramid vision transformer. Comput. Vis. Media **8**(3), 415–424 (2022)
37. Xu, W., Xu, Y., Chang, T., Tu, Z.: Co-scale conv-attentional image transformers. In: Proceedings of the IEEE/CVF International Conference on Computer Vision, pp. 9981–9990 (2021)

38. Yu, F., Koltun, V.: Multi-scale context aggregation by dilated convolutions. arXiv preprint arXiv:1511.07122 (2015)
39. Yuan, L., et al.: Tokens-to-Token ViT: training vision transformers from scratch on imagenet. In: Proceedings of the IEEE/CVF International Conference on Computer Vision, pp. 558–567 (2021)
40. Zhang, H., Hu, W., Wang, X.: ParC-Net: position aware circular convolution with merits from ConvNets and transformer. In: Avidan, S., Brostow, G., Cissé, M., Farinella, G.M., Hassner, T. (eds.) ECCV 2022. LNCS, vol. 13686, pp. 613–630. Springer, Cham (2022). https://doi.org/10.1007/978-3-031-19809-0_35

Syntax-Aware Complex-Valued Neural Machine Translation

Yang Liu and Yuexian Hou[✉]

College of Intelligence and Computing, Tianjin University, Tianjin, China
{lauyon,yxhou}@tju.edu.cn

Abstract. Syntax has been proven to be remarkably effective in neural machine translation (NMT). Previous models obtained syntax information from syntactic parsing tools and integrated it into NMT models to improve translation performance. In this work, we propose a method to incorporate syntax information into a complex-valued Encoder-Decoder architecture. The proposed model jointly learns word-level and syntax-level attention scores from the source side to the target side using an attention mechanism. Importantly, it is not dependent on specific network architectures and can be directly integrated into any existing sequence-to-sequence (Seq2Seq) framework. The experimental results demonstrate that the proposed method can bring significant improvements in BLEU scores on two datasets. In particular, the proposed method achieves a greater improvement in BLEU scores in translation tasks involving language pairs with significant syntactic differences.

Keywords: Neural machine translation · Attention mechanism · Complex-valued neural network

1 Introduction

In recent years, neural machine translation (NMT) has benefited from the sequence-to-sequence (Seq2Seq) framework and attention mechanism [1,12,13,19]. NMT has shown effective improvements over statistical machine translation (SMT) models in various language pairs. The attention-based encoder-decoder architecture encodes the source language sentence into a sequence of hidden real-valued vectors and then computes their weighted sum based on the attention mechanism to generate the target language sentence predictions in the decoder [5].

Syntax information has been widely used and proven effective in SMT [4,11,23], and researchers have also attempted to incorporate syntax information into NMT [6,17,24]. Several studies have demonstrated the significance of syntax information, which is also briefly discussed in this work. For example, in the sentence "He saw her duck", according to the syntactic analysis results shown in Fig. 1, when "duck" is used as an attributive of "her", it means "a duck". In this case, the dependency relationship between "duck" and "her" is *poss* (possessive). However, when "duck" is used as the predicate of "her", it means "to

L. Iliadis et al. (Eds.): ICANN 2023, LNCS 14258, pp. 474–485, 2023.
https://doi.org/10.1007/978-3-031-44192-9_38

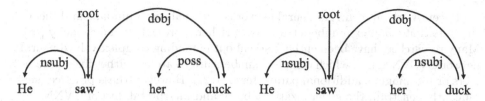

Fig. 1. An example that illustrates how different syntactic dependency structures can lead to a change in the meaning of a sentence.

dodge", "to avoid", or "to duck down". In this case, the dependency relationship between "duck" and "her" is *nsubj* (noun subject). This suggests that syntactic information greatly affects the meaning of words.

A considerable number of researchers have integrated syntactic information into NMT to enhance translation performance. Most of these studies integrated syntax on the source side [6,17]. However, in reality, the syntactic dependencies differ across different languages. Therefore, previous research lacked matching of syntactic dependencies across different languages. As shown in Fig. 2, consider the Chinese sentence "他在公园里散步。" and its English translation "He went for a walk in the park." These two sentences convey the same meaning, which is describing someone walking in the park. However, from the perspective of syntactic analysis, they are not exactly the same.

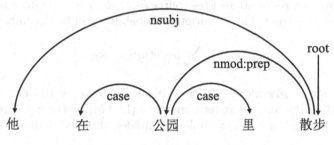

(a) Syntactic dependencies in Chinese.

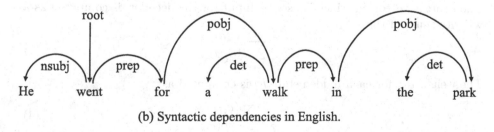

(b) Syntactic dependencies in English.

Fig. 2. An example that illustrates how the same sentence meaning can have different syntactic dependency structures in different languages.

Recent work on recurrent neural networks and analysis of fundamental theory suggests that complex numbers may have a richer representational capacity [18]. Many researchers have been enthusiastic about extending complex-valued neural networks (CVNNs), in which complex numbers are treated as either fixed parameters or meaningless additional parameters [21, 22]. However, these practices significantly constrain the generalization ability and interpretability of CVNNs.

In this work, syntactic information from different languages is embedded into CVNNs. The complex-valued attention mechanism is used to score complex-valued hidden vectors, aiming to jointly learn the attention scores of both words and syntax. This approach does not depend on specific model architectures and can be applied to any existing Seq2Seq architecture. Our core idea is that the same word with different syntactic dependencies can have different meanings. This complex word embedding approach can alleviate to some extent translation errors caused by polysemy. We conducted experiments on Chinese-to-English and English-to-German translation tasks. Experimental results show that our approach is very effective, especially for long sentences.

2 Background

2.1 Neural Machine Translation

A typical neural machine translation system is an attention-based Encoder-Decoder architecture, which models the conditional probability $p(y|x)$ by computing the source sentence $x_1, ..., x_n$ to the target sentence $y_1, ..., y_m$. An encoder is used to obtain a representation of the source sentence, and a decoder generates one target word at a time. The conditional probability can be decomposed as:

$$\log p(y|x) = \sum_{j=1}^{m} \log p(y_j|y_{<j}, s) \tag{1}$$

A recurrent neural network (RNN) is typically chosen as the encoder and decoder, including the long short-term memory (LSTM) or the gated recurrent unit(GRU). Taking RNN as an example, the hidden state h_t at time t is:

$$h_t = \tanh(W_{ih}x_t + b_{ih} + W_{hh}h_{t-1} + b_{hh}) \tag{2}$$

where x_t is the input at time t, and h_{t-1} is the hidden state at time $t - 1$. The context vector c_i, which is used as input for the decoder, is computed as a weighted sum of these h_t:

$$c_i = \sum_{j=1}^{n} \alpha_{ij}h_j \tag{3}$$

The weight α_{ij} for each hidden state h_j is computed as:

$$\alpha_{ij} = \frac{\exp(e_{ij})}{\sum_{k=1}^{n} \exp(e_{ik})} \tag{4}$$

where $e_{ij} = a(s_{i-1}, h_j)$ is an alignment model, and s_{i-1} represents the hidden state of the decoder at time $i - 1$.

2.2 Complex-Valued Neural Network

A complex number can be represented as $z = a + ib$, where a is the real part and b is the imaginary part, and i is the imaginary unit. In CVNNs, a complex-valued vector can be represented as:

$$h = x + iy \tag{5}$$

where x and y are real-valued vectors. A complex-valued matrix can be represented as:

$$W = A + iB \tag{6}$$

where A and B are real-valued matrices. The calculation rule for the product of a complex-valued matrix and a complex-valued vector is as follows:

$$Wh = (Ax - By) + i(Bx + Ay) \tag{7}$$

It can be expressed in matrix notation as follows:

$$\begin{bmatrix} \Re(Wh) \\ \Im(Wh) \end{bmatrix} = \begin{bmatrix} A & -B \\ B & A \end{bmatrix} \begin{bmatrix} x \\ y \end{bmatrix} \tag{8}$$

A complex-valued activation function (e.g. ReLU) can be represented as:

$$\mathbb{C}\mathrm{ReLU}(z) = \mathrm{ReLU}(\Re(z)) + i\mathrm{ReLU}(\Im(z)) \tag{9}$$

3 Proposed Approach

In this section, we will provide details about the approach we have proposed (the basic structure is shown in Fig. 3). We refer to it as Syntax-Aware Complex-Valued Neural Machine Translation (SynCoNMT). For simplicity, we first agree to use the following notation to represent the general complex-valued form of a tensor:

$$\mathbb{C}(z) = \Re(z) + i\Im(z) \tag{10}$$

where z can be a tensor of arbitrary shape. $\Re(z)$ and $\Im(z)$ respectively represent the real and imaginary parts of the complex tensor z.

3.1 Syntax Embedding

In this work, we use CVNNs to represent words and syntactic information as the real and imaginary parts of complex-valued vectors, respectively. We refer to this embedding as Syntax Embedding (SE). The word vectors and dependency vectors are obtained from the word and dependency lookup tables, respectively. The SE of a word w, denoted as $\mathbb{C}(s_{ij})$, represents the meaning of the word w_i in a specific syntactic dependency relation d_j, and is defined as follows:

$$\mathbb{C}(s_{ij}) = w_i + id_j = \Re(s_{ij}) + i\Im(s_{ij}) \tag{11}$$

Furthermore, the meaning of word w_i under the dependency relations d_j and d_k can be represented by two embeddings, $\mathbb{C}(s_{ij})$ and $\mathbb{C}(s_{ik})$, which have the same real part but different imaginary parts.

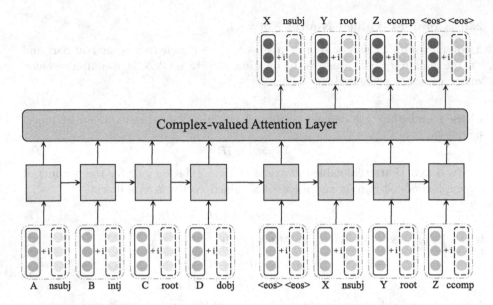

Fig. 3. Syntax-Aware Complex-Valued Neural Machine Translation. The words and their syntactic information are represented as complex-valued vectors with real and imaginary components respectively, and the entire network is computed using complex-valued operations.

3.2 Complex-Valued Neural Machine Translation

The SynCoNMT that we propose receives complex-valued syntactic embeddings (as described in Sect. 3.1) and predicts the conditional probability distribution of the target word. The encoder and decoder use a complex-valued RNN architecture for computation. Specifically, the hidden state $\mathbb{C}(h_t)$ at time t is:

$$\mathbb{C}(h_t) = \mathbb{C}\tanh(\mathbb{C}(W_{ih}x_t) + \mathbb{C}(b_{ih}) + \mathbb{C}(W_{hh}h_{t-1}) + \mathbb{C}(b_{hh})) \qquad (12)$$

The complex-valued context vector $\mathbb{C}(c_i)$ is computed as the weighted sum of the hidden states $\mathbb{C}(h_t)$ using complex-valued attention scores, as follows:

$$\mathbb{C}(c_i) = \sum_{j=1}^{n} \mathbb{C}(\alpha_{ij})\mathbb{C}(h_j) \qquad (13)$$

The weight $\mathbb{C}(\alpha_{ij})$ for each complex-valued hidden state $\mathbb{C}(h_j)$ is computed as:

$$\mathbb{C}(\alpha_{ij}) = \mathbb{C}\text{Softmax}(\mathbb{C}(e_{ij})) \qquad (14)$$

where $\mathbb{C}(e_{ij}) = \mathbb{C}\text{align}(\mathbb{C}(s_{i-1}), \mathbb{C}(h_j))$ is a complex-valued alignment model that follows the complex-valued computation rules described in Sect. 2.2. The complex-valued attention scores weight both the word vectors and syntax vectors, allowing the decoder to focus on both semantic and syntactic information simultaneously.

3.3   Syntax-Based Loss Function

The model we proposed simultaneously predicts words and syntax and uses the predicted words as the final translation result. We use two complex-valued fully connected layers to map the decoder's hidden state s_i to the word and dependency space respectively:

$$\hat{y}_w = |\mathbb{C}\text{Linear}_w(\mathbb{C}(s_i))| \tag{15}$$

$$\hat{y}_d = |\mathbb{C}\text{Linear}_d(\mathbb{C}(s_i))| \tag{16}$$

where $| \cdot |$ represents the computation of the modulus of each element in a complex-valued vector. We jointly compute the loss of predicting words and syntax dependencies using the cross-entropy loss function. The formalization is as follows:

$$\mathcal{L} = \alpha\mathcal{L}_w(y_w, \hat{y}_w) + (1 - \alpha)\mathcal{L}_d(y_d, \hat{y}_d) \tag{17}$$

where α is a hyperparameter, $\hat{y}_*$ is the predicted distribution of word or dependency, and the loss terms $\mathcal{L}_w(y_w, \hat{y}_w)$ and $\mathcal{L}_d(y_d, \hat{y}_d)$ are given by (18) and (19), respectively:

$$\mathcal{L}_w(y_w, \hat{y}_w) = -\sum_{i=1}^{|V|} y_w^{(i)} \log(\hat{y}_w^{(i)}) \tag{18}$$

$$\mathcal{L}_d(y_d, \hat{y}_d) = -\sum_{i=1}^{|D|} y_d^{(i)} \log(\hat{y}_d^{(i)}) \tag{19}$$

where $|V|$ and $|D|$ are the sizes of the word lookup table and the dependency lookup table respectively.

4   Experiments

4.1   Settings

We conducted experiments on two datasets. First, we trained on a dataset of 1.25 million sentence pairs from the LDC corpora[1] for Chinese-to-English sentence pairs. Then, we used NIST MT02 as the development set and NIST MT03, 04, 05, and 06 as the test sets. We also conducted experiments using 4.43 million sentence pairs from the WMT'14 for the English-to-German sentence pairs, with newstest2012 as the development set and newstest2013, newstest2014, and newstest2015 as the test sets. All languages use SpaCy [8] for tokenization and syntactic dependency parsing. Finally, we always use a single sentence as a reference for evaluation using case-insensitive 4-gram BLEU score [15].

For the hyperparameters of the model, all hidden states are set to 512 dimensions. The word embeddings and dependency embeddings dimensions for both the source and target languages are set to 512. Training continues until there is no improvement in the BLEU score on the development set for 5 consecutive epochs.

---

[1] LDC2002E18, LDC2003E07, LDC2003E14, Hansards portion of LDC2004T07, LDC2004T08, and LDC2005T06.

4.2   Baseline Systems

To evaluate our proposed method, we compared it with relevant NMT methods:

Chen et al. (2017a) [2]: Propose a tree-coverage model that makes attention depend on the syntax of the source language.

Chen et al. (2017b) [3]: By incorporating source dependency information to enhance source representations.

BahdanauNMT [1]: The standard NMT model uses an attention mechanism (global attention).

LoungNMT [13]: Following the work of [1], local attention is employed to improve the performance of NMT translation.

4.3   Evaluating SynCoNMT

Table 1 and Table 2 respectively show the translation results of SynCoNMT proposed in Sect. 3 on Chinese-to-English and English-to-German translation tasks. We implemented SynCoNMT-B and SynCoNMT-L based on the baseline models BahdanauNMT [1] and LoungNMT [13], respectively, to demonstrate the effectiveness of the proposed approach. Although the syntax-based method proposed by Chen et al. (2017a) [2] does not always outperform attention-based methods, it indicates that syntactic information is valuable for NMT.

In the Chinese-to-English translation task, SynCoNMT improved the performance of BahdanauNMT and LoungNMT by an average of 1.28 and 0.80 BLEU points, respectively. This indicates that SynCoNMT can effectively enhance the translation performance of NMT. Similarly, in the English-to-German translation task, SynCoNMT improved the performance of BahdanauNMT and LoungNMT by an average of 1.61 and 0.75 BLEU points, respectively. This suggests that SynCoNMT is a robust method.

Specifically, compared to the syntax-based method proposed by Chen et al. (2017a) [2], SynCoNMT achieved higher BLEU scores, indicating that incorporating syntactic information into CVNNs is valuable.

It is noteworthy that despite LoungNMT being more effective than BahdanauNMT in the baseline, SynCoNMT performed better on BahdanauNMT than on LoungNMT. This suggests that syntactic embedding is more effective when considering the overall sentence information, as the syntactic tree is essentially a tree structure with a holistic nature.

4.4   Effect of Translating Long Sentences

We grouped similar-length sentences in the test sets of both tasks to evaluate BLEU performance. For instance, the sentence length "30" denotes sentences with source lengths between 20 to 30. Then, we calculated the BLEU score for each group, and the results are shown in Fig. 4(a) and Fig. 4(b). SynCoNMT consistently produced higher BLEU scores than the baseline BahdanauNMT and LoungNMT on sentences of different lengths in both translation tasks. Particularly, in terms of performance on longer sentences, SynCoNMT-B achieved significantly higher BLEU scores than other methods. This is because our method

Table 1. The results of SynCoNMT on Chinese-to-English translation tasks.

Models	MT03	MT04	MT05	MT06	AVG.
Chen et al. (2017a)	35.64	36.63	34.35	30.57	34.30
Chen et al. (2017b)	35.91	38.73	34.18	33.76	35.64
BahdanauNMT	35.24	37.49	34.60	32.48	34.95
LoungNMT	35.57	37.85	34.93	32.74	35.27
SynCoNMT-B	**36.27**	**39.02**	**35.71**	**33.91**	**36.23**
SynCoNMT-L	36.09	38.97	35.65	33.57	36.07

Table 2. The results of SynCoNMT on English-to-German translation tasks.

Models	newstest2013	newstest2014	newstest2015	AVG.
Chen et al. (2017a)	20.78	19.43	20.37	20.19
Chen et al. (2017b)	20.91	19.35	20.57	20.28
BahdanauNMT	20.23	18.67	19.78	19.56
LoungNMT	20.74	19.00	20.15	19.96
SynCoNMT-B	**21.89**	**20.72**	**20.91**	**21.17**
SynCoNMT-L	21.43	20.54	20.17	20.71

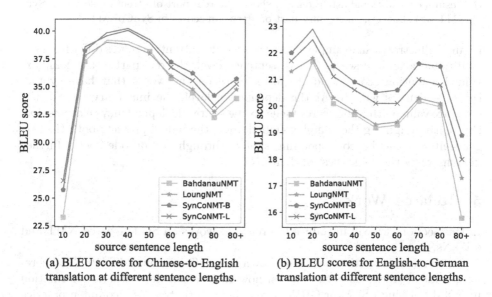

(a) BLEU scores for Chinese-to-English translation at different sentence lengths.

(b) BLEU scores for English-to-German translation at different sentence lengths.

Fig. 4. The performance of SynCoNMT on different sentence lengths.

focuses more on syntactic matching between the source and target sentences, rather than just considering the syntactic structure of one side (either the source or target). Moreover, the use of complex embeddings allows for joint word and syntax constraints on the predicted output, improving the performance of NMT.

4.5 Complex-Valued Attention

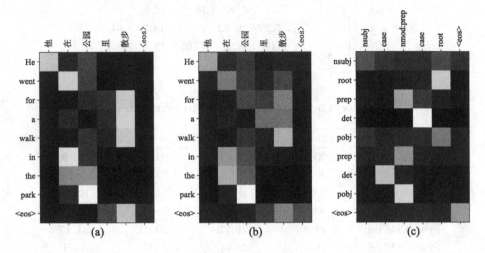

Fig. 5. The x-axis and y-axis of each figure respectively represent the words or dependencies in the target language (English) and the source language (Chinese). (a) shows the results of traditional attention. (b) shows the real part of attention scores in SynCoNMT. (c) shows the imaginary part of attention scores in SynCoNMT.

Figure 5 illustrates an example where the complex attention scores differ from the traditional attention scores. At the sentence level, the real part of the complex-valued attention scores tends to focus more on the words that have syntactic dependencies with it. At the dependency level, the imaginary part of the complex-valued attention scores focus on the syntactic dependency relationships. By jointly weighting the complex embeddings, the model predicts both the target sentence and its corresponding syntax through the decoder. This further demonstrates the robustness of SynCoNMT.

5 Related Work

In this section, we will introduce the relevant works on Syntax-based NMT and CVNNs.

Syntactic information has been shown to be effective in SMT [10,23]. Therefore, a lot of work has been done on how to incorporate syntactic information into NMT. Using LSTM or GRU to model syntactic trees is a common practice [9,14]. Hashimoto et al. [6] proposed combining head information with sequential words as input and modeling syntactic information using latent dependency graphs. Chen et al. [3] used convolutional neural networks to represent dependency trees. Wu et al. [24] integrated syntactic information through multiple Bi-RNNs. Syntax-based NMT research is very active, but previous methods have focused on modeling syntactic information in the source language while ignoring syntactic information in the target language.

CVNNs have received increasing attention in recent years because they can capture the interrelationships between real and imaginary parts within a single network. One of the early works on CVNNs is the complex backpropagation algorithm proposed by Hirose [7]. This algorithm extends the backpropagation algorithm to the complex domain, enabling the training of CVNNs. Inspired by Hirose's work, Zhang et al. [25] proposed complex-valued convolutional neural networks. Popa et al. [16] proposed complex deep belief networks. Virtue et al. [20] proposed an approach for fingerprint recognition using CVNNs, which demonstrated better performance than its real-valued counterpart. Zhu et al. [26] proposed a quaternion-based convolutional neural network and demonstrated its superiority in image classification and object detection tasks.

However, to the best of our knowledge, CVNNs have not yet been applied to the Seq2Seq architecture of NMT. Therefore, inspired by the exciting work in CVNNs, we investigated the application of CVNNs in NMT.

6   Conclusion

In this paper, we present SynCoNMT, which employs complex-valued modeling of syntactic information to improve the performance of NMT. Our approach not only outperforms its real-valued counterpart but also outperforms other syntax-based NMT approaches. In addition, unlike approaches that only consider syntax on the source side, SynCoNMT considers syntactic mappings on both the source and target sides. Experiments and analysis demonstrate the effectiveness of our approach. In the future, we will explore how to apply our approach to other tasks.

References

1. Bahdanau, D., Cho, K., Bengio, Y.: Neural machine translation by jointly learning to align and translate. arXiv preprint arXiv:1409.0473 (2014)
2. Chen, H., Huang, S., Chiang, D., Chen, J.: Improved neural machine translation with a syntax-aware encoder and decoder. In: Proceedings of the 55th Annual Meeting of the Association for Computational Linguistics, Vancouver, Canada (Volume 1: Long Papers), pp. 1936–1945. Association for Computational Linguistics (2017). https://doi.org/10.18653/v1/P17-1177. https://aclanthology.org/P17-1177
3. Chen, K., et al.: Neural machine translation with source dependency representation. In: Proceedings of the 2017 Conference on Empirical Methods in Natural Language Processing, Copenhagen, Denmark, pp. 2846–2852. Association for Computational Linguistics (2017). https://doi.org/10.18653/v1/D17-1304. https://aclanthology.org/D17-1304

4. Chiang, D.: Hierarchical phrase-based translation. Comput. Linguist. **33**(2), 201–228 (2007). https://doi.org/10.1162/coli.2007.33.2.201
5. Cho, K., van Merriënboer, B., Bahdanau, D., Bengio, Y.: On the properties of neural machine translation: encoder-decoder approaches. In: Proceedings of SSST-8, Eighth Workshop on Syntax, Semantics and Structure in Statistical Translation, Doha, Qatar, pp. 103–111. Association for Computational Linguistics (2014). https://doi.org/10.3115/v1/W14-4012. https://aclanthology.org/W14-4012
6. Hashimoto, K., Tsuruoka, Y.: Neural machine translation with source-side latent graph parsing. In: Proceedings of the 2017 Conference on Empirical Methods in Natural Language Processing, Copenhagen, Denmark, pp. 125–135. Association for Computational Linguistics (2017). https://doi.org/10.18653/v1/D17-1012. https://aclanthology.org/D17-1012
7. Hirose, A.: Continuous complex-valued back-propagation learning. Electron. Lett. **20**(28), 1854–1855 (1992)
8. Honnibal, M., Montani, I.: spaCy: industrial-strength natural language processing in Python (2020). https://doi.org/10.5281/zenodo.1212303
9. Kokkinos, F., Potamianos, A.: Structural attention neural networks for improved sentiment analysis. In: Proceedings of the 15th Conference of the European Chapter of the Association for Computational Linguistics, Valencia, Spain (Volume 2, Short Papers), pp. 586–591. Association for Computational Linguistics (2017). https://aclanthology.org/E17-2093
10. Li, J., Resnik, P., Daumé III, H.: Modeling syntactic and semantic structures in hierarchical phrase-based translation. In: Proceedings of the 2013 Conference of the North American Chapter of the Association for Computational Linguistics: Human Language Technologies, Atlanta, Georgia, pp. 540–549. Association for Computational Linguistics (2013). https://aclanthology.org/N13-1060
11. Liu, Y., Liu, Q., Lin, S.: Tree-to-string alignment template for statistical machine translation. In: Proceedings of the 21st International Conference on Computational Linguistics and 44th Annual Meeting of the Association for Computational Linguistics, Sydney, Australia, pp. 609–616. Association for Computational Linguistics (2006). https://doi.org/10.3115/1220175.1220252. https://aclanthology.org/P06-1077
12. Luong, M.T., Manning, C.: Stanford neural machine translation systems for spoken language domains. In: Proceedings of the 12th International Workshop on Spoken Language Translation: Evaluation Campaign, Da Nang, Vietnam, pp. 76–79 (2015). https://aclanthology.org/2015.iwslt-evaluation.11
13. Luong, T., Pham, H., Manning, C.D.: Effective approaches to attention-based neural machine translation. In: Proceedings of the 2015 Conference on Empirical Methods in Natural Language Processing, Lisbon, Portugal, pp. 1412–1421. Association for Computational Linguistics (2015). https://doi.org/10.18653/v1/D15-1166. https://aclanthology.org/D15-1166
14. Miwa, M., Bansal, M.: End-to-end relation extraction using LSTMs on sequences and tree structures. In: Proceedings of the 54th Annual Meeting of the Association for Computational Linguistics, Berlin, Germany (Volume 1: Long Papers), pp. 1105–1116. Association for Computational Linguistics (2016). https://doi.org/10.18653/v1/P16-1105. https://aclanthology.org/P16-1105
15. Papineni, K., Roukos, S., Ward, T., Zhu, W.J.: Bleu: a method for automatic evaluation of machine translation. In: Proceedings of the 40th Annual Meeting of the Association for Computational Linguistics, Philadelphia, Pennsylvania, USA, pp. 311–318. Association for Computational Linguistics (2002). https://doi.org/10.3115/1073083.1073135. https://aclanthology.org/P02-1040

16. Popa, C.-A.: Complex-valued deep belief networks. In: Huang, T., Lv, J., Sun, C., Tuzikov, A.V. (eds.) ISNN 2018. LNCS, vol. 10878, pp. 72–78. Springer, Cham (2018). https://doi.org/10.1007/978-3-319-92537-0_9

17. Shi, X., Padhi, I., Knight, K.: Does string-based neural MT learn source syntax? In: Proceedings of the 2016 Conference on Empirical Methods in Natural Language Processing, Austin, Texas, pp. 1526–1534. Association for Computational Linguistics (2016). https://doi.org/10.18653/v1/D16-1159. https://aclanthology.org/D16-1159

18. Trabelsi, C., et al.: Deep complex networks. In: International Conference on Learning Representations (2018). https://openreview.net/forum?id=H1T2hmZAb

19. Vaswani, A., et al.: Attention is all you need. In: Advances in Neural Information Processing Systems, vol. 30 (2017)

20. Virtue, P., Stella, X.Y., Lustig, M.: Better than real: complex-valued neural nets for MRI fingerprinting. In: 2017 IEEE International Conference on Image Processing (ICIP), pp. 3953–3957. IEEE (2017). https://doi.org/10.1109/ICIP.2017.8297024

21. Wang, B., Li, Q., Melucci, M., Song, D.: Semantic Hilbert space for text representation learning. In: The World Wide Web Conference, WWW 2019, pp. 3293–3299. Association for Computing Machinery, New York (2019). https://doi.org/10.1145/3308558.3313516

22. Wang, B., Zhao, D., Lioma, C., Li, Q., Zhang, P., Simonsen, J.G.: Encoding word order in complex embeddings. arXiv preprint arXiv:1912.12333 (2019)

23. Williams, P., Koehn, P.: Syntax-based statistical machine translation. In: Proceedings of the 2014 Conference on Empirical Methods in Natural Language Processing: Tutorial Abstracts, Doha, Qatar. Association for Computational Linguistics (2014). https://aclanthology.org/D14-2005

24. Wu, S., Zhou, M., Zhang, D.: Improved neural machine translation with source syntax. In: Proceedings of the Twenty-Sixth International Joint Conference on Artificial Intelligence, IJCAI 2017, pp. 4179–4185 (2017). https://doi.org/10.24963/ijcai.2017/584

25. Zhang, Z., Wang, H., Xu, F., Jin, Y.Q.: Complex-valued convolutional neural network and its application in polarimetric SAR image classification. IEEE Trans. Geosci. Remote Sens. **55**(12), 7177–7188 (2017). https://doi.org/10.1109/TGRS.2017.2743222

26. Zhu, X., Xu, Y., Xu, H., Chen, C.: Quaternion convolutional neural networks. In: Ferrari, V., Hebert, M., Sminchisescu, C., Weiss, Y. (eds.) ECCV 2018. LNCS, vol. 11212, pp. 645–661. Springer, Cham (2018). https://doi.org/10.1007/978-3-030-01237-3_39

Traffic Flow Prediction Based on Multi-type Characteristic Hybrid Graph Neural Network

Yuhang Wang and Hui Gao[✉]

University of Electronic Science and Technology of China, Chengdu, China
202121080403@std.uestc.edu.cn, huigao@uestc.edu.cn

Abstract. In the traffic flow prediction task, how to obtain the complex spatial-temporal correlation in the traffic data is a hard nut to crack. This paper proposes a novel Multi-Type Characteristics Hybrid Graph Neural Network (MTCHGNN) to capture these complex dependencies. First, previous studies have shown that limited representations of given graph structures with incomplete relationships may restrict the performance of those models. So we construct the novel graph generation module to obtain a multi-type characteristic hybrid graph structure, which can not only describe the short-term spatial-temporal relationships between nodes in the traffic road network but also be effective for long-term dynamic changes with specific road conditions. Second, our spatial-temporal feature extraction architecture utilizes a multi-semantic graph attention network to capture features in every time step, which can discriminatively aggregate the information with multiple receptive fields according to the complex spatial-temporal dependencies between nodes. We evaluate our proposed approach on real-world datasets, and superior performance is achieved over state-of-the-art baselines.

Keywords: Spatial-Temporal · Graph Neural Network · Traffic forecasting

1 Introduction

Traffic flow prediction is indispensable in Intelligent Transportation Systems (ITS), which aims to forecast future traffic flow by given historical conditions and underlying road networks. Unlike general time series prediction, traffic data contains complex spatial-temporal information. From a macro perspective, the original road network contains spatial information (e.g., direction, distance), while the temporal properties of the nodes are implicitly stored in the traffic data (e.g., functionally identical communities have similar time patterns) [24]. The traffic data also shows homomorphic wide-dynamic congestion during rush hours and stable traffic pattern deviations between weekdays and weekends, which means the current state is related to the recent time steps and connects with the certain moments of the previous day or week [10]. At the micro level,

L. Iliadis et al. (Eds.): ICANN 2023, LNCS 14258, pp. 486–497, 2023.
https://doi.org/10.1007/978-3-031-44192-9_39

traffic data show dynamic and complex fluctuations, and there are significant differences in the traffic state at any given time [6]. Figure 1 indicates the complex spatial-temporal correlation in traffic data.

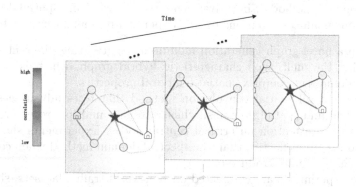

Fig. 1. It is an example of a partial graph in the road network. The solid lines indicate the original connection between nodes, and the dashed lines represent implicit connections. In every time step, the central node should have more influence on the surrounding nodes, making them highly similar. Meanwhile, the temporal correlation should be considered, although there is no link in the original networks. In different time steps, the correlation between nodes is weak because of the dynamically changing road conditions while being highly similar at certain moments because of the periodicity.

In recent years, GNN-based methods [11,27,28] have successfully applied in traffic flow prediction task because of the graph-like structure of the road network. A vital component of the GNN-based approach is to model the robust graph structures that describe complex spatial-temporal relationships between nodes. Nevertheless, existing methods [9,11,13] do not fully model the complex spatial-temporal relationships and are insufficiently discussed when exploring long-term dependencies between nodes. So we construct the graph generation module, which has a spatial graph from the inherent characteristics in the road network, utilize all recording data to construct a temporal graph that contains implicit similarity between nodes, and use the attention mechanism to capture dynamics changes in data. The module's output is the multi-type characteristic hybrid graph, which is helpful to capture the complex spatial-temporal correlation. In addition, many advanced graph neural network frameworks (spatial domain) have been proposed, such as GIN [25], Graphomer [26], GraphSNN [21], and excellent results have been achieved in other applications of graphs, but existing state-of-the-art methods [6,10] use graph spectral convolutions and their variants in traffic flow prediction. Graph spectral convolution may be more suitable for static graphs because they have a wider receptive field than spatial domain methods and have better mathematical properties. However, the major drawback of the spectral approach is that it is graph-dependent, as it learns filters that are a function of the particular graph Laplacian, which constrains the operation to a fixed graph structure [7]. After considering traffic data's periodic and dynamic characteristics, each input data has its graph containing complex spatial-temporal correlation, not a fitted graph structure, which may be more suitable for spatial methods. Considering those properties, we design a modified spatial convolution method fusing advantages from spectral and spatial domains. To sum up, our main contributions to this paper can be summarized as follows:

- We design a novel graph generation module for aggregating different graphs and getting the multi-type characteristic hybrid graph, which is powerful enough to represent complex spatial-temporal properties.
- We design a novel spatial convolution method that fuses advantages from both spectral and spatial domains, which can gain multiple receptive fields and focus more attention on critical central nodes. Experiments show that our method is more effective than the spectral domain method when complex dynamic changes are introduced.
- Extensive experiments are conducted on real-world traffic datasets, showing that our model outperforms existing baseline models. Meanwhile, we discuss the performance of our model with multi-scale information (e.g., daily or weekly information) inputs. Unlike many previous models, the results show that our model can use multi-scale information to obtain excellent results and does not require additional modules.

2   Related Works

2.1   Traffic Flow Prediction with Traditional Methods

Statistical methods are used for traffic flow prediction, such as vector autoregression model (VAR) [29] and autoregressive integrated moving average (ARIMA) [22]. Machine learning methods include k-nearest neighbors algorithm (KNN) [18], support vector machine (SVM) [8]. These models are limited by considering time information without considering spatial features. Therefore, Deep learning approaches have been proposed, which are widely used in other challenging tasks. ConvLSTM [16] combines convolutional neural network (CNN) and Long Short Term Memory (LSTM) to model spatial and temporal relations, CLTFP [23] firstly attempts to align spatial-temporal regularities. Although impressive results have been achieved, all of the mentioned methods ignore the non-Euclidean structure of traffic road networks, so they are unsuitable for traffic tasks with graph-structured information.

2.2   Traffic Flow Prediction with Graph Models

The traffic road network can be treated as a directed graph, so it is natural to use GNN-based models to capture features from traffic data. STGCN [27] makes the complete convolution on graph-structure data, which reveals the potential of graph neural networks for traffic flow prediction tasks. Graph WaveNet [24] designs a self-adaptive matrix to replace the original adjacent matrix. STGRAT

[9] combines the graph attention [20] and standard attention mechanism, indicating that graph spatial convention has great potential for traffic flow prediction. ASTGCN [6] introduces an attention mechanism to capture the dynamics spatial-temporal correlation. However, its shallow architecture limits its performance. DSTAGNN [10] makes a deeper attention mechanism and gets excellent results, but the inherent information has been dropped, which may harm the model's performance. STSGCN [17] builds the spatial graph with multi-neighborhood time steps. STFGNN [11] follows the idea of STSGCN, which constructs a spatial-temporal fusion graph as a predefined graph that mix the static adjacent graph and temporal graph generated by DTW algorithm [1]. STGODE [5] tries to improve model performance by alleviating the oversmooth problem in graph neural networks and achieves specific results. However, the spatial-temporal dependencies only came from the static graph structure in the above three methods, which may lose potential dynamic information.

3   Method

3.1   Preliminaries

Problem Definition. We define the road network as a graph $\mathcal{G} = (V, E, \mathcal{A})$, where V is a set of N nodes; E is a set of edges; $\mathcal{A} \in \mathbb{R}^{N \times N}$ is a adjacency matrix contains edge weight information. For each time step, the traffic status can be regarded as a graph signal $X^t \in \mathbb{R}^{N \times C}$, where N is the number of nodes and C is the number of features. $\mathcal{X} = (X^{t-m}, X^{t-m+1}, \cdots, X^{t-1}) \in \mathbb{R}^{N \times C \times M}$ denotes the value of all graph signal over previous m time slices. Following the previous traffic forecasting framework, given $\mathcal{X}$ and road network $\mathcal{G}$, our goal is to learn a mapping function $\mathcal{F}$ to predict the traffic observation of next T time steps $\mathcal{X}_p = (X^{t+1}, X^{t+2}, \cdots, X^{t+T}) \in \mathbb{R}^{N \times C \times T}$, as follow:

$$[X^{t-m}, X^{t-m+1}, \cdots, X^{t-1}; \mathcal{G}] \xrightarrow{\mathcal{F}} [X^{t+1}, X^{t+2}, \cdots, X^{t+T}]. \tag{1}$$

3.2   Network Architecture

The proposed MTCHGNN is shown in Fig. 2. The overall framework of our model consists of several Spatial-Temporal (ST) layers and an output layer. Each ST layer contains two components, Graph Generation and Feature Extraction. After going through several ST layers, we use the output layer, which contains two fully connected layers, to generate the prediction. The details of the ST layer are discussed in the following subsections.

Graph Generation Module. Multi-Graph convolutional network [2] applied in bike prediction indicates that multiple-type hybrid graphs may contain richer information, which can improve the model's performance. Inspired by that, we construct the complex spatial-temporal relationship between nodes from different perspectives, mixing them as the hybrid graph.

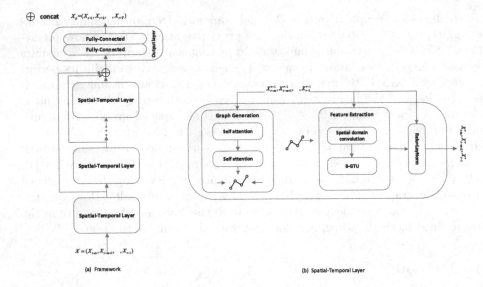

Fig. 2. (a) is the framework of the MTCHGNN, consisting of several Spatial-Temporal Layers and an Output layer that contains two Fully-connected layers. (b) is the detail of the Spatial-Temporal Layer, where the Graph Generator constructs the graph structure and Feature Extraction captures features from the spatial and temporal dimensions.

Statical Adjacency Matrix Construction. Firstly we construct the statical matrix. In this work, the spatial adjacency matrix is constructed by the inherent property of the road network. It is defined as:

$$\mathcal{A}^s = \begin{cases} exp(-\frac{d_{ij}^2}{\delta^2}), & if \ d_{ij} > 0 \\ 0, & otherwise, \end{cases} \tag{2}$$

where d_{ij} is the distance from node i to node j. δ^2 is the variance of all values of distance. A^s is a digraph, which contains the direction and distance of the road.

Temporal similarities between nodes also provide a wealth of information and should be considered. We utilize Wasserstein Distance [14] to measure the minimum effort taken to reconfigure a probability distribution to another, which was proposed in DSTAGNN [10]. The Wasserstein Distance between two nodes n_1 and n_2 can be defined as:

$$d_{wasserstein}(n_1, n_2) \triangleq inf \int_x \int_y \gamma(x, y) \cos t(n_1, n_2) dx dy, \tag{3}$$

where $\gamma(x, y)$ is the joint probability distribution function of two nodes and $cost(n_1, n_2)$ is the function describe the cost from n_1 probability distribution to n_2 probability distribution. The temporal adjacency matrix A^t is defined as:

$$\mathcal{A}^t = \begin{cases} 1 - d_{wasserstein}(i, j), & if \ 1 - d_{wasserstein}(i, j) > \mu \\ 0, & otherwise, \end{cases} \tag{4}$$

where μ is the threshold to control the sparsity of the matrix.

Complex Dynamic Graph Generation. Matrix A^s and A^t are static graphs that cannot describe the dynamic changes between nodes. We capture periodic and dynamic from raw data. Self-attention mechanisms [19] are used to generate dynamic graph structures. We get the Q_1^r, K_1^r, V_1^r where $Q_1^r, K_1^r, V_1^r \in \mathbb{R}^{c^{(r-1)} \times M \times d_s}$ by embedding the output of the previous ST layer. Through a standard attention layer, the data is transferred into $head_i^r \in \mathbb{R}^{c^{(r-1)} \times M \times N}$. In order to enrich the expression, we use a multi-head attention mechanism. The first attention mechanism with n heads can be defined as:

$$MultiHead(Q_1^r, K_1^r, V_1^r) = Concat(head_1, head_2, \cdots, head_n)$$
$$s.t. \ head_i = Attention(Q_1^r, K_1^r, V_1^r), \tag{5}$$

where $Attention()$ is a single attention layer. We put the results of the attention mechanism into a fully connected layer to make the last dimension $N \times n$ to N. Then we aggregate the feature and time dimension, ready for the input of the subsequent attention mechanism. The second attention differs from the standard attention mechanism, where the input dimension is consistent with the output dimension. The input will be translated into graph structures. So we modify the attention mechanism, only using two vectors Query(Q_2^r) and Key(K_2^r) where $Q_s^r, K_s^r \in \mathbb{R}^{N \times d_s}$ are the embedding from the output of the fully connected layer. We generate H dynamic graphs in parallel, which enrich the representation of semantics. It can be represented as:

$$D^h = softmax(\frac{Q_2^r(K_2^r)^T}{\sqrt{d_t}})$$
$$D = [D^1, D^2, \cdots, D^H]. \tag{6}$$

Multi-graph Fusion. We fuse static graphs and dynamic graphs, making the module choose the proportion of different types of graphs and get the multi-type characteristic hybrid graph. Our experiments show that the hybrid graph is more potent than any single graph. It can be described as:

$$S^h = (W_{dg}^h D^h + W_{sg}^h A^s + W_{tg}^h A^t)$$
$$S = [S^1, S^2, \cdots, S^H], \tag{7}$$

where $W_{dg}^h, W_{sg}^h, W_{tg}^h \in \mathbb{R}^{N \times N}$ are learnable parameters. The output of the graph generation module is H multi-type characteristic hybrid graphs, where the number of H is consistent with the subsequent multi-semantic graph attention network.

Spatial-Temporal Feature Extraction. We utilize a multi-semantic graph attention networks to capture features in every time steps and use the bi-directional gated convolution on each node.

Multi-semantic Graph Attention Network. Graph spectral convolution may be more suitable for fixed graph structures [7] due to its mathematical nature. After considering traffic data's periodic and dynamic characteristics, each input data has its graph containing complex spatial-temporal correlation. So using spatial convolution instead of spectral convolution on graph data is natural. We use an improved graph attention network to operate at each time step. One advantage of graph spectral convolution represented by ChebNet is that by using high-order polynomials approximation, the graph spectral convolution can aggregate the information from multi-hop neighborhoods, whereas graph spatial convention usually only focus on 1-hop neighborhood. We exploit a multi-head attention mechanism based on multi-semantic graphs to simulate this property of graph spectral convolution. The multi-semantic attention is defined as:

$$Y_t^r = GAT(\sum_{h=0}^{H} GAT(X^{(r-1)}, S^h), \sum_{h=0}^{H} S^h), \tag{8}$$

where $Y_t^r \in \mathbb{R}^{N \times c^r}$ is the output of multi-semantic attention in time step t, $GAT()$ indicates a single graph attention layer [20] and $X^{(r-1)}$ is the output of the previous ST layer in every time steps. We put different semantic graphs in different heads and use adding operators instead of concat operators, stimulating the process of chebyconv. Finally, we aggregate all the information through a graph attention layer.

Bi-directional Gated Convolution. STFGNN [11] utilizes a gated convolution capture feature in the temporal dimension, which was first proposed in 2017 [3]. However, unidirectional 1D convolution may have information-forgetting problems when facing long sequences. So we improve the structure and develop the bi-directional gated convolution (B-GTU). The input of the bi- directional gated convolution is $Y_t^r \in \mathbb{R}^{N \times M \times c^r}$ and $\bar{Y}_t^r \in \mathbb{R}^{N \times M \times c^r}$ is the reverse of X^r in temporal dimension. B-GTU can be denoted as:

$$Z = \Phi(\theta_1 * Y_t^r + b_1) \odot \sigma(\theta_2 * \bar{Y}_t^r + b_2), \tag{9}$$

where $\theta_1, \theta_2 \in \mathbb{R}^{1 \times S \times c^r \times c^r}$ are two independent 1D convention operation. The output $Z \in \mathbb{R}^{N \times (M-S+1) \times c^r}$. In order to extract features of different scales, we use three parallel B-GTU modules with different receptive fields. We concat the output of three B-GTU and get the output $Z_{concat} \in \mathbb{R}^{N \times (3M-S_1-S_2-S_3+3) \times c^r}$ where S_1, S_2, S_3 are different kernel size. Through a fully connected layer, we get the final output $Z^r_{out} \in \mathbb{R}^{N \times M \times c^r}$.

4   Experiments

4.1   Datasets

We validate our model on three real road traffic datasets, PEMS03, PEMS04, and PEMS08 [27] from California, which are widely used to verify the performance of different models. PEMS03 is the data containing 358 detectors from January to June 2017. PEMS04 is the traffic data containing 307 detectors from January to February 2018. PEMS08 is the traffic data containing 170 detectors, and the time was from July to August 2016. The original traffic data is aggregated into the 5-minute interval from the raw data. So the time of day was divided into 288-time windows.

4.2 Baseline Methods

1. DCRNN [12] Diffusion convolutional recurrent neural network, which combines graph convolution and RNN.
2. STGCN [27] Spatio-Temporal Graph Convoluntional Networks, which is a graph convolution network based on the spectral method.
3. ASTGCN [6] Attention Based Spatial Temporal Graph Convolutional Networks, which introduces spatial and temporal attention mechanisms into model.
4. STSGCN [17] Spatial-temporal synchronous graph convolutional network, which includes local spatial-temporal subgraph modules.
5. STFGNN [11] Spatial-temporal fusion graph neural network, which uses a spatial-temporal fusion graph to complement the spatial correlation.
6. STGODE [5] Spatial-temporal graph ode network, which applies continuous graph neural network to alleviate the oversmooth problem in graph neural networks.
7. GMSDR [13] Multi-Step Dependency Relation, which is a brand new variant of recurrent neural network and get excellent performance.

4.3 Experiment Settings

We split the data with a ratio of 6:2:2 on all data into training, validation, and test sets. To be fair with previous works, We set the previous time length $M = 12$, and the size of the predicting window is $T = 12$, which means we aim to predict the traffic flow over one hour in the future by using the previous hour. All experiments are trained and tested on a GPU NVIDIA Geforce RTX3090.

The model contains 4 ST layers; the number of attention heads and GAT heads are all 3. The size of the parallel B-GTU convolution kernel is $S_1, S_2, S_3 = 3, 5, 7$. Feature dimensions in each component are all 32. We train our model using Adam optimizer with a learning rate of 0.0001, and Huber loss is our loss function. Training epochs are 100, and the batchsize is 32. In this paper, the mean absolute error (MAE), the mean absolute error (MAPE), and the root mean squared error (RMSE) are used to measure the performance of models.

4.4 Experiment Results and Analysis

Table 1 shows the result of our model and baseline methods with three metrics that many previous studies adopted. It can be seen that our model has achieved

Table 1. Performance comparison of our model and baseline models on three different datasets. It shows the average results of each datasets.

Datasets	Metric	DCRNN	STGCN	ASTGCN(r)	STSGCN	STFGNN	STGODE	GMSDR	MTCHGNN
PEMS03	MAE	18.18	17.49	17.69	17.48	16.77	16.50	<u>15.78</u>	**15.34**
	MAEP(%)	18.91	17.15	19.40	16.78	16.30	16.69	<u>15.33</u>	**14.84**
	RMSE	30.31	30.12	29.66	29.21	28.34	27.84	<u>26.82</u>	**26.79**
PEMS04	MAE	24.70	22.70	22.93	21.19	<u>19.83</u>	20.84	21.69	**19.25**
	MAEP(%)	17.12	14.59	16.56	13.90	<u>13.02</u>	13.77	14.63	**12.96**
	RMSE	38.12	35.55	35.22	33.65	<u>31.88</u>	32.82	33.28	**31.14**
PEMS08	MAE	17.86	18.02	18.61	17.13	16.64	16.81	<u>16.36</u>	**15.35**
	MAEP(%)	11.45	11.40	13.08	10.96	10.60	10.62	<u>10.28</u>	**10.10**
	RMSE	27.83	27.83	28.16	36.80	36.22	25.97	<u>25.58</u>	**24.37**

_ denotes the best indicator in baselines.

the best results in all indicators on the three datasets. Since GMSDR lacks critical data processing on the PEMS04 dataset, its result may be inaccurate. However, we compared the result on the other two datasets declared in GMSDR, and our model still performed better in all metrics. Multi-type characteristic hybrid graphs we generated have richer information to represent the complex spatial-temporal correlation between nodes and are suitable for the model's performance. In addition, our spatial-temporal feature extraction can capture the dynamic change of data for both short-term and long-term. We will discuss this in detail in the next part.

4.5   Model Results with Multi-Scale Inputs

Previous studies have not explored their model's performance under multi-scale inputs(weekly and daily input). However, intuitively, traffic data shows a high degree of periodic variation. Meanwhile, ASTGCN and its following works [4,15] have proved with experiments that adding periodic information is good for traffic flow prediction task. In this part, We explore whether our model can extract features from multi-scale information and get better results. We add the data from the daily-periodic and weekly-periodic segments, whose definitions are the same as ASTGCN. Three semantic inputs are concated into one model without changing any other components. So only the dimension of input M is expanded from 12 to 36, which differs from ASTGCN and its subsequent studies. They usually use three parallel architectures to extract information at different scales, which would triple the model's size and introduce additional fusion modules. Table 2 shows that in all three datasets, a model with multi-scale inputs performs better at all metrics. It indicates that our model can utilize data from data at multiple scales and obtain better results than the model only with recent input, Although multi-scale inputs have a more complex spatial-temporal correlation.

4.6   Ablation Experiments

We performed ablation experiments on the PEMS08 dataset, and Table 3 shows the results. We use models with multi-scale inputs because the data contain more

Table 2. Ability of our model to extract features from multi-scale inputs

Datasets	Model	MAE	MAPE	RMSE
PEMS03	MTCHGNN	15.34	14.84	26.79
	MTCHGNN(P)	**15.15**	**14.71**	**26.50**
PEMS04	MTCHGNN	19.25	12.96	31.14
	MTCHGNN(P)	**18.96**	**12.80**	**30.92**
PEMS08	MTCHGNN	15.35	10.10	24.73
	MTCHGNN(P)	**14.38**	**9.62**	**23.55**

(p) denotes the model with multi-scale inputs.

Table 3. Comparison of the results of different model strategies

A^s	A^t	D	Cheb(K=3)	GAT(H=3)	GAT(H=1)	GCN	B-GTU	GTU	MAE	MAPE	RMSE
✓	✓	✓		✓			✓		**14.38**	**9.62**	**23.55**
	✓	✓		✓			✓		14.53	10.24	23.61
✓		✓		✓			✓		14.46	9.89	23.60
✓	✓			✓			✓		15.10	10.32	24.50
✓	✓	✓	✓				✓		14.41	9.77	23.67
✓	✓	✓			✓		✓		14.40	9.96	23.72
✓	✓	✓				✓	✓		14.48	9.94	23.77
✓	✓	✓		✓				✓	14.58	10.06	23.59

D denotes the graph generated by attention mechanism.

complex dependencies than single-segment inputs. First, we explored the effect of different graph structures on the results. We discard the graph A^s, D, or A^t individually. From the experimental results, D has a great help in improving the model's ability, much more than the static graphs. Meanwhile, the inherent graph structure of the road network may be more critical than graphs constructed by other methods. After combining these graphs, the model achieves the best results. It indicates that a hybrid graph containing complex spatial-temporal correlation between nodes can benefit to model's performance. We then comprehensively explore the expressive power between spatial and spectral convolution without changing other components of our model. First, chebconv is selected to replace our GAT layer with the hyper-parameter K = 3, which has outstanding performance in the previous studies [6,27]. Compared with our multi-semantic graph with head 3, the results of our components are better than chebconv in all three metrics. We also use GCN to replace our GAT layer, which can be thought of as using a first-order polynomial to fit the Laplacian matrix of the graph. Experiments show that our GAT (H = 1) layer is still more powerful than GCN. Experiments verify our idea that after considering traffic data's periodic and dynamic characteristics, each input data has its graph containing complex spatial-temporal correlation, not a fitted graph structure, which may be more suitable for spatial methods. Finally, we replace our bi-directional gated convolution with the unidirectional gated convolution. The experiments show that the bi-directional structure is more expressive than the unidirectional structure in long sequence feature extraction.

5   Conclusion

In this paper, we utilize our graph generation module to obtain the multi-type characteristic hybrid graph and propose the Spatial-Temporal Feature Extraction which contains a multi-semantic graph attention networks to capture features in every time steps and use the bi-directional gated convolution on each node. The results of the experiments prove the efficiency of the MTCHGNN. We also explore the model's performance under different scale inputs without any extra components, which was not discussed in the previous benchmark. For future work, we plan to utilize more powerful graph neural networks to apply traffic flow prediction task to enhance the model's performance.

References

1. Berndt, D.J., Clifford, J.: Using dynamic time warping to find patterns in time series. In: KDD Workshop, Seattle, WA, USA, vol. 10, pp. 359–370 (1994)
2. Chai, D., Wang, L., Yang, Q.: Bike flow prediction with multi-graph convolutional networks. In: Proceedings of the 26th ACM SIGSPATIAL International Conference on Advances in Geographic Information Systems, pp. 397–400 (2018)
3. Dauphin, Y.N., Fan, A., Auli, M., Grangier, D.: Language modeling with gated convolutional networks. In: International Conference on Machine Learning, pp. 933–941. PMLR (2017)
4. Duan, Y., Chen, N., Shen, S., Zhang, P., Qu, Y., Yu, S.: FDSA-STG: fully dynamic self-attention spatio-temporal graph networks for intelligent traffic flow prediction. IEEE Trans. Veh. Technol. **71**(9), 9250–9260 (2022)
5. Fang, Z., Long, Q., Song, G., Xie, K.: Spatial-temporal graph ode networks for traffic flow forecasting. In: Proceedings of the 27th ACM SIGKDD Conference on Knowledge Discovery & Data Mining, pp. 364–373 (2021)
6. Guo, S., Lin, Y., Feng, N., Song, C., Wan, H.: Attention based spatial-temporal graph convolutional networks for traffic flow forecasting. In: Proceedings of the AAAI Conference on Artificial Intelligence, vol. 33, pp. 922–929 (2019)
7. Hechtlinger, Y., Chakravarti, P., Qin, J.: A generalization of convolutional neural networks to graph-structured data. arXiv preprint arXiv:1704.08165 (2017)
8. Jeong, Y.S., Byon, Y.J., Castro-Neto, M.M., Easa, S.M.: Supervised weighting-online learning algorithm for short-term traffic flow prediction. IEEE Trans. Intell. Transp. Syst. **14**(4), 1700–1707 (2013)
9. Kim, K., Jin, S., Ko, S., Choo, J.: STGRAT: a spatio-temporal graph attention network for traffic forecasting (2020)
10. Lan, S., Ma, Y., Huang, W., Wang, W., Yang, H., Li, P.: DSTAGNN: dynamic spatial-temporal aware graph neural network for traffic flow forecasting. In: International Conference on Machine Learning, pp. 11906–11917. PMLR (2022)
11. Li, M., Zhu, Z.: Spatial-temporal fusion graph neural networks for traffic flow forecasting. In: Proceedings of the AAAI Conference on Artificial Intelligence, vol. 35, pp. 4189–4196 (2021)
12. Li, Y., Yu, R., Shahabi, C., Liu, Y.: Diffusion convolutional recurrent neural network: data-driven traffic forecasting. arXiv preprint arXiv:1707.01926 (2017)
13. Liu, D., Wang, J., Shang, S., Han, P.: MSDR: multi-step dependency relation networks for spatial temporal forecasting. In: Proceedings of the 28th ACM SIGKDD Conference on Knowledge Discovery and Data Mining, pp. 1042–1050 (2022)

14. Panaretos, V.M., Zemel, Y.: Statistical aspects of Wasserstein distances. Ann. Rev. Stat. Appl. **6**, 405–431 (2019)
15. Shi, X., Qi, H., Shen, Y., Wu, G., Yin, B.: A spatial-temporal attention approach for traffic prediction. IEEE Trans. Intell. Transp. Syst. **22**(8), 4909–4918 (2020)
16. Shi, X., Chen, Z., Wang, H., Yeung, D.Y., Wong, W.K., Woo, W.: Convolutional LSTM network: a machine learning approach for precipitation nowcasting. In: Advances in Neural Information Processing Systems, vol. 28 (2015)
17. Song, C., Lin, Y., Guo, S., Wan, H.: Spatial-temporal synchronous graph convolutional networks: a new framework for spatial-temporal network data forecasting. In: Proceedings of the AAAI Conference on Artificial Intelligence, vol. 34, pp. 914–921 (2020)
18. Van Lint, J., Van Hinsbergen, C.: Short-term traffic and travel time prediction models. Artif. Intell. Appl. Crit. Transp. Issues **22**(1), 22–41 (2012)
19. Vaswani, A., et al.: Attention is all you need. In: Advances in Neural Information Processing Systems, vol. 30 (2017)
20. Veličković, P., Cucurull, G., Casanova, A., Romero, A., Lio, P., Bengio, Y.: Graph attention networks. arXiv preprint arXiv:1710.10903 (2017)
21. Wijesinghe, A., Wang, Q.: A new perspective on "how graph neural networks go beyond Weisfeiler-Lehman?". In: International Conference on Learning Representations (2021)
22. Williams, B.M., Hoel, L.A.: Modeling and forecasting vehicular traffic flow as a seasonal Arima process: theoretical basis and empirical results. J. Transp. Eng. **129**(6), 664–672 (2003)
23. Wu, Y., Tan, H.: Short-term traffic flow forecasting with spatial-temporal correlation in a hybrid deep learning framework. arXiv preprint arXiv:1612.01022 (2016)
24. Wu, Z., Pan, S., Long, G., Jiang, J., Zhang, C.: Graph WaveNet for deep spatial-temporal graph modeling. arXiv preprint arXiv:1906.00121 (2019)
25. Xu, K., Hu, W., Leskovec, J., Jegelka, S.: How powerful are graph neural networks? arXiv preprint arXiv:1810.00826 (2018)
26. Ying, C., et al.: Do transformers really perform badly for graph representation? In: Advances in Neural Information Processing Systems, vol. 34, pp. 28877–28888 (2021)
27. Yu, B., Yin, H., Zhu, Z.: Spatio-temporal graph convolutional networks: a deep learning framework for traffic forecasting. arXiv preprint arXiv:1709.04875 (2017)
28. Zheng, C., Fan, X., Wang, C., Qi, J.: GMAN: a graph multi-attention network for traffic prediction. In: Proceedings of the AAAI Conference on Artificial Intelligence, vol. 34, pp. 1234–1241 (2020)
29. Zivot, E., Wang, J.: Vector autoregressive models for multivariate time series. In: Zivot, E., Wang, J. (eds.) Modeling Financial Time Series with S-PLUS®, pp. 385–429. Springer, New York (2006). https://doi.org/10.1007/978-0-387-32348-0_11

Whisker Analysis Framework for Unrestricted Mice with Neural Networks

Zhijie Tan[1(✉)], Shengwei Meng[2], Yujia Tan[3], Yiqun Wu[3], Yi Li[3], Tong Mo[1], and Weiping Li[1]

[1] School of Software and Microelectronics, Peking University, Beijing, China
besttangent@stu.pku.edu.cn, {motong,wpli}@ss.pku.edu.cn
[2] School of Computer Science, Beijing University of Posts and Telecommunications, Beijing, China
mengshengwei@bupt.edu.cn
[3] Zhongnan Hospital of Wuhan University, Wuhan University, Wuhan, China
{tanyujia,2018305230017,2015283030165}@whu.edu.cn

Abstract. Whiskers of rats and mice form an important tactile system. Non-invasive analysis of the movement pattern of whiskers can inspire the development of research including the tactile perception of rodents. However, the whiskers of mice are very slender and easily confused with body hair or video background. At the same time, the vibration frequency of whiskers is very high, and the vibration process may produce artifacts or motion blurs. In addition, the movement pattern analysis of whiskers needs to exclude the ego-motion of the head for unrestricted mice. In this paper, we propose WAFUM (Whisker Analysis Framework for Unrestricted Mice) to provide a visual analysis model for the movement pattern of whiskers in a non-invasive way with neural networks. In the first step, this model detects the region where the whiskers are located, makes semantic segmentation of the whiskers, and generates the pose of the whisker group by clustering. The second step is to recover the head pose through key point detection and tracking. Finally, the model combines the results of the former two steps to recover the ego-motion mode of whiskers. The experimental part demonstrates that with the help of neural networks, whisker tracking for the unrestricted mice can be completed using a consumer-grade smartphone in a non-invasive way while all of the other fragile traditional algorithms fail.

Keywords: Whisker segmentation · Neural network · Pose estimation

1 Introduction

Normally, a mouse has 31 whiskers of varying lengths. These whiskers together constitute the precise tactile system of mice and are important sensory organs of mice [4,14,17]. The study of the movement pattern of mice whiskers can help to reveal the development of the tactile system of mice, or as an important characterization of mental diseases such as autism in mice [18]. The study on the movement pattern of whiskers includes invasive methods, semi-invasive methods, and

L. Iliadis et al. (Eds.): ICANN 2023, LNCS 14258, pp. 498–510, 2023.
https://doi.org/10.1007/978-3-031-44192-9_40

non-invasive methods. Invasive methods include using electromyography which cannot record shapes and positions of the whiskers [9], fixing a high-contrast marker on the whiskers whose weight will directly affect the movement state of the whiskers [25] or cutting off some of the whiskers [6,8] which will directly affect the motion state of the whiskers. These invasive methods generally affect the mental state of mice [12]. The semi-invasive method is mainly manifested in the need to fix the head or body of mice, including the use of linescan imaging [10] or linear light sheet [1] which only focuses on cross lines, and the use of high-speed cameras based on visual image processing [19]. These methods cannot rule out the effect of ego-motion on mice heads, so the head must be fixed with external equipment. However, the semi-invasive method also affects the normal whisker movement pattern of mice. The non-invasive method does not have any impact on the daily behavior of mice. Usually, the visual image analysis method is directly used to restore poses, shapes, and other key information about the whiskers. Based on the image sequence, the movement patterns or states of the whiskers can be analyzed, which has a good development potential [3].

Using high-speed photography to recover the motion state and related information of whiskers also has some challenges. Firstly, high-speed photography itself brings a very large amount of data, which requires image analysis methods being fully automated and fast, including whisker detection, segmentation, and motion pattern analysis [3], [19]. Secondly, the whisker itself is relatively thin and has a fast vibration frequency which makes the whisker itself easy to be confused with the body hair, and it is common to produce motion blurs in the movement process [4], [20]. Consequently, it is very challenging to detect or track whiskers without dedicated expensive cameras. Finally, the movement of the whisker itself also receives the influence of the head movement of mice [6]. If only the head of the mouse is fixed, it has an impact on the mental state of the mouse itself, which is not in line with the daily-life habits of mice, and cannot get effective data about the whiskers.

Thanks to the great breakthrough of deep learning technology in medical image detection and segmentation, some traditional algorithms that need to carefully design visual features are quickly replaced by the deep learning model based on CNNs (Convolutional Neural Networks) or transformers [21,24]. These traditional algorithms are usually very sensitive to noise while the calculation speed is relatively slow [19]. They usually require a carefully designed light environment [3], expensive professional shooting equipment [22], and tedious experimental steps [19]. As shown in Fig. 3, the traditional algorithm only works on the region which contains the whiskers while WAFUM uses the clarity of the general picture taken by the mobile phone containing the mouse's body. At the same time, the proposed model does not require experienced experts in computer vision to set additional parameters, such as whisker width, whisker shape, etc. [3], only simple image annotations are needed. There are usually two ideas for such tasks as industrial flaw detection similar to whisker detection [26]. One is a two-stage segmentation method [16], which first extracts the region of whiskers, and then uses the semantic segmentation method to extract the pixel positions of whiskers. The other is directly semantic segmentation in the original image to obtain the mask of whiskers [11]. The first method will relatively lose certain computational efficiency and background information, but it has a higher detection rate and more accurate segmentation result for such a relatively thin object as whiskers. Therefore, this paper designs a model of object detection and semantic segmentation to obtain the precise shape of the whiskers. However, since the final generation is the classification of each pixel, it is necessary to further use RANSAC (RANdom SAmple Consensus) [7] to generate the pose information of whiskers. To obtain the motion information of whiskers in a non-fixed state, this paper uses the method of keypoint detection and tracking [15] to recover the motion information of the mouse head. Then the key points of the mouse model are marked. To simplify the model, the model assumes that the triangular surface composed of these three key points and the whiskers are always in the same horizontal plane, and the whiskers and the head are rigidly connected. In this way, by detecting and tracking the key points on the mouse, the pose information of the head can be recovered by solving a system of equations, and the pose of the whiskers in the non-fixed state can be calculated.

This paper presents a non-invasive visual method for the analysis of whiskers based on neural networks, namely WAFUM. This method only needs a mobile phone to support high-speed photography, which has good adaptability and can promote the research of mice whiskers in most laboratories. The experimental results prove the effectiveness and accuracy of the segmentation method. In addition, the vibration frequency of whiskers annotated manually is compared to prove the effectiveness of this model.

The main contributions of this paper are summarized as follows:

- A complete analyzing framework of whisker movement pattern under the unrestricted state is proposed, which can automatically process massive data generated by high-speed photography at high frequency, while only one cheap consumer-level shooting device is needed.
- Using the object detection and semantic segmentation method based on neural networks, a novel method for effective detection and segmentation of whiskers in mice is designed.
- To our best knowledge, WAFUM brings the first 3D whisker tracker for the rodents without any invasive methods including restricting the head/body in a small space, fixing the head, attaching high-contrast markers to the whiskers, or trimming the whiskers.

2   Methodology

The main process of WAFUM includes image data preprocessing, whisker transition estimation in the world frame, head transition estimation in the world frame, and whisker ego-motion estimation in the head frame. Figure 1 visualizes the pipeline of WAFUM.

Before describing the method of this part, some abbreviations, acronyms, and concepts in the following part and figures are defined as follows. For a video

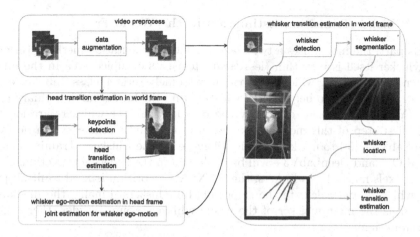

Fig. 1. Pipeline of WAFUM. Firstly, the raw images are converted into the gray images with the histogram equalization algorithm in the video preprocess part. Secondly, whisker transition estimation in the world frame is completed by a two-stage segmentation algorithm and the RANSAC algorithm. Thirdly, keypoint detection and tracking are used for head transition estimation in the world frame. Finally, a joint estimation is designed for whisker ego-motion estimation in the head frame.

consisting of image frames, this article specifies that the frame at time t is F_t, then the video can be written as a set $V \{F_1, F_2, ..., F_n\}$, where n is the time of the last frame. For the main whisker at the time of $t-1$ and t, the whole moving process is shown in Fig. 2. P_{LE} is the left eye, P_{RE} is the right eye, and P_{Nose} is the nose. These three points form a triangle and this triangle is on the head plane. P_1 is the interaction of main whisker and the triangle and P_2 is another endpoint of main whisker. P_1^t means the location of P_1 at the time of t and the same to the remains. The world frame is a right-handed orthonormal frame that will never be modified. The head frame is a right-handed orthonormal frame. Its XoY plane is which plane the triangle consisting of P_{LE}, P_{RE}, and P_{Nose} is on. The pose of an object in the world frame like a whisker is a 6D vector, which can be marked as:

$$P_{world}^{whisker} = (x_{world}^{whisker}, y_{world}^{whisker}, z_{world}^{whisker}, \alpha_{world}^{whisker}, \beta_{world}^{whisker}, \gamma_{world}^{whisker}) \quad (1)$$

In (1), $x_{world}^{whisker}$, $y_{world}^{whisker}$, $z_{world}^{whisker}$ is the 3D location in world frame and $\alpha_{world}^{whisker}$, $\beta_{world}^{whisker}$, $\gamma_{world}^{whisker}$ is the 3D heading angle in world frame.

The transition of an object in the world frame like a whisker is a 6D vector, which can be marked as:

$$T_{world}^{whisker} = (\Delta x_{world}^{whisker}, \Delta y_{world}^{whisker}, \Delta z_{world}^{whisker}, \Delta\alpha_{world}^{whisker}, \Delta\beta_{world}^{whisker}, \Delta\gamma_{world}^{whisker}) \quad (2)$$

In (2), $\Delta x_{world}^{whisker}$, $\Delta y_{world}^{whisker}$, $\Delta z_{world}^{whisker}$ is the 3D location variation in world frame and $\Delta\alpha_{world}^{whisker}$, $\Delta\beta_{world}^{whisker}$, $\Delta\gamma_{world}^{whisker}$ is the 3D heading angle variation in the world frame. In Fig. 2, $head^t$ means the head frame at the time of t.

2.1   Whisker Transition Estimation in the World Frame

In this part, the model uses a two-stage whisker segmentation method. Because the whisker itself is very thin (less than $5\,\mu m$), its occupied area in the image is often less than 5%, which leads to an extremely serious class imbalance. To balance the pixel ratio between the whiskers and the background, a binary classifier (YOLOv5) is used to identify the region where the whiskers are located in the first step of this model. Next, we use a semantic segmentation network (DeepLabV3+ [5]) to mark all pixels belonging to the whiskers. Training details of YOLOv5 and DeepLabV3+ will be explained in the experiment section. Then for all pixels marked as whiskers, the RANSAC algorithm is used to fit all possible whiskers and calculate the slopes of the whiskers. Finally, the median is selected as the main whisker of the whole whisker group. Besides, there exists an assumption:

Assumption 21. *The whisker group is considered as one whisker, which is called the main whisker and abbreviated as mw.*

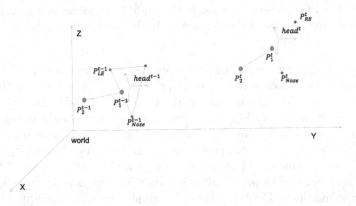

Fig. 2. A brief introduction to mouse movement from time t-1 to t. The world frame is fixed while the head frame is always changing. P_{LE} is the left eye, P_{RE} is the right eye and P_{Nose} is the nose. P_1 is the interaction of main whisker and the triangle and P_2 is another endpoint of main whisker. The whisker motion in the world frame consists of head motion and whisker ego-motion.

Details of the RANSAC algorithm for fitting out all of the lines are as follows: **Step 1**: Select any two of the segmented pixels, and restore the number of other pixels whose distance towards the line decided by these two pixels is less than a distance threshold as *inliers_num*. **Step 2**: Check whether the *inliers_num* in Step 1 is more than ever. If yes, then restore the inliers and parameters of this line. If the repeats number reaches the maximum trials of the RANSAC algorithm, go to Step 3 or return to Step 1. **Step 3**: Check whether the *inliers_num* in Step 2 is more than a number threshold of inliers. If yes, then restore the inliers and parameters of this line and delete all of the inliers from the pixel set. Then return to step 1. If no, exit the whole algorithm. The main whisker transition is calculated by:

$$T^{mw}_{world} = P^{mw}_{world,t} - P^{mw}_{world,t-1} \tag{3}$$

The variation in the z-axis in (3) is omitted in the next part because of assumption 23. '-' in (3) only means calculating the variation between two poses especially if we use quaternion to represent the rotation angles. '-' is not a simple arithmetic operation.

2.2   Head Transition Estimation in the World Frame

In this part, DeepLabCut [15] was used as the pose estimation tool in this model. Firstly, the mice were marked with key points, and a total of three key points were used. Next, we tracked these key points and complete the pose estimation of the head. Training details of DeepLabCut will be described in the experiment section. These three key points include the mouse's left eye, right eye, and nose. Assumption 22 is proposed as follows:

Assumption 22. *These three key points in mice form a rigid triangle (three sides of the triangle are rigid rods without deformation).*

As shown in Fig. 2, this triangle satisfies the following conditions: The distance between any two of P_{LE}, P_{RE}, and P_{Nose} will not change during motion. The triangles made up of P_{LE}, P_{RE}, and P_{Nose} will not change in shape and size during motion. With assumption 22, the z coordinate can be calculated by solving the following ternary quadratic equation where d(.,.) means the distance between two points which are fixed:

$$\left.\begin{array}{l}(x^{LE} - x^{RE})^2 + (y^{LE} - y^{RE})^2 + (z^{LE} - z^{RE})^2 = d(P^{LE}, P^{RE}) \\ (x^{LE} - x^{Nose})^2 + (y^{LE} - y^{Nose})^2 + (z^{LE} - z^{Nose})^2 = d(P^{LE}, P^{Nose}) \\ (x^{Nose} - x^{RE})^2 + (y^{Nose} - y^{RE})^2 + (z^{Nose} - z^{RE})^2 = d(P^{Nose}, P^{RE})\end{array}\right\} \tag{4}$$

The head transition in the world frame is calculated by:

$$T^{head}_{world} = P^{head}_{world,t} - P^{head}_{world,t-1} \tag{5}$$

2.3   Whisker Ego-motion Estimation in Head Frame

In this part, WAFUM uses the result of whisker transition estimation in the world frame part and head transition estimation in the world frame part for joint estimation. Before the whisker ego-motion estimation, there are 3 assumptions:

Assumption 23. *The main whisker is always at the same plane which is decided by the triangle consisting of P_{LE}, P_{RE}, P_{Nose}.*

Assumption 24. *The main whisker is a rigid rod.*

Assumption 25. P_1 *is a fixed half point and it never slides on the segment consisting of* P_{LE}, P_{Nose}.

The whisker transition of ego-motion in the head frame is calculated by:

$$T_{head}^{mw} = T_{world}^{mw} - T_{world}^{head} \tag{6}$$

3   Experiments

3.1   Dataset

The dataset for the whisker segmentation is recorded by Huawei P20 Pro which has a SOC of Hisilicon Kirin 970, 6 GB RAM & 128 GB ROM, and a camera consisting of a CMOS of Sony IMX 600 (1.73 in., 3648 * 2736 pixels) and an aperture of f1.8. The resolution of images in the dataset is 1920 * 720 and the shooting frequency is 960 Hz. The camera is 17.5 cm away from the ground, and the center of the camera imaging plane is aligned with the center of the glass dish. The camera imaging plane is parallel to the horizontal plane. The dataset contains 12 motion sequences, each of which contains 306 images. 10 images of every sequence are annotated for object detection and semantic segmentation. For the annotation part, the unclear images are omitted and the bounding box (bbox) covers the whiskers very tightly. 3 to 6 adjacent whiskers are segmented in every annotated image. Whiskers in every sequence are chosen to be consistent unless the whiskers are shadowed or extremely blurred. 90 images form the training set, 20 images form the verification set and the remaining is the test set.

The dataset for the head keypoints detection is generated by choosing sequence 01 as the training set. 20 images are marked with P_{LE}, P_{RE}, P_{Nose}. When creating the dataset, *imgaug* in the config of the DeepLabCut[1] is set to true. *Outlieralgorithm* is set to be *manual* which means the user can label whether the current frame is abnormal(an outlier) or not. *Refine_labels* is set to be true so the labels can be re-assigned and optimized. *Merge_datasets* is set to be true then the optimized results will be merged into the original dataset.

3.2   Training Details of Neural Networks

All neural networks are trained on 4 Nvidia V100. The model names, backbones, decode_head, training time and inference time of every neural network are described in Table 1. The parameters of YOLOv5 are using the default settings[2] except for the batch size and maximum training epochs. The batch size is set to 16 and maximum epochs are set to 1000. Early stopping is used. FCN, FPN, DeepLabv3, SegFormer, PSPNet, ANN in WAFUM are using the default settings in[3] except for the maximum training epochs. The maximum training

---

[1] https://github.com/AlexEMG/DeepLabCut.
[2] https://github.com/ultralytics/yolov5.
[3] https://github.com/open-mmlab/mmsegmentation.

Table 1. The model names, backbones, decode_head, training time and inference time of neural networks used in the experiment section.

models	backbone	decode_head	Training (min)	Inference (ms)
FCN	HRNet18	FCNHead	51.4	29.2
FPN	ResNet50	FPNHead	192.2	62.3
DeepLabv3	ResNet50	ASPPHead	134.7	51.8
SegFormer	*MixVisionTransformer*	SegFormerHead	187.4	43.7
PSPNet	ResNet50	PSPHead	201.1	66.2
ANN	ResNet50	FCNHead	235.8	56.4
YOLOv5	CSPDarknet	FPNHead	123.6	6.4
DeepLabCut	ResNet50	–	1566.6	25.0

epochs are set to 300 or 600, while 600 is the default value. If the users are short of waiting time or computation resources, they can choose 300 for instead. The training fraction of DeepLabCut is set to 0.95 which means 95% of the original data will be used as the training dataset. The $default\_net\_type$ is $ResNet50$. The batch size is set to 8.

Table 2. The comparison of one-stage algorithms and two-stage algorithms for the whisker segmentation.

	epochs	300			600		
	models	mIoU	mAcc	mDice	mIoU	mAcc	mDice
One-stage	FCN	49.91	50.00	49.95	49.91	50.00	49.95
	FPN						
	DeepLabv3						
	SegFormer						
	PSPNet						
	ANN						
Two-stage (Ours)	YOLOv5+FCN	77.08	84.74	85.28	78.90	89.13	86.75
	YOLOv5+FPN	81.38	92.03	88.65	77.36	92.64	85.54
	YOLOv5+DeepLabv3	**81.91**	**92.23**	**89.04**	**83.03**	91.13	**89.85**
	YOLOv5+SegFormer	49.26	50.00	49.63	49.26	50.00	49.63
	YOLOv5+PSPNet	74.36	87.83	82.99	81.79	91.10	88.95
	YOLOv5+ANN	78.80	91.00	86.68	71.50	**92.75**	80.81

3.3   Why the Whisker Segmentation Needs a Two-Stage Algorithm?

The results of the one-stage algorithms in Table 2 are the same. Because none of these algorithms succeeds to segment any whisker in the original image, these algorithms divide all of the pixels into the background. And this wrong segmentation leads to a result that the segmentation accuracy of the background is 1.0 and for the whiskers, the accuracy is 0.0. Thus, the mAcc is 0.5. The IoU and Dice for the background can never be 1.0 except for all of the background pixels and the whisker pixels are classed correctly.

Table 2 states an obvious result that these one-stage algorithms (FCN, FPN, etc.) can not detect any whisker in the original image without the whisker detection stage. In contrast, with YOLOv5 as the whisker detection model, most models can achieve an ideal mIOU, mAcc and mDice. SegFormer seems to be the outlier. It can be explained by that the SegFormer uses MixVisionTransformer as the backbone. The Transformer network can hardly converge without a large amount of image data. And the training dataset in this experiment section only consists of nearly 100 images. The one-stage algorithm suffer heavily from the class-imbalance in the original image. The whisker pixels occupy less than 1% area and the background pixels seem too much. The two-stage algorithm works on the region only containing the entire whiskers. The percent of whisker pixels can increase to 20% or more. Therefore, the two-stage algorithm is unavoidable for the whisker segmentation task.

3.4   Why the Traditional Algorithms Fail?

This part will discuss the comparison between WAFUM, Whiskertracking [23], Whiskeras [3], Whiskeras 2.0 [2] and Whiskertracker [13] on our dataset. All of the traditional algorithms [2, 3, 13, 23] above failed to segment or track any of the whiskers from our raw images which are recorded by the mobile phone.

The traditional computer vision algorithms usually assumes that the whiskers have sharp edges. The brightest (or darkest) pixels must be the background. The image itself has no or few noise, artifacts or moire. However, the facts in our dataset are the whiskers in these images have no sharp edges. The brightest (or darkest) pixels are not only the background, but also might be the noise. The images taken with mobile phones are full of noise, moire, and artifacts.

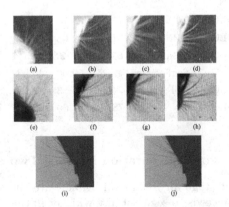

Fig. 3. The comparison of the images in our dataset and traditional dataset

When the facts are conflicted with the assumptions, the failure seems natural. Taking the background removal algorithm which are commonly used by Whiskeas and other algorithms as an example, Fig. 3(a–d) are the original images chosen from our dataset. Figure 3(e–h) are the generated images after using the background removal algorithm. The matching relation are in the manner of (a)–(e), ... , (d)–(h). Figure 3(i–j) are the images used by the traditional algorithms like Whiskeas. It can be seen that the background removal algorithm is completely losing its magic in the dataset obtained in this paper. The brightest/darkest pixels in the Fig. 3(e–h) can be the noise except for the background. In fact, the erosion, dilation, low-pass filter and other traditional computer vision algorithms widely used in the previous whisker segmentation algorithms not only rely heavily on prior parameter settings, but also cannot process images containing a large number of moire, artifacts, and noise.

When the traditional algorithms even can not segment the whiskers in the image of our dataset, it is impossible to track any whisker. Assuming that these algorithms can use our segmented whiskers, these whisker tracking methods can not be modified slightly to support the whisker tracking. Considering the following common restrictions in the previous algorithms: "one whisker": The whiskers are trimmed to the only one. "fixed head": The head are fixed. "2D movement": The mice can only move in the same plane. For the algorithms with restriction "one whisker", the tracking methods in these algorithms do not exist in fact. They only complete the whisker segmentation. For the multi-whiskers, these algorithms can not complete the segmentation or the tracking. For the algorithms with restriction "fixed head", the ego-motion of the head is not estimated. Because the mice in the dataset are not head-fixed, the whisker movement can not escape the influence of the head movement. For the algorithms with restriction "2D move", the precise estimation for the whisker vibration angle will be influenced when the head moves in the Z-axis. Therefore, to our best knowledge, as the first 3D whisker tracker without nearly any restrictions, the dataset seems too difficult for the previous algorithms.

3.5   Overall Vibration Performance on All the Sequences

All sequence results for vibration frequency show an error range of $(-2, +3)$. The most severe problem is because of assumption 21 that the main whisker in the current frame is not always the same as the previous frame. The problem may increase the predicted frequency with a sudden jump of slopes. And this sudden jump will increase the estimated frequency. So the estimated frequency are higher than the groundtruth averagely. Seq 12 is an outlier, because the vibration range is very small and it can hardly to find out it should be a vibration cycle. WAFUM performs very well on the whisker sequence of low frequency and a little worse for the sequence of high frequency. It can be explained by the fact that when the whiskers vibrate at a high frequency, the mouse is thought to move its head at the same time to explore the space. Then the error of the complete framework will increase because both head estimation error and whisker estimation error increase. Another reason is that the raw images (1920 * 720) captured by Huawei

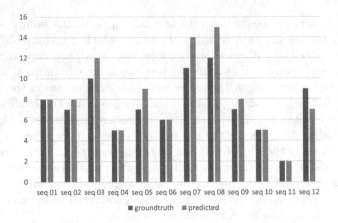

Fig. 4. Overall vibration performance on all the sequences

P20 Pro for the high-frequency sequence are not clear enough. However, another evidence for such performance is that we manually count the frequency from the rotation angle image like Fig. 4 and this will improve the final result.

4   Conclusions

This paper presents a novel algorithm for analyzing the motion pattern of mice whiskers in a free-moving state with cheap devices. It can automatically process the huge amount of image data generated by high-speed photography, semantically segment the shape of whiskers from the image using a two-stage algorithm, and use the RANSAC algorithm to calculate the pose information of whiskers. After that, the mouse head pose is restored using the detection and tracking of key points. Finally, the motion pattern of the mouse's whisker is restored by combining the mouse's head pose with the mouse's whisker pose in the world frame. Experiments demonstrate the effectiveness of the two-stage segmentation algorithm.

References

1. Harvey, M.A., Bermejo, R., Philip Zeigler, H.: Discriminative whisking in the head-fixed rat: optoelectronic monitoring during tactile detection and discrimination tasks. Somatos. Motor Res. **18**(3), 211–222 (2001)
2. Arvanitis, P., Betting, J.H.L.F., Bosman, L.W.J., Al-Ars, Z., Strydis, C.: WhiskEras 2.0: fast and accurate whisker tracking in rodents. In: Orailoglu, A., Jung, M., Reichenbach, M. (eds.) SAMOS 2021. LNCS, vol. 13227, pp. 210–225. Springer, Cham (2022). https://doi.org/10.1007/978-3-031-04580-6_14
3. Betting, J.H.L., Romano, V., Al-Ars, Z., Bosman, L.W., Strydis, C., De Zeeuw, C.I.: WhiskEras: a new algorithm for accurate whisker tracking. Front. Cell. Neurosci. **14**, 588445 (2020)
4. Carvell, G.E., Simons, D.J.: Biometric analyses of vibrissal tactile discrimination in the rat. J. Neurosci. **10**(8), 2638–2648 (1990)

5. Chen, L.-C., Zhu, Y., Papandreou, G., Schroff, F., Adam, H.: Encoder-decoder with atrous separable convolution for semantic image segmentation. In: Ferrari, V., Hebert, M., Sminchisescu, C., Weiss, Y. (eds.) ECCV 2018. LNCS, vol. 11211, pp. 833–851. Springer, Cham (2018). https://doi.org/10.1007/978-3-030-01234-2_49

6. Clack, N.G., et al.: Automated tracking of whiskers in videos of head fixed rodents. PLoS Comput. Biol. **8**(7), e1002591 (2012)

7. Derpanis, K.G.: Overview of the RANSAC algorithm. Image Rochester NY **4**(1), 2–3 (2010)

8. Dooley, J.C., Glanz, R.M., Sokoloff, G., Blumberg, M.S.: Self-generated whisker movements drive state-dependent sensory input to developing barrel cortex. Curr. Biol. **30**(12), 2404–2410 (2020)

9. Hill, D.N., Bermejo, R., Zeigler, H.P., Kleinfeld, D.: Biomechanics of the vibrissa motor plant in rat: rhythmic whisking consists of triphasic neuromuscular activity. J. Neurosci. **28**(13), 3438–3455 (2008)

10. Jadhav, S.P., Wolfe, J., Feldman, D.E.: Sparse temporal coding of elementary tactile features during active whisker sensation. Nat. Neurosci. **12**(6), 792–800 (2009)

11. Johnson, J.W.: Adapting mask-RCNN for automatic nucleus segmentation. arXiv preprint arXiv:1805.00500 (2018)

12. Kelly, M.K., Carvell, G.E., Kodger, J.M., Simons, D.J.: Sensory loss by selected whisker removal produces immediate disinhibition in the somatosensory cortex of behaving rats. J. Neurosci. **19**(20), 9117–9125 (1999)

13. Knutsen, P.M., Derdikman, D., Ahissar, E.: Tracking whisker and head movements in unrestrained behaving rodents. J. Neurophysiol. **93**(4), 2294–2301 (2005)

14. Knutsen, P.M., Pietr, M., Ahissar, E.: Haptic object localization in the vibrissal system: behavior and performance. J. Neurosci. **26**(33), 8451–8464 (2006)

15. Mathis, A., et al.: DeepLabCut: markerless pose estimation of user-defined body parts with deep learning. Nat. Neurosci. **21**(9), 1281–1289 (2018)

16. Meng, L., Zhang, Q., Bu, S.: Two-stage liver and tumor segmentation algorithm based on convolutional neural network. Diagnostics **11**(10), 1806 (2021)

17. O'Connor, D.H., Clack, N.G., Huber, D., Komiyama, T., Myers, E.W., Svoboda, K.: Vibrissa-based object localization in head-fixed mice. J. Neurosci. **30**(5), 1947–1967 (2010)

18. Pan, L., et al.: A short period of early life oxytocin treatment rescues social behavior dysfunction via suppression of hippocampal hyperactivity in male mice. Mol. Psychiatry 1–15 (2022)

19. Perkon, I., Košir, A., Itskov, P.M., Tasič, J., Diamond, M.E.: Unsupervised quantification of whisking and head movement in freely moving rodents. J. Neurophysiol. **105**(4), 1950–1962 (2011)

20. Rahmati, N., et al.: Cerebellar potentiation and learning a whisker-based object localization task with a time response window. J. Neurosci. **34**(5), 1949–1962 (2014)

21. Razzak, M.I., Naz, S., Zaib, A.: Deep learning for medical image processing: overview, challenges and the future. In: Dey, N., Ashour, A.S., Borra, S. (eds.) Classification in BioApps. LNCVB, vol. 26, pp. 323–350. Springer, Cham (2018). https://doi.org/10.1007/978-3-319-65981-7_12

22. Romano, V., et al.: Potentiation of cerebellar Purkinje cells facilitates whisker reflex adaptation through increased simple spike activity. Elife **7**, e38852 (2018)

23. Sreenivasan, V., Esmaeili, V., Kiritani, T., Galan, K., Crochet, S., Petersen, C.C.: Movement initiation signals in mouse whisker motor cortex. Neuron **92**(6), 1368–1382 (2016)

24. Valanarasu, J.M.J., Oza, P., Hacihaliloglu, I., Patel, V.M.: Medical transformer: gated axial-attention for medical image segmentation. In: de Bruijne, M., et al. (eds.) MICCAI 2021. LNCS, vol. 12901, pp. 36–46. Springer, Cham (2021). https:// doi.org/10.1007/978-3-030-87193-2_4

25. Venkatraman, S., Elkabany, K., Long, J.D., Yao, Y., Carmena, J.M.: A system for neural recording and closed-loop intracortical microstimulation in awake rodents. IEEE Trans. Biomed. Eng. **56**(1), 15–22 (2008)

26. Virupakshappa, K., Marino, M., Oruklu, E.: A multi-resolution convolutional neural network architecture for ultrasonic flaw detection. In: 2018 IEEE International Ultrasonics Symposium (IUS), pp. 1–4. IEEE (2018)

Adaptive Segmentation Network for Scene Text Detection

Guiqin Zhao$^{(\boxtimes)}$

School of Computer Science and Technology, University of Chinese Academy of
Sciences, Beijing 100049, China
zhaoguiqin20@mails.ucas.edu.cn

Abstract. Inspired by deep convolution segmentation algorithms, scene
text detectors break the performance ceiling of datasets steadily. However, these methods often encounter threshold selection bottlenecks and
have poor performance on text instances with extreme aspect ratios. In
this paper, we propose to automatically learn the discriminate segmentation threshold, which distinguishes text pixels from background pixels
for segmentation-based scene text detectors and then further reduces
the time-consuming manual parameter adjustment. Besides, we design
a Global-information Enhanced Feature Pyramid Network (GE-FPN)
for capturing text instances with macro size and extreme aspect ratios.
Following the GE-FPN, we introduce a cascade optimization structure
to further refine the text instances. Finally, together with the proposed threshold learning strategy and text detection structure, we design
an Adaptive Segmentation Network (ASNet) for scene text detection.
Extensive experiments are carried out to demonstrate that the proposed
ASNet can achieve the state-of-the-art performance on four text detection benchmarks, *i.e.*, ICDAR 2015, MSRA-TD500, ICDAR 2017 MLT
and CTW1500. The ablation experiments also verify the effectiveness of
our contributions.

Keywords: Text detection · Adaptive segmentation

1 Introduction

Scene text detection has become very popular in the computer vision community,
the performance of scene text detectors on various text detection datasets is
constantly refreshed. But there are still many problems to be solved to realize
accurate text detection in the real-world scenarios [17]. Here, we focus on two
general problems: discriminate segmentation threshold selection and extreme
aspect ratio.

Discriminate Segmentation Threshold Selection. For the segmentation-
based text detectors, the segmentation threshold used to distinguish text pixels
from background pixels is indispensable. To achieve the best detection performance, researchers need to manually set different thresholds for the algorithm
on different datasets. It is often very time-consuming and laborious especially

© The Author(s), under exclusive license to Springer Nature Switzerland AG 2023
L. Iliadis et al. (Eds.): ICANN 2023, LNCS 14258, pp. 511–522, 2023.
https://doi.org/10.1007/978-3-031-44192-9_41

when the dataset is huge, and difficult to select the appropriate threshold for open application scenarios. Therefore, it is urgently needed to obtain an appropriate segmentation threshold without performance feedback from the test set. DBNet [13] first raises the concept of adaptive threshold, but it still follows the previous method of manually selecting the threshold in the inference stage. Our method takes a further step to learn and adopt the adaptive segmentation threshold in the inference stage and achieves good performance.

Extreme Aspect Ratio. Most text detection algorithms extract text features by various convolutions. It is usually limited by the size of the receptive field, so it is difficult for them to obtain sufficient information for the accurate detection of long text instances. Most regression-based methods, such as EAST [30] and RRD [14], face the problem of inaccurate regression caused by the lack of receptive field. Mask TextSpotter [18] and DeepText [29] follow a Mask R-CNN [8]-style framework to alleviate the problem of inaccurate single-stage regression due to insufficient receptive field. LOMO [26] and MOST [10] construct a cascade structure to get accurate text detection by iterative regression.

To solve these two problems, we propose an Adaptive Segmentation Network (ASNet) for accurately detecting text in real-world scenarios. Specifically, for the first problem, we propose the discriminate segmentation threshold which contains two concepts of threshold: the dataset level threshold (DTH) and the image level threshold (ITH). The network we designed can automatically learn the dataset level threshold and learn the way to predict the image level threshold in the training process, which can be directly used in the inference stage. The performance of the threshold we learned is comparable to the performance of the manually selected threshold. For the second problem, we introduce a cascade structure to the proposed ASNet so that the network can overcome the problem of the insufficient receptive field by iteratively refining the location of the text instance. Meanwhile, we introduce the self attention mechanism to the Feature Pyramid Network (FPN) [15] to form the Global-information Enhanced Feature Pyramid Network (GE-FPN), which increases the receptive field and further improves the performance of the proposed network. The contributions of this paper are three-fold:

– We propose an Adaptive Segmentation Network (ASNet) for scene text detection that can alleviate the dilemma of segmentation threshold selection and alleviate the problem of insufficient receptive field in the text detection task.
– We propose the adaptive segmentation threshold which contains two concepts of learnable thresholds, namely dataset level threshold and image level threshold, which promotes the performance of the proposed network and avoids manually selecting segmentation thresholds in the inference stage.
– We introduce the self attention mechanism and the cascade structure to the proposed ASNet, which expands the receptive field of ASNet and further improves the performance.

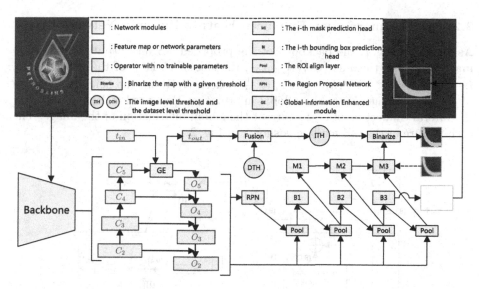

Fig. 1. Workflow of the proposed ASNet in the inference stage. $C_i, i \in \{2,3,4,5\}$ denotes the multi-scale feature maps extracted by the backbone. $O_i, i \in \{2,3,4,5\}$ denotes the multi-scale feature maps output from GE-FPN. The generation of the DTH is described in Eq. 1 and the fusion block and the generation of the ITH is described in Eq. 2.

2 Methodology

2.1 Overview

The proposed ASNet is composed of a ResNet 50 [9] backbone, a Global-information Enhanced Feature Pyramid Network (GE-FPN), a Region Proposal Network (RPN) [20], and a cascade head.

The overall architecture of the proposed ASNet is shown in Fig. 1. First, we extract the multi-scale feature maps with a ResNet-50 backbone, and then the multi-scale feature maps are feed into the GE-FPN to be better aggregated. Meanwhile, the dataset level threshold (DTH) and the image level threshold (ITH) are generated in the forward propagation of the Global-information Enhanced module (GE) in the GE-FPN. Second, we input the multi-scale feature maps into the Region Proposal Network (RPN) to obtain a series of proposals, which are then input into the cascade head together with the multi-scale feature maps to obtain the score, bounding box and mask of the text instances. Then, we binarize the mask of the text instances that achieve high score with the image level threshold. Finally, We use the bounding box predicted by the last bounding box prediction head to map the binary mask back to the original size of the image and get the final detection result.

2.2   Global-Information Enhanced Feature Pyramid Network

As shown in Fig. 1, the backbone of the proposed ASNet outputs four feature maps, we name them as $\{C_i\}_{i\in\{2,3,4,5\}}$, the size of C_i is $\frac{1}{2^i}$ of the input image, i.e., $C_i \in \mathbb{R}^{B\times C\times h_i\times w_i}$, $h_i = \frac{H}{2^i}$, $w_i = \frac{W}{2^i}$, where H, W are the height and width of the input image. We add a Global-information Enhanced (GE) module after the lateral connection of C_5 to extract the global information of the image. The architecture of the GE module is shown in Fig. 2.

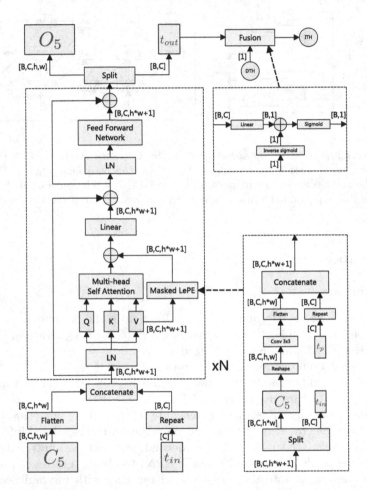

Fig. 2. Architecture of the Global-information Enhanced module. For better expression, we annotate the shape of the feature map. $C_5 \in \mathbb{R}^{B\times C\times h\times w}$, $h = h_5 = \frac{H}{32}$, $w = w_5 = \frac{W}{32}$, where H, W are the height and width of the input image. LN denotes the Layer Normalization.

As we can see in Fig. 2, firstly, we flatten C_5 and combine it with t_{in} by concatenation operation, where $t_{in} \in \mathbb{R}^C$ is a trainable vector of the network.

Secondly, we apply Layer Normalization (LN) for the features and then feed it into Multi-head Self Attention module. Since t_{in} does not have positional relationship with the pixels on C_5, we use Masked LePE for position encoding. Then, we apply Layer Normalization (LN) for the features and then feed it into the Feed Forward Network [21]. We repeat the GE module for N times, and N is 2 in our experiments. Finally, the features encoded by GE module are split into O_5 and t_{out}, where O_5 is used to enhance the global information of the original FPN and t_{out} is used to predict the image level threshold.

2.3   Cascade Structure

Most text detection algorithms based on Mask R CNN [8], such as Mask Textspotter [18] and DeepText [29], are faced with the problem that the single-step bounding box regression for text instance is not accurate enough. Inspired by Cascade R-CNN [2] and HTC [4], we establish a multi-step bounding box regression head. As shown in Fig. 1, firstly, we input the proposals output by RPN into ROI align layer and obtain the text features. Secondly, we input the text features into the first bounding box head B1 to obtain the refined bounding box prediction. Then, we input the refined bounding box prediction into ROI align layer and obtain the text features for the second bounding box head B2 and the first mask head M1. We repeat this procedure for three times to obtain more accurate detection results.

2.4   Adaptive Segmentation Threshold Learning

Segmentation threshold can be used to binarize the probability map of the text instances into the binary mask. The optimal segmentation thresholds for different images or different datasets are often different. Besides, it is very cumbersome and impractical to manually select segmentation thresholds to obtain the optimal. In this regard, we propose the adaptive discriminate threshold which contains the dataset level threshold and the image level threshold.

The dataset level threshold (DTH) is a trainable parameter of the proposed ASNet. In the training stage, the DTH for each datasets can be learned through the back propagation algorithm. In the inference stage, we fix the DTH learned in the training stage and use it as a candidate segmentation threshold for the binarization of the predicted probability map.

The image level threshold (ITH) is a value obtained by adding an offset to the DTH. Inspired by ViT [7] and DETR [3], we obtain the predicted offset for the test image through a predefined token t_{in}, which is a trainable parameter of the proposed ASNet. To better explain how DTH and ITH are generated, we use t_D and t_I to represent the DTH and the ITH respectively, $t_{out} \in \mathbb{R}^{B \times C}$ represents the feature vector fused with global information in Fig. 2 and $t_d \in \mathbb{R}$ is a trainable parameter of the proposed ASNet. The generation process for t_D

and t_I can be formulated as follows:

$$t_D = \text{Sigmoid}(t_d) \in \mathbb{R}[0,1], \tag{1}$$

$$t_I = \text{Sigmoid}(t_d + \text{Linear}_{C \to 1}(t_{out})) \in \mathbb{R}[0,1]^B, \tag{2}$$

where $\text{Linear}_{C \to 1}$ denotes a linear projection that project the channels of t_{out} (C) to 1.

2.5 Adaptive Threshold Loss

We propose a novel Adaptive Threshold Loss to supervise both the text instance probability maps and the two-level segmentation thresholds at the same time. The loss function of mask branch for a single text instance which has matched the ground truth of a certain text instance can be formulated as follows:

$$\mathcal{L}_{ath}(m, \hat{m}, t_D, t_I) = \mathcal{L}_{SCEL}(m, \hat{m})$$
$$+ \alpha \mathcal{L}_{DL}(\text{Step}(m, t_D), \hat{m}) + \beta \mathcal{L}_{DL}(\text{Step}(m, t_I), \hat{m}), \tag{3}$$

$$\mathcal{L}_{SCEL}(m, \hat{m}) = -\frac{1}{h_m w_m} \sum_{i=1}^{h_m} \sum_{j=1}^{w_m} [\hat{m}_{ij} \log m_{ij} + (1 - \hat{m}_{ij}) \log(1 - m_{ij})], \tag{4}$$

$$\mathcal{L}_{DL}(x, y) = 1 - \frac{2 \cdot \text{sum}(xy)}{\text{sum}(x) + \text{sum}(y)}, \tag{5}$$

$$\text{Step}(x, y) = \frac{1}{1 + \exp[-k(x-y)]}, \tag{6}$$

where $m \in \mathbb{R}[0,1]^{h_m \times w_m}$ is the predicted probability map of the mask branch, $\hat{m} \in \mathbb{Z}[0,1]^{h_m \times w_m}$ is the ground truth of a certain text instance mask which matches this proposal. α and β are used to balance the importance of the three losses, we set $\alpha = \beta = 0.5$ in our experiments. The Step function equals to the Step function in DBNet [13], we set $k = 50$ in our experiments. As proved in DBNet, the Step function is a continuous approximation of the Binarize function, *i.e.*, $\text{Binarize}(m, t) = \text{I}[m > t]$, where I is the characteristic function. In the training stage, we use Step function to replace Binarize function so that the network can obtain the ability of predicting the image level segmentation threshold for each image through backward propagation.

2.6 Optimization

The loss function for the proposed ASNet can be formulated as:

$$\mathcal{L} = \mathcal{L}_{RPN} + \sum_{i=1,2,3} \lambda_i (\mathcal{L}_{score,i} + \gamma_b \mathcal{L}_{bbox,i} + \gamma_m \mathcal{L}_{mask,i}), \tag{7}$$

where $\mathcal{L}_{RPN}$ denotes the loss for the Region Proposal Network, $\mathcal{L}_{score,i}$ and $\mathcal{L}_{bbox,i}$ denote the text score loss and bounding box regression loss for the i-th bounding box prediction head Bi in Fig. 1, $i = 1, 2, 3$. $\mathcal{L}_{mask,i}$ is the mask loss for the i-th mask prediction head Mi in Fig. 1.

3 Experiments

We conducted quantitative experiments on four public benchmarks: ICDAR 2015 [11], MSRA-TD500 [25], ICDAR 2017 [19] and CTW1500 [16] to verify the effectiveness of the proposed algorithm and the effectiveness of the proposed components.

3.1 Implementation Details

The backbone of the proposed method is the ResNet-50 which is pre-trained on ImageNet [6]. For experiments that introduce additional data, the proposed ASNet is first pre-trained on Cocotext v2 [22] for 80 epochs, then it is fine-tuned separately on the dataset which we report the results for 160 epochs. For experiments that do not introduce additional data, we train ASNet for 160 epochs on ICDAR 2015 and CTW1500 respectively. We train 1200 epochs on MSRA-TD500. The data augmentation contains color jitter, random rotation, random horizontal flipping, random scale, random crop, and padding to 800 × 800. In the inference stage, we resize the long dimension of test images to 640, 1920, 1600 and 640 for MSRA-TD500, ICDAR2015, ICDAR2017 and CTW1500 respectively.

3.2 Straight Text Detection Results

To verify the detection performance of the proposed ASNet on straight text, we make an extensive comparison with the recent state-of-the-art methods on three text detection datasets, i.e., ICDAR 2015, MSRA-TD500 and ICDAR 2017.

Table 1. Comparison with recent state-of-the-art methods on ICDAR 2015 [11] and MSRA-TD500 [25]. We fixed the backbone of all the compared methods to ResNet-50. 'Ext.' denotes extra training data, † denotes using DCN [5] in backbone.

Methods	Paper	Ext.	ICDAR2015			MSRA-TD500		
			R (%)	P (%)	F (%)	R (%)	P (%)	F (%)
PAN [24]	ICCV'19		77.8	82.9	80.3	77.3	80.7	78.9
PAN [24]	ICCV'19	✓	81.9	84.0	82.9	83.2	85.7	84.5
PSENet [23]	CVPR'19	✓	84.5	86.9	85.7	–	–	–
CRAFT [1]	CVPR'19	✓	84.3	89.8	86.9	78.2	88.2	82.9
LOMO [26]	CVPR'19	✓	83.5	91.3	87.2	–	–	–
DB† [13]	AAAI'20	✓	83.2	91.8	87.3	79.2	91.5	84.9
DRRG [27]	CVPR'20	✓	84.7	88.5	86.6	82.3	88.1	85.1
FCENet [31]	CVPR'21		84.2	85.1	84.6	–	–	–
MOST [10]	CVPR'21	✓	87.3	89.1	88.2	82.7	90.4	86.4
TextBPN [28]	ICCV'21	✓	–	–	–	84.5	86.6	85.6
ASNet	Ours		83.5	90.0	86.6	76.3	**95.3**	84.7
ASNet	Ours	✓	**88.9**	**91.9**	**90.4**	**88.1**	93.1	**90.6**

ICDAR 2015 mainly focuses on multi-oriented text in natural scenes. As shown in Table 1, the proposed ASNet achieves SOTA performance on ICDAR2015. If compared with the methods without pre-training, the proposed ASNet outperforms the previous SOTA method FCENet by 2.0% (86.6% *vs.* 84.6%) in F-measure. If compared with the algorithm with pre-training, the proposed ASNet can still outperforms the previous SOTA method MOST by 2.2% (90.4% *vs.* 88.2%) in F-measure. The result shows that the proposed ASNet can achieve good detection performance for the text instances in natural scenes.

MSRA-TD500 is a multilingual dataset containing many extreme long text instances. As shown in Table 1, the proposed ASNet achieves SOTA performance on MSRA-TD500. If compared with the methods without pre-training, the proposed ASNet outperforms the previous SOTA method PCR by 2.3% (84.7% *vs.* 82.4%) in F-measure. If compared with the algorithm with pre-training, the proposed ASNet can still outperforms the previous SOTA method GNNets by 2.1% (90.6% *vs.* 88.5%) in F-measure. The result shows that the proposed ASNet is capable of detecting text instances with extreme aspect ratio.

ICDAR 2017 is a dataset containing multilingual text instances. As shown in Table 1, the proposed ASNet achieves SOTA performance on ICDAR 2017. The result shows that the proposed ASNet can detect text instances of different languages well (Table 2).

Table 2. Comparison with recent state-of-the-art methods on ICDAR 2017 [19] test set.

Methods	Paper	Ext.	ICDAR2017		
			R (%)	P (%)	F (%)
PSENet [23]	CVPR'19	✓	68.2	73.8	70.9
CRAFT [1]	CVPR'19	✓	68.2	80.6	73.0
LOMO [26]	CVPR'19	✓	60.6	78.8	68.5
DB† [13]	AAAI'20	✓	67.9	83.1	74.7
DRRG [27]	CVPR'20	✓	61.0	75.0	67.3
MOST [10]	CVPR'21	✓	72.0	82.0	76.7
ASNet	Ours	✓	**74.5**	**84.2**	**79.1**

3.3 Curve Text Detection Results

CTW1500 is a widely used dataset for arbitrarily-shaped text detection. As shown in Table 3, the proposed ASNet achieves SOTA performance on CTW1500. If compared with the methods without pre-training, the proposed

ASNet outperforms the previous SOTA method TextBPN by 0.3% (84.3% *vs.* 84.0%) in F-measure. If compared with the methods with pre-training, the proposed ASNet outperforms the previous SOTA method TextBPN by 0.2% (85.2% *vs.* 85.0%) in F-measure.

Table 3. Comparison with recent state-of-the-art methods on CTW1500.

Methods	Paper	Ext.	ICDAR2017		
			R (%)	P (%)	F (%)
DRRG [27]	CVPR'20	✓	83.0	85.9	84.5
FCENet [31]	CVPR'21		80.7	85.7	83.1
TextBPN [28]	ICCV'21		80.6	87.7	84.0
TextBPN [28]	ICCV'21	✓	83.6	86.5	85.0
ASNet	Ours		82.4	86.2	84.3
ASNet	Ours	✓	82.4	**88.1**	**85.2**

3.4 Ablation Study

We conducted ablation studies on the ICDAR 2015 dataset, shown in Table 4. The baseline of the proposed ASNet is Mask R-CNN, whose result is referred from open-mmocr [12].

Table 4. Ablation studies on ICDAR 2015 under the protocol of IoU@0.5. The Aug in the table denotes data augmentations we used in the training stage.

Cascade	DTH	ITH	GE	Aug	R (%)	P (%)	F (%)
					78.30	87.20	82.50
✓					78.43	**90.75**	84.14
	✓				82.67	86.63	83.41
	✓	✓			80.84	87.68	84.12
			✓		81.46	86.46	83.89
	✓	✓	✓		81.42	88.07	84.61
✓	✓	✓	✓		80.98	90.58	85.51
✓	✓	✓	✓	✓	**83.53**	89.99	**86.64**

Cascade Structure. As shown in Table 4, compared with the baseline, the cascade structure can bring relative improvements of 3.55% (90.75% *vs.* 87.20%) in Precision on ICDAR 2015 while keep the Recall nearly unchanged (78.43% *vs.* 78.30%), which shows that the multi-step bounding box regression process can significantly improves the precision of detecting text instances.

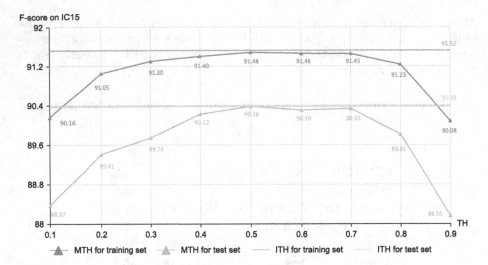

Fig. 3. Performance comparison between the image level threshold (ITH) and manually selected threshold (MTH) on the training set and test set of ICDAR 2015. TH denotes the segmentation threshold used to binarize the predicted text instance probability map.

Global-Information Enhanced Module. As shown in Table 4, the addition of the Global-information Enhanced module after the lateral connection of C_5 of the FPN brings relative improvements of 3.16% (81.46% *vs.* 78.30%) in Recall and 1.39% (83.89% *vs.* 82.50%) in F-measure on ICDAR 2015. The results shows that GE module can effectively enhance the receptive field of the original FPN and makes the network capable of detecting text instances with extreme aspect ratio.

Adaptive Segmentation Threshold. As shown in Table 4, with DTH, the model achieve relative improvements of 0.91% (83.41% *vs.* 82.50) in F-measure on ICDAR 2015. With ITH, the model can bring relative improvements of 0.71% (84.12% *vs.* 83.41%), which shows that adaptive threshold is more effective than a fixed threshold. Moreover, in order to verify the effectiveness of the adaptive segmentation threshold in the inference stage, we compared the F-measure performance of the model using the image level threshold and the manually selected threshold at an interval of 0.1 on ICDAR 2015. As shown in Fig. 3, When testing on the training set or on the testing set, ITH can achieve better or equivalent performance.

4   Conclusions

In this paper, we propose to automatically learn the adaptive segmentation threshold for segmentation-based scene text detectors, which can not only assist the training process of the network but also help to select segmentation threshold in the inference stage. Meanwhile, we introduce the self attention mechanism into our method and propose the Global-information Enhanced Feature Pyramid Network (GE-FPN), which expands the receptive field of the network and improves the performance of the network. The experiments demonstrate that the proposed ASNet achieves state-of-the-art performance on ICDAR 2015, MSRA-TD500, ICDAR 2017 MLT and CTW1500.

References

1. Baek, Y., Lee, B., Han, D., Yun, S., Lee, H.: Character region awareness for text detection. In: IEEE CVPR, pp. 9365–9374 (2019)
2. Cai, Z., Vasconcelos, N.: Cascade R-CNN: delving into high quality object detection. In: IEEE CVPR, pp. 6154–6162 (2018)
3. Carion, N., Massa, F., Synnaeve, G., Usunier, N., Kirillov, A., Zagoruyko, S.: End-to-end object detection with transformers. In: Vedaldi, A., Bischof, H., Brox, T., Frahm, J.-M. (eds.) ECCV 2020. LNCS, vol. 12346, pp. 213–229. Springer, Cham (2020). https://doi.org/10.1007/978-3-030-58452-8_13
4. Chen, K., et al.: Hybrid task cascade for instance segmentation. In: IEEE CVPR, pp. 4974–4983 (2019)
5. Dai, J., et al.: Deformable convolutional networks. In: IEEE CVPR, pp. 764–773 (2017)
6. Deng, J., Dong, W., Socher, R., Li, L., Li, K., Fei-Fei, L.: ImageNet: a large-scale hierarchical image database. In: IEEE CVPR, pp. 248–255 (2009)
7. Dosovitskiy, A., et al.: An image is worth 16×16 words: transformers for image recognition at scale. In: ICLR (2021)
8. He, K., Gkioxari, G., Dollar, P., Girshick, R.: Mask R-CNN. In: IEEE ICCV (2017)
9. He, K., Zhang, X., Ren, S., Sun, J.: Deep residual learning for image recognition. In: IEEE CVPR, pp. 770–778 (2016)
10. He, M., et al.: MOST: a multi-oriented scene text detector with localization refinement. In: IEEE CVPR, pp. 8813–8822 (2021)
11. Karatzas, D., et al.: ICDAR 2015 competition on robust reading. In: IEEE ICDAR, pp. 1156–1160 (2015)
12. Kuang, Z., et al.: MMOCR: a comprehensive toolbox for text detection, recognition and understanding. arXiv preprint arXiv:2108.06543 (2021)
13. Liao, M., Wan, Z., Yao, C., Chen, K., Bai, X.: Real-time scene text detection with differentiable binarization. In: AAAI, vol. 34, pp. 11474–11481 (2020)
14. Liao, M., Zhu, Z., Shi, B., Xia, G.S., Bai, X.: Rotation-sensitive regression for oriented scene text detection. In: IEEE CVPR, pp. 5909–5918 (2018)
15. Lin, T.Y., Dollár, P., Girshick, R., He, K., Hariharan, B., Belongie, S.: Feature pyramid networks for object detection. In: IEEE CVPR, pp. 2117–2125 (2017)
16. Liu, Y., Jin, L., Zhang, S., Luo, C., Zhang, S.: Curved scene text detection via transverse and longitudinal sequence connection. Pattern Recognit. **90**, 337–345 (2019)
17. Long, S., He, X., Yao, C.: Scene text detection and recognition: the deep learning era. IJCV **129**(1), 161–184 (2021)
18. Lyu, P., Liao, M., Yao, C., Wu, W., Bai, X.: Mask textspotter: an end-to-end trainable neural network for spotting text with arbitrary shapes. In: ECCV, pp. 67–83 (2018)

19. Nayef, N., et al.: ICDAR 2017 robust reading challenge on multi-lingual scene text detection and script identification-RRC-MLT. In: IEEE ICDAR, vol. 1, pp. 1454–1459 (2017)
20. Ren, S., He, K., Girshick, R., Sun, J.: Faster R-CNN: towards real-time object detection with region proposal networks. In: NeurIPS, vol. 28 (2015)
21. Vaswani, A., et al.: Attention is all you need. In: NuerIPS, pp. 5998–6008 (2017)
22. Veit, A., Matera, T., Neumann, L., Matas, J., Belongie, S.: COCO-text: dataset and benchmark for text detection and recognition in natural images. arXiv preprint arXiv:1601.07140 (2016)
23. Wang, W., et al.: Shape robust text detection with progressive scale expansion network. In: IEEE CVPR, pp. 9336–9345 (2019)
24. Wang, W., et al.: Efficient and accurate arbitrary-shaped text detection with pixel aggregation network. In: IEEE CVPR, pp. 8440–8449 (2019)
25. Yao, C., Bai, X., Liu, W., Ma, Y., Tu, Z.: Detecting texts of arbitrary orientations in natural images. In: IEEE CVPR pp. 1083–1090 (2012)
26. Zhang, C., et al.: Look more than once: an accurate detector for text of arbitrary shapes. In: IEEE CVPR, pp. 10552–10561 (2019)
27. Zhang, S.X., et al.: Deep relational reasoning graph network for arbitrary shape text detection. In: IEEE CVPR, pp. 9699–9708 (2020)
28. Zhang, S., Zhu, X., Yang, C., Wang, H., Yin, X.: Adaptive boundary proposal network for arbitrary shape text detection. In: IEEE ICCV, pp. 1285–1294. IEEE (2021)
29. Zhong, Z., Jin, L., Huang, S.: DeepText: a new approach for text proposal generation and text detection in natural images. In: IEEE ICASSP, pp. 1208–1212 (2017)
30. Zhou, X., et al.: EAST: an efficient and accurate scene text detector. In: IEEE CVPR, pp. 5551–5560 (2017)
31. Zhu, Y., Chen, J., Liang, L., Kuang, Z., Jin, L., Zhang, W.: Fourier contour embedding for arbitrary-shaped text detection. In: IEEE CVPR, pp. 3123–3131 (2021)

How to Extract and Interact? Nested Siamese Text Matching with Interaction and Extraction

Jianxiang Zang$^{(\boxtimes)}$ and Hui Liu

Shanghai University of International Business and Economics, Shanghai, China
{21349110,liuh}@suibe.edu.cn

Abstract. Text matching is a core problem in Natural Language Processing, and one popular approach is the Siamese model. To enhance the performance of the Siamese matching model, researchers have proposed diverse network blocks, which can be divided into Information Interaction Blocks and Feature Extraction Blocks based on their functions. Traditional approaches, employing a pipeline-based arrangement for these blocks, encounter limitations when it comes to capturing focused semantics via local reasoning. To better systematize these two types of blocks, we propose a nested Siamese text matching framework, with the introduction of the Interaction Extraction Module (IEM) and the Function Amplification Module (FAM). Specifically, the IEM acts as a Feature Extraction or Information Interaction Block, nested within both the FAM and the model structure itself. IEM assumes the responsibility for global matching within the model while FAM leverages the Late Attention and nested IEMs to sharpen local matching and reasoning capabilities. Through our experiments, the performance of this nested Siamese model has proven to be superior to that of other pipeline-based Siamese matching models.

Keywords: Text Matching · Nested Siamese Framework · Information Interaction · Feature Extraction

1 Introduction

The purpose of text matching is to predict the level of semantic similarity between a pair of text sequences [2,3,7,16,21]. One of the popular methods for text matching is the Siamese model, which employs dual encoders to encode two texts separately and fuse them at the matching layer. In order to enhance the performance of the Siamese matching model, previous studies have proposed various network blocks to capture matching information of different granularity in sentences [3,10,12,14,19,24,27].

We categorize these blocks based on their functions into *Information Interaction Blocks* and *Feature Extraction Blocks*. Tensor cross-fusion [3,12,19,27] is the most versatile Information interaction Block, capable of capturing semantic focal points such as entities and behaviors. Pooling fusion [3,10,19,24], on

© The Author(s), under exclusive license to Springer Nature Switzerland AG 2023
L. Iliadis et al. (Eds.): ICANN 2023, LNCS 14258, pp. 523–535, 2023.
https://doi.org/10.1007/978-3-031-44192-9_42

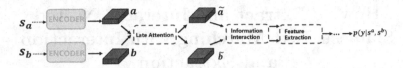

Fig. 1. Widely adopted Siamese text matching model employs a pipeline-based arrangement for Feature Extraction and Information Interaction Blocks.

the other hand, is the most universal Feature Extraction Block. It enhances the model's global control over semantics and improves the model's level of generalization. As the Information Interaction Block and Feature Extraction Block have distinct functional orientations, their arrangement within the model significantly impacts the system's overall performance. Figure 1 illustrates the widely adopted Siamese text matching framework [3,10,12,14,19] wherein the Feature Extraction and Information Interaction Blocks are arranged in a pipeline manner within the model. The present pipeline-based arrangement encounters limitations in exclusively enhancing the model's global matching capabilities at the sentence-pair level, struggling to tackle the challenge of improving localized matching, reasoning capacities, and proficiency in focusing on vital semantic information.

In this paper, deviant from the archetypal pipeline-based Siamese text matching models, we present **NIE-Match**[1], a **N**ested Siamese text matching framework that incorporates **I**nformation **I**nteractions and Feature **E**xtractions. The key components of the framework are the *Function Amplification Module* (FAM) and the *Interaction Extraction Module* (IEM). IEM acts as a Feature Extraction or Information Interaction Block, nested within both the FAM and the model structure itself. IEM assumes the responsibility for global matching within the model while FAM leverages the Late Attention and nested IEMs to sharpen local matching and reasoning capabilities. To examine the effect of NIE-Match on models encoded by traditional deep networks and pre-trained models, we conduct experiments using BiLSTM and BERT as encoder, respectively.

Our main contributions resides in the following aspects:

- We have divided the introduced blocks in the Siamese matching model into two functional categories: the Information Interaction Block and the Feature Extraction Block. This has enhanced the interpretability of the previous Siamese model.
- Deviant from the archetypal pipeline-based Siamese text matching models, we propose a Nested Siamese text matching framework NIE-Match. Specifically, we introduce the Function Module (IEM) and Function Amplifier (FAM) to the Siamese text matching model, which not only ensured global information consistency but also sharpened the local reasoning capabilities.
- Through experimentation, we have identified the optimal combination of FAM and IEM in NIE-Match, which outperforms other pipeline-based baselines in terms of performance.

---

[1] Code and appendix available: https://github.com/hggzjx/nie_match.

2   Related Work

With the emergence of deep learning and the introduction of Siamese match-ing models, the approach to the text matching task has transitioned from fea-ture engineering to structure engineering. Researchers began using convolutional networks [6,22] and recurrent networks [16,25] as Siamese encoders to obtain embeddings of sentence pairs for fine-grained level matching. Subsequent studies have integrated rich Late Attention mechanisms and interactive matching lay-ers into Siamese models [3,17]. In recent years, Transformer-based pre-trained encoders have gained widespread use for text semantic matching tasks [23], achieving remarkable results [4,18,26]. Similarly, a large number of Late Atten-tion strategies have been introduced to enhance the performance of Siamese models based on Transformer encoding, such as the cross-attention layer [8], the MLP layer [13], and the transformer layer [2].

Previous studies have proposed blocks in order to enhance the performance of models. We divide them into Feature Extraction Blocks and Information Interac-tion Blocks according to function. Tensor cross-fusion is the most classic Infor-mation Interaction Block, which not only retains the original information of the vectors, but also captures the differences and commonalities between the text vectors [3,12,19,27]. Pooling fusion is the most common Feature Extrac-tion Block, which uses max pooling or average pooling to extract features from semantic vectors of the sentence pair [3,10,19,24].

As referred in Sect. 1, approaches above involve arranging these blocks in a pipeline style [3,10,12,14,19], leading to limitations. To address this issue, we propose a Nested Siamese text matching framework NIE-Match.

3   Methodology

The four sub-figures of Fig. 2 illustrate the different aspects of the NIE-Match framework. Figure 2(a) illustrates the design of the Model Structure. Figure 2(b) depicts the two encoder options available in the model, BiLSTM and BERT. Figure 2(c) and 2(d) highlight the key components of the model: FAM and IEM. The IEM acts as a Feature Extraction or Information Interaction Block, nested within both the FAM and the Model Structure itself. IEM assumes the respon-sibility for global matching within the model while FAM leverages the Late Attention and nested IEMs to sharpen local matching and reasoning capabili-ties. We propose two forms of FAM and IEM, which can be combined in different ways to create various model strategies.

3.1   Model Structure

The model's primary structure takes an input sentence pair, represented by either two sentence embeddings or two sequences of sentence tokens denoted as s^a and s^b. The objective during training is to develop a classifier ξ that can compute the conditional probabilities $P(y|s^a, s^b)$ necessary to predict the relationship between the output sentence pairs, with the output probabilities guiding the prediction process.

$$P(y|\boldsymbol{s}^a, \boldsymbol{s}^b) = \xi(\boldsymbol{s}^a, \boldsymbol{s}^b) \tag{1}$$

$$y = \arg\max_{y \in Y} P(y|\boldsymbol{s}^a, \boldsymbol{s}^b) \tag{2}$$

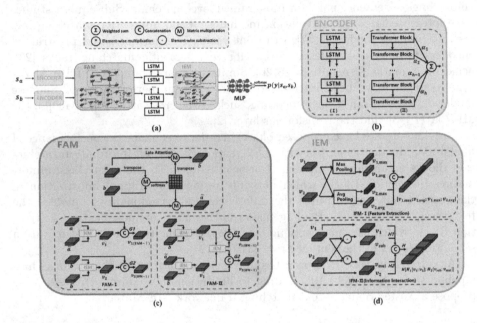

Fig. 2. Overview of NIE-Match. (a) Model Structure; (b) Encoder; (c) Function Amplification Module (FAM), comprising two options; (d) Interaction Extraction Module (IEM), comprising two options.

The labels $y \in Y$ denote the semantic relationships between the input sentence pairs, either match, not match or a collection of varying levels of matching degrees.

The model first employs two independent Siamese encoders to encode $\boldsymbol{s}^a$ and $\boldsymbol{s}^b$, resulting in encoded vectors $\boldsymbol{a} = (\boldsymbol{a}_1, \boldsymbol{a}_2 \dots \boldsymbol{a}_{l_a})$ and $\boldsymbol{b} = (\boldsymbol{b}_1, \boldsymbol{b}_2 \dots \boldsymbol{b}_{l_b})$. $\boldsymbol{a}_i$ and $\boldsymbol{b}_j$ are embeddings of l-dimensional vectors. The encoded vectors of the sentence pairs are processed by the FAMs to obtain vectors $\boldsymbol{v}_{1(\text{FAM})}$ and $\boldsymbol{v}_{2(\text{FAM})}$ with enhanced local reasoning. These obtained vectors are then further inferred by using a BiLSTM layer.

$$\boldsymbol{v}_{1(\text{FAM})}, \boldsymbol{v}_{2(\text{FAM})} = \text{FAM}(\boldsymbol{a}, \boldsymbol{b}) \tag{3}$$

Finally, the vectors enhanced with local reasoning from FAM are concatenated and matched using the IEM module in model structure, which then feed the results into a fully connected layer for final classification. Here the $\text{MLP}(\cdot)$ is the multi-layers perceptron.

$$v = \text{IEM}(\text{BiLSTM}(v_{1(\text{FAM})}), \text{BiLSTM}(v_{2(\text{FAM})})) \tag{4}$$

$$P(y|s^a, s^b) = \text{softmax}(\text{MLP}(v)) \tag{5}$$

3.2 Encoder

We employ two encoders with shared weights to map the tokens or embeddings of sentences into continuous vectors and obtain $a = \text{Enc}(s_a)$ and $b = \text{Enc}(s_b)$. We aim to investigate the effect of NIE-Match on models that use traditional deep networks and pre-trained models as encoders. So we use BiLSTM and BERT as encoders, respectively.

$$\text{Enc}_{\text{BiLSTM}}(s^a) = \text{BiLSTM}(s^a), \quad \text{Enc}_{\text{BiLSTM}}(s^b) = \text{BiLSTM}(s^b) \tag{6}$$

Additionally, for BERT as encoder, we utilize the weighted sum of all word hidden states from different Transformer blocks as the final contextual representation of the input words in the sentences.

$$\alpha_h = \frac{\exp(F_1(\text{TrBlock}^h(s^a)))}{\sum_{h=1}^{H} \exp(F_1(\text{TrBlock}^h(s^a)))}, \quad \beta_h = \frac{\exp(F_2(\text{TrBlock}^h(s^b)))}{\sum_{h=1}^{H} \exp(F_2(\text{TrBlock}^h(s^b)))} \tag{7}$$

$$\text{Enc}_{\text{BERT}}(s^a) = \sum_{h=1}^{H} \alpha_h \text{TrBlock}^h(s^a), \quad \text{Enc}_{\text{BERT}}(s^b) = \sum_{h=1}^{H} \beta_h \text{TrBlock}^h(s^b) \tag{8}$$

where, $\text{TrBlock}^h(\cdot)$ represents the semantic representation of the hth Transformer Block.

3.3 Function Amplification Module

FAM is a functional amplifier to enhance information interaction or feature extraction by leveraging Late Attention and nested IEM, thereby refining local matching and reasoning capabilities. Given two input sentences vectors a and b, FAM obtains two semantic representations $v_{1(\text{FAM})}$ and $v_{2(\text{FAM})}$ that have been sufficiently enhanced with information.

There are two main training paradigms for text matching. The first is the Siamese model, which encodes sentence pairs and enhances the fusion of information independently for the two sentence vectors. The second is the Cross model [15,23], which encodes sentence pairs and enhances the information fusion both jointly. Inspired by these two training paradigms, we proposed two candidate FAM structures, *FAM-I* and *FAM-II*.

Late Attention. The Late Attention in enables full information interaction between sentence pairs. First, the dot product of a and b is calculated and normalized using the softmax operation to obtain the similarity matrix between each sentence vector.

$$m_{ji}^b = \frac{\exp(a_i^T \cdot b_j)}{\sum_{k=1}^{l_b} \exp(a_i^T \cdot b_k)}, \quad m_{ij}^a = \frac{\exp(a_i^T \cdot b_j)}{\sum_{k=1}^{l_a} \exp(a_k^T \cdot b_j)} \tag{9}$$

Here similarity matrix m_{ji}^b measures the b's j^{th} position's impact on the ith position of a. The function of m_{ij}^a is similar with Eq. 9. Next, the similarity matrix will be used as weights to obtain $\widetilde{a}$ and $\widetilde{b}$ as shown in Eq. 10.

$$\widetilde{a}_i = \sum_{j=1}^{l_b} m_{ji}^b \cdot b_j, \quad i \in [1, ... l_a], \quad \widetilde{b}_j = \sum_{i=1}^{l_a} m_{ij}^a \cdot a_i, \quad j \in [1, ... l_b] \tag{10}$$

where $\widetilde{a}_i$ is the weighted sum of $\{b_j\}_{j=1}^{l_b}$ with m_{ji}^b. Intuitively, the purpose of Late Attention is to use the elements in $\{b_j\}_{j=1}^{l_b}$ that are related to $\widetilde{a}_i$ to represent $\widetilde{a}_i$. The same is performed for each word in the s^b with Eq. 10.

FAM-I. For FAM-I, our objective is to enable local reasoning on both the sentence vector and its representation, which have been enhanced through Late attention. FAM-I first performs IEM operation on the vectors $<a, \widetilde{a}>$, and vectors $<b, \widetilde{b}>$ to obtain enhanced vectors v_1', v_2'. These enhanced vectors are then concatenated with a,b to obtain the final enhanced vectors of sentence pairs after information enhancement by FAM-I module. The IEM operation will be discussed in detail in Sect. 3.4.

$$v_1' = \text{IEM}(a, \widetilde{a}), \quad v_2' = \text{IEM}(b, \widetilde{b}) \tag{11}$$

$$v_{1(\text{FAM--I})} = G_1([a; v_1']), \quad v_{2(\text{FAM--I})} = G_2([b; v_2']) \tag{12}$$

where G_1, G_2 are single-layer feedforward networks with independent parameters. [;] is the concatenation operation.

FAM-II. For FAM-II, our argument is that utilizing a joint representation of sentence pairs, similar to the Cross model, from the beginning of the process may facilitate more comprehensive information fusion in local reasoning. FAM-II performs IEM operation on vectors $<a, b>$ and vectors $<\widetilde{a}, \widetilde{b}>$ separately to obtain enhanced vectors v_1'', v_2''. It then performs an IEM operation between v_1'' and v_2'', and concatenates the result with v_1'' and v_2'' respectively, to obtain final enhanced encodings of the sentence pair.

$$v_1'' = \text{IEM}(\widetilde{a}, \widetilde{b}), \quad v_2'' = \text{IEM}(a, b) \tag{13}$$

$$v_{1(\text{FAM--II})} = G_1([v_1''; \text{IEM}(v_1'', v_2'')]), \quad v_{2(\text{FAM--II})} = G_2([v_2''; \text{IEM}(v_1'', v_2'')]) \tag{14}$$

3.4   Interaction Extraction Module

The Interaction Extraction Module (IEM) is a function module that is both used independently in the model and as a component in the Function Amplification Module. There are two kinds of IEM, *IEM-I* and *IEM-II*. IEM-I serves as a Feature Extraction Block while IEM-II operates as an Information Interaction Block. Given the input vectors v_1 and v_2, IEMs obtain a fixed-length vector $v_{(IEM)}$ through feature extraction or information interaction.

IEM-I. IEM-I is designed as a Feature Extraction Block that is devised to extract comprehensive global feature information from sentences. It involves the computation of both average and maximum pooling values of the sentence vector in isolation, followed by the concatenation of these four pooled vectors to derive the final vector.

$$v_{1,\max} = \max_{i=1}^{l_1} v_{1,i}, \quad v_{1,\mathrm{avg}} = \frac{\sum_{i=1}^{l_1} v_{1,i}}{l_1} \tag{15}$$

$$v_{2,\max} = \max_{j=1}^{l_2} v_{2,j}, \quad v_{2,\mathrm{avg}} = \frac{\sum_{j=1}^{l_2} v_{2,j}}{l_2} \tag{16}$$

$$v_{(IEM-I)} = [v_{1,\max}; v_{1,\mathrm{avg}}; v_{2,\max}; v_{2,\mathrm{avg}}] \tag{17}$$

IEM-II. IEM-II is designed as an Information Interaction Block, intended to capture critical semantic focal points present in sentence pairs. It is accomplished by employing element-wise subtraction and multiplication techniques to extract both difference and commonality information, respectively. Specifically, the subtraction operation is utilized to capture the dissimilarities between the sentence pairs, while the multiplication operation is employed to highlight areas of commonality. The final result is obtained by concatenating these tensors, as shown in Formula 19.

$$v_{\mathrm{sub}} = v_1 \ominus v_2, \quad v_{\mathrm{mul}} = v_1 \otimes v_2 \tag{18}$$

$$v_{(IEM-II)} = H([H_1([v_1; v_2]); H_2([v_{\mathrm{sub}}; v_{\mathrm{mul}}])) \tag{19}$$

where H, H_1, H_2 are single-layer feedforward networks. $\ominus$ denotes element-wise subtraction and $\otimes$ denotes element-wise multiplication.

4   Experiments

Our study assesses the performance of our models in comparison to baseline models using three text semantic matching datasets: QQP [9], MRPC [5], and SNLI [1]. The architecture of NIE-Match is predicated upon the FAM, we denote NIE-Match-I as the implementation that employs FAM-I and NIE-Match-II as the implementation that employs FAM-II.

Table 1. Model blocks and experimental results of different text semantic matching models (Accuracy). FEB denotes Feature Extraction Block, while IIB denotes Information Interaction Block.

Model	Model Blocks				Datasets		
	Encoder	Late Attention	FEB	IIB	QQP	MRPC	SNLI
BiMPM [24]	BiLSTM	✓	✓		88.2	–	82.9
ESIM [3]	BiLSTM	✓	✓	✓	87.8	74.4	88.0
DRCN [11]	BiLSTM	✓	✓	✓	87.1	75.0	89.0
RE2 [27]	BiLSTM	✓		✓	87.8	75.2	88.9
NIE-Match	BiLSTM	✓	✓	✓	**89.1**	**76.1**	**89.0**
Siamese BERT [19]	BERT		✓	✓	81.8	71.9	83.8
ColBERT [10]	BERT	✓	✓		86.3	74.2	87.1
Sentence T5 [14]	T5	✓	✓	✓	90.3	77.9	–
NIE-Match	BERT	✓		✓	**90.5**	**76.3**	**88.7**

4.1　Main Result

Table 1 shows the model blocks and performance of both baselines and NIE-Match. It is worth noting that the optimal strategy for NIE-Match is presented, while subsequent experiments provide a detailed account of the selection process for the optimal FAM and the optimal combination of FAM and IEM strategies. As is shown in Table 1, when similar functional blocks are present, our model outperforms other pipeline-based baselines in terms of performance.

4.2　Effect of Function Amplification Module

Ablation Study. As a functional amplifier, FAM offers abundant local matching and reasoning capabilities. Table 2 shows the performance of the model before and after the introduction of the two FAMs for the two encoders (BiLSTM and BERT), as well as the level of enhancement. Our results suggest that the introduction of FAM leads to an improvement in performance for both encoders, with a more pronounced effect on traditional deep neural network encoders. This may be due to the fact that pre-trained language models, such as BERT, have already captured a significant amount of semantic information through their multi-layer attention mechanisms, whereas traditional deep neural network encoders can benefit more from the additional semantic information provided by the FAM.

Robustness Experiment. Based on Table 2, FAM-II provides a more significant enhancement for the model. To test its generalization ability, we conduct robustness experiments[2]. We use a common toolkit[3] to perform transformations,

---

[2] In the robust experimental setup, we referred to the work of [28].

[3] https://www.textflint.io.

Table 2. Results of ablation study. The numbers in bold represent whether the level of enhancement is significant (using signed rank sum test [20]; $p < 0.05$).

FAM	Encoder	QQP	MRPC	SNLI
		Ori.->FAM (improve)	Ori.->FAM (improve)	Ori.->FAM (improve)
FAM-I	BiLSTM	85.84->88.90 (**3.06**)	73.23->76.02 (**2.79**)	85.68->88.41 (**2.73**)
	BERT	87.41->89.57 (2.16)	74.47->76.91 (2.44)	85.59->88.12 (2.53)
FAM-II	BiLSTM	85.84->89.14 (**3.30**)	73.23->76.11 (**2.88**)	85.40->89.04 (**3.64**)
	BERT	87.41->90.46 (**3.05**)	74.47->77.11 (2.64)	85.83->88.71 (**2.88**)

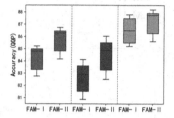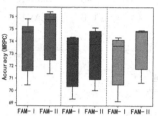

Fig. 3. Robustness Experimental results. Each box represents the distribution of accuracy data for a group. The red, blue, yellow boxes indicate BackTrans, SwapWord, Overlap respectivly. (Color figure online)

including BackTrans, SwapWord, and Overlap. We test 6 models of NIE-Match-I and 6 models of NIE-Match-II, with each model framework corresponding to the best-performing IEM combinations and three encoding methods (BiLSTM with Word2vec, BiLSTM with Glove, and BERT) in three transformation scenarios. As shown in Fig. 3, the NIE-Match-II model maintains superior performance compared to NIE-Match-I, indicating that FAM-II offers both better performance and stronger robustness.

4.3   Effect of Interaction Extraction Module

Different IEM choices within the Model Structure and FAM result in varied model framing strategies. To determine the optimal IEM arrangement for superior performance, we evaluate each strategy using Siamese BiLSTM and BERT encoders. Six strategies, based on different IEM choices, are tested on two model frameworks and presented in Table 3.

Figure 4 displays the performance of different model strategies, which is the average of NIE-Match-I and NIE-Match-II. Based on the results shown in Fig. 4, we can conclude that for BiLSTM-encoded models, the ST-3 strategy, which includes a Feature Extraction Block enabling full extraction of global features in sentence pairs, is optimal. Conversely, for BERT-encoded models, the ST-4 strategy, which captures interactive information, is preferred, as BERT already extracts a significant amount of feature information from sentences through multi-layered attention and feed-forward neural networks during pre-training.

Table 3. The strategies formed by the varying choices of IEM in FAM and model structure. IEM (FAM) is the IEM in FAM, IEM (Structure) is the IEM in the Model Structure

Strategy	IEM (FAM)	IEM (Structure)
ST-1	–	IEM-I
ST-2	–	IEM-II
ST-3	IEM-II	IEM-II
ST-4	IEM-II	IEM-I
ST-5	IEM-I	IEM-II
ST-6	IEM-I	IEM-I

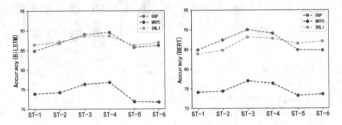

Fig. 4. Results of the multi-combination strategy experiments on the NIE-Match framework with BiLSTM and BERT as encoders.

4.4 Case Study

In order to provide an intuitive comparison of the nested Siamese matching model's advantages over pipeline-based models, we employ trained NIE-Match (BERT) and ColBERT [10] models to independently encode sentence pairs from the QQP dataset (test) and subsequently compute the similarity matrices between these encoded pairs. As demonstrated in Fig. 5, NIE-Match directs the model's attention towards crucial terms such as 'book', 'aspiring entrepreneur', 'people you have never met', 'influence', and 'life', which play a significant role in assessing sentence similarity. This can be attributed to NIE-Match's distinctive nested structure that adeptly balances global matching and local reasoning. Consequently, in comparison to the pipeline-based ColBERT model, NIE-Match exhibits a heightened ability to concentrate on essential semantic information within the text.

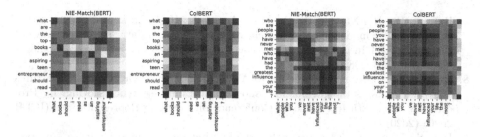

Fig. 5. Similarity matrix between sentence pairs encoded by ColBERT and NIE-Match, with darker colors indicating higher semantic similarity.

5 Conclusion

In this paper, we propose a nested Siamese text matching framework that incorporates the concepts of Feature Extraction Block and Information Interaction Block. Specifically, we introduce the functional module IEM and the functional amplifier FAM into the Siamese model, resulting in significant and consistent improvements in performance.

In the future, we hope to introduce weak labels and design additional auxiliary tasks to capture more fine-grained matching information, which will enhance the performance of Siamese matching models.

References

1. Bowman, S., Angeli, G., Potts, C., Manning, C.D.: A large annotated corpus for learning natural language inference. In: Proceedings of the 2015 Conference on Empirical Methods in Natural Language Processing, pp. 632–642 (2015)
2. Cao, Q., Trivedi, H., Balasubramanian, A., Balasubramanian, N.: DeFormer: decomposing pre-trained transformers for faster question answering. In: Proceedings of the 58th Annual Meeting of the Association for Computational Linguistics, pp. 4487–4497 (2020)
3. Chen, Q., Zhu, X., Ling, Z.H., Wei, S., Jiang, H., Inkpen, D.: Enhanced LSTM for natural language inference. In: Proceedings of the 55th Annual Meeting of the Association for Computational Linguistics (Volume 1: Long Papers), pp. 1657–1668 (2017)
4. Devlin, J., Chang, M.W., Lee, K., Toutanova, K.: BERT: pre-training of deep bidirectional transformers for language understanding. In: Proceedings of the 2019 Conference of the North American Chapter of the Association for Computational Linguistics: Human Language Technologies, Volume 1 (Long and Short Papers), pp. 4171–4186 (2019)
5. Dolan, B., Brockett, C.: Automatically constructing a corpus of sentential paraphrases. In: Third International Workshop on Paraphrasing (IWP2005). Asia Federation of Natural Language Processing (2005)
6. Hu, B., Lu, Z., Li, H., Chen, Q.: Convolutional neural network architectures for matching natural language sentences. In: Advances in Neural Information Processing Systems, vol. 27 (2014)

7. Huang, P.S., He, X., Gao, J., Deng, L., Acero, A., Heck, L.: Learning deep structured semantic models for web search using clickthrough data. In: Proceedings of the 22nd ACM International Conference on Information & Knowledge Management, pp. 2333–2338 (2013)
8. Humeau, S., Shuster, K., Lachaux, M.A., Weston, J.: Poly-encoders: architectures and pre-training strategies for fast and accurate multi-sentence scoring. In: Proceedings of the 8th International Conference on Learning Representations (ICLR 2020) (2020)
9. Iyer, S., Dandekar, N., Csernai, K., et al.: First Quora dataset release: question pairs. Data (2017). quora.com
10. Khattab, O., Zaharia, M.: ColBERT: efficient and effective passage search via contextualized late interaction over BERT. In: Proceedings of the 43rd International ACM SIGIR Conference on Research and Development in Information Retrieval, pp. 39–48 (2020)
11. Kim, S., Kang, I., Kwak, N.: Semantic sentence matching with densely-connected recurrent and co-attentive information. In: Proceedings of the AAAI Conference on Artificial Intelligence, vol. 33, pp. 6586–6593 (2019)
12. Li, D., et al.: VIRT: improving representation-based models for text matching through virtual interaction. CoRR abs/2112.04195 (2021). https://arxiv.org/abs/2112.04195
13. Liu, H., Dai, Z., So, D., Le, Q.V.: Pay attention to MLPS. In: Advances in Neural Information Processing Systems, vol. 34, pp. 9204–9215 (2021)
14. Ni, J., et al.: Sentence-T5: scalable sentence encoders from pre-trained text-to-text models. In: Findings of the Association for Computational Linguistics: ACL 2022, pp. 1864–1874 (2022)
15. Nogueira, R.F., Cho, K.: Passage re-ranking with BERT. CoRR abs/1901.04085 (2019). https://arxiv.org/abs/1901.04085
16. Palangi, H., et al.: Deep sentence embedding using long short-term memory networks: analysis and application to information retrieval. IEEE/ACM Trans. Audio Speech Lang. Process. 24(4), 694–707 (2016)
17. Pang, L., Lan, Y., Guo, J., Xu, J., Wan, S., Cheng, X.: Text matching as image recognition. In: Proceedings of the AAAI Conference on Artificial Intelligence, vol. 30 (2016)
18. Raffel, C., et al.: Exploring the limits of transfer learning with a unified text-to-text transformer. J. Mach. Learn. Res. 21, 1–67 (2020)
19. Reimers, N., Gurevych, I.: Sentence-BERT: sentence embeddings using Siamese BERT-networks. In: Proceedings of the 2019 Conference on Empirical Methods in Natural Language Processing and the 9th International Joint Conference on Natural Language Processing (EMNLP-IJCNLP), pp. 3982–3992 (2019)
20. Rey, D., Neuhäuser, M.: Wilcoxon-signed-rank test. In: Lovric, M. (ed.) International Encyclopedia of Statistical Science, pp. 1658–1659. Springer, Heidelberg (2011). https://doi.org/10.1007/978-3-642-04898-2_616
21. Rücklé, A., Pfeiffer, J., Gurevych, I.: MultiCQA: zero-shot transfer of self-supervised text matching models on a massive scale. In: Proceedings of the 2020 Conference on Empirical Methods in Natural Language Processing (EMNLP), pp. 2471–2486 (2020)
22. Shen, Y., He, X., Gao, J., Deng, L., Mesnil, G.: A latent semantic model with convolutional-pooling structure for information retrieval. In: Proceedings of the 23rd ACM International Conference on Conference on Information and Knowledge Management, pp. 101–110 (2014)

23. Vaswani, A., et al.: Attention is all you need. In: Advances in Neural Information Processing Systems, vol. 30 (2017)
24. Wang, Z., Hamza, W., Florian, R.: Bilateral multi-perspective matching for natural language sentences. In: Proceedings of the 26th International Joint Conference on Artificial Intelligence, pp. 4144–4150 (2017)
25. Wu, Y., Wu, W., Xing, C., Zhou, M., Li, Z.: Sequential matching network: a new architecture for multi-turn response selection in retrieval-based chatbots. In: Proceedings of the 55th Annual Meeting of the Association for Computational Linguistics (Volume 1: Long Papers), pp. 496–505 (2017)
26. Xiong, L., et al.: Approximate nearest neighbor negative contrastive learning for dense text retrieval. In: Proceedings of the 8th International Conference on Learning Representations (ICLR 2020) (2020)
27. Yang, R., Zhang, J., Gao, X., Ji, F., Chen, H.: Simple and effective text matching with richer alignment features. In: Proceedings of the 57th Annual Meeting of the Association for Computational Linguistics, pp. 4699–4709 (2019)
28. Zou, Y., et al.: Divide and conquer: text semantic matching with disentangled keywords and intents. In: Findings of the Association for Computational Linguistics: ACL 2022, pp. 3622–3632 (2022)

Label-Guided Graphormer for Hierarchy Text Classification

Song Li, Jingjing Huo, Wenqiang Xu, Maozong Zheng, Kezun Zhang, Hong Chen, and Xuan Lin[✉]

AntGroup, No. 556 Xixi Road, Hangzhou, China
`daxuan.lx@antgroup.com`

Abstract. Hierarchical text classification (HTC), a subtask of multi-label classification, remains a challenging problem due to its complex label topology hierarchy. Although various methods have been proposed for modeling hierarchical information in recent research, less attention has been paid to techniques that utilize label information hidden in the training data, which can be potentially beneficial for hierarchical classification. In this paper, we focus on enhancing label representations from the perspective of contextual interactions and semantic complements, which refer to label co-occurrences and keywords respectively. And a Label-guided Graphormer (LGraphormer) is proposed for the purpose of integrating these promising features. The final prediction is performed by feeding its output embeddings into a text encoder in a hierarchy-aware manner. Our extensive experiments show that the proposed approach achieves state-of-the-art performance on three widely used public datasets, demonstrating the effectiveness of our methodology. Our code is available at: https://github.com/ContentTech/LGraphormerHTC.git.

Keywords: hierarchical text classification · data information · label represent enhancement · Graphormer net

1 Introduction

Hierarchical text classification (HTC) is a special case of multi-label classification that intends to classify text based on its label hierarchy [13,23]. It has been widely used in various applications, including but not limited to intent classification in the search engine, news classification [6], scientific paper classification [8], *etc*. Due to its large-scale, imbalanced, and structured hierarchy characteristics, HTC remains a challenging problem [18], which has attracted a lot of studies recently.

In general, solutions for HTC can be categorized into local and global approaches [23]. The local methods typically construct a model for each individual node or layer and subsequently make predictions along a top-down topological path, but the increased parameters tend to cause exposure bias [5]. In contrast, the global methods typically make predictions for the entire hierarchy

L. Iliadis et al. (Eds.): ICANN 2023, LNCS 14258, pp. 536–547, 2023.
https://doi.org/10.1007/978-3-031-44192-9_43

through a single model. Initially, it ignored the impact of hierarchical information and regarded HTC as a common multi-label classification. Following the proposal of incorporating hierarchical information into text encoders by [23] in 2020, subsequent research in the global category has primarily focused on exploring the intersection between hierarchies and text encoders [1,17]. More recently, graph neural networks (GNNs) have been introduced to encode hierarchy in [18], with the resulting output being injected into BERT for further prediction, achieving state-of-the-art performance on three popular public datasets. Despite the frequent use of hierarchy-based methods in recent years, there has been limited attention given to incorporating label information retrieved from the dataset, which has been demonstrated to be useful in multi-label classification tasks, as evidenced by [9].

In this paper, we propose a method to enhance label representation by incorporating co-occurrences and keywords as contextual interactions and semantic complements. In previous work, label embeddings are typically learned from the label semantics [4,18], but only the label names are utilized, leading to suboptimal performance for the task without explicit label names [8]. To alleviate this problem, we extract keywords through the unsupervised TF-IDF algorithm and use them as a supplement to label semantics. Additionally, label co-occurrence relations have been widely used in multi-label classification [12,22], we believe such relations can also benefit HTC. So, we obtain the label co-occurrence matrix based on the proportion of the label pairs and use it as a sub-graph of hierarchy.

However, encoding various label information, including hierarchy, semantics, and co-occurrence, remains a challenging problem due to their different structural properties. For instance, independent label information, like semantics, can be formed as a sequence, whereas interactive information, like co-occurrence, is more appropriately represented as a matrix. To fuse them together, we propose the LGraphormer, which is inspired by graph net Graphormer [21]. Graphormer leverages a transformer block to encode information and achieves state-of-art performance in many graph-related tasks. Based on its capability of integrating sequence and matrix features, we adopt it to encode the aforementioned information and obtain outstanding feature representations. To perform the final prediction, we feed the output embeddings of LGraphormer into BERT in a layer-aware way following the action in [18]. Extensive experiments demonstrate the effectiveness of our proposed method.

We summarize our main contributions as follows:

- The proposed approach seeks to enhance the label representation by means of leveraging information retrieved from the dataset. More specifically, we explore co-occurrences as contextual interactions and use keywords as semantic complements.
- The LGraphormer is proposed as a solution to address the challenge of effectively integrating the information with diverse structural properties. Its flexibility enables the easy extension to incorporate more label features.
- We conduct extensive experiments on three public datasets and achieve state-of-art performance, demonstrating the effectiveness of the proposed method.

2   Related Work

The HTC task, aiming to model the large-scale, imbalanced, and structured hierarchy [3], is still a challenging task. Compared to the multi-label task, HTC focuses on using the hierarchy information to improve the model performance. Recent research based on the hierarchy modeling methods can be grouped into: the local and the global approaches.

The local approaches generally need to build models for every node or layer and perform the up-down classification following the hierarchy tree. Kazuya et al. [5] propose to apply the CNN net to the up-layer of the hierarchy tree through fine-tuning technology. Shimura et al. [15] optimizes the classification parameters of the child node using the parent node to alleviate the data imbalance problem.

The global approach can be treated as a special multi-label classification with topological hierarchy information. Plenty methods have been exploited, including recursive regularization [20], reinforcement learning [10], capsule network [11] and meta-learning [19]. Zhou et al. [23] proposes to treat the hierarchy as a directed graph and encode the hierarchy using the GCN graph net, then put the result into a text encoder. Chen et al. [1] regard HTC as a matching problem and map the text and label into the same embedding space through contrastive learning. Jiang et al. [4] try to learn static label embedding and do the prediction through a generation way. Wang et al. [17] proposes to generate the positive samples through graph net and incorporate the hierarchy by contrastive learning. More recently, Wang et al. [18] introduce the prompt-tuning approach to the HTC task.

3   Problem Definition

As for any HTC, we can define the topological hierarchy as set $\mathcal{H} = (\mathcal{Y}, E)$, $\mathcal{H}$ is the labels set (hierarchy tree nodes), E represents the edges set of the hierarchy. The task of HTC is to model the classification from the input text x to the hierarchy label set $\nu \in \mathcal{Y}$. As all labels are structured as a tree graph, apart from the root node, each node has only one father, and labels of one layer have the same depth. Since it is a sub-task of multi-label classification, the model prediction can be one or more paths of $\mathcal{H}$.

4   Methodology

This part will introduce a new hierarchy-aware classification model, which adopts the LGraphormer to encode all label information, including hierarchy, keywords, and co-occurrences, as shown in Fig. 1.

4.1   Hierarchy-Aware Classification Model

To leverage the hierarchy information, similar to [18], we apply the hierarchy-aware soft prompt mechanism. For general text classification, the Model's

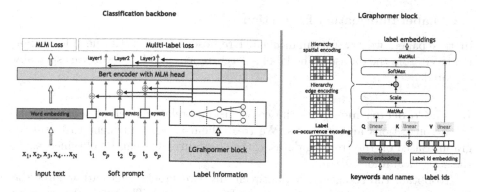

Fig. 1. The hierarchy-aware model encodes different label information using LGraphormer. The left part shows the classification backbone and the right LGraphormer block. The spatial and the edge features are extracted from the hierarchy label tree; The label's co-occurrence relations and keywords are retrieved from the dataset; All the label features are incorporated by the attention block of LGraphormer. The obtained label embeddings are fed into the BERT in a layer-awar manner to finish the final classification.

inputs will be formed as "[CLS]x[SEP]", the classification head is built based on the hidden embedding of [CLS]. Differently, we modify the template as "[CLS]x[SEP][V1][PRED]...[VL][PRED]", where the [VL] is the soft prompt which can be learned during training, L is the depth number of hierarchy tree; [PRED] is a special token to build the layer-aware prediction head.

The BERT [16] is adopted as a text encoder in this paper. We use its embedding layer to convert the token to embedding and form inputs as:

$$T = [x_1, x_2, \cdots, x_N, t_1, e_p, \cdots, t_L, e_p] \tag{1}$$

where $X = [x_1, x_2, \cdots, x_N]$ is the token embedding; e_p is embedding for [PRED] and is initialized by the [MASK] of BERT. $\{t_m\}_{m=1}^L$ is the layer-aware prompt embedding, which is randomly initialized. For clarity, later parts will ignore the [CLS] and [SEP].

The hidden embeddings can be obtained after the BERT encoder:

$$H = [h_1, h_2, \cdots, h_N, h_{t_1}, h_p^1, \cdots, h_{t_L}, h_p^L] \tag{2}$$

where h_i is the hidden embedding for x_i; h_p^m the hidden embedding of e_p corresponding to m-th layer.

In terms of verbalizer, we create a learnable virtual word for each label. Inputting label l_i into the LGraphormer block will produce more informative embedding v_i. To finish the label prediction, as shown in left part of Fig. 1, we build an independent prediction head for each layer, which means one [PRED] is responsible for only one layer. Based on that, the model can learn the dependency between layers in a better way [18].

4.2   Label Information Extraction

In this paper, we try to enhance label representations with the information retrieved from the dataset. The label co-occurrences and keywords are especially explored.

Label Co-occurrences. As the co-occurrence relations reflect more complicated connections among labels, We treat them as a supplement to hierarchy graph. Based on the training dataset, the co-occurrences can be obtained using the statistical information.

To obtain the co-occurrence between any two labels, this part ignores the hierarchy constraint, and treats every node as one label. The total label number is marked as M. Considering any two labels l_i and l_j, the proportion of l_j in l_i samples can be computed as:

$$R_{l_j \in l_i} = \frac{num_{l_i \cap l_j}}{num_{l_i}} \tag{3}$$

where $i, j \in [1, \cdots M]$, $num_{l_i \cap l_j}$ means the label number with both l_i and l_j, num_{l_i} the sample number of l_i. Setting the l_i as row index and l_j as column index, we can get the co-occurrence matrix among all labels.

To reduce the effect of observation errors, this paper split the float into several buckets:

$$R_{ij} = \text{INT}(R_{l_j \in l_i} \times \Omega) \tag{4}$$

where the Ω is the bucket number. We use the $\Omega = 10$ in this paper. It is easy to notice that the proportion will be 10 if l_j is the child of l_i, and the number will be larger than 0 if there is a link between the labels. Thus we believe the matrix can contain more information than the hierarchy.

Label Semantics. The importance of label semantics have been explored in previous approaches [4,18]. But only the label names are focused, leading to poor performance on the task without meaningful name, such as RCV1-V2 task [8]. To solve this problem, we extract keywords from the training set to supplement semantic information.

The unsupervised algorithm DF-IDF is used in this paper for its low computation consumption. We define the HTC train samples as S $=$ [$s_1, s_2, \cdots, s_N$], and total number is N. Each sample can be described as s_i = [$token_1$, $token_2, \cdots, token_{\text{Lenth}}$], and the TF-IDF score for the token can be computed as :

$$score_{token} = \frac{f_{token}}{Length} \times \log(\frac{N}{1 + num_{token \in s}}) \tag{5}$$

where f_{token} is the appearing times of the *token* in sample s_i; *Length* the sample's total length; N the total number of samples in dataset; $num_{token \in s}$ the number of the samples that contain the *token*. Setting the subset with the l_i as $S_{sub} = [s_1, s_2, \cdots, s_n]$, the weight of the keywords can be obtained by summarizing TF-IDF scores:

$$weight_{token} = \sum_{token \in s_1}^{s_n} score_{token} \tag{6}$$

Arranging the tokens in descending order according to the weight, the top-N words are the keywords of the label l_i. Repeating the above process can generate the keywords for all labels. Since they are calculated from a statistical distribution, there may be a bias between the keyword and the true meaning of the label. Therefore, it is best to use them as a complement to label names. It means that only the name is used if the meaningful label name exists, or the keywords are added.

4.3   Label-Guided Grahpormer

To incorporate the label information including hierarchy, co-occurrence, and semantics, the LGraphormer is proposed based on the graphormer layer, which uses an attention block to encode information.

Firstly, the label embedding is initiated by the semantics and id embedding, as shown in right part of Fig. 1:

$$f_i = label\_id\_emb(l_i) + token\_emb(st_{l_i}) \tag{7}$$

where $label\_id\_emb()$ puts every label a learnable embedding with d_h dimension; $token\_emb()$ is the embedding layer of BERT. Commonly the token embedding weight is utilized to initialize the label, in contrast, we share the token embedding of BERT with the label semantics to make its embedding more instructive. Repeating the equation for all labels can get all embeddings, and stacking them will make a sequence matrix F with dimension $M \times d_h$, which will be fed into the Graphormer layer in a later step.

To leverage the hierarchy information and the co-occurrence relationship, we modify the attention block to cover all label information. Based on the hierarchy tree graph, the path and distance between nodes are first extracted. There is only one shortest path between any two labels $[e_1, e_2, \cdots, e_D]$, and the distance between the two is $\phi(l_i, l_j) = D$. In combination with the co-occurrence matrix computed above, we modify the Query-Key matrix in the attention block as :

$$A_{ij} = \frac{(f_i W_Q)(f_j W_K)^T}{\sqrt{d_h}} + c_{ij} + b_{\phi(l_i,l_j)} + r_{R_{ij}} \tag{8}$$

where the A_{ij} is the value in position (i, j); The first part of the equation is a standard operation of self-attention, the Query and Key are mapped by two weight matrix W_Q and W_K with a dimension of $d_h \times d_h$. c_{ij} is the spatial encoding. We put every tree edge a learnable parameter w_{e_n}, and encoding the path as $c_{ij} = \frac{1}{D}\sum_{n=1}^{D} w_{e_n}$. $b_{\phi(l_i,l_j)}$ is the distance encoding, which gives a learnable parameter based on distance $\phi(l_i, l_j)$. $r_{R_{ij}}$ is the encoding of co-occurrence, a learnable parameter built based on the R_{ij} in the matrix.

A softmax operation is then performed on the obtained weight matrix A, followed by multiplying the Value and linking the last layer's output F, finally, the normalization layer is added to generate the result:

$$F_{\text{output}} = LayerNorm(softmax(A)V + F) \tag{9}$$

where F_{output} is the output of the Graphormer layer; And V is the value of attention mechanism. The Graphormer layer utilized here is a modified version, more detail about the original one can be found in [21].

Based on the process above, we can get the label embedding $\mathbf{f}_i$, which covers the hierarchy information, semantics, and co-occurrences etc. As the text encoder is organized in layer-aware as shown way in Fig. 1, we need to group the label embeddings according to the hierarchy layers and obtain the mean embedding :

$$g_{t_m} = \frac{1}{N} \sum_{l_n \in \nu_m} \mathbf{f}_{l_n} \tag{10}$$

where ν_m is the label set of layer m; N the label number in layer m; $\mathbf{f}_{l_n}$ the output of the LGraphormer corresponding to the label l_n. We add it to the prompt embedding of Eq. 1 and input them into the text encoder BERT:

$$t_m = t_m + g_{t_m} \tag{11}$$

where g_{t_m} is the mean label embedding of Eq. 10.

4.4   Loss Function

To get a better result, we fine-tune the classification based on the pre-trained model BERT and keep the MLM task. During training, 15% tokens are randomly masked and become the targets of MLM, so its loss function can be built as:

$$\mathcal{L}_{\text{CE}} = -\log \frac{e^{s_{y_t}}}{\sum_{i=1}^{C} e^{s_{y_i}}} \tag{12}$$

where y_t is the token target, $s_{y_t} = \mathbf{v}_t^T h_p + b_{tm}$, $\mathbf{v}_t$ is the token embedding, b_{tm} a learnable bias term. It is a standard cross entropy loss (CE loss), and the model is optimized by maximizing the target's output score.

In contrast, the HTC is a kind of multi-label classification task, which often uses the binary cross-entry loss (BCE loss) to optimize the model. But the loss puts every label as a two classes problem, ignoring the relations between labels. To improve, we utilize the Zero-bounded Multi-label Cross Entropy Loss (ZMLCE) proposed in [18] to optimize the model. Similar to the CE loss, it optimizes the model by maximizing the target's prediction score too. The difference is that the ZMLCE loss holds a zero anchor, which makes the prediction score larger than zero for positive targets, and lower than zero for negative targets. Based on the hidden embedding h_p^m, the loss function for the layer m can be built as

$$\mathcal{L}_{\text{ZMLCE}} = \log(1 + \sum_{l_i \in \nu_m^n} e^{s_{l_i}}) + \log(1 + \sum_{l_i \in \nu_m^p} e^{-s_{l_i}}) \tag{13}$$

where $s_{l_i} = \mathbf{v}_i^T h_p^m + b_{im}$, $\mathbf{v}_i^T$ the label embedding, b_{im} a learnable bias term; ν_m^n represents the negative targets set; ν_m^p the positive targets set.

Finally, a multi-task loss is formed to optimize the model jointly:

$$\mathcal{L}_{\text{all}} = \sum_{m=1}^{L} \mathcal{L}_{\text{ZMLCE}}^m + \frac{1}{N} \sum_{n=1}^{N} \mathcal{L}_{\text{CE}}^n \qquad (14)$$

where L the layer number of the hierarchy; N the masked token number of MLM task; When inferring, the labels can be obtained by the prediction scores larger than zero.

5   Experiment

Table 1. Data details of the three public datasets. Label_num means the total label number of hierarchy. Avg_labels presents the average label number per sample.

Dataset	Depth	Label_num	Avg_labels	Train	Dev	Test
NYT	8	166	7.6	23345	5834	7292
WOS	2	141	2.0	30070	7518	9397
RCV1-2	4	103	3.24	20833	2316	781265

Table 2. F1 scores on 3 datasets. Best results are in boldface.

model	NYT		WOS		RCV1-V2	
	Micro-F1	Macro-F1	Micro-F1	Macro-F1	Micro-F1	Macro-F1
TextRCNN (2020) [23]	70.83	56.18	83.55	76.99	81.57	59.25
HiAGM (2020) [23]	74.97	60.83	85.82	80.28	83.96	63.35
HTCInfoMax (2021) [2]	–	–	85.58	80.05	83.51	62.71
HiMatch (2021) [1]	–	–	86.20	80.53	84.73	64.11
BERT (2022) [17]	78.24	66.08	85.63	79.07	85.65	67.02
BERT+HiAGM (2022) [17]	78.64	66.76	86.04	80.19	85.58	67.93
BERT+HTCInfoMax (2022) [17]	78.75	67.31	86.30	79.97	85.53	67.09
BERT+HiMatch (2021) [1]	–	–	86.70	81.06	86.33	68.66
HGCLR (2022) [17]	78.86	67.96	87.11	81.20	86.49	68.31
HGBL (2022) [4]	80.47	70.19	87.36	82.00	87.23	**71.07**
HPT (2022) [18]	80.42	70.42	87.16	81.93	87.26	69.53
ours	**81.30**	**71.78**	**87.65**	**82.31**	**87.51**	69.42

5.1 Experiment Setup

Datasets and Evaluation Metrics. The proposed method is tested on three popular public datasets: NYTimes (NYT) [14], Web_of_Science (WOS) [7] and RCV1-V2 [8]. The statistical details of datasets are listed in Table 1. In addition, the labels for both NYT and WOS have meaningful names, while labels for RCV1-V2 are meaningless names consisting of randomly selected letters. Following the data processing of previous work [1,18,23], we measure the experimental results with Macro-F1 and Micro-F1.

Baselines. A variety of hierarchical text classification baselines are introduced in this part for systematic comparisons, including HiAGM [23], HTCInfoMax [2], HiMatch [1], HGCLR [17], HGBL [4] and HPT [18]. The HiAGM and HTCInfoMax mainly focus on joining the hierarchy information, HiAGM proposes a hierarchy-aware model to get label mixed features through soft attention and HTCInfoMax improves it by maximizing text-label mutual information. The HiMatch and HGCLR introduce contrastive learning into HTC, the former treats it as a matching problem to maximize the embedding similarity between the text and hierarchy; the latter produces positive samples through a new graph net and incorporates the hierarchy by using contrastive learning. The HGBL trains a static embedding for every label through BERT layers and then classifies the hierarchy by a generation method. Recently, HPT introduces prompt-tuning into HTC and obtains an obvious improvement. Noticing from [4,18], the pre-trained model BERT-based methods commonly have a better performance compared to LSTM, as listed in Table 2.

Implement Details. We use the Pytorch platform to build the end-to-end model, whose backbone is chosen as the pre-trained model bert-base-uncased following previous work [1,18]. And one layer of LGraphormer is utilized to incorporate label information including hierarchy, label semantics, co-occurrences etc. The train batch size is set to 16, adam as the optimizer, and start learning rate as 1e-4. And the learning rate is updated by ReduceLROnPlateau, if no higher Macro-F1 occurs within 3 epochs, the learning rate is halved. Dev data is evaluated every epoch, and if a higher Macro-F1 is not reached for 6 epochs, early-stopping will be performed. Furthermore, we set bucket 10 for the co-occurrence matrix and select 5 keywords for each label to achieve better performance.

5.2 Main Results

Table 2 shows the comparison between baselines and our method. The proposed method achieves state-of-art performance on NYT and WOS and reaches almost the SOTA on RCV1-V2. That proves the effectiveness of the proposed method, which enhances the label representations by the information retrieved from dataset.

In comparison with others, our method has more advantages. The HGCLR incorporates the hierarchy through contrastive learning, but the direct injecting method utilized in our method seems more effective. The HGBL tries to obtain static label embedding from the hierarchy and the label names, we enhance label representations from the perspective of contextual interactions and semantic complements, which refers to label co-occurrences and keywords respectively. And a simple graph net is utilized in HPT to encode hierarchy, we improve it to Graphormer to fuse various information with different properties and get better label representations. Based on the improvements, our method reaches the state-of-art performance.

Among the three datasets, NYT owns the most hierarchy layers, which means the most complicated hierarchy structure. Nevertheless, our method can still obtain significant improvements, reaching 81.30% for Micro-F1 and 71.78% for Macro-F1, which demonstrates the advantage of the method in dealing with complex hierarchies. Although it is noted that Micro-F1 of RCV1-V2 achieves the best but Macro-F1 does not exceed HGBL, which may be caused by its more serious data imbalance problem.

5.3   Ablation Study

Table 3. Ablation result on 3 datasets. r.m. stands for remove. r.p. stands for replaced with.

model	NYT		WOS		RCV1-V2	
	Micro-F1	Macro-F1	Micro-F1	Macro-F1	Micro-F1	Macro-F1
ours	**81.30**	**71.78**	**87.65**	**82.31**	**87.51**	**69.42**
r.m. keywords	–	–	–	–	86.87	68.36
r.m. name	80.91	71.12	87.03	81.90	86.73	68.33
r.m. co-ocurrence	80.82	71.11	86.68	81.17	86.45	68.09
r.p. GAT	80.51	70.96	86.53	81.05	86.74	68.10

To demonstrate the effectiveness of our approach, an ablation study is performed by stepwise removing the proposed strategies. And the experiments are conducted on three datasets to show the universality (Table 3).

The test firstly removes the keywords from the RCV1-V2 as it lacks the label names. The result shows an obvious drop in both Macro-F1 and Micro-F1, proving that keywords can be a supplement for the label semantics and contribute to the classification. Then we remove the label names for three datasets (RCV1-V2 uses the designed mark as its name), in this way all semantics are removed, and the indexes drop again. Further, we removed the co-occurrences and another drop appeared accordingly. All the above phenomenons demonstrate that enhancing label embeddings by the information obtained from dataset can further improve the HTC task.

Besides, we replace Graphormer to a simpler graph net GAT [18]. It is noticed that both Micro-F1 and Macro-F1 for NYT and WOS appear obvious reduction, while that for the RCV1-V2 shake a bit. The results shows that improving the graph net can be beneficial to HTC as well.

6   Conclusion

In this paper, we propose to enhance label representations from the perspective of contextual interactions and semantic complements, which refers to label co-occurrences and keywords respectively. Especially, the co-occurrence matrix is computed based on the proportion of label pairs and used as a subgraph of hierarchy; the keywords are extracted using the unsupervised algorithm TF-IDF and treated as a complement of label semantics. To fuse the information with different structural properties, we propose the LGraphormer and achieve more informative label embeddings. The final prediction is finished by feeding the embeddings into BERT in a layer-aware manner. Compared to other approaches, our method achieves the state-of-arts on all three popular public datasets, demonstrating the improvement of the proposed method.

Acknowledgements. We thank all the anonymous reviewers for their valuable suggestions.

References

1. Chen, H., Ma, Q., Lin, Z., Yan, J.: Hierarchy-aware label semantics matching network for hierarchical text classification. In: The 59th Annual Meeting of the Association for Computational Linguistics (ACL 2021) (2021)
2. Deng, Z., Peng, H., He, D., Li, J., Yu, P.S.: HTCInfoMax: a global model for hierarchical text classification via information maximization (2021)
3. Devlin, J., Chang, M.W., Lee, K., Toutanova, K.: BERT: pre-training of deep bidirectional transformers for language understanding (2018)
4. Jiang, T., Wang, D., Sun, L., Chen, Z., Zhuang, F., Yang, Q.: Exploiting global and local hierarchies for hierarchical text classification (2022)
5. Kazuya, S., Jiyi, L., Fumiyo, F.: HFT-CNN: learning hierarchical category structure for multi-label short text categorization. In: In Proceedings of the 2018 Conference on Empirical Methods in Natural Language Processing (2018)
6. Kowsari, K., Brown, D.E., Heidarysafa, M., Meimandi, K.J., Barnes, L.E.: HDL-Tex: hierarchical deep learning for text classification. IEEE (2017)
7. Kowsari, K., Brown, D.E., Heidarysafa, M., Meimandi, K.J., Gerber, M.S., Barnes, L.E.: Web of science (hierarchical text classification) (2017)
8. Lewis, D.D., Yang, Y., Rose, T.G., Fan, L.: RCV1: a new benchmark collection for text categorization research. J. Mach. Learn. Res. **5**(2), 361–397 (2004)
9. Liu, X., Wang, S., Zhang, X., You, X., Wu, J., Dou, D.: Label-guided learning for text classification (2020)
10. Mao, Y., Tian, J., Han, J., Ren, X.: Hierarchical text classification with reinforced label assignment (2019)
11. Peng, H., et al.: Hierarchical taxonomy-aware and attentional graph capsule rcnns for large-scale multi-label text classification. Institute of Electrical and Electronics Engineers (IEEE), no. 6 (2021)

12. Pengfei, G., Dedi, L., Lijiao, Z., Yue, L., Yinglong, M.: A three-phase augmented classifiers chain approach based on co-occurrence analysis for multi-label classification (2022)
13. Pham, T., Nguyen, V., Tran, V., Nguyen, T., Ha, Q.: A semi-supervised multi-label classification framework with feature reduction and enrichment*. J. Inf. Telecommun. 1(2), 141–154 (2017)
14. Sandhaus, P.: The New York times annotated corpus overview (2008)
15. Siddhartha, B., Cem, A., Francisco, P., Kostas, T.: Hierarchical transfer learning for multi-label text classification. In: In Proceedings of the 57th Conference of the Association for Computational Linguistics, pp. 6295–6300. Association for Computational Linguistics, Florence (2019)
16. Vaswani, A., et al.: Attention is all you need. arXiv (2017)
17. Wang, Z., Wang, P., Huang, L., Sun, X., Wang, H.: Incorporating hierarchy into text encoder: a contrastive learning approach for hierarchical text classification (2022)
18. Wang, Z., Wang, P., Liu, T., Cao, Y., Sui, Z., Wang, H.: HPT: hierarchy-aware prompt tuning for hierarchical text classification. arXiv e-prints (2022)
19. Wu, J., Xiong, W., Wang, W.Y.: Learning to learn and predict: a meta-learning approach for multi-label classification. In: Proceedings of the 2019 Conference on Empirical Methods in Natural Language Processing and the 9th International Joint Conference on Natural Language Processing (EMNLP-IJCNLP) (2019)
20. Yang, G.Y.: Recursive regularization for large-scale classification with hierarchical and graphical dependencies. In: SIGKDD Explorations Null (CDaROM) (2013)
21. Ying, C., Cai, T., Luo, S., Zheng, S., Liu, T.Y.: Do transformers really perform bad for graph representation? (2021)
22. Zhang, X., Zhang, Q.W., Yan, Z., Liu, R., Cao, Y.: Enhancing label correlation feedback in multi-label text classification via multi-task learning (2021)
23. Zhou, J., Ma, C., Long, D., Xu, G., Liu, G.: Hierarchy-aware global model for hierarchical text classification. In: Association for Computational Linguistics (2020)

Text Semantic Matching Research Based on Parallel Dropout

Zhuangzhuang Li[1,2], Zengzhen Shao[2(✉)], Jianxin Xiao[1,2], Zixiao Yu[1,2], and Xu Zhang[1,2]

[1] School of Information Science and Engineering, Shandong Normal University, Jinan 250014, China
[2] School of Data Science and Computer Science, Shandong Women's University, Jinan 250002, China
shaozengzhen@163.com

Abstract. Text semantic matching is a fundamental task in natural language understanding, and has a wide range of applications in information retrieval, question and answer systems, reading comprehension, and machine translation. Currently, a better way to do text semantic matching tasks is to extract word vectors or sentence vectors with BERT and then fine-tuning them, but the commonly used fine-tuning methods suffer from the overfitting problem. We propose a bi-directional long short-term memory-parallel dropout model (BiLSTM-PD), which combines word vectors and sentence vectors to improve feature vectors quality and uses parallel dropout to reduce overfitting. First, word vectors and sentence vectors are generated using the pre-trained model, BiLSTM converts the word vectors into sentence vectors, and the sentence vectors generated by BiLSTM are combined with the sentence vectors generated by the pre-trained model to form the final sentence vectors representation; then, four dropout functions are used to randomly discard a portion of the neurons of the sentence vectors to obtain four subsets, and then a linear layer is used to transform the four subsets of dimensionality and calculate the average value, and then use the Softmax and Argmax functions to calculate the predicted value of each batch to know whether the two sentences are similar. Experiments on two text semantic matching datasets and detailed analyses demonstrate the effectiveness of our model.

Keywords: Text semantic matching · BERT · BiLSTM · Parallel dropout

1 Introduction

Text semantic matching refers to comparing the semantic similarity between two pieces of text to determine whether they have the same meaning or express similar meanings. In recent years, significant progress has been made in the application of pre-trained models for the semantic matching of text pre-trained models can learn linguistic representations by training on large-scale data to provide higher-quality semantic features for downstream tasks. Among them,

L. Iliadis et al. (Eds.): ICANN 2023, LNCS 14258, pp. 548–559, 2023.
https://doi.org/10.1007/978-3-031-44192-9_44

feature-based matching [21] and interaction-based matching [18] are the two main applications of pre-trained models for text semantic matching.

The feature-based matching method refers to encoding two sentences separately to obtain their sentence vectors representations and then processing these sentence vectors by simple fusion to obtain the final matching result. The feature-based matching approach can effectively avoid the problem of information overload and has good computational efficiency at the same time. However, the independent encoding of two sentences in a sentence pair may lead to the neglect of the interaction information between sentences, which affects the matching accuracy. We usually use interactive matching methods to better use the interaction information between sentences. The interactive matching method refers to splicing two texts together as a single text for classification. This method can obtain richer semantic information and thus improve the matching accuracy. For example, in question-answer systems, the correlation between the question and the text can be better captured by stitching the question and the text together.

In this study, we propose the BiLSTM-PD model. The model combines word vectors and sentence vectors to improve the quality of feature vectors, uses parallel dropout to reduce overfitting, and uses interactive matching methods to obtain richer semantic information. Experiments on two semantic matching datasets show that the present model achieves excellent performance. The contribution of this paper includes three parts:

1. Combining word vectors and sentence vectors to ensure a higher quality representation of feature vectors.
2. Parallel dropout is proposed to reduce overfitting by parallel operations.
3. The results show that the BiLSTM-PD model can improve the performance of semantic matching and can also be easily integrated into other interaction-based text semantic matching models to improve accuracy.

2   Related Work

2.1   Text Semantic Matching

Text semantic matching aims to determine the semantic relationship between two text sequences. In earlier work, researchers mainly used keyword-based matching methods such as TF-IDF [12] and BM25 [11]. These methods rely on manually defined features and often fail to assess the semantic relevance of the text. With the development of deep learning techniques, researchers have started to propose various neural models to solve the text semantic matching problem. These models use deep learning techniques such as recurrent neural networks (RNN) [9] and convolutional neural networks (CNN) [10] to encode text sequences and then compare the encoded text sequences to determine the similarity between them. Their recurrent neural networks are mainly used for sequence modeling and can handle variable-length input sequences adaptively. They are widely used in the field of text semantic matching. There are also some improved models based on RNNs, such as Siamese [17], which classifies two text sequences by encoding them separately through the same RNN and then stitching them together for the task of text semantic matching. With the emergence of pre-trained models, the field of text semantic matching has also started to apply this technique. Pre-trained models can automatically learn rich semantic information by performing unsupervised learning on a large-scale text corpus to improve the performance of text semantic matching. BERT [5] is a representative model among them, which achieves extremely high performance by learning bidirectional contextual representations through a joint training task. Subsequent researchers have also proposed various improved models based on BERT, such as RoBERTa [15] and ALBERT [13].

2.2 Dropout

Dropout is a regularization technique commonly used in deep learning to reduce the complexity of the network by dropping some random neurons during training, thus reducing the risk of overfitting. Dropout was first proposed by Hinton et al. [8], one of the reasons for model overfitting is that the relationship between neurons is too complex, and dropout can prevent the relationship between neurons from being too complex by randomly dropping some neurons. Dropout is implemented in a simple way, i.e., some neurons are randomly dropped with a certain probability p in each training so that they are not involved in forward and backward propagation. This allows the network to be more robust during training and improves generalization. In addition to the original dropout technique, there are some improved methods. For example, DropConnect [19], which replaces random dropout with random disconnections, can increase the capacity of the network while reducing overfitting, and DropBlock [6], which replaces random dropout with random block dropout, can further reduce the risk of overfitting. However, these methods generally use only one dropout, while the parallel dropout we use works better by using multiple dropouts to randomly discard a portion of the neurons in the sentence vectors.

3   Method

Text semantic matching can be viewed as a classification task to find labels $y \in Y = \{similar, dissimilar\}$ for a given sentence pair (S_a, S_b). Figure 1 shows our model BiLSTM-PD for this task, and the model structure includes an input layer, a feature extraction layer, a dropout layer, and an output layer. In the following, we describe the components of the model.

3.1   Input Layer

Given two text sequences $S_a = \{w_1^a, ..., w_l^a\}$ and $S_b = \{w_1^b, ..., w_l^b\}$, we need to add an [cls] at the beginning of the sentence and [sep] in the middle and at the end of the two sentences, $S_{a,b} = [[cls] \, S_a \, [sep] \, S_b \, [sep]]$. Here, w_i^a and w_j^b represent the i-th and j-th word in the sequences; [cls] denotes the beginning

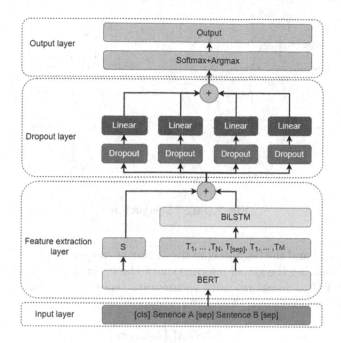

Fig. 1. General framework of the model

of the sequence and is used for the classification task; [*sep*] is used to separate two sentences or paragraphs in the input sequence so that BERT can distinguish them. We use $S_{a,b}$ as the input of BERT.

3.2 Feature Extraction Layer

The feature extraction layer consists of two parts, BERT and BiLSTM. The main work of this layer is that BERT generates word vectors and sentence vectors, BiLSTM converts the word vectors into sentence vectors, and the sentence vectors generated by BiLSTM are combined with the sentence vectors generated by the pre-trained model to form the final sentence vectors representation the structure of BiLSTM is shown in Fig. 2.

BERT: BERT is a pre-trained natural language processing model with a Transformer-based neural network at its core, whose goal is to map text data into vector representations by learning large amounts of unlabeled text data. We input $S_{a,b}$ to the BERT layer to obtain a vector representation S of the entire sentence pair and a vector representation x_t of each word, $x_t = [T_1, ..., T_N; T_1, ..., T_M]$, and we use x_t as input to the BiLSTM.

BiLSTM: The BiLSTM [7] consists of a combination of a forward LSTM [23] and a backward LSTM, using the forward LSTM and the backward LSTM to

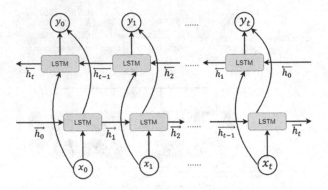

Fig. 2. BiLSTM structure

traverse the end and the beginning of the sequence, respectively, with the aim of efficiently capturing the global information of the input sequence. In this paper, we use BiLSTM to transform word vectors into sentence vectors. The BILSTM is calculated as follows:

$$\overrightarrow{h_t} = LSTM\left(\overrightarrow{h_{t-1}}, x_t\right) \tag{1}$$

$$\overleftarrow{h_t} = LSTM\left(\overleftarrow{h_{t-1}}, x_t\right) \tag{2}$$

$$H = \left[\overrightarrow{h_t}, \overleftarrow{h_t}\right] \tag{3}$$

where x_t is the input data at moment t, $\overrightarrow{h_t}$ and $\overrightarrow{h_t}$ is the output of the forward LSTM hidden layer and the output of the reverse LSTM hidden layer, respectively, and H is the output after the two are connected. The sentence vectors H is obtained by BILSTM processing, and the sentence vectors H is combined with the sentence vectors S generated by BERT to obtain the sentence vectors C, $C = [S, H]$.

3.3 Dropout Layer

The dropout layer consists of four dropout functions and four linear layers. Since the four dropout functions randomly discard a part of the neurons of the sentence vectors, the sentence vectors produce four subsets after the dropout layer. The dropout layer is computed as follows:

$$v_i = d_i\left(C\right), i \in [1, 2, 3, 4] \tag{4}$$

$$u_i = l_i\left(v_i\right), i \in [1, 2, 3, 4] \tag{5}$$

$$z = mean\left(u_1, u_2, u_3, u_4\right) \tag{6}$$

C represents the sentence vectors, d_i represents the four dropout functions; v_i represents the four subsets of the sentence vectors; l_i represents the four linear layers; u_i represents the four probability vectors mapped to the predicted label space. u_i is averaged to obtain z, and the probability vectors z goes to the output layer for the next processing step.

3.4   Output Layer

The output layer consists of a Softmax function and an Argmax function.

$$f = argmax\,(softmax\,(z))\tag{7}$$

Softmax is the function that generates the vectors of probability distribution and Argmax is the function that determines the location of the maximum value. Z obtains the probability distribution vectors by Softmax function, and then obtains the predicted label vectors f for each Batch by Argmax function, with the value of f being 0 or 1. The accuracy of this Batch is obtained by comparing the predicted labels with the true labels.

Table 1. Datasets Statistics.

Datasets	Type	Train	Dev	Test
BQ	Positive	50.0k	5.0k	5.0k
	Negative	50.0k	5.0k	5.0k
LCQMC	Positive	138.5k	4,4k	6.2k
	Negative	100.1k	4,4k	6.2k

Table 2. Parameter Setting.

Hyperparameter	Value
Batch size	32
Epoch number	10
Optimizer	ADAMW
Learning rate	2e-05
Lr decay rate	0.01
Max char len	50
BiLSTM output size	384
Word embedding size	768

4   Experimental Setup

4.1   Datasets

The model was evaluated on two semantic matching datasets, including BQ [1], and LCQMC [14]. BQ is a question matching dataset for the banking and finance domain with data from question pairs in the customer service logs of online banking, while LCQMC is a large-scale open-domain Chinese question matching dataset constructed from Baidu Know. All datasets are divided into training, validation, and test data. Datasets statistics of BQ and LCQMC are shown in Table 1.

4.2   Parameter Setting

The parameters are set as shown in Table 2. The batch size of the dataset is fixed at 32. The initial learning rate is 2e-05, which decreases at a rate of 0.01 during the training period. Also, we adjust the output dimension of the BiLSTM hidden layer to 384. Finally, we use the ADAMW optimizer to modify all trainable parameters.

4.3   Evaluation Metrics

To evaluate the effectiveness of the model, the evaluation metrics for text semantic matching include accuracy (ACC) rate and F1 score (F1).

4.4   Contrast Model

We compare our model with recent work, including state-of-the-art neural network models and BERT-based approaches. DIIN [16] extracts relevant information from input sequences by a self-attention mechanism in the absence of RNNs or CNNs. ESIM [2] extracts information from text sequences using a bidirectional LSTM and models the relationship between sequences by a self-focusing mechanism. BiMPM [20] uses multi-angle matching and fusion. RE2 [22] employs richer features for the alignment process to improve performance. For the pre-trained approach, we consider BERT, RoBERTa, PERT [4], and MacBERT [3].

5   Experimental Results

5.1   Comparison Results and Discussion

Table 3 shows the results of the BQ dataset. All baselines are divided into two groups, the first group is four neural network-based methods and the second group is four pre-trained model-based methods. The pre-trained model-based methods show superior performance compared to the traditional neural matching models. For example, BERT outperformed ESIM by 1.95% and 0.95% in terms of accuracy and F1, respectively. MacBERT outperformed RE2 by 4.47% and 3.53% in terms of accuracy and F1, respectively. And the BiLSTM-PD model using MacBERT as the base model outperformed all eight models. For example, BiLSTM-PD is 1.82% and 2.30% higher than RoBERTa in terms of accuracy and F1, respectively. The possible reasons are that our model uses BiLSTM, which can better integrate the contextual information of the input sequences,

Table 3. Experimental results of accuracy on the BQ datasets.

Model	Acc(%)	F1(%)
DIIN [16]	82.45	83.19
ESIM [2]	81.74	82.25
BiMPM [20]	80.47	81.82
RE2 [22]	80.23	80.74
BERT [5]	83.69	83.20
RoBERTa [15]	83.48	83.00
PERT [4]	84.08	83.63
MacBERT [3]	84.70	84.27
BiLSTM-PD(MacBERT)	**85.30**	**85.30**

combining word vectors and sentence vectors can extract richer semantic features.

Table 4 shows the results of the LCQMC dataset. The method based on pre-trained models showed superior performance compared to the traditional neural matching models. For example, RoBERTa outperforms DIIN in terms of accuracy and F1 by 1.83% and 0.60%, respectively. PERT outperforms BiMPM in terms of accuracy and F1 by 2.71% and 1.35%, respectively. And the BiLSTM-PD model using MacBERT as the base model outperformed all eight models. For example, BiLSTM-PD outperforms MacBERT in terms of accuracy and F1 by 0.63% and 0.68%, respectively. Overall, our models achieved the best results on the LCQMC dataset.

Table 4. Experimental results of accuracy on the LCQMC dataset.

Model	Acc(%)	F1(%)
DIIN [16]	83.57	84.23
ESIM [2]	84.34	85.48
BiMPM [20]	83.72	84.63
RE2 [22]	84.23	84.97
BERT [5]	86.23	85.72
RoBERTa [15]	85.40	84.83
PERT [4]	86.43	85.98
MacBERT [3]	86.69	86.22
BiLSTM-PD(MacBERT)	**87.32**	**86.90**

To explore the effectiveness of our models, we combined BiLSTM-PD with the four pre-trained models to compare the results with the original pre-trained models and calculated the improvement in accuracy and F1, with bolded numbers indicating significant changes. As can be seen in Table 5 and Table 6, the accuracy and F1 of all pretrained models steadily improved on both datasets, and the improvement was particularly significant on the two pretrained models, RoBERTa and MacBERT. The results show that converting word vectors into sentence vectors by BiLSTM and combining the sentence vectors generated by BiLSTM with those generated by BERT and using four dropout functions to randomly discard a portion of the neurons of the sentence vectors can effectively improve the model and can be well integrated with the pre-trained model.

Table 5. Experimental results of accuracy on the BQ and LCQMC datasets.

Model	BQ	LCQMC
	Ori.→BiLSTM-PD(change)	Ori.→BiLSTM-PD(change)
BERT	83.69 →84.14 (**0.45**)	86.23 →86.25 (0.02)
RoBERTa	83.48 →83.96 (**0.48**)	85.40 →86.87 (**1.47**)
PERT	84.08 →84.11 (0.03)	86.43 →86.46 (0.03)
MacBERT	84.70 →85.30 (**0.60**)	86.69 →87.32 (**0.63**)

Table 6. Experimental results of F1 on the BQ and LCQMC datasets.

Model	BQ	LCQMC
	Ori.→BiLSTM-PD(change)	Ori.→BiLSTM-PD(change)
BERT	83.20 →83.41 (0.21)	85.72 →86.01 (0.29)
RoBERTa	83.00 →83.56 (**0.56**)	84.83 →85.52 (**0.69**)
PERT	83.63 →83.87 (0.24)	85.98 →86.24 (0.26)
MacBERT	84.27 →85.30 (**1.03**)	86.22 →86.90 (**0.68**)

5.2 Ablation Experiments

The main modules of the BiLSTM-PD model are the BiLSTM and the dropout layer, and the dropout layer has two important parameters, so we designed two ablation experiments.

Number of Dropout Samples: We choose 6 quantities of 0, 1, 2, 4, 8, and 16 respectively. We can see from Fig. 3 that the error rate tends to decrease and then increase as the number of dropout samples increases, which indicates that too many or too few dropout samples will make the model less effective. When the number of dropout samples is 4, the error rate of both data sets is the lowest, so it is better to choose 4 as the number of dropout samples in the experiment.

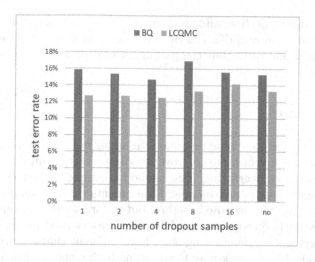

Fig. 3. Error rate of different dropout sample numbers

Dropout Ratio: We choose five probabilities, 10%, 30%, 50%, 70%, and 90%. Here we show how the multiple samples loss of BQ and LCQMC datasets works with different loss rates:{10%, 10%, 10%, 10%}, {10%, 10%, 30%, 30% }, {30%, 30%, 30%, 30%}, {10%, 30%, 50%, 70%}, {10%, 30%, 70%, 90% }, {30%, 50%, 70%, 90% }, {70%, 70%, 70%, 70% }, {70%, 70%, 90%, 90% }, {90%, 90%, 90%, 90% }, with mean values of 10%, 20%, 30%, 40%, 50%, 60%, 70%, 80%, and 90%, respectively. Figure 4 shows the test set error rates for different dropout ratios. Regardless of the dropout ratio setting, parallel dropout outperforms no dropout. Dropout ratio from 10% to 90%, the Test error rate shows a wave-like

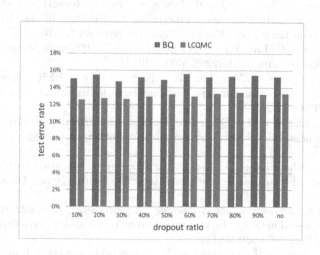

Fig. 4. Error rate of different dropout ratio

growth followed by a decline, and the test set error rate reached its lowest at an average dropout ratio of 30%. The overall change in the test error rate is not significant, which indicates that the parameter of dropout ratio has little effect on the model.

6   Conclusion

In this study, we propose a text semantic matching model that combine word vectors and sentence vectors to improve feature vectors quality and uses parallel dropout to reduce overfitting. The method is simple and effective, and easy to combines with pre-trained models. Experiments on two semantic matching datasets show that the proposed method outperforms the previously proposed model. However, the pre-trained models and datasets used in our work are all in Chinese, and since different languages have different characteristics and processing methods, future work may focus on modifying the models appropriately according to language characteristics to apply to other language datasets.

References

1. Chen, J., Chen, Q., Liu, X., Yang, H., Lu, D., Tang, B.: The BQ corpus: a large-scale domain-specific Chinese corpus for sentence semantic equivalence identification. In: Proceedings of the 2018 Conference on Empirical Methods in Natural Language Processing, pp. 4946–4951 (2018)
2. Chen, Q., Zhu, X., Ling, Z.H., Wei, S., Jiang, H., Inkpen, D.: Enhanced LSTM for natural language inference. In: Proceedings of the 55th Annual Meeting of the Association for Computational Linguistics (Volume 1: Long Papers), pp. 1657–1668 (2017)
3. Cui, Y., Che, W., Liu, T., Qin, B., Wang, S., Hu, G.: Revisiting pre-trained models for Chinese natural language processing. In: Findings of the Association for Computational Linguistics: EMNLP 2020, pp. 657–668 (2020)
4. Cui, Y., Yang, Z., Liu, T.: PERT: pre-training BERT with permuted language model, arXiv preprint arXiv:2203.06906 (2022)
5. Devlin, J., Chang, M.W., Lee, K., Toutanova, K.: BERT: pre-training of deep bidirectional transformers for language understanding, arXiv preprint arXiv:1810.04805 (2018)
6. Ghiasi, G., Lin, T.Y., Le, Q.V.: Dropblock: a regularization method for convolutional networks. In: Advances in Neural Information Processing Systems, vol. 31 (2018)
7. Graves, A., Schmidhuber, J.: Framewise phoneme classification with bidirectional LSTM and other neural network architectures. Neural Netw. **18**(5–6), 602–610 (2005)
8. Hinton, G.E., Srivastava, N., Krizhevsky, A., Sutskever, I., Salakhutdinov, R.R.: Improving neural networks by preventing co-adaptation of feature detectors, arXiv preprint arXiv:1207.0580 (2012)
9. Hou, B.J., Zhou, Z.H.: Learning with interpretable structure from gated RNN. IEEE Trans. Neural Netw. Learn. Syst. **31**(7), 2267–2279 (2020)

10. Huang, P.S., He, X., Gao, J., Deng, L., Acero, A., Heck, L.: Learning deep structured semantic models for web search using clickthrough data. In: Proceedings of the 22nd ACM International Conference on Information & Knowledge Management, pp. 2333–2338 (2013)
11. Kadhim, A.I.: Term weighting for feature extraction on Twitter: a comparison between BM25 and TF-IDF. In: 2019 International Conference on Advanced Science and Engineering (ICOASE), pp. 124–128. IEEE (2019)
12. Kim, D., Seo, D., Cho, S., Kang, P.: Multi-co-training for document classification using various document representations: TF-IDF, LDA, and Doc2Vec. Inf. Sci. **477**, 15–29 (2019)
13. Lan, Z., Chen, M., Goodman, S., Gimpel, K., Sharma, P., Soricut, R.: Albert: a lite BERT for self-supervised learning of language representations. In: International Conference on Learning Representations (2019)
14. Liu, X., et al.: LCQMC: a large-scale Chinese question matching corpus. In: Proceedings of the 27th International Conference on Computational Linguistics, pp. 1952–1962 (2018)
15. Liu, Y., et al.: RoBERTa: a robustly optimized BERT pretraining approach, arXiv preprint arXiv:1907.11692 (2019)
16. Mirakyan, M., Hambardzumyan, K., Khachatrian, H.: Natural language inference over interaction space: ICLR 2018 reproducibility report. arXiv preprint arXiv:1802.03198 (2018)
17. Mueller, J., Thyagarajan, A.: Siamese recurrent architectures for learning sentence similarity. In: Proceedings of the AAAI Conference on Artificial Intelligence, vol. 30 (2016)
18. Rao, J., Liu, L., Tay, Y., Yang, W., Shi, P., Lin, J.: Bridging the gap between relevance matching and semantic matching for short text similarity modeling. In: Proceedings of the 2019 Conference on Empirical Methods in Natural Language Processing and the 9th International Joint Conference on Natural Language Processing (EMNLP-IJCNLP), pp. 5370–5381 (2019)
19. Wan, L., Zeiler, M., Zhang, S., Le Cun, Y., Fergus, R.: Regularization of neural networks using DropConnect. In: International Conference on Machine Learning, pp. 1058–1066. PMLR (2013)
20. Wang, Z., Hamza, W., Florian, R.: Bilateral multi-perspective matching for natural language sentences. In: Proceedings of the 26th International Joint Conference on Artificial Intelligence, pp. 4144–4150 (2017)
21. Wu, Z., et al.: An efficient Wikipedia semantic matching approach to text document classification. Inf. Sci. **393**, 15–28 (2017)
22. Yang, R., Zhang, J., Gao, X., Ji, F., Chen, H.: Simple and effective text matching with richer alignment features. In: Proceedings of the 57th Annual Meeting of the Association for Computational Linguistics, pp. 4699–4709 (2019)
23. Yu, Y., Si, X., Hu, C., Zhang, J.: A review of recurrent neural networks: LSTM cells and network architectures. Neural Comput. **31**(7), 1235–1270 (2019)

Towards Better Core Elements Extraction for Customer Service Dialogue Text

Shengjie Ji[1,2], Chun Chen[1,2], and Fang Kong[1,2(✉)]

[1] Laboratory for Natural Language Processing, Soochow University, Suzhou, China
{20215227043,20195227037}@stu.suda.edu.cn, kongfang@suda.edu.cn
[2] School of Computer Science and Technology, Soochow University, Suzhou, China

Abstract. Customer service conversations are usually short, but contain rich information, such as product details, customer demands and some emotions. Therefore, it is crucial to extract the core elements to fully understand the dialogue. Different from written texts, in the dialogue text, it can be challenging to differentiate between target elements and others, and the proportion of core elements is relatively low. In this paper, we propose a boundary enhanced span classification model with negative sampling strategy to address this issue. On the one hand, the enhancement of boundary representation improves the model's ability to identify core element boundaries. On the other hand, the negative sampling strategy improves the model's ability to recognize negative cases in different dialogue scenarios. Experimental results on the Jingdong customer service corpus demonstrate the effectiveness of our approach.

Keywords: Core Element Extraction · Span Classification · Dialogue Text · Negative Sampling

1 Introduction

Information Extraction (IE) aims to identify predefined information with special meanings, such as entities, events or relations. It plays an significant role in understanding natural language texts. Depending on the characteristics of content and the particularity of task, Information Extraction may have specific definitions. In this paper, we are committed to extracting the core elements on dialogue text.

Our work is centered on the Jingdong dataset, which comprises multiple rounds of dialogue in Jingdong customer service. This kind of dialogue texts tends to be colloquial, short and with concise semantics. Due to the background of e-commerce, these texts are also riddled with noise, such as URL links and memes. These features not only add a burden to label and organize the dataset, but also make it difficult for the model to identify the boundaries of core elements.

Considering the application of element extraction to downstream tasks, we define three core elements on the dialogue text: Object (OBJ), Action (ACT)

© The Author(s), under exclusive license to Springer Nature Switzerland AG 2023
L. Iliadis et al. (Eds.): ICANN 2023, LNCS 14258, pp. 560–571, 2023.
https://doi.org/10.1007/978-3-031-44192-9_45

and Modifiability (MOD), which are highly associated with the semantics of the dialogue text. This kind of core elements is different from traditional named entities, which usually have a unique definition, such as words with PER (person) or LOC (location) tags labeled as the same tag in any sentence. However, the core elements defined in Jingdong dataset may have disparate representations in different sentences. For example, the OBJ in the first sentence shares the same word with the ACT in the second sentence in Fig. 1. This illustrates that a single word can possess diverse meanings in distinct contexts, ultimately resulting in different tags.

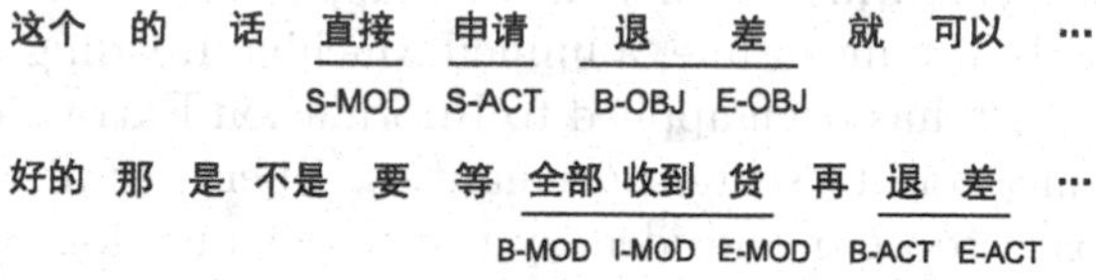

这个 的 话 直接 申请 退 差 就 可以 …
　　　　　S-MOD S-ACT B-OBJ E-OBJ

好的 那 是 不是 要 等 全部 收到 货 再 退 差 …
　　　　　　　　　　　B-MOD I-MOD E-MOD B-ACT E-ACT

Fig. 1. Example of the core elements defined in dialogue.

In general, there are two challenges in extracting the core elements of the Jingdong dataset: (1) The colloquial dialogue text has simple semantics, and the annotation of the dataset is difficult, which puts forward higher requirements for the model. (2) Unlike traditional named entities, the three core elements defined on Jingdong dataset are strongly correlated with the semantics of the dialogue texts and cannot be clearly distinguished.

To address the challenges mentioned above, we propose a boundary enhanced span classification with negative sampling strategy. For the first challenge, a boundary enhanced encoder can be employed to extract the structural feature inside the dialogue sentence, which is composed by a Star-Transformer layer and a GAT layer. Meanwhile, we add an auxiliary task to predict the head and tail the core elements, which is benefit to learning the boundary information explicitly. To tackle with the second challenge, we use the span classification instead of traditional sequence labeling, which can cooperate with semantic information to identify three elements. A negative sampling will also be applied in our work to distinguish between the target elements and other words in the sentence, which can also ensure relatively competitive performance when the dataset is limit in scale. Comparative experiments on the JD dataset can prove the reliability of our method.

2 Related Work

Similar with Named Entity Recognition, our work is devoted to identifying the predefined elements in dialogue text, in which there exists an intrinsic semantic connection among the three core elements.

A common approach to Named Entity Recognition is sequence labeling model based on a bidirectional LSTM [1,7–9,15] which is also widely used in Relation Extraction and Event Extraction [14,20]. In recent years, with the development of named entities, methods based on span classification have gradually been applied in this area. Fu et al. [5] compare the performance of sequence labeling to span classification under Named Entity Recognition task. They found that SEQLAB-based models are better at dealing with those entities that are long and with low label consistency, while SPANNER systems do better in sentences with more Out-of-Vocabulary (OOV) words and entities with medium length. Tan et al. [17] employ the span classification on Nested Entity Recognition. Li et al. [10] propose a span-based model for joint overlapped and discontinuous named entity recognition. In the meantime, a unified Machine Reading Comprehension (MRC) framework [12] has been applied to Information Extraction tasks, which can match label meaning to sentence semantics. Eberts et al. [4] also use the span-based approach to filter and identify the target mention, which is feed to the relation classification layer.

Considering the application of Information Extraction model in real life, Peng et al. [16] focus on Chinese medical insurance industry, and Zeng et al. [20] work on the dialogue text in criminal law.

In this paper, we utilize a span-based framework associated with negative sampling strategy to better identify the predefined core elements. In addition, we propose a boundary enhancement module to accommodate special conversational texts in Jingdong dataset.

3   Model

Figure 2 shows the general architecture of our boundary enhanced span classification model, which is composed of three parts: token embedding layer, boundary enhanced encoder and the softmax decoder of span classification.

3.1   Token Embedding Layer

From the perspective of Chinese dialogue text, we integrate word embedding with char embedding to obtain contextual representation. For a given sentence, we represent each character by looking up the pre-trained word embeddings[1] [11]. Then, the sequence of character embeddings contained in a word will be feed into a bi-direction GRU layer [3].

Considering that there are a large number of neologisms and exclusive terms in the dialogue, we employ Jieba[2] for word segmentation and then leverage BERT [2] to obtain word embeddings.Additionally, we also incorporate the powerful Part-of-Speech tagging capabilities of StanfordCoreNLP[3] to enhance token

---

[1] https://github.com/Embedding/Chinese-Word-Vectors.
[2] https://github.com/fxsjy/jieba.
[3] https://stanfordnlp.github.io/CoreNLP.

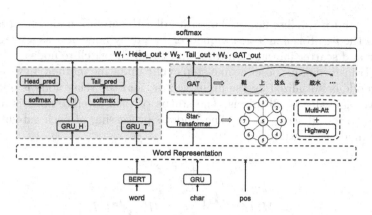

Fig. 2. The general architecture of our boundary enhanced model under span classification with negative sampling.

representation. The final token representation is obtained as Eq. 1–3:

$$x_i^w = BERT(word_i) \tag{1}$$

$$x_i^c = GRU(e(char_i)) \tag{2}$$

$$x_i = [x_i^w; x_i^c; pos_i] \tag{3}$$

where [;] denotes concatenation, and pos_i is the Part-of-Speech tagging of $word_i$.

3.2   Boundary Enhanced Encoder

As shown in Fig. 2, the encoder mainly consists of three parts, i.e., GRU-based head and tail representation layer, Star-transformer based contextual embedding layer, and GAT-based dependency embedding layer.

Star-Transformer. Transformer [18] employs h attention heads to implement self-attention on an input sequence separately. Given a sequence of vectors X, we use a query vector Q to soft select the relevant information with attention:

$$Att(Q, K, V) = softmax(\frac{QK^T}{\sqrt{d_k}})) \cdot V \tag{4}$$

$$K = XW^K, V = XW^V \tag{5}$$

$$MulAtt = (z_1 \oplus z_2 \oplus \cdots \oplus z_h) \cdot W^o \tag{6}$$

$$z_i = Att(QW_i^Q, KW_i^K, VW_i^V) \tag{7}$$

where $\oplus$ denotes concatenation, and W^* are learnable parameters.

Compared with the traditional Transformer, Star-Transformer [6] abandons redundant connections and has an approximate ability to model the long-range dependencies. The topological structure of Star-Transformer is made up of one relay node and n satellite nodes. The state of i-th satellite node represents the feature of the i-th token in a text sequence. The relay node acts as a virtual hub to gather and scatter information from and to all the satellite nodes.

Star-Transformer proposes a time-step cyclic updating method, in which each satellite node is initialized by the input vector, and the relay node is initialized as the average value of all tokens. The status of each satellite node is updated according to its adjacent nodes. The update processing of each satellite node and relay node is shown in Eq. 8–10:

$$C_i^t = [h_{i-1}^{t-1}; h_i^{t-1}; h_{i+1}^{t-1}; e^i; s^{t-1}] \tag{8}$$

$$h_i^t = MulAtt(h_i^{t-1}, C_i^t, C_i^t) \tag{9}$$

$$s^t = MulAtt(s^{t-1}, [s^{t-1}; H^t], [s^{t-1}; H^t]) \tag{10}$$

where C_i^t denotes contextual information of i-th.

GAT. In this work, we employ the dependencies between words to construct graph neural networks. Note that the dependency is directional, and the current word is only related to the word with shared edge. This kind of directed linkage further obtains the internal structural information of the entity, enriching the sequential representation.

The adjacency matrix depicted in Fig. 3 serves as a powerful visualization of the relationships between relevant words. Specifically, our adjacency matrix is composed of four sub-matrixes as following:

(1) a matrix from directional dependency relation. For example, $matrix_1[0][4] = 1$ means token 0 depends on token 4.
(2) a matrix to enhance self-information of each token in a sentence, only $matrix_2[i][i] = 1$.
(3) a matrix that represents the left-to-right orientation relationship in a sentence, only $matrix_3[i][i+1] = 1$.
(4) a matrix that represents the right-to-left orientation relationship in a sentence, only $matrix_4[j+1][j] = 1$.

where $matrix[i][j] = 1$ indicates the connection between node i and node j.

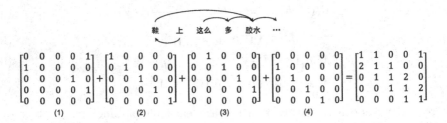

Fig. 3. Components of the adjacency matrix.

Subsequently, Graph Attention Networks (GAT) [19] which utilizes masked self-attention layers to assign different importance to neighbouring nodes, is an excellent fit for our work:

$$e_{ij} = att(W\vec{h}_i, W\vec{h}_j) \tag{11}$$

$$\alpha_{ij} = softmax_j(e_{ij}) \tag{12}$$

$$= \frac{exp(e_{ij})}{\sum_{k \in N_i} exp(e_{ik})} \tag{13}$$

$$= \frac{exp(LeakyReLU(\vec{a}^T[Wh_i \oplus Wh_j]))}{\sum_{k \in N_i} exp(LeakyReLU(\vec{a}^T[Wh_i \oplus Wh_k]))} \tag{14}$$

Moreover, a GAT operation with K independent attention heads can be expressed as:

$$\vec{h}'_i = \sigma(\frac{1}{K}\sum_{k=1}^{K}\sum_{j \in N_i} \alpha_{ij}^k W^k \vec{h}_j) \tag{15}$$

where the attention coefficients e_{ij} and α_{ij} represent the importance of node j to node $i. \oplus$ denotes concatenation. W and $\vec{a}$ are learnable parameters. N_i is the neighborhood of node i and σ is the activation function.

3.3 Head and Tail Representation

Additionally, two independent GRU [3] layers are utilized to perform head and tail predictions for entities, and their hidden features are combined with the output of the GAT layer:

$$H_h = GRU_{head}(x_i) \tag{16}$$

$$H_t = GRU_{tail}(x_i) \tag{17}$$

$$H = W_1 \cdot H_h + W_2 \cdot H_t + W_3 \cdot H_{GAT} \tag{18}$$

where W_1, W_2, W_3 are learnable parameters, and H is the final input for CRF.

Mention boundary recognition is not only the task we need to deal with, but also a perfect natural assistance with the elements extraction, which transform perspectives from the specific semantics of the mention to the general semantics. The final multi-task loss function is composed of the categorical cross-entroy loss for boundary detection and entity categorical label prediction:

$$L_{multi} = L_{head} + L_{tail} + L_{label} \tag{19}$$

3.4 Span Classification with Negative Sampling

Although the boundary enhanced encoder can extract semantic features from the dialogue text, the pre-defined core elements cannot be distinguished clearly, especially when training data is insufficient. To this end, we incorporate a negative sampling approach which enable us to identify the necessary elements based on various semantics and attain comparable results even in situations where training data is comparatively insufficient [13].

Span Classification. The three kinds of core elements we defined on the Jing-dong dataset are of variable lengths and indivisible from the surrounding spans, so methods based on sequence labeling cannot fully leverage their advantages in this scenario. For example, the MOD in the second sentence of Fig. 1 is a phrase consisting of verbs and nouns, which cannot be easily distinguished from other non-entity spans. To this end, our work is based on span classification which directly employ a softmax layer as the decoder. At the same time, the span-based framework can work with the boundary enhanced encoder well, whose goal is to recognize the difference between the target elements and the surrounding tokens.

Negative Sampling. For the reason that the three core elements defined in this paper are strongly correlated with the context, similar words may be labeled differently in different sentences. In other words, the same token may no longer express the same meaning of core elements in different dialogue scenarios. To this end, we introduce negative sampling strategy with the mention of smoothing this discrepancy. We collect negative spans in random and merge them with positive samples into a candidate set to participate in training, which can give our model the ability to distinguish between positive and negative samples in different scenarios.

Given the positive elements set P, we first obtain all the negative instance candidates, and then merge a collection of positive and negative samples, as formulas 20–22 show.

$$N = \{(i,j,O)|(i,j,l) \notin P, 1 \leq i \leq j \leq n, l \in L\}, \tag{20}$$

$$N_{number} = int(p * n) \tag{21}$$

$$All = P \cup N \tag{22}$$

where L is the label set. n is the length of the sentence, and p is the negative sampling rate.

4   Experiments

4.1   Dataset

We collect relevant dialogue text in Jingdong customer service, which is a typ-ical e-commerce field. It contains multi-type dialogue contents such as product detail consultation, coupon acquisition, order logistics inquiry, and return and exchange transactions. It is a typical non-written text, which has a large number of memes and URL links, and the colloquial characteristics are prominent. We have labeled each sentence with multiple tags such as intent, emotion, object, action, modifiaility, and sentence rewriting, which can be applied to a variety of natural language processing tasks.

This paper will be experimented with the core elements of the dialogue text on the Jingdong dataset. We pre-define three kind of core elements on the Jing-dong dialogue text: Object (OBJ), Action (ACT) and Modifiaility (MOD), which are highly associated with semantics of sentence. Object represents the subject expressed in a sentence. The Modifiaility indicates that the mention is used to decorate the subject object. Action is the core element that is semantically assigned to the subject object. Figure 1 depicts two examples of this annotation paradigm.

In total, we label 317129 conversation sentences with core elements tags, which are partitioned into three parts: training set, validation set and test set with proportions of 90%, 5%, and 5%, respectively. We further split the training set into five sub-training sets with different sizes in the ratio of 1:2:3:4:5 through random sampling strategy. Table 1 and Table 2 provide detailed statistics on the label distribution in the Jingdong dataset.

Table 1. Statistics of Jingdong datasets.

	train1	train2	train3	train4	train5	dev	test	all
sentence	57083	114166	171249	228324	285416	15856	15857	317129
word	375311	754081	1131474	1509314	1885251	105857	104954	2096062
labeled word	152386	304383	456739	609990	761232	43218	41810	846260
label rate	40.60%	40.36%	40.37%	40.42%	40.38%	40.83%	39.84%	40.37%

Table 2. Detailed statistics of Jingdong datasets.

	train1	train2	train3	train4	train5	dev	test	all
OBJ	9450	18568	27889	37241	46432	2569	2621	51622
ACT	49034	98184	147069	196103	245181	13667	13664	272512
MOD	35512	71152	107022	142934	178320	9991	9835	198146
ALL	93996	187904	281980	376278	469933	26227	26120	522280

4.2   Results and Analysis

To verify the effectiveness of our proposed model on dialogue texts, we conduct three sets of experiments on Jingdong dataset: sequence labeling with LSTM encoder, negative-sampled span classification with LSTM encoder, and negative-sampled span classification with boundary enhanced model. We use Accuracy (ACC), Precision (P), Recall (R) and F1 score (F1) as evaluation metrics.

Table 3 shows the results of our proposed boundary enhanced model under span classification on the Jingdong dataset, where the number of sentences from training set 1 to training set 5 is increased in turn. The best performance on training set 5 is 90.47% in Acc, and 87.30% in F1. Detailed performance of each element has been shown in Table 4. It's clear that the recognition of ACT is higher than OBJ, about 10.91%.

Table 3. Performance of boundary enhanced model under span classification with negative sampling method.

	Acc (%)	P (%)	R (%)	F1 (%)
train1	85.65	84.63	84.54	84.58
train2	88.31	84.98	86.36	85.67
train3	89.56	86.42	86.60	86.51
train4	89.89	86.33	87.40	86.86
train5	**90.47**	**86.52**	**88.09**	**87.30**

Table 4. Detailed performance of boundary enhanced model under span classification with negative sampling method.

	ACT			MOD			OBJ		
	P (%)	R (%)	F1 (%)	P (%)	R (%)	F1 (%)	P (%)	R (%)	F1 (%)
train1	87.21	89.56	88.37	83.46	80.05	81.72	75.04	75.27	75.15
train2	87.92	90.55	89.21	82.85	83.21	83.03	77.22	76.40	76.81
train3	89.37	90.42	89.89	84.42	83.57	83.99	78.33	78.15	78.24
train4	88.63	91.34	89.96	85.20	84.33	84.76	78.26	78.38	78.32
train5	89.59	91.28	**90.43**	84.58	85.53	**85.05**	78.00	81.11	**79.52**

To verify the effectiveness of the application of span classification framework and boundary enhanced model, we conduct experiments on sequence labeling framework and LSTM model. Table 5 shows the performance of LSTM model under sequence labeling and span classification framework. We can see that span classification with negative sampling method is higher than sequence labeling on all evaluation metrics, where the gap of the best F1 result is 6.1%. As an application on dialogue text in e-commerce scenario, the sequence labeling model achieved the best F1 of 70.87% on training set 5. The span classification framework got 74.97% on the smallest training set 1, which is 3.61% higher than sequence labeling. The comparison between sequence labeling and span classification in Table 5 illuminates the effectiveness of span classification on the extraction of core elements, which also demonstrates that negative sampling strategy can not only learn the positive samples, but also have the ability to distinguish between positive and negative samples in dialogue text.

Figure 4 plots the F1 values on three models, which can also be seen on Table 3 and Table 5. The abscissa coordinate means five datasets of different sizes, and the ordinate coordinate represents the F1 value. We can see from Fig. 4 that the performance shows a upward trend from training set 1 to training set 5. An steepest increase in performance occurs under the sequence labeling framework when transitioning from training set 1 to training set 5, resulting in a 5.45% improvement. While the performance exhibits a relatively slow upward trend when converting from small training set to large training set under the

Table 5. Performance of LSTM model under sequence labeling and span classification framework.

	LSTM on sequence labeling				LSTM on span classification			
	Acc (%)	P (%)	R (%)	F1 (%)	Acc (%)	P (%)	R (%)	F1 (%)
train1	77.32	68.67	62.46	65.42	80.81	69.56	81.31	74.97
train2	78.05	69.59	64.08	66.73	81.66	69.82	83.87	76.20
train3	78.69	70.23	66.19	68.15	81.60	70.40	84.21	76.69
train4	78.76	70.36	66.70	68.48	82.18	70.75	84.31	76.94
train5	79.37	73.10	68.77	70.87	81.75	70.30	85.04	76.97

span classification frame with negative sampling strategy, and the gap between training set 1 and training set 5 is only 2% and 2.72%. Therefore, the span classification of the negative sampling can achieve comparable result in small training set, greatly reducing resource consumption.

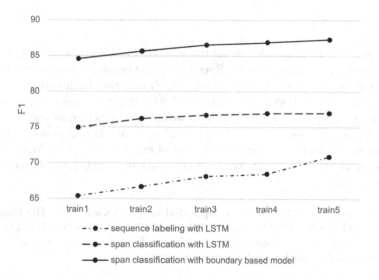

Fig. 4. Comparison of F1 value on five training sets under three models.

By comparing the result of LSTM and the boundary enhanced model under span classification framework in Table 3 and Table 5, we can find that the boundary enhanced model brings about 10% improvement on F1 value. Table 6 depicts the number of recognition errors of the LSTM based model and our Boundary enhanced model under sequence labeling and span classification framework, including Type Error (TE), Unrecognized Error (UE) and Boundary Error (BE). As the dataset gradually expands, Type Error (TE) decreases on all of the three models. Notably, our boundary enhanced span classification model with negative sampling strategy only has 331 boundary errors, which is 456 fewer than the LSTM model under span classification. Similarly, the boundary errors under sequence labeling is 893, which is 106 more than the same LSTM model under span classification. It proves that our boundary enhanced span classification model can identify the boundary of core elements pre-defined.

Table 6. Recognition errors of three models.

	Seq-LSTM			Span-LSTM			Span-Boundary		
	TE	UE	BE	TE	UE	BE	TE	UE	BE
train1	10572	8216	1260	5509	9947	847	4349	4344	412
train2	10097	8030	1165	4822	10103	790	3814	4271	356
train3	9529	8027	1118	4691	9841	770	3708	3798	332
train4	9383	8027	1082	4704	9737	798	3522	3865	347
train5	8645	7099	893	4518	10022	787	3334	3846	331

5   Conclusion

In this paper, we focus on identifying three pre-defined core elements in dialogue text of Jingdong customer service. Specifically, we employ a boundary enhanced model to serve the spoken dialogue text, which contains both explicit head and tail boundary information and dependency-based implicit boundary information. What's more, a span classification framework with negative sampling strategy is used to recognize the core elements in dialog, which is highly correlated with the semantics of sentence. The effectiveness of our method for dialogue text can be demonstrated through extensive experiments by using different models and training set sizes.

Acknowledgement. This work was supported by the National Key RD Program of China under Grant No. 2020AAA0108600, Projects 61876118 and 61976146 under the National Natural Science Foundation of China and the Priority Academic Program Development of Jiangsu Higher Education Institutions.

References

1. Chiu, J.P., Nichols, E.: Named entity recognition with bidirectional LSTM-CNNs. Trans. Assoc. Comput. Linguist. **4**, 357–370 (2016)
2. Devlin, J., Chang, M.W., Lee, K., Toutanova, K.: BERT: pre-training of deep bidirectional transformers for language understanding. arXiv preprint arXiv:1810.04805 (2018)
3. Dey, R., Salem, F.M.: Gate-variants of gated recurrent unit (GRU) neural networks. In: 2017 IEEE 60th International Midwest Symposium on Circuits and Systems (MWSCAS), pp. 1597–1600. IEEE (2017)
4. Eberts, M., Ulges, A.: Span-based joint entity and relation extraction with transformer pre-training. arXiv preprint arXiv:1909.07755 (2019)

5. Fu, J., Huang, X., Liu, P.: Spanner: named entity re-/recognition as span prediction. arXiv preprint arXiv:2106.00641 (2021)
6. Guo, Q., Qiu, X., Liu, P., Shao, Y., Xue, X., Zhang, Z.: Star-transformer. arXiv preprint arXiv:1902.09113 (2019)
7. Hammerton, J.: Named entity recognition with long short-term memory. In: Proceedings of the Seventh Conference on Natural Language Learning at HLT-NAACL 2003, pp. 172–175 (2003)
8. Huang, Z., Xu, W., Yu, K.: Bidirectional LSTM-CRF models for sequence tagging. arXiv preprint arXiv:1508.01991 (2015)
9. Lample, G., Ballesteros, M., Subramanian, S., Kawakami, K., Dyer, C.: Neural architectures for named entity recognition. arXiv preprint arXiv:1603.01360 (2016)
10. Li, F., Lin, Z., Zhang, M., Ji, D.: A span-based model for joint overlapped and discontinuous named entity recognition. arXiv preprint arXiv:2106.14373 (2021)
11. Li, S., Zhao, Z., Hu, R., Li, W., Liu, T., Du, X.: Analogical reasoning on Chinese morphological and semantic relations. In: Proceedings of the 56th Annual Meeting of the Association for Computational Linguistics (Volume 2: Short Papers), pp. 138–143. Association for Computational Linguistics (2018). https://aclweb.org/anthology/P18-2023
12. Li, X., Feng, J., Meng, Y., Han, Q., Wu, F., Li, J.: A unified MRC framework for named entity recognition. arXiv preprint arXiv:1910.11476 (2019)
13. Li, Y., Liu, L., Shi, S.: Empirical analysis of unlabeled entity problem in named entity recognition. arXiv preprint arXiv:2012.05426 (2020)
14. Luan, Y., Wadden, D., He, L., Shah, A., Ostendorf, M., Hajishirzi, H.: A general framework for information extraction using dynamic span graphs. arXiv preprint arXiv:1904.03296 (2019)
15. Ma, X., Hovy, E.: End-to-end sequence labeling via bi-directional LSTM-CNNs-CRF. arXiv preprint arXiv:1603.01354 (2016)
16. Peng, S., et al.: A dialogue-based information extraction system for medical insurance assessment. arXiv preprint arXiv:2107.05866 (2021)
17. Tan, C., Qiu, W., Chen, M., Wang, R., Huang, F.: Boundary enhanced neural span classification for nested named entity recognition. In: Proceedings of the AAAI Conference on Artificial Intelligence, vol. 34, pp. 9016–9023 (2020)
18. Vaswani, A., et al.: Attention is all you need. In: Advances in Neural Information Processing Systems, vol. 30 (2017)
19. Veličković, P., Cucurull, G., Casanova, A., Romero, A., Lio, P., Bengio, Y.: Graph attention networks. arXiv preprint arXiv:1710.10903 (2017)
20. Zeng, Y., Yang, H., Feng, Y., Wang, Z., Zhao, D.: A convolution BiLSTM neural network model for Chinese event extraction. In: Lin, C.-Y., Xue, N., Zhao, D., Huang, X., Feng, Y. (eds.) ICCPOL/NLPCC -2016. LNCS (LNAI), vol. 10102, pp. 275–287. Springer, Cham (2016). https://doi.org/10.1007/978-3-319-50496-4_23

UIT: Unifying Pre-training Objectives for Image-Text Understanding

Guoqiang Xu[1,2(✉)] and Shenggang Yan[1]

[1] Northwestern Polytechnical University, Xian, Shanxi, China
beowolftheone@163.com
[2] Jiangsu Automation Research Institute, Lianyungang, Jiangsu, China

Abstract. In the recent past, pre-trained models in vision-language research have witnessed a dramatic increase. However, most of these models are typically pre-trained independently, following either a contrastive, image-to-text generative, or text-to-image generative objective. This paper presents a unique framework, UIT, which fuses these pre-training objectives using a unicoder-decoder architecture that comprises an image unicoder, a text unicoder, and a bi-modal decoder. The image/text unicoders can interchange between encoding and decoding roles for different tasks, offering versatility and shared understanding that enhances both image-to-text and text-to-image transformations. UIT outshines existing models in a variety of tasks, such as retrieval, captioning, VQA, and SNLI-VE, demonstrating particular prowess in zero-shot situations. It delivers notable results in tasks like zero-shot ImageNet classification, zero-shot text-to-image synthesis, and zero-shot captioning.

1 Introduction

In the domain of vision-and-language learning, foundational models have primarily focused on three approaches. Firstly, the development of visual representation pre-training using correlated textual descriptions and contrastive losses [13,14,33,34], where two unimodal encoders process image and text separately. These pre-trained dual-encoder models support downstream tasks like zero-shot image classification and image-text retrieval, while also enhancing the visual encoders' capacity for image processing tasks like classification. Secondly, the pre-training of image-encoder and text-decoder models with Image-to-Text (I2T) token generation loss [1,5,27,32] has led to generative models that excel in vision-and-language tasks such as Visual Question Answering and image captioning. Thirdly, models have been pre-trained with Text-to-Image (T2I) token generation loss [3,4,17,37], which utilize VQ-VAE and GAN models [26,35] to tokenize raw images into image tokens and treat text-to-image generation as a sequence-to-sequence task. These models have demonstrated strong performance in text-based image generation tasks (Fig. 1).

The majority of these models focus on a single objective, with only a few incorporating two objectives, such as CoCa [36], OFA [29], and UnifiedIO [12]. Notably, all three objectives share the same pre-training data source image-text pairs. The knowledge they acquire should complement one another, with contrastive learning emphasizing high-level multimodal matching and image or text generation necessitating more detailed image-text representations. Furthermore, joint pre-training allows for partially shared computational graphs, leading to more efficient optimization and deployment.

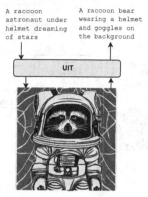

Fig. 1. Running example of UIT

This study introduces a unified framework called "Unifying Pre-Training Objectives for Image-Text Understanding" (UIT), which combines bi-modal and bi-contrastive learning, image-to-text generation, and text-to-image generation. UIT consists of an image unicoder, a text unicoder, and a cross-attention decoder. Image and text unicoders are structurally similar to Transformers but can alternate between unimodal image and text encoding and decoding, respectively, only differing in input embeddings and attention masks. When optimizing contrastive objectives, the image and text unicoders function as encoders, while during text and image generation loss optimization, the unicoders operate in encoding and auto-regressive decoding modes, with the cross-attention decoder fusing and generating features. This setup allows efficient knowledge sharing between encoding and decoding, improving both T2I and I2T generation, and unifying all three pre-training paradigms.

UIT is trained on large-scale noisy web-crawled image-text data and image annotation data, with labels treated as text. The pre-trained UIT demonstrates strong capabilities in unimodal visual understanding, image-text matching, image-text understanding, and text-to-image generation. For example, UIT achieves 82.5% accuracy in zero-shot ImageNet classification, 9.3 FID in zero-shot text-to-image generation, and a 44.5 CIDEr score in zero-shot image-to-text captioning. After fine-tuning, UIT further attains 86.34% linear probing accuracy on ImageNet, 4.58 FID on text-to-image generation, and a 78.20 VQA score.

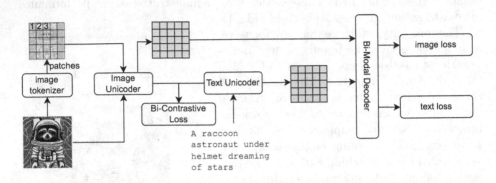

Fig. 2. Pipeline of UIT

2   The UIT Model

We initiate by illustrating the process of input handling and proceed to discuss the design of the model, which incorporates our introduced unicoder module. This component possesses the combined benefits of unimodal encoding and decoding. Finally, an in-depth explanation of the pre-training procedure is presented.

2.1   Input

With the aim to accommodate a range of tasks, our model is designed to support three distinct forms of input: tokens of text, distinct image tokens, and unprocessed images. In accordance with the conventional procedure in preceding studies [11,16,36], SentencePiece model is utilized to tokenize the text inputs based on a vocabulary of 64k, which was trained on the selected pretraining datasets.

Distinct Image Tokens. UIT creates images through an autoregressive technique, necessitating the transformation of 2D images into a series of image tokens [6,7,9,17,37]. In alignment with Parti [37], a pretrained and static ViT-VQGAN [35] is utilized as the tokenizer. Specifically, each image with the size of 256×256 is tokenized into a 32×32 grid of image tokens, offering 8,192 image token categories in the code book. These categories are appended to the existing text vocabulary as supplementary tokens. During inference, to create images, we sequentially decode the image tokens and input them into the ViT-VQGAN decoder for the reconstruction of the original image. Unprocessed Image. For tasks related to image comprehension and image-text comprehension, we also input unprocessed images to retain the original pixel information. Subsequently, each image is separated into non-overlapping sections in line with the established process in ViTs. By default, unless stated otherwise, the image resolution is set at 288×288 and the patch size at 18×18.

2.2 Structure

The architecture of UIT, illustrated in Fig. 2, is composed of one unicoder each for images and text, and a cross-attention decoder. We refer to these components as unicoders, as they can function as either encoders or decoders, depending on the requirements of each task. The concept of text and image unicoders is motivated by studies such as [2,8,38], which have shown that a single Transformer model is capable of performing both bidirectional encoding for understanding tasks and autoregressive decoding for generation tasks. In our use case, unicoders, when operating in the decoding mode, can leverage the shared knowledge from the encoding process to produce unimodal autoregressive features. This forms an effective basis for the bimodal generative goal. Experimental ablation further confirms that unicoders enhance both text-to-image (T2I) generation and multimodal understanding.

Image Unicoder. Lately, Vision Transformers (ViT) have risen to prominence as an effective method for encoding image features. Transformers are employed as decoders in autoregressive image token generation. These two operations are combined in our image unicoder. This unicoder functions in two ways: (1) In encoding mode, each 2D image patch is transformed into a feature vector using a learnable linear projection layer, in line with ViT. These projected features are fed into a series of Transformer layers to obtain encoded image features, using a bidirectional attention mask. (2) In decoding mode, the image unicoder translates the raw image into image tokens and initializes an embedding layer from where token embeddings are indexed. The Transformer layers used in the encoding mode are reused in the decoding mode, but with a causal cone-shaped attention mask. Both modes share the Transformer layers' parameters, the difference lying in input handling and attention masks. We believe that, compared to conventional image encoders, the added decoding mode can leverage shared knowledge gained during image encoding to generate image autoregressive features, thus improving text-to-image generation.

Text Unicoder. Similar to the image unicoder, the text unicoder offers encoding and decoding modes that reuse the Transformer parameters. Both modes employ the same tokenizer and embedding layer to extract token features, as they have identical input formats. A causal attention mask is applied in decoding mode. Previous research provides two options for text encoding: a bi-directional mask or a causal mask. Our empirical observations did not reveal significant performance differences between the two, so we defaulted to the causal mask in our experiments.

Bi-modal Decoder. The bi-modal decoder functions as a fusion and generation module, following the structure of the cross-attention decoder. During text generation, the input is the text autoregressive feature from the text unicoder in decoding mode, with encoded image features serving as cross-attention data. In contrast, during image generation, the image token autoregressive feature from the image unicoder in decoding mode is used as input and cross-attends to encoded text features. Unlike in text generation, where a simple causal mask is used, image generation employs a cone-shaped masked sparse attention to reduce the memory and computational requirements of long image token sequences.

2.3   Initial Training Phase

The initial training phase of the Unimodal Image-Text (UIT) model comprises three key objectives: contrastive loss for image and text, Image-to-Text (I2T) generation loss, and Text-to-Image (T2I) generation loss. This section elaborates these losses, along with providing an overview of our model scaling and initialization strategy.

Contrastive Loss Function. Raw images and text are fed into the image and text unicoders, respectively, for encoding, generating encoded image and text features. For text, akin to the approach adopted by CLIP [15] and ALIGN [11], the feature vector of the CLS token tagged at the end of the input sequence is utilized as the global representation. For images, the unicoder outputs a feature sequence. These are aggregated by applying an attention pooler in the lines of [36], which is a single multi-head attention layer having one learnable query and unicoder output features as the key and value. After procuring the global features of image and text, a bi-contrastive loss is deployed to optimize the paired image-text in relation to others in the same batch:

$$\mathcal{L}_{\text{Con(text2image)}} = -\frac{1}{N} \sum_{i=1}^{N} \log \frac{\exp\left(\frac{x_i^\top y_i}{\tau}\right)}{\sum_{j=1}^{N} \exp\left(\frac{x_i^\top y_j}{\tau}\right)}$$

$$\mathcal{L}_{\text{Con(image2text)}} = -\frac{1}{N} \sum_{i=1}^{N} \log \frac{\exp\left(\frac{y_i^\top x_i}{\tau}\right)}{\sum_{j=1}^{N} \exp\left(\frac{y_i^\top x_j}{\tau}\right)} \tag{1}$$

$$s.t. \quad \mathcal{L}_{\text{Con}} = \mathcal{L}_{\text{Con(text2image)}} + \mathcal{L}_{\text{Con(image2text)}}$$

Here, x_i and y_j symbolize the normalized global embeddings of i-th image and j-th text, respectively. τ is a trainable temperature parameter that modifies the scale of the loss.

I2T and T2I Generation Loss. We frame the two generation tasks as token generation problems. As illustrated in Fig. 2, the image unicoder, text unicoder, and Bimodal decoder are linked to execute two tasks flawlessly by merely alternating the unicoders' working modes. A cross-entropy loss is imposed on the Bi-modal decoder to maximize the conditional likelihood of the accurate token under the forward auto-regressive factorization. The losses for I2T and T2I generation are expressed as:

$$\mathcal{L}_{\text{I2T}} = -\sum_{t=1}^{T} \log P_\theta \left(y_t \,|\, y_1, \ldots, y_{t-1}, I\right)$$

$$\mathcal{L}_{\text{T2I}} = -\sum_{t=1}^{T} \log P_\theta \left(x_t \,|\, x_1, \ldots, x_{t-1}, T\right) \tag{2}$$

$$s.t. \quad \mathcal{L}_{\text{Total}} = \mathcal{L}_{\text{I2T}} + \mathcal{L}_{\text{T2I}}$$

To clarify, the parameters in Eq. 2 are defined as follows:

- $\mathcal{L}_{\text{I2T}}$: This loss is encountered while predicting text tokens y_t given the image I and preceding text tokens $y1, \ldots, y_{t-1}$.
- $\mathcal{L}_{\text{T2I}}$: This loss is encountered while predicting image tokens x_t given the text T and preceding image tokens $x1, \ldots, x_{t-1}$.
- P_θ: This denotes the conditional probability function parameterized by θ, which represents the model parameters.
- y_t: It is the tth text token in the sequence.
- x_t: It is the tth image token in the sequence.
- $y_1, \ldots, y_{t-1}$: These are the preceding text tokens in the sequence before the tth token.
- $x_1, \ldots, x_{t-1}$: These are the preceding image tokens in the sequence before the tth token.
- I: This is the supplied image used for conditioning in the image-to-text task.
- T: This is the supplied text used for conditioning in the text-to-image task.

Classifier-Free Guidance for T2I. In our model, we incorporate classifier-free guidance (CFG) [10] during the T2I generation. Specifically, in the training process, we randomly mask conditioning vectors or input text tokens at a certain probability (in our case, 10%). During inference, we calculate two predictions: one conditional, $I(z, T)$, and one unconditional, $I(z)$, differing solely in text input: while the conditional prediction $I(z, T)$ takes the original text tokens as input, the unconditional prediction $I(z)$ is fully masked. We then interpolate $I(z, c)$ and $I(z)$ to derive the final generated image:

$$I = I(z) + \alpha(I(z, T) - I(z)), \tag{3}$$

In this formula, α is a hyperparameter to adjust the scale of classifier-free guidance, set at 2.0 by default. Final Loss. Finally, we sum up these three losses to optimize the model end-to-end:

$$\mathcal{L}_{\text{UIT}} = \lambda_{\text{Con}} \mathcal{L}_{\text{Con}} + \lambda_{\text{I2T}} \mathcal{L}_{\text{I2T}} + \lambda_{\text{T2I}} \mathcal{L}_{\text{T2I}} \tag{4}$$

Here, $\lambda_{\text{Con}}, \lambda_{\text{I2T}}, \lambda_{\text{T2I}}$ represent scalar coefficients for the contrast loss, Image-to-Text loss, and Text-to-Image loss, respectively. In our experiments, we set $\lambda_{\text{Con}} = 1, \lambda_{\text{I2T}} = 1, \lambda_{\text{T2I}} = 1$.

2.4 Model Scaling and Initialization

Similar to most modern Transformer models, the UIT model can be scaled along the dimensions of model depth, width, and input sequence length, while controlling the computational resources (i.e., FLOPs) and memory footprints. We adopt an empirical scaling law to tune these dimensions coherently, following a rule of thumb that favors more layers over wider layers or longer sequences given a fixed compute budget.

For model initialization, we leverage the recent findings in large language model training [15]. More specifically, we employ a hybrid initialization approach where the unicoders are initialized with pretrained language and vision models (like GPT-3 for text unicoder and ViT for image unicoder) and the bimodal decoder is randomly initialized [19–25,28,30,31]. This approach not only provides a good initialization point that understands the raw input modalities but also shortens the convergence time by utilizing the inductive biases from pretraining.

2.5   Post-training Adaptation Phase

Upon completion of the primary training regimen, we implement a further adaptation phase, refining the model on specialized tasks such as image generation guided by text, and modifications to images based on textual instructions. The specificities of this adaptation phase are designed to enhance the UIT model's aptitude for these tasks and can vary based on the task's unique requirements. The procedural details are elucidated in the experimental section for each task.

In conclusion, the UIT model offers a cohesive and adaptable architecture for a variety of text-image application scenarios. By tapping into the combined strength of representational learning and generative modeling, it significantly streamlines the learning process and the implementation of multimodal applications, pushing the boundaries of text-image comprehension and generation.

3   Experimental Evaluation

This section commences with a description of the data and the optimization process used for pre-training (Sect. 3.1). Subsequent sections, Sect. 3.2 and Sect. 3.3, present the main findings of the zero-shot evaluation and the fine-tuning assessment, respectively. Each evaluation probes three capabilities: (1) visual understanding, (2) image captioning and multimodal understanding, and (3) text-to-image synthesis. Section 3.4 involves an ablation study of the various components of UIT to substantiate our design choices.

3.1   Details of Pre-training

The pre-training of UIT leverages a composite of ALIGN, JFT-4B, and WebLI datasets. ALIGN and JFT-4B datasets cater to the contrastive and image-to-text (I2T) loss, while the WebLI and ALIGN datasets are combined for the text-to-image (T2I) generation loss. For T2I generation, WebLI is favored owing to its extensive depiction of visual specifics. The optimization of T2I loss is achieved by sampling 1,024 image-text pairs from ALIGN and WebLI, and contrastive and I2T losses with 30,720 image-text pairs from ALIGN and JFT. UIT-Base/Large is subjected to pre-training for 1M steps, deploying the Adafactor optimizer with a weight decay parameter set to 0.04. The learning rate is incrementally heated to $4.5e-5$ over the first 6,000 steps, and then subjected to an exponential decay starting from the 100,000th step. The pre-training procedure is completed in approximately 14 days on a GTX V100 32GB setup. The model is further refined over an additional 50k steps with 576×576 high-resolution raw images serving as input for the image encoder.

Table 1. Comparison of various models with randomly perturbed data

M	VB	IU ImageNet Linear Probing	ITU					CC MS-COCO T2I Generation (FID ↓)
			VQ		SV		MCC (CIDEr)	
			td	ts	d	t		
CLIP	Scratch	85.35	-	-	-	-	-	-
ALIGN	Scratch	85.52	-	-	-	-	-	-
UNITER	Faster-RCNN	-	73.95	74.13	79.32	79.29	-	-
VinVL	Faster-RCNN	-	76.67	76.52	-	-	130.92	-
CLIP-ViL	CLIP	-	76.62	76.53	80.57	80.36	134.11	-
ALBEF	PT. ViT	-	75.79	75.97	80.74	80.84	-	-
BLIP	PT. ViT	-	78.12	78.27	-	-	136.83	-
SimVLM	PT. ResNet	-	80.16	80.29	86.07	86.18	143.12	-
OFA	PT. ResNet	-	81.91	82.14	91.11	91.04	145.08	10.47
X-LXMERT 19	Faster-RCNN	-	-	-	-	-	122.55	29.94
CoCa-2.1B	Scratch	-	79.95	80.16	87.11	87.08	143.28	-
PALI-17B	PT. ViT	-	84.12	84.48	-	-	148.98	-
Parti-20B	-	-	-	-	-	-	-	3.37
UIT-Base	Scratch	83.55	76.15	76.45	85.53	85.24	135.19	5.13
UIT-Large	Scratch	86.34	78.08	78.20	86.19	85.97	139.65	4.58

3.2 Zero-Shot Evaluation on Applications

UIT exhibits remarkable performance across a variety of zero-shot tasks, encompassing image classification, image-text retrieval, image captioning, and text-to-image generation. In zero-shot image classification, UIT-Large attains an accuracy of 82.5% on ImageNet, thus outperforming formidable baselines like CLIP and ALIGN. In the case of zero-shot image-text retrieval, UIT-Large surpasses prior models in 5 out of 8 metrics applied on Flickr and MS-COCO datasets. In the zero-shot image captioning task, UIT-Base/Large yields a CIDEr score of 42.0/44.5 on MS-COCO. Lastly, for zero-shot text-to-image generation, UIT-Large achieves a FID score of 9.3 on MS-COCO, outclassing even larger-scale models such as DALL-E 2 and Make-A-Scene (Table 2).

3.3 Fine-Tuning on Downstream Tasks

The research demonstrates the transferability of the Unified Image-Text (UIT) model across multiple downstream tasks in the fields of image understanding, image-text understanding, and text-guided content creation. For image

Table 2. Comparative Results for Diverse Zero-Shot Tasks

Job	Framework	Parameter	Collection	Score (%)
Picture Classification	UIT-Large	Accuracy	ImageNet	82.5
	CLIP	-	-	-
	ALIGN	-	-	-
Image-Text Recovery	UIT-Large	-	Flickr & MS-COCO	-
Picture Captioning	UIT-Base	CIDEr	MS-COCO	42.0
	UIT-Large	CIDEr	MS-COCO	44.5
	SimVLM	CIDEr	MS-COCO	32.2/32.4
Text-to-Picture Generation	UIT-Large	FID	MS-COCO	9.3
	DALL-E 2	-	-	-
	Make-A-Scene	-	-	-

Table 3. Task Ablation. Con. denotes contrastive loss

Tasks			Assessment		
Con	T2P	P2T	ZS IN	VQA	ZS IG. ($\downarrow$)
✓	-	-	70.8	-	-
-	✓	-	-	-	12.5
-	-	✓	-	68	-
-	✓	✓	-	65.3	13.1
✓	✓	✓	71.2	66.8	13.2

Table 4. Module Ablation

Module		Assessment		
Image	Text	VQA	ZS Cap	ZS IG. ($\downarrow$)
Encoder	Encoder	65.8	32.8	13.7
Unicoder	Encoder	66.5	36.8	13.2
Encoder	Unicoder	67.7	35.1	13.6
Unicoder	Unicoder	66.8	37.8	13.4

understanding, a linear probing approach was taken on ImageNet. This process involved fixing all the parameters of the image unicoder in UIT and only training a linear classifier for image recognition. In this experiment, UIT-Large was able to outperform well-established baselines like CLIP and ALIGN by approximately 1%. Regarding image-text understanding, tasks requiring this ability were categorized into Visual Question Answering (VQA), SNLI-VE, and image captioning. All parameters of UIT were fine-tuned for these tasks, and the model was evaluated on the validation/test sets. In the fine-tuning for image captioning, the predictions computed by UIT were made in the same way as in zero-shot image captioning. The results, as detailed in Table 5, show that UIT can achieve competitive CIDEr scores against other models.

In alignment with previous research methodologies [32,36], our approach applies the Visual Question Answering (VQA) task as a classifying challenge among the top 3,129 recurring answers in the training dataset. This process entails passing the original image through the image unicoder in encoding mode, while the accompanying question is managed by the text unicoder in decoding mode. The subsequent step engages the Bimodal decoder to leverage the text decoding features and cross-attend to the encoded image attributes. The eventual output from the Bi-modal decoder serves as the unified global feature. To

Table 5. Ablation on initialization

Model	Evaluation		
	ZS IN.	VQA	ZS IG. ($\downarrow$)
Init. Text Unicoder from CoCa	75.4	68.4	11.4
Train from Scratch	75.1	68.6	11.5

deduce the answer, a linear classifier is trained on this global feature. Based on the data in Table 1, it is evident that UIT delivers a commendable performance compared to other Vision-Language Pretraining (VLP) models.

When it comes to SNLI-VE, the procedure mirrors the VQA fine-tuning. The final token output feature of the Bi-modal decoder is extracted and a linear classifier is applied to forecast the three relations. As per Table 1, UIT demonstrates its capability to outclass robust VLP models and register outstanding performance. It is important to note that, unlike OFA which uses both image and text premises as inputs, other models, including UIT, only rely on image premises.

As for Text-to-Image Generation, our study follows the methodologies set forth by [18,37]. We fine-tune UIT on the MS-COCO training dataset and assess the Frechet Inception Distance (FID) score on a random sample of 30k from the test set.

a panda astronaut walking with swagger on mars in an infinite universe, syntheware digital art

a group of teddy bears are having pizza at night in times square

A husky dog wearing sunglasses, orange beret and green turtleneck

Fig. 3. Qualitative results of zero-shot text-to-image generation from UIT-Large.

3.4 Ablation

In this segment, we undertake an in-depth analysis of the design elements present in UIT. The majority of these ablation studies are carried out on UIT-Base, under a minimized batch size and a truncated training timeline. Particularly, the total batch size stands at 4,352, with 4,096 reserved for the contrastive and I2T loss, and the remaining 256 set aside for T2I loss. Furthermore, the entire training step spans 200k, and is devoid of high-resolution pre-training. The tasks we have chosen for this analysis include zero-shot ImageNet Classification (ZS IN.) for evaluating image comprehension, fine-tuned VQA or MS-COCO zero-shot Captioning (ZS Cap.) for multimodal comprehension, and MS-COCO zero-shot text-to-image generation (ZS IG.) for image generation. We employ CIDEr to measure ZS Cap. result, while FID (with lower scores indicating superior performance) is used to assess the ZS IG. result.

In the context of **Training Objectives**, we examine the implications of three training objectives: contrastive loss, I2T loss, and T2I loss, as well as their mutual influence. The findings are presented in Table 3. A few key insights that can be gathered include: (1) A comparison of the initial and final rows reveals that Bi-modal generation objectives can slightly enhance image comprehension beyond the contrastive loss, improving zero-shot ImageNet accuracy by 0.4%. (2) A scrutiny of the second, third, and fourth rows displays that the two generation losses - I2T loss and T2I loss - have a minor conflicting impact. Upon the addition of T2I loss, the VQA accuracy dips by 2.7, whereas the introduction of I2T loss causes the zero-shot image generation FID score to increase by 0.6. (3) A comparison of the fourth and fifth rows indicates that while the contrastive loss augments vision-language comprehension, it has no effect on image generation. Altogether, these findings underscore the feasibility of harmoniously integrating three essential objectives within a single framework.

Under the **Loss Weight** subheading, considering the three objectives, we undertake an ablation of varying weights for them, selecting the optimal one as the default setup for all experiments.

With regard to **Unicoder vs. Encoder**, prior Vision-Language projects have conventionally adopted an encoder-decoder pipeline, where the encoder processes image/text features, and the Bi-modal decoder amalgamates these and facilitates generation. In contrast, we introduce unicoder as an alternative to encoder, capable of both encoding and decoding unimodal representations via shared parameters. In this part, we undertake an ablation of image and text unicoders against image and text encoders. It's crucial to note that the unicoder doesn't contribute additional parameters to the encoders because encoding and decoding in unicoder utilize the same parameters. Table 4 demonstrates that both the image unicoder and text unicoder can deliver superior performance over the encoders, and their combined usage brings about the best balance between image generation and multimodal comprehension.

In **Train From Scratch**, we initialize the text unicoder with a pre-trained unimodal text decoder from CoCa. We also undertake a trial to train all from scratch. To minimize potential discrepancies due to CoCa's significantly larger batch size, all models in this comparison are trained with an unshrunk batch size. As per Table 5, utilizing pre-trained weight from CoCa marginally improves zero-shot ImageNet recognition and text-to-image generation by 0.3% and 0.1, respectively. However, it does not enhance VQA. This comparison confirms the feasibility of training UIT entirely from scratch without significant performance degradation.

3.5 Visualization

We create visual representations of both successful and unsuccessful image generations by UIT-Large, using prompts from PartiPrompt. As shown in Fig. 3, UIT is capable of generating high-quality, widely applicable, open-domain images derived from text.

4 Conclusion

In this work, we introduce a unified vision-language foundational model, UIT, which integrates three key objectives: Bi-modal contrastive learning, image-to-text generation, and text-to-image generation. Composed of an image unicoder, a text unicoder, and a cross-attention decoder, UIT possesses the capability to toggle between two modes: unimodal image/text encoding and decoding. The model is trained on extensive, noisy web-crawled image-text data as well as image annotation data. UIT exhibits potent zero-shot capabilities and transferability in diverse domains, including unimodal visual comprehension, image-text alignment, image-text comprehension, and text-guided image content creation.

References

1. Alayrac, J.B., et al.: Flamingo: a visual language model for few-shot learning. Adv. Neural. Inf. Process. Syst. 35, 23716–23736 (2022)
2. Bao, H., et al.: UniLMv2: pseudo-masked language models for unified language model pre-training. In: International Conference on Machine Learning, pp. 642–652. PMLR (2020)
3. Chang, H., et al.: Muse: text-to-image generation via masked generative transformers. arXiv preprint arXiv:2301.00704 (2023)
4. Chang, H., Zhang, H., Jiang, L., Liu, C., Freeman, W.T.: MaskGIT: masked generative image transformer. In: Proceedings of the IEEE/CVF Conference on Computer Vision and Pattern Recognition, pp. 11315–11325 (2022)
5. Chen, X., et al.: PaLI: a jointly-scaled multilingual language-image model. arXiv preprint arXiv:2209.06794 (2022)
6. Ding, M., et al.: CogView: mastering text-to-image generation via transformers. Adv. Neural. Inf. Process. Syst. 34, 19822–19835 (2021)
7. Ding, M., Zheng, W., Hong, W., Tang, J.: CogView2: faster and better text-to-image generation via hierarchical transformers. arXiv preprint arXiv:2204.14217 (2022)
8. Dong, L., et al.: Unified language model pre-training for natural language understanding and generation. In: Advances in Neural Information Processing Systems, vol. 32 (2019)

9. Gafni, O., Polyak, A., Ashual, O., Sheynin, S., Parikh, D., Taigman, Y.: Make-a-scene: scene-based text-to-image generation with human priors. In: Avidan, S., Brostow, G., Cissé, M., Farinella, G.M., Hassner, T. (eds.) ECCV 2022. LNCS, vol. 13675, pp. 89–106. Springer, Cham (2022). https://doi.org/10.1007/978-3-031-19784-0_6

10. Ho, J., Salimans, T.: Classifier-free diffusion guidance. arXiv preprint arXiv:2207.12598 (2022)

11. Jia, C., et al.: Scaling up visual and vision-language representation learning with noisy text supervision. In: International Conference on Machine Learning, pp. 4904–4916. PMLR (2021)

12. Lu, J., Clark, C., Zellers, R., Mottaghi, R., Kembhavi, A.: Unified-IO: a unified model for vision, language, and multi-modal tasks. arXiv preprint arXiv:2206.08916 (2022)

13. Mu, N., Kirillov, A., Wagner, D., Xie, S.: SLIP: self-supervision meets language-image pre-training. In: Avidan, S., Brostow, G., Cissé, M., Farinella, G.M., Hassner, T. (eds.) ECCV 2022. LNCS, vol. 13686, pp. 529–544. Springer, Cham (2022). https://doi.org/10.1007/978-3-031-19809-0_30

14. Radford, A., et al.: Learning transferable visual models from natural language supervision. In: International Conference on Machine Learning, pp. 8748–8763. PMLR (2021)

15. Radford, A., et al.: Language models are unsupervised multitask learners. OpenAI Blog **1**(8), 9 (2019)

16. Raffel, C., et al.: Exploring the limits of transfer learning with a unified text-to-text transformer. J. Mach. Learn. Res. **21**(1), 5485–5551 (2020)

17. Ramesh, A., et al.: Zero-shot text-to-image generation. In: International Conference on Machine Learning, pp. 8821–8831. PMLR (2021)

18. Saharia, C., et al.: Photorealistic text-to-image diffusion models with deep language understanding. Adv. Neural. Inf. Process. Syst. **35**, 36479–36494 (2022)

19. Tang, X., et al.: Hyperbolic code retrieval: a novel approach for efficient code search using hyperbolic space embeddings. arXiv preprint arXiv:2308.15234 (2023)

20. Tang, X., et al.: Multilevel semantic embedding of software patches: a fine-to-coarse grained approach towards security patch detection. arXiv preprint arXiv:2308.15233 (2023)

21. Tang, X., Sun, T., Zhu, R., Wang, S.: CKG: dynamic representation based on context and knowledge graph. In: 2020 25th International Conference on Pattern Recognition (ICPR), pp. 2889–2895. IEEE (2021)

22. Tang, X., Tian, H., Kong, P., Liu, K., Klein, J., Bissyande, T.F.: App review driven collaborative bug finding. arXiv preprint arXiv:2301.02818 (2023)

23. Tang, X., Zhu, R., Sun, T., Wang, S.: Moto: enhancing embedding with multiple joint factors for Chinese text classification. In: 2020 25th International Conference on Pattern Recognition (ICPR), pp. 2882–2888. IEEE (2021)

24. Tian, H., et al.: Is ChatGPT the ultimate programming assistant-how far is it? arXiv preprint arXiv:2304.11938 (2023)

25. Tian, H., et al.: Is this change the answer to that problem? correlating descriptions of bug and code changes for evaluating patch correctness. In: Proceedings of the 37th IEEE/ACM International Conference on Automated Software Engineering, pp. 1–13 (2022)

26. Van Den Oord, A., Vinyals, O., et al.: Neural discrete representation learning. In: Advances in Neural Information Processing Systems, vol. 30 (2017)

27. Wang, J., et al.: GIT: a generative image-to-text transformer for vision and language. arXiv preprint arXiv:2205.14100 (2022)

28. Wang, L., et al.: Delving into commit-issue correlation to enhance commit message generation models. CoRR abs/2308.00147 (2023). https://doi.org/10.48550/arXiv.2308.00147

29. Wang, P., et al.: Unifying architectures, tasks, and modalities through a simple sequence-to-sequence learning framework. arXiv preprint arXiv:2202.03052 (2022)

30. Wang, S., Tang, D., Zhang, L.: A large-scale hierarchical structure knowledge enhanced pre-training framework for automatic ICD coding. In: Mantoro, T., Lee, M., Ayu, M.A., Wong, K.W., Hidayanto, A.N. (eds.) ICONIP 2021. CCIS, vol. 1517, pp. 494–502. Springer, Cham (2021). https://doi.org/10.1007/978-3-030-92310-5_57

31. Wang, S., Tang, D., Zhang, L., Li, H., Han, D.: HieNet: bidirectional hierarchy framework for automated ICD coding. In: Bhattacharya, A., et al. (eds.) DASFAA 2022. LNCS, vol. 13246, pp. 523–539. Springer, Cham (2022). https://doi.org/10.1007/978-3-031-00126-0_38

32. Wang, Z., Yu, J., Yu, A.W., Dai, Z., Tsvetkov, Y., Cao, Y.: SimVLM: simple visual language model pretraining with weak supervision. arXiv preprint arXiv:2108.10904 (2021)

33. Yao, L., et al.: FILIP: fine-grained interactive language-image pre-training. arXiv preprint arXiv:2111.07783 (2021)

34. You, H., et al.: Learning visual representation from modality-shared contrastive language-image pre-training. In: Avidan, S., Brostow, G., Cissé, M., Farinella, G.M., Hassner, T. (eds.) ECCV 2022. LNCS, vol. 13687, pp. 69–87. Springer, Cham (2022). https://doi.org/10.1007/978-3-031-19812-0_5

35. Yu, J., et al.: Vector-quantized image modeling with improved VQGAN. arXiv preprint arXiv:2110.04627 (2021)

36. Yu, J., Wang, Z., Vasudevan, V., Yeung, L., Seyedhosseini, M., Wu, Y.: CoCa: contrastive captioners are image-text foundation models. arXiv preprint arXiv:2205.01917 (2022)

37. Yu, J., et al.: Scaling autoregressive models for content-rich text-to-image generation. arXiv preprint arXiv:2206.10789 (2022)

38. Zhou, L., Palangi, H., Zhang, L., Hu, H., Corso, J., Gao, J.: Unified vision-language pre-training for image captioning and VQA. In: Proceedings of the AAAI Conference on Artificial Intelligence, vol. 34, pp. 13041–13049 (2020)

Author Index

L. Iliadis et al. (Eds.): ICANN 2023, LNCS 14258, pp. 587–589, 2023.
https://doi.org/10.1007/978-3-031-44192-9

Printed in the United States
by Baker & Taylor Publisher Services